Winston Churchill
A Biographical Companion

Winston Churchill
A Biographical Companion

Chris Wrigley

ABC-CLIO

Santa Barbara, California
Denver, Colorado
Oxford, England

Frontispiece photograph: Library of Congress

Library of Congress Cataloging-in-Publication Data
Wrigley, Chris.
    Winston Churchill : a biographical companion / Chris Wrigley.
        p.   cm. — (ABC-CLIO biographical companions)
    Includes bibliographical references and index.
    ISBN 0-87436-990-8 (hard cover : alk. paper)—ISBN 1-57607-539-7 (eBook)
    1. Churchill, Winston, Sir, 1874–1965—Encyclopedias.   2. Prime
ministers—Great Britain—Biography—Encyclopedias.   3. Great
Britain—Politics and government—20th century—Encyclopedias.
I. Title.   II. ABC-CLIO biographical companion
DA566.9.C5 W75   2002
941.084'092—dc21

                                                            2002002178

07   06   05   04   03   02   10 9 8 7 6 5 4 3 2   1 (cloth)

ABC-CLIO, Inc.
130 Cremona Drive, P.O. Box 1911
Santa Barbara, California 93116-1911

*This book is also available on the World Wide Web as an eBook. Visit www.abc-clio.com for
details.*

This book is printed on acid-free paper ∞.

Manufactured in the United States of America

ABC-CLIO BIOGRAPHICAL COMPANIONS

Adolf Hitler, by David Nicholls

Andrew Johnson, by Glenna R. Schroeder-Lein and Richard Zuczek

Benjamin Franklin, by Jennifer L. Durham

George Washington, by Frank E. Grizzard, Jr.

James K. Polk, by Mark E. Byrnes

Joseph Stalin, by Helen Rappaport

Napoleon, by David Nicholls

Queen Victoria, by Helen Rappaport

Susan B. Anthony, by Judith E. Harper

Thomas Jefferson, by David S. Brown

———————

ABC-CLIO Biographical Companions are encyclopedic guides to the lives of men and women who have had a significant impact on the social, political, and cultural development of the Western world. Each volume presents complete biographical information in an easily accessible format. An introduction and a chronology provide an overview, while the A-to-Z entries amplify a myriad of topics related to the person. A collection of documents and extensive illustrations give the reader an acute sense of the individual's life and times.

For Maggie Walsh,

With love

CONTENTS

Winston Churchill: A Biographical Companion, 1

PREFACE

Winston Churchill looms large over the history of Britain in the first five-and-a-half decades of the twentieth century. He was a man of many careers. His life intersected with those of many politicians, statesmen, and leaders of the armed forces. This book provides a guide to many people who played a part in his life and to other aspects of his life. It provides some depth of coverage on the well-known, and some nearly unknown, individuals who were selected for inclusion rather than a brief consideration of a large number of people. Hopefully, the entries are an enjoyable read.

Churchill deserves such treatment. He was one of the twentieth century's great figures, one of those who made a difference to major events. His career still arouses great interest and even fierce controversy. This book provides a biographical guide to a major political career and to other aspects of Churchill's colorful and varied life.

ACKNOWLEDGMENTS

Like other authors of books of this kind, I owe much to the many authors of important works relating to the entries. These authors can be found at the end of the entries under "Suggestions for further reading." I am also much indebted to the meticulous scholarship of Sir Martin Gilbert and to the late Randolph Churchill for their work on the official history and its companion volumes. I hope that those who enjoy reading about Churchill will find some information new to them, drawn from my own researches for over thirty years in the era of Churchill.

I am very grateful again to Su Spencer for her skillful work in turning my manuscript into a form ready for publishing. I have also been brought to the finishing line by the encouragement and enthusiasm for the book shown by Dr. Robert Neville, my editor at ABC-CLIO in Oxford, UK.

INTRODUCTION

Born in Blenheim Palace on 30 November 1874, Winston Spencer Churchill was the son of Lord and Lady Randolph Churchill and the grandson of the duke of Marlborough. He was born into aristocratic politics, Conservative politics, at a high social level. He did not have to pursue a career as a politician, although he felt impelled to do so.

As the elder son of a younger son of a duke, he expected to have to make his way in the world. There were obvious careers for the sons who were not heirs to titles: the church, the army, and politics prominent among them. Winston Churchill favored the army and politics. He briefly even considered a career in the church. Churchill as a modern Thomas à Beckett, asserting the rights of the church, is a might-have-been to ponder!

Churchill went into the army because his poor early educational performance made it seem a career to which he might win entry. His path was Sandhurst, not a university. Given his later outstanding use of the English language, not least in his many books, this was either a serious failure of the private education system or he markedly underachieved.

From fairly early on, he had desired a political career, and from his teens, he was a man with a mission. This was to vindicate his much admired father, whose political career took a terminal downward spin from December 1886 when he resigned as chancellor of the exchequer. Winston's filial piety led him to believe that his father had been done-down by the evil machinations of jealous rivals rather than that his father, who had become highly temperamental and unpredictable, had committed political suicide. Moreover, in seeking to be his father's champion, like some knight of old, he was also seeking to win his father's respect, and even love (at least before Lord Randolph's death in 1895), and also that of his mother. When he was a child, neither parent gave him the love and attention he craved, his father being too busy in politics, his mother too involved in society.

Churchill, then, aspired to achieve success in politics, to carry on where his father had left off. From early on in his adult life, he sought glory in battle as a means of securing a position in politics while he was young. He had surprising confidence that in action he would be fated to survive largely intact. He was fearless, even reckless, in the face of danger, and he did survive the Northwest Frontier of India, the Battle of Omdurman, the Boer War, and later the Western Front.

He also sought fame through best-selling books. He initially sought to follow Benjamin Disraeli's example, writing a novel titled *Savrola*. Although published in 1900, it was the first book he had begun, its completion being delayed by his accounts of the Malakand Field Force and Sir Herbert Kitchener's campaign in the Sudan. In 1900, Winston Churchill seriously considered writing a play about the Boer War, but his mother argued against this on grounds that it would be in bad taste. Earlier, Disraeli had been quite explicit about his publications' being a career move. Thus, in June 1834, Disraeli had written to his sister, "I must publish yet more, before the attention which I require can be obtained." In the case of the young Churchill, he also sought attention. As with the young Disraeli, the money that his military and other books brought in was also important.

Churchill was familiar with the early struggles of major politicians of the past, such as Disraeli, to make a start in British politics. He was especially familiar with Disraeli's career, not least because of his connections with his own family. Disraeli, who enjoyed aristocratic company, visited Blenheim Palace and encouraged Lord Randolph Churchill in the early stages of his political career. Winston Churchill throughout his career spoke of his belief in "Tory Democracy," an ill-defined variety of Conservatism much referred to in rhetoric stemming from Disraeli and Lord Randolph Churchill. He believed in it much more than his father ever did. Winston Churchill loyally backed the Conservative Party's Primrose League, founded by his father in honor of the memory of Disraeli. He made his first political speech at one of its meetings held at Claverton Down, near Bath, in 1897. For Winston Churchill, "Tory Democracy" signified an attachment to social reform and social cohesion. Winston Churchill was also like Disraeli and his father in often being blunt and explicit about his ambitions. Such brazen ambition alienated many from Lord Randolph Churchill and many were disconcerted by this aspect of his elder son.

Aristocratic politics involved making full use of family connections. Lord Salisbury, the Conservative Party leader, did not hesitate to reward many of his relatives with government places, so much so that there was a widespread jest of his later government's being dubbed "The Hotel Cecil," a play on his family name (Cecil) and that of a high-quality hotel. Both Lord Randolph and his son Winston made full use of their family connections and the allure of their social status. When Winston Churchill first stood for Parliament for Oldham in 1899, the local Conservatives were well pleased that he won the promise of his cousin "Sunny," the duke of Marlborough, to speak on his behalf.

Lady Randolph's social connections were repeatedly mobilized on behalf of both her sons. Winston Churchill vociferously required this help from his mother and of his other connections. He bluntly wrote to his mother on 10 January 1898, "It is a pushing age, we must shove with the best." He echoed this advice to his brother on 4 December 1898: "You can't push too much in all things." His single-minded self-advancement was a contrast to many of the middle classes' upbringing, which esteemed reticence and curbed excessive egotism with such phrases as "You are only one pebble on the beach." Churchill, however, was confident, as he put it, in his destiny to achieve fame. On first meeting the young Violet Bonham Carter, he observed, "We are all worms. But I do believe that I am a glow-worm."

On the same occasion, Churchill held forth on how short human life was and how much had to be crammed quickly into a limited number of years. Churchill's hyperactivity was driven early on by a fear that he would die young, his father having died not long before his forty-sixth birthday. In the event, he lived to be ninety, dying seventy years to the day after his father. This belief that time was short was shared by his great political associate, David Lloyd George, whose father had died even younger, at forty-three, and who was something of a hypochondriac.

Both Churchill and Lloyd George were remarkably frank with their future wives, telling them in no uncertain terms that they would take second place behind their political ambitions. Although the Churchills' marriage had its shaky times, Clementine Churchill provided Winston with the love and support he greatly needed and was truly the rock on which his career rested after 1908. Churchill often caused his wife great anxiety and stress. This he demonstrated through his disregard for his own safety, as displayed in his pre–First World War love of flying. He also showed it with the way he emulated his mother in the grandiose spending of money, whether it be buying Chartwell in 1922 or gambling in casinos; an unfortunate characteristic that was in turn emulated by their son Randolph. This extravagance even included very expensive finely woven silk underclothes. Years of anxiety over being able to pay minor household bills put great strain on Clementine and resulted in many marital arguments. In one such argument, Mary Soames has recalled, her mother even threw a dish of spinach at her husband. Churchill's optimism that all would come well with his finances was encouraged by the sums he earned from his writings and his North American lecture tours.

Clementine Churchill also disliked and distrusted many of her husband's political cronies. She probably rightly saw his close association with F. E. Smith, Lord Beaverbrook, and Brendan Bracken as politically damaging associations, especially the first two. Churchill created his own male club world, epitomized in The Other Club, made up of people of whom Churchill approved. In a way, he was a little reminiscent of a feudal lord, with his entourage of supporters enjoying his largesse. His circle came to include many able, young Conservative M.P.s. However, this style of politics resulted in meals becoming political or book-research occasions. In this, he followed Lloyd George, who had conducted famous political breakfasts. Winston and Clementine Churchill rarely had dinners alone, especially during the Second World War. They often went their own ways, on holidays and even over Christmas. Yet, for all the strains, the marriage mattered to both.

When Clementine Hozier married Winston Churchill, he was a Liberal minister. She was from a Liberal family background and was, as Violet Bonham Carter later observed, "a better natural Liberal than Winston." Churchill, nevertheless, had some strong Liberal sympathies, which he held throughout his career. On 6 April 1897, he wrote to his mother that were it not for the issue of Home Rule for Ireland he would be a Liberal. He was greatly attracted to the politics of Lord Rosebery, which combined imperialism with domestic social reform. After the turn of the century, Rosebery advocated the politics of national efficiency, involving a dumping of the old party obsessions in favor of making efficient industry, education, and politics. At the end of the Second World War, faced with a powerful Labour Party, Churchill sought a national Conservative-Liberal electoral alliance. He did secure a straight fight with Labour in the Colne Valley for his old friend Violet Bonham Carter, a leading Liberal, in the 1951 general election, and he spoke for her on 15 October.

It was often suggested that Churchill held few political principles for long. He had not only "ratted" from his party (left the Conservatives in 1904), but had "re-ratted" (returned in 1924). Perhaps it is more striking how several of his principles, held most doggedly, disrupted his career. This was so with Free Trade, the empire and India, and belief in the monarchy.

Churchill's economic policies were for long the orthodoxies established in the nineteenth century or earlier. He had a deep and firm belief in the efficacy of free market forces, as unfettered as possible. When he was extending the intervention of the state into social welfare in the 1908–1911 period, he took pains to be explicit that the changes in the labor market were at the margin, protecting a minority who were unable to compete, and that the measures would not affect overall the operation of the free market. In a major speech on 11 October 1906, he commented, "The existing organization of society is driven by one mainspring—competitive selection. It may be a very imperfect organization of society, but it is all we have got between us and barbarism."

Until the 1930s, he was committed to Free Trade. This was also a central tenet of the British Liberal Party from the days of Richard Cobden and William Gladstone to the early 1930s. Free Trade was a policy that Conservative leaders from mid century had accepted, though in some cases mostly keeping reservations private. When Joseph Chamberlain launched a protectionist campaign in 1903, under the euphemistic title of "tariff reform," Churchill became a leading figure in the Free Food League. His stance on Free Trade led to his departure from the Conservative Party in 1904.

Churchill also supported another bulwark of Liberal economic policy: adherence to the Gold Standard. Before 1914 Britain, as the country that exported the highest proportion of its manufactured goods and the most capital, benefited from exchange rates fixed to gold. However, when in 1925 Churchill returned sterling to the Gold Standard at the prewar parity to the dollar, he received heavy criticism, not least from the economist J. M. Keynes in his *The Economic Consequences of Mr. Churchill* (1925). Churchill himself had had doubts, being concerned that as usual British finance was being helped at the expense of British industry, but continued with an economic course indicated by his predecessors since 1919.

Throughout his career, Churchill was antisocialist. He commented in a speech on 11 November 1906, "I am convinced that it is necessary to maintain the individual ownership of property, and I do not believe that we will get [high] productivity unless we interest every individual." Churchill was often hostile to middle-class intellectuals who were socialists but was less critical of non-Communist trade unionists such as Ernest Bevin and David Kirkwood. Although Churchill was hostile to democratic socialism, he was vehemently opposed to communism. He began making his mark as a potential leader of the Right wing of the Conservative Party during his period as the dedicated supporter of the White armies fighting Bolshevik Russia, 1918–1920. He

added to it in his vigorous opposition to the Labour Party being permitted to form a minority government in 1924 and by his robust action during the General Strike, 1926.

In opposing communism, Churchill was a property-owning democrat who opposed dictatorship, not least in the name of the proletariat. In opposing organized labor, Churchill was revealing one side of his ingrained aristocratic paternalism. He was genuinely sympathetic and eager to help working people who fell on hard times. But it was assistance on his terms, and he felt that they should be grateful. He did not like it if working people operated through organizations that made demands. Although he praised moderate trade unionism in relatively quiet times, as in 1900–1909 and 1945–1955, he took a firmer line when trade union demands were accompanied by disorder or when they challenged the existing social order. As home secretary in 1910–1911, he was responsible for public order and so took a firm law-and-order line; in 1926 he believed that the General Strike was a serious challenge to the British constitution.

In facing such challenges, Churchill's army career influenced his behaviour. In serious labor unrest in South Wales and Liverpool, he was not on the side of the employers or the strikers; if he was on the side of anyone, he was concerned for the troops or police brought in to preserve or reestablish law and order. In these instances, as at the siege of Sidney Street, East London, in January 1911, and also at Antwerp in 1914, he was especially interested in the operational side of matters.

Churchill's reverence for the British constitution was marked by an old-fashioned romantic, even fawning, respect for the monarchy. When in office, he made much of his role as the king's servant, and, later, the queen's servant. This did not stop him from pressing his case on occasion, to the annoyance of King Edward VII or even

King George V. In 1936, he damaged his political reputation in seeking too long to uphold Edward VIII's preferences in the 1936 abdication crisis. Clementine Churchill, who felt that her husband was wrong over Edward VIII and Mrs. Simpson, warned him that Baldwin was in tune with public opinion. When the Churchills attended the coronation of King George VI and Queen Elizabeth, Churchill was moved to tears when the royal couple made their vows, saying to his wife that Baldwin had been right and Mrs. Simpson "wouldn't have done." With the accession of Queen Elizabeth II, he delighted in playing the venerable elder statesman to the young queen, following Lord Melbourne in this role 115 years earlier after the accession of Queen Victoria.

Churchill's political outlook also included a lifelong commitment to the British Empire. He saw action in India, the Sudan, and South Africa. Like Disraeli, he saw India as the pearl in the crown of the empire; Churchill was criticized by many in the 1930s who believed his understanding of India had not progressed since the 1890s, when he had served there in the army. Churchill had supported the moderate Indian reforms brought forward after the First World War and had condemned General Reginald Dyer for the Amritsar massacre, 1919. He set back his ministerial career by eight years when he left the Opposition front bench in January 1931 over the viceroy's decision to release Mahatma Gandhi from prison and by his vigorous opposition to putting the prospect of eventual self-government "before the gleaming eyes of the excitable millions" in India. He applied his formidable powers of language to denouncing Indian nationalists, just as earlier he had condemned "the foul baboonery of Bolshevism."

Churchill's career was marked by his strong regard for the United States, which he regarded almost as an honorary U.K. dominion. From his American mother he had imbued a transatlantic culture. She had initiated and edited the *Anglo-Saxon Review.* Under the Anglo-Saxon name, she observed in its first preface, "just laws, high purpose, civilizing influence, and a fine language have been spread to the remotest regions." Lady Randolph and Winston Churchill tended to see the English-speaking peoples as having evolved into a highly effective race. Winston Churchill long wished to recount the history of these peoples, the British, the Americans, and the people of the dominions, and began his *A History of the English Speaking Peoples* in the mid-1930s. When the first volume was published in 1956, he offered the book as "a personal view on the processes whereby English-speaking peoples throughout the world have achieved their distinctive position and character." Also, after referring to the Anglo-American alliance in the Second World War, he referred to the cold war era, commenting that whether things went well or not, there was "a growing feeling that the English-speaking peoples might point a finger showing the way."

In the late 1930s, Churchill had faith that the United States would enter the war. In contrast, Neville Chamberlain was pessimistic. Churchill as prime minister focused much effort on trying to convince the United States that Britain could and would fight, if helped with the necessary resources. His great speeches were aimed at opinion leaders in the United States as well as at the morale of the British people.

Churchill also had a strong affection for France, for its people and for its culture. He had been impressed by the French army before the First World War, attending maneuvres in September 1907, and on the Western Front during the First World War. Having himself served in the trenches he thereafter shared the feeling of a special camaraderie between those who had survived that experience. In the 1920s, he hoped for French concessions on the Treaty of Versailles to reduce tension with Germany, but by the later 1930s, after Adolf Hitler had come to power in Germany, he argued for an Anglo-French military alliance. With the invasion of France and the crumbling of French resistance in 1940, he offered union between the two countries. Later, in spite of clashes with Charles de Gaulle, Churchill generally backed de Gaulle and the Free French, in spite of Franklin D. Roosevelt's doubts.

After the Second World War, Churchill, anxious about Soviet Russia, spoke of the need for "a kind of united states of Europe" at Zurich in September 1945. Churchill still put the empire first, but he did attend the early meetings of the United Europe Movement and the Council of Europe and was a president of the European Movement. In the foreword he contributed to the European Movement's book, *European Movement and the Council of Europe* (1949), he wrote not only of its peaceful moral conception but also that its "physical strength will be such that none will dare molest her tranquil sway."

Churchill drew much strength from his deep sense of history and from his long experience. Lord Woolton later recalled Churchill commenting, "The longer you can look back, the further you can look forward." Churchill in making his defiant speeches in 1940 was aware of Queen Elizabeth I's oratory at Tilbury in the face of the threatened Spanish invasion of 1588, when she declared to her troops that she was resolved "to live or die amongst you all, to lay down . . . my honour and my blood even in the dust." It was a speech he printed in the second volume of *A History of the English Speaking Peoples* (1956).

Churchill combined his courage and his sense of the past with his formidable use of the English language. Lord Halifax later wrote of Churchill as the voice of the British people's "indomitable refusal to accept the verdict of reason" in 1940, commenting that he was "the unflinching spokesman, in language that will live wherever men speak the English tongue." He

added that working on speeches with Churchill was "a good education in the use of English—monosyllables wherever possible, and always Anglo-Saxon derivatives in preference to Latin."

Churchill provided unambiguous and well-focused leadership to Britain during the Second World War. Although a great imperialist, he could see no future for Britain and its empire in a world where Nazi Germany dominated continental Europe. Although Professor John Charmley and others have challenged the assumptions he made in 1940–1941, most historians have agreed with Churchill's view. He epitomized British defiance and the will to fight on.

This is not to say he had no drawbacks as a leader. He presided over several major failures, not least the loss of the *Prince of Wales* and the *Repulse* off Malaya and the surrender of Singapore. He was inclined to come to hasty judgements on the effectiveness of commanding officers, being hard, for example, on Auchinleck. It is said that an effective prime minister needs to be a good butcher; Churchill, on occasion, could be too good at dispatching senior officers. He could also be unforgiving to those who gave him unpalatable advice, whether they be major or lesser figures. For a while, he ostracized Sir Walter Monckton for his advice on the governorship of Malta; and in 1941 he ended the civil service career of Frank Pick, the deputy head of London Transport, when he refused to massage the statistics of aircraft losses in the way Churchill wished.

Nevertheless, Churchill was a great war leader. Harry Hopkins reported to Roosevelt in January 1941, "Churchill is the gov't in every sense of the word—he controls the grand strategy and often the details—labour trusts him—the army, navy, air force are behind him to a man." Churchill commanded respect from the Allies and was a sufficiently powerful personality to uphold Britain's place at the later major wartime conferences, even as Roosevelt was recognizing the economic and relative military weakening of Britain. Although Churchill famously stated that he did not intend to preside over the liquidation of the British Empire, he was the British leader when the war sapped the empire's strength and undercut its prestige, especially in the Far East.

Lord Hankey felt that Churchill should have retired gracefully after the 1945 general election defeat. The publication in 1966 of the diaries of Lord Moran, Churchill's doctor, which covered 1940–1960, harmed his later reputation, especially for his last government. Not surprisingly, his doctor's diaries related much ill-health and despondency concerning his declining health in old age. This view was combated by the collection of memoirs of those who had worked with him, *Action This Day* (ed. J. Wheeler-Bennett, 1968), and later by Anthony Seldon's reassessment of his 1951–1955 government *(Churchill's Indian Summer,* 1981). Although Seldon claimed too much in arguing that "he has some claim to be regarded as the most considerable British Prime Minister since the war," Churchill's last government should not be seen as a failure, nor his role in it, at least until his serious stroke in late June 1953. In retrospect, Churchill's concern to show that the Conservatives were not the enemy of organized labor has been much criticized by historians and later Conservative politicians as being damaging in terms of inflation. Indeed, some made this criticism at the time.

Churchill was a major international figure after the Second World War. He genuinely believed that he could do much through summit diplomacy to mitigate the dangers of the cold war. He succeeded in securing a major conference with President Dwight D. Eisenhower and the French at Bermuda in June 1953, but he failed to gain agreement for a summit conference with Joseph Stalin's successors. Eisenhower recalled of Churchill in Bermuda in his *The White House Years: Mandate for Change* (1963), "Although the years had aged the Prime Minister, adding in the process a new weapon to his defensive armament—a partial deafness that he seemed to turn on and off to suit his purposes—time had not dulled his mind or tongue."

Churchill was obsessed by history; he often ruminated about the lessons of history, the development of Britain through the ages and, perhaps, above all, his own place in history. Isaiah Berlin in his essay, "Mr. Churchill in 1940" (1949), observed, "The clear, brightly coloured vision of history, in terms of which he conceives both the present and the future, is the inexhaustible source from which he draws the primary stuff out of which his universe is so solidly built." Churchill sought fame all his adult life and he greatly surpassed his father. Greatness became him well. But, as he always feared he would, he faded fast after the pursuit and tenure of power ended in 1955. When Lady Violet Bonham Carter visited him in July 1960 and commented on his "voracious appetite for life," he replied that it had gone since he had left office five years earlier.

By the time of his death in 1965, Churchill was a legendary figure. His state funeral on 30 January 1965 was a major national event, just as that of the duke of Wellington had been over a century earlier. Churchill's was seen by millions as it was televised, a five-hour major broadcast. Churchill commemoratives were produced in huge quantities, matching or surpassing the volume of output in honor of Abraham Lincoln, William Ewart Gladstone, Benjamin Disraeli, and David Lloyd George. His memory has been honored by statues from Brunei to Nova Scotia, from Fulton to Washington, D.C., from Copenhagen and Oslo to Luxemburg. Places have been named after him in France and in numerous other countries, and hundreds of stamps have been issued in his honor.

In 1964, the British historian A. J. P. Taylor marked Churchill's ninetieth birthday with an essay that concluded, "He was the saviour of his country and the saviour of freedom throughout the world." Revisionist historians have come and gone, but for most, Churchill's wartime leadership, for all its faults, was his finest hour and the struggle against Nazi Germany was crucial for freedom and democracy.

Winston Churchill

A Biographical Companion

Abbey Division of Westminster By-Election (1924)

The Abbey division of Westminster was a very safe Conservative seat. In the 1922, 1924, 1929, and 1935 general elections, the Conservative candidate gained between 74 and 80.8 percent of all votes cast; in the 1918, 1923, and 1931 general elections, the Conservative was returned without a contest. In a by-election in 1921, an Anti-Waste candidate (one demanding less public expenditure and being to the political right of a Conservative candidate supporting the coalition government of David Lloyd George) polled just under 35 percent of the vote. In a by-election in March 1924, Winston Churchill came within forty-three votes (35.8 to 35.9 percent of the votes cast) of beating the Conservative candidate.

When the Conservatives under Stanley Baldwin lost their majority in the House of Commons in the December 1923 general election, and with Churchill unsuccessful as a Liberal candidate, the Labour Party was the largest of the Opposition parties. Though the Labour and Liberal parties had both opposed tariffs, the main issue in the election, Churchill urged the Liberals to combine with the Conservatives to prevent Labour from forming a government. In February 1924, the London *Times* published a letter from Churchill urging Liber-

als in Burnley not to vote Labour in a by-election in which there was no Liberal candidate. He followed this by announcing that as an Independent, he would contest a by-election in the Abbey Division of Westminster. Baldwin personally was willing to help Churchill secure the official Conservative nomination but, after discussing the matter with Austen Chamberlain, a former Conservative Party leader and a colleague of Churchill's in Lloyd George's governments, decided that it was too soon for Churchill to change his party allegiance back to the Conservatives. Churchill's own approaches were unsuccessful. Apparently, he was invited to address the Abbey constituency Conservative Association at a selection meeting on the condition that he accepted the decision of the selectors. This he declined to do. The local Liberals ran a candidate explicitly to block Churchill.

During the campaign, some prominent Conservatives, notably Leo Amery, campaigned against Churchill, but others supported him. After Amery published a letter in the *Times* supporting Otho Nicholson, the official candidate, Arthur Balfour, the former Conservative leader and prime minister, published a letter wishing Churchill success. The controversy surrounding Churchill's candidature secured a high voter turnout for a by-election: 61.6 percent compared with 38.5 percent in the same constituency for the 1921 by-election.

The Conservative leadership successfully found Churchill a safe seat. He accepted the Conservative invitation to stand as the Constitutionalist candidate for Epping on 11 September 1924.

Suggestions for further reading:
Cook, Chris. 1973. "By-Elections of the First Labour Government." In *By-Elections in British Politics,* edited by Chris Cook and John Ramsden. London: Macmillan.
Cowling, Maurice. 1971. *The Impact of Labour 1920–1924.* Cambridge: Cambridge University Press.
Craig, F. W. S. 1969. *British Parliamentary Election Results 1918–1949.* Glasgow: Political Reference Publications.
Gilbert, Martin. 1976. *Winston S. Churchill.* Vol. 5. London: Heinemann.

Abdication Crisis (1936)

Winston Churchill seriously damaged his political reputation in persistently championing Edward VIII during the abdication crisis. Churchill allowed his romantic attachment to the monarchy and his personal liking for Edward to cloud his judgement.

Churchill, like most politicians and members of London's genteel society, knew of King Edward VIII's happy yet illicit relationship with Mrs. Wallis Simpson. In July 1936, when consulted by the king's legal adviser, Walter Monckton, Churchill advised strongly against Mrs. Simpson's seeking a divorce from her second husband. This was not advice appreciated by Wallis Simpson and Edward, and she went ahead to secure her divorce. On 16 November 1936, three weeks after Mrs. Simpson secured the decree nisi, the king informed Stanley Baldwin that he intended to marry her. Baldwin, the cabinet, and senior members of both houses of Parliament expressed their opposition. Churchill told Lord Salisbury privately that he shared this view and wished to advise the king that many had made great sacrifices for their country in the war, there-fore the king should do so also by not marrying Mrs. Simpson. Churchill also hoped that Beaverbrook would be successful in convincing Mrs. Simpson to withdraw her petition for divorce before it was made absolute, thereby ending the crisis. When the king and Mrs. Simpson made clear their intention to marry, Baldwin, with the backing of the leaders of the other political parties, was emphatic that the king would have to abdicate if he persisted with this intention.

On 3 December 1936, the king asked Baldwin whether he could consult Churchill, "an old friend with whom he could talk freely." This he did the next day. Early on 4 December, Baldwin, having declined the king's request to make a public broadcast, deeming it to be "thoroughly unconstitutional," urged the king to make a very quick decision. Churchill saw the king that evening, offering as his main advice that the king should "have full time for his decision." He also urged that the king should not leave the country and he should have his physicians check that he was in a fit state to make such a decision. Churchill saw Lord Beaverbrook, another supporter of the king, and sent Baldwin a full account of the meeting.

Churchill also released a statement to the press, published on 6 December, which argued that the king must be granted time for his decision. Baldwin and his colleagues, however, wanted a quick decision, at the very least before Christmas. Beaverbrook shrewdly told Churchill on 5 December that "Our cock won't fight." Churchill, after talks at Chartwell with friends, among them Robert Boothby and Archibald Sinclair, suggested to the king as a possible solution a statement to the effect that the king would not marry contrary to the advice of his ministers, a situation that would not occur until April 1937 when Mrs. Simpson's divorce became absolute. The king, however, felt that this would only postpone matters, his resolve to marry Mrs. Simpson being firm.

Churchill, not knowing the king's response to this solution, went to the House of Commons on 7 December. When he rose during question time to argue that the House should take "no irrevocable step" before receiving a full statement, and to justify his own actions, he was howled down. Even most of his usual supporters felt his intervention was a grave misjudgment that was damaging to the king's position. Boothby estimated that only seven members of Parliament would have supported him. Some members suspected Churchill, as well as Beaverbrook, of taking up the king's cause to politically embarrass Baldwin.

Churchill was shattered by such a serious rebuff. At the time it was felt that he had undone two years' work of steadily restoring himself to the forefront of British politics; but it is most likely that the impact of this political misjudgment was not that bad, other than initially. Churchill informed Lord Salisbury on 9 December that his main difference with Baldwin and his colleagues was that he judged an abdication to be a far graver disaster than they did. In fact, Churchill had misjudged the strength of the king's determination to marry Mrs. Simpson and that he had no intention of changing his mind. In spite of Mrs. Simpson's offering on 9 December to withdraw her petition for divorce, the king signed a deed of abdication on 10 December. Baldwin took it to the House of Commons that afternoon. In the debate that followed, Churchill said that all recrimination and controversy should now end and that he accepted that the king had abdicated "freely, voluntarily, spontaneously, in his own time and in his own way." Leopold Amery noted in his diary that Churchill had "in an admirably phrased little speech executed a strategical retreat."

When Churchill lunched with Edward at his home, Fort Belvedere, on 11 December, he gave advice on Walter Monckton's draft of Edward's broadcast to the nation.

According to Edward, Churchill had tears in his eyes and quoted some lines of verse by Andrew Marvell on the beheading of King Charles I. He was in tears again at Chartwell when he heard Edward's address to the nation broadcast on the radio. In later private correspondence, Churchill expressed his belief that the abdication had been "altogether premature and probably quite unnecessary."

Related entries:
Edward VII, King; Monckton, Walter Turner

Suggestions for further reading:
Beaverbrook, Lord. 1966. *The Abdication of King Edward VIII*. Edited by A.J.P. Taylor. London: Hamish Hamilton.
Gilbert, Martin. 1976. *Winston S. Churchill*. Vol. 5. London: Heinemann.
Windsor, Duke of. 1951. *A King's Story*. London: Cassell.
Ziegler, Philip. 1990. *King Edward VIII*. London: Collins.

Addison, Christopher (Viscount Addison of Stallingborough, 1869–1951)

Between 1910 and 1922, Churchill and Viscount Addison maintained amicable relations as fellow reforming Liberals and then as Liberal coalitionist supporters of David Lloyd George. Their main difference was over intervention in Bolshevik Russia. Churchill was by far the more charismatic figure, yet Addison also enjoyed a long ministerial career (1914–1951), but as a member of the Labour Party after he had left the Liberals.

Christopher Addison was born in Hogsthorpe, Lindsey, in east Lincolnshire on 19 June 1869. His father was a tenant farmer. He moved on to a larger farm at Stallingborough, near Grimsby. Christopher Addison bought the Hogsthorpe farm in 1919 and then managed it. Educated at a local school in Wainfleet and then at Trinity College, Harrogate, he went on to study medicine in Sheffield and at St. Bartholomew's Hospital in London. After working briefly as a doctor, he taught at Sheffield Medical School and then, when Sheffield University was established in 1897, he was its first holder of the Arthur Jackson Chair of Anatomy. In 1901, he returned to London to posts at Charing Cross Hospital and St. Bartholomew's.

Addison was radicalized by his work among those suffering ill-health in the East End and other parts of London. His first wife, Isobel MacKinnon Gray, whom he married in 1902, was a Christian socialist and was therefore supportive of his radical politics. In 1907, he became the Liberal candidate for Hoxton, in the East End, winning the seat in the January 1910 general election. In the House of Commons, he provided an expert link between Lloyd George and the medical profession during the controversies over the introduction of National Health Insurance in 1911. Addison also advocated labor, negotiating with Churchill (as home secretary) the creation of a Union of City Hawkers.

During the First World War, Addison entered junior office as parliamentary secretary to the Board of Education. His career ascended when, in May 1915, he joined Lloyd George at the Ministry of Munitions as an under secretary of state. Addison was not only Lloyd George's loyal lieutenant in that office but also the person in the House of Commons who sounded out Liberal members of Parliament as to whether they would support a Lloyd George government. Addison himself lost faith in Herbert Henry Asquith, the Liberal prime minister from 1908 to 1916, over the failure to secure a Home Rule settlement after the Easter Rising in Dublin in 1916. In Lloyd George's government, Addison was initially minister of munitions, a post he held from December 1916 until Churchill succeeded him on 17 July 1917. Addison was supportive when

Lloyd George strengthened the Liberal part of the coalition government and saw Churchill's return as especially important, offering on 4 June 1917 to have the ministry's estimates organized quickly "so as to pave the way for Winston if you wished him to follow me." Addison moved on to head the new Ministry of Reconstruction. He also continued to be one of the main organizers of Lloyd George's support within the Liberal Party, and he and Churchill usually agreed about political issues.

In January 1919, Addison became president of the Local Government Board and prepared the way for the Ministry of Health. This was set up in June 1919, with Addison as its first minister. Churchill supported Addison's housing program, but they differed over intervention in Bolshevik Russia. That apart, their relations were good and they both supported "fusion," the continuance of Lloyd George's coalition government with the coalition Liberals and coalition Conservatives merged. However, when Addison's housing program came under Conservative attack for its cost, Lloyd George no longer fully supported him and he resigned from the government in July 1921.

After the fall of Lloyd George's government in 1922, Addison moved to the Labour Party (standing unsuccessfully as a Labour candidate in the 1924 general election), while Churchill and several other coalition Liberals moved to the Conservative Party. In the 1929 general election, Addison was elected M.P. for Swindon and returned to junior office as parliamentary secretary to the Ministry of Agriculture, succeeding as minister there in June 1930. He lost his Swindon seat in the 1931 general election, regained it in a by-election in 1934, but lost it in the 1935 general election. In 1937, he was elevated to the House of Lords as Baron Addison of Stallingborough.

In the House of Lords, Addison was a notable critic of appeasement. Through Wing Commander Charles Torr Anderson, one of Churchill's advisers on defense, Addison was briefed on matters concerning power. Anderson informed Addison in March 1938 that Churchill deemed him "a good ally to have." Addison in turn gave input into the Labour Party leadership's thinking on air defense.

Addison was the Labour Party's leader in the House of Lords from 1940 to 1951. Churchill offered him no ministerial post but did offer him in 1941 the post of vice chairman of the Development Commission, to assist agricultural policy. Addison declined, concentrating on his role in the House of Lords. With the return of Labour to office under Clement Attlee, Addison was close to the prime minister and successively held the posts of secretary of state for dominion affairs (1945–1947), secretary of state for Commonwealth relations (1947), lord privy seal (1947–1951), and finally, succeeded Herbert Morrison as lord president of the council (1951).

Before the October 1951 general election, Addison learned that he was terminally ill. He died on 11 December 1951.

Suggestions for further reading:
Gilbert, Martin. 1975. *Winston S. Churchill.* Vol. 4. London: Heinemann.
Minney, R. J. 1958. *Viscount Addison, Leader of the Lords.* London: Odhams.
Morgan, Kenneth, and Jane Morgan. 1980. *Portrait of a Progressive: The Political Career of Christopher, Viscount Addison.* Oxford: Clarendon Press.

Adenauer, Konrad (1876–1967)

Churchill was able to do business with Konrad Adenauer as an anti-Nazi, anticommunist, conservative politician. Churchill took care to treat Adenauer and West Germany with respect, saying of him in the House of Commons on 11 May 1953 that he may well be "the wisest German statesman since the days of Bismarck."

Konrad Adenauer was born in Cologne in 1876. After studying at the Universities of Freiburg, Munich, and Bonn, he became a lawyer in Cologne. From 1917 to 1933, he was chief burgomaster of Cologne and from 1920 until 1933 president of the Prussian State Council. He was a leading figure in the Catholic Centre Party. He was dismissed from all his offices by the Nazis and imprisoned in 1934 and 1944. At the end of the Second World War, he was a founder of the Christian Democratic Party and was briefly chief burgomaster of Cologne again. From September 1949 to October 1963, when he retired, he was the first federal chancellor of West Germany, and from 1951 until 1955, he was foreign minister as well.

Adenauer was resolutely hostile to the Soviet Union. His policy was, as he put it, "The part of Germany not occupied by Russia is an integral part of Western Europe." Churchill and Adenauer met in London in December 1957, where Churchill spoke warmly of the need for better Franco-German relations and tried to reassure that any détente with the Soviet Union would not be at the expense of West Germany. Adenauer was in no hurry for German reunification, resisting suggestions of a reunited neutral Germany, instead wanting a West Germany linked into Western Europe with eventually a reunited Germany of similar political complexion. He did what he could to persuade Churchill and other Western leaders to admit West Germany into membership of Western organizations, including the setting up of a European Defence Community with West Germany a member.

Churchill wanted to see Adenauer remain in office in West Germany. This tempered his enthusiasm in 1953 for trying to improve relations with the Soviet Union by way of negotiating a reunited neutralized Germany. The Foreign Office was told by one of Adenauer's advisers that Adenauer was "scared stiff" by Churchill's attitude at this time.

For all this, Adenauer was not as great a "Cold Warrior" as many West German politicians. Like Churchill, he was enthusiastic about building good Franco-German relations and he was keener than Churchill to move toward European integration.

Generally, Adenauer respected Churchill. This respect was reflected when Adenauer went out of his way to visit the ailing ex-premier at Roquebrune on 13 February 1958, and in his London home on 18 November 1959; and also when Adenauer sent Churchill gifts for his eightieth and eighty-fifth birthdays. Adenauer retired in 1963 and died in 1967.

Suggestions for further reading:
Gilbert, Martin. 1988. *Winston S. Churchill.* Vol. 8. London: Heinemann.
Schwarz, Hans-Peter. 1995. "Churchill and Adenauer." In *Winston Churchill: Studies in Statesmanship,* edited by R.A.C. Parker. London: Brasseys.
Young, John. 1996. *Winston Churchill's Last Campaign: Britain and the Cold War 1951–1955.* Oxford: Oxford University Press.

Admiralty, First Lord of (1911–1915)

Churchill became first lord of the admiralty on 25 October 1911. The post was then especially attractive to him given Anglo-German naval rivalry. He had long been a firm believer that British security should be dependent on a powerful navy. The main exception to his championing such a view was in 1908–1909, when he had joined David Lloyd George in resisting an immediate increase in dreadnought building from four to six. He and Lloyd George had rightly felt that fears over increased German battleship building were false alarms (though after the First World War, he conceded that the extra British naval building that arose from this panic had proved very valuable in the later part of the war).

In the aftermath of the Agadir crisis of July 1911, Churchill had taken a great interest in naval and military matters. Because of this, as well as his political drive, Herbert Henry Asquith chose him rather than Lord Haldane to succeed Reginald McKenna at the admiralty in October 1911.

Churchill readily took to the navy and immersed himself in naval matters. In his first eighteen months as first sea lord he spent 182 days at sea. He also visited all the major ships and the various naval dockyards and other naval establishments. In involving himself in policy issues and the efficient running of the navy, he was far more proactive than his recent predecessors. However, this led to controversy, as the sea lords felt with some cause, that Churchill was interfering in their areas of responsibility. There was also outrage at Churchill's proneness to consult junior officers and to back their views against those of their superiors, thereby undercutting naval discipline. Such friction was at its worst mostly in the first two years; later there was growing respect for Churchill's drive and his championing of the navy's interests.

During Churchill's first tenure of the post of first lord, there were several notable reforms. One major reason for the change of political leadership there was Asquith's determination that a naval war staff should be set up and that the admiralty should prioritize the army's need to transport six divisions to France upon British involvement in a European war. Churchill removed the first sea lord, Sir Arthur Wilson, who was obstructive of these policies, and he converted the navy war council into an admiralty war staff, which was in effect from 8 January 1912. He also replaced the board of the admiralty, bringing in Admiral Sir Francis Bridgeman as first sea lord, Vice Admiral Prince Louis of Battenberg as second sea lord, and Captain William Pakenham as fourth sea lord.

In pressing ahead with reforms, Churchill was advised by Admiral "Jackie" Fisher, who had retired as first sea lord a year before Churchill became first lord of the admiralty.

British politician and First Lord of the Admiralty Winston Churchill with Mrs. Churchill and General Bruce Hamilton during army maneuvers on Salisbury Plain (Hulton/Archive)

Churchill would have brought the seventy-one-year-old admiral back from retirement if it had been politically feasible; but Fisher had upset too many people and his long-running feud with Lord Charles Beresford had been damaging to the navy. With Fisher's advice and encouragement Churchill improved the pay and conditions of the sailors (who had had only a one-penny-a-day pay increase since 1852), established the Royal Navy Staff College to train junior officers, founded the Royal Naval Air Service, built a class of fast battleships ("destroyers") that were oil-powered and equipped with large weapons, and accelerated the move from coal power to oil power.

Churchill, as first lord of the admiralty, now became an advocate of increased battleship building. Churchill had learned in advance from Kaiser Wilhelm II, via Sir Ernest Cassel, details of the proposed 1912 German Naval Law and informed Sir Edward Grey that "the facts are grim." He felt that unless the Germans made their six-year program a twelve-year one, the British program should be increased. In Glasgow on 9 February 1912, Churchill gave a major speech in which he said British naval power was defensive and essential for her safety, whereas for Germany it was a luxury because she was a great power through her army. He also went on to declare a policy of laying down two Dreadnoughts for each German one above the levels of the 1911 German Naval Law. He also offered Germany a "naval holiday," a temporary halt to accelerating naval construction.

Although the North Sea was the vital area for Britain, there was also concern about the Mediterranean. Without an alliance with France, Britain's pre-Dreadnought battleships would be outclassed by Austrian and Italian Dreadnoughts, a concern even if Austrian and Italian building was aimed at each other. Churchill, meeting with Lord Kitchener in Malta on 4 July 1912, had been willing to maintain two or three battle cruisers and four armored cruisers in the Mediterranean. The Committee of Imperial Defence required more so that it could maintain a one-power Mediterranean standard; Churchill succeeded in gaining cabinet approval for four battle cruisers and four armored cruisers, deemed to be sufficient to defeat any force that Austria could muster.

For Britain, the naval position in the Mediterranean worsened during the Italian war with Turkey in 1911–1912. The Italians gained naval bases at Tobruk in Tripoli and at the Dodecanese Islands, which could threaten the routes to the Suez Canal. Matters were made worse in November 1912 when Germany established a Mediterranean squadron. In response, Britain helped modernize the Turkish fleet and, on 17 July 1912, Churchill agreed to Anglo-French naval discussions on the condition that they would be without prejudice to each country's freedom of action. The French planned to send their new Dreadnoughts to the Mediterranean, and the British navy would protect the French Atlantic and Channel coasts. The naval conversations resulted in an agreement on 10 February 1913, which at least prepared the way for an alliance. In May 1914, after repeated requests from Russia, the cabinet agreed to naval conversations with Russia, but there were no great advantages for Britain.

In March 1913, Churchill repeated his offer of a "naval holiday" when bringing forward estimates that were 2.7 percent higher than those of the previous year and provided for five Dreadnoughts, eight light cruisers, sixteen destroyers, and several submarines. By that autumn there was greater pressure for greater naval expenditure in 1914–1915. In May 1913, the Canadian Senate rejected Sir Robert Borden's naval bill to build three Dreadnoughts for the defense of the British Empire. Italy built four Dreadnoughts, making a total of fourteen (with Austria) in the Mediterranean. In a speech at Manchester on 18 October 1913, Churchill repeated his "naval holiday" offer. At the Guildhall in London on 10 November 1913 he warned that the next naval estimates would be greatly increased given the other countries' naval building.

Churchill's demands for increased naval estimates led to a clash with his erstwhile ally, David Lloyd George. The chancellor of the exchequer made public his views that there was no need for increased armaments expenditure when Anglo-German relations were improving. Churchill and the sea lords were prepared to resign if the cabinet did not approve four new Dreadnoughts. For some weeks it seemed possible that the cabinet would fall apart over the naval estimates. The crisis ended in February 1914 with a compromise, a rise of 5.6 percent over the original 1913–1914 estimates and a promise to make a substantial reduction the following year. This compromise favored Churchill's views more than those of Lloyd George.

Ahead of the outbreak of war, on 26 July 1914, Churchill and Prince Louis of Battenberg stopped the Third Fleet from dispersing after practicing mobilization in the English Channel. The next day, Churchill prepared the navy to be ready for war should it occur; this included sending the First Fleet from the Isle of Wight to the North Sea and taking the measures necessary to appoint Vice Admiral Sir John Jellicoe the commander in chief if war broke out, replacing Sir George Callaghan earlier than had been arranged.

With the outbreak of war, the navy secured the swift transportation of the British Expeditionary Force to France, although other naval activities were more mixed in their success. A chapter of muddles caused the German battle cruiser *Goeben* and the light cruiser *Breslau* to pass through the eastern Mediterranean and reach Constantinople. In the North Sea, in spite of poor work by the war staff, the navy came off well in an engagement with German ships off Heligoland on 28 August 1914. At the Battle of Coronel, off South America, Sir Christopher Cradock's naval force was beaten by Admiral von Spee's modern cruisers and light cruisers on 1 November 1914. Churchill and Fisher responded with determination and decisiveness, sending two capital ships with all haste to the south Atlantic. In December, the British naval force sank all but one of von Spee's force off the Falklands. The following month, on 23 January 1915, Beatty failed to destroy a German force near the Dogger Bank, but again the Germans were discouraged from venturing into the North Sea. In addition to supervising the war at sea, Churchill took an active role in the defense of Antwerp. As Vice Admiral Sir Peter Gretton has commented, Churchill displayed "as-tonishing activity" in the opening months of the war and, as before, "took a more active part in the day-to-day running of the war at sea than any first lord in history." Gretton felt that, given the feebleness of the naval war staff, decisive and efficient leadership was needed.

The Churchill-Fisher combination came to grief, however, over the Gallipoli campaign.

Related entries:
Antwerp; Battenberg, Prince Louis Alexander of; Fisher, John Arbuthnot; Gallipoli

Suggestions for further reading:
Churchill, Randolph S. 1967 and 1969. *Winston S. Churchill.* Vol. 2 and companion vol. 2, part 3. London: Heinemann.
Churchill, Winston S. 1923. *The World Crisis.* Vols. 1 and 2. London: Thornton Butterworth.
Gretton, Vice Admiral Sir Peter. 1968. *Former Naval Person: Winston Churchill and the Royal Navy.* London: Cassell.
Mackay, Ruddock F. 1973. *Fisher of Kilverstone.* Oxford: Clarendon Press.
Marder, Arthur. 1961 and 1965. *From the Dreadnought to Scapa Flow.* Vols. 1 and 2. Oxford: Oxford University Press.
Roskill, Stephen. 1977. *Churchill and the Admirals.* London: Collins.
Wiemann, F. W. 1971. "Lloyd George and the Struggle for the Navy Estimates of 1914." In *Lloyd George: Twelve Essays,* edited by A. J. P. Taylor. London: Hamish Hamilton.

Admiralty, First Lord of (1939–1940)

Winston Churchill served as first lord of the admiralty for a second time from 3 September 1939 until 10 May 1940, this time in Neville Chamberlain's wartime National government. He was also a member of the war cabinet. On his appointment, the board of the admiralty signaled the fleet, "Winston is back." For Churchill, this marked not just an experienced politician's return after nearly a quarter of a century but also a vindication.

Winston Churchill as the first lord of the admiralty addressing the men of HMS **Exeter,** *after its return to Plymouth from the Battle of the River Plate and the sinking of the German battleship* **Admiral Graf Spee.** *(Hulton/Archive)*

Churchill's first sea lord was Admiral Sir Albert Dudley Pound (1877–1943), a less eccentric figure than Admiral Lord Fisher, who had proved to be Churchill's nemesis in 1915. Churchill later described his relationship with Pound as one of "friendship and mutual confidence." Churchill took vigorous control of the admiralty from the outset, sending out a constant stream of minutes that often exhorted action or sought information.

Although not advocating a return to the Dardanelles, Churchill's mind was fertile with schemes for naval action. These included "forcing a passage into the Baltic," seizing Narvik, the port for Swedish iron ore exports, and mining Norwegian territorial waters. He was also vigorous in proclaiming naval successes and losses, begin-

ning with the sinking of U-boats, but also the loss of the aircraft carrier *Courageous* in September 1939. In October, he reported the horrific loss of the *Royal Oak* and 786 men in Scapa Flow, when a U-boat breached the defenses; but in December he could report the brave action of three cruisers against the German battleship the *Graf Spee,* and in February 1940 the release of 299 prisoners from the *Altmark.*

Churchill and the navy failed to block or seriously impede the German invasion of Norway. However, the navy did destroy ten German destroyers in Narvik Fjord. The Allied campaign in central Norway weakened, and in late April 1940 the navy evacuated the troops from there. Disappointment over Norway provided the issue on which opposition to the Chamberlain government could focus, leading to Chamberlain's resignation on 9 May 1940.

Suggestions for further reading:
Churchill, Winston S. 1948. *The Second World War.* Vol. 1. London: Cassell.
Gilbert, Martin. 1983. *Winston S. Churchill.* Vol. 6. London: Heinemann.

Agadir (July 1911)

Churchill ascribed his belief in the bad intentions of Germany as stemming from the time of the Agadir crisis, July 1911. Then Churchill felt that Germany's action had put her in the wrong and made it necessary for Britain to give France diplomatic support, and even join France if the crisis led to war between Germany and France.

In May 1911 the French, who saw Morocco as their sphere of influence, occupied Fez. This move was intended to protect Europeans when a revolt erupted against the Sultan. The kaiser and his ministers, believing that the declaration of a French protectorate over all Morocco was imminent, sent the gunboat *Panther* to Agadir on 1 July, ostensibly to protect German commercial interests and citizens. The British were concerned not only that it was an affront to France but also that the Germans hoped to establish a naval base near the entrance of the Mediterranean, close to Gibraltar.

On 21 July 1911, in a major speech at the Mansion House, London, David Lloyd George warned Germany that Britain would not hold out for peace at any price if she were "treated where her interests were vitally affected as if she were of no account." When the German ambassador complained to Sir Edward Grey, the foreign secretary, Grey felt Germany might make a surprise attack on the British fleet and warned Reginald McKenna, the first lord of the admiralty, to alert the navy. Soon after, Churchill initiated the guarding of naval explosive magazines in London.

The Agadir crisis stimulated Churchill's interest in national defense. On 13 August 1911, he wrote a lengthy memorandum titled "Military Aspects of the Continental Problem" for the Committee of Imperial Defence's meeting on 23 August. In the memorandum he predicted that a German attack would have the French army falling back on Paris and the south by the twentieth day, but thereafter the German army would be extended to the full, and so vulnerable, by the fortieth day. In this situation it would be crucial for Britain to raise a substantial army. In the summer of 1914, Churchill's broad predictions proved correct.

Churchill's alertness contrasted with the remarkable unpreparedness of the admiralty during the Agadir crisis. This contrast most probably influenced Herbert Henry Asquith in moving Churchill to the admiralty later in 1911.

Suggestions for further reading:
Churchill, Randolph S. 1967. *Winston S. Churchill.* Vol. 2. London: Heinemann.
Churchill, Winston S. 1923. *The World Crisis.* Vol. 1. London: Thornton Butterworth.
Marder, Arthur. 1961. *From the Dreadnought to Scapa Flow.* Vol. 1. Oxford: Oxford University Press.

Air, Secretary of State for (1919–1921)

At David Lloyd George's request, Churchill took on responsibility for the Air Ministry as well as the war office from 10 January 1919. Churchill took considerable interest in the military side of aviation, but was less energetic in his support of the civil side.

Having been forbidden during the war, civil aviation resumed after the First World War on 1 May 1919. That month, Churchill invited his predecessor as secretary for air, Lord Weir, to chair a standing committee on civil aviation, which focused initially on imperial air routes. The key routes, given the limited performance of aircraft then, went via Egypt to South Africa and via Egypt to India and Australia. Churchill was unable to extract from the treasury the money needed to develop these routes, and a break in many services occurred by the end of February 1921. Sir Frederick Sykes, whom Churchill had removed as chief of the air staff and made air member in charge of civil aviation, later expressed bitterness about Churchill's absorption in military aviation at the expense of civil.

Churchill appointed Sir Hugh Trenchard as chief of the air staff. When Trenchard hesitated, feeling that there would be policy differences, Churchill suggested they both write notes on their policies and exchange them. Trenchard wrote his, but Churchill said that he had not had time to write notes but saw nothing to disagree with in Trenchard's. Soon after his appointment, Trenchard offered to resign because of ill-health, but Churchill insisted he take time to recuperate and then return.

Churchill was keen to develop air power for the cheaper yet effective defense of the British Empire. He believed air power would be especially important in the Middle East, where long lines of communication were difficult and expensive to protect. It had been used to the RAF's satisfaction against the "Mad Mullah" in Somaliland in 1919–1920. In February 1920, Churchill asked Trenchard to produce a scheme for the Air Ministry to control Mesopotamia by relying on airplanes, armored cars, and well-defended bases. Reliance on air power was adopted for Mesopotamia, with Churchill offering to save the government millions of pounds over army control. At the Cairo Conference, March 1921, Churchill and Trenchard outlined plans to reduce expensive military garrisons in Mesopotamia and to use eight squadrons of aircraft to achieve air control of the area. British airpower in the area was also deemed vital to back Emir Abdullah in Trans-Jordan. After Churchill

had left the Air Ministry (1 April 1921), from 1 October 1922 the Royal Air Force (RAF) took over the defense of Iraq under a treaty between Britain and Iraq made in conformity with the expectations of League of Nations for areas under mandates.

In 1922, during the government's drive for economies, Churchill was successful in resisting the proposals of Sir Eric Geddes's committee on reducing expenditure to break up the RAF and return its parts to the army and the navy.

Suggestions for further reading:
Boyle, Andrew. 1962. *Trenchard: Man of Vision.* London: Collins.
Gilbert, Martin. 1975. *Winston S. Churchill.* Vol. 4. London: Heinemann.
Reader, W. J. 1968. *Architect of Air Power: The Life of the First Viscount Weir of Eastwood, 1877–1959.* London: Collins.
Townshend, Charles. 1986. "Civilization and 'Frightfulness': Air Control in the Middle East between the Wars." In *Warfare, Diplomacy and Politics,* edited by C. J. Wrigley. London: Hamish Hamilton.

Alcohol

Winston Churchill enjoyed high-quality alcohol, especially champagne, brandy, and whisky. At lunchtime, he drank beer, especially with beef. A huge cigar and a large whisky and soda or a brandy were almost trademarks. He began heavy drinking as a young man in India. He drank too much for his own good, but was rarely out of control. One of his tragedies was that his son, Randolph, followed in this habit and it helped to undermine his career in politics.

In the early part of the Second World War, President Franklin D. Roosevelt and other Americans were concerned about the scale of his drinking. However, those who worked with Churchill claimed that his drinking was less heavy than many believed. His wartime private detective, Inspector W. H. Thompson, later wrote, "During a long evening of conferences, successive visitors would find Mr Churchill with a glass of whisky and soda at his elbow; but more often than not it would be the same drink which remained forgotten and hardly touched throughout the whole session."

One of his wartime secretaries, Marian Holmes, later recalled, "He was a regular drinker. He drank quite a lot of brandy after a huge meal. He drank with food. That was the point. . . . He never drank to the point of being worse for wear. I remember him once saying, 'I have taken more out of alcohol, than alcohol has taken out of me.' And that really summed it up."

Yet other accounts describe gargantuan quantities of alcohol consumed. Oliver Harvey recorded of one evening, when Churchill had clashed with Sir Anthony Eden, "The quantities of liquor he consumed—champagne, brandies, whiskies— were incredible."

Displaying loyalty, his staff later understated his consumption of alcohol; but even their comments suggest a problem. By 1953, Churchill was promising his doctor that he would cut down his alcohol consumption, but even then he joked that he was substituting cointreau for brandy.

Suggestions for further reading:
Clayton, Tim, and Phil Craig. 1999. *Finest Hour.* London: Hodder and Stoughton.
Harvey, John, ed. 1978. *The War Diaries of Oliver Harvey.* London: Collins.
Moran, Lord. 1966. *Winston Churchill: The Struggle for Survival, 1940–1965.* London: Constable.
Thompson, W. H. 1951. *I Was Churchill's Shadow.* London: Christopher Johnson.

Aldershot

Winston Churchill was based at Aldershot with the 4th Hussars from February until September 1895. At the beginning of 1894, Winston had written to Colonel John Palmer Brabazon (nicknamed by women "Beautiful Bwab" because of his good looks and inability to pronounce "r"), one of his mother's admirers, expressing his wish to join his cavalry regiment. Lord Randolph Churchill had wanted his son to join an infantry regiment but, with his death in January 1895, the way was clear for Winston to pursue his preference. So Lady Randolph pressed Brabazon, and then the duke of Cambridge, to allow Winston to join the 4th Hussars as he wished. Very soon, on 20 February 1895, Winston was commissioned and posted to the 4th Hussars.

He had already visited the regiment, staying with Brabazon from a Saturday until a Monday in late April 1894, and again on later occasions. He also knew Aldershot. While at Harrow, he had camped for the best part of a week at Aldershot at the end of the summer term, 1891. On 8 April 1892, he had won the Public School Fencing Championship at Aldershot (one of the many occasions when his father was too busy to travel to support him).

Churchill arrived at the regiment on 19 February 1895, even before his own room was prepared. He wrote to his mother that he had arranged with a local contractor to "furnish it palatially" with rented goods. He also noted that there were many Harrovians in the regiment.

At Aldershot, he improved his horse riding and indulged in both polo playing and steeplechasing. He also aroused controversy when he took part in a point-to-point race for the 4th Hussars Subalterns' Challenge Cup on 20 March 1895. Subsequently, the National Hunt Committee's stewards declared the race null and void. He was also involved in a campaign to persuade a man not to join the regiment and then, when he did, to leave it.

By October 1895, the 4th Hussars had marched to Hounslow, ahead of nine years' service in India. From Hounslow, Churchill took leave to go to New York and Cuba.

Related entries:
Churchill, Lady Randolph; Cuba

Suggestions for further reading:
Churchill, Randolph S. 1966. *Winston S. Churchill.* Vol. 1. London: Heinemann.
Churchill, Winston S. 1930. *My Early Life.* London: Thornton Butterworth.
Martin, Ralph G. 1972. *Lady Randolph Churchill.* Vol. 2. London: Cassell.

Alexander, Albert Victor (1885–1965)

Albert Victor Alexander was the big Cooperative movement figure in the Labour Party from the 1920s to the 1950s. He held office three times as first lord of the admiralty. In speaking up for the navy, Churchill and Alexander shared a common concern.

Alexander was born on 1 May 1885 in Weston-Super-Mare. After becoming a member of the Weston Cooperative Society in 1908, he moved up, being elected to its board in 1910 and becoming its vice president in 1919. He worked as a clerk in local government until 1920, when he became parliamentary secretary to the Cooperative Congress. As such, he ensured that the Cooperative movement's political concerns were presented in Whitehall. In November 1921, he was selected as prospective parliamentary candidate for Sheffield Hillsborough and won the seat in the 1922 general election. This he held from 1922–1931 and from 1935–1950 (when he was elevated to the House of Lords). In the first Labour government (1924), Alexander was parliamentary under secretary to the Board of Trade and in the second (1929–1931) he entered the cabinet as first lord of the admiralty. In this position, he vigorously rebutted accusations from Churchill in June 1930 that he had weakened Britain's naval strength. In a debate on the estimates on 21 July 1930, he observed of Churchill that his speeches were "always entertaining. . . . But he has learned nothing from his experience of the Great War."

In 1936, both Alexander and Churchill were critical of the National government's policies toward Germany on naval matters. Thereafter, as former first lords, they often both spoke up for the navy. Alexander, unlike many of his Labour colleagues, preferred Churchill to Lord Halifax as Chamberlain's successor. When Churchill became prime minister, his first appointment after the war cabinet was Alexander as first lord of the admiralty, the post Churchill was vacating. However, Churchill as first lord had demanded to be in the war cabinet. As prime minister, he created and took the post of minister of defense, chaired the defense committee of the cabinet, and kept the service ministers out of the war cabinet. Alexander and the other service ministers were left to organize and administer the forces for which they were responsible. Churchill on occasion noted the views of Alexander and the first sea lord, Sir Dudley Pound. This was so when they persuaded Churchill not to supply tanks to Egypt via the Mediterranean but rather send them on the longer, but safer, Cape route. Alexander, with Pound and Lord Beaverbrook, also convinced Churchill of the unpleasant need to fire on the French fleet off Oran, to prevent the fleet from being used by Germany.

During the Second World War, Churchill and Alexander had a good relationship, and they met nearly every day. Alexander never posed a political threat to Churchill. He offered capable, solid administration and commonsense advice. Like Ernest Bevin, Alexander was a down-to-earth Labour man whom Churchill found reliable. He might well have echoed Viscount Wavell's 1946 assessment of Alexander: "Straight, sensible and honest. The very best type of British Labour." In 1945, as chancellor of Bristol University, Churchill presented both Alexander and Bevin with honorary doctorates.

Alexander continued as first lord of the admiralty under Clement Attlee (1945–1946) before being appointed to the newly separate post of defense minister (1946–

1950) and then chancellor of the Duchy of Lancaster (1950–1951). His political career ended as Labour's leader in the House of Lords, 1955–1964.

Suggestions for further reading:
Roskill, Stephen. 1977. *Churchill and the Admirals.* London: Collins.
Tilley, John. 1995. *Churchill's Favourite Socialist: A Life of A. V. Alexander.* Manchester, UK: Holyoake Books.

Alexander of Tunis, Field Marshal Earl the Honorable Harold Rupert Leofric George (1891–1969)

Harold Alexander was in command of the British Expeditionary Force at the time of the evacuation from Dunkirk in 1940; was commander in chief in North Africa from November 1942; and from November 1944, he was Supreme Allied Commander in the Mediterranean.

Alexander was the third son of Lord Caledon. Educated at Harrow and Sandhurst, he was commissioned into the Irish Guards in 1911. He served on the Western Front during the First World War. He was wounded at the first Battle of Ypres, November 1914; received the Military Cross for his part in the Battle of Loos, September 1915; was given the DSO (Distinguished Service Order) for his part in the later stages of the Battle of the Somme, 1916; and took part in the major battles of 1917 and 1918. He volunteered to serve in Latvia, fighting the Bolsheviks at the end of the war. During the interwar years, he served at the Staff College and in India on the Northwest Frontier.

Alexander came to prominence in 1940 when he was put in charge of the outer defense of Dunkirk before the evacuation of British troops. In this he displayed courage and good organization. He also brought himself to Churchill's notice when he sent the premier's nephew, Johnny Churchill, to see his uncle and press for small boats to be sent so that troops could be brought back across the English Channel. On 22 June 1940, not long after his return from Dunkirk, Alexander joined Churchill at Chequers. His next active service was in Burma, where he organized the retreat from Rangoon into India, ahead of rapidly advancing Japanese forces.

In August 1942, Alexander succeeded General Sir Claude Auchinleck as commander in chief Middle East, with Bernard Montgomery as the Eighth Army Commander under him. After the successful second Battle of El Alamein, Alexander (in early 1943) was appointed ground forces commander in North Africa, commander Eighteenth Army Group, and deputy supreme commander to General Dwight Eisenhower. He reorganized the Allied forces and conducted a highly successful campaign in Tunisia. He attacked in May 1943, defeating the Axis forces in North Africa. He reported to Churchill on 13 May 1943, "All enemy resistance has ceased. We are masters of the North African shores."

Alexander was less successful in Sicily, where he did not sufficiently control his two colorful subordinates, General Montgomery and General George Patton. Yet Sicily was taken within thirty-eight days. The Allied advance in Italy was slower than had been hoped, with a war of attrition at Monte Cassino. Nevertheless, his forces took Rome on 4 June 1944, ahead of the Normandy landings. In November, he became supreme allied commander, Mediterranean Theatre. His spring offensive in 1945 led to the defeat of the German forces in Italy.

Alexander was appointed to the rank of field marshal in 1944, created a viscount in 1946, and admitted to the Order of Merit in 1959. He served as governor general of Canada, 1946–1952. Churchill appointed him minister of defense from 1 March 1952 until 18 October 1954, when he retired at his own request. Churchill had held the post himself in 1951–1952. Alexander provided eminence without a political challenge to Churchill. With Alexander in the post, Churchill continued to dominate policy making in this area. Overall, Alexander proved an ineffective cabinet minister and politician. Sir John Colville commented of Alexander, "He was Churchill's *beau idéal* of a soldier and the admiration was mutual."

Related entries:
Auchinleck, Field Marshal Sir Claude John Eyre; Montgomery, Bernard Law

Suggestions for further reading:
Colville, Sir John. 1985. *The Fringes of Power: Downing Street Diaries 1939–1955.* London: Hodder and Stoughton.
Hillson, Norman. 1952. *Alexander of Tunis.* London: W. H. Allen.
Jackson, W. G. F. 1971. *Alexander of Tunis as Military Commander.* London: Batsford.
Nicolson, Nigel. 1973. *Alex: The Life of Field-Marshal Earl Alexander of Tunis.* London: Weidenfeld and Nicolson.
North, John, ed. 1962. *The Alexander Memoirs 1940–1945.* London: Cassell.
Reid, Brian Holden. 1991. "Alexander." In *Churchill's Generals,* edited by John Keegan. London: Weidenfeld and Nicolson.
Seldon, Anthony. 1981. *Churchill's Indian Summer: The Conservative Government 1951–1955.* London: Hodder and Stoughton.

Amery, Leopold Charles Maurice Stennett (1873–1955)

*L*eopold Amery was a leading Conservative politician whose career was marked by his dedication to the causes of tariff reform and the British Empire. He and Churchill clashed over the issue of tariffs but were both early champions of rearmament in the 1930s. Churchill described Amery as "the straightest man in public life." Churchill and Amery were acquaintances (rather than warm friends) from Harrow, where Amery was one year ahead.

Amery was born on 22 November 1873 at Gorakhpur in northwest India, the eldest of three sons of Charles Frederick Amery and Elizabeth Amery. His father worked for the Indian Forest Department. His mother was Hungarian; she had left Hungary after the failure of the revolution in 1848. After Harrow, Amery went to Oxford—to Balliol College in 1892, and in 1897 he was elected a fellow of All Souls College. He then worked for the London *Times* as a war correspondent during the Boer War, and as a leader writer. He was editor and principal author of *The Times History of the War in South Africa, 1899–1902.* 7 vols. London: *Times,* 1900–1909. He was greatly influenced on imperial matters by Alfred Milner and on tariff reform by Joseph Chamberlain. Through Chamberlain's son Neville he secured the nomination for the South Birmingham (Sparkbrook) constituency, which he represented from 1911 to 1945.

Amery's career took off in the wake of Lord Milner's entry into David Lloyd

Undated portrait of Leopold Amery (Hulton/Archive)

George's war cabinet in December 1916. Then Amery became an assistant secretary to the war cabinet. From 1919 he held a junior ministerial office, initially under Milner and briefly, in 1921, under Churchill at the colonial office; thereafter at the admiralty, as parliamentary and financial secretary. Although Churchill remained loyal to Lloyd George in October 1922, Amery was one of the junior ministers who worked for the fall of the coalition government and its replacement by a Conservative government.

Churchill and Amery clashed over tariffs in the 1920s and differed, but less markedly, over imperial policy. Amery was first lord of the admiralty, 1922–1923, and the secretary of state for the dominions and colonies, 1924–1929. Churchill, who returned to office as chancellor of the exchequer from 1924 to 1929, remained a free trader while Amery pressed hard for protection. Amery always felt that Churchill's appointment by Stanley Baldwin "had converted his government into just that kind of Whig coalition which I had hoped the Tory party had escaped by breaking away from Lloyd George in 1922." In the 1930s, they were both out of office and both were early proponents of rearmament and vehement antiappeasers. When Chamberlain's government was crumbling, on 7 May 1940 Amery made one of the most famous conclusions to a twentieth-century speech in the House of Commons. Echoing Oliver Cromwell's words on dismissing the Long Parliament in 1653, Amery called for a real national government and told Chamberlain, "You have sat too long here for any good you have been doing. In the name of God go!"

In Churchill's wartime coalition government (1940–1905) and his caretaker government (May–July 1945), Amery was secretary of state for India. In the mid-1930s, Amery and Churchill had disagreed over India, Amery supporting moves to dominion status for India and Churchill opposing any form of Indian self-govern-ment. During the war, Amery was again far more radical than Churchill or the viceroy, Lord Linlithgow. He wanted to motivate the Indians by promising them independence after the war. Churchill was vehemently opposed to this and, in July 1940, vigorously intervened to stop any such move, bringing Amery to the brink of resignation. Churchill himself drafted a statement promising India dominion status at some unspecified time in the future, the "August offer" of 1940. This, as Churchill expected, would be rejected by the Indian leaders. Churchill later blamed Amery for the giving away (as he saw it) of India. Churchill and Amery did agree in wishing to oppose the United States from interfering in the affairs of the British Empire. During the war, however, Amery was often exasperated by what he felt was Churchill's inability to grasp various issues regarding India, such as those regarding a separate Muslim state and Anglo-Indian finance. He even passed a note in the cabinet room to Sir Archibald Wavell, the new viceroy, that Churchill "knows as much of the Indian problem as George III did of the American colonies." Although he admired Churchill in other respects, Amery thought the prime minister was off balance when he dealt with India.

In the 1945 general election, Amery lost his seat. Churchill offered to secure him a peerage, but Amery declined, not wishing to harm his son Julian's political career. Amery strongly supported Churchill's sentiments in favor of a united Europe and expressed approval at Zurich in September 1946 when he became a vice president of the United Kingdom Council of European Movement. When Amery died in 1955, Churchill paid tribute to "a great patriot."

Suggestions for further reading:
Amery, L. S. 1953 and 1955. *My Political Life*. 3 vols. London: Hutchinson.
Barnes, John, and David Nicholson, eds. 1980 and 1988. *The Leo Amery Diaries*. 2 vols. London: Hutchinson.

Louis, W. R. 1992. *In the Name of God Go! Leo Amery and the British Empire in the Age of Churchill.* New York and London: W. W. Norton.

Anderson, Sir John (Viscount Waverley, 1882–1958)

Sir John Anderson, 25 August 1945 (Hulton/Archive)

Sir John Anderson was one of the war cabinet ministers on whom Churchill most relied during the Second World War. He was an efficient but not colorful man and was never a warm friend of Churchill's (Clementine Churchill did not like him, either). Nevertheless, Churchill recognized his abilities and greatly relied on his efficient and effective work.

John Anderson was born in Edinburgh on 8 July 1882, the son of David Alexander Pearson Anderson and his wife, the former Janet Kilgour Briglemen. His father was a skilled printer who ran a stationer's shop; his mother was the daughter of a businessman in engineering and granddaughter of a German sailor. Anderson was educated at George Watson's College for Boys and won an Edinburgh University bursary. He graduated with first-class honors in mathematics and national philosophy. He went on to study chemistry at Leipzig. Because he wished to marry, he decided to take the civil service examinations, but before doing so he returned to Edinburgh University to take courses in economics and political science. In 1905, he took the civil service examinations and topped the list of successful candidates. He was appointed to a post in the colonial office in October 1905. He moved on to work for the National Insurance Commission, becoming its secretary in 1913. In 1917, he became secretary to the new Ministry of Shipping, a role that later involved him in providing advice on shipping matters at the Paris Peace Conference in 1919. After two other posts and a knighthood, in autumn 1919 he became chairman of the Inland Revenue. He then served as joint under secretary to the lord lieutenant of Ireland from 1920 to 1922; he became the permanent under secretary at the home office from 1922 to 1932; and was governor of Bengal from 1932 to 1937.

On Sir John Anderson's return to England, he was adopted as the National Government candidate for the Scottish universities, a by-election brought about by the death of Ramsay MacDonald. He won the seat on 28 February 1938. In May 1938, he was appointed chairman of a committee looking into "various aspects of the problem of transferring persons from areas which are likely to be exposed to continuous air attack." After the publication of the *Report of Committee on Evacuation* (1938), Anderson was the obvious person to reassure the public that the government took air-raid precautions seriously. When he entered the government as lord privy seal on 31 October 1938, Chamberlain named him the minister for civilian defense. With the outbreak of war, Anderson became home secretary with the additional post of minister of home security.

When Churchill became prime minister, he appointed Anderson lord president of the council, a position that enabled him to take responsibility for the home front while Churchill concentrated on his role as war leader. Churchill had worked with Anderson during the General Strike in 1926, when Anderson had displayed his exceptional organizational abilities in a crisis. He made Anderson a member of his war cabinet and put him at the head of a committee to overlook "the larger issues of economic policy," urging him "to take the lead prominently and vigorously in this committee." His role soon broadened and he was deemed to be, with Churchill and Ernest Bevin, one of the three key ministers of the central period of the war. General Jan Christian Smuts, the South African statesman, saw him as the equivalent of Milner in the First World War, a safe pair of hands to run the administrative machine.

With the sudden death of Sir Kingsley Wood, the chancellor of the exchequer, in September 1943, Churchill moved Anderson to that position. His first task was to introduce the pay-as-you-earn (PAYE) system of taxation, which his predecessor had prepared. In early 1945, when Churchill and Sir Anthony Eden were leaving the country for Yalta, Churchill advised King George VI to appoint Anderson should they both die, emphasizing that he was an Independent National member of Parliament. Anderson remained chancellor of the exchequer during Churchill's "caretaker government." He was acting head of the government while Churchill and Eden were at the Potsdam Conference.

Anderson held his seat in 1945. Although an Independent, he served in Chur-

chill's shadow cabinet and was an effective Opposition speaker in the House of Commons. With the abolition of the university seats, Anderson's career in the Commons ended. He declined Clement Attlee's thrice-made offer of a peerage and Churchill's of a safe Conservative seat. After his 1951 victory, Churchill offered Anderson a peerage and the post of chancellor of the Duchy of Lancaster. He rejected the post but accepted a viscountcy, which was announced in the New Year honors list of 1952. He continued with his lucrative directorships and other business positions. In 1957, Queen Elizabeth II conferred the Order of Merit on him.

John Anderson died on 4 January 1958. Churchill wrote to his widow, "John was a man of great courage, and his services to our country were of the highest order."

Suggestions for further reading:
Gilbert, Martin. 1986. *Winston S. Churchill*. Vol. 7. London: Heinemann.
Wheeler-Bennett, Sir John W. 1962. *John Anderson: Viscount Waverley*. London: Macmillan.

Antwerp

Antwerp, Belgium's largest port, depended on Dutch goodwill for access via the River Scheldt to the North Sea. In the early weeks of the First World War, there were fears that the Dutch might enter the war on Germany's side. This did not occur. However, it was evident that before long German forces would attack Antwerp.

From 9 September 1914, Churchill arranged for naval guns and ammunition to be sent to Antwerp for its defense. At Lord Kitchener's request, Churchill sent Admiral Henry Oliver to Antwerp in late September. He disabled thirty-eight German merchant ships by having explosives placed in their propelling machinery; this action allayed fears that they might be used in an invasion of Britain. Kitchener and Herbert Henry Asquith were especially anxious to reinforce Antwerp with heavy artillery and armed forces. Kitchener feared that the early German capture of Antwerp would lead to their soon taking the whole North Sea coast as far as Calais, thus threatening the British Expeditionary Force.

Matters became critical on 2 October 1914. The Belgian government doubted its ability to defend Antwerp much longer. With Asquith away in Cardiff, Kitchener and Sir Edward Grey, the foreign secretary, decided to consult Churchill. As he traveled from London to Dover on his way to Dunkirk, Churchill's train was reversed twenty miles from London; he joined Kitchener, Grey, Sir William Tyrrell, Grey's private secretary, and Prince Louis of Battenberg, the first sea lord, late that night. At this meeting, Churchill learned of a telegram that reported the Belgian government's decision to leave Antwerp the next day. At his suggestion, it was agreed to send the Royal Marine Brigade immediately from Dunkirk to Antwerp, with army reinforcements to follow. It was also agreed that Churchill should go to Antwerp, not Dunkirk, and report to Kitchener his views on how much longer Antwerp could resist the German attack. Churchill's presence would also stiffen the defenders' will to resist. Asquith, on his return, agreed that the Belgian withdrawal from Antwerp at that time was "a mad decision, quite unwarranted by the situation," and felt that Churchill would stiffen resistance but that his going in person was "one of the many unconventional incidents of the war."

Yet it worked. Antwerp held out until 10 October, and Churchill succeeded in stiffening the Belgian will to resist by his presence and by promising, and delivering, marine reinforcements. However, with no other troops immediately available, he had to use two naval brigades that he had created in August and were still in training. In asking Kitchener to send the brigades, he did specify that they should be "minus recruits." This exclusion was not made, and Churchill was criticized for sending in raw recruits to Antwerp. Churchill displayed bravery in touring Antwerp's defenses; one famous eyewitness account describes him wearing a naval hat and imperturbably smoking a large cigar while shells burst nearby.

Expected back at the admiralty on 5 October, that morning Churchill sent a telegram to Asquith, offering to resign from the cabinet and take command of the British forces relieving and defending Antwerp. According to Asquith, the cabinet received news of his offer "with a Homeric laugh." Kitchener, unlike the politicians, took it seriously, offering to commission Churchill as a lieutenant general and place him in charge of operations. Asquith recalled Churchill on 6 October because General Henry Rawlinson was arriving at Antwerp that afternoon. Churchill returned during the night of 6–7 October.

The cost of the marines' involvement at Antwerp were 57 dead and 158 wounded; 936 men were taken prisoner by the Germans and a further 1,500 men, who crossed into the Netherlands, were interned for the rest of the war.

Churchill was virulently criticized by the right-wing press—the London *Morning Chronicle* and the London *Daily Mail*. He rightly rebutted critics by pointing out that he acted in line with the policy of Asquith, Grey, and Kitchener and that there were no alternative troops immediately available. However, his colleagues felt that he glorified active service and (in the words of David Lloyd George) had "behaved in a rather swaggering way." Nevertheless, he had stiffened Belgian resistance when this appeared important, militarily and politically (as a message of Britain's support to a wronged neutral), and had displayed courage and determination.

Related entry:
Kitchener, Horatio Herbert

Suggestions for further reading:
Gilbert, Martin. 1971. *Winston S. Churchill*. Vol. 3. London: Heinemann.
Marder, Arthur J. 1965. *From the Dreadnought to Scapa Flow*. Vol. 2. Oxford: Oxford University Press.

Appeasement

*I*f not Churchill's finest hour, then some not far off were his hours in opposition to appeasement. It would be wrong to suggest that he was always consistently hostile to appeasement, but he nearly always was. Over the four to five years before the outbreak of the Second World War in Europe, Churchill was courageously and defiantly hostile to appeasing Adolf Hitler, even though it kept him out of cabinet office and might have cost him the Conservative Party nomination for his parliamentary seat.

Appeasement was the term applied to the British and French governments' attempts to satisfy Germany's grievances through a series of concessions. This policy began under Stanley Baldwin, with acquiescence in Hitler's occupation of the Rhineland in 1936, and reached its apogee under Neville Chamberlain at Munich in 1938.

For some on the imperial right of the British Conservative Party, Hitler and the Nazis were a threat to the British Empire. Churchill was vigorous in condemning Nazism in the House of Commons in November 1933, warning against "a philosophy of blood lust." Then he was isolationist. In November 1934, he made a major speech in the Commons in which he expressed his concern that Britain's air defenses were inadequate. Having given Baldwin ample warning of his speech, Baldwin himself responded emolliently. After Churchill returned to the theme in March 1935, Baldwin involved Churchill and Churchill's prickly protégé, Professor Frederick Lindemann, in the Air Defence Research Sub-Committee of the Committee of Imperial Defence and in the Air Ministry's scientific committee, respectively. Churchill's hopes of office were kept alive by Baldwin.

Churchill was unlikely to win the support of the Left while he was still praising Benito Mussolini and General Francisco Franco. However, Churchill was willing to talk the language of the League of Nations because he wanted to back the covenant with the threat of the French army and the British navy. For him, collective security represented an armed alliance. Churchill annoyed the Left by his lack of indignation when Mussolini invaded Abyssinia. However, he joined in criticism of Franco after the bombing of British ships in Spanish harbors in June 1938.

Churchill was optimistic for a while that a solution could be reached that would maintain Czechoslovakia and yet satisfy the Sudeten Germans. He, Lindemann, and Archibald Sinclair were unduly impressed by Konrad Henlein, chairman of the Sudeten German Party from 1933 to 1938, who was very much Hitler's man. However, Churchill was not under any illusions about Czechoslovakia for long. By August 1938 he was pressing Lord Halifax, the foreign secretary, to work for a joint warning by Britain, France, and Russia to Germany against a German invasion of Czechoslovakia. After Chamberlain's Munich agreement with Hitler, Churchill was vigorous in deploring it as "a total and unmitigated defeat" and in calling for greater rearmament. Churchill condemned his own party leader's policy, and was himself denounced by Chamberlain loyalists in his own constituency.

Churchill's stance was vindicated when Hitler seized the rest of Czechoslovakia in March 1939. Chamberlain carefully tried to resurrect appeasement to avoid war and also to keep Churchill out of office. Churchill, in April 1939, was still keen to join the government and help facilitate rapid rearmament. Chamberlain was equally keen to keep him out, and his supporters put forth the argument that Churchill's inclusion in the government would not help to avoid war but would be more likely to bring it about. Chamberlain's keeping Churchill out of office indicated to Soviet leaders that Chamberlain did not wish to make a final break with Germany. When war was unavoidable in early September 1939, however, Chamberlain did bring Churchill into his government.

As the historian R. A. C. Parker has observed, Churchill and Chamberlain shared common aims. "Both intended to preserve the independence of Britain and its Empire. Their methods were totally different."

Related entries:
Baldwin, Stanley; Chamberlain, (Arthur) Neville; Halifax, Earl of; Hoare, Sir Samuel John Gurney

Suggestions for further reading:
Gilbert, Martin. 1976. *Winston S. Churchill.* Vol. 5. London: Heinemann.
Parker, R. A. C. 1993. *Chamberlain and Appeasement: British Policy and the Coming of the Second World War.* London: Macmillan.
———. 2000. *Churchill and Appeasement.* London: Macmillan.
Stewart, Graham. 1999. *Burying Caesar: Churchill, Chamberlain and the Battle for the Tory Party.* London: Weidenfeld and Nicolson.

Ashley, Maurice Percy (1907–1994)

When Winston Churchill wrote a biography of the duke of Marlborough in 1929, he hired the young Maurice Ashley as his part-time research assistant. Ashley, who was of radical political inclinations, came to like and admire Churchill. He later helped Churchill with the seventeenth-century section of his *History of the English Speaking Peoples.*

Maurice Ashley was born on 4 September 1907, the son of Sir Percy Walter Llewellyn and Doris (née Hayman) Ashley. He was educated at St. Paul's School, London, and New College, Oxford, where he earned first-class honors in modern history in 1929.

After graduating, Ashley was approached by Keith Feiling (Randolph Churchill's tutor) of Christ Church, who asked Ashley whether he would be interested in becoming Winston Churchill's historical research assistant for his work on the duke of Marlborough. The post would be half-time at £300 per annum. Ashley was appointed after lunching with Churchill, Feiling, and Professor Frederick Lindemann in Lindemann's rooms in Christ Church.

Churchill expected to employ Ashley for two years for a two-volume book, but the two years became four (1929–1933) and the life of Marlborough became four volumes. Churchill's cousin, the ninth duke of Marlborough, gave Churchill, and so Ashley, access to the then closed papers of his ancestor, which were held at Blenheim Palace. Ashley visited other archives, including some in Vienna. Ashley often discussed the work in progress with Churchill at Chartwell. He later recalled, "We would invariably do an hour's work before lunch, an hour or two after tea." Then, after dinner and a game of backgammon, "about eleven pm the day's work would really begin."

Although Maurice Ashley was Churchill's main research assistant from 1929 to 1933, he also employed Lieutenant John Hely Owen (1883–1970) to advise on naval matters and Lieutenant Colonel Ridley Pakenham Pakenham-Walsh (1888–1966) to advise on military matters, which included visiting the sites of Marlborough's battles. After Ashley had finished, Churchill employed John Wheldon (b. 1911), a Balliol graduate, to be his resident research assistant at Chartwell from February 1934 to the autumn of 1935. He in turn was succeeded by F. W. D. Deakin (b. 1913), a fellow and lecturer at Wadham College, from April 1936 to the autumn of 1939.

After 1933, Ashley continued to help Churchill with his historical writing and, with Edward Marsh and others, he checked proofs. In 1939, when Churchill began working on his *History of the English Speaking Peoples,* Ashley was one of those he turned to for help with briefing papers. He supplied 10,000-word papers on Oliver Cromwell and on the Stuarts. In 1948, when Ashley sent a copy of one of his books to Churchill, he commented, "I shall always remember with gratitude that I learned more of the art of writing history from working for you than I did from my Oxford professors."

Ashley combined his work for Churchill with doctoral research, which resulted in his first book, *Financial and Commercial Policy Under the Cromwellian Protectorate* (1934). After working for Churchill, Ashley joined the editorial staff of the *Manchester Guardian* (1933–1937) and the London *Times* (1937–1939). He was editor of *Britain Today* (1939–1940) before serving in the army in the Grenadier Guards, then Intelligence Corps. After the Second World War, he was deputy editor (1946–1958), then editor (1958–1967) of *The Listener.* He was later a research fellow in the Department of Social Sciences and Economics, Loughborough University of Technology (1968–1970). Editor of *The Listener* at the time of Churchill's death, he published his own memories of Churchill and also wrote an introduction to *Tributes Broadcast by the BBC* (1965). He also published the substantial *Churchill as Historian* (1968). He was made a CBE (Commander of the British Empire) in 1978. He died on 26 September 1994.

Suggestions for further reading:
Ashley, Maurice. 1968. *Churchill as Historian.* London: Secker and Warburg.
Gilbert, Martin. 1976 and 1988. *Winston S. Churchill.* Vols. 5 and 8. London: Heinemann.

Asquith, Herbert Henry (First Earl of Oxford and Asquith, 1852–1928)

Asquith, as Liberal prime minister (1908–1916) and Liberal Party leader (1908–1926), was important in ad-

British Prime Minister Herbert Henry Asquith, 1894 (Hulton/Archive)

vancing Churchill's political career before the First World War. Churchill in these years admired Asquith, especially during the December 1910 general election. However, in May 1915, Asquith sacrificed Churchill (and Lord Haldane) when he formed a coalition government. Thereafter from 1917, while a Liberal, Churchill was one of David Lloyd George's leading supporters.

Herbert Henry Asquith, the younger son of a Morley (West Yorkshire) wool manufacturer, Joseph Dixon Asquith, was born on 12 September 1852. The family were Congregationalists. His father died in 1861; he was thirty-five. Asquith and his brother were brought up by their mother's family, initially by their wealthy grandfather, William Williams, and after his death by their uncle, John Williams. The boys were educated at the City of London School.

From there, Asquith won a classical scholarship to Balliol College, Oxford. There he gained first class honors, was elected to a prize fellowship, and shone in debating at the Oxford Union. He chose a career as a lawyer because this was the major route to a career in politics for those without money. As a poorly paid barrister, Asquith supplemented his income by writing for the *Spectator* and the *Economist*. Asquith came to the attention of William Gladstone's attorney general, Sir Henry James, through his legal work. In 1886, Asquith was elected to Parliament for East Fife, his predecessor having been against Irish Home Rule and for this reason deselected by the Gladstonian Liberals (but stood as Liberal Unionist).

Asquith soon came to the fore in politics. He served as home secretary from 1892 to 1895, and had he been sufficiently wealthy, he might well have succeeded Sir William Harcourt as Liberal leader in 1899. During the Boer War, Asquith became increasingly associated with Lord Rosebery and the Liberal Imperialists. With Sir Edward Grey and R. B. Haldane, he plotted to force Sir Henry Campbell-Bannerman to go to the House of Lords when a Liberal government was formed. This failed in December 1905, but Asquith became chancellor of the exchequer and succeeded Campbell-Bannerman as prime minister and Liberal leader in May 1908.

When Churchill made his maiden speech in the House of Commons on 18 February 1901, Asquith was one of the major politicians who was present to hear Lord Randolph's son. Asquith warmly congratulated him on it when he spoke. Churchill mixed socially with several leading Liberal Imperialists, including Lord Rosebery, Churchill's uncle, Lord Tweedmouth, and Sir Edward Grey. When he gave a lecture at St. Andrews University in September 1901, Asquith took the chair.

Churchill naturally had more contact with Asquith after he crossed the floor of the House of Commons on 31 May 1904

and joined the Liberal Party. They had ministerial connections from December 1905, when Churchill was an under secretary at the colonial office and Asquith was chancellor of the exchequer. Churchill took part in the proceedings of the cabinet committee, of which Asquith was a prominent member, by reviewing the proposals for constitutional settlements in South Africa. Asquith requested that Churchill prepare a cabinet paper on the Transvaal Constitution.

When Asquith became prime minister, he had no hesitation in judging Churchill worthy of a place in his cabinet. On 4 March 1908, Asquith had written to his wife after an interview with the king, "I said that Winston had every claim to cabinet rank and that he had behaved very well when twice passed over for Loulou [Lewis Harcourt] and [Reginald] McKenna, both of whom had inferior claims." After Campbell-Bannerman's resignation, Churchill was considered for the colonial office and the Local Government Board, but Asquith in the end nominated him to be president of the Board of Trade.

Asquith admired Churchill's energy, though at times felt that he pressed himself forward too much. When Lord Crewe, Lord Elgin's successor as colonial secretary, was offended by frequent advice from Churchill, Asquith observed of one Churchill letter, "A typical missive, born of froth out of foam." Asquith also saw Churchill as something of an uncouth barbarian in terms of classical education. Yet there is much, at least in regard to Churchill, in the judgement of J. A. Spender, joint author of the official biography of Asquith: "There was in the early years a paternal quality in his relations to Lloyd George and Winston Churchill. He was greatly attracted by both; he liked their exuberance and vitality, and when they got into scrapes, was apt to look on with amused indulgence."

During the House of Lords crisis, 1909–1910, Churchill was a vigorous opponent of the upper house. Like many other Liberals, he was surprised to learn after the first of the two 1910 general elections that Asquith had not secured from the king a pledge to create enough peers to overturn the House of Lords's veto should the Liberals win the election. However, in the second election, Churchill was greatly impressed by Asquith's leadership, informing him that his speeches "stood out in massive pre-eminence." He was not alone in judging the December 1910 election to be Asquith's finest hour.

Earlier, in the January–February 1909 cabinet arguments over whether to build six or four Dreadnoughts, Churchill was on Lloyd George's side of the argument, urging four. Asquith supported those who wanted six, and became irritated by the campaigns of Churchill and Lloyd George for the smaller building program. By 1911, Churchill was very concerned about the prospects of a war with Germany and was urging Asquith to ensure that Britain was prepared. On 13 September 1911, he wrote to Asquith asking whether the admiralty was ready to fight a major battle with the German fleet. He left the prime minister in no doubt that he would like to leave the Home Office for the admiralty. When Churchill stayed with Asquith at Archerfield, Scotland, he secured the offer of first lord of the admiralty.

Asquith supported Churchill at the admiralty. While Churchill was in this post, they had greater personal contact. They spent a month together on the admiralty yacht, *Enchantress,* each of the three summers before the outbreak of the First World War. Between 22 May and early June 1912, they cruised in the Mediterranean and, at Malta, discussed with Lord Kitchener naval policy concerning war in the Mediterranean. In January 1914, there was another crisis over naval estimates, this time with Lloyd George and Churchill in position. Asquith skilfully postponed meetings and allowed Lloyd George and Churchill to come to an agreement, which met Churchill's concerns.

On 30 July 1914, Churchill secured Asquith's permission to send the First Fleet to its war station in the safety of the North Sea. Asquith's admiration for Churchill's vigor was tried in October 1914 by Churchill's desire to resign from the cabinet so that he could stay in Antwerp and take command of its defense. The prime minister ordered him back to England. Asquith backed the naval attack in the Dardanelles, but distanced himself from Churchill and Admiral Lord Fisher when things went wrong.

In the construction of a coalition government in May 1915, Churchill and Lord Haldane were the two most prominent Liberals that Asquith sacrificed. Asquith followed Gladstone in believing that a good prime minister needed to be a good butcher. Afterwards Asquith observed of Churchill, "To speak with the tongue of men and angels, and to spend laborious days and nights in administration, is no good if a man does not inspire trust." He did offer Churchill the chancellorship of the Duchy of Lancaster, which kept him in the cabinet and on the war council, but gave him no departmental responsibility.

Asquith supported Churchill's wish in July 1916 to accept Kitchener's invitation to go to Gallipoli and give a ministerial assessment of conditions there and prospects for victory. However, the Conservative coalition ministers objected. Thereafter, Churchill pressed Asquith to allow the publication of admiralty papers, which Churchill believed would vindicate his part in the Dardanelles campaigns. By late October 1915, Churchill felt marginalized from the making of war policy and offered Asquith his resignation. Asquith pressed him to stay until he, Asquith, had made a policy statement on the Dardanelles in the Commons on 2 November 1915. This statement disappointed Churchill, and after the Dardanelles committee ended its work, he pressed his resignation. This ended the ten years' work in government together for Asquith and Churchill, but both expressed their continued personal friendship.

Nevertheless, their paths differed. Churchill joined Lloyd George's governments in 1917–1922 and so was against Asquith's mainstream Liberal group in the bitter Liberal feuds of these years. After Liberal reunion over tariffs in 1923, Churchill soon broke with Asquith and the Liberals over Asquith's decision after the 1923 general election to ask Labour to form a government. By this time, Churchill was making himself the preeminent antisocialist British politician. When in 1926 he took a vigorous stance against the General Strike, he was delighted with Asquith's hostility to the strike (a hostility that ended Asquith's leadership of the Liberal Party).

Asquith, who had lost his East Fife seat in the 1918 general election but had won a by-election for Paisley in 1920, ended his career in the House of Commons when he lost his seat in the 1924 general election. He accepted a peerage in January 1925, becoming Earl Oxford and Asquith; in the same year, he was also awarded the Order of the Garter and the Freedom of the City of London. He died on 15 February 1928.

For Churchill in the prewar years, Asquith was an older politician whom he could look up to. Churchill enjoyed his older colleague's conversation, so full of classical and historical learning, and he admired Asquith's concise and legalistic powers. Churchill judged him a great peacetime prime minister, but one who lacked the necessary urgency and dynamism in war.

Related entries:

Asquith, Margot; Bonham Carter, Lady Violet; Campbell-Bannerman, Sir Henry; Gallipoli; Grey, Sir Edward; Haldane, Richard Burdon

Suggestions for further reading:

Cassar, George H. 1994. *Asquith as War Leader.* London: Hambledon Press.

Churchill, Randolph S. 1967. *Winston S. Churchill.* Vol. 2. London: Heinemann.
Churchill, Winston S. 1927. *Great Contemporaries.* London: Thornton Butterworth.
Gilbert, Martin. 1971, 1975, and 1976. *Winston S. Churchill.* Vols. 3–5. London: Heinemann.
Jenkins, Roy. 1964. *Asquith.* London: Collins.
Koss, Stephen. 1976. *Asquith.* London: Allen Lane.
Spender, J. A., and Cyril Asquith. 1932. *Life of Herbert Henry Asquith, Lord Oxford and Asquith.* 2 vols. London: Hutchinson.

Asquith, Margot (Countess of Oxford and Asquith, 1864–1945)

Winston Churchill and Margot Asquith knew each other well from the 1890s. Both strong characters, there was more often friction than friendship, especially when Churchill threatened the political position of Herbert Henry Asquith, both during his premiership and after, when Churchill supported David Lloyd George or returned to the Conservatives. Churchill often found Margot Asquith an unattractive personality, too forceful, often eccentric and indiscreet, and he sometimes went out of his way to avoid her.

Emma Alice Margaret (but always known as Margot) Tennant was born on 2 February 1864 at "The Glen" in Peebleshire, Scotland, the sixth daughter of Charles and Emma (née Winslow) Tennant. Her father was a self-made millionaire businessman. The Tennants were strong Liberal Party supporters and Sir Charles Tennant was a Liberal member of Parliament from 1879 to 1886. He was made a baronet in 1885. Mrs. Gladstone and Lord Rosebery stayed with the Tennants on the eve of one of William Gladstone's speeches in Glasgow in 1880. On 10 May 1894, Margot Tennant married Herbert Henry Asquith, then the home secretary, whose first wife had died in

1891. Asquith married Margot for love, but as an impecunious politician, his lifestyle was enhanced when Sir Charles Tennant settled the then large sum of £5,000 a year on Margot. It was also changed by Margot's love of society as well as of politics.

Margot Asquith was fiercely loyal to her husband and deeply suspicious of younger, thrusting politicians such as Churchill and Lloyd George. Given to writing indiscreet and even embarrassing notes to leading politicians, she was sometimes supportive, sometimes critical of Winston Churchill. She was also critical of him to others. Thus, in 1909, at the time Churchill and Lloyd George were pressing for economy in naval expenditure, she commented of Churchill that it was "all part and parcel of his erratic temperament and lack of judgement." Many of her sharp words about Winston Churchill got back to him.

Clementine Churchill was equally loyal to her husband and was outraged when Asquith demoted him in 1915. Asquith recorded of one meeting between the Clementine and Margot, "Clemmie came here before dinner and I gather from Margot's account they had a very bad and almost Billingsgate half hour" (Billingsgate fish market is noted for its rough-and-ready types and bad language).

In 1920 and 1922, Margot Asquith published her autobiography in two volumes. Deemed very indiscreet at the time, although mild by later standards, they caused a sensation. Winston Churchill gave the first volume a generally favorable review in the London *Daily Mail,* observing that it was written "with art, and, what is better unconscious art" and recollected her riding as a "feather-weight daredevil" with the Melton Mowbray and other hunts in the 1890s. Her second volume included references to Churchill, including her meeting with Joseph Chamberlain in early 1910, when she recorded him as saying, "Winston is the cleverest of all the young men, and the mistake Arthur made was letting him

go." He also featured in her *More Memories* (1933) and received a slender chapter in her *Off the Record* (1943).

Margot Asquith remained intensely loyal to her husband after his fall from the premiership in December 1916. She was bitter toward those Liberals who supported Lloyd George. When Winston Churchill and Edwin Montagu lost their seats in the November 1922 general election, she exulted, "Serves them right." After Asquith lost his Paisley seat, he became a peer in 1925 and she the Countess of Oxford and Asquith. She died on 28 July 1945.

Related entries:
Asquith, Herbert Henry; Bibesco, Princess Elizabeth Charlotte Lucy; Bonham Carter, Lady Violet

Suggestions for further reading:
Asquith, Margot. 1920 and 1922. *The Autobiography of Margot Asquith.* London: Thornton Butterworth.
Bennett, Daphne. 1984. *Margot: A Life of the Countess of Oxford and Asquith.* London: Gollancz.
Oxford, Margot. 1933. *More Memories.* London: Cassell.
Oxford and Asquith, the Countess of. 1943. *Off the Record.* London: Muller.
Soames, Mary. 1979. *Clementine Churchill.* London: Cassell.

Astor, Lady Nancy Witcher Langhorne (1879–1964)

Lady Astor and Winston Churchill were strongly opinionated people who frequently clashed. They were both strong antisocialists and anticommunists and they both embraced Anglo-American unity. However, Churchill was very much out of sympathy with Lady Astor's Christian Science, temperance, and feminist views, as well as her support for appeasement in the 1930s.

Nancy Langhorne was born on 19 May 1879 in Danville, Virginia. Her father,

Chiswell Dabney Langhorne, had made a fortune through railway development. In 1897, she married Robert Gould Shaw II, a rich Bostonian who drank heavily. The marriage was dissolved in 1903. She left the United States for England in 1904, taking with her their much-loved son, Robert Gould Shaw III. She married Waldorf Astor in 1906; the couple became the parents of four sons and a daughter. In 1914, Lady Astor was converted to Christian Science, a belief she advocated vigorously.

Winston and Clementine Churchill had been friendly with Waldorf and Nancy Astor before the First World War. Churchill first visited them at Cliveden in May 1907, but had not been pleased with Nancy Astor's taste for seating too many guests at a table. Nancy Astor later recalled of Churchill then, "If seated next to a person he did not fancy, he would not utter a word." The Churchills visited Cliveden on other occasions during those years. In 1912, when Clementine Churchill was recuperating from an illness, the Astors lent her their house at Sandwich where she and her children enjoyed the ocean for several weeks.

Winston Churchill and Nancy Astor eventually came to dislike one another. They both held strong views. She deplored loose morals, drinking, and smoking. Churchill was a major sinner in her eyes on the last two counts. Although Churchill was loyal to Clementine, Nancy Astor felt that he had married unwisely. She wrote before the marriage, "The girl Winston Churchill is [to] marry is *lovely* but v. stupid. As poor as a rat—but nice." For Churchill's part, he disapproved of her becoming a member of Parliament in 1919 and ignored her for two years. When she complained to him about his icy behavior he responded, "I find a woman's intrusion into the House of Commons as embarrassing as if she burst into my bathroom when I had nothing with which to defend myself, not even a sponge." She quickly replied, "Winston, you're not handsome enough to have worries of that kind."

Churchill was also repelled by her Christian Science proselytizing, her temperance campaigns (which included pressing for prohibition in Britain in the 1920s), and her constant heckling of other members of Parliament in the House of Commons.

Churchill was highly critical of Nancy Astor and George Bernard Shaw for accepting a Soviet invitation to tour Russia in 1931. In a private interview with Joseph Stalin, Nancy Astor pressed him about why he had "slaughtered so many Russians." When he asked about Churchill, she replied, "Oh, he's finished!" On their return, Churchill rebuked them for not publicly condemning the tyranny and the gulags. When he published *Great Contemporaries* in 1937, he added to an August 1929 *Pall Mall* essay on George Bernard Shaw a section on his Russian trip and denounced Nancy Astor with some vehemence. This was on the lines that she "enjoys the best of all worlds . . . a leader of fashionable society and of advanced feminist democracy" and observed that "she combines a kindly heart with a sharp and wagging tongue." Stalin spoke of her visit and her comments on Churchill when Churchill visited him in Moscow in August 1942.

Churchill was also highly critical of Nancy Astor's attitude toward Hitler, who, she noted, did not drink or smoke. Nancy Astor was long a supporter of Chamberlain and appeasement, even heckling Churchill when he spoke out against the Munich settlement. However, in the vote of no confidence in Chamberlain on 8 May 1940, she was one of thirty-three Conservative members of Parliament who voted with the Opposition.

During the Second World War, she and Waldorf Astor, who was then mayor of Plymouth, did much to help maintain morale. When Winston and Clementine Churchill toured the recently bomb-damaged city on 2 May 1941, Churchill was deeply moved by the horrible sights. Nancy Astor, abrasive as ever, commented very audibly, "It's all very well to cry, Winston, but you got to do somethin'."

Waldorf Astor successfully pressed his wife to stand down from Parliament in 1945. She was pleased when her sons, John Jacob, Michael, and William, became Conservative M.P.s. In May 1959, Nancy Astor was made a Freeman of the City of Plymouth. She died on 2 May 1964.

With regard to Churchill, she is probably best remembered for being the butt of one of his best witticisms. According to Consuelo Vanderbilt Balsan, the first wife of the ninth duke of Marlborough, Nancy Astor and Winston Churchill had a row at Blenheim: "Nancy, with a fervour whose sincerity could not be doubted, shouted, 'If I were your wife I would put poison in your coffee.' Whereupon Winston, with equal heat and sincerity answered, 'And if I were your husband I would drink it.'"

Suggestions for further reading:
Balsan, Consuelo Vanderbilt. 1952. *The Glitter and the Gold.* New York: Harpers.
Collis, Maurice. 1960. *Nancy Astor.* New York: Dutton.
Grigg, John. 1980. *Nancy Astor: Portrait of a Pioneer.* London: Sidgwick and Jackson.
Masters, Anthony. 1981. *Nancy Astor.* London: Weidenfeld and Nicolson.
Musolf, Karen J. 1999. *From Plymouth to Parliament: A Rhetorical History of Nancy Astor's 1919 Campaign.* London: Macmillan.
Sykes, Christopher. 1972. *Nancy: The Life of Lady Astor.* New York: Harper and Row.

Atlantic Charter (August 1941)

The Atlantic Charter was agreed by Churchill and President Franklin D. Roosevelt at the Placentia Bay conference, held off the Newfoundland coast from 9 to 12 August 1941. The name "Atlantic Charter" was that given to the joint declaration by the London *Daily Herald.*

The United States was still neutral. In July 1941, Roosevelt urged Churchill to dispel rumors within the United States that Britain had been making secret promises of territory after the war to sympathetic countries, in the manner of the secret treaties of the First World War. Churchill responded by having Sir Alexander Cadogan draft a list of democratic principles for the postwar settlement. This draft declaration was given to Roosevelt on 10 August. Churchill sent a telegram outlining the proposals to London for the war cabinet to consider. Its assent, following a meeting in the early hours of 12 August, was sent back to Churchill immediately. The war cabinet did add a call for "improved labour standards, economic advancement and social security."

The Charter contained eight major principles declared to be held by both countries: (1) no territorial aggrandizement; (2) no territorial changes without the free consent of the peoples concerned; (3) the right to self-government; (4) equal access for all to the world's raw materials and equal opportunity to trade; (5) improved labor standards, economic advancement, and social security; (6) after the destruction of the Nazi tyranny, a lasting peace to enable people to live free from fear and want; (7) freedom to travel on the high seas; and (8) the abandonment of the use of force, with peace guaranteed by a permanent system of general security.

Churchill was uneasy about the third principle, fearing that it could be applied to the British Empire. He was especially anxious about India, Nigeria, and East Africa. He also warned that, if interpreted broadly, it could be used in Palestine by the Arabs to the great disadvantage of the Jews. There was also some concern in the Conservative Party about the fourth principle, which undercut imperial preference.

The Atlantic Charter was endorsed at the White House on 1 January 1942 in a joint declaration by twenty-six countries pledging military and economic cooperation against Germany and her allies. As well as the United States and Britain, the signatories were the USSR, Australia, Belgium,

Canada, China, Costa Rica, Cuba, Czecho-slovakia, the Dominican Republic, El Salvador, Greece, Guatemala, Haiti, Honduras, India, Luxembourg, the Netherlands, New Zealand, Nicaragua, Norway, Panama, Poland, South Africa, and Yugoslavia. These countries were later joined by Bolivia, Brazil, Chile, Colombia, Ecuador, Egypt, Ethiopia, France, Iceland, Iraq, Lebanon, Liberia, Mexico, Paraguay, Persia, Peru, the Philippines, Saudi Arabia, Syria, Turkey, Uruguay, and Venezuela. These forty-eight countries were to be the nucleus of the United Nations organization, founded in April–June 1945.

Related entries:
Placentia Bay Conference; Roosevelt, Franklin Delano

Suggestions for further reading:
Gilbert, Martin. 1983. *Winston S. Churchill.* Vol. 6. London: Heinemann.
Kimball, Warren F. 1997. *Forged in War: Churchill, Roosevelt and the Second World War.* London: Harper Collins.
Wilson, Theodore A. 1991. *The First Summit: Roosevelt and Churchill at Placentia Bay.* 2d ed. Lawrence, KS: University of Kansas.

The detonation of the first atomic bomb in New Mexico, 16 July 1945 (Library of Congress)

Atomic Bomb

For Churchill, the preparation of the atomic bomb was one of the great secrets of the Second World War. He insisted on very few people knowing of it. Once the weapon was used, Churchill felt that the end justified the terrible effects. After the war, he firmly believed that the atomic bomb had deterred Soviet expansionism in Western Europe.

Radioactivity was discovered in France in 1896 and thereafter research relating to atomic energy was conducted in several countries. British moves to investigate the possibilities of an atomic bomb followed from the research of two refugee physicists at Birmingham University, Otto Frisch and Rudolph Peierls. The MAUD Committee

(the letters hid no acronym), set up in April 1940 under George Thomson, a physicist, reported in July 1941 that an atomic bomb was feasible. Further British nuclear research was code-named Tube Alloys. Scientists from the United States visited Britain in 1941 and recommended that the United States should make an atomic bomb. The U.S. development was code-named the Manhattan project. General Leslie Groves, who was at the head of the project in Washington, later commented, "Prime Minister Churchill was probably the best friend that the Manhattan project ever had."

In June 1942, Churchill had discussed the atomic bomb with President Franklin D. Roosevelt at Roosevelt's home, Hyde Park, and had agreed that it should be a joint venture. Sir John Anderson, who had been put in charge of development in Britain, reported to Churchill that the scale of the production plant would be too great for Britain in the midst of the war; he recommended that production be in the United States, but that it would remain a joint venture. However, in January 1943, Anderson informed Churchill that the U.S. authorities had banned further exchanges of information and now deemed it entirely a U.S. venture. Churchill responded by requesting Anderson to estimate the cost of Britain carrying out research and beginning production on her own. But because the United States had secured all the Canadian production of uranium and heavy water for the next two years, Britain did need to work with the United States. On 26 May 1943, Churchill, in Washington, raised the issue with Roosevelt, who agreed to resume the exchange of information.

Churchill and Roosevelt agreed to a memorandum on atomic weapons in mid-August 1943 at Hyde Park. After stating that neither country would use atomic weapons against the other, they agreed not to use them against others nor to provide others with information concerning atomic weapons, except with the consent of the other.

In March 1944, Churchill resisted Anderson's view that information concerning atomic weapons should be discussed in the war cabinet and the defense committee. He was even more emphatic in rejecting Anderson's suggestion that Stalin and the Soviet Union should be informed. In November 1944, he declined to provide the Chiefs of Staff with more information concerning the bombing of German of targets linked to atomic research.

The atomic bomb was discussed by Churchill and Roosevelt at Hyde Park in September 1944, after the Quebec Conference. Churchill had taken Lord Cherwell (Professor Frederick Lindemann) with him as his expert. They knew that an atomic bomb would be ready by August 1945, and they tentatively agreed that it should be used against Japan.

Churchill raised the matter of British atomic research development with President Roosevelt on the last occasion he saw him, on the USS *Quincy,* off Alexandria, on 16 February 1945. Churchill remained determined to keep the atomic secret a matter for as few people as possible, declining in March 1945 to share knowledge of it with General Charles de Gaulle of France.

After the atomic bomb was dropped on Japan, Churchill said its use would be debated in the future but he felt he could defend its use to "my Maker." He believed that the atom bomb had deterred the Soviet Union from trying to take over Western Europe after 1945.

In his final premiership, Churchill made clear that he was following Clement Attlee's government when continuing to develop a British atomic bomb. During talks with President Harry Truman in Washington in January 1952, Churchill secured agreement that U.S. forces in East Anglia would not use atomic weapons without the agreement of the British government. He was against the use of atomic weapons in the Korean War.

Churchill and President Dwight D. Eisenhower discussed atomic weapons at the Bermuda Conference in December 1953. Churchill regretted that atomic information was no longer exchanged between the United States and Britain. Eisenhower was emphatic that he viewed atomic weapons as conventional weapons by that time, whereas Churchill viewed them as something terrible and distinct. Churchill was afraid that the United States might use atomic weapons on China. He returned to his theme of the desirability of more exchange of atomic information between the United States and Britain when he visited Eisenhower in Washington in June 1954.

Related entries:
Eisenhower, Dwight David; Roosevelt, Franklin Delano; Quebec Conference, Second; Yalta Conference

Suggestions for further reading:
Gilbert, Martin. 1986 and 1988. *Winston S. Churchill.* Vols. 7 and 8. London: Heinemann.

Gowing, Margaret. 1964. *Britain and Atomic Energy 1939–1945*. London: Macmillan.

Attlee, Clement Richard (First Earl Attlee, 1883–1967)

Portrait of Clement Richard Attlee, 1945 (Library of Congress)

Clement Attlee was Churchill's efficient deputy prime minister during the Second World War. Churchill generally respected his wartime role, commenting that he was "a faithful colleague who served his country well." However, Churchill was prone to underestimate Attlee, just as he underestimated Baldwin. His criticism, "Mr. Attlee is a very modest man. But then he has much to be modest about" is well-remembered. Yet, Attlee, Labour Party leader, 1935–1945, was a capable politician and an able prime minister, 1945–1951.

Attlee was born in Putney on 3 January 1883, the son of Henry Attlee, a very successful London solicitor. He grew up in a wealthy household, one imbued with Christian and philanthropic values. He was educated at Haileybury, a public school (the British public school, so-called because it prepares students for public life, is the counterpart of the private school in the United States), and University College, Oxford. Trained as a barrister, he practiced law briefly. From 1912, he was a tutor in social services at the London School of Economics, his qualification coming from devoted social work in the East End of London, self-financed through his private income.

Attlee's experiences of poverty in East London converted him to socialism. He joined the two democratic socialist bodies, the Fabian Society in 1907, and the Independent Labour Party (ILP) in 1908, soon becoming secretary of the Stepney branch. With the outbreak of the First World War, he volunteered for the army, returning as Major Attlee, a title he used in politics for much of the interwar period. In 1919, he was selected as prospective Labour candidate for Stepney, and he was mayor of that borough in 1919. Elected to Parliament in 1922, he became one of Ramsay MacDonald's parliamentary private secretaries; in the first Labour government (1924), he was under secretary at the War Office. In the late 1920s, he served on the Simon Commission, which reviewed the constitutional future of India. Attlee served in Ramsay MacDonald's second Labour government (1929–1931) as chancellor of the Duchy of Lancaster (1930–1931) and postmaster general (1931).

Attlee really came to the fore in the 1931 general election; he managed to hold his seat, but nearly all the leading Labour Party figures who did not follow Ramsay MacDonald into the National government lost theirs. He became deputy leader of the parliamentary Labour Party, then having only fifty-two M.P.s, and devoted long hours to opposition in the House of Commons, including eight months as acting leader when George Lansbury was ill. After Lansbury resigned as leader in 1935, Attlee became leader.

Attlee served in Gallipoli and always defended Churchill's vision there. He later commented that only "incredible blunders marred Churchill's fine strategic conception." Attlee was strongly opposed to Churchill's die-hard views on India, and during the abdication crisis in 1936, he supported Stanley Baldwin. From 1936, Attlee, along with Ernest Bevin and Hugh Dalton, moved to change Labour's policy on defense. Attlee deplored Hitler's occupation of the Rhineland and established a Labour Party Defence Committee. He supported Anthony Eden when he resigned as foreign secretary in 1938 and, ahead of the Munich agreement, he called on Chamberlain to take a firm stance in support of Czechoslovakia. Churchill welcomed the Labour Party's public statement on this, telephoning Attlee and congratulating him on having "done honour to the British nation." With the Munich Agreement, Attlee condemned Chamberlain's policy, observing that his feelings "were akin to those I felt on the night that we evacuated the Gallipoli Peninsula." When Attlee and Herbert Morrison sounded out Conservative dissidents about whether they would act with Labour and Liberal members of Parliament on foreign issues against the government, only Churchill was willing.

In May 1940, Attlee led the attack on the Chamberlain government's conduct during the war at a two-day debate on the failure of the British expedition to Norway. After the government's majority fell from some 250 to 81, Attlee was primarily concerned about getting Chamberlain out and was willing to accept Lord Halifax or Churchill, but Attlee's personal preference was most probably for Churchill. Attlee's decisive role in May 1940 was to make it absolutely clear that Chamberlain had to go. When Churchill accepted the premier-

ship, he quickly offered Attlee and his Labour Party colleagues two places in a small war cabinet of five or six, as well as substantial numbers of other positions in the government. Attlee was a war cabinet member throughout the war, with the posts of lord privy seal (1940–1942), dominions secretary (1942–1943) and lord president of the council (1943–1945). He acted as if he were deputy prime minister from the beginning, but was formally given the title on 19 February 1942, and chaired, or served on, all the most important wartime committees.

Attlee's major contribution during the war was in domestic policy. Attlee, with Ernest Bevin, minister of labor (May 1940–1945) and Herbert Morrison, home secretary (October 1940–1945), set the tone of wartime planning and welfare. The home front, with prospects of postwar reconstruction, became something of a Labour preserve. Attlee was considered an efficient chairman of meetings, being famous for his brevity and sharp focus on the issue in hand, unlike Churchill, who indulged in monologues and digressions. In 1945, he commented to Churchill, "I must remind the Right Honourable Gentleman that a monologue is not a decision." On 19 January 1945, Attlee wrote a lengthy letter to Churchill in which he complained that Churchill wasted busy ministers' time by being ill-prepared, disregarding agreements arrived at by colleagues in committee, and paying excessive attention to the views of Lord Beaverbrook and the Conservative politician Brendan Bracken. Churchill was outraged and consulted Beaverbrook and Bracken, who said that Attlee was right; he then complained to his wife, who replied, "I admire Mr. Attlee for having the courage to say what everyone is thinking." A calmer Churchill replied to Attlee that he would "always endeavour to profit by your counsels."

With the defeat of Germany in May 1945, Attlee initially hoped that Churchill's wartime coalition would be maintained until the defeat of Japan. However, he found that the predominant mood in the Labour Party was to leave the coalition and fight an autumn election. Churchill called the election on 5 July 1945. Churchill made an early mistake when, on 4 June in a campaign broadcast, he warned that the election of Labour would lead to the introduction of a Gestapo and that small savers would see their money disappear. Attlee ridiculed such views and campaigned on social reconstruction and, more specifically, on implementing the Beveridge Report. Labour won a landslide victory and Attlee became the first Labour prime minister with a majority in the House of Commons.

Attlee took office between the ends of the wars with Germany and Japan. With the war with Japan ending, Attlee wrote to Churchill to offer "to you, as leader from the darkest hours through so many anxious days, my congratulations on this crowning result of your work." He paid similar tribute in the House of Commons, on 16 August 1945, the day after Japanese acceptance of defeat, commenting that Churchill's "place in history is secure."

Attlee and Churchill kept each other informed on such matters as atomic weapons. Churchill played a part in securing Britain a U.S. loan in 1946. He also informed Attlee of U.S. reactions to his draft Fulton speech and to responses after it. Churchill also cleared with Attlee the use of government records in his war memoirs.

As prime minister and leader of the Opposition, Attlee and Churchill often clashed in Parliament from 1945 to 1955. One of the early and most memorable occasions was when Churchill moved a vote of censure in the House of Commons on 5 and 6 December and Attlee made a very effective reply. To Churchill's complaint that the government, unlike the Conservatives, put country before party, Attlee referred to Churchill's Gestapo speech. He derided

Churchill's speech, saying that it amounted to one complaint: "Why, when you were elected to carry out a socialist programme, did you not carry out a Conservative programme? To the Right Hon. Gentleman everything that is Conservative is normal, anything that sees a changing world, and wishes to change it, must be wrong."

Similarly, about Churchill's stance over the granting of independence to India in 1947, Attlee was firm and succinct in rebutting his attacks. Attlee observed in the House of Commons of Churchill, "I think his practical acquaintance with India ended some fifty years ago. He formed some strong opinions—I might almost say prejudices—then. They have remained with him ever since." Churchill was not at his best as leader of the Opposition; Attlee's incisiveness and lack of histrionics was frequently an effective weapon to puncture Churchill's lengthy and high-flown speeches.

Although Churchill did not wish for Attlee as a personal friend, he generally respected him. In his last premiership, with Attlee as leader of the Opposition, he maintained good relations. When the Freedom of the City of London was presented to Attlee on 20 November 1953, Churchill praised Attlee's premiership for its "formidable and costly rearmament programme," including atomic weapons, "which have enabled the nations of the free world to confront Communist aggression." Clement and Violet Attlee were guests at Clementine Churchill's seventieth birthday party at 10 Downing Street on 1 April 1955; they were also guests three days later when Queen Elizabeth II and the duke of Edinburgh dined at 10 Downing Street on Churchill's last evening as prime minister. Churchill included Attlee on the list of those receiving copies of his *A History of the English Speaking Peoples.*

Attlee paid a fulsome and thoughtful tribute to Churchill's career on 30 November 1954, when Parliament honored Churchill on his eightieth birthday. After Churchill's death, Attlee paid a further tribute to Churchill in the House of Lords, and, although frail himself, he attended the funeral service in St. Paul's Cathedral.

Attlee accepted a peerage when he stood down as Labour Party leader in 1955. Earlier, in 1945, he had been made a Companion of Honour, and in 1951 he had been awarded the Order of Merit. In 1956, he was enrolled as a Knight of the Garter. Lady Attlee died in June 1964 and Clement Attlee died on 8 October 1967.

Related entries:
Bevan, Aneurin; Bevin, Ernest; Cripps, Sir (Richard) Stafford

Suggestions for further reading:
Attlee, Earl. 1954. *As It Happened.* London: Heinemann.
Brookshire, Jerry. 1966. *Clement Attlee.* Manchester, UK: Manchester University Press.
Burridge, Trevor. 1985. *Clement Attlee: A Political Biography.* London: Cape.
Gilbert, Martin. 1976–1988. *Winston S. Churchill.* Vols. 5–8. London: Heinemann.
Harris, Kenneth. 1982. *Attlee.* London: Weidenfeld and Nicolson.
Pearce, Robert. 1997. *Attlee.* London: Longman.

Auchinleck, Field Marshal Sir Claude John Eyre (1884–1981)

General Sir Claude Auchinleck, nicknamed "the Auk," was commander in chief Middle East in June 1941 until November 1942. Churchill removed him because he was impatient with Auchinleck's cautious approach in fighting Field Marshal Erwin Rommel in North Africa.

Auchinleck was born at Aldershot on 21 June 1884, the son of a professional soldier, Lieutenant Colonel John Claude Alexander Auchinleck (from Ireland, of Scottish ancestry). After Sandhurst, Auchinleck served in the Indian army from 1903. During the

First World War, he fought in Mesopotamia, in the unsuccessful attempts to relieve Kut in 1916 and in the successful campaign of 1917, which took Kut and Baghdad. He returned from India in early 1940 and was sent, at Churchill's instigation, to command all troops in northern Norway. He arrived on 11 May 1940, shortly after the "phoney war" had ended, and tried to strengthen the forces around Narvik. With the retreat in France, Auchinleck was ordered to withdraw from Norway. This he did after taking Narvik on 28 May 1940. Churchill was angered by the delay in attacking Narvik, deeming it "a shocking example of costly over-caution and feebleness," a poor contrast with the vigor shown by the German forces. However, the prime blame was attributed to General Mackesy, who was in charge before Auchinleck's arrival.

Churchill was more impressed by Auchinleck when he dealt with a revolt in Iraq. After a period as general officer commanding the Southern Command, Auchinleck returned to India as commander in chief. Auchinleck rightly anticipated serious problems for Britain from prominent German-supporting politicians in Iraq. Auchinleck rejected suggestions to delay in sending forces to Basra, after the pro-German, former prime minister, Rashid Ali, seized power in Baghdad in early April 1941. The British forces landed at Basra without opposition, and Auchinleck's decisiveness impressed Churchill. Churchill and Field Marshal Sir John Dill, chief of the Imperial General Staff, privately designated Auchinleck as Sir Archibald Wavell's eventual successor as commander in chief Middle East. On 20 June 1941, Churchill replaced Wavell with Auchinleck.

Like Wavell before him, Auchinleck was pressured by Churchill and other ministers to take the offensive before he felt he was adequately prepared to do so. Auchinleck greatly respected Churchill as a leader but, as he later observed, he lacked a realization of "the practical difficulties of supply and transport and munitions and tanks." Auchinleck launched his big offensive, "Crusader," on 18 November 1941, which secured the relief of Tobruk by 7 December. However, in January 1942, Rommel successfully counterattacked. Churchill became angered by Auchinleck's unwillingness to launch a major offensive until June, when he would have numerical superiority over Rommel. Before that occurred, Rommel attacked again on 26 May, taking Tobruk as he advanced on Egypt. Auchinleck relieved his Eighth Army commander and took personal command. In July, Auchinleck successfully stopped Rommel at the first Battle of Alamein.

Churchill replaced Auchinleck in August 1942 with General Alexander. Churchill said that removing Auchinleck was "like killing a magnificent stag." This decision has generally been judged as unfairly harsh. Auchinleck's main error, in hindsight, was that he delayed too long in taking over direct control of the Eighth Army. Churchill offered Auchinleck a newly divided Middle East Command, covering Palestine, Syria, Persia, and Iraq. Auchinleck declined this offer and returned to India. He resumed the post of commander in chief there from June 1943 (until independence in 1947), mobilizing resources for the Burma campaign. He was knighted in 1940, promoted to field marshal in 1946, and declined a peerage in 1947. Auchinleck died on 23 March 1981.

Related entries:
Montgomery, Bernard Law; Wavell, Field Marshal Archibald Percival

Suggestions for further reading:
Connell, John. 1959. *Auchinleck*. London: Collins.
Gilbert, Martin. 1994. *The Churchill War Papers*. Vol. 2, *Never Surrender*. London: Heinemann.
Parkinson, Roger. 1977. *The Auk: Auchinleck, Victor at Alamein*. London: Granada.
Warner, Philip. 1981. *Auchinleck: The Lonely Soldier*. London: Buchan and Enright.
———. 1991. "Auchinleck." In *Churchill's Generals*, edited by John Keegan. London: Weidenfeld and Nicolson.

Aviation (1909–1919)

Churchill was quick to see the importance of the airplane. In January 1909, he was a vocal exponent of its potential military value; he even became a keen aviator himself for a while. Churchill had been impressed by the use of balloons during the Boer War (1899–1902). He had witnessed Lord Roberts's effective use of them in his march into Boer territory in 1900.

In January 1909, when serving on the Committee of Imperial Defense's subcommittee on aerial navigation, Churchill urged Lord Haldane, the secretary of state for war, to ensure that Sir Hiram Maxim and Orville Wright were consulted. Churchill himself was full of the potential of airplanes, including for bombing naval bases, after an hour and a half discussion with Maxim. Maxim was formally consulted, but Wright was not. When the Aerial League of the British Empire (like the earlier Navy League, it described itself as a "strictly nonparty organization") held its first big meeting at the Mansion House, London, on 5 April 1909, Churchill sent a letter of support that was read to the assembly.

As first lord of the admiralty, Churchill founded the Royal Naval Air Service. At the outbreak of the First World War, the navy had some 50 aircraft to the army's roughly 150. Admiral Fisher shared and encouraged his enthusiasm, observing to Churchill on 10 November 1911, "*Aviation supersedes small cruisers and Intelligence vessels.*" Churchill required both land and seaplanes, the latter's role including torpedo operations against battleships. Churchill also favored the navy's developing airships, but this was agreed upon too late for an airship to be available for operations with the fleet in the North Sea early in the First World War.

Churchill, like the Labour leader James Ramsay MacDonald, was for a while an enthusiastic aviator. He began flying lessons in late 1912 or early 1913, and he was so keen that he would go up as many as ten times a day. One of his many instructors, Captain Gilbert Wildman-Lushington, was killed on 2 December 1913 when landing a plane. This accident alarmed Clementine Churchill and some of Churchill's friends. When the experienced aviator Gustav Hamel vanished over the Channel on 28 May 1914 on the way to give an air demonstration, at Churchill's request, near Portsmouth, Churchill gave up flying until he became minister of munitions in 1917. He resumed his flying lessons in the summer of 1919, hoping to qualify for a pilot's license. However, on 18 July 1919, he had a serious crash when taking off from Croydon airport with Colonel A. J. L. Scott. He was badly bruised and gave up learning to fly. He never earned a flying certificate, nor did he ever fly solo.

In the last stages of the First World War, Churchill acknowledged that with a shortage of manpower, the air force was a lower priority than the army. He also prioritized tank production above aircraft manufacture. After the war, on 10 January 1919, Churchill was made secretary of state for war and air. In the 1920s, when he was earning much money from journalism, he wrote two pieces on flying for *Nash's Pall Mall:* "In the Air" (June 1924), and "Why I Gave Up Flying" (July 1924).

Related entry:
Air, Secretary of State for

Suggestions for further reading:

Churchill, Randolph S. 1967 and 1969. *Winston S. Churchill.* Vol. 2 and companion vol. 2, part 3. London: Heinemann.
Churchill, Winston S. 1923–1931. *The World Crisis.* 5 vols. London: Thornton Butterworth.
Driver, Hugo. 1998. *The Birth of Military Aviation: Britain, 1903–1914.* Suffolk, UK: Royal Historical Society and Boydell and Brewer.
Gilbert, Martin. 1975. *Winston S. Churchill.* Vol. 4. London: Heinemann.
Gollin, Alfred. 1984. *No Longer an Island: Britain and the Wright Brothers, 1902–1909.* London: Heinemann.

B

Baldwin, Stanley (Earl Baldwin of Bewdley, 1867–1947)

Churchill often underestimated Baldwin as a politician. Outwardly often appearing indolent, Baldwin could be wily and was skillful at projecting the image of an honest, straightforward Englishman. Churchill thought him second-rate and broke away from the Conservative leadership in early 1930 over India, rearmament, and the abdication of King Edward VIII. For Baldwin, Churchill's stances on these issues confirmed his view that Churchill frequently lacked good political judgement.

Stanley Baldwin was born at Lower Park, Bewdley, on 8 August 1867, the only child of Alfred and Louisa Baldwin. Alfred Baldwin, an able youngest son, effectively ran the family business, which centered on the iron trade. Louisa was the daughter of a Wesleyan minister, George Browne Macdonald. Stanley was educated at Harrow and Trinity College, Cambridge. From 1888, he worked in the family firm, which was run on benign paternalist lines. He succeeded his father as Conservative member of Parliament for Bewdley. His father held the seat in 1892–1908, and he won it in an uncontested by-election, representing Bewdley until his peerage in 1937. He had stood unsuccessfully for Kidderminster in 1906.

Baldwin served on the back benches until he became the parliamentary private secretary of the Conservative leader, Andrew Bonar Law, after the formation of David Lloyd George's coalition government in December 1916. From June 1917 until April 1921, Baldwin was financial secretary to the treasury. He entered the cabinet as president of the Board of Trade in April 1921, but by autumn 1922 he was considering resigning because he disliked the cynicism of Lloyd George and his associates and wanted the coalition to end. At the Carlton Club meeting on 19 October 1922, which resulted in the collapse of the government, he was the only cabinet minister hostile to Lloyd George and the coalition, commenting "a dynamic force is a terrible thing: it may crush you, but it is not necessarily right." In the ensuing Bonar Law government, he was chancellor of the exchequer, and on 22 May 1923 he became prime minister, serving 1923–1924, 1924–1929, and 1935–1937.

Churchill usually underestimated Baldwin's skills as a politician. Baldwin was often in tune with the sentiments of Conservative backbenchers and the Conservative-inclined sector of the electorate. Churchill, who had become a cabinet minister within a month of Baldwin's arrival in the House of Commons, tended to judge Baldwin as a second-rate figure who lacked charisma. By the time Baldwin reached the

Stanley Baldwin at his desk, March 1923 (Hulton/Archive)

cabinet, Churchill had moved to the Right in the coalition government. He and Baldwin agreed on many issues, and both deplored the recognition of Soviet Russia (except with unlikely conditions satisfied) and opposed the chairing by a nongovernment figure (Sir Eric Geddes) of the committee reviewing and cutting public expenditure. Yet Churchill remained a supporter and friend of David Lloyd George, while Baldwin had come to detest him.

Churchill and Baldwin were on opposite sides at the end of the coalition government in 1922. Baldwin was horrified by the willingness of Lloyd George and Churchill to go to war with Turkey at the time of the Chanak crisis and allied himself with George Curzon in his efforts to avoid British involvement in war in Asia Minor or Gallipoli. Before the Carlton Club meeting, Churchill unwisely tried to bully Baldwin into remaining loyal to the coalition. Baldwin's wife, Lucy, recorded in her diary that after Churchill had harangued her husband for some time, he then shouted, "There'll be some pretty mud-slinging," to which the hitherto silent Baldwin had riposted, "That would be a pity because some pretty big chunks could come from the other side." Baldwin went on to become chancellor of the exchequer, and Churchill lost his parliamentary seat.

In December 1923, Baldwin risked a year-old Conservative parliamentary majority by calling a general election on the issue of tariffs. He lost, and a minority Labour government took office in January 1924. Churchill was alarmed at the prospect of a socialist government and moved ever closer to a return to the Conservative Party. With his return to Parliament in late October 1924, and Baldwin's return to office,

Baldwin took the bold step of making Churchill chancellor of the exchequer. Baldwin and his advisers felt it was better to have Churchill within the government rather than outside it, where he could organize dissent. Also, Churchill in a senior post was not likely to return to Lloyd George. Indeed, Churchill on being offered his father's old post declared that Baldwin had given him higher office than Lloyd George had. Baldwin supported Churchill as chancellor of the exchequer, and on such matters as relations with the Soviet Union they often warmly agreed.

After the Conservative defeat in the 1929 general election, Churchill drifted away from Baldwin, Neville Chamberlain, and the other Conservative leaders. In October 1929, Baldwin urged the Conservative leaders to join with Labour in supporting eventual dominion status for India. After the matter was debated in the House of Commons on 7 November, Samuel Hoare reported in a letter, "Throughout the debate Winston was almost demented with fury and since the debate has scarcely spoken to anyone." He did not expect, nor was he given, office in the 1931 National government, in which Baldwin and the Conservatives held eleven of the sixteen cabinet posts. He remained separated from the Conservative leadership over his calls for rearmament as well as on India. In the 1935 general election, Baldwin promised "no great armaments." After the election, Churchill's hopes of returning to the admiralty under Baldwin were dashed.

Baldwin was more ready to listen to Churchill than was his successor, Neville Chamberlain. Nevertheless, Baldwin felt strongly that Churchill lacked "judgement and wisdom." On rearmament, Baldwin was wrong. But over the abdication crisis of 1936, many would have agreed with Baldwin, perhaps even Clementine Churchill. Many believed that Churchill was using the crisis to oust Baldwin, but they underestimated Churchill's strong monar-chical views. By the time Baldwin retired, on 28 May 1937, Churchill was very pleased to see him go and later often disparaged him as a leader.

Baldwin was made a Knight of the Garter, and a little later, on 8 June 1937, an earl. He died on 13 December 1947.

Related entries:
Appeasement; Chamberlain, (Arthur) Neville; Chanak

Suggestions for further reading:
Ball, Stuart. 1988. *Baldwin and the Conservative Party: The Crisis of 1929–1931*. New Haven: Yale University Press.
Gilbert, Martin. 1975, 1976, and 1988. *Winston S. Churchill*. Vols. 4, 5, and 8. London: Heinemann.
Middlemas, Keith, and John Barnes. 1969. *Baldwin*. London: Weidenfeld and Nicolson.
Williamson, Philip. 1999. *Stanley Baldwin*. Cambridge: Cambridge University Press.

Balfour, Arthur James, First Earl (1848–1930)

Arthur James Balfour was a landed Conservative of the old style, with whom Winston Churchill usually got on well. Nevertheless, Churchill felt that Balfour had failed to give decisive leadership over the tariffs issue in 1903–1904, and he left the Conservative Party. In office in Liberal governments (1905–1915), Churchill favored keeping Balfour informed on defense issues through the Committee of Imperial Defence and more generally on admiralty matters. He was pleased that it was Balfour, not another Conservative, who succeeded him as first lord of the admiralty in May 1915.

Balfour was born at Whittinghame, East Lothian, Scotland, on 25 July 1848, the eldest son and fourth child of James Maitland Balfour and his wife, Lady Blanche Harriet Gascoyne-Cecil, second daughter of the second marquis of Salisbury. Hence Balfour

Arthur James Balfour with Winston Churchill, both members of the wartime coalition cabinet, May 1915 (Hulton / Archive)

was a nephew of the third marquis of Salisbury, prime minister in 1885–1886, 1886–1892, and 1895–1902. He therefore had most powerful political connections and also benefited from being a wealthy landowner in his own right. Educated at Eton and Trinity Hall, Cambridge, Balfour developed philosophical and scientific interests. He published books of philosophy, beginning with *A Defence of Philosophic Doubt* (1879). He was elected unopposed as M.P. for Hertford in 1874, a seat under his uncle's influence. He soon embarked on probably the longest ministerial career in modern British politics, beginning as his uncle's parliamentary private secretary, 1878–1880, and then becoming a minister in every Conservative or coalition government from 1885 to 1929. Nicknamed at Cambridge "Pretty Fanny" for his collection of china and his apparently gentle, even precious disposition, he showed his toughness as chief secretary for Ireland (1887–1891) and earned in Irish Nationalist eyes the sobriquet "Bloody Balfour." He made a mark in the Commons in 1880–1885 through his association with Lord Randolph Churchill, though in his "Fourth Party" phase of maverick opposition he nevertheless remained a major conduit of Commons information to his uncle. As leader of the House of Commons, 1891–1892, 1895–1902, he was rightly seen by many as preparing to succeed his uncle as prime minister.

When Churchill reached the House of Commons, Balfour took an interest in Lord Randolph's son, taking care to hear his maiden speech. Balfour was one of those whose conversation Winston Churchill greatly enjoyed; he was also a good listener, an exceedingly endearing trait for Churchill. Although Churchill attacked Balfour, his own leader, over the handling of the later stages of the Boer War and over his responses to Joseph Chamberlain's tariff reform campaign, Balfour remained good humored in his personal relations with Churchill. This did not deter him from vigorously attacking Churchill politically after he had crossed the floor of the House of Commons to the Liberals, as over the proposed South African settlement and the Liberal government's criticisms of Lord Milner. Balfour, like Herbert Henry Asquith, enjoyed cross-party friendships, but he could still perform effectively as a partisan party politician.

Churchill, while in Asquith's governments (1908–1915), was happy to involve Balfour further in defense matters, Balfour remaining a member of the Committee of Imperial Defence after the fall of his government. Balfour admired Churchill's vigor at the admiralty, especially at the outbreak of the First World War. When, in May 1915, Asquith made it clear that Churchill would not continue at the admiralty, he pressed strongly for Balfour to be his successor and was delighted when Balfour was made first lord. However, before long, Churchill was complaining of Balfour's lack of vigor, observing to Jack Seely in August 1916 that his successor at the admiralty epitomized "the art of doing nothing with mighty rewards."

Back in office under Lloyd George, Churchill again had Balfour as a ministerial colleague. Balfour was foreign secretary from December 1916 to October 1919, and lord president of the council from October 1919 to October 1922; Churchill held offices beginning with minister of munitions from July 1917. Churchill and Balfour backed Lloyd George strongly, both being optimistic in the dark days after the German offensive on the Western Front of 21 March 1918. Churchill was also supportive of Balfour's backing for the creation of a Jewish state, initially with the Balfour Declaration in 1917. On the issue of intervention in Russia against the Bolsheviks, however, Churchill was a hawk and deplored Balfour's relaxed attitude toward the Bolsheviks. Churchill was also impatient with the more cautious approach of Balfour and Curzon to reaching an agreement with King Feisal over Iraq in 1921.

Churchill again served with Balfour in Stanley Baldwin's government of 1924–1929. Balfour was not initially a minister but returned to the position of lord president of the council upon Curzon's death in April 1925. Balfour, who had been on the Committee of Imperial Defence from the outset of the government, became chairman after Curzon died. He felt that Churchill's case for a Ministry of Defence was flawed because the post would be too much for one minister to control. He also opposed Churchill's

"Ten Year Rule," the assumption in planning that no major war would occur for a decade.

Churchill and Balfour remained friends until the latter's death on 19 March 1930. Churchill much appreciated Balfour's warm praise of his 1928 budget. He consulted Balfour about the Paris Peace Conference (1919) chapter of *The World Crisis: The Aftermath,* and later sent him a copy of the book. Balfour responded on 6 March 1929 by praising the work as "Five volumes of immortal history." Churchill wrote an elegant yet substantial portrait of Balfour in the *Strand,* April 1931, which he revised for *Great Contemporaries* (1937), adding to it further information concerning the 1903 resignations from Balfour's government. After the fall of the government, Churchill visited him at his brother's house at Fishers Hill, Woking, where he lived during his last months.

Related entries:
Bonar Law, Andrew; Chamberlain, Joseph Austen

Suggestions for further reading:
Churchill, Randolph S. 1967. *Winston S. Churchill.* Vol. 2. London: Heinemann.
Churchill, Winston S. 1937. *Great Contemporaries.* London: Thornton Butterworth.
Dugdale, Blanche E. C. 1936. *Arthur James Balfour, First Earl of Balfour.* 2 vols. London: Hutchinson.
Egremont, Max. 1980. *Balfour.* London: Collins.
MacKay, Ruddock F. 1985. *Balfour: Intellectual Statesman.* Oxford: Oxford University Press.
Young, Kenneth. 1963. *Arthur James Balfour.* London: Bell.
Zebel, Sydney H. 1973. *Balfour: A Political Biography.* Cambridge: Cambridge University Press.

Bangalore

Bangalore was a major military base in southern India, in the Madras presidency. At over 3,000 feet above sea level, it has a pleasant climate. Churchill went there with the 4th Hussars in October 1896 and finally left Bangalore and the army in early 1899.

He lived comfortably, waited on by Indian servants, in a bungalow that he rented with two other subalterns, Hugo Baring and Reginald Barnes. His main leisure interest was polo, which he played most days from 5:00 P.M. onward. He also read the works of Edward Gibbon and Thomas Macaulay, Adam Smith's *Wealth of Nations,* many volumes of *The Annual Register* from 1874 onward, as well as works by Rudyard Kipling and others. He also enjoyed growing roses and collecting butterflies.

It was in Bangalore that he met Pamela Plowden, daughter of an Indian civil servant based at Hyderabad. He was much enamored of her at their first meeting in October 1896. She was, as Randolph Churchill observed, "the first great love of his life."

After August 1897, Churchill used Bangalore as a base for his travels to war zones and for playing polo, but as time went on, he visited it less often.

British statesman and author Winston Leonard Spencer Churchill became a keen polo player during his time as a subaltern in Bangalore, 1896–1897. (Hulton/Archive)

Suggestions for further reading:
Churchill, Randolph S. 1966. *Winston S. Churchill*. Vol. 1. London: Heinemann.
Churchill, Winston S. 1930. *My Early Life*. London: Thornton Butterworth.

Barnes, George Nicholl (1859–1940)

George Barnes was the kind of "patriotic Labour" figure that Churchill admired. He was an old-style skilled trade unionist, a type of Labour Party person that Churchill was happier with than he was with socialist intellectuals. However, in 1917–1919, friction occurred between them, above all concerning Soviet Russia.

Barnes was born at Lochee, Forfarshire, on 2 January 1859, the son of a journeyman machinist. When he was seven, his family moved south, and he received elementary education at Ponder's End, Middlesex, until going to work at eleven. He was apprenticed as an engineer in Lambeth and Dundee. He found employment in London, joined the Amalgamated Society of Engineers (ASE), and became an active socialist and cooperator. He became secretary of the ASE in 1896, a post he held until 1908. He ran unsuccessfully for Parliament for the Independent Labour Party in 1895 but was elected for Glasgow Blackfriars as a Labour Representation Committee candidate in 1906. Barnes was chairman of the parliamentary Labour Party in 1910–1911, but did not shine in the role of leader.

With the First World War, Barnes was part of the prowar majority. In the autumn of 1914, he served on a committee that reviewed the system of war pensions. When Lloyd George formed a government in 1916, Barnes became minister of pensions. When Arthur Henderson resigned from the war cabinet over his wish to attend a socialist conference in Stockholm (to help bolster Alexander Kerensky's position in Rus-

sia), Barnes took his place. Like Henderson before him, Barnes gave the government expertise in industrial relations, and in 1917 he was in charge of the major government enquiry into industrial unrest following the May 1917 engineering strikes.

Churchill, as minister of munitions, worked with Barnes over labor matters from 1917 to 1918. There was friction between them when Barnes, with Lord Milner, was much involved in sorting out the problems of differential wages between skilled, semiskilled, and unskilled workers over a 12.5 percent wage award to engineering workers in October 1917. Barnes even blamed Churchill for the unrest when speaking in Glasgow in mid-January 1918, although in his autobiography he conceded that Churchill had "made an honest effort to rectify" the problem.

Barnes, who had been steadily moving politically to the right in the Labour movement, resigned from the Labour Party at the end of the war; this enabled him to stay on in the coalition government. In the 1918 general election, he was part of that "patriotic Labour" that called for the hanging of the German kaiser. He held his seat against the Labour Party.

However, in David Lloyd George's postwar coalition, Barnes played a liberal role. He attended the Paris Peace Conference in 1919 as the government's Labour representative. He was an able advocate of the League of Nations, and he played a major role in the creation of the International Labour Organization (ILO). He clashed with Churchill over Russia; Barnes was among those ministers in mid-1919 who were critical of British military intervention and wanted an early end to it. He also urged moderation in Ireland.

After the ILO was set up and a permanent Labour Office established in Geneva, Barnes, in January 1920, resigned from the government. Faced with the likely loss of his parliamentary seat to a resurgent Labour Party, Barnes did not contest the

1922 general election. In retirement, he remained active in support of the ILO and in the cooperative movement. By the mid-1930s, he was a supporter of Harold Macmillan's Next Five Years Group. He died on 2 April 1940.

Suggestions for further reading:

Barnes, G. N. 1924. *From Workshop to War Cabinet.* London: Herbert Jenkins.

Churchill, Winston S. 1929. *The Aftermath.* London: Thornton Butterworth.

Nield, Barbara. 1977. "Barnes, George Nicoll." In vol. 4 of *Dictionary of Labour Biography,* edited by J. M. Bellamy and J. Saville. London: Macmillan.

Battenberg, Prince Louis Alexander of (First Marquess of Milford Haven, 1854–1921)

Churchill got on well with Prince Louis of Battenberg, at least until wartime. Prince Louis was generally judged to be the ablest senior officer in the navy before the First World War, although he was not as forceful nor as brilliant as Lord Fisher. For Churchill, this was an advantage, enabling him, as first lord of the admiralty, to have his way more readily than he would had he had Fisher to contend with.

Born at Graz, Austria, 26 May 1854, Prince Louis was the eldest son of Prince Alexander of Hesse and grandson of Louis II, grand duke of Hesse-Darmstadt. Through the friendship between his mother, formerly the Countess Julia Theresa von Haucke, and Princess Alice, daughter of Queen Victoria, he grew up in Britain and became a naturalized citizen. He joined the Royal Navy as a cadet in 1868. As a lieutenant, he took part in the bombardment of Alexandria in July 1882 and the subsequent occupation. After several promotions, he became director of naval intelligence at the admiralty, 1902–1915. He

was made a rear admiral in 1904. After several years of command at sea, he returned to the admiralty as second sea lord in 1911. The following year, Churchill appointed him first sea lord. In 1911, Herbert Henry Asquith had passed Prince Louis over after sounding out Lloyd George who (according to Lord Esher) "was horrified at the idea of a German holding the supreme place."

Prince Louis reached the top of the Royal Navy because he was very capable. Because Queen Victoria and King Edward VII took an interest in his career, however, he was by no means hindered by his royal connections. In 1884, he married his cousin, Princess Victoria, the daughter of Louis IV of Hesse-Darmstadt and Princess Alice. Like Edward VII, Prince Louis spoke with a pronounced German accent, and this German background resulted in his being undermined when war occurred with Germany in 1914.

On 26 July 1914, as war approached, Prince Louis stopped the demobilization of the fleet after the end of a test mobilization of part of it. Churchill was away at Overstrand, near Cromer, with Clementine and their children. He approved Prince Louis's action by telephone and returned to London. Although Prince Louis played such a large part in preparing the navy for war, his loyalty was questioned by many when war broke out.

Churchill also had some reservations about Prince Louis in the post of first sea lord during wartime. He felt that Prince Louis lacked the imagination of Lord Fisher, and he had also been a reluctant supporter of Churchill over Antwerp. Churchill saw the prime minister on 27 October 1914, both agreeing that Prince Louis should go. Prince Louis, subjected to many vile attacks on his loyalty, was willing to go. He resigned on 29 October 1914. His wish to be admitted to the privy council was granted on 5 November 1914.

In July 1917, at the request of King George V, Prince Louis relinquished his German titles, adopted the surname Mountbatten, and was raised to the peerage as marquess of Milford Haven, earl of Medina and Viscount Alderney. He died on 11 September 1921.

Suggestions for further reading:
Churchill, Randolph S. 1967. *Winston S. Churchill*. Vol. 2. London: Heinemann.
Gilbert, Martin. 1971. *Winston S. Churchill*. Vol. 3. London: Heinemann.
Hurd, Archibald. 1927. "Mountbatten, Louis Alexander, First Marquess of Milford Haven." In *Dictionary of National Biography 1912–1921*, edited by H. W. C. Davis and J. R. H. Weaver. Oxford: Oxford University Press.
Marder, Arthur, 1961. *From the Dreadnought to Scapa Flow*. Vol. 1. Oxford: Oxford University Press.

Battle of Britain (1940)

The Battle of Britain, the aerial warfare from July to October 1940, followed the Battle of France. After the fall of Belgium, the Netherlands, and France, Adolf Hitler turned the Luftwaffe on to the task of defeating the RAF and so preparing the way for the invasion of Britain. The RAF lost many planes and pilots but they inflicted sufficiently heavy losses on the German planes that the threat of invasion was averted. Between 10 July and 31 October 1940, 1,733 German aircraft were destroyed and 915 British fighters were lost (with 449 pilots killed).

Churchill was exultant at the courage and success of British fighter pilots during the summer of 1940, and visited Fighter Command headquarters at Stanmore on 15 August to receive more details about the air battles over Britain. He followed this visit with two more, on 31 August and 15 September, this time to No. 11 Fighter Group headquarters at Uxbridge. He was moved and impressed by what he saw. He spoke movingly in the House of Commons on 20 August of the gratitude that Britain and the free world should feel for the bravery of the British airmen. This he encapsulated in some of his most famous words: "Never in the field of human conflict was so much owed by so many to so few."

Lady Violet Bonham Carter wrote to him, commenting of this sentence that it "will live as long as words are spoken and remembered. Nothing so simple, so majestic and so true has been said in so great a moment of human history."

Suggestions for further reading:
Addison, Paul, and Jeremy Crang, eds. 2000. *The Burning Blue*. London: Pimlico.
Gilbert, Martin. 1983. *Winston S. Churchill*. Vol. 6. London: Heinemann.

BBC (British Broadcasting Corporation)

Winston Churchill's relationship with the BBC was strained. He was outraged by its claims to neutrality in the General Strike (1926) and Suez Crisis (1956). He was equally indignant that he was kept off the air for much of the 1930s. He was suspicious that the BBC was filled with "reds," especially early in the cold war. Yet his wartime broadcasts have become part of history, an important aspect of his ability to boost the nation's morale.

The British Broadcasting Company, Ltd. was established on 18 October 1922. This was done under the auspices of the postmaster general because the post office was the licensing authority for radio stations. It was formed from some 200 manufacturers and shareholders. In December 1926, the British Broadcasting Corporation was formed under royal charter as a public service body required to act in the public interest and funded by radio license fees. From 1923 to 1938, the managing director of the company, and then the corporation, was John Reith. In 1925, 1,6454,000 radio licences were issued, rising to 8,951,000 in 1940 and 9,710,000 in 1945.

Churchill was quick to grasp the political importance of radio. He wanted to mobilize it against the General Strike in 1926, but John Reith refused to allow it to become a direct agent of the government. Reith also refused Churchill's request that the right-wing trade union leader James Havelock Wilson be allowed to broadcast against the strike.

In 1928 Churchill, as chancellor of the exchequer, was allowed to broadcast on the subject of his budget. John Reith noted in his diary, "He delivered a good defence of the budget, supposed to be non-controversial but it was not." Given the imminence of a general election, he was not permitted to broadcast on his 1929 budget.

Churchill was outraged to find himself frequently blocked from broadcasting on the radio as he moved away from the Conservative Party's mainstream in the 1930s. In February 1931, he was turned down when he asked to broadcast on India. In December 1929, he even offered to pay the BBC £100 to broadcast for half an hour on politics, but was firmly told by Reith that its license forbade taking payment for broadcasting. Yet, even in the 1930s, he did broadcast on a few occasions, including in the series *"Whither Britain?"* and *"The Causes of War,"* as well as on India in 1935 and the Mediterranean in October 1938. Churchill even broadcast on Radio Toulouse (which could be received in Britain) in 1938.

Churchill began his premiership in 1940 hostile to the BBC, apparently even referring to it as "an enemy within the gates, doing more harm than good." Churchill saw that two advisers were appointed and a reconstituted board of governors included Lady Violet Bonham Carter. However, Churchill's wartime broadcasts had a big impact on morale during the war. By November 1942, Churchill had broadcast thirty-three times since the outbreak of the war in September 1939.

After the war, Churchill thought the BBC was broadcasting too many communist speakers. In a letter to Herbert Morrison, in 1948, he warned that the communists were a conspiracy, not a party. He also warned the BBC to be alert to communist infiltration.

Churchill was also critical of the BBC's monopoly, resenting his few broadcasts in the 1930s. He was exasperated by the BBC's neutrality during the Suez crisis, 1956.

Suggestions for further reading:
Briggs, Asa. 1961, 1965, and 1970. *The History of Broadcasting in the United Kingdom*. Vols. 1–3. Oxford: Oxford University Press.
Gilbert, Martin. 1988. *Winston S. Churchill*. Vol. 8. London: Heinemann.

Beatty, David (Earl, 1871–1936)

Beatty was the brave, swashbuckling type of naval man whom Churchill admired. Repeated fast promotions and marriage to a wealthy woman encouraged Beatty to become arrogant and to disregard his superiors' views, but Churchill was not put off by this aspect of Beatty. He also warmed to him as a wealthy man of society, who also enjoyed hunting.

David Beatty was born on 17 January 1871 at Stapeley, Cheshire, the second son of David Longfield and Katherine Beatty (formerly Sadleir). From an early age, he was eager to join the navy. When he was thirteen he went to the naval cadet training establishment, the *Britannia*. On graduating at fifteen, he joined the *Alexandra,* the flagship of the Mediterranean Fleet, commanded by the duke of Edinburgh (Queen Victoria's second son) until 1889. He had further contact with royalty when he served on the royal yacht *Victoria and Albert* for Queen Victoria's summer cruise in July 1892. His other postings included serving on the *Trafalgar*. In 1896, that ship's former commander, Stanley Colville, was put in charge of the gunboats used in Sir Herbert Kitchener's campaign to retake the Sudan in 1896. Colville asked for Beatty to join him. When Colville was seriously wounded on the way to Dongola, Beatty took command. After a spell of leave, Beatty returned and was in action for much of the time between October 1897 and the Battle of Omdurman in August 1898. Churchill had seen Beatty at a distance when he and another officer were walking along the bank of the Nile and Beatty, on a gunboat, offered them a drink, throwing them a bottle of champagne. Churchill also wrote of Beatty and the gunboats in his *The River War* (1899). Beatty went on with Kitchener to Fashoda.

Beatty returned from Egypt a famous figure. He was made a Companion of the Distinguished Service Order and promoted to commander at an unusually early age. Posted to China, he saw action in the Boxer Rising, 1900. For his service and bravery, he was promoted to captain in 1900, although he was not yet thirty. In 1910, he was promoted to rear admiral, the youngest since the eighteenth century. His career continued to advance rapidly when Churchill became first lord of the admiralty.

On 8 January 1912, Churchill appointed Beatty his naval secretary. Beatty provided Churchill with memoranda on a range of issues, there being then no effective naval staff. Beatty backed Churchill's moves to create a naval war staff. Churchill promoted Beatty to the command of the Battle Cruiser Squadron, effective 1 March 1913. When Britain entered the First World War, Beatty was in northern waters, prepared to scout for the Grand Fleet under Sir John Jellicoe.

Early on in the war, Beatty was successful. In late August 1914, Beatty and his battle cruisers successfully rescued Reginald Tyrwhitt and his flagship at Heligoland Bight, turning a potential defeat into a victory. In January 1915, he scored a limited success off the Dogger Bank. His promo-

tion to vice admiral was confirmed in August 1915. Beatty's career reached a climax in the Battle of Jutland, 31 May–1 June, 1916. There Jellicoe showed sensible caution and Beatty showed boldness and bravery, but did not excel at signaling (one of his major tasks being to provide information to the Grand Fleet).

In November 1916, Jellicoe became first sea lord and Beatty was promoted to acting admiral (at forty-five) and given command of the Grand Fleet. Beatty took a keen interest in combating submarines and was an advocate of convoys. On 1 January 1919, Beatty was promoted to admiral. He was also made an earl and appointed to the Order of Merit in 1919. That November, he became first sea lord, retiring in 1927. He died on 11 March 1936 and was buried in St. Paul's Cathedral on 16 March.

Related entry:
Fisher, John Arbuthnot

Suggestions for further reading:
Chalmers, Rear Admiral W. S. 1951. *The Life and Letters of David, Earl Beatty.* London: Hodder and Stoughton.
Gilbert, Martin. 1971. *Winston S. Churchill.* Vol. 3. London: Heinemann.
Marder, Arthur. 1961–1970. *From the Dreadnought to Scapa Flow.* 5 vols. Oxford: Clarendon Press.
Roskill, Stephen. 1980. *Admiral of the Fleet Earl Beatty: The Last Naval Hero.* London: Collins.

Beaverbrook, Lord (William Maxwell Aitken, 1879–1964)

Churchill and Lord Beaverbrook's friendship often blew hot and cold. Churchill, like so many others, found Beaverbrook's company fun and uplifting. Yet Beaverbrook was often predictably unpredictable as a political supporter, often eager to ride his own political hobbyhorses. As a friend, Beaverbrook was often very

Canadian-born British publisher and politician Lord Beaverbrook, c. 1952 (Hulton/Archive)

generous, especially when people suffered adversity. This was true of his relationship with Churchill.

Max Aitken was born at Vaughan, Maple, Ontario, on 25 May 1879, the third son of William Cuthbert and Jane Aitken. William Aitken, a Presbyterian minister, had emigrated to Canada from Scotland. Max's mother was the daughter of Joseph Noble, a farmer and storekeeper. Leaving the local school at sixteen, he moved from working in a law firm to selling insurance and then bonds. After much business dealing, he was a dollar millionaire by 1907. In July 1910, he and his wife moved to England. Through Andrew Bonar Law's support, he secured the Conservative nomination for Ashton-under-Lyne. He won the seat in the December 1910 general election. He was given a knighthood in June 1911 and made a baronet in January 1916. He received a peerage in December 1916.

Beaverbrook met Churchill through their mutual friend F. E. Smith, the Conser-

vative M.P. for Liverpool Walton, probably in March or April 1911. Aitken, aware of the financial success of Churchill's post–Boer War lecture tour in the United States, offered in late April or early May to organise a visit to Canada for him. Churchill declined. However, Churchill was soon trying to arrange a meeting between Aitken and David Lloyd George, and in December 1911 tried to secure for Aitken a place as a British commissioner to investigate the trade resources of the British Empire, a move that Herbert Henry Asquith, the prime minister, firmly blocked. Clementine Churchill long viewed Aitken, like F. E. Smith, as a likely bad influence on her husband.

When war became imminent in late July 1914, Churchill talked about the political situation with Smith and Aitken, all three interested in the possibility of a coalition government. Bonar Law was not thinking that way. Asquith did not need to for some nine months, as nearly all his ministers supported Britain's entry into the war. Ironically, when Asquith did form a coalition, Churchill's removal from the admiralty was a major Conservative Party demand in spite of Aitken's pleas to Bonar Law. In December 1916, Lloyd George deputed Aitken to break the news to Churchill that the Conservatives still insisted on his exclusion from senior office.

In January 1918, a few months after Churchill's return to government as minister of munitions, he sounded Beaverbrook out about his becoming director of finance in that ministry. Beaverbrook declined. The next month, Lloyd George appointed Beaverbrook minister of information and chancellor of the Duchy of Lancaster. He had a minor tussle with Churchill over who would be in charge of trips to show influential munitions workers the Western Front. Beaverbrook conceded that the selection of who should go should rest with munitions, but all other aspects would be handled by his ministry. Later in the year, when Lloyd George was preparing for a general election, he secured Churchill's help in gaining a promise from Beaverbrook to support the coalition in his newspaper, the London *Daily Express.*

After the First World War, Beaverbrook and Churchill's friendship cooled for some months over intervention in Russia, which Beaverbrook opposed. They were brought together again by Duff and Diana Cooper, who invited them to a dinner party on 4 November 1919. Thereafter, Churchill, Beaverbrook, and the earl of Birkenhead (formerly F. E. Smith) were frequent dining companions. Beaverbrook, always generous to his friends, presented Churchill with a set of the *Dictionary of National Biography* in July 1921.

Churchill and Beaverbrook fell apart again with the 1922 general election. Beaverbrook had supported his friend and mentor, Bonar Law. Worse still, he had used his newspapers and had personally intervened in the East Dorset constituency to oust Churchill's cousin, Freddy Guest. After the death of Bonar Law in October 1923, Churchill sent his condolences to Beaverbrook and they resumed contact. On 12 November 1923, Beaverbrook invited Churchill, Lloyd George, Birkenhead, and Austen Chamberlain to Cherkley for a weekend, where they discussed the new political situation after Stanley Baldwin had come out in favor of protection. In fact, Baldwin's campaign divided the old coalitionists, and Churchill soon abandoned the Liberal Party for Baldwin and the Conservative Party. Beaverbrook appears to have been the shrewder assessor of likely political outcomes in early December 1923. He successfully bet Churchill £5 to £4 that Labour would form a government in 1924, and £15 to £5 that Asquith would not be prime minister in 1924.

Churchill dined with Beaverbrook on 5 November 1924, the evening of his return to high office. Birkenhead, also present, revealed that he had been appointed secretary of state for India. Churchill at first declined to tell Beaverbrook the office he had been given. Birkenhead remonstrated, "You've been consulting with Max for weeks past in the most intimate way—you've been taking his help and advice and support. You were ready enough to appeal to him in your despair and now you neglect him in your hour of triumph." Beaverbrook rightly guessed Churchill had promised Clementine not to reveal what was still secret.

Beaverbrook deplored Churchill's decision to restore Britain to the Gold Standard at the pre-1914 parity. He commissioned J. M. Keynes to write a series of critical articles in the *Evening Standard,* "The Economic Consequences of Mr. Churchill." Churchill was outraged, and again their friendship went into temporary abeyance. This time, their friendship was renewed through their interest in writing recent history. Churchill sent Beaverbrook proofs of the third volume of *The World Crisis;* Beaverbrook reciprocated with those of the first volume of *Politicians and the War.* Beaverbrook staunchly defended Bonar Law and Lloyd George when he read Churchill's proofs, while Churchill wanted changes concerning himself.

Churchill and Beaverbrook clashed over the General Strike, 1926. Beaverbrook felt that the strike could have been averted and disliked Churchill's bellicose outlook on the dispute. He liked even less Churchill's attempt to requisition the *Express*'s newsprint and its buildings. Beaverbrook had a major row with Churchill and secured the support of William Joynson-Hicks, the home secretary, who alone could sign a requisition order. Nevertheless, they continued to exchange proofs and Beaverbrook was present at Churchill's fifty-second birthday party on 30 November 1926. There relations remained good during 1927 and 1928.

By 1929, Beaverbrook was ready to launch his Empire Free Trade campaign. He despised Baldwin but rightly felt that

Neville Chamberlain, not Churchill, would succeed him if he was deposed as leader. By 1932, he was thinking that Churchill might retire from Parliament. However, Beaverbrook was out of sympathy with Churchill on India and not interested in his biography of the duke of Marlborough, although they both supported King Edward VIII during the abdication crisis. Churchill later commented to Beaverbrook that perhaps they had both been wrong about that. Beaverbrook was notably wrong over the coming of war in 1939, repeatedly insisting that it could be averted.

Churchill wanted Beaverbrook brought into wartime government. In November 1939, he pressed Chamberlain to put Beaverbrook in charge of food. When Churchill became prime minister, Beaverbrook became one of his closest advisers, probably his most important friend of similar standing in politics (Anthony Eden, Harold Macmillan, and others being markedly younger). In November 1940, Churchill made Beaverbrook minister for aircraft production and a member of his war cabinet. Churchill also used Beaverbrook as his personal envoy to Stalin and his companion on several major trips abroad. These trips included going to Tours when France collapsed in 1940 and attending Churchill's meeting with President Franklin D. Roosevelt at Placentia Bay in August 1941.

After his role at air production during the Battle of Britain ended, Beaverbrook's closeness to Churchill was politically more significant than his government posts. He was a prominent member of the small group of political figures whom Churchill often saw after midnight. His wartime posts after aircraft production (2 August 1940–1 May 1941) were minister of state (and still in the war cabinet May–June 1941), minister of supply (29 June 1941–4 February 1942), minister of war production (4–19 February 1942), and, after an interlude brought about by ill-health, lord privy seal (24 September 1943–26 July 1945).

In May 1942, Churchill nearly replaced Lord Halifax with Beaverbrook as ambassador in Washington. He even sounded Roosevelt out, through his special envoy, Harry Hopkins. However, Beaverbrook put a major condition on taking the post: that Churchill would make a commitment to the Second Front. Churchill refused. Beaverbrook launched his Second Front Now campaign, utilizing the *Daily Express* and also left-wing speakers, eager to assist the Soviet Union's offensive. Beaverbrook denied that he intended the campaign to result in Churchill's removal.

Beaverbrook returned to office in September 1943. When Churchill fell ill in North Africa in late 1943, Beaverbrook joined him in Marrakesh and kept him company as well as attending military conferences. He resumed his role as a very influential political adviser to Churchill. A. J. P. Taylor, in his biography of Beaverbrook, headed the chapter on his last period of office (1943–1945) "Court Favorite Again," which sums up well his position with regard to Churchill.

Beaverbrook played a major role in the 1945 general election campaign, which proved disastrous for the Conservative Party. Beaverbrook expected the Conservatives, helped by Churchill's prestige, to win. The campaign strategy was directed by Beaverbrook, Brendan Bracken, and James Stuart, the chief whip. Beaverbrook focused on Churchill, presumably as any other Conservative election strategist would have done, and was not responsible for Churchill's counterproductive abuse of the Labour Party. Beaverbrook sent Churchill his resignation from office the day before voting took place. Just before the result, when Churchill was in Berlin, Beaverbrook wrote to him commenting, "The only asset the Tories have got is in Berlin anyway."

Beaverbrook withdrew from active politics for the most part. He was distrusted within the Conservative Party, his only close associate being Brendan Bracken, who was equally distrusted. In 1947, Beaverbrook opposed the American economic loan to Britain. He had earlier opposed the policies of J. M. Keynes that led to the Bretton Woods proposals, 1944, on postwar monetary and financial arrangements.

Churchill often availed himself of Beaverbrook's hospitality and stayed at Beaverbrook's homes in Jamaica and the South of France. Churchill was staying with Beaverbrook in the Mediterranean at La Capponcina on 23 August 1949 when he had a stroke, a matter Beaverbrook kept out of the press. Beaverbrook thereafter took pains to help and protect Churchill, although politically they were apart; Beaverbrook was hostile to Churchill's wish to draw closer to Europe and still wanted to strengthen Empire links. Beaverbrook's last political campaign was against British entry into the European Common Market.

Churchill continued to see Beaverbrook into old age. He wrote to wish Beaverbrook a happy eighty-fourth birthday in May 1963, and went to a dinner to celebrate the birthday on 25 May 1962. He also lunched with Beaverbrook at Cherkley on 3 June 1962. Beaverbrook wrote warmly to Clementine Churchill on her husband's eighty-ninth birthday. Beaverbrook died on 9 June 1964.

Related entries:
Bonar Law, Andrew; Bracken, Brendan

Suggestions for further reading:
Chisholm, Anne, and Davie Michael. 1992. *Beaverbrook: A Life.* London: Hutchinson.
Gilbert, Martin. 1971–1988. *Winston S. Churchill.* Vols. 3–8. London: Heinemann.
Taylor, A. J. P. 1972. *Beaverbrook.* London: Hamish Hamilton.
Young, Kenneth. 1966. *Churchill and Beaverbrook.* London: Eyre and Spottiswoode.

Benn, Tony (Anthony Wedgwood Benn, 1925–)

Churchill, the grandson of a duke, declined to enter the House of Lords.

In 1953, he supported the young Tony Benn in his endeavors to disclaim his rights to a peerage, and reaffirmed his stance on behalf of Benn in 1959, 1960, and 1961.

Tony Benn was born on 3 April 1925 at 40 Grosvenor Road, Westminster, London, the second son of William Wedgwood and Margaret Eadie Benn. His father was a Liberal M.P., 1906–1926, and Labour M.P., 1928–1931 and 1935–1941. He served as secretary of state for India, 1929–1931, and as Viscount Stansgate, secretary of state for air, 1945–1946. His mother was the daughter of Daniel Turner Holmes, a schoolmaster and a Liberal M.P., 1910–1918. Educated at Westminster School and New College, Oxford, Benn joined the RAF in 1943 after one year at Oxford. He returned to his university studies after the war before working for the BBC. He was elected to Parliament for Bristol South-East in a by-election, in succession to Sir Stafford Cripps. He represented the constituency from 1950 to 1960 and from 1963 to 1983. Between 1960 and 1963 he fought to disclaim his father's peerage. His father died on 17 November 1960.

Benn had hoped the problem for him of a peerage would be solved by reform of the House of Lords, something that Churchill hoped in 1953 might be achieved through the agreement of the two main parties. Churchill wanted reform, but the parliamentary Labour Party voted against such an approach to the issue. After the failure in 1953 of a Peers Bill by a Labour M.P., Benn tried to secure the passage of a Personal Bill, which would allow him individually to renounce a peerage. This failed, as did an attempt in the House of Lords by his father in 1955. Benn then tried to abolish the House of Lords and replace its main function with the privy council.

After his father died, Benn vigorously fought his exclusion from the House of Commons. He was backed by his constituency Labour Party, and succeeded in gaining some all-party support for his cause. He was greatly helped by Churchill's willingness in late 1959 to let him use his earlier letter to try to convince Harold Macmillan to support a change in the law. When in February 1961 Benn asked whether Churchill would give him further support when he fought the by-election to be held in his Bristol constituency, he was informed that Churchill had withdrawn from the controversy but was willing to reaffirm his 1953 letter. Later, Churchill contributed £10 to Benn's election fund. Benn's campaign team put out 10,000 copies of Churchill's letters to households in Bristol South-East. Benn was supported by 23,275 voters, to 10,231 for the Conservative candidate. Benn, nevertheless, was excluded from the House of Commons. When Benn was ordered to pay £8,000 costs of the election petition, an appeal raised the money, and again Churchill contributed. With the Peerage Act of July 1963, the Conservative M.P. for Bristol South-East resigned his seat and Benn overwhelmingly won the ensuing by-election.

Tony Benn went on to hold major ministerial offices in the Labour governments of 1964–1970 and 1974–1979. After boundary changes, he fought a new Bristol seat, Bristol East, in 1983 but lost. By this time, the leader of the Labour left, he was triumphantly reelected to the House of Commons in March 1984 for Chesterfield, a seat he held until his retirement in 2001.

When the Royal Historical Society held a conference entitled "Churchill in the Twenty-first Century" in London in January 2001, Tony Benn spoke at a "round table, witness" session, with Lady Soames, Lord Carrington, and Lord Deedes (the last two being the only surviving members of Churchill's 1951–1955 government). Benn was incisive and amusing on the subject of Churchill, recounting not only Churchill's support of his battle to avoid becoming a peer but also commenting on his father's clashes with Churchill over India and his

brother's letter from Churchill. In the Second World War, his brother was reported as saying that he would rather be bombed than be evacuated to the United States, and Churchill sent him a handwritten letter of appreciation and a copy of *My Early Life*.

Suggestions for further reading:
Benn, Tony. 1994. *Year of Hope: Diaries, Letters and Papers 1940–1962*. Edited by Ruth Winston. London: Hutchinson.
———. 2001. "Churchill Remembered." In *Transactions of the Royal Historical Society*, 6th ser., vol. II, pp. 393–397.
Browne, Alfred. 1983. *Tony Benn: The Making of a Politician*. London: W. H. Allen.
Jenkins, Robert. 1980. *Tony Benn: A Political Biography*. London: Writers and Readers Publishing Cooperative.
Lewis, Russell. 1978. *Tony Benn: A Critical Biography*. London: Associated Business Press.

Berlin, Sir Isaiah (1909–1997)

Churchill admired Isaiah Berlin's wartime press summaries from Washington during the Second World War and consulted him over chapters of *The Gathering Storm*. Berlin wrote a notably eulogistic essay on Churchill in 1949, best known under its later title, *Mr. Churchill in 1940*.

Isaiah Berlin was born in Riga, Latvia (then Livonia in the Russian Empire), on 6 June 1909. He was the only child of Mendel and Mussa Marie Berlin. His father was a businessman dealing in timber. During the First World War, the family moved to Andreapol, then to Petrograd. Berlin was educated at home, drawing on the family's library. He grew up with Leonard Schapiro, later also a notable academic in Britain. In October 1920, the family left Petrograd for Riga, and then, in early 1921, moved to England. He was educated at St. Paul's School, London, and Corpus Christi College, Oxford. In October 1932, Berlin became a tutor in philosophy at New College and the following month became the first Jew elected to All Souls. Berlin was a Zionist all his adult life.

In 1941, Berlin worked in New York for the Ministry of Information, building up support for Britain among trade unions, black organizations, and Jewish groups. In New York, he became friendly with Chaim Weizmann. Berlin provided press surveys first for the Ministry of Information and from 1942 for the foreign office (he was based in the British embassy in Washington, D.C.). Berlin's reports were read by Churchill, Anthony Eden, and other cabinet officials and senior officials in Whitehall. In January 1944, Churchill enquired who wrote the reports (which went out under the ambassador's name) and was informed, "Mr. Berlin, of Baltic Jewish extraction, by profession a philosopher." Berlin had met Churchill earlier, albeit very briefly, when taking a cable to him in the White House in August 1943. On 9 February 1944, the Churchills invited Irving Berlin to lunch, muddling him with Isaiah Berlin. Churchill was bewildered when, after asking his guest what was the most important thing he had written, Berlin replied, "White Christmas." This case of mistaken identity became a favorite wartime anecdote in London and Washington.

When Berlin returned to Oxford in 1946, he enjoyed a sizeable reputation. He was already being dubbed "the cleverest man in England." He was one of the people William Deakin recommended Churchill turn to for advice on *The Gathering Storm*. Churchill took Berlin's advice seriously and revised his text appropriately; he thanked Berlin with a £220 honorarium.

In 1949, Berlin wrote a major appreciation of Sir Winston Churchill on the publication of *The Gathering Storm*. The essay first appeared as "Mr. Churchill and F.D.R." in the *Atlantic Monthly* and the *Cornhill Magazine*. It was republished as a small book titled *Mr. Churchill in 1940*

(London: John Murray, 1965) after Churchill's death. In it, he rebutted earlier criticism of Churchill's prose as "a false front, a hollow sham." He argued, "Mr. Churchill sees history—and life—as a great Renaissance pageant." During the Second World War, the seriousness of the situation required a "heightened tone," of which his "archaisms of style" were "indispensable ingredients." In praising both Churchill and Franklin D. Roosevelt, he saw Roosevelt as "a typical child of the twentieth century and of the New World," while Churchill "remains a European of the nineteenth century." Berlin concluded his essay praising Churchill as "an orator of prodigious powers, the saviour of his country, a mythical hero who belongs to legend as much as to reality, the largest human being of our time." This was praise a little reminiscent of that of J. M. Keynes on David Lloyd George, but without negative features. Churchill, when he read Berlin's essay, simply observed, "Too good to be true," but he wrote that Christmas to Berlin observing that he had read it "with so much pleasure."

Isaiah Berlin was much criticized for his eulogy of an active Conservative politician. Berlin admired Churchill, but was not himself a Conservative. Apparently he voted Labour in the 1945 general election and, because of Labour's policy in Palestine, Liberal in the 1950 general election.

Berlin's international fame as a philosopher and intellectual grew during the 1950s and 1960s. In 1957, he succeeded G. D. H. Cole as Chichele professor of Social and Political Theory and in 1965 he became the first principal of Iffley College, which, through Berlin's fundraising abilities, became Wolfson College, a post he held in 1966–1975. He remained active as an internationally renowned scholar, and enjoyed his presidency of the British Academy, 1974–1978. He received a knighthood in 1957 and the Order of Merit in 1971. He died on 5 November 1997.

Suggestions for further reading:
Berlin, Isaiah. 1965. *Mr. Churchill in 1940.*
    London: Methuen.
Gilbert, Martin. 1986 and 1988. *Winston S.
    Churchill.* Vols. 7 and 8. London: Heinemann.
Ignatieff, Michael. 1998. *Isaiah Berlin: A Life.*
    London: Chatto and Windus.

Related entries:
Bevin, Ernest; Truman, Harry S.

Suggestions for further reading:
Bullock, Alan. 1983. *Ernest Bevin: Foreign Secretary
    1945–1951.* London: Heinemann.
Davison, W. Phillips. 1958. *The Berlin Blockade.*
    Princeton: Princeton University Press.
Gilbert, Martin. 1988. *Winston S. Churchill.* Vol. 8.
    London: Heinemann.
Tusa, Ann, and John Tusa. 1988. *The Berlin
    Blockade.* London: Hodder and Stoughton.

Berlin Blockade
(June 1948–May 1949)

The Berlin blockade, with the ensuing Berlin airlift of June 1948 to May 1949, was one of the most serious early incidents in the cold war. The crisis arose after Joseph Stalin was angered by U.S., British, and French plans for their occupied zones of Germany, and specifically by the introduction of a new currency. Stalin imposed a road and rail blockade on Berlin, itself divided but an island within the Soviet zone of Germany.

From the outset of the crisis, Churchill praised Ernest Bevin's firm response to Soviet intimidation, pleased there was no further "Munich." However, in late July 1948, he was concerned that the Berlin crisis could slide into World War Three. In the House of Commons in December 1948, he praised Bevin and his colleagues for the great success of the Berlin airlift. On 31 March 1949, in a wide-ranging speech in Boston, Churchill spoke of the importance of the Berlin airlift and commented that Soviet Russia was "something quite as wicked but in some ways more formidable" than Nazi Germany.

The Berlin blockade reinforced Churchill's belief that a determined stance, backed by overwhelming strength, would deter the Soviet Union and avoid a third world war. On returning to office in 1951, he felt that since the Berlin airlift, the deterrents had become more powerful and a major war was less likely. For him and others, the crisis over Berlin was a turning point in the early cold war.

Bermuda Conference
(December 1953)

The Bermuda Conference between the United States, Britain, and France, was held on 4–8 December 1953. The conference dealt with Soviet policy after Joseph Stalin, Korea, the setting up of a European Defence Community, and atomic energy policy.

The conference had long been intended. Churchill believed that he, rather than any other English politician, had the prestige to bring about better international understanding if a summit conference could be arranged. After the death of Stalin on 5 March 1953, Churchill was eager to arrange such a meeting. On 21 April, he telegraphed President Dwight D. Eisenhower urging such a meeting of "the three victorious Powers, who separated at Potsdam in 1945." Eisenhower was discouraging, but after an approach from the French, he urged that France be included in a meeting between the United States and Britain. Churchill suggested that this meeting be held in Bermuda. However, a French political crisis and then Churchill's serious stroke on 23 June delayed the meeting.

Churchill left London for Bermuda by air at midnight on 1 December 1953. He was accompanied by Anthony Eden, Sir Norman Brook, John Colville, Lord Cherwell (Professor Lindemann), Christopher Soames, and Lord Moran. After arriving in

Joseph Laniel, Dwight D. Eisenhower, and Sir Winston Churchill at the Ocean Club in Bermuda prior to the opening of the Three Power Conference, 7 December 1953 (Hulton/Archive)

Bermuda, Churchill returned to the airport on the third to greet Joseph Laniel and Georges Bidault, the French prime minister and foreign secretary; and on the fourth to greet President Eisenhower and his secretary of state, John Foster Dulles.

The conference was marked by Eisenhower's taking a grimmer view of Soviet intentions after Stalin. Churchill argued for NATO (North Atlantic Treaty Organization) to be strong but that the West reassure the Russians that they need not fear another invasion and that wider contacts and trade should be encouraged. Eisenhower saw no need to change policy toward the Soviet Union, which he believed remained committed to a "policy of destroying the Capitalist free world by all means, by force, by deceit or by lies." The British and Americans, meeting apart from the French, also differed over a proposed response to a future breach of the truce in Korea. To the

concern of Churchill and Eden, Eisenhower made it clear that he was prepared to use atomic weapons. Whereas Churchill believed such weapons to be of a new and different dimension to conventional weapons, Eisenhower saw them as a further development in conventional weapons.

The British and French differed over the proposed European Defence Community, the French not wishing to join. Churchill argued that the only realistic alternative in that case was to bring West Germany into NATO. This was not an alternative favored by the United States at that time, who preferred a "peripheral defence" of Europe, relying on their bases stretching from Iceland to Turkey.

Before Eisenhower left, Churchill urged him to stop the United States supplying arms to Egypt. Churchill ended the conference disappointed that it was not leading to a summit conference with the Soviet

Union. Churchill left Bermuda by air on the evening of 10 December, the same day that Clementine Churchill, accompanied by Mary Soames, accepted on his behalf the Nobel Prize for literature in Stockholm.

Related entry:
Eisenhower, Dwight David

Suggestions for further reading:
Colville, John. 1985. *The Fringes of Power.* London: Hodder and Stoughton.
Gilbert, Martin. 1988. *Winston S. Churchill.* Vol. 8. London: Heinemann.
Young, John. 1996. *Winston Churchill's Last Campaign: Britain and the Cold War 1951–1955.* Oxford: Clarendon Press.

both to well-established artistic and society figures and to members of the younger generation. One of the most frequent visitors to Faringdon in the 1940s was Clarissa Churchill. Berners claimed that Emmeline Pocock, the leading figure in his *Far from the Madding War* (London: Constable, 1941) was based on her.

Suggestions for further reading:
Amory, Mark. 1998. *Lord Berners: The Last Eccentric.* London: Chatto and Windus.
Betjeman, John. 1959. "Lord Berners." In *Dictionary of National Biography: 1941–1950,* edited by L. G. Wickham Legg and E. T. Williams. Oxford: Oxford University Press.
Rowse, A. L. 1989. *Friends and Contemporaries.* London: Methuen.

Berners, Lord (Gerald Hugh Tyrwhitt, 1883–1950)

Gerald Hugh Tyrwhitt was born 18 September 1883. He was educated at Eton and traveled in Europe before joining the diplomatic service, 1910–1920. He began as honorary attaché to the British embassy at Constantinople before moving on to Rome. Winston Churchill apparently upset some of the Constantinople staff with his rudeness while staying in the embassy in summer 1910. The young Gerald Tyrwhitt made the patronizing observation, "I fancy he can't help it." Later, in the early 1920s, as Lord Berners, he was a fellow member of a house party in the South of France with Winston Churchill, both of them painting. It was said that when Churchill threw away unsatisfactory paintings, Berners recovered them and painted over them.

He inherited the title of Berners in 1918, and with the title, valuable estates. Berners was a notable composer, a writer of mostly witty, light short novels, and a painter. Perhaps above all, he was a colorful social figure, holding court at his home, Faringdon, near Oxford. Berners was host

Bertie, Lady Gwendeline Theresa Mary (1885–1941)

Winston and Clementine Churchill always got on well with Churchill's sister-in-law, Lady Gwendeline (formerly Bertie). Their children spent much time together and the sisters-in-law, although very different in temperament, were good friends.

Lady Gwendeline Theresa Mary Bertie was born in 1885, a daughter of the 7th earl of Abingdon and his second wife, Gwendeline Mary Dormer. "Goonie" (the nickname by which she was best known) was a friend of both Jack and Winston Churchill. Jack wrote to Winston in Africa on 14 November 1907 that "a very wonderful thing has happened. Goonie loves me." They married on 7 August 1908. Their first child, John George, was born on 31 May 1909. He was followed by Peregrine (1913) and Clarissa (1920).

Goonie and Clementine Churchill were great friends. They spent much of July and August 1914 with their children at Overstrand, near Cromer. A year later, they lived together in harmony at 41 Cromwell

Road, South Kensington, when Churchill left the admiralty and felt the need to economize. That summer, he rented Hoe Farm, near Godalming, and, after watching Goonie painting, decided to try himself. One of his earliest paintings was of Goonie. Thereafter, the two families frequently came together at Christmas and other times. Jack and Goonie were gentler souls than Winston and Clementine. Clementine observed on one occasion that her sister-in-law acted as her safety valve when she was angry with Winston.

Her health declined in 1940 through cancer. She died in early July 1941. On 10 July, she was buried in the cemetery at Bladon, where Lord and Lady Randolph Churchill were buried, and where Jack, Winston, and Clementine Churchill were later buried.

Suggestions for further reading:
Churchill, Randolph S. 1967. *Winston S. Churchill.* Vol. 2. London: Heinemann.
Gilbert, Martin. 1971–1983. *Winston S. Churchill.* Vols. 3–6. London: Heinemann.
———. 2000. *The Churchill War Papers.* Vol. 3. London: Heinemann.
Hough, Richard. 1990. *Winston and Clementine: The Triumph of the Churchills.* London: Bantam Press.
Soames, Mary. 1979. *Clementine Churchill.* London: Cassell.
———, ed. 1998. *Speaking for Themselves: The Personal Letters of Winston and Clementine Churchill.* London: Doubleday.

Bevan, Aneurin (1897–1960)

Churchill admired Bevan's considerable skills as an orator and debater, but he deplored Bevan's class bitterness. Perhaps Churchill liked even less Bevan's criticisms of his and his government's conduct of the Second World War. He referred to Bevan's wartime opposition when he castigated Bevan as minister of health, 1945–1951.

Aneurin Bevan was born on 15 November 1897 at 32 Charles Street, Tredegar, Monmouthshire, the sixth of the ten children of David and Phoebe Bevan. His father was a miner, a Methodist, and a lover of music and books. His mother was the daughter of John Prothero, a blacksmith. Educated at Sirhowy elementary school, he began work at the Ty-tryst colliery when he was fourteen. He was an active trade unionist, a radical who was kept out of the coal mines by the employers for much of the time after 1921. He was elected to the Tredegar District Council in 1922, the Monmouthshire County Council in 1928, and to the House of Commons for Ebbw Vale, the seat he represented until his death, in 1929.

Churchill was one of the targets of Bevan's maiden speech in the House of Commons in July 1929. In a debate on the Labour government's interim proposals for unemployment, Bevan criticized Churchill for demanding that the minority government should act cautiously, then, complaining that its measure was insufficient, made a

Labour M.P. Aneurin Bevan, minister of health, leaving 10 Downing Street after a cabinet meeting on the general election date, 10 January 1950. (Hulton/Archive)

jibe about Churchill's "chameleon-like character in politics." Churchill later congratulated him on an effective debating speech.

In the late 1930s, Bevan was impressed by Churchill's stand against appeasement. He wrote in August 1940 of Churchill, "All the manifold gifts of the first parliamentarian of the time could do nothing against the servile limpets of the Tory Party machine." Although he praised Churchill as "the unchallenged leader and spokesman of the British people," he felt it vital to ensure the government was subject to criticism. In an article titled "The Problem of Mr Churchill" in *Tribune,* July 1941, he observed of Churchill, that "if speeches could win a war, then we have as good as won," but went on to criticize the content of Churchill's speech. He observed of Churchill's denunciation of his critics, "Apparently it was a greater offence to point out the defects in policy than to be guilty of them." He complained, "This is a one-man government." Bevan continued to oppose aspects of the government's war policy, not least the threat to close the London *Daily Mirror* over a cartoon by Zec. He was also prominent in calling for an early Second Front in Europe. Churchill responded to Bevan's opposition by calling him "a squalid nuisance."

With Labour's election victory, Bevan became minister of health. Churchill attacked him with vigor, repaying Bevan's wartime criticisms. Churchill often criticized Bevan with venom, complaining of his class-war attitudes. When the National Health Service came into being in July 1948, Bevan stated in a speech that he considered the Tory Party "lower than vermin." Churchill responded by condemning Bevan as "the Minister of Disease," asking whether "morbid hatred" was "a form of mental disease."

Yet for all his bitterness, Churchill respected Bevan's abilities as a speaker. On one occasion, listening to Bevan in the House of Commons, Churchill regretted that there were no such skillful speakers on the Conservative side.

Bevan's ministerial career ended as minister of labor, January–April 1951. He resigned from Attlee's government over the introduction of prescription charges to the National Health Service. He and his supporters, the Bevanites, were opponents of the Labour Party leadership for several years. Bevan returned to the leadership of the party as shadow colonial secretary, then foreign secretary and, in 1959, deputy leader. He died on 6 July 1960.

Suggestions for further reading:
Foot, Michael. 1962 and 1973. *Aneurin Bevan.* Vols. 1 and 2. London: MacGibbon and Kee and Davis-Poynter.
Smith, Dai. 1993. *Aneurin Bevan and the World of South Wales.* Cardiff, UK: University of Wales Press.

Beveridge, Sir William (1872–1963)

Beveridge was a social researcher, a civil servant, an academic, and a Liberal politician. In 1908, Churchill turned to him for advice on labor exchanges. In 1942 and afterwards, Churchill was politically embarrassed by the level of popular support for Beveridge's report on a contributory, near comprehensive social welfare system.

William Beveridge was born in Rangpur, Bengal, on 5 March 1872, the second child and elder son of Henry and Annette Beveridge. His father was a district sessions judge in Bengal who had worked for the East India Company because his father's bookselling and publishing business had gone bankrupt. His mother was the daughter of William Ackroyd, a Stourbridge businessman. Educated at Charterhouse and Balliol College, Oxford, he was elected the Stowell Civil Law Fellow at University College, Oxford, a position he held until

1910. From 1903–1905 he was subwarden at Toynbee Hall, the university settlement in East London, where he studied poverty at close quarters. From 1906 to 1908, he was a leader writer for the *Morning Post*.

Churchill, who was full of how Liberalism might deal with poverty and unemployment, was impressed by Beveridge's four articles, "Social Reform: How Germany Deals with It" in the *Morning Post* in September 1907. When Churchill took over at the Board of Trade, Beveridge, who was in the building one day, provided the civil servants with several publications and memoranda he had written concerning labor exchanges. The result was that Churchill in the summer of 1908 secured Beveridge's employment at the Board of Trade to help prepare the legislation on labor exchanges. Both Beveridge and Churchill saw labor exchanges as a preliminary to compulsory unemployment insurance. After the Labour Exchanges Act was passed, Beveridge became director of labor exchanges.

Beveridge continued to be employed in the Board of Trade until 1916. From 1916–1918 he was second secretary at the Ministry of Food, becoming permanent secretary in 1919. He was knighted in 1919. He left the civil service for an academic career, serving as director of the London School of Economics and Politics, 1919–1937, and master of University College, Oxford, 1937–1945.

In 1941, Arthur Greenwood, minister without portfolio and a member of the war cabinet, was in charge of preliminary plans for reconstruction and invited Beveridge to chair an interdepartmental committee of civil servants to look into future social services. The resulting report, which became known as the Beveridge Report, recommended the consolidation and the extension of existing provision, with the intended result that citizens should be covered for the risks of life from the cradle to the grave. The report presumed that government management of the economy would ensure near full employment and that a National Health Service would be set up. The report memorably spoke of dealing with the "five giants on the road of reconstruction": want, ignorance, squalor, idleness, and disease.

The Beveridge Report was published in December 1942. It became a surprise wartime bestseller, also being translated and published in other countries. It offered the British people "jam tomorrow" at the time of hardship and general austerity. Beveridge promoted his report with vigor. The Conservative Party was lukewarm; Churchill was anxious about the cost and did not wish to promise too much for peacetime reconstruction given the disillusionment after the end of the First World War when a "Land Fit for Heroes" did not materialize. In contrast, the Labour Party took it up and soon became associated with its fulfilment, which was one element in the party's 1945 general election victory.

Beveridge himself was a Liberal. He was elected to Parliament under the wartime truce for Berwick-upon-Tweed in 1944, but he was defeated in the 1945 general election. He was created a baron in 1946, taking the title of Baron Beveridge of Tuggal. He died on 16 March 1963.

Suggestions for further reading:
Beveridge, Lord. 1953. *Power and Influence: An Autobiography.* London: Hodder and Stoughton.
Harris, José F. 1977. *William Beveridge: A Biography.* Oxford: Clarendon Press.

Bevin, Ernest (1881–1951)

*E*rnest Bevin was a major contributor to the success of Churchill's wartime government. Bevin, Britain's most powerful trade union leader and a big man in both senses, could stand up to Churchill and argue his case. He was called the Labour

British foreign secretary Ernest Bevin (left), at the first meeting of the United Nations General Assembly at Central Hall, Westminster, London, with British Prime Minister Clement Attlee, 10 January 1946 (Hulton/Archive)

Party's Churchill. Winston Churchill in Opposition generally approved of Bevin's main policies as foreign secretary, Bevin also being strongly anticommunist.

Ernest Bevin was born in Winsford, Somerset, on 7 March 1881, the youngest of the seven children of Diana Mercy Bevin, formerly Tidboald. She had married William Bevin, an agricultural laborer, and moved to South Wales, but had returned without him four years before Ernest's birth. Bevin was brought up in poverty, his mother working as a domestic servant and a midwife so that she could feed the family of eight. She died when Bevin was eight and he was brought up in Devon by his sister and her husband. He attended Winsford Church School; then with his move to Devon, he attended Morchard Bishop Church School, Colebrook Board School, and Hayward Boys' School,

Crediton, leaving when he was eleven. He moved from job to job, living in Bristol from the age of thirteen. He was an active Baptist for some years, then became a socialist. He became secretary of the Bristol Right to Work Committee in 1908 and unsuccessfully ran for Bristol City Council in 1909. In 1910 he organized carters as a branch of the Dockers' Union. He was notably successful and from 1911 became one of the union's regional organizers, rising to be one of three national organizers in 1914. After the First World War, Bevin worked toward amalgamating transport workers' trade unions; on 1 January 1922, the Transport and General Workers' Union was formed, with Bevin as its secretary.

As a trade union leader, Bevin was often critical of Churchill in the interwar years. He deplored Churchill's role in intervention in Russia, the return to the Gold Standard at the prewar parity in 1925, and Churchill's activities during the General Strike, 1926. However, like Churchill, he was hostile to Adolf Hitler and Fascism, observing at the 1936 Labour Party conference that the trade unions had been smashed in Germany and Austria and stating the case for rearmament.

When Churchill formed his wartime government, Bevin's inclusion was very important for Churchill and for the trade union movement. George Isaacs, M.P., a trade unionist and Attlee's future minister of labor, later commented that "the fact that in Bevin they had a personality who could meet the prime minister on level terms" was "a necessary condition for the partnership." Churchill soon came to appreciate Bevin's toughness and determination and within five months he included him in the war cabinet. In a speech in the House of Commons on 29 July 1941, Churchill paid tribute to Bevin's massive contribution to securing high industrial production.

After the 1945 general election, Bevin was foreign secretary until March 1951. Churchill admired his firm anticommunist stance. He kept Bevin and Attlee informed of U.S. reactions to his draft Fulton speech and to the delivered speech. As leader of the Opposition, Churchill found much to criticize in Bevin's conduct of foreign affairs but believed that he was right about the big issues. He paid a fulsome tribute to Bevin when he stood down as foreign secretary.

Bevin became lord privy seal on 9 March 1951, but his health was deteriorating rapidly; he died on 14 April 1951. Churchill recommended his widow for an honor, and in 1952 she became Dame Florence Bevin. When Churchill College was being founded, the Transport and General Workers' Union donated £50,000 to build a memorial library to Bevin.

Related entries:
Attlee, Clement Richard; Fulton Speech

Suggestions for further reading:
Bullock, Alan. 1960, 1967, and 1983. *The Life and Times of Ernest Bevin.* 3 vols. London: Heinemann.
Gilbert, Martin. 1983, 1986, and 1988. *Winston S. Churchill.* Vols. 6–8. London: Heinemann.
Weiler, Peter. 1993. *Ernest Bevin.* Manchester, UK: Manchester University Press.
Wrigley, Chris. 2001. "Churchill and the Trade Unions." In *Transactions of the Royal Historical Society,* 6th ser., vol. II, pp. 273–293.

Bibesco, Princess Elizabeth Charlotte Lucy (1897–1945)

Churchill was friendly with the Asquith family, especially before 1915. He remained friends with Violet Asquith (later Bonham Carter) all his life. He also knew her half-sister, Elizabeth, meeting her frequently at various social functions.

Elizabeth Charlotte Lucy Asquith was born at 20 Cavendish Square, London, on 26 February 1897. She was the elder child of Herbert Henry Asquith, the former Liberal home secretary and future prime minister, and Margaret (Margot), his second wife (formerly Tennant). Asquith had four children by his first wife, who died in 1891. Elizabeth was intelligent and attractive, but overshadowed by her mother. When she wished to marry a young American diplomat without money, Hugh Gibson, in December 1916, Margot was outraged. However, in 1919, her parents readily accepted her engagement to the Roumanian diplomat, Prince Antoine Bibesco (1878–1952). They married at St. Margaret's, Westminster, in May 1919, a lavish wedding that her parents could not fully afford. In 1921, the Bibescos went with their daughter Priscilla, born in 1920, to Roumania's New York embassy, and thereafter served in embassies in other countries. Elizabeth was not happy in her marriage and drank too much alcohol as a solace. At the outbreak of the Second World War, she returned to Roumania.

She died in early April 1945, shortly before the war in Europe ended.

Related entries:
Asquith, Herbert Henry; Asquith, Margot; Bonham Carter, Lady Violet

Suggestions for further reading:
Bennett, Daphne. 1984. *Margot.* London: Gollancz.
Bonham Carter, Mark, and Mark Pottle, eds. 1996. *Lantern Slides: The Diaries and Letters of Violet Bonham Carter 1904–1914.* London: Weidenfeld and Nicolson.
Pottle, Mark, ed. 1998. *Champion Redoubtable: The Diaries and Letters of Violet Bonham Carter 1914–1945.* London: Weidenfeld and Nicolson.

Birdwood, Field Marshal Lord William Riddell (1865–1951)

Birdwood was a senior military officer at Gallipoli, whose camp commandant was Jack Churchill. Birdwood had known Winston Churchill earlier, in India and in South Africa.

Birdwood was born in India on 13 September 1865 at Kirkee, Poona, the second son of Herbert Mills Birdwood, under secretary to the government of Bombay. He was brought up in England, educated at a dame school in Cheltenham, Clifton College, and Sandhurst. He served in India from 1885. He first met Winston Churchill in a polo tournament between the 11th Bengal Lancers and the 4th Hussars (in late 1896 or early 1897). Birdwood went to South Africa in November 1899, taking part in the Battle of Colenso, December 1899. Birdwood next met Churchill when the latter, soon after his escape from the Boers, joined the troops in their camp before Colenso in his dual roles of a war correspondent and an officer in the South Africa Light Horse. Birdwood later recalled that "his description of all his adventures filled us with admiration and delight." Churchill also joined Birdwood at the head of the cavalry squadrons entering Ladysmith when it was relieved on 28 February 1900. From 1900–1909, Birdwood worked with Lord Kitchener, and from 1905–1909 was his military secretary.

From 1912, Birdwood was secretary to the government of India in the army department and a member of the governor general's legislative council. With the outbreak of the First World War, he helped to organize the supply of Indian army units to France, Egypt, and Mesopotamia. In November 1914, Kitchener appointed Birdwood to command Australian and New Zealand troops. In February 1915, Kitchener sent Birdwood to the Dardanelles to report on the naval attack. Birdwood reported back that naval action was unlikely to succeed on its own. By the time a combined naval and military attack on the Gallipoli Peninsula was launched, Birdwood argued against it, given that the possibility of surprise had gone. Sir Ian Hamilton went ahead, and Birdwood commanded the Anzac troops. He was in executive command of the successful evacuation of Gallipoli. In Robert Rhodes James's judgement, "Birdwood was one of the very few British commanders to leave Gallipoli with an increased reputation."

Birdwood accompanied his Anzac Corp to France in March 1916. He was promoted to general in 1917 and became commander of the Fifth Army in May 1918. Jack Churchill stayed with him from Gallipoli until 1919, mostly as his assistant military secretary.

After the war, Birdwood commanded the Northern Army in India, 1920–1924, and became commander in chief of the Indian army, 1925–1930. After retiring from the army, he became master of Peterhouse College, Cambridge (1930–1938). Birdwood was created a baronet in 1919, promoted to field marshal in 1925, and was created Baron Birdwood of Anzac and

Totnes in 1938. As chancellor of Bristol University, Churchill conferred an honorary doctorate on him in 1935. Churchill wrote the foreword to Birdwood's autobiography, *Khaki and Gown,* published in December 1941. Birdwood died on 17 May 1951.

Related entries:
Churchill, John Strange Spencer; Gallipoli; Hamilton, Sir Ian Standish Monteith; Kitchener, Horatio Herbert

Suggestions for further reading:
Birdwood, Field Marshal Lord. 1941. *Khaki and Gown: An Autobiography.* London: War, Lock and Co.
Churchill, Randolph S. 1966. *Winston S. Churchill.* Vol. 1. London: Heinemann.
James, Robert Rhodes. 1971. "Birdwood, William Riddell." In *Dictionary of National Biography 1951–1960,* edited by E. T. Williams and H. M. Palmer. Oxford: Oxford University Press.

Birkenhead, Earl of (Frederick Edwin Smith, 1872–1930)

For many years, F. E. Smith was Winston Churchill's closest friend. Churchill viewed him as his most brilliant contemporary and greatly enjoyed his company. Together they founded The Other Club. Churchill enjoyed Smith's enthusiasm for high living and his buccaneering approach to politics. However, Clementine Churchill worried with good reason about Smith's being a major source of encouragement to her husband to be extravagant.

Frederick Edwin Smith was born at Birkenhead on 12 July 1872, the eldest son of Frederick and Elizabeth Smith. His father was an estate agent, a barrister, and a local Conservative politician, becoming mayor of Birkenhead a month before his death in 1888. His mother was the daughter of Edwin Taylor, a local rate collector. He was educated at Birkenhead School and Wadham College, Oxford, achieving first class honors in jurisprudence. Elected a fellow of Merton College, he taught law there and at Oriel College, 1897–1900. He was called to the bar in 1899. He practiced law in Liverpool and was a major local Conservative speaker. He made his name in a number of highly publicized trials in London. In the January 1906 general election, he was elected for Liverpool, Walton.

Among the depleted ranks of Conservative M.P.s in the 1906 Parliament, Smith stood out. Six-foot-one-inch in height, good-looking, and very self-assured, he exercised a sharp wit and savage tongue on his opponents. He attacked the Liberal ministers with all the vigor and flair that Lord Randolph Churchill had exhibited in the early 1880s. He lived an extravagant lifestyle, earning great sums at the bar and spending equal or more sums quickly. He enjoyed high society. In mid-1906, Churchill and Smith were introduced in the House of Commons, and they became life-long friends.

Clementine Churchill often criticized her husband's friendship with Smith. She rightly felt that Smith encouraged him in reckless extravagance and excess. In the pre–First World War period, she deplored the way they both lost large sums gambling when at camp as officers of the Oxfordshire Yeomanry. They also drank too much and smoked too many cigars. When Margaret and F. E. Smith had a son on 7 December 1907, he was christened Frederick Winston Furneaux Smith, and Winston Churchill was his godfather. When Clementine and Winston Churchill had a son in 1910, he was christened Randolph Frederick Spencer Churchill, and F. E. Smith was his godfather.

In the pre-1914 House of Commons, Churchill, David Lloyd George, and F. E. Smith were among the best speakers. They were not hindered by friendship from making hard-hitting party speeches, with Smith often savaging Churchill and Lloyd George. In 1911, Churchill and Smith formed The Other Club, which facilitated cross-party dining even in the midst of heated party politics. Churchill was often Smith's guest at his London home, 32 Grosvenor Gardens, or at his country house in Charlton, near Oxford.

After the outbreak of war in 1914, Lord Kitchener had Smith appointed director of the Press Bureau. He was responsible for the highly controversial area of censoring press reports concerning the army and navy. Smith moved on to the role of recording officer to the Indian Corps, 1914–1915. Unlike Churchill, he did not press for frontline service on the Western Front. In May 1915, Smith became solicitor general in Asquith's coalition government, receiving a knighthood with the post. When Carson resigned as attorney general in October 1915, Smith succeeded him, joining the cabinet. He remained attorney general under Lloyd George until January 1919.

While Churchill was in France, Smith wrote to him about the latest political gossip. He also visited him, taking gifts of brandy and cigars. On one occasion when he visited Churchill, in January 1916, the military authorities arrested Smith because he had failed to obtain the necessary pass. Churchill appreciated Smith's continuing friendship, not least because he championed Churchill's return to political office.

In January 1919, Lloyd George promoted Smith to lord chancellor, with Smith taking the title earl of Birkenhead. Birkenhead was a reforming lord chancellor, and he also played an influential role in the government. With Churchill, he was a particularly close associate of Lloyd George, the prime minister. Both Churchill and Birkenhead played important roles in the negotiations on Ireland in 1921. He was prominent in the group of leading Conservatives who remained loyal to Lloyd George and the coalition government, and were ousted by the Carlton Club meeting in October 1922.

In 1924 Baldwin brought back the leading coalition-supporting Conservatives. Birkenhead returned as secretary of state for India, from November 1924 until October 1928. Churchill also returned to office, as chancellor of the exchequer. In 1928, Birkenhead was offered the lord chancellorship again, but declined. Later in the year he retired from office, anxious to earn more money to settle his debts and to provide for his children.

Sadly, Birkenhead squandered his great gifts. In January 1920 Lord Riddell had noted in his diary that he was "very clever and brilliant, but drinks too much. Far more than is good for him." By 1928 he was exhausted and his health was undermined. He died on 30 September 1930.

According to Clementine Churchill, her husband wept when he learned of his death, saying repeatedly, "I feel so lonely." At The Other Club on 30 October 1930, Churchill paid tribute to his fellow founder-member who had attended seventy-eight out of ninety-four dinners since the club was founded, saying that he had been his dearest friend. Later, he wrote an essay on Birkenhead in the *News of the World,* 1 March 1936, which was revised for *Great Contemporaries* (1937).

Related entries:
Lloyd George, David; The Other Club

Suggestions for further reading:
Birkenhead, the Earl of. 1933 and 1935. *Frederick Edwin, the Earl of Birkenhead.* 2 vols. London: Thornton Butterworth.
Campbell, John. 1983. *F. E. Smith: First Earl of Birkenhead.* London: Jonathan Cape.
Soames, Mary. 1979. *Clementine Churchill.* London: Cassell.

Black and Tans (1919–1922)

The Black and Tans were the larger of two bodies of men recruited to reinforce the Royal Irish Constabulary. Their name derived from the color of their uniform. The other body was the Auxiliaries, an elite group of former British army officers. Some 12,000 Black and Tans were recruited between December 1919 and 1921, whereas some 1,500 Auxiliaries were recruited. Many of those recruited to the Black and Tans were former soldiers. The Black and Tans were responsible for numerous atrocities against nationalist communities during their involvement in the British forces' struggle against the Irish Republican Army. Arthur Henderson, the leading Labour Party politician, condemned the violence of the British government's forces in Ireland, comparing this to the effect of turning "a mad dog loose in the public streets."

Churchill supported David Lloyd George in approving the setting up of the Black and Tans as a counterterrorist body. According to Thomas Jones, the deputy secretary of the cabinet, Churchill felt that before a settlement was reached in Ireland, "It was necessary to raise the temperature of the conflict to a real issue and shock, and trial of strength." When General Henry Wilson, chief of the Imperial General Staff, protested to Churchill about the Black and Tans' reprisals, Churchill refused to condemn them, even talking (according to Wilson) of them as "honourable and gallant officers." Both he and Lloyd George publicly denounced IRA (Irish Republican Army) assassinations, Churchill at Dundee on 16 October 1920 declaring the government's resolve "to break up the murder gang in Ireland."

In November 1920, Churchill urged Lloyd George to require all males in Ireland to carry identity cards and all those traveling between Ireland and Britain to have passports. With Lloyd George, Churchill, and other ministers as obvious assassination targets, Scotland Yard assigned Detective Sergeant Walter. H. Thompson to guard Churchill.

In May 1921, Churchill was one of five ministers (all Liberal coalitionists) who favored trying to negotiate a truce with the leaders of Sinn Fein, but the five were outvoted in cabinet.

Churchill continued to defend the conduct of the Black and Tans in 1920–1921 in the House of Commons in April 1922. With the Irish settlement in December 1921, the Black and Tans and the Auxiliaries were disbanded. Churchill's gave his support to a gendarmerie that was recruited from these men for Palestine. In October 1922, General H. H. Tudor wrote to Churchill stating that the Black and Tans had been successful in Palestine, having "a great influence already in keeping things quiet."

Related entries:
French, Sir John Denton Pinkstone; Thompson, Walter H.

Suggestions for further reading:
Gilbert, Martin. 1975. *Winston S. Churchill*. Vol. 4. London: Heinemann.
Townshend, Charles. 1979. *The British Campaign in Ireland 1919–1921*. Oxford: Clarendon Press.

Bladon

Bladon church was the parish church for Blenheim Palace. Lord Randolph Churchill was buried there on 28 January 1895, and Lady Randolph Churchill was buried beside him on 2 July 1921. Their younger son, John, was also buried there in late February 1947.

Winston Churchill had first intended to be buried at Chartwell; however, on 15 December 1959, he told his solicitor that he wished to be buried with his father at Bladon.

On 30 January 1965, after the state funeral with the service in St. Paul's Cathedral, Churchill's body was taken by the launch *Havengore* down the Thames to Festival Pier, then on the locomotive *Winston Churchill* from Waterloo to Long Handborough. From Long Handborough station his body was taken to Bladon churchyard and buried next to his father, mother, and brother.

Related entries:
Churchill, John Strange Spencer; Churchill, Lady Randolph; Churchill, Lord Randolph Henry Spencer

Suggestion for further reading:
Gilbert, Martin. 1988. *Winston S. Churchill.* Vol. 8. London: Heinemann.

Blenheim Palace

Blenheim Palace, near Woodstock, Oxfordshire, was built for the first duke of Marlborough by Sir John Vanbrugh (1664–1726), the architect and playwright, from money and land granted in 1705 by Queen Anne. It was named after the duke's 1704 victory at Blenheim. Queen Anne herself had chosen Vanbrugh and taken an interest in the design. It was built as both a private home and a national monument. In 1710, the building was only half completed at a cost of £134,000 against Vanbrugh's original estimate of £100,000. By 1712, it was still not complete, though £220,000 had been spent and £45,000 was owed. After the first duke's death, the building was completed in 1725 by his widow, Sarah, Duchess of Marlborough.

Winston Churchill was born in a downstairs room at Blenheim on 30 November 1874. He wrote warmly of Blenheim Palace in a passage in his book *Lord Randolph Churchill.* He much enjoyed staying with his relatives there, including the 1893 Christmas he spent there (a year after his cousin had succeeded as the ninth duke at the age of nearly twenty-one), and resumed visits after his return from the Western Front in 1916. It was at Blenheim that he proposed to Clementine Hozier on 11 August 1908 and where the couple spent the first two days of their honeymoon in mid-September 1908. Their stays at Blenheim were interrupted for some two years after a row between Clementine Churchill and the duke over her warm support and correspondence with David Lloyd George concerning a fiery land speech in October 1913. This family row was settled by 1916, in which year Winston and Clementine Churchill spent Christmas at Blenheim. As well as many Christmases, another notable visit was in August 1958 to mark the fiftieth anniversary of their engagement. After his state funeral, Winston Churchill was buried within a mile of his birthplace, next to his parents and his brother, Jack, in Bladon churchyard.

Blenheim Palace was also the venue for one of Churchill's major post–Second World War speeches, given in August 1947 to a rally of west country Conservatives. Randolph Churchill (1911–1968) wrote about Blenheim in his *Fifteen Famous English Homes* (London: Derek Verschoyle, 1954).

Suggestions for further reading:
Churchill, Randolph S. 1966 and 1967. *Winston S. Churchill.* Vols. 1 and 2. London: Heinemann.
Gilbert, Martin. 1971 and 1988. *Winston S. Churchill.* Vols. 3 and 8. London: Heinemann.
Sherwood, Jennifer, and Nikolaus Pevsner. 1974. *Oxfordshire.* Harmondsworth, UK: Penguin.
Soames, Mary. 1979. *Clementine Churchill.* London: Cassell.

Board of Trade, President of (1908–1910)

Churchill was president of the Board of Trade, 12 April 1908 until 14 February 1910. When Herbert Henry Asquith became prime minister, he promoted Churchill into the cabinet, giving him the post that had been filled with distinction by his friend and mentor, David Lloyd George. Asquith had offered him the admiralty and possibly the Local Government Board, but

Churchill declined the former as it was held by his uncle, Lord Tweedmouth. His years at the Board of Trade marked the apogee of his reputation as a radical social reformer.

Even before going to the Board of Trade, Churchill had taken an interest in social policy. He had spoken on the subject during his Tory Democrat days. In 1906, he reviewed Upton Sinclair's classic exposé of labor conditions in the Chicago meatpacking industry, *The Jungle,* for T. P. O'Connor's weekly journal. From autumn 1906, he called for more state intervention to ensure minimum standards of living and working conditions and to control the railways. In 1907, he helped Charles Masterman, a Liberal M.P. who focused on social reform, in preparing an article that included discussion of social problems. In this period he most probably read articles by Sidney and Beatrice Webb and William Beveridge on social issues. In January 1908, he asked Arthur Wilson Fox of the Board of Trade for advice concerning Germany's development of labor exchanges and social security.

On taking office, Churchill investigated the issue of labor exchanges, which led to the Labour Exchanges Act, 1909. He also took up the issue of low-paid labor ("sweated labour") much of it being female labor, which resulted in the Trade Boards Act, 1909. Churchill also took up the matter of unemployment insurance, which became Part 2 of the National Insurance Act, 1911.

Churchill, like Lloyd George before him, intervened to try to settle industrial disputes under the provisions of the Conciliation Act of 1896. He made considerable efforts to establish a new sliding-scale agreement in the cotton industry. He also encouraged the spread of boards of conciliation in industry. Between late 1907 and the end of 1909, sixty-seven new boards were established.

Churchill also introduced several bills to assist industries. These industries included shipping, insurance, and electric lighting.

Related entries:
Lloyd George, David; Trade Boards Act

Suggestions for further reading:
Addison, Paul. 1992. *Churchill on the Home Front.* London: Jonathan Cape.
Churchill, Randolph S. 1967. *Winston S. Churchill.* Vol. 2. London: Heinemann.
Gilbert, Bentley B. 1966. *The Evolution of National Insurance in Britain.* London: Michael Joseph.
Pelling, Henry. 1989. *Winston Churchill.* 2d ed. London: Macmillan.
Wrigley, Chris. 1982. "The Government and Industrial Relations." In *A History of British Industrial Relations 1875–1914,* edited by Chris Wrigley. Brighton, Sussex, UK: Harvester.

Boer War (1899–1902)

Winston Churchill became internationally famous through his bravery under fire on an armored train in November 1899 and his subsequent escape from Boer captivity in Pretoria. He also wrote twenty-two substantial dispatches for the *Morning Post,* which became the basis for two of his books. He returned to Britain in 1900 with the fame he had long yearned for, and successfully contested a seat in Oldham in the 1900 general election.

The first Boer War of 1881 had seen William Gladstone's government concede independence to the Boer republics of the Transvaal and the Orange Free State, though Britain claimed suzerainty over them (in effect, a right of veto over their external affairs). By the late nineteenth century, Britain had growing anxieties about all of South Africa, a crucial strategic area on the route to India. With the discovery of gold and diamonds in the Boer republics, the balance of power in South Africa swung toward the Boer states. The republics' leaders were hostile to Britain and eagerly transported much of their trades through Portuguese territory, not British South Africa. There was also increasing friction between immigrant white labor (uitlanders) and the Boer authorities,

British statesman and author Winston Churchill during his service in the South African Light Horse, 1899 (Hulton/Archive)

with the British taking up the cause of the non-Boers. An attempt made by Cecil Rhodes's associate, Dr. Jameson, to precipitate an uprising against the Boers in December 1895 ended in a fiasco and caused Rhodes to resign as premier of Cape Colony.

The British colonial secretary, Joseph Chamberlain, and the government's representative in South Africa, Sir Alfred Milner, appear to have believed that war was inevitable and failed to negotiate a peaceful settlement. In October 1899, fearing British intentions, the Boers made a preemptive military strike into British Natal. The British army initially suffered a series of defeats in "Black Week," 9–15 December 1899, and British troops were besieged at Ladysmith, Mafeking, and Kimberley. By June 1900, British forces had lifted the sieges and had gone on to capture the Boer capitals of Johannesburg and Pretoria. Thereafter, the war was marked by prolonged Boer guerrilla resistance and stern measures taken by Lord Kitchener to eradicate support for Boer forces.

On 31 October 1899, Winston Churchill arrived at Cape Town to write reports on the war for the *Morning Post*. He then traveled by armored train toward the front. On 15 November, the train was ambushed near Frere, and part of it derailed. Churchill saved the railway engine by leading a group of men to clear the track, though under enemy fire. Churchill was taken prisoner and moved to Pretoria, where he was held in the State Model School. He escaped on 12 December 1899 and made his way by train to Laurenco Marques, Portuguese territory to the east of Pretoria. He returned to Durban by steamer on 23 December.

He remained in South Africa for a further six months. He wrote reports of military action at the Tugela River, Spion Kop, Hassar Hill, and Potgieter's Ferry. He was among the first to enter Ladysmith and Pretoria. He was with Sir Ian Hamilton in his campaigns in the Orange Free State and the Transvaal. He left South Africa on 4 July, traveling on the *Dunottar Castle*, the ship he had traveled out on.

Related entries:
Botha, Louis; Milner, Alfred; Smuts, Jan Christian

Suggestions for further reading:
Churchill, Randolph S. 1966. *Winston S. Churchill*. Vol. 1. London: Heinemann.
Churchill, Winston S. 1900. *London to Ladysmith*. London: Longmans, Green.
———. 1900. *Ian Hamilton's March*. London: Longmans, Green.
———. 1930. *My Early Life*. London: Thornton Butterworth.
Woods, Frederick, ed. 1972. *Young Winston's Wars*. London: Seeley Service.

Bonar Law, Andrew (1858–1923)

Andrew Bonar Law was not Churchill's preferred kind of politician.

He was too dour, lacking in exuberance or apparent vitality. Although a prime minister (1922–1923) and a ministerial colleague of Churchill, he was not one of those Churchill wrote about and included in his collection *Great Contemporaries* (1937). Yet the two men's relationship became warmer after the First World War.

Andrew Bonar Law, the son of a Presbyterian minister of Ulster background, James Law, was born in rural New Brunswick, Canada, on 16 September 1858. After his mother's death in 1861, perhaps when he was six, Bonar Law went to Scotland to live with his aunt at Helensburgh, near Glasgow. After leaving school, he worked for his mother's family firm, Kidston and Sons, merchant bankers. In 1885, the Kidstons lent him the money to buy a partnership in Jacks and Company, traders in iron and steel, and Bonar Law made the firm very profitable. In 1900, he won the Glasgow, Blackfriars seat. After Balfour became prime minister in 1902, Bonar Law became parliamentary secretary to the Board of Trade. He came out as a strong supporter of Joseph Chamberlain and tariff reform. Losing his seat in the 1906 general election, he was reelected in a by-election for Dulwich and was soon included as a Conservative and Unionist front bench speaker.

Under Balfour's leadership, Churchill was in the opposing, free trade, section of the Conservative Party to Bonar Law. When Bonar Law left his safe seat of Dulwich to argue the tariff reform case in Manchester Northwest in the December 1910 general election, Churchill campaigned in the constituency against him. Bonar Law lost, but his courageous campaign made him a potential candidate for leader, and he was consoled with the safe seat of Bootle in a by-election in February 1911. In November 1911, he succeeded Arthur James Balfour as leader of the Conservatives and Liberal Unionists. Thereafter, he and Churchill were vigorous opponents over Ulster and Home Rule, both strongly denouncing the other.

In the House of Commons on 30 April 1912, on the second reading of the Home Rule Bill, Churchill accused Bonar Law of "almost treasonable activity." In turn, at a Unionist rally at Churchill's birthplace, Blenheim, Bonar Law denounced the government of being "a revolutionary committee." Yet, for all this, Churchill tried to find a compromise solution acceptable to the Irish Nationalists and Ulster. Bonar Law, stiffened by Sir Edward Carson, was determined that nothing but the exclusion of Ulster from the Home Rule Bill would satisfy them. The outbreak of the First World War prevented likely civil war in Ireland.

Bonar Law and most of the Conservative leadership (other than Balfour) were firm in requiring that Churchill be removed from the admiralty when Herbert Henry Asquith's coalition government was formed. Churchill's attempt on 20 May 1915 to impress on Bonar Law the wisdom of his conduct at the admiralty got nowhere. Bonar Law became colonial secretary, and Churchill became chancellor of the Duchy of Lancaster. Bonar Law opposed Churchill's going to Gallipoli at Lord Kitchener's invitation in July 1915 and he increasingly opposed the continuation of that campaign. After Churchill resigned from the government, Bonar Law often made savage replies to Churchill's speeches in the House of Commons.

When David Lloyd George brought Churchill into his government in July 1917, many prominent Conservatives were outraged. Bonar Law, though hostile to Churchill's appointment declined to make a major issue of it, fearing a long-excluded Churchill would end up invigorating an Asquithian opposition. After the 1918 general election, Bonar Law accepted that Churchill should have a major post in the new government. Thereafter, Churchill's relations with Bonar Law were generally good. Churchill was genuinely sorry when ill-health forced Bonar Law to resign from Lloyd George's government in March

1921. When Churchill's daughter Marigold died in August 1921, Bonar Law was among those who sent his sincere condolences.

Bonar Law's health was sufficiently strong for him to be prime minister for seven months (October 1922–May 1923) after he had provided leadership to a Conservative revolt against Lloyd George's coalition government. He died on 30 October 1923.

Related entries:
Balfour, Arthur James; Beaverbrook, Lord; George, David Lloyd

Suggestions for further reading:
Adams, R. J. Q. 1999. *Bonar Law.* London: Murray.
Blake, Robert. 1955. *The Unknown Prime Minister.* London: Eyre and Spottiswoode.
Churchill, Randolph S. 1967. *Winston S. Churchill.* Vol. 2. London: Heinemann.
Gilbert, Martin. 1971 and 1975. *Winston S. Churchill.* Vols. 3 and 4. London: Heinemann.
Ramsden, John. 1978. *The Age of Balfour and Baldwin, 1902–1940.* London: Longmans.

Bonham Carter, Lady Violet (Baroness Asquith of Yarnbury, 1887–1969)

Churchill's long friendship with Lady Violet Bonham Carter had several downs—when they clashed on political issues—but far more ups. In *Great Contemporaries* (1937), he referred to her as a "wonderful being" and praised her gifts of oratory, observing that the aged ex-premier Asquith "found in his daughter a champion redoubtable even in the first rank of party orators." Churchill especially appreciated her company after the Second World War, when so many of his other friends died.

Helen Violet Asquith was born in London on 15 April 1887, the fourth child of five of Herbert Henry and Helen Kelsall Asquith. Her father was a barrister and M.P., a future Liberal Party leader, and prime minister. Her mother, who died in 1891, was the daughter of a Manchester physician. Educated privately, she was a keen reader. She venerated her father and, after his death, defended his reputation with the utmost vigor. She also came very close to hero worship with Winston Churchill, whom she met in 1906. In 1915, she married her father's principal private secretary, Maurice Bonham Carter. They had four children, and two of them were active in Liberal politics. Mark Bonham Carter was briefly a Liberal M.P. and later a Liberal peer, and Laura married Jo Grimond, Liberal Party leader in 1956–1967, and played an active part in Liberal affairs. Sir Maurice Bonham Carter died on 7 June 1960.

Violet Bonham Carter wrote her recollections of Churchill in her book on the period up to the fall of her father from the premiership in 1916. *Winston Churchill as I Knew Him* (1965) was generally well received. However, the British historian A. J. P. Taylor, writing in the *New York Review of Books,* 3 June 1965, observed that many of her stories about Churchill come from other books. More vivid on Churchill are her diaries, published in three volumes in 1995–2000.

She first met Churchill in the summer of 1906 at a dinner party given by Lady Wemyss. When she said that she was nineteen, Churchill replied that he was already thirty-two, and then held forth on the theme of the shortness of human life. She always remembered his words, "We are all worms. But I do believe that I am a glow-worm." She first heard him speak at a public meeting on 22 November 1910 and was greatly impressed. When Churchill was at the admiralty, she was perceptive in noting in May 1912 that "his enthusiasms became obsessions." She also commented in October 1913, "Winston is disconcerting because he is so self absorbed," but added that if someone caught his attention he could be very appreciative.

After her father's fall from office in 1916, Violet Bonham Carter supported him politically, and Churchill's career went in other directions. She did not share Churchill's horror at the thought of a minority Labour government taking office in 1924, nor would she press her father to keep them out. She was right in predicting to Churchill, "I think the Labour Govt. will suffer from the timidity and inefficiency of its members not from their violence." She was hurt when Churchill wrote to criticize a reference to himself in Asquith's posthumous memoirs but failed to express sympathy over the death of her father. He wrote a fulsome apology, acknowledging he was ashamed.

In the 1930s, she was a prominent supporter of Churchill in his opposition to appeasement. She joined him in spring 1936 in forming the focus in Defence of Freedom and Peace and was one of three support speakers to Churchill at the public meeting the group held in Albert Hall on 3 December 1936. She was widely judged to be one of the most effective political speakers of the period. She was deemed by one observer to have been as "hard as steel" when opposing the Munich agreement, 1938, and was delighted when Churchill became prime minister.

From 1943, Churchill hoped for a Conservative-Liberal coalition against Labour, and he courted Violet Bonham Carter's support for such a policy. By early 1944, she was well aware that the political tide in Britain was running powerfully to the Left. By late in the war, her admiration for Churchill as war leader and her affection for him as an old friend were strong. In the excitement of victory in Europe, she wrote to him on 8 May, beginning the letter "Beloved Winston" and ending it "your devoted Violet." Nevertheless, she made it clear that in the 1945 general election she would be an opponent. She came third in the Wells constituency.

After 1945, Violet Bonham Carter was a much appreciated friend of both Winston and Clementine Churchill. She even entered the upper-crust silly nicknames used of family and close friends, her sobriquet from at least June 1945 being Churchill's "bloody duck." She was platonically very fond of him in their later years. In 1950, she noted in her diary that she would have liked to help him politically: "I also longed to do what he asked for my great love's sake and because this might be the last thing he would ever ask me that I could do."

In response to his renewed requests for a Conservative-Liberal electoral agreement, however, she knew that she could not sway the other leading Liberals. In 1951, Churchill supported her standing against Labour, without a Conservative candidate, for Colne Valley in the 1951 general election. Churchill even went to her constituency on 15 October and spoke in her support; nevertheless, she lost by 2,189 votes. Had she been elected, Churchill would have offered her the post of minister of education. In the June 1953 honors list she was gazetted as a Dame of the British Empire (DBE).

Violet Bonham Carter saw much of Churchill during the last fifteen years of his life. He was delighted with her chapter, "Winston Churchill as I Know Him" in *Winston Spencer Churchill: Servant of Crown and Commonwealth,* edited by Sir James Marchant (1954). As a woman whose life was spent in politics, she understood his obsession with politics. After one of her many visits to him after his retirement, she noted his sad comment (in July 1960) that he had had no appetite for life since 1955. Her last visit was on 14 January 1965, when she saw him resting in bed and noted in her diary "his beloved face looked at peace."

Although she was not elected to the House of Commons, Violet Bonham Carter was a major force in Liberal politics. She was president of the Liberal Party in 1945 and was president of the Women's Liberal Federation, 1923–1925 and 1939–1945, and a major advocate of Britain's entry into the Common Market. She was frequently on television as a politician and as a commentator on current affairs. In 1964, she was made a life peer, becoming Baroness Asquith of Yarnbury, and was active in the House of Lords. She died on 19 February 1969.

Related entries:
Asquith, Herbert Henry; Bibesco, Princess Elizabeth Charlotte Lucy

Suggestions for further reading:
Bonham Carter, Jane. 1998. "Violet Bonham Carter." In *Dictionary of Liberal Biography,* edited by Duncan Brack. London: Politico's Publishing.

Bonham Carter, Mark, and Mark Pottle, eds. 1996. *Lantern Slides: The Diaries and Letters of Violet Bonham Carter 1904–1914.* London: Weidenfeld and Nicolson.

Bonham Carter, Violet. 1965. *Winston Churchill as I Knew Him.* London: Eyre and Spottiswoode and Collins.

Pottle, Mark, ed. 1998. *Champion Redoubtable: The Diaries and Letters of Violet Bonham Carter 1914–1945.* London: Weidenfeld and Nicolson.

———. 2000. *Daring to Hope: The Diaries and Letters of Violet Bonham Carter 1946–1969.* London: Weidenfeld and Nicolson.

Boothby, Robert John Graham (Lord Boothby, 1900–1986)

Churchill admired the young Robert Boothby, perhaps seeing something of himself in his self-confident, almost buccaneering approach to politics. However, Boothby was not willing to fetch and carry for Churchill and spoke out on the issues of the day. In the 1930s Boothby was at the fore of the antiappeasers who backed Churchill.

Robert Boothby was born in Edinburgh on 12 February 1900, the son of Robert Tuite and Mabel Augusta Boothby. His father was the manager of the Scottish Provident Institution and a director of the Royal Bank of Scotland. His mother was the daughter of Henry Hill Lancaster, an Edinburgh advocate. Educated at Eton and Magdalen College, Oxford, Boothby embarked on a legal career in 1922. His father was a friend of Stanley Baldwin, and through the Conservative and Unionist headquarters in Edinburgh, he was offered Orkney and Shetland to fight in the 1923 general election. He came within 811 votes of his Liberal opponent. In the 1924 general election, he won East Aberdeenshire from the Liberals and held it until he went to the House of Lords in 1958.

Boothby, when young, had admired David Lloyd George's coalition government, 1916–1922, and Lloyd George and Churchill in particular. He first met Churchill when he and Birkenhead spoke at the Oxford Union. From the start as an M.P., he made a mark as a liberal Conservative, speaking up for the unemployed and for moderate trade unionism and against a return to the Gold Standard at the prewar parity. In spite of his criticisms of Churchill as chancellor of the exchequer, Churchill made him his parliamentary private secretary in late 1926 and secured his election to The Other Club in 1928. Boothby, however, was very much his own man and not willing to put serving Churchill first and last. He later observed of Churchill, "He saw and lived life in terms of himself."

Boothby, with Harold Macmillan, Oliver Stanley, and John Loder, published *Industry and the State: A Conservative View,* in April 1927. This advocated much intervention in the economy, outraging many Conservatives. Churchill, however, took up one proposal: to derate industry. Boothby accompanied Churchill in 1927 to Italy. Boothby differed from Churchill, deploring his vigorous anti-Soviet policy, and he offered his resignation to Churchill in December 1928. Churchill rejected the offer, as he did on other occasions.

After the 1929 general election defeat of the Conservatives, Boothby and Churchill differed over India. However, Boothby and

Churchill came together again on the issue of rearmament. Indeed, in July 1927, Boothby had complained publicly of Churchill's parsimony in the matter of defense expenditure. Boothby was alarmed by Adolf Hitler from the time he secured power, and was at the fore in opposing the German reoccupation of the Rhineland, the Hoare–Laval Pact, and Munich.

When Churchill became prime minister, Boothby received junior office as under secretary at the Ministry of Food. He was effective in the post, but resigned in October 1940 after a select committee of the House of Commons criticized his prewar connection with emigré Czech financial claims. In referring the matter to a select committee, Churchill probably overreacted. Boothby then served with Bomber Command and later worked with the Free French. Churchill's major contact with Boothby after Boothby's resignation was to beseech him to speak in favor of the government on 1 July 1942 when a motion of no confidence was debated in the House of Commons. Two years later, Boothby aroused Churchill's wrath by trying to debate in the House of Commons Churchill's refusal to let Charles de Gaulle go to France in June 1944.

Boothby continued to be his own man after the Second World War. In December 1945, he denounced the American economic loan as "an economic Munich" and divided the House of Commons, even though Churchill, leader of the Opposition, did not want this to happen. However, Boothby and Churchill worked together in favor of Western European unity, but Boothby was bitterly disappointed when he was given no ministerial post in 1951. Churchill did send him as a Conservative Party representative to the European Consultative Assembly at Strasbourg, a role he maintained until 1957. In December 1952, Churchill invited Boothby to dine at Chartwell and the 1953 coronation honors list posted him for a knighthood. Boothby, a

skillful orator, moved Churchill to tears with his fine address at Duff Cooper's memorial service in 1954, but otherwise their political relationship was marked by clashes. After Churchill's retirement, Boothby was not given office under Anthony Eden, who apparently commented that he did not want Charles James Fox in his government. Boothby was made one of the first life peers in 1958.

In Churchill's retirement Boothby visited him on several occasions in the Smoking Room of the House of Commons or at his London home. He had dinner with Churchill in January 1965 shortly before Churchill died. Boothby died on 16 July 1986.

Suggestions for further reading:
Boothby, Robert. 1947. *I Fight to Live*. London: Gollancz.
———. 1978. *Recollections of a Rebel*. London: Hutchinson.
Gilbert, Martin. 1976, 1983, 1986, and 1988. *Winston S. Churchill*. Vols. 5–8. London: Heinemann.
Rhodes, James Robert. 1991. *Bob Boothby: A Portrait*. London: Hodder and Stoughton.

Botha, Louis (1862–1919)

Louis Botha was the type of valiant foe Winston Churchill greatly admired. A formidable enemy during the Boer War, Botha went on to lead South Africa and to display his loyalty to Britain during the First World War.

Louis Botha was born in Natal in 1862, the son of a cattle rancher. His maternal grandfather, Gerrit van Rooyen, had been a leading supporter of General Marthinius Pretorius, the Boer leader of mid-century. After fighting Zulus, he was granted substantial land to farm in the Vryheid district of the Transvaal. He had been opposed to the Boer preemptive strike against Britain, abstaining in the vote. Nevertheless, he distinguished himself in the early stages of the war and was promoted to general after the Battle of Ladysmith, 30 October 1899.

Botha was in charge of the Boer force that ambushed the armored train on which Churchill traveled when he was seeking to see fighting. Botha's men captured fifty-eight of those who had been on the train, including Churchill. Churchill later became wrongly convinced that Botha had personally captured him.

Botha went on to become internationally famous as a Boer general. He was the victor against General Sir Redvers Buller at the Battle of Colenso, ten miles southeast of Ladysmith, on 15 December 1899. He went on to retake Spion Kop, 24–25 January 1900. Botha commanded the last Boer army in action and succeeded in beating Major Hubert Gough at Blood River Port in Natal in September 1901. Botha was one of the Boer leaders who negotiated peace terms with the British in 1902.

With the Liberal government's grant of self-government to the states in South Africa, Botha, like Jan Christian Smuts, was willing to work with Britain. Churchill deplored Lord Milner's moves to smash the Boers because he thought the Boers should be "the rock" on which British influence in the area should be based. Botha became the premier of the Transvaal in 1907 after the Boer Het Volk Party won a majority of five in the first elections after the war. Churchill paid a warm tribute to Botha when Botha attended the 1907 Colonial Conference. There were even untrue rumors that Churchill and Botha's daughter were romantically attached.

Botha became the first prime minister of the Union of South Africa; he died in office in 1919. In the First World War, he displayed his loyalty to Britain in suppressing a pro-German Boer revolt and also in a successful campaign in German Southwest Africa. He attended the Paris Peace Conference and signed the Treaty of Versailles.

Related entries:
Boer War; Smuts, Jan Christian

Suggestions for further reading:
Churchill, Randolph S. 1966 and 1967. *Winston S. Churchill*. Vols. 1 and 2. London: Heinemann.
Nasson, Bill. 1999. *The South African War*. London: Arnold.
Pakenham, Thomas. 1979. *The Boer War*. London: Weidenfeld and Nicolson.

Bracken, Brendan (1901–1958)

Brendan Bracken was the most consistent supporter of Winston Churchill during the 1930s and served in his wartime government as minister of information. Clementine Churchill initially did not care for him, feeling that he was a self-seeking hanger-on. Perhaps she had also heard the widespread but false rumor that he was Churchill's son through another relationship. By the later part of the Second World War she recognized Bracken's strong loyalty to her husband and was genuinely upset by his death.

Brendan Bracken was born on 15 February 1901, the second son of Joseph Kevin and Hannah Bracken. His father, a sculptor and builder, was a Fenian, a founder of the Gaelic Athletic Association, and also a supporter of Charles Stuart Parnell. He died when Brendan was three. Bracken was brought up by his mother, the former Hannah Ryan, who had no interest in nationalist politics, and her mother. Although he loved reading, the young Bracken was notably mischievous. In early 1916, he was sent to Australia, where he made contact with a cousin who was a priest. He continued to read widely but upset his Catholic contacts by his blatant lack of faith. Nevertheless, he took to signing his name "Brendan Newman Bracken." He returned to Ireland in the second half of 1919, but soon moved on to England. A year later, he presented himself as nearly four years younger then he was and as an Australian orphan at Sedbergh for what was to be a final term of schooling. He acquired what he felt he needed to rise in England, a public-school tie. While teaching, he made contact with the local Independent Conservative M.P., and made a mark proclaiming the merits of the British Empire. In late 1922, he began working for Oliver Locker Lampson's *Empire Review,* a monthly. Through this journal he became friendly with J. L. Garvin, the editor of the London *Observer,* and Winston Churchill, from mid-1923.

Bracken visited Churchill at Hosey Rigge, a house rented by Churchill while work was being carried out on Chartwell. He was soon Churchill's main assistant in Churchill's unsuccessful campaign as an Anti-Socialist candidate in Leicester West in the 1923 general election. When Brendan Bracken edited the *Illustrated Review,* he secured an essay by Churchill on free trade, and also a story by Garvin. He turned it into a successful magazine under the title *English Life.* John Masefield wrote a vindication of the Gallipoli campaign for the newly titled magazine, and Churchill also contributed articles to *English Life.*

By the time of the March 1924 by-election, Bracken had appointed himself in effect Churchill's assistant. He again devoted himself to Churchill's campaign and secured a letter of support for Churchill from Arthur Balfour. However, not long after Churchill was appointed chancellor of the exchequer, Bracken and Churchill fell out. Bracken continued to champion Churchill in *English Life* and also in the *Banker,* which he founded in January 1926. He even printed Clementine Churchill's portrait in *English Life.* He was also secretary, while Churchill was chairman, of a committee raising funds for a memorial to Lord Stevenson.

Bracken prospered as a director of the publishers Eyre and Spottiswoode. In 1928, he was instrumental in persuading them to buy the *Financial News,* a half share in the *Economist,* the *Investors Chronicle,* and the *Liverpool Journal of Commerce.* The following year, he took over the medical journal, the *Practitioner.*

In 1929 Bracken, with an invented résumé, was selected as Conservative candidate for North Paddington and won the seat by 528 votes. He soon became associated with Churchill, defending his record as chancellor of the exchequer and supporting his stance on India. Bracken also cultivated and encouraged Winston Churchill's son Randolph. In the 1931 general election, Churchill spoke at Bracken's main political rally. Bracken was returned with a majority of 14,304 votes.

In the 1930s, Bracken became the loyalist of Churchill's small group of supporters. Bracken and Robert Boothby kept Churchill informed of political developments when he was writing at Chartwell or visiting the United States. Bracken put up with Churchill's bad moods and often managed to raise his flagging spirits. After the 1935 general election, in which he was returned with a majority of 7,228, Bracken mobilized such business friends as W. S. Robinson and Sir Henry Strakosch to provide details of German rearmament. While Bracken supported Churchill through thick and thin, Churchill attended Conservative Party functions in Bracken's constituency.

With Churchill's return to office as first lord of the admiralty, Bracken became his parliamentary private secretary. Although Churchill was impeccably loyal to Neville Chamberlain, Bracken aired his hostility to the appeasers still in office. When Chamberlain's government was doomed, Bracken pressed Churchill hard not to offer to serve under Lord Halifax. With Churchill as prime minister, Bracken was made a member of the privy council but was given no formal office. He continued to act as Churchill's assistant. In September 1940, he moved into 10 Downing Street, where he was one of Churchill's small circle of advisers. Later in the year, he was a godfather to Randolph's son, Winston.

Churchill trusted Bracken. Bracken was one of the few during the Second World War who would stand up to Churchill and argue with him when he felt he was wrong. He often gave good political advice, especially when Lord Beaverbrook pressed him to take the Conservative Party leadership when Chamberlain resigned. Occasionally, Bracken was indiscreet. He spoke of the sinking of the French fleet at Oran before it was publicly announced, thereby forcing an earlier statement than had been intended.

When Duff Cooper resigned as minister of information in mid-1941, Beaverbrook successfully pressed for Bracken to succeed Cooper. Bracken was appointed on 21 July 1941, but Churchill was fearful that the post might end Bracken's political career. Bracken aimed to provide the public with information on the war, expecting a free press to be a patriotic and responsible press. Churchill, however, expected the press to criticize neither him nor the government and often expected Bracken or Francis Williams, the controller of censorship, to prevent criticism. To their horror, Churchill urged the suppression of the London *Daily Mirror* because of a cartoon by Zec that offended him.

Bracken was very much Churchill's man and he declined offers of other ministerial posts. The Ministry of Information gave him access to the prime minister when he needed it. Moreover, within a year he was deemed one of the most successful ministers in the government. Nevertheless, there was some hostility toward him, as well as Lord Beaverbrook and Lord Cherwell, from disgruntled Conservative backbenchers who felt the three were too much Churchill's cronies.

Anthony Eden and other ministers appreciated Bracken's role in handling Churchill when he had rash or foolish ideas. Often Churchill would rage at him, but then think again. Bracken was also a valuable conciliator when other ministers or officials clashed. In the latter part of the war,

when Churchill was ill but tried to carry on regardless, Bracken was the person who could say, "Winston, if you go on playing the fool like this you are going to die."

In the last days of Churchill's wartime coalition government and during his brief caretaker government, Brendan Bracken was notably vigorous in party political matters. Because he was opposed to the 1944 Bretton Woods agreement, he declined the office of president of the Board of Trade but accepted first lord of the admiralty. During the 1945 general election, Beaverbrook and his press ran a strong Conservative campaign, which included much reporting of Bracken's speeches; but Bracken lost his seat by 6,545 votes. He then tried to console Churchill on the Conservative Party defeat, observing that without Churchill as leader it would have been vastly worse.

Churchill succeeded in securing him the Conservative nomination for a by-election in Bournemouth in November 1945, which Bracken won with a much reduced majority (from 20,312 to 6,454). Bracken resumed his business interests. He took the lead in opposing the Gas Bill in early 1948. Generally, however, Bracken represented a right-wing free-market Toryism. His sympathies were with Beaverbrook, who had left active politics, and acted as a go-between for Beaverbrook and Churchill.

Bracken played a vigorous role in the 1950 general election campaign. He was a candidate in the safer Conservative Bournemouth East, and won by a majority of 14,787.

When Churchill returned to office in 1951, Bracken was offered the colonial office, and then less onerous domestic posts, but he declined due to poor health. In late 1951, he announced that he intended to resign his seat. He was made a peer in the 1952 New Year's honors list, Viscount Bracken of Christchurch. Although he retired from active politics, he did give Churchill advice and support when Churchill suffered a second stroke in June 1953.

Bracken's later interests included setting up *History Today* in 1951. When Robert Rhodes James, then an undergraduate at Worcester College, had an essay on Lord Randolph Churchill accepted in early 1955, Bracken sent a copy to Churchill. He also accompanied Churchill on several occasions to The Other Club at the Savoy. He was a trustee of the Chartwell Trust, and as such was exasperated by the bad behavior of Randolph Churchill.

Bracken was one of the two major figures in Michael Foot's 1944 polemic, *Brendan and Beverley* (published under the pseudonym "Cassius"). He was also featured as the brash adventurer Rex Mottram in Evelyn Waugh's *Brideshead Revisited* (1945).

Bracken died on 8 August 1958. Churchill was upset by the news of his death, and repeated several times, "Poor dear Brendan." Clementine Churchill was also upset by his death. The main beneficiary of his will was Churchill College, Cambridge. Churchill, Beaverbrook, and others subscribed over £40,000 to the Brendan Bracken Memorial Fund, which set up a reading room in his honor and was attached to the library of Churchill College, Cambridge.

Suggestions for further reading:
Boyle, Andrew. 1973. *Poor Dear Brendan*. London: Hutchinson.
Gilbert, Martin. 1976–1988. *Winston S. Churchill*. Vols. 5–8. London: Heinemann.
Lysaght, Charles Edward. 1979. *Brendan Bracken*. London: Allen Lane.
Soames, Mary. 1979. *Clementine Churchill*. London: Cassell.

Bridges, Edward Ettingdene (Baron, 1892–1969)

As wartime prime minister, Churchill soon began to appreciate the work of Edward Ettingdene Bridges as secretary to the war cabinet and his dedication to securing efficient and effective administration during the Second World War. As for Bridges, he soon came to admire Churchill as a "really great man" who inspired others to emulate his own stamina, courage, and endurance.

Edward Bridges was born at Yattendon Manor, Berkshire, on 4 August 1892. He was the son of Robert Seymour and Mary Monica Bridges. His father was later poet laureate (1913–1930). His mother was the daughter of the leading architect Alfred Waterhouse. He had two elder sisters. He was educated at Eton and Magdalen College, Oxford (1911–1914). Bridges was wounded in March 1917 while serving on the Western Front, and he worked in the treasury before returning to his regiment. After the war, he returned to the treasury, in 1935 becoming head of the division that overlooked defense expenditure. In 1938, he succeeded Sir Maurice Hankey as secretary to the cabinet and to the Committee of Imperial Defence. Bridges's role was reduced to a more manageable scale by Churchill in 1940. Churchill did not have much to do with Bridges until he became prime minister. Then, Bridges later recollected, his attitude was usually "welcoming friendliness combined with outspoken comment." He also testified to a new sense of purpose and greater pace of work in government with Churchill's arrival.

Bridges found Churchill liked to work closely with a group of senior ministers, armed forces officers, and civil servants. They worked in Whitehall, in Churchill's home, and even in his bedroom, and he confided in them. Bridges wrote of Churchill's candor as a result of "the special relationship between Churchill and those who worked closely for him." He also noted that Churchill usually expected applause, not criticism, and that those wishing to influence him needed to impress on him that not only were they on his side but were trying to help his cause. Bridges felt Churchill's "Action This Day" minutes reminded those who received them that Churchill was watching over their performances. They also helped in his speeding up of government. Bridges gave his considered verdict that "From May 1940 to . . . the middle of 1942 were the greatest years of Churchill's life." Churchill paid fulsome tribute to Bridges in his *The Second World War,* Vol. 3 (1949), portraying him as the ideal, hard-working, and self-sacrificing civil servant.

Attlee appointed Bridges secretary to the treasury in 1946. He played an important role in the negotiations to secure the postwar U.S. loan. He was also deeply involved in the postwar overhaul of the civil service. He retired in 1956, but continued, as one of "the good and the great," to chair major committees until 1968. He was created a baron in 1957 and invested as a Knight of the Garter in 1965. He died in Guildford on 27 August 1969.

Related entries:
Brook, Norman Craven; Hankey, Sir Maurice Pascal Alers

Suggestions for further reading:
Gilbert, Martin. 1983 and 1986. *Winston S. Churchill.* Vols. 6 and 7. London: Heinemann.
Trend, Lord. 1981. "Bridges, Edward Ettingdene, First Baron Bridges." In *The Dictionary of National Biography 1961–1970,* edited by E. T. Williams and C. S. Nicholls. Oxford: Oxford University Press.
Wheeler-Bennett, Sir John. 1968. *Action This Day: Working with Churchill.* London: Macmillan.

Brodrick, William St. John Freemantle (Earl of Midleton, 1856–1942)

Although St. John Brodrick was a sincere and able Conservative politician, he lacked charisma. Churchill opposed Broderick's proposed army reforms, adopting a stance explicitly based on that of his father, Randolph Churchill, when he resigned in 1886. He was equally critical of Brodrick's role in recalling Lord Curzon, the viceroy of India, in 1905.

St. John Brodrick was born in London on 14 December 1856, the eldest son of William and Augusta Mary Brodrick. His father was later the eighth Viscount Midleton. His mother was a daughter of Sir Thomas Francis Freemantle, later first Baron Cottesloe. Educated at Eton and Balliol College, Oxford, he was returned unopposed for the safe Conservative seat, West Surrey, in 1880. From 1885 to 1906, he represented Guildford. He held junior office in Lord Salisbury's governments of 1886–1892 and 1895–1900, in the latter being under secretary of state for war and then for foreign affairs. After the 1900 general election, Salisbury promoted him to secretary of state for war, in the midst of the Boer War.

Churchill, newly elected to the House of Commons, naturally spoke in debates on military matters, not hesitating to refer to his own experiences of war. On 12 March 1901, he made a particularly effective speech in the House of Commons over a motion to set up an inquiry into the dismissal of Major General Sir Henry Colville. In it, he argued powerfully that the military authorities must have the right to determine dismissals. Brodrick congratulated Churchill on his success, writing, "May I say you will never make a better speech than you made tonight."

Brodrick, however, very soon found Churchill a vigorous and persistent critic of his proposed army reforms. Brodrick's proposals centered on the creation of six army corps, three of regular soldiers but three of militia and volunteers. This would entail recruiting a further 50,000 to the militia and cost overall an additional £5 million. Churchill criticized the scheme; he said that it was unlikely to make the army stronger, that it was not effective use of £5 million, and that strengthening the navy, not the army, was a greater priority.

After a series of speeches outside of Parliament, Churchill made a major speech in the debate in the House of Commons on 13 May 1901, for which he drew on his father's letter of resignation of December 1886. Brodrick could respond with the observation that Churchill had "a hereditary desire to run imperialism on the cheap." Churchill published his speeches on the army in *Mr. Brodrick's Army,* a 104-page book published by Arthur L. Humphreys in April 1903 and sold for one shilling.

While preparing his biography of Lord Randolph Churchill, Churchill needed (under the terms of his father's literary settlement) to consult the secretary of state for India and also the foreign secretary. Brodrick, in spite of their recent political conflict, was helpful.

Brodrick was moved to the India office in October 1903, with his successor greatly watering down his proposed army reforms. Brodrick was unfortunate to be secretary of state when Curzon and Lord Kitchener feuded. Brodrick put up with much from Curzon, and not just over the clash with Kitchener, before Curzon was recalled in 1905. Churchill was on Curzon's side, condemning Kitchener and Brodrick in his *Great Contemporaries* (1937). Brodrick later observed of Churchill's comments that he "was justly entitled to make on the facts before him," but in his autobiography set out to rebut his assessment. He argued that Curzon's clash with Kitchener "merely stereotyped the conviction of the whole cabinet that, despite Curzon's ability and knowledge and service, his continuance in India was a danger to the Empire."

Brodrick lost his seat in the 1906 general election. His father died in 1907, and he entered the House of Lords as the ninth Viscount Midleton. A big Irish landowner, at Midleton, County Cork, he became the leader of the southern Unionists. In 1917 he sought, through the Irish Convention, to bring a settlement to the Irish conflicts by securing a united, autonomous Ireland but within the British Empire. After the convention's failure, he declined Lloyd George's offer of the lord-lieutenancy of Ireland because he refused to be responsible for introducing conscription and Home Rule in tandem in Ireland. In July 1921, after seeing the Irish statesman Eamon de Valera, he successfully urged Lloyd George to accept a truce in Ireland; but Midleton was disappointed with the resulting settlement. He died on 13 February 1942.

Related entries:
Curzon, George Nathaniel; Kitchener, Horatio Herbert; *Mr. Brodrick's Army*

Suggestions for further reading:
Atkins, J. B. 1959. "Brodrick (William) St. John (Freemantle)." In *Dictionary of National Biography 1941–1950,* edited by L. G. Wickham Legg and E. T. Williams. Oxford: Oxford University Press.
Churchill, Randolph S. 1967. *Winston S. Churchill.* Vol. 2. London: Heinemann.
Midleton, the Earl of. 1939. *Records and Reactions 1856–1939.* London: Murray.
Woods, Frederick. 1963. *A Bibliography of the Works of Sir Winston Churchill.* London: Nicholas Vane.

Brook, Norman Craven (Lord Normanbrook, 1902–1967)

Churchill and Norman Craven Brook built up a good relationship during the Second World War. This was strengthened by Brook's advice and help with *The Second World War.* During Churchill's 1951–1955 government, Brook was the official on whom Churchill relied most. By then it was very much a special relationship, with Brook a great admirer of Churchill.

Norman Brook was born in Bristol on 29 April 1902, the son of Frederick Charles and Annie Brook. His father was a tax assessor. Educated at Wolverhampton Grammar School and Wadham College, Oxford, he embarked on a career in the civil service in 1925. He was principal private secretary then personal assistant to Sir John Anderson, 1938–1942. He was a deputy secretary of the cabinet, 1942–1945. He succeeded Sir Edward Bridges as secretary to the cabinet at the beginning of 1947, a post he held until 1956, when he succeeded Bridges as secretary to the treasury. It was while he was deputy secretary to the cabinet that Brook developed a good relationship with Churchill, which strengthened further after the war.

Churchill was pleased that Brook could be the civil servant to vet his use of official documents in his war memoirs. Bill Deakin later recalled of Brook that he often visited Chartwell to advise on the memoirs and he testified, "He was a man of limitless integrity. . . . He was the most responsible and most learned witness." Brook made no serious objections on behalf of the cabinet office to his many requirements in reproducing official papers. In the case of volume 4, Brook suggested the title *(The Hinge of Fate)* and revised a chapter, his new version being dubbed by Churchill "a masterpiece."

Churchill and Brook worked together well during Churchill's 1951–1955 government. Brook was more proactive in offering advice, even on political matters, than Bridges. Unlike Bridges, Brook was made a member of The Other Club, a good sign that Churchill liked Brook socially. After Churchill's serious stroke in 1953, Brook was one of those invited to Chartwell. Lord Moran noted of Brook on 30 June, "Winston likes him and they talked for a long time." Brook was one of Churchill's advisers before and during the December 1953 Bermuda Conference. After Churchill retired, Brook continued to keep him informed of major developments, including the Suez crisis, 1956.

Later, in his recollections of Churchill, he vigorously rebutted Lord Moran's suggestions that Churchill was in physical and mental decline and had been even before

1945. He agreed, however, that from his stroke in 1953 he was engaged in "a struggle to preserve his life and thereafter a struggle to remain in office." He paid tribute to Churchill's immense willpower and determination to overcome the effects of the stroke.

Brook succeeded Bridges as secretary to the treasury in 1956, where he served until he retired in 1962. He was created a baron in 1963. He was chairman of the governors of the BBC, 1964–1967. He died on 15 June 1967.

Related entries:
Bridges, Edward Ettingdene; The Other Club

Suggestions for further reading:
Colville, John. 1981. *The Churchillians.* London: Weidenfeld and Nicolson.
Gilbert, Martin. 1983–1988. *Winston S. Churchill.* Vols. 6–8. London: Heinemann.
Seldon, Anthony. 1981. *Churchill's Indian Summer.* London: Hodder and Stoughton.
Trend, Lord. 1981. "Brook, Norman Craven, Baron Normanbrook." In *The Dictionary of National Biography 1961–1970,* edited by E. T. Williams and C. S. Nicholls. Oxford: Oxford University Press.
Wheeler-Bennett, Sir John. 1968. *Action This Day: Working with Churchill.* London: Macmillan.

Brooke, Field Marshal Sir Alan (Viscount Alanbrooke, 1883–1963)

Sir Alan Brooke was chief of the General Staff from December 1941 to January 1946; as such, he was one of those who worked closest with Churchill during the Second World War. Sir John Colville later wrote of him in these years that he was "at once spellbound and exasperated by Churchill."

Brooke, born 23 July 1883, was the ninth and youngest child of Sir Victor Brooke, the third baronet, of Colebrooke, Fermanagh. The Brookes were major Ulster landown-

Sir Alan Brooke, Dwight D. Eisenhower, Sir Bernard L. Montgomery, John B. Anderson, and Omar N. Bradley in Germany, 25 March 1945 (Library of Congress)

ers. His nephew Basil Stanlake Brooke (1888–1973), the fifth baronet, was a major Unionist politician and prime minister of Northern Ireland, 1943–1963, and created a viscount (Brookeborough) in 1952. Churchill had been friendly with Brooke's brothers, especially Victor, at Harrow. He was born and brought up at Pau, in the south of France, where the family owned a villa, and he spoke fluent French and German. After attending the Royal Military Academy at Woolwich, he joined the Royal Field Artillery. He served in India and Ireland before 1914. In the First World War, he served on the Western Front, being notable for producing a "creeping barrage" during the Battle of the Somme, 1916. During the interwar years he was for a period an instructor at the Staff College, Camberley, and later at the Imperial Defence College. Promoted to general in 1938, at the outbreak of war he was commander in chief, Southern Com-

mand, and commander of II Corps of the British Expeditionary Force. He saw action in France. Shortly after his return to Britain, he was appointed commander in chief, Home Forces, and in this he position organized defenses against the expected German invasion.

In December 1941, Brooke replaced Dill as chief of the General Staff. As professional head of the army, he was the most important strategic adviser to Churchill and the war cabinet. Brooke played a key role in securing Anglo-American cooperation for the war in North Africa and acted as a buffer between Churchill and the commanders in the field. Brooke also made the case that a successful invasion of France could not safely take place until 1944, when it was hoped the German army would be further weakened in Russia and the cross-continental communications would be adversely affected by strategic bombing. He curbed Churchill's enthusiasm to maintain General Alexander's forces in Italy so that they could march on Vienna. He also disagreed vigorously with Churchill over the Far East. Brooke wanted the British contribution to be part of the U.S. amphibious attack on the Philippines, the Marianas, and Formosa, but Churchill wanted a distinct British campaign to recover Burma, Malaya, and Singapore.

When accepting Churchill's offer of the post of chief of the Imperial General Staff, Brooke was aware of what was ahead of him. In his diary, 16 November 1941, he wrote, "I have the greatest respect and affection for him, so that I hope I may be able to stand the storms of abuse which I may well have to bear frequently." Churchill exasperated Brooke by his accusatory style of cross-examining colleagues for their views and advice, by his taste for intervening in operational details properly left to the commanders in the field, and by his predilection of holding meetings at all hours and having unreasonable expectations of his subordinates. Yet, as he emphasized when the first volume of his diaries was prepared for publication in 1956, he felt Churchill was "quite the most wonderful man I have ever met" and was one of the rare "human beings who stand out head and shoulders above all others." In spite of their mutual irritation on occasions, Churchill greatly respected Brooke, even commenting on one occasion, "I love that man."

Churchill offered Brooke the post of commander in chief, Middle East, when he was replacing General Auchinleck. Churchill also spoke of his becoming supreme allied commander for the invasion of France in 1944, but Churchill, to Brooke's regret, readily agreed to President Franklin D. Roosevelt's request that this role should go to General Eisenhower. Instead, Brooke remained at Whitehall, though he left as quickly as he could after the war, in January 1946.

He was knighted in 1940, promoted to field marshal in 1944, created a baron in 1945, and a viscount in 1946; he became a Knight of the Garter, also in 1946. He served as chancellor of Queen's University, Belfast, from 1949, and was in charge of Queen Elizabeth II's coronation parade (as lord high constable of England). He was also a director of the Midland Bank and several companies. He died on 17 June 1963.

Suggestions for further reading:
Alanbrooke, Viscount. 2000. *War Diaries*. London: Weidenfeld.
Bryant, Arthur. 1957. *The Turn of the Tide.* London: Collins.
———. 1959. *Triumph in the West.* London: Collins.
Colville, Sir John. 1985. *The Fringes of Power: Downing Street Diaries 1939–1955.* London: Hodder and Stoughton.
Fraser, David. 1982. *Alanbrooke.* London: Collins.
———. 1991. "Alanbrooke." In *Churchill's Generals,* edited by John Keegan. London: Weidenfeld and Nicolson.
Ismay, Lord. 1960. *Memoirs.* London: Heinemann.

Brooke, Rupert (1887–1915)

Winston Churchill admired Rupert Brooke as the modern poet hero. Perhaps he saw him as his age's Lord Byron. He certainly admired his determination to fight for his country with no expectation of surviving. When Brooke died, Churchill was genuinely upset, not least as Brooke's two short-lived wartime ventures were Churchill's Antwerp and Dardanelles campaigns.

Rupert Chawner Brooke was born on 3 August 1887 in Rugby, Warwickshire. His father, William Parker Brooke, was a schoolmaster at Rugby School, and Rupert studied there from the age of fourteen. His mother was Mary Ruth Brooke (formerly Cotterill). He went up to Cambridge in October 1906, to King's College, where his uncle, Alan Brooke, was dean (and later provost), and his father a fellow. At Cambridge, he joined the Fabian Society and was elected to the Apostles (the Cambridge Conversazione Society). After leaving Cambridge in 1909, he lived nearby at Grantchester and wrote poetry. In 1912, he went to London and, with his patron Eddie Marsh, launched *Georgian Poetry*. In 1913, he traveled to North America and the South Pacific, returning in June 1914.

Marsh had spoken warmly of Brooke to Winston Churchill over several years. However, they met for the first time only on 30 July 1914, at a dinner party given by Herbert Henry Asquith at Downing Street. With war imminent, Churchill offered to secure Brooke a commission. After Britain entered the European war, Brooke took up this offer and became a second lieutenant in the Royal Naval Division. In late September, he lunched with Churchill and Marsh, and was told by Churchill of his determination to hold the northern French ports from Dunkirk to Le Havre. Soon after he began training in early October, he and Arthur Asquith were among the new recruits dispatched to Antwerp. Back in London on 9 October 1914, he and Asquith saw Churchill and informed him of their experiences.

Brooke dined with Churchill and Marsh at the admiralty on 14 February 1915. After Marsh left, Brooke and Churchill talked late into the night. Brooke confided that he did not expect to survive the Dardanelles expedition. Churchill was very buoyant, having great faith in the navy's firepower. Winston and Clementine Churchill also saw Brooke when the king reviewed the Royal Naval Division at Blandford on 25 February 1915. Margot Asquith, who was also present, wrote in her diary of her delight at seeing Brooke and Arthur Asquith "with walking sticks standing in front of their men looking quite wonderful." She added, "Rupert is a beautiful young man."

Churchill and the Asquiths urged General Sir Ian Hamilton to do what he could to look after Brooke, but Brooke declined a safe staff post. Brooke died on 23 April at Lemnos of blood poisoning brought about by a mosquito bite when he was in Egypt. Winston Churchill wired his brother Jack, "Endeavour if your duties allow to attend Rupert Brooke's funeral on my behalf. We shall not see his like again." He wrote a fulsome tribute to Brooke, which was published in the London *Times* on 26 April 1915. Churchill's paean of praise to Brooke became a major part Brooke's image as the archetypal Edwardian; a patriotic, golden young man struck down in his prime as part of Britain's noble sacrifice: "Joyous, fearless, versatile, deeply instructed, with classic symmetry of mind and body, he was all that one would wish England's noblest sons to be."

Although recently ousted from the admiralty, Churchill was genuinely moved by Brooke's death. On 25 May 1915, Marsh wrote to Violet Asquith that at dinner the previous evening, Churchill, amidst talking of his own woes, "had suddenly broken out *à propos* of nothing, . . . that nothing had grieved him, or went on grieving him, so much as Rupert's death" and he upbraided Marsh for not introducing him earlier to Brooke.

Suggestions for further reading:
Gilbert, Martin. 1971. *Winston S. Churchill*. Vol. 3. London: Heinemann.
Hassall, Christopher. 1959. *Edward Marsh: Patron of the Arts, a Biography*. London: Longman.
———. 1964. *Rupert Brooke*. London: Faber.
Jones, Nigel. 1999. *Rupert Brooke: Life, Death and Myth*. London: Richard Cohen.

Brownrigg, Rear Admiral Sir Douglas Egremont Robert (1867–1939)

Brought out of retirement, Rear Admiral Sir Douglas Brownrigg was chief naval censor throughout the First World War. He worked with Churchill while he was at the admiralty, 1914–1915, and they were in near daily contact during the Dardanelles campaign.

Brownrigg, the son of the third baronet, was born on 26 July 1867. He succeeded his father in 1900. He entered the navy in 1881, and served in the Sudan in 1884. He was promoted to commander in 1902 and captain in 1907. He was naval attaché in Tokyo and Peking in 1910–1912, before retiring in 1913. He was approached in spring 1914 to take on the post of chief censor of radio-telegraphy in the event of mobilization for war.

Brownrigg's accounts of Churchill's working habits in 1914–1915 are comparable to the better-known accounts of him as prime minister, 1940–1945. Like Admiral Fisher, the first sea lord, Churchill had high expectations of his staff; he wanted them to carry out things quickly and for them to work long and often antisocial hours as he did. Brownrigg noted that after Churchill was succeeded by Arthur Balfour, the hours worked lessened.

Churchill drove himself hard. Brownrigg enjoyed working for him, but observed that he was "a whale for work" and "a little thoughtless of others." If Brownrigg was unable to check censor matters with Churchill during the working day, then Churchill would call in to his office at 1:30 A.M. on his way to bed. During the Dardanelles campaign, Brownrigg and his staff sent to his bedside the cable and radio messages that had come in during the night. Brownrigg then attended Churchill's bedside at 9:15 A.M. Churchill would be sitting up in a huge bed, a stenographer sitting at its foot and piles of dispatch boxes nearby. Churchill himself always had "an enormous Corona Corona in his mouth," a glass of warm water on his bedside table, and a notepad on his knee.

Brownrigg admired Churchill's skill with language and his "flair for framing communiqués," some of which he considered masterpieces. He felt that Churchill was something of a gambler who withheld bad news for a time in the hope it could be published with good news. In the case of the sinking of the *Audacious*, 27 October 1914, Churchill wanted to announce its loss in the Commons, but the first sea lord, Admiral Lord Fisher, dissuaded him; its loss was not announced until after the Armistice.

When Churchill left the admiralty in 1915, he saw individually all the heads of departments. Brownrigg recorded that his departure "was extraordinarily dignified and won him a great deal of sympathy, even amongst those over whom he had at times ridden rough-shod." He wrote to Churchill expressing his conviction that "your knowledge, energy and pluck" would ensure before long that he would be brought back into a public position. In 1916, after much criticism of the two official communiqués issued after the Battle of Jutland, Brownrigg invited Churchill to give his view of the battle and provided him with the official material to read in the admiralty. Brownrigg deemed this to be the greatest mistake of his life, as the press denounced both the giving of Churchill favored access to material and Churchill for giving his views.

Brownrigg retired for a second time on 2 March 1919, having wound up the office of naval censor; that year he had been promoted to rear admiral. He was a director of the Fairfield Shipbuilding and Engineering Company.

Suggestions for further reading:
Brownrigg, Rear Admiral Sir Douglas. 1920. *Indiscretions of the Naval Censor.* London: Cassell.
Gilbert, Martin. 1972. *Winston S. Churchill.* Companion vol. 3, part 2. London: Heinemann.

Burns, John Elliott (1858–1943)

Churchill and John Elliott Burns served together in the Liberal governments from December 1905 until Burns resigned in August 1914 at the outbreak of the First World War. Burns, who had been a fiery socialist speaker and trade union hero, by this time appeared to be an old-fashioned Radical and a man jealous of the social reforms accomplished by Churchill and David Lloyd George.

Burns was born on 20 October 1858, the son of Alexander and Barbara Burns. His father was a Scottish engineer who moved to London in the 1850s. John Burns grew up in straightened circumstances, one of nine children. Leaving school at ten or eleven, he was a model of self-education and self-help. He funded his own apprenticeship as an engineer. By 1878, he was active in radical politics; after two years working for the United African Company, he returned to London in 1881 a committed socialist. He became the greatest working-class orator in London in the 1880s and 1890s. Initially, he was a major figure in the Marxist Social Democratic Federation (SDF) and he was prominent in the big unemployment and other demonstrations of the 1880s.

Burns drifted away from the SDF's leadership and the Battersea branch of the SDF became in effect his own support organization. He won the Battersea seat in the first London County Council elections in early 1889. Later in the year, he became internationally famous as one of the leaders of the great 1889 London dock strike. At the first socialist May Day demonstration in London, he was the huge crowd's most popular speaker. In 1892, he was elected to Parliament for Battersea, a seat he held until he retired in 1918. However, during the 1890s, he drifted away from independent socialism and became an eminent Lib-Lab M.P., opposing the Boer War and tariffs. With the formation of Sir Henry Campbell-Bannerman's government in 1905, he was appointed president of the Local Government Board.

Burns as president of the Local Government Board (1905–1914) was resistant to radical new ideas and sympathetic to the orthodoxies held by his senior civil servants. He espoused the self-help beliefs typical of the skilled workers of his era, exemplified in his pamphlet, *Brains Better Than Bets or Beer: A Straight Tip to the Workers* (1902). Burns's inertia in regard to producing imaginative schemes to reduce unemployment left ample scope for Churchill to innovate. Burns's energies were more often than not focused on trying to ensure measures that excluded "scroungers" from benefiting.

Burns took an early interest in the son of Lord Randolph and Lady Churchill. After Churchill made his major speech on 13 May 1901 criticizing William Brodrick's expenditure on the army, Burns wrote to Lady Randolph praising his speech and expressing the hope "that he will go further in the career he has chosen." Some eight years later, Burns was hostile to the reform politics of Churchill and Lloyd George, partly out of jealousy and partly out of antipathy to their brand of New Liberalism. Burns was very much an old-style Radical, hostile to the People's Budget of 1909 and hostile to increased expenditure on armaments. He resigned from his post of president of the Board of Trade (1914) on the outbreak of the First World War.

Burns withdrew from politics at the end of the First World War; in retirement, he enjoyed his library, especially his impressive collection on the history of London. He died on 24 January 1943. A memorial service was held at the St. Margaret's, Westminster, with James Stuart, M.P., the government's chief whip representing Churchill, and Clement Attlee and Viscount Samuel among those present. When an appeal was set up for a memorial, Churchill donated £5. The resulting portrait of Burns by George Leech was unveiled by Ernest Bevin on 6 November 1943.

Related entries:
Asquith, Herbert Henry; Hardie, James Keir

Suggestions for further reading:
Brown, Kenneth D. 1977. *John Burns.* London: Royal Historical Society.
Churchill, Randolph S. 1967. *Winston S. Churchill.* Vol. 2. London: Heinemann.
Kent, William. 1950. *John Burns: Labour's Lost Leader.* London: Williams and Norgate.

Butler, Richard Austen ("Rab") (Baron Butler of Saffron Walden, 1902–1982)

Churchill admired "Rab" Butler's abilities, even though he was closely associated with Neville Chamberlain and appeasement. Butler had risen apparently effortlessly on the inside of the Conservative Party and continued to do so until Churchill's retirement, after which he was so accustomed to having advancement fall into his lap that he was unable to fight to secure the premiership. Butler, having disagreed with Churchill over India and appeasement, came to admire him after a few months of his wartime premiership.

Richard Austen Butler was born on 9 December 1902 at Attock in northwest India, the son of Montagu and Ann Butler. His father was a revenue official. The young Rab (as he was known) seriously injured his right arm in a riding accident in 1909, leaving it damaged for the rest of his life. He left India for school in England in 1911. After Marlborough, he studied at Pembroke College, Cambridge. Like his father, he became president of the Cambridge Union. After graduating, he was given a fellowship by Corpus Christi College. He married a wealthy woman, Sydney Elizabeth Courtauld, in April 1926. While away on a world tour, Butler's relatives sought to arrange the Conservative nomination for Saffron Walden for him, the Courtaulds being a very substantial employer there. He was selected at the age of twenty-four and elected at twenty-six. Even before being elected,

his uncle, Sir Geoffrey Butler, M.P., secured him the post of unpaid private secretary to Sir Samuel Hoare, the secretary of state for air. He quickly made his mark as a loyal supporter of the Conservative Party leadership. With the formation of the 1931 national government, he became parliamentary private secretary to Hoare, now secretary of state for India. Churchill commented that Butler's appointment was "a curious, and maybe fortunate, coincidence."

Butler later observed, "My own career . . . exemplifies the advantages of the long hand . . . the steady influence one may exert by being at all times on the inside." In this he was in marked contrast to Churchill, 1931–1939. Butler was promoted to under secretary at the India office in November 1932. As such, he had to face Churchill's vigorous criticisms of government policy on Indian constitutional reform. Churchill, with characteristic generosity, praised Butler's performances at the time of the India Bill's passage in 1935.

After nine months as under secretary at the Ministry of Labour, Butler was appointed under secretary at the foreign office, with his superior, Lord Halifax, not in the House of Commons. However, Neville Chamberlain took charge of foreign affairs in the Commons. Although Butler was considered to be a success, he became closely associated with Chamberlain and appeasement. He warmly supported the Munich agreement. He was dismayed when Chamberlain fell. Churchill reappointed Butler and Lord Halifax to the foreign office. He continued as under secretary under Anthony Eden. Butler came to admire Churchill, and Churchill recognized Butler as one of the ablest younger ministers.

On 20 July 1941, Churchill appointed Butler president of the Board of Education. When Churchill appointed him, he told him not only "I think you can leave your mark there" but also, "I should not object if you could introduce a note of patriotism into the schools. Tell the children that Wolfe won Quebec." Early on, Churchill made it clear that he did not want political controversy stirred up during the war and hence no controversial Education Bill. Butler nevertheless pressed ahead, introducing his bill in December 1943. When an amendment requiring equal pay for male and female teachers was passed in the Commons, Churchill and Bevin gave Butler their robust support, with Churchill making the removal of the new clause a matter of confidence in the government. The 1944 Education Act (or "Butler's Education Act") was the major social legacy of Churchill's wartime government.

In Churchill's 1945 "caretaker" government, Butler was appointed minister of labor and national service, in succession to Ernest Bevin. With the Conservative defeat in 1945, Butler became one of Churchill's most reliable lieutenants in the House of Commons. Butler also continued to rebuild the Conservative Party organization. In November 1945, Churchill appointed Butler the head of the Conservative Party Research Department. He also appointed him chairman of his Industrial Policy Committee, which consulted businessmen and even some trade unionists and produced the *Industrial Charter.* Churchill was less than enthusiastic for a document that the Conservative Party's right wing deemed to be "milk and water socialism." After the 1950 general election, Butler was Churchill's negotiator with Lady Violet Bonham Carter in an unsuccessful attempt to arrange a pact against Labour at the next election.

With the Conservative victory in the 1951 general election, Churchill appointed Butler to be his chancellor of the exchequer. Curiously, Churchill appointed the elderly Sir Arthur Salter as minister of state for economic affairs ("the best economist since Jesus Christ," according to Churchill) and Lord Cherwell as paymaster general to help him. Early on when Butler was chancellor, there was friction between him and Churchill, Butler believing that Churchill had

not supported him adequately when he had wished to float the pound and make sterling convertible (OPERATION ROBOT). By late 1952, Butler chaired cabinet meetings when both Churchill and Eden were away. When Churchill suffered a serious stroke in June 1953, Butler effectively took charge of the government for three months (Eden also being ill). In August 1954, Churchill considered moving Eden to domestic affairs and Butler to the foreign office, but Eden preferred not to move.

After Churchill's retirement, Butler remained at the forefront of Conservative politics for a further nine years. He served as lord privy seal and leader of the House of Commons, 1955–1957, home secretary, 1957–1962, first secretary of state, 1962–1963, and foreign secretary, 1963–1964. Butler was passed over as Conservative Party leader in 1957 and 1963. In January 1965, he accepted the nomination to the mastership of Trinity College, Cambridge, and a life peerage. He died on 9 March 1982.

Related entries:
Chamberlain, (Arthur) Neville; Education Act; Industrial Charter; Macmillan, (Maurice) Harold

Suggestions for further reading:
Butler, Lord. 1971. *The Art of the Possible.* London: Hamish Hamilton.
Cosgrave, Patrick. 1981. *R. A. Butler: An English Life.* London: Quartet.
Gilbert, Martin. 1986 and 1988. *Winston S. Churchill.* Vols. 7 and 8. London: Heinemann.
Howard, Anthony. 1987. *RAB: The Life of R. A. Butler.* London: Cape.
Sparrow, Gerald. 1965. *"RAB": Study of a Statesman.* London: Odhams.

Buxton, Sydney Charles (Earl Buxton, 1853–1934)

ydney Buxton was a Radical minister in the Liberal governments during 1905–1914, and was Winston Churchill's successor at the Board of Trade. He was a Radical of an older kind, but nevertheless was more radical than most Liberals on labor matters. He was an associate of Herbert Henry Asquith and Sir Edward Grey, not David Lloyd George and Churchill.

Sydney Buxton was born on 25 October 1853 into a notable Quaker brewing family. His grandfather, Sir Thomas Foxwell Buxton, had been a leader in the struggle for the emancipation of slaves. His father, Charles Buxton, was a Liberal M.P. Educated at Clifton College and Trinity College, Cambridge, Sydney Buxton entered Liberal politics young, running successfully for the seat of Westminster in the 1876 London School Board election. He was reelected in 1879, but defeated in 1882. As a member of the London School Board and in print, he made his name as a Gladstonian keen to economize on public expenditure.

Buxton stood unsuccessfully in the 1880 general election. He published *A Handbook to Political Questions of the Day and the Arguments on Either Side* (1880), which reached eleven editions (and many editions of a cheap, brief *Manual*). He was elected to Parliament for Peterborough in a by-election in June 1883. Buxton soon made a name for himself as a leading figure of the London Municipal Reform League. He also wrote books, notably *Finance and Politics, An Historical Study 1783–1885*, 2 vols. (1888), and later, *Mr. Gladstone as Chancellor of the Exchequer* (1901). Buxton lost his Peterborough seat in November 1885 but was elected in the July 1886 general election for the East London seat of Poplar. He served on the Royal Commission on Elementary Education, 1886–1888. With the return of Gladstone to office, he served as under secretary at the colonial office (1892–1895). Like Churchill after him, he shined in the House of Commons because the secretary of state was a peer, Lord Ripon.

Buxton became one of the Liberal Party's experts on labor matters. As Poplar's M.P., he had been involved in supporting the dock workers in the great 1889 London dock strike. He was a warm advocate of Boards of Conciliation and Arbitration and also of factory legislation. He also was seen by Sidney and Beatrice Webb as a coming man of London and national Radicalism, along with Herbert Asquith, Richard Burdon Haldane, Sir Edward Grey, and A. H. D. Acland, and one who mattered in the development of Liberal policy toward sweated labor, factory legislation, and unemployment.

When the Liberals took office, Buxton, who might have expected to become president of the Board of Trade, entered the cabinet as postmaster general, 1905–1910. He was eclipsed by the dynamic Radical duo of Lloyd George (1905–1908) and Winston Churchill (1908–1910). Contrary to Randolph Churchill's view in *Winston S. Churchill,* vol. 2 (p. 314), Buxton was more radical than John Burns or Herbert Gladstone; but he was alarmed by Lloyd George's rhetoric in the 1909–1910 clashes with the House of Lords. Representing Poplar, he was acutely aware of unemployment; and in October 1908, backed by Lloyd George and Churchill, he pressed for the government to support a proposal for the levying of a special rate to help those out of work. In 1910, he succeeded Churchill at the Board of Trade and was responsible for carrying through Churchill's innovatory work on unemployment insurance with Lloyd George, the chancellor of the exchequer. Buxton was also responsible for conciliation (if requested) during the labor unrest of 1910–1914. When dock strikes were threatened in South Wales in 1910 and in London in 1911, Churchill, as home secretary, offered Buxton advice and demanded action.

In 1914, Buxton became governor general of South Africa. Like his predecessor, Herbert Gladstone, he was elevated to a viscountancy, becoming Viscount Buxton of Newtimber. He served there during the turbulent years of the First World War and its aftermath (1914–1920). On his return, he was made an earl. In February 1921, at Churchill's invitation, he chaired a committee on the constitutional development of Southern Rhodesia. In 1924, he declined to be considered as a successor to his friend Lord Grey as Liberal leader in the House of Lords. In 1926, during the Liberal rifts over the General Strike, he sided with Asquith and Grey against Lloyd George. He died on 15 October 1934.

Suggestions for further reading:
Churchill, Randolph S. 1967. *Winston S. Churchill*. Vol. 2. London: Heinemann.
Waley, Daniel. 1999. *A Liberal Life: Sydney, Earl Buxton, 1853–1934*. Sussex, UK: Newtimber Publications.

C

Cadogan, Sir Alexander Montagu George (1884–1968)

Sir Alexander Cadogan was permanent under secretary at the foreign office during Churchill's second period at the admiralty (1939–1941) and his first premiership (1940–1945). They were both from aristocratic backgrounds, the first Earl of Cadogan having served under the first duke of Marlborough at his great battles. Cadogan and Churchill got on well together, each aware of the other's strong points.

Alexander Cadogan was born on 24 November 1884, the youngest of nine children of the fifth Earl of Cadogan and his wife, daughter of the Earl of Craven. The fifth earl had held junior office under Benjamin Disraeli and cabinet office under Lord Salisbury. Alexander was educated at Eton and Balliol before entering the diplomatic service. He was posted to Constantinople and Vienna before the First World War. During the First World War he worked in the foreign office. After the war, he attended the Peace Conference and from 1923 was head of the League of Nations section of the foreign office. In 1934, Cadogan, with his family, went as British minister to China for two years. In 1936, he returned to be senior deputy under secretary at the foreign office. At the beginning of 1938, he succeeded Sir Robert Vansittart as permanent under secretary of state for foreign affairs.

Churchill features frequently in Cadogan's wartime diaries. They saw each other many times at various meetings, both when Churchill was at the admiralty and when he was prime minister. He worked well with Churchill but was perceptive about him. On 29 May 1940 he noted, "W. S. C. rather theatrically bull-doggish. . . . That is Winston's fault—theatricality." His diaries mention Churchill enjoying his role of boosting morale, walking around with a big cigar, and often giving "V for Victory" signs.

Although Cadogan generally admired Churchill, like Clement Attlee, he could be exasperated with his approach to meetings. On 13 March 1944, Cadogan complained in his diary, "Quite regardless of the lateness of the hour, P.M. indulged his capacity for non-conduct of business." After Churchill's defeat in the 1945 general election, Cadogan wrote expressing his admiration for Churchill's wartime leadership. Churchill responded on 5 August 1945 with praise for Cadogan's wartime contribution, observing in old-fashioned style, "You have indeed played a man's part in this glorious struggle."

In February 1946, Cadogan left the foreign office to be Britain's first permanent representative to the United Nations. He retired in 1950. He was the first civil servant to receive the Order of Merit. In 1952, at Jock Colville's suggestion, Churchill chose Cadogan to be chairman of the BBC's board of governors, a post he held until late 1957. He died on 9 July 1968.

Suggestions for further reading:
Dilks, David, ed. 1971. *The Diaries of Sir Alexander Cadogan 1938–1945*. London: Cassell.
Gilbert, Martin. 1983–1988. *Winston S. Churchill*. Vols. 6–8. London: Heinemann.

Cairo Conference (November 1943)

The conference (code name Sextant) was held in Cairo in late November 1943. Churchill reached Cairo on 21 November and stayed in the villa of Lord Moyne (as Walter Edward Guinness he had been Churchill's junior minister at the treasury in the 1920s), Britain's resident minister. Seven squadrons of aircraft, eighty-two anti-aircraft guns, five troops of infantry, armored cars, and a radar warning system were deployed to protect Churchill and President Franklin D. Roosevelt. The conference sessions began on 23 November and ended on 26 November. On 27 November, Churchill and Roosevelt flew on separately to Tehran for a conference with Joseph Stalin.

In spite of a serious security breach in mid-November when the United Press issued a dispatch rightly speculating that the meeting would be held at Mena House, half a mile from the Giza pyramids, the conference went ahead as planned. The Cairo Conference focused on the Far East and it also enabled the Americans and British to discuss in advance the meeting with Stalin in Tehran.

Roosevelt and Chiang Kai-Shek, Chinese general and statesman, successfully pressed for an amphibious assault on the Andaman Islands south of Burma (OPERATION BUCCANEER). Churchill also promised a military offensive in northern Burma with Orde Wingate's groups causing disruption deep behind Japanese lines. There was also further commitment to the Mediterranean offensive and to supporting partisan forces in Yugoslavia, Greece, and Albania.

Roosevelt wanted to support Chiang Kai-Shek against both the Japanese and internal communism. OPERATION BUCCANEER and OPERATION ANAKIM were intended to open supply routes to China. However, the war aim of the restoration of lost Chinese territory required Stalin's agreement.

After the Tehran Conference, Churchill and Roosevelt returned to Cairo and resumed discussions between 2 and 7 December 1943. Because Roosevelt reluctantly recognized during the second phase of the Sextant talks that there were not enough landing craft to invade southern France as well as the Andaman Islands, OPERATION BUCCANEER was canceled. With Roosevelt and Churchill fully committed to OPERATION OVERLORD, the cross-channel invasion of northern Europe, Roosevelt, at the resumed Cairo talks, indicated his decision to appoint General Dwight D. Eisenhower to command the operation.

On 23 November, during the first phase of the Cairo Conference, Churchill and Sarah Churchill, his daughter, enjoyed showing Roosevelt the pyramids and the sphinx. Churchill, Sarah Churchill, and Anthony Eden were among Roosevelt's guests for a Thanksgiving Day (25 November) dinner, and the president carved the turkey. Churchill and his daughter gave a dinner in honor of Chiang Kai-Shek at the Villa Casey.

Suggestions for further reading:
Gilbert, Martin. 1986. *Winston S. Churchill*. Vol. 7. London: Heinemann.
Kimber, Warren F., ed. 1984. *Churchill and Roosevelt: The Complete Correspondence*. Vol. 2. London: Collins.
Loewenheim, F. L., H. D. Langley, and M. Jonas, eds. 1957. *Roosevelt and Churchill: Their Secret Wartime Correspondence*. London: Barrie and Jenkins.

Campbell-Bannerman, Sir Henry (1836–1908)

In his young Tory M.P. phase, Churchill had been scathing of Henry Campbell-Bannerman and his "methods of barbarism" speech during the Boer War. Then Churchill had accused him of smearing British generals. However, even before Churchill crossed the floor to the Liberals, he appreciated some of the Liberal leader's qualities. Campbell-Bannerman fostered and supported Churchill in his first ministerial post at the colonial office.

Henry Campbell was born on 7 September 1836 at Kelvinside, an eighteenth-century house, on the River Kelvin, near Glasgow, the second son of James Campbell and his wife, the former Janet Bannerman. His father was a successful businessman and his mother the daughter of a prosperous Manchester manufacturer. Educated at Glasgow High School, Glasgow University, and Trinity College, Cambridge, he went into the family firm. He was more interested in foreign travel and being commander of a company of the Lanarkshire Rifle Volunteers than being a businessman. He read widely and discussed Radical and Chartist politics. In 1868, he ran as a Radical against a moderate Liberal for Stirling Burghs in a by-election. He polled well. He won the seat in the autumn general election and held it until his death forty years later. In 1871, he was left a legacy providing he took the name Bannerman, which he did. He secured office in Gladstone's and Rosebery's governments as financial secretary to the War Office, 1871–1874 and 1880–1882, secretary to the admiralty, 1882–1884, chief secretary for Ireland, 1884–1885, and secretary of state for war, 1886 and 1892–1895. He was given a knighthood in 1895. He became the Liberal Party leader in the House of Commons in 1899 and prime minister in 1905–1908.

Campbell-Bannerman, having seen the rise and fall of Lord Randolph Churchill, took an early interest in his son's political career. He sent him a note of praise on his maiden speech in the House of Commons. He was one of the Liberal leaders who dined with Churchill, Hugh Cecil, and their associates in 1902. Campbell-Bannerman's avoidance of strident opposition in the Commons to Chamberlain's tariff proposals made it easier for Churchill and other Conservative Free Traders to oppose them. In May 1903, Churchill wrote to Campbell-Bannerman making it clear he would be willing to cooperate in opposing tariffs. In June 1904, Churchill crossed the floor of the House of Commons and joined the Liberals. When Campbell-Bannerman formed a government in December 1905, he offered Churchill the post of financial secretary to the treasury, but Churchill pushed for under secretary to the colonies, the post just vacated by his cousin the duke of Marlborough; it put Churchill to the fore in major uproars in the House of Commons over South African issues. Campbell-Bannerman supported Churchill when the king complained of the vigor with which he had responded to Milner's bitter attacks on the government.

Churchill was much involved with the 1907 Colonial Conference. Campbell-Bannerman presided over the opening, thereafter Lord Elgin took the chair. Churchill, however, arranged and attended the festivities put on for the various prime ministers, making the most of the speech-making opportunities they occasioned.

When Churchill learned in East Africa that Campbell-Bannerman's health was deteriorating, he was sorry; he observed that the prime minister had been "a good friend who has always shown me kindness." Campbell-Bannerman resigned as prime minister on 5 April and died at 10 Downing Street on 22 April 1908.

Related entries:
Asquith, Herbert Henry; Grey, Sir Edward; Haldane, Richard Burdon

Suggestions for further reading:
Churchill, Randolph S. 1967. *Winston S. Churchill.* Vol. 2. London: Heinemann.
Spender, J. A. 1923. *The Life of the Right Hon. Sir Henry Campbell-Bannerman.* 2 vols. London: Hodder and Stoughton.
Wilson, John. 1973. *CB: A Life of Sir Henry Campbell-Bannerman.* London: Constable.

Cartland, John Ronald Hamilton (1907–1940)

Ronald Cartland was a young Conservative M.P. who was a strong supporter of Winston Churchill in Parliament, 1935–1940. He died in action near Dunkirk in 1940.

Ronald Cartland was born on 7 January 1907, the first son and second child of Bertram and Mary Cartland, both from wealthy families. The Cartland wealth was mostly lost with the 1903 financial crash of the Fishguard Railway. Bertram Cartland became founder and honorary secretary of the Pershore Primrose League, then a paid provincial secretary (as such being a Conservative Party organizer in the 1910 elections) and secretary to Bolton Eyres Monsell, Conservative M.P. for South Worcestershire. Bertram Cartland served with distinction on the Western Front in the First World War, being an acting colonel when killed while resisting a major German offensive on 27 May 1918.

Ronald and his younger brother Anthony were brought up by their mother. Their elder sister, Barbara Cartland (1901–2000) earned money from writing novels and also from articles for Lord Beaverbrook's newspapers. Winston Churchill was among those with whom she lunched, an encounter she recalled in her autobiography *We Danced All Night* (1970). Their mother also earned extra money by running a knitwear shop in the mid-1920s. After education at Charterhouse and brief employment in the cashier's department of a City of London firm, Ronald Cartland worked in the Education Department and in other positions in the Conservative Central office, 1927–1935. In 1935, he was elected M.P. for the Birmingham constituency of King's Norton.

Ronald Cartland visited Germany in August 1935. He returned convinced that the Germans hated the English; he thought that they would annex Austria and would embark on war with Britain. In Parliament, he quickly joined with Duncan Sandys, Alan Lennox-Boyd, and other young Conservatives to press the national government over aspects of empire and foreign and defense policy. They were dubbed the new Fourth Party by the press. Churchill welcomed their efforts. Duncan Sandys, his son-in-law, kept him informed. When Lord Walmer formed a Conservative Special Areas Committee to press for more vigorous responses to the problems of bad employment, Ronald Cartland was its secretary and its members included Winston Churchill, Duncan Sandys, Alan Lennox-Boyd, and Robert Boothby. Cartland continued thereafter to press for more action on unemployment.

When Anthony Eden resigned as foreign secretary, Ronald Cartland was one of the few Conservative M.P.s who, like Winston Churchill, spoke in the House of Commons in Eden's support. He also supported Winston Churchill in his calls for an independent committee of enquiry into air rearmament. On 3 July 1938, Ronald Cartland accompanied Winston Churchill to the Austin aircraft factory in his King's Norton constituency. Afterwards, Cartland observed, "The men were thrilled to see him. I've never seen such enthusiasm. Its not surprising—he has such presence—such personality—also the man in the street realises that he has been right in everything he has said since 1933. Those in high places say he's finished—I don't believe it. He has a following in the country far bigger than those in Westminster think."

Like Winston Churchill, Anthony Eden, Leo Amery, and Duff Cooper, Ronald Cartland was unimpressed by Neville Chamberlain's Munich settlement. After Munich, this group was joined by others such as Richard Law, Harold Macmillan, Lord Walmer, Ronald Tree, and Harold Nicolson in opposing appeasement. Cartland believed that those over forty had faith in Neville Chamberlain to keep Hitler and Stalin at bay, but those under forty supported Churchill because "he has the vitality, the enthusiasm and the progressive mind of youth." In an adjournment debate in the House of Commons on 3 August 1939, Cartland made the most effective Conservative speech critical of Chamberlain, winning Churchill's warm praise. As a result, Cartland was in danger of deselection by his Conservative association, but the outbreak of war ended such a move.

At the outbreak of war, Ronald Cartland joined his regiment, the 53d Worcestershire Yeomanry Anti-Tank Regiment, and went to France in early January 1940. He was delighted by Churchill's accession to the premiership: "He may yet save civilisation." In the retreat to Dunkirk, he fought a rearguard action at Cassel and was killed on 30 May 1940 as his troops made for the coast. His brother Anthony was also killed in a rearguard action near Dunkirk.

After the news of Ronald Cartland's death, Churchill, Eden, Amery, Clement Attlee, Brendan Bracken, Sandys, and others paid fulsome tributes to his memory. When Barbara Cartland published the biography of her brother, Winston Churchill contributed a preface (dated 7 November 1941) in which he commented, "At a time when our political life had become feckless and dull, he spoke fearlessly for Britain."

Suggestions for further reading:
Cartland, Barbara. 1942. *Ronald Cartland*. London: Collins.
Gilbert, Martin. 1976 and 1983. *Winston S. Churchill*. Vols. 5 and 6. London: Heinemann.

Casablanca Conference (January 1943)

The conference (codename Symbol) was held in Casablanca in January 1943. Churchill arrived on 12 January and left on 25 January, staying at the Villa Mirador. The conference sessions began on 15 January and ended on 24 January. It was mostly an Anglo-American conference because Joseph Stalin was unwilling to leave Russia when he was winning at Stalingrad. General Charles de Gaulle arrived on 22 January and agreed to talk with General Giraud, Churchill hoping that de Gaulle would recognize Giraud's authority in North Africa.

The Casablanca Conference centered on talks about the opening of a second front in Europe to force Germany to remove some troops from Russia. Churchill wanted to move from North African success to southern Europe, beginning with an invasion of Sicily (OPERATION HUSKY). Churchill and his advisers argued that an invasion of northern Europe in 1943 would be premature, and they opposed the alternative of concentrating instead on the Pacific. Nevertheless, the Combined Chiefs of Staff did agree to establish a combined staff in London to plan a large-scale invasion of northern Europe in 1944.

At Casablanca, Churchill and President Franklin D. Roosevelt also gave priority to defeating the U-boats in the Atlantic and to intensifying the bombing offensive on Germany. There was also agreement to recover Burma and to increase aid to China. Churchill warmly endorsed Roosevelt's declaration that peace could come to the world only with the unconditional surrender of Germany, Italy, and Japan.

Roosevelt left early on 25 January. Churchill relaxed by climbing the tower of the Villa Taylor and painting the Atlas Mountains, the only picture he painted during the war. That evening he left by air for Cairo.

Winston Churchill, Franklin D. Roosevelt, Charles de Gaulle, and other military leaders, 1943 (Library of Congress)

Related entries:
Cairo Conference; De Gaulle, General Charles André Joseph Marie; Roosevelt, Franklin Delano

Suggestions for further reading:
Gilbert, Martin. 1986. *Winston S. Churchill.* Vol. 7. London: Heinemann.
Kimball, Warren F., ed. 1984. *Churchill and Roosevelt: The Complete Correspondence.* Vol. 2. London: Collins.

Cassel, Sir Ernest Joseph (1852–1921)

Sir Ernest Cassel was a good friend to the Churchills. He had been a friend of Lord and Lady Randolph Churchill and he was a very good friend to Winston Churchill. He provided much good financial advice and also lent him money.

Born at Cologne on 8 March 1852, he was the youngest of three children of Jacob and Amalia Cassel. His father had a small banking business. He left school at fourteen and worked for another bank; from 1869 to 1871, he worked in Liverpool and Paris. After he left France because of the Franco-Prussian war, he worked in finance in London. He became a British citizen in 1878, by which time he was well on his way to amassing a fortune. He became one of the most respected and wealthiest financiers in the City of London. From 1898 to 1910, he had his own headquarters in the city. Through his horse racing interests, he became friendly with the Prince of Wales. He was knighted by Queen Victoria in 1899 and received further honors from King Edward VII.

Cassel's friends included Lord Randolph Churchill. When Winston performed poorly in army exams, Lord Randolph considered putting him into business through his connection with either Cassel, Horace Farquharson, or Nathaniel Rothschild should he fail again. Winston's brother Jack began his career as a stockbroker working for Ernest Cassel. Cassel also helped Winston Churchill to advance socially by introducing him to important figures at various social occasions. Winston Churchill also turned to Cassel to invest on his behalf the earnings from his books.

Churchill also availed himself of Cassel's hospitality for holidays. In 1902, he took a trip up the Nile with the Cassels, along with several leading society and political figures. He also stayed at Cassel's villa in Switzerland for part of the summer of 1904 (when he was writing the biography of his father) and for a fortnight in the summer of 1906. When Churchill married, Cassel gave him £500 as a wedding present.

When Churchill was first lord of the admiralty before the First World War, Cassel acted as an intermediary between Churchill and Kaiser Wilhelm of Germany. Through Cassel, the kaiser provided Churchill with advance details of the 1912 German Navy Law. After the kaiser had rebuffed Churchill's proposal of a "Naval Holiday," Churchill made conciliatory comments in a letter to Cassel intended to be seen by the kaiser. Churchill also benefited from Cassel's German connections, meeting through him men such as the major German shipowner Albert Ballin. Cassel suffered from First World War anti-German sentiment in Britain but he had many friends in high places to testify to his loyalty.

During the war, Churchill continued to benefit from his family's friendship with Cassel. Cassel both loaned him substantial sums of money and also administered on his behalf $20,000 of investments in the United States. Sir Ernest Cassel died on 21 September 1921.

Suggestions for further reading:
Churchill, Randolph S. 1966 and 1967. *Winston S. Churchill*. Vols. 1 and 2. London: Heinemann.

Gilbert, Martin. 1971. *Winston S. Churchill*. Vol. 3. London: Heinemann.

Cecil, Lord Edgar Algernon Robert Gascoyne (Viscount Cecil of Chelwood, 1864–1958)

Churchill and Robert Cecil were well-acquainted for much of their lives but were often active political opponents. Even when together in Baldwin's second government, their views differed on defense matters. Nevertheless, especially in later life, their relationship was marked by warmth and respect.

Edgar Algernon Robert Cecil was born in London on 14 September 1864, the third son of the marquis of Salisbury and his wife, the former Georgina Alderson. He was known by his third name, Robert (or by family and friends as "Bob"). Educated at Eton and University College, Oxford, Robert Cecil became a barrister in 1887 and was appointed a queen's counsel in 1899. Like his brother Hugh, he was a Conservative Free Trader. He was elected to Parliament for a safe London Conservative seat, East Marylebone, 1906–1910, but left because of opposition from tariff reformers. He unsuccessfully stood in the two 1910 general elections but won Hitchin in a 1911 by-election, holding the seat until he accepted a peerage in 1923.

As political opponents, Churchill and Cecil did not spare each other. Churchill vigorously denounced Cecil in July 1913 over his vehement role in the Marconi scandal. Cecil spoke of Churchill's having "a dark and tortuous mind" in April 1914 at a rally in Hyde Park in support of Ulster. Cecil was not impressed by Churchill's performance in office in the early part of the First World War. He complained in April 1915, "Winston with all his ability and qualities has done very badly. His craving for applause makes him boastful of success and so timid about failures that he conceals all unpalatable news that he can."

With the formation of a coalition government in May 1915, Robert Cecil became parliamentary under secretary at the foreign office and was made a privy councillor. In February 1916, he entered the cabinet, adding to his foreign office post that of minister of blockade. In Lloyd George's wartime government, Arthur Balfour was foreign secretary, but Cecil was given the title of assistant secretary of state. In November 1918, he resigned over the disestablishment of the Welsh Church. He went in the British delegation to the Paris Peace Conference and took up what became the great cause of his political career, the League of Nations. He was shocked by Churchill's "exceedingly militarist . . . point of view" with regard to intervention in Russia. With Baldwin's first government (1923–1924), Robert Cecil became lord privy seal, with special responsibility for League of Nations matters. In Baldwin's second government (1924–1929), he again had responsibility for affairs concerning the League of Nations, but this time with the post of chancellor of the Duchy of Lancaster. However, he resigned in October 1927 over the government's policy on naval disarmament. In this, his main opponent was Churchill, who wrote a warm letter praising his dignified resignation on such a matter of principle.

In later life, Cecil came to appreciate Churchill's stance on defense. He observed, "A great mistake I made was in not working with Winston, who I think was really strongly in favor of the League, subject to his overmastering belief in force as the only effective agent in international affairs." When Churchill published his war memoirs, he was delighted by Cecil's review, which began, "This is a wonderful book by a wonderful man."

Cecil was president of the League of Nations Union, 1923–1945, and honorary life president of the United Nations Association, 1945–1958. He received the Nobel Peace Prize in 1937 and was made a Companion of Honour in 1956. He died on 24 November 1958.

Related entries:
Balfour, Arthur James, First Earl; Cecil, Lord Hugh Richard Heathcote

Suggestions for further reading:
Cecil of Chelwood, Viscount. 1941. *A Great Experiment*. London: Cape.
———. 1949. *All the Way*. London: Hodder and Stoughton.
Churchill, Randolph S. 1967. *Winston S. Churchill*. Vol. 2. London: Heinemann.
Rose, Kenneth. 1975. *The Later Cecils*. London: Macmillan.

Cecil, Lord Hugh Richard Heathcote (Baron Quickswood, 1869–1956)

*L*ord Hugh Cecil was an aristocratic friend who much influenced Churchill in his brief years as a Conservative M.P. at the start of the twentieth century. However, Cecil's strident opposition to constitutional reform in 1910 ended their close friendship for three decades.

Hugh Cecil was born at Hatfield on 14 October 1869, the fifth son of the third Marquis of Salisbury and his wife, the former Georgina Alderson. He was nicknamed "Linky" because his family deemed his shambling gait resembled that of the so-called missing link. Yet he was intellectually very bright, reading widely in the family library as well as at Eton and University College, Oxford. He gained first class honors in history and was a fellow at Hertford College, Oxford, 1891–1936. He held very strong Anglican beliefs, but was dissuaded from a clerical career by his mother. Instead, he was elected Conservative M.P. for Greenwich, 1895–1906, and for Oxford University 1910–1937.

Churchill and Hugh Cecil first met in 1898. The young Winston Churchill was very taken aback to be out-argued by Hugh Cecil and his friends, all reactionary Conservative M.P.s. Once elected to Parliament, he joined this group, nicknamed Hughligans, although unlike Hugh Cecil he had no taste for political rows over Anglican doctrine. However, both were ardent Free Traders. Though Churchill left the Conservative Party, Hugh Cecil remained but became isolated in it. A tariff reformer stood against him in 1906, and, having lost his seat, Andrew Bonar Law even said that he would rather lose a Conservative seat in a by-election than see Cecil returned.

Returned to Parliament in 1910, Hugh Cecil was a leader of uproar in the House of Commons over the Parliament Bill. Although Churchill urged preserving the ancient constitution by making it fair, Hugh Cecil urged the king to play an active political role, as in the past, to defeat the Liberals. In 1912, he published *Conservatism* and sent Churchill a copy.

In 1936, Hugh Cecil became provost of Eton, a post he held until 1944. In December 1940, Churchill wrote to offer to propose his name for a barony. He accepted, taking the name Quickswood, a long demolished house near Hatfield in which one of his distant ancestors had kept a mistress. Thereafter, Hugh Cecil and Winston Churchill revived their old friendship. When Churchill sent him his war memoirs, he responded by writing, "It is a most interesting performance only matched by Julius Caesar." He died on 10 December 1956.

Related entry:
Cecil, Lord Edgar Algernon Robert Gascoyne

Suggestions for further reading:
Churchill, Randolph S. 1967. *Winston S. Churchill*. Vol. 2. London: Heinemann.

Rose, Kenneth. 1975. *The Later Cecils.* London: Macmillan.

Chamberlain, (Arthur) Neville (1869–1940)

During the 1920s and during the first year of the Second World War, Churchill and Chamberlain had much respect for each other. They clashed in the 1930s, primarily over rearmament. After becoming prime minister, Churchill treated Chamberlain with much consideration and respect. After his death, he kept in touch with Anne Chamberlain, his widow, and included her at his farewell dinner at 10 Downing Street in 1955.

Neville Chamberlain was born on 18 March 1869 at Edgbaston, Birmingham, the only son of Joseph and Florence Chamberlain. Florence Kenrick was Joseph's second wife. Neville had an older half-brother, Austen. He was educated at Rugby and Mason College (later Birmingham University). When he was twenty-one, he ran the family sisal plantation in the Bahamas for seven years before he returned to business in Birmingham. Elected to Birmingham City Council in 1911, he made a big impact and became lord mayor from 1916 to 1917. He was made director general of national service in 1917 by David Lloyd George; unfortunately, Lloyd George disliked him and he resigned after seven months. He was elected to Parliament for Birmingham Ladywood in the 1918 general election. He refused suggestions of office under Lloyd George and was anticoalition. When Bonar Law was prime minister, Chamberlain became postmaster general, October 1922 to February 1923, and paymaster general, February to March 1923, and then entered the cabinet as minister of health. After Stanley Baldwin became prime minister he was promoted to chancellor of the exchequer, August 1923 to

British statesman and Prime Minister Neville Chamberlain at Heston Airport on his return from Munich after meeting with Adolf Hitler, making his "Peace in Our Time" address, 30 September 1938 (Hulton/Archive)

January 1924. After the return to office of the Conservatives in November 1924, he was offered the exchequer again but preferred to return to the Ministry of Health until the fall of the government in 1929. At the Ministry of Health, Chamberlain established a reputation as a reformer, with a major Housing Act in 1923 to his credit.

From early on as an M.P., Chamberlain admired Churchill's parliamentary skills. His preference for a return to the Ministry of Health opened the way for Churchill to become chancellor of the exchequer, and Chamberlain continued to admire Churchill in this office. Churchill took big views, but Chamberlain was industrious in mastering details. In August 1925, Chamberlain wrote to Stanley Baldwin, "What a brilliant creature! . . . I like his humour and

his vitality. I like his courage. . . . But not for all the joys of Paradise would I be a member of his staff! Mercurial!"

By early 1929, Baldwin and Chamberlain could conceive of a situation where in a hung Parliament in which Lloyd George held the balance, Churchill would become Conservative leader and take office with Lloyd George. However, Labour took office later that year. To Chamberlain's surprise, Churchill removed himself from the Conservative leadership, primarily over India. In the National government, under Ramsay MacDonald then Baldwin, Chamberlain was minister of health again, from August to November 1931, then chancellor of the exchequer. As chancellor, he was pressed by Churchill over rearmament. In 1932, as the country began to pull out of the world recession, Chamberlain emphasized that other risks would have to take second place to the needs of economic recovery.

Churchill had some hopes of a return to office when Baldwin retired in May 1937. He seconded the motion nominating Chamberlain to be leader of the Conservative Party. Chamberlain as prime minister gave a stronger, more decisive lead than had Baldwin. He preferred Churchill out of his government than in it. By the time of Munich he seems to have known of Churchill's campaigns against him, at least with Jan Masaryk, the Czech minister in London, as he appears to have had transcripts of their telephone messages. Chamberlain firmly resisted Churchill's attempt in November 1938 to establish a Ministry of Supply, Churchill being supported in a vote only by Brendan Bracken and Harold Macmillan, of Conservative M.P.s.

With the outbreak of war, Chamberlain brought Churchill into his war cabinet as first lord of the admiralty. Churchill worked loyally with Chamberlain in the early phase of the Second World War. When the House of Commons displayed a substantial lack of confidence in Chamberlain in a two-day debate on 7 and 8 May 1940, Lloyd George advised Churchill "not to allow himself to be converted into an air-raid shelter to keep the splinters from hitting his colleagues."

Few things became Churchill better than the consideration he showed Chamberlain after his fall from the premiership. After returning from Buckingham Palace to be sworn in as prime minister, he wrote to Chamberlain to say he was proud to have won his confidence and friendship since the outbreak of war and that he would benefit from his advice. Churchill appointed him lord president of the council. In this position, Chamberlain chaired economic committees dealing with agriculture and food, trade, transport, and shipping. Churchill kept Chamberlain informed, and invited him and his wife to dinner on 30 May 1940.

Churchill turned down Chamberlain's offer to resign as leader of the Conservative Party. He argued that not being a party leader was an advantage as head of a national government. However, when Chamberlain's health collapsed, Churchill did accept the post in October 1940. Chamberlain resigned from the government in late September 1940. He declined offers of a peerage or the Order of the Garter, preferring, like his father, to die as "Mr. Chamberlain." He died on 9 November 1940. Churchill paid a moving tribute to him to a meeting of the M.P.s and was moved to tears at his funeral in Westminster Abbey on 14 November 1940.

Related entries:
Appeasement; Baldwin, Stanley; Hoare, Sir Samuel John Gurney

Suggestions for further reading:
Dilks, David. 1984. *Neville Chamberlain*. Vol. 1, *1869–1929*. Cambridge: Cambridge University Press.
Dutton, David. 2001. *Neville Chamberlain*. London: Arnold.
Feiling, Keith. 1947. *The Life of Neville Chamberlain*. London: Macmillan.
Gilbert, Martin. 1976 and 1983. *Winston S. Churchill*. Vols. 5 and 6. London: Heinemann.
Parker, R. A. C. 1993. *Chamberlain and Appeasement*. London: Macmillan.

Chamberlain, Joseph (1836–1914)

Churchill, who had admired Joseph Chamberlain as the imperialist colonial secretary of 1895–1903, vigorously opposed Chamberlain's crusade for tariffs. Churchill's belief in free trade ran so deep that he broke with the Conservative Party rather than support economic protection.

Joseph Chamberlain was born at Camberwell Grove, London, on 8 July 1836, the eldest son of Joseph and Caroline Chamberlain. His father ran the family boot and shoe manufacturing business. His mother was the daughter of Henry Harben, a provision merchant. After education at University College School, he joined the family firm when he was sixteen. When he was eighteen, he represented his father's interests in his uncle's expanding screw-manufacturing business in Birmingham. He worked for Nettleford's for twenty years, leaving a wealthy man. He was elected to Birmingham City Council in 1869 and to the first school board in 1870. He became chairman of the National Education League that year, championing nonconformist views. He was elected mayor of Birmingham in 1873, 1874, and 1875. He was a major proponent of municipal action to improve social conditions. He won a Birmingham parliamentary seat in a by-election in 1876. Chamberlain became president of the Board of Trade in 1880–1885 and president of the Local Government Board, 1886, in Gladstone's second and third governments. He broke with Gladstone and the Liberal Party over Irish Home Rule.

Chamberlain and Lord Hartington led the Liberal Unionists. In 1895, on being offered senior office by Lord Salisbury, he requested the secretaryship of state for the colonies. He played a major role in Salisbury's government at the peak of Britain's imperial prestige. He was a major protagonist in the events leading to the outbreak of the Boer War in 1899. Salisbury was succeeded as prime minister by his nephew, Arthur Balfour, in 1902. In 1903, Chamberlain launched his tariff reform campaign, intending it to strengthen the British Empire, protect British industry and employment, and provide funds for old-age pensions and other social reforms without taxing hard the middle and upper classes.

Chamberlain had admired Lord Randolph Churchill and his talk of "Tory Democracy" in the early 1880s. However, he had been critical of his wilder attacks on Salisbury from 1887 onward. Young Winston Churchill eagerly cultivated his father's political contemporaries; in early 1896 he was at a dinner party where Chamberlain was also a guest and they discussed South Africa. In 1899, Churchill sought letters of introduction to important people in South Africa. On 4 October, Chamberlain promised to write to Alfred Milner to ask "his good offices for the son of my old friend." After Churchill's adventures in South Africa, Chamberlain wrote to him, congratulating him both on his escape from the Boers and on the quality of his newspaper reports on the war. After his election to Parliament for Oldham, Churchill spent two days at Chamberlain's home, Highbury, in Birmingham. When he gave a lecture on the Boer War in Birmingham in November 1900, Chamberlain chaired the meeting. He was present, and praised Churchill's maiden speech in the House of Commons on 18 February 1901.

Chamberlain was one of the notables whom Churchill, Hugh Cecil, and the other "Hughligans" invited to dinner. After the meal, in April 1902, Chamberlain told his young Conservative hosts, "I will give you a priceless secret. Tariffs! There are the politics of the future, and of the near future." However, when Chamberlain launched his tariff campaign on 15 May 1903, Churchill was quick to condemn his move; thereafter they were vigorous opponents on the issue.

Nevertheless, Joseph Chamberlain cooperated fully with Winston Churchill when he was preparing the biography of his father. In September 1904, Churchill dined at Highbury with Chamberlain, who reminisced for hours about the politics of Lord Randolph's time. He also warned Churchill to be prepared for much abuse, which Chamberlain had endured, for changing political sides. Churchill published a portrait of Chamberlain in *Pall Mall*, February 1930, which he reprinted in *Great Contemporaries*, 1937.

Chamberlain suffered a serious stroke on 11 July 1906. He died on 2 July 1914.

Related entries:
Chamberlain, (Arthur) Neville; Milner, Alfred

Suggestions for further reading:
Amery, Julian. 1951 and 1969. *The Life of Joseph Chamberlain.* Vols. 4–6. London: Macmillan.
Churchill, Randolph S. 1966 and 1967. *Winston S. Churchill.* Vols. 1 and 2. London: Heinemann.
Marsh, Peter T. 1994. *Joseph Chamberlain: Entrepreneur in Politics.* New Haven: Yale University Press.

Chamberlain, Joseph Austen (1863–1937)

Austen Chamberlain was a leading politician for the first three decades of the twentieth century and one with whom Churchill usually could work well. Chamberlain, unlike his father, had a strong sense of fair play and of political rectitude. After Chamberlain was passed over for foreign secretary in late 1935, Churchill summed him up in words that have stuck: "He always plays the game, and never wins it." They were both politically sons of their fathers, at least initially. In December 1913, Chamberlain wrote to Churchill, "Our fathers were friends in spite of political differences and I hope that you and I can preserve our friendship through like difficulties." This they mostly managed to do.

Born on 16 October 1863, Austen Chamberlain was the eldest son of Joseph Chamberlain, the leading Birmingham and then national politician. He was educated at Rugby, Trinity College, and Cambridge University. He was very much his father's political heir. He was elected M.P. for Worcestershire East in 1892 and from 1914 represented his father's constituency, West Birmingham. He entered the cabinet as postmaster general in 1900 and was promoted to chancellor of the exchequer (1903–1905) during the early stages of the Conservative and Unionist divisions over his father's campaign for tariffs.

On 11 August 1903, before Joseph Chamberlain left Arthur Balfour's government that September, Churchill and John Seely gave a dinner at the House of Commons for leading Conservatives and Unionists. Balfour and Austen Chamberlain were present. However, civil war soon broke out within the party. Joseph Chamberlain soon telling Austen that at the next general election he felt it essential to get rid of "the foes in our own household—the Churchills, Seelys, Bowles, etc."

After Churchill had joined the Liberals, Austen Chamberlain and Churchill clashed over the 1909 budget and the ensuing constitutional crisis over the powers of the House of Lords as well as over Ireland. In November 1913, Churchill tried to defuse the political conflict over Ireland by talking with Austen Chamberlain on the admiralty yacht *Enchantress*. He suggested that Herbert Henry Asquith and the government was willing to exclude Ulster from Home Rule. Soon after, when Asquith spoke at Leeds in a firmer sense, Austen Chamberlain complained to Churchill about Asquith's tougher tone. On 8 December 1913, Chamberlain dined at Churchill's house with Lord Morley and F. E. Smith. Chamberlain came away impressed that both Churchill and Morley were eager for Asquith to move quickly to secure a settlement of the issue.

However, their relations deteriorated as party conflict over Ulster worsened in 1914. When in April 1914 Chamberlain moved a vote of censure on the government over the Curragh incident and Ulster generally, Churchill denounced the recent Ulster gunrunning and commented that his motion was "uncommonly like a vote of censure by the criminal classes on the police." In September 1914, relations reached rock bottom; Chamberlain was outraged when the government put forward an amending bill, which would allow the 1914 Home Rule Bill to come into force after the war. He called off a speech that Churchill was due to give in Birmingham, commenting he could not appear on a political platform with him. For Chamberlain, Asquith was "trading on the patriotism of his opponents" and he observed to Churchill, "You have destroyed our belief in the honor of public men."

Conservative and Unionist bitterness toward Churchill over Ulster in 1913–1914 underlay their hostility to him in office during the war. In their view, Antwerp and Gallipoli were but additions to an existing indictment. When David Lloyd George formed a government in December 1916, Austen Chamberlain was one of the Conservative leaders who made their participation in the government conditional on Churchill's exclusion.

After the end of the war, Churchill, as secretary of state for war, and Chamberlain, as chancellor of the exchequer, had their disagreements. Chamberlain was orthodox in his approach, keen to economize. He was concerned at the cost of Churchill's demobilization plans and more generally pressed Churchill to keep military expenditure within £110 million for the first postwar year. Later, in 1924–1929, Churchill was to urge similar restraint on Chamberlain and other colleagues.

After Chamberlain succeeded Andrew Bonar Law as leader of the Conservative Party he disappointed many of the Conservative Party backbenchers in the House of Commons and activists in the country. For the anticoalition Tories, he was deemed to be too close to those they felt had no principles: Lloyd George, Churchill, and F. E. Smith. He was leader only for eighteen months until the fall of Lloyd George's coalition government in October 1922.

Under Stanley Baldwin's leadership of the Conservative Party (1923–1937), Chamberlain became a respected elder statesman who usually spoke up for orthodox Conservatism. As such, after at first vigorously supporting Churchill's candidature for the Abbey Division of Westminster in

1924, he came to feel that Churchill was being precipitate in making a move back toward the Conservative Party. He felt that Churchill's promotion to chancellor of the exchequer in 1924 was premature, having himself suggested to Baldwin that Churchill might return to the colonies. However, his brother Neville, when declining the exchequer in favor of health, suggested Churchill as chancellor of the exchequer to Baldwin. Baldwin surprised most people by appointing him to that senior post.

As chancellor of the exchequer, Churchill pressed Chamberlain, the foreign secretary (1924–1929), to pursue economical policies. Very soon he was pressing him to secure substantial sums toward the repayment of war debts from France and Italy. He also pressed Austen Chamberlain in December 1924 to advise the cabinet that war with Japan was not "among the reasonable possibilities to be taken into account in the next 10, 15 or 20 years."

In the mid-twenties, Churchill was less pro-French than Chamberlain He was against giving unilateral guarantees to France against German aggression, arguing instead that Germany's eastern grievances should be remedied by revisions to the Treaty of Versailles, 1919. Churchill was backed by Chamberlain in 1928 when he urged the Committee of Imperial Defence to maintain the Ten Year Rule, that war was unlikely for ten years, so that defense expenditure could be moderated. Churchill's and Chamberlain's views converged in the mid-1930s, with Churchill urging British support for France as their concern about Nazi Germany grew. From 1933 to 1937, Churchill and Chamberlain often acted together to press the government to respond more vigorously to the threat of Adolf Hitler.

Churchill and Chamberlain were friends for much of 1900–1937. After Chamberlain supported Churchill over naval expenditure in mid-1925, Churchill began signing his letters "Yours ever." Chamberlain responded,

"It is a solemn form of signature, but after so many years of friendship I follow your example with confidence." Nevertheless, they continued to have their differences, notably over India in the early 1930s. Chamberlain was one of those who read through draft chapters of *The World Crisis* for Churchill in the late 1920s. When Chamberlain died on 16 March 1937, Churchill was genuinely shocked and upset.

Suggestions for further reading:
Churchill, Randolph S. 1967. *Winston S. Churchill.* Vol. 2. London: Heinemann.
Dutton, David. 1985. *Austen Chamberlain: Gentleman in Politics,* Bolton, UK: Ross Anderson Publications.
Gilbert, Martin. 1971, 1975, and 1976. *Winston S. Churchill.* Vols. 3, 4, and 5. London: Heinemann.
Petrie, Sir Charles. 1939 and 1940. *The Life and Letters of the Right Hon. Sir Austen Chamberlain.* 2 vols. London: Cassell.
Self, Robert C., ed. 1995. *The Austen Chamberlain Diary Letters.* Cambridge: Cambridge University Press.

Chanak

The Chanak crisis of September–October 1922 was one of the major causes of the collapse of David Lloyd George's coalition government on 19 October 1922. Churchill, then secretary of state for the colonies, had warned against a Turkish military revival and the necessity of relying on Greek forces, but when the crisis came, he was a staunch supporter of Lloyd George.

As one part of the Treaty of Sèvres, 20 August 1920, Smyrna and its hinterland were given to Greece to administer for five years, after which a plebiscite would be held to determine the area's future. The Turks under Kemal Ataturk refused to ratify the treaty and took military action against Greece. The Turkish forces captured Smyrna on 9 September 1922, and in October advanced on Chanak (now Cannakale) on the Dardanelles. This was part of a neutral zone of the Straits and was garrisoned by British troops. Lloyd George ordered his troops to repel the Turks, but the local British commander, General Tim Harington, made an agreement with the Turkish forces on 11 October. This undercut the 1920 treaty, giving the Turks back much territory but providing for the neutralization of the Dardanelles and the Bosphorus. These arrangements were the basis of the Treaty of Lausanne, 1923.

Churchill had been sympathetic to Turkish control of Asia Minor, but he believed European Turkey should be kept under Allied control, not least the Gallipoli Peninsula. General Harington had urged the retention of the garrison at Chanak as a rearguard, with the main British concern to defend the Gallipoli Peninsula. Lloyd George and Churchill had been shocked by further massacres of Armenians in 1921 and by much destruction in Smyrna. They hoped for Greek, Serbian, and Roumanian troops as well as British. Churchill appealed to Australia, New Zealand, and other dominions for troops. Only New Zealand and Newfoundland offered help immediately, with Australia offering help later. The London *Daily Mail* denounced the Chanak policy, arguing that no British or empire lives should be lost "in order that Mr. Winston Churchill may make a new Gallipoli."

The British began reinforcing Chanak, with Turkish troops close by and within the neutral zone, refusing to leave but not opening fire. Lloyd George felt a withdrawal would seriously damage the prestige of the British Empire, whereas Churchill warned that a defeat would be even worse. Ataturk rejected British requests to withdraw his troops from the neutral zone. The government decided to issue an ultimatum demanding the withdrawal of Turkish forces, or British forces would fire. Churchill hoped that the ultimatum would ensure negotiations. Harington delayed delivering it because he felt there was no immediate danger of an attack at Chanak and that Ataturk was willing to negotiate. Churchill, in drafting the cabinet's approval of this policy, added the observation that the cabinet did not "believe that repeated concessions and submissions to victorious orientals is the best way to avert war." Harington reached agreement with General Ismet at the Mudania Conference, 3–11 October 1922.

Lloyd George and Churchill's willingness for war attracted much political criticism. The former Conservative Party leader, Andrew Bonar Law, warned in a letter published in the London *Times*, 7 October 1922, that Britain needed French support: "We cannot act alone as the policeman of the world." To dissident Conservatives, this appeared to indicate Bonar Law's willingness to emerge from retirement.

Twelve days later, the result of a by-election at Newport was announced. The independent Conservative won a formerly coalition Liberal seat. Later that morning, Conservative M.P.s met at the Carlton Club and voted to withdraw from the coalition government. Lloyd George resigned as prime minister in the afternoon. Churchill lost his Dundee seat in the subsequent general election.

Related entries:
Curzon, George Nathaniel; Bonar Law, Andrew

Suggestions for further reading:
Gilbert, Martin. 1975. *Winston S. Churchill.* Vol. 4. London: Heinemann.
Harington, General Sir Charles. 1940. *Tim Harington Looks Back.* London: Murray.
Walder, David. 1969. *The Chanak Affair.* London: Hutchinson.

Chancellor of the Duchy of Lancaster (1915)

Churchill was chancellor of the Duchy of Lancaster for nearly six months, from 25 May until 12 November 1915. Bonar Law, leader of the Conservative Party, made it clear on the formation of Herbert Henry Asquith's coalition government that Churchill must leave the admiralty. Both David Lloyd George and Churchill suggested to Asquith that Churchill should become secretary of state for the colonies. However, Asquith made a bad political misjudgment in keeping Bonar Law out of the top jobs and giving him the colonial office. Churchill was given instead the Duchy of Lancaster, usually a post for senior politicians on their way out or promising young politicians on their way up.

Churchill was pleased that he remained a member of the war council (now named the Dardanelles Committee) and, to a certain extent, that he was still by some ten years the youngest member of the cabinet. When, in November 1915, Asquith reconstituted the Dardanelles Committee as a war committee having fewer members and excluding Churchill, Churchill decided to resign, doing so in a letter on 12 November 1915. In his resignation speech on 15 November, Churchill emphasized that, in spite of criticism to the contrary, in all important decisions at the admiralty he had had the first sea lord's agreement in writing.

Suggestion for further reading:
Gilbert, Martin. 1971. *Winston S. Churchill.* Vol. 3. London: Heinemann.

Chancellor of the Exchequer (1924–1929)

Churchill was chancellor of the exchequer from 6 November 1924 until 4 June 1929, taking over thirty-eight years after his father had held the office. Churchill was very disappointed when Lloyd George did not appoint him to the post in succession to Sir Austen Chamberlain in April

1921. Churchill was delighted in 1924 to unpack his father's chancellor's robes, which his mother had carefully stored.

Churchill was surprised that Stanley Baldwin appointed him immediately on his return to the Conservative Party. Baldwin had given first refusal of the post to Neville Chamberlain, who had been chancellor of the exchequer during Baldwin's first government of seven month's duration. Chamberlain preferred to return to being minister of health and he suggested to Baldwin that Conservative Party objections to Churchill's having the exchequer would be no worse than Churchill's returning to the admiralty, another possibility. Baldwin, who was carefully bringing back into office the leading coalition Conservatives, preferred to have Churchill in office than leading backbench discontent.

Churchill's time at the treasury was not one of his most successful periods in office. It was not an area where he had innovative ideas, though he was as ever good at expressing matters in vivid language. The return to the Gold Standard in 1925 at the prewar parity between the pound and the dollar most probably damaged the recovery of exports. Here, he carried out the consensus view of the time, even if he had doubts within two years.

He was also orthodox in determining to be a frugal chancellor of the exchequer by holding down levels of public expenditure and reducing income tax. Although the defense budget rose from £105 to £113 million in 1923–1929, a period of static or falling prices, Churchill supported rolling forward the Ten Year Rule, which presumed that financial planning should assume no major war for ten years or until there was a serious threat. In the 1930s, the appeasers argued that he was responsible for rearmament starting from a low level, though he could counter that the arrival in power of Hitler constituted such a threat as was always conceived as triggering the end of the ten-year premise.

At the time, Churchill's tenure of the exchequer was generally judged to have been a success. He, along with Neville Chamberlain and Douglas Hogg, was mentioned as a possible successor to Baldwin. However, his stance on India removed him from the leadership of the Conservative Party before it returned to office in 1931.

Related entries:
Baldwin, Stanley; Chamberlain, (Arthur) Neville

Suggestion for further reading:
Gilbert, Martin. 1976. *Winston S. Churchill*. Vol. 5. London: Heinemann.

Chartwell Manor

In the autumn of 1922, Churchill bought Chartwell Manor, near Westerham in Kent and some twenty-five miles from Westminster. After extensive renovation and extension work, he and his family lived in it until a few months before his death, his last stay there being in October 1964.

The name came from a spring, the Chart Well, which rises on one side of a valley, and there were farms on the site from medieval times. After John Campbell-Colquhoun bought the property in 1848, the farmhouse was upgraded into a Victorian country mansion. When William Campbell-Colquhoun died on 15 June 1922, the property needed substantial work, especially the extensive dry rot in its northern wing. Campbell-Colquhoun's brother, Captain Archibald Campbell-Colquhoun, lived in Dunbarton and did not want to live at Chartwell. The house and nearly eighty acres had been put up for auction in July 1921, but had not reached its reserve of £6,500. In September 1922, Churchill negotiated with the estate agents, Knight, Frank and Rutley, over the £5,500 asking price, offering £4,800. When he raised this to £5,000, his offer was accepted (on 24

British statesman Winston Churchill at home in the study of his Chartwell estate in Kent, 25 February 1939 (Hulton/Archive)

September 1922) and the sale was completed that November. Soon after his offer was accepted, he took his children, Diana, Sarah, and Randolph, to see it, only telling them after they had voiced enthusiastic approval that he had already bought it.

Churchill paid for Chartwell in the short term by raising a mortgage and loans and by selling the Londonderry Arms. In the longer term, it was paid for by the first volume of *The World Crisis*. In September 1922, he had contracts for £9,000 from Thornton Butterworth, £5,000 from its American publisher, and £5,000 from the *Times* for serial rights. With additional contracts under negotiation, he was confident he could cover the purchase price and the alterations he required.

Churchill spent some £18,000 in improving the building. This included reconstructing much of the front of the house and adding a wing at right-angles to the main building, which contained a dining room, a drawing room, and Clementine Churchill's bedroom. In 1923, while the reconstruction of Chartwell was underway, Churchill rented a nearby house, Hosey Rigg (which he called "Cosy Pig"), from where it was easy to check the building work at Chartwell. Hosey Rigg had had an earlier famous resident, Lewis Carroll, at the time he wrote *Alice's Adventures in Wonderland*. The Churchills moved into Chartwell in 1924.

Churchill loved the view from Chartwell Manor, across the two lakes on his land— filled from the Chart Well—and to the Weald of Kent beyond. He enjoyed walking in the garden after lunch, feeding the fish in his pond, or watching the wildfowl on the lakes. He spent much of the summer of 1925 at Chartwell, working on the garden. He built a dam and, from 1925 to 1932, built most of a large brick wall himself. On the strength of this work, he joined the Amalgamated Union of Building Trade Workers as an adult apprentice. He also carried out other bricklaying, notably on "Wellstreet," a house on the estate. The Churchills also set out a grass tennis court, much used by Clementine Churchill. After the Second World War, this was turned into a croquet lawn. Winston Churchill played croquet as if he were playing polo, swinging the stick with one hand. They also had a circular heated outside swimming pool built in the 1930s.

Painting was a major way in which Churchill relaxed at Chartwell and elsewhere. He had his own studio, a separate building at the bottom of the orchard (next to Orchard House, in which Winston and Clementine Churchill lived in the early part of the Second World War). The studio had been one of several dilapidated buildings. He continued to improve this building by enlarging it and putting in bigger windows. In 1946, he had Robert Southon, a local builder, construct a mobile painting platform for his studio. He kept many of his paintings in the studio, where he displayed them on its walls. The building was a comfortable retreat equipped with a comfortable armchair and an open fire.

Churchill could also retreat to his study. This was on the first floor of the main part of the house. Churchill's architect, Philip Tilden, removed the old ceiling, leaving bare the beams and rafters of the old farmhouse. He put in a Tudor doorway with a molded architrave. As well as bookcases, Churchill's study contained a mahogany table, on which he wrote. For some years, he also used an upright desk, which had belonged to Benjamin Disraeli (and which his son, Randolph Churchill, used from 1962 to 1968). In his study at Chartwell, Churchill finished *The World Crisis* and wrote all or most of *Marlborough; The Second World War; A History of the English Speaking Peoples;* and *Thoughts and Adventures.* Most of his books were housed in the library on the ground floor.

Chartwell Manor was closed during the Second World War. Because it was thought a possible target for enemy aircraft, the lakes were camouflaged with brushwood until September 1945. Before the war, in early 1937, Winston Churchill had written to his wife to suggest selling Chartwell now that their children had either left home or soon would do so. In the summer of 1945, Churchill resolved to sell Chartwell. A group of his friends, led by Lord Camrose, felt that Chartwell should be bought for the National Trust, with the condition Churchill should be permitted to live there in privacy for the rest of his life. On 29 November 1946, Churchill received £43,800 for the property, and he took a fifty-year lease for £350 a year. In December, Churchill bought two farms close to Chartwell, Parkside Farm (for £10,250) and Chartwell Farm (for £22,545).

After his death, the National Trust opened Chartwell to the public. With the assistance of Lady Churchill and her daughter, Mrs. Mary Soames, the house was restored to its state as a family home (changes made to cope with Sir Winston Churchill's final years were removed). It was opened to the public in the summer of 1966. Between then and the end of October 1966, nearly 150,000 people visited the property, and by July 1987 the total had reached 3,329,073.

Related entries:
Londonderry Arms Hotel; *Painting as a Pastime*

Suggestions for further reading:
Fedden, Robin. 1969. *Churchill at Chartwell.* Oxford: Pergamon Press.
Gilbert, Martin. 1975, 1976, 1977, and 1988. *Winston S. Churchill.* Vols. 4, 5, and 8, and companion vol. 4, part 3. London: Heinemann.
Soames, Mary. 1990. *Winston Churchill: His Life as a Painter.* London: Collins.

Churchill, Clarissa (Countess of Avon, 1920–)

Clarissa Churchill is Winston Churchill's only niece. She is the daughter of his brother John Spencer Churchill and Lady Gwendeline Spencer Churchill. She and her brothers, John and Peregrine, were frequently in the company of Winston and Clementine Churchill and their children.

Clarissa Churchill was born on 28 June 1920. She and her brothers spent many Christmases at Chartwell up to 1933 and also in 1936. During the Second World War, she worked in the communications department of the foreign office. She often visited her aunt and uncle at Downing Street.

On 14 August 1952, she married Anthony Eden, who had divorced his first wife. She had first met him when she was sixteen. Both her parents being dead, she told Clementine Churchill first of her engagement. Winston Churchill insisted that she hold the wedding reception at 10 Downing Street, and Clementine returned early from Capri to organize the reception. Their wedding present was a check for £500.

Related entries:
Bertie, Lady Gwendeline Theresa Mary; Churchill, John Strange Spencer; Eden, Sir (Robert) Anthony

Suggestions for further reading:
Colville, John. 1985. *The Fringes of Power.* London: Hodder and Stoughton.
Gilbert, Martin. 1988. *Winston S. Churchill.* Vol. 8. London: Heinemann.
Rhodes, James Robert. 1986. *Anthony Eden.* London: Macmillan.

Churchill, Clementine (Lady Spencer-Churchill, 1885–1977)

Clementine Churchill provided the rock of emotional stability that Winston Churchill lacked earlier in his career. She restrained, or at least lessened, his overbearing tendencies and his financial irresponsibilities. She was prone to anxiety and did not care for the limelight, but she had courage and determination. The historian A. J. P. Taylor commented, "Clementine Churchill proved the perfect wife for Winston Churchill; no woman had a more difficult assignment."

Clementine Hozier was born on 1 April 1885 at 75 Grosvenor Street, London, the second daughter of Colonel Henry and Lady Blanche Ogilvy Hozier. After leaving the army in 1874, Henry Hozier became secretary to Lloyds of London, the insurance underwriters. He ran unsuccessfully as Liberal candidate for Woolwich in 1885. The Hozier's marriage ended in separation in 1891. Clementine and her elder sister were educated at a school in Moray Place, Edinburgh, before joining their mother and two younger children in London. Clementine learned French and lived with her mother, sisters, and brother in Dieppe for nearly a year from 1899 to 1900. There the family befriended the painter Walter Sickert. After the death from typhoid fever of Clementine's older sister, the family returned to England. Clementine completed her formal education at Berkhamsted High School, passing the Higher School Certificate in French, German, and biology in 1903. In 1904 she lived with a German family in Berlin.

Clementine first met Winston Churchill at a ball given by Lord and Lady Crewe in the summer of 1904. He asked his mother to introduce him, but was tongue-tied when she did. She became engaged to two men, Sidney Peel and Lionel Earle, but terminated the engagements. She met Winston Churchill a second time in March 1908 at a dinner party given by her aunt, Lady St. Helier. This time he was fluent and focused his attention on her. After further meetings, Clementine was invited to Blenheim Palace for a house party, 10–12 August 1908. He proposed to her at the Greek temple beside the lake. They married on 12 September 1908 at St. Margaret's,

Westminster. The best man was Lord Hugh Cecil and the bridesmaids were her sister, Nellie Hozier, her cousins, Venetia Stanley and Madeline Whyte, her friend Horatia Seymour, and Winston Churchill's cousin, Clare Frewen. The register was signed by David Lloyd George, the chancellor of the exchequer. Afterwards they spent a few days at Blenheim Palace before traveling in Italy and staying with Baron de Forest at Eichorn in Austria.

Clementine was intelligent and determined but of a quiet nature. Violet Asquith, who much admired Winston Churchill, wrote unkindly at the time of their engagement, "His wife could never be more to him than an ornamental sideboard as I have often said and she is unexacting enough not to mind not being more." Clementine was Liberal in politics but was not keen to take a high political profile herself, preferring to spend her time on family matters, playing tennis, or visiting art galleries. She remained loyal to Winston during his shift into Conservative politics in the 1920s.

They first lived at 12 Bolton Street in London, Winston's bachelor apartment. In early 1909 they bought a nine-year lease on 33 Eccleston Square, Victoria, London, where Diana was born on 11 July that year. She was a good and even frugal manager of household finance. In contrast Winston had an aristocratic profligacy in money matters, was grandiose in expenditure, and was prone to gambling. While Clementine brought up their young children, she often had the solace of the company of her sister-in-law, "Goonie" Churchill, the wife of Winston's brother Jack.

In later life Clementine said her happiest years with her husband were during his Radical phase. She stood up for Asquith and Lloyd George against the sneers of her husband's aristocratic relatives. In October 1913 she even left Blenheim Palace indignantly when the duke criticized her action of replying to Lloyd George on Blenheim Palace writing paper. However, she came to

be bitter about Lloyd George, feeling he should have stopped Asquith from demoting her husband in May 1915, and that he should have brought her husband back into high office when the new government was formed in December 1916.

With Winston Churchill's departure from the admiralty in 1915, they left Admiralty House. As their home was rented to Sir Edward Grey, they moved (after an interval in Arlington Street) into 41 Cromwell Road, South Kensington, the home of Jack and Goonie Churchill. Clementine, Goonie, and their children lived there while Jack and Winston were away on war service. Later, Clementine and Winston moved back to 33 Eccleston Square and bought a house, Lullenden, in the country at East Grinstead, Sussex. Clementine and the children spent the latter part of the war there, out of London. Toward the end of the war, when the lease on Eccleston Square expired, they lived at 3 Tenterden Street, near Hanover Square, London, where Marigold was born on 15 November 1918. A year later they sold their East Grinstead house to General Sir Ian Hamilton. For awhile, from 15 October 1919 until 1920 they stayed with Freddie Guest and his family at Templeton, Roehampton; Guest was then coalition Liberal chief whip and politically close to his cousin, Winston Churchill. In 1920 the Churchills bought 2 Sussex Square, London, moving in late summer, and in September 1922 they acquired Chartwell.

The worst family crisis of the Churchills' lives occurred in August 1921. While at Broadstairs their daughter Marigold, then two years and nine months old, developed septicemia and died. They were both devastated by her death. In October 1922 Winston Churchill fell ill with appendicitis and underwent an operation. As a result Clementine spoke on his behalf in Dundee in the 1922 general election. She continued to support him as he moved back to the Conservative Party. Her main political activities were to support him in his Epping constituency. She helped to raise funds for the Conservative Association and spoke at local events.

Clementine supported her husband during his years out of office in the 1930s. She had briefly been fascinated by Benito Mussolini when she met him in Rome in 1926, even keeping a signed photograph of him for awhile in the drawing room at Chartwell. By the early 1930s she shared her husband's alarm concerning the threat of Adolf Hitler and Nazi Germany. In contrast, she strongly disagreed with Winston over Edward VIII and Mrs. Wallis Simpson. She rightly felt that Stanley Baldwin was taking the stance that was in line with British public opinion.

Clementine's health was often not strong. From the early days of her marriage she had vacationed with her children but without her husband. Overstrand, a village close to Cromer, Norfolk, was a favored destination. In 1938 Clementine went to the Caribbean with Lord Moyne and a Royal Commission inquiring about social conditions in the West Indies. Clementine and Winston were also sometimes apart over Christmas during and after the Second World War.

In the Second World War Clementine Churchill gave her husband the support he needed to endure the strain. More than that, she was one of the very few who could tell him bluntly when he was being too overbearing with colleagues. As early in his wartime premiership as 27 June 1940 she wrote to him saying, "I have noticed a deterioration in your manner . . . you are not as kind as you used to be," and urged that he combine with his "terrific power" the qualities of "urbanity, kindness and if possible Olympic calm." Later, she supported Clement Attlee when he was critical of the way Churchill was verbose when chairing wartime meetings.

Clementine spent much time during the war answering letters from the general public. She conducted an investigation into the conditions in air-raid shelters, confirming that they were as bad as her correspondents suggested. Her husband pressed for action on her findings. Clementine was eager to help Russia after Hitler had invaded in June 1941, and accepted the Red Cross's invitation to head the aid to Russia appeal. This role took her to Moscow, Leningrad, Stalingrad, Yalta, Odessa, and Kursk from March until May 1945. Her other wartime work included being president of the Young Women's Christian Association's Wartime Fund from February 1941, and being an active member of the Committee for the Fulmer Chase Maternity Home. In early 1944 Clementine believed that the Second World War would see the end of their lives together, predicting Winston would die at its end. She added, "You see, he's seventy and I'm sixty and we're putting all we have into this war, and it will take all we have."

Toward the end of the war Clementine looked for a new London home, hoping her husband would soon retire. Early in 1945 they admired 28 Hyde Park Gate, Kensington, London, and bought the property later in the year. With Labour's landslide victory in the 1945 general election, Clementine consoled her husband. Her daughter Mary described Clementine as "riding the storm with unflinching demeanour."

After the Second World War Clementine Churchill took up other good causes. In January 1949 she was elected chairman of the National Hostels Committee of the Young Women's Christian Association (YWCA) and was very active in its affairs. She resigned after her husband became prime minister again, but became a vice president of the YWCA. Later, she made major charitable appeals on the radio, in 1959 for World Refugee Year and in 1961 for buildings of New Hall, Cambridge, a women's college.

However, a major concern was her husband's health, especially after his first stroke on 24 August 1949. She had more serious cause for concern after his major stroke on

23 June 1953. She had her own health problems, ranging from a major gynecological operation in May 1951 to neuritis in her right arm and shoulder. She was pleased when her husband set a retirement date for 5 April 1955, but recognized that retirement would upset him, saying to her daughter Mary, "It's the first death—and for him, a death in life." After he left the premiership, she found it harder to readjust to a quieter lifestyle and became prey to anxiety and depression. Her health picked up somewhat in 1956 and they enjoyed their golden wedding celebrations in 1958. She also enjoyed her involvement in improving the gardens of Chartwell, especially as the house and grounds were no longer their financial responsibility but of the National Trust.

After Winston Churchill's death on 24 January 1965, Clementine decided to leave both Chartwell and 28 Hyde Park Gate. She went to rest in the Caribbean in February and March, returning shortly before her eightieth birthday. She moved into a flat at 7 Princes Gate, London, in September. In May, on the recommendation of Prime Minister Harold Wilson, Clementine was made a life peer. She sat on the cross benches and voted in favor of the abolition of the death penalty. She took great interest in the development of Churchill College, Cambridge, and advocated the admission of women (which occurred from 1972). She became a trustee of Lord Attlee's Memorial Foundation in 1966 and president of the National Benevolent Fund for the Aged in 1972.

In her last years she read or had read to her the volumes of the official biography of Winston Churchill, and did the same with the chapters up to the early part of the First World War of her daughter Mary's biography of her.

She died on 12 December 1977.

Related entries:
Churchill, Diana Spencer; Churchill, Marigold Frances; Churchill, Mary; Churchill, Randolph Frederick Edward Spencer; Churchill, Sarah Millicent Hermione

Suggestions for further reading:
Churchill, Randolph S. 1967. *Winston S. Churchill,* Vol. 2. London: Heinemann.
Fishman, Jack. 1963. *My Darling Clementine.* London: W. H. Allen.
Gilbert, Martin. 1971, 1975, 1976, 1983, 1986, and 1988. *Winston S. Churchill,* Vols. 3–8. London: Heinemann.
Soames, Mary. 1979. *Clementine Churchill.* London: Cassell.

Churchill, Diana Spencer (1909–1963)

Diana Churchill committed suicide before her parents' deaths, her death shocking both of them, though its impact was lessened in their old age. Her later years were marked by mental breakdowns, with alcohol worsening her lot. Yet she was strong on others' behalf, including her sister Sarah and her brother Randolph. When she was recovering from a breakdown in 1955, Winston Churchill wrote to Clementine Churchill of Diana, "She is very dear to me."

Diana, born on 11 July 1909 at 33 Eccleston Square, was Winston and Clementine Churchill's first child. She, like her brother Randolph, was an ill-disciplined child who upset a stream of nannies. In 1920, she was sent with Sarah to Nottingham Hill High School. Later, she went to a finishing school in Paris, run by the Protestant sisters Ozanne. She was a small, attractive girl.

On 12 December 1932, Diana married John Milner Bailey, the son of her father's friend Sir Abe Bailey, a millionaire South African mineowner. The marriage crumbled after a year and they were divorced in 1935. Relations with her mother, which had not been very good, deteriorated. She was much closer to her father and her sister, Sarah. When Churchill was spending New Year's Eve 1934 alone at Chartwell, Diana

L–R: Tom Mitford (Clementine's cousin and only brother of the Mitford sisters), Winston Churchill, Freddie Birkenhead, Clementine Churchill, her daughter Diana Churchill and son Randolph Churchill, and comedian Charlie Chaplin at the Churchill home, Chartwell, Kent, July 1931 (Hulton/Archive)

surprised him by joining him there. The following month, she and Sarah went to Liverpool to help their brother Randolph in the Liverpool Wavertree by-election. They also helped him in another by-election, West Toxteth, later in the year.

Diana married the Conservative politician Duncan Sandys in 1935. The marriage resulted in three children, Celia (later married to Michael Kennedy, then Dennis Walters), Edwina (later married to Piers Dixon), and Julian. Before the Second World War, Diana was an air-raid warden in London and during it she served as an officer in the Women's Royal Naval Service (WRNS) in London. Being there, she was able to visit and support her parents during the stresses of the war.

In 1953, Diana's health was undermined by a severe nervous breakdown. This was followed by lengthy and often painful treatment, including electrical shocks. Although she did not get on well with her mother, she found her father a reassuring and stable presence. Her sister wrote of her in November 1955, "She has a feeling of having been greatly wronged. This is not specific, it does not relate to any one person, or even any special time in her life; but this feeling persists, accompanied by a feeling of unfulfilment and lack of recognition." It was not easy to live in the shadow of an overachieving father.

When Diana and Duncan Sandys separated in 1956–1957, she then lived with her daughters in Chester Row, London. They were divorced in 1960. Diana gave her sister Sarah much support in her troubles and also many other people from mid-1962, when she began working for the Samaritans in

London. She became a friend of the Reverend Chad Varah, the founder of the organization. She died from an overdose of sleeping pills on the night of 19–20 October 1963. Her parents were too unwell to go to her funeral, but they went to the memorial service held at St. Stephens, Walbrook, in the City of London, which housed the headquarters of the Samaritans.

Related entries:
Churchill, Clementine; Churchill, Mary; Churchill, Randolph Frederick Edward Spencer; Churchill, Sarah Millicent Hermione; Sandys, Edwin Duncan

Suggestions for further reading:
Churchill, Sarah. 1981. *Keep on Dancing.* London: Weidenfeld and Nicolson.
Gilbert, Martin. 1988. *Winston S. Churchill.* Vol. 8. London: Heinemann.
Hough, Richard. 1998. *Winston and Clementine: The Triumph of the Churchills.* London: Bantam Press.
Soames, Mary. 1979. *Clementine Churchill.* London: Cassell.

Churchill, John Strange Spencer ("Jack") (1880–1947)

Winston's younger brother was born in Dublin on 4 February 1880. He was named after one of his godfathers, Lieutenant Colonel John Strange Jocelyn, the third son of the earl of Roden and the owner of a large estate. Jack and Winston were close, though very different in character. Winston was an achiever or, indeed, an overachiever. On the prospect of going to study at Oxford University, Jack tellingly commented that he liked "the idea of going . . . where Winston had not been." He often felt that he lived in his elder brother's shadow.

Like Winston, Jack often implored both his parents to visit him at his boarding schools more frequently. He was also close to and loyal to his nanny, Mrs. Elizabeth Ann Everest. When he was older, Lady Randolph tended to rely on him rather than Winston to do things for her. Like Winston, he depended emotionally on his mother; but, unlike Winston, he found it difficult to accept her second and third marriages. At school, Jack was more studious than Winston, but generally considered less intelligent. After leaving Harrow in 1897, he spent a year in Paris. After much indecision about a career, he found a job as a stockbroker in the City of London through the influence of his mother with the major financier Ernest Cassel.

He left work to join the army and served in the Boer War and the First World War. In the Boer War, he secured a lieutenancy in the South African Light Horse Brigade. He was wounded in action in February 1900 and was mentioned in dispatches. In the First World War, he served as a major in the Queen's Own Oxfordshire Hussars in France, Gallipoli, and then France again.

On 7 August 1908, he married Lady Gwendeline ("Goonie") Bertie (1885–1941), who was the daughter of the seventh earl of Abingdon. It seems that she had once seen Winston as an eligible match. The following May, their first child, John George Spencer (1909–), was born, followed later by Henry Winston Spencer, known as Peregrine (1913–), and Clarissa (1920–). For over a year, from late June 1915, after Winston Churchill's loss of his post at the admiralty in the formation of the Asquith coalition government in May 1915, he and his family shared his brother's house at 41 Cromwell Road, London, with his sister-in-law and her children (his brother was serving in France).

Jack and Winston remained close until Jack's death on 23 February 1947. During the Second World War, after Jack's house was blown up, he lived with his brother at 10 Downing Street, either in the house itself or in its annex. Winston was very saddened by the death of his younger brother—as he put it—"after 67 years of brotherly love."

Related Entries:
Bertie, Lady Gwendeline Theresa Mary;
    Churchill, Lady Randolph; Everest, Mrs.
    Elizabeth Ann

Suggestions for further reading:
Churchill, Randolph S. 1966. *Winston S.
    Churchill.* Vol. 1. London: Heinemann.
Churchill, Winston S. 1996. *His Father's Son: The
    Life of Randolph Churchill.* London:
    Weidenfeld and Nicolson.
Colville, John. 1985. *The Fringes of Power:
    Downing Street Diaries.* London: Hodder and
    Stoughton.
Gilbert, Martin. 1971. *Winston S. Churchill.* Vol. 3.
    London: Heinemann.

Churchill, Lady Randolph (1854–1921)

Lady Randolph Churchill had a major influence on Winston, much more than her husband (for all Winston's adulation of him). Although she was not present as much as he wished when he was young, she was his major adviser and reliable friend when he was a young man. She energetically used her very impressive network of top society connections on his behalf, advancing his career very substantially in the period before he achieved government office in December 1905.

Jeanette—always known as Jennie—Jerome was born on 9 January 1854 in Brooklyn, New York. Her father, Leonard Jerome, after working as a partner in a family law firm and for sixteen months (1852–1853) as U.S. consul in Trieste, was a successful speculator, winning and losing fortunes on Wall Street. He became a millionaire for awhile through shrewd dealing during the financial panic of 1857. Leonard Jerome was something of a womanizer, and his daughter's nickname "Jennie" was in memory of his friendship with the famous Swedish singer Jenny Lind.

In 1867, when Jennie was thirteen, her mother, Clara, and her daughters moved to Paris. There the Jerome women lived on the edge of court life until fleeing to London shortly before the Prussians besieged the city in 1870. Clara Jerome and her three daughters relocated in London, taking part in the various fashionable seasons. On 12 August 1873, during Cowes Week, at a dance on HMS *Ariadne* in honor of the Prince of Wales and the future Czar Alexander III of Russia, Jennie Jerome met Lord Randolph Churchill. He proposed to her that week. They were married less than a year later, after a long wrangle between their fathers over the details of the marriage settlement. The marriage took place in Paris at the British embassy on 15 April 1874.

Lady Randolph Churchill was twenty when Winston was born on 30 November 1874. Winston had been born prematurely after Lady Randolph, at least seven months pregnant, had slipped and fallen while out walking with a shooting party at Blenheim Palace on 24 November and had been shaken up in a pony carriage traveling over rough ground on 28 November. Whether this was all part of an elaborate effort to disguise a conception that had preceded their marriage can never be proved or disproved. However, much is known about Lord Randolph to suggest that it is not unlikely, especially given that in such a well-documented life no record exists of Winston's weight at birth. On 4 February 1880, she gave birth to a second son, John Strange (known as Jack).

Lady Randolph's first marital home was a house at 1 Curzon Street, London, rented during the summer of 1874 before they took up a thirty-seven-year lease on one of the duke of Marlborough's houses, at 48 Charles Street. Both houses are in Mayfair, in the vicinity of Hyde Park, Green Park, and the Mall, an area both fashionable and convenient for Parliament. Her married life was initially centered on the social whirl of London society, with the adulterous Prince of Wales at its heart. After a major row in 1876 concerning Lord Randolph's elder

A young Winston Churchill (right), with his mother, the American heiress Jennie Jerome (Lady Randolph), and his brother Jack, 1889 (Hulton/Archive)

brother, the duke of Blandford, who was openly living with Lady Aylesford (who had earlier had an affair with the Prince of Wales), the Prince of Wales ensured that Lord and Lady Randolph Churchill were ostracized from high society.

Soon after, Lord and Lady Randolph Churchill, with Winston, accompanied the duke and duchess of Marlborough to Ireland. Lord Randolph's father was lord lieutenant of Ireland from 11 December 1876 until the fall of Benjamin Disraeli's government in April 1880. Lord Randolph was his unofficial and unpaid private secretary in Dublin from early 1877. Winston's earliest memories included those of his parents when they hunted in Ireland. In 1930, in *My Early Life,* he recalled that his mother "always seemed to me a fairy princess" who shone for him "like the Evening Star." He

also remembered watching his grandfather make a speech when unveiling the statue of Field Marshal Sir Hubert Gough, first Viscount Gough (1779–1869), in February 1880.

On their return to London, Lord and Lady Randolph Churchill lived at 29 St. James's Place, next door to Sir Stafford Northcote, the Conservative leader in the House of Commons. Back in London, Lady Randolph helped and supported her husband in his increasingly successful political career. She saw less of Winston, a lonely school boy at Ascot, Brighton, and then Harrow, than he wished. In spring 1882, when Lord Randolph's illness had become severe, she rented a cottage near Wimbledon; when he recovered, they went to stay with the Jeromes in New York. His recurrent illnesses demanded much attention from Lady Randolph, and this reinforced her tendency to put looking after him above responding to Winston's frequent calls for attention and affection.

With Lord Randolph's growing success in politics in the early 1880s, the Churchills were welcomed back into society. The Prince of Wales resumed social intercourse with them. They were invited several times to the royal lodge at Sandringham, Lady Randolph often visiting on her own. Lord Randolph was in poor health and often went abroad with male friends, without Lady Randolph. Presumably with her husband's acquiescence, she had affairs not only with the Prince of Wales but also with several society figures, including the dashing Austrian, Count Kinsky, and perhaps also Lord Dunraven, Count Herbert von Bismarck, the marquis de Breteuil, Henry Cust, and Colonel John Palmer Brabazon.

When Lord Randolph accepted the secretaryship of state for India in June 1885, Lady Randolph ran his campaign in Woodstock in the resulting by-election. She canvassed energetically with her mother-in-law, the dowager duchess of Marlborough. By this time, Lady Randolph was already playing a prominent role in the Primrose League, set up by Lord Randolph and his associates as a Conservative Party social organization in memory of Disraeli. After her husband's death, she remained an active member. Winston made his first public speech at a meeting of the Bath Primrose League at Claverton Down, 26 July 1897.

In June 1894, Lady Randolph took her husband, who was declining into insanity, on what was intended to be a world tour. Lord Randolph's rapid deterioration caused them to interrupt the tour and return to London, where he died on 24 January 1895. Lady Randolph was then forty years old. The horrors of Lord Randolph's final phase brought Winston and his brother Jack closer to their mother. During his early twenties, Winston's main confidante was his mother, to a degree surprising in one of his age.

Lady Randolph utilized society friends, such as Colonel Brabazon, to forward Winston's career. Brabazon advised her how to secure a place for him in the 4th Hussars. She introduced Winston to numerous influential people, including Lord Salisbury. She also exercised her influence to have accusations against Winston of malpractice in horse racing dropped and to secure support against an accusation of homosexuality. Bourke Cockran, with whom Lady Randolph had an affair after her first husband's death, looked after Winston on his first trip to the United States in 1895. He was then en route to Cuba, where he observed the nationalist uprising from the Spanish side. She secured Arthur Balfour's help to find a publisher for *The Malakand Field Force*. Lady Randolph also successfully appealed to a range of eminencies to assist Winston in securing a place on Lord Kitchener's campaign in the Sudan.

By late 1898, Winston was also helping his mother; he assisted her in her plans to publish a literary magazine by meeting and discussing details with John Lane of the Bodley Head. This enterprise, the *Anglo-Saxon Review,* was intended to give her a more positive interest in life other than the ephemeral whirl of society. After Winston resigned his commission in the army in 1899, he helped his mother prepare the first issue; the journal ran to ten issues.

When Winston first stood for Parliament at Oldham in 1899, Lady Randolph's presence was a great draw. She was treated as a celebrity and on one occasion spoke before 200 women members of the Primrose League. During the Boer War, Lady Randolph chaired a committee to raise American money to fund a hospital ship. The ship, the *Maine,* and its crew were supplied by an American millionaire, Bernard Nadel Baker, and Lady Randolph's committee funded the conversion. She sailed with the ship to Cape Town and on to Durban. There, she spoke with the wounded, who were brought from Spion Kop and other battles. She also met her two sons and visited Chievely, in the war zone, and Ladysmith after it had been relieved.

On 28 July 1900, she married George Cornwallis-West (1874–1951), a man sixteen days older than Winston. She had first met him in June 1898 at Warwick Castle, among the countess of Warwick's guests, when she was entertaining the Prince of Wales. Cornwallis-West's parents had vehemently opposed the match, as had the Prince of Wales and many of Lady Randolph's society friends. Thoughts of marriage were abandoned before the Boer War, but renewed after Lady Randolph's return with the hospital ship in late April 1900. Winston was far from enthusiastic about the marriage, but loyally supported his mother, his brother being less acquiescent. The date of the wedding was fixed so that Winston could be present on his return from the war. After the wedding, she still enjoyed the privilege of retaining the name Lady Randolph Churchill; but she put a notice in the *Times* stating that she wished to be known as Mrs. George Cornwallis-West.

Winston successfully pressed his mother to break her honeymoon to help him fight Oldham again, this time in the 1900 general election. She secured Joseph Chamberlain to speak for him, and had the pleasure of seeing her oldest son elected to Parliament at the age of twenty-six. She shared Winston's Free Trade views, and in late 1903, vigorously condemned the Randolph Churchill branch ("habitation") of the Primrose League for providing a platform for the secretary of the Tariff Reform League. She helped Winston again in the 1906 general election, when he won a Manchester seat.

In spite of a happy start, her marriage with George Cornwallis-West broke down, and she filed for a divorce in January 1913. As soon as the divorce became absolute, Cornwallis-West married the famous actress, Mrs. Patrick Campbell, within the

hour. Afterwards, Lady Randolph placed a notice in the *Times* to say that she now wished to be known as Jennie Spencer-Churchill.

In the pre–First World War years, she remained active. She wrote and went to two plays: *His Borrowed Plumes,* performed at Hicks' Theatre, London, in July 1909; and *The Bill,* performed at the Glasgow Repertory Theatre in March 1913. She also set up what was in effect an ancestor of the "theme park," the re-creation of "Shakespeare's England," in a major exhibition at Earl's Court. During the First World War, she again organized facilities for wounded soldiers. She chaired the committee that raised money for the American Women's War Hospital at Paignton, Devon, and also worked on books for the war effort, translating *My Return to Paris* (from French to English) and editing *Women's War Work.*

On 1 June 1918, Jennie Spencer-Churchill married Montagu Phippen Porch (1877–1964). He was forty-one (three years younger than Winston) and she was sixty-four. They had met at the wedding of her nephew, Hugh Frewen, in Rome in the early summer of 1914. They saw each other several times in subsequent days, but became engaged in early 1918 when he was on leave from his regiment. Although Winston was "very surprised," he again supported his mother and was the first to sign the marriage register. After this marriage, she made it clear that she wished to be known again as Lady Randolph Churchill rather than Mrs. Montagu Porch. At the end of the war, Montagu Porch resigned from the Nigerian Civil Service and shared in her society life in London and France.

Following a bad fall, a broken ankle, gangrene, and complications, Lady Randolph died on 29 June 1921. She was buried at Bladon, near Oxford, next to Lord Randolph. Later, both Winston and Jack were buried with them. She was an energetic woman of many talents. Although her devotion to society took her away from Winston when he was young and in need of attention, she used her social networks vigorously to advance her son's army career and, later, his political career. She provided bad examples, not least in managing money, but during his earlier adult life she was a much-needed rock of support, both practical and emotional. For many years she was both his mother and his best friend.

Related entries:
Churchill, John Strange Spencer; Churchill, Lord Randolph Henry Spencer

Suggestions for further reading:
Churchill, Peregrine, and Julian Mitchell. 1974. *Jennie: Lady Randolph Churchill.* London: Collins.
Cornwallis-West, Mrs. George. 1908. *The Reminiscences of Lady Randolph Churchill.* London: Arnold.
Leslie, Anita. 1969. *Jennie: The Life of Lady Randolph Churchill.* London: Hutchinson.
Martin, Ralph. 1969 and 1971. *Lady Randolph Churchill.* 2 vols. London: Cassell.
Sandys, Celia. 1994. *From Winston with Love and Kisses: The Young Churchill.* London: Sinclair Stevenson.

Churchill, Lord Randolph Henry Spencer (1849–1895)

Winston's father was Lord Randolph Churchill, the second surviving son of the seventh duke of Marlborough. He was twenty-five when Winston, his oldest son, was born. Winston worshipped his father, and craved affection and attention. Lord Randolph's interest in his son was intermittent and he often showed him a cold dislike. This, perhaps, was a good example of the jealousy that some fathers have for their first-borns when they feel displaced in their wives' affections.

Lord Randolph Churchill was born on 13 February 1849. From early on, he was a spirited but volatile boy. In his early years at Eton, he misbehaved with vigor. He went on to Merton College, Oxford, where he narrowly missed gaining first class honors.

Lord Randolph, as second son of the seventh duke of Marlborough, grew up in a network of top Conservative connections. Benjamin Disraeli often visited Blenheim, and Lord Randolph admired much of Disraeli's politics (even if Disraeli was not as influential on Lord Randolph as Winston later suggested). Lord Salisbury also visited Blenheim, and in November 1880 spoke at a Conservative rally in Lord Randolph's constituency, Woodstock. Lord Randolph also often associated with Arthur Balfour in the early 1880s, when Balfour sometimes joined Lord Randolph, John Eldon Gorst, and Sir Henry Drummond Wolff in serious opposition to the Liberal government in the House of Commons (the group being known as the "Fourth Party"). Lord Randolph was elected to Parliament in 1874 for Woodstock, a seat where the influence of the duke of Marlborough was strong. After Woodstock (1874–1885) he represented South Paddington (1885–1895).

Lord Randolph's political career was brief but spectacular. From an early age, he had been notably temperamental, often rude and aggressive. Such traits became even more marked after a serious illness in 1882, which may have marked the onset of symptoms of syphilis.

In the general election of 1886 that followed the defeat of William Gladstone's first Home Rule Bill, Lord Randolph famously denounced Gladstone's proposal as one "to gratify the ambition of an old man in a hurry." Lord Randolph was aware that he was living on limited time himself; he was often a young man in a hurry, aspiring to the premiership before an expected early death. His son Winston, aware of the early deaths of his father and uncle, felt that he also had to be quick to achieve political eminence.

Lord Randolph's politics, like his moods, were often variable. He often spoke for the landed interest and for Fair Trade (i.e., protection), yet he also spoke the language of Tory Democracy. He was a popular speaker in Tory Lancashire, and he appealed directly (to the horror of Lord Salisbury) to the Conservative Party activists.

He was unpredictable; for the Conservative Party leadership, a charismatic "loose cannon." He frequently attacked Gladstone and other Liberal leaders in markedly unrestrained language. Yet he was also vitriolic about Conservative leaders, especially Sir Stafford Northcote, and not always in private.

Nevertheless, his position in the Conservative Party was sufficiently strong for Lord Salisbury to offer him the post of secretary of state for India in his first government (June 1885–January 1886) and chancellor of the exchequer in his second government (formed August 1886). Becoming chancellor of the exchequer at thity-seven suggested he had a great political future. However, he was not tamed by office, remaining unpredictable and rarely a good team player. In December 1886, he precipitately ended his ministerial career by resigning over the defense estimates. Whether Lord Randolph had greater aims, such as the leadership of the Conservative Party, or ousting Lord Iddesleigh (formerly Northcote) from the foreign office, it is clear is that he overestimated the strength of his political position. His ill-judged and reckless resignation certainly consigned him to the margins of politics.

By the early 1890s, as the progress of syphilis undermined his faculties, he was increasingly a sad shadow of his former self in the House of Commons. He took some consolation in keeping racehorses, with Lord Dunraven as his partner. In this venture he was successful. He died on 24 January 1895, seventy years to the day before the death of his son Winston.

Related entries:
Churchill, John Strange Spencer; Churchill, Lady Randolph

Suggestions for further reading:
Churchill, Winston S. 1906. *Lord Randolph Churchill*. 2 vols. London: Macmillan.
Foster, Roy. 1981. *Lord Randolph Churchill*. Oxford: Clarendon Press.
Quinault, R. E. 1979. "Lord Randolph Churchill and Tory Democracy." *Historical Journal* (April): pp. 141–165.
Rhodes, James Robert. 1959. *Lord Randolph Churchill*. London: Weidenfeld and Nicolson.
Rosebery, Lord. 1906. *Lord Randolph Churchill*. London: Humphreys.

Churchill, Marigold Frances (1918–1921)

Marigold Frances was the fourth child of Winston and Clementine Churchill, born on 15 November 1918. Like her sister Sarah, she had red hair. She was an energetic little girl who loved to sing. Her parents nicknamed her "Duckadilly."

Marigold was susceptible to throat infections and coughs. On holiday at Broadstairs in August 1921, she became very ill and died on 23 August.

Suggestion for further reading:
Soames, Mary. 1979. *Clementine Churchill*. London: Cassell.

Churchill, Mary (Lady Mary Soames, 1922–)

Mary Churchill was Winston and Clementine Churchill's youngest child and is the sole surviving child. Growing up in Chartwell, she saw much of her parents; she remained geographically close to them for the first ten years of her marriage, when she and her husband lived at Chartwell Farm. She has written major works about her parents.

Mary Churchill was born in London on 15 September 1922, the fifth child of Winston and Clementine Churchill. Educated at local schools at Chartwell, and by a French tutor during summer school holidays, she took on part-time work with the Red Cross and at a canteen after the outbreak of the Second World War. After her father became prime minister, she was based at Chequers, helping the Women's Voluntary Service in Aylesbury. In September 1941, she joined the Auxiliary Territorial Service after training at Aldermaston and Oswestry; she was then posted to an antiaircraft battery at Enfield. Later, when she was attached to a battery in Hyde Park, London, her father would visit the battery. Subsequently, the battery was redeployed in various parts of southern England.

From 1943, Mary Churchill accompanied her father on some of his official engagements. She was with him, her mother, and her sister Sarah when he received the Freedom of the City of London on 30 June. She also acted as her father's aide-de-camp at the Quebec Conference, 1943. Before the conference, Churchill showed her Niagara Falls, and she accompanied him to President Franklin D. Roosevelt's home, Hyde Park. After the conference, Mary and her mother went with Churchill on his short fishing holiday at Lac des Neiges, and then on to Washington, 1–12 September.

In January 1945, Mary Churchill accompanied her antiaircraft battery to defend Brussels. That July, she took her leave entitlement so that she could join her parents for a week's holiday at the Château de Bordaberry, Hendaye, near Bordeaux and the Spanish frontier. On their return, she accompanied her mother to the election count in her father's constituency on 26 July. She and the other members of her family did their best to console her father in the Conservative general election defeat. Before she returned to her unit, she went with her parents to the theater to see Noel Coward's *Private Lives,* which they all enjoyed.

Mary Churchill was demobilized on 1 April 1946. She often accompanied her parents when they received honors. In July, she and her sister Sarah saw the king invest her mother as a Dame Grand Cross of the Order of the British Empire for her major services during the Second World War. In September, she accompanied her parents to Brussels and then Paris. While at the Paris embassy, she met Christopher Soames, then the assistant military attaché. They married on 11 February 1947. They lived at Chartwell Farm for ten years, with Christopher Soames initially managing the farms, before moving to Hamsell Manor, near Tunbridge Wells, in 1957.

While the Soameses lived at Chartwell Farm, Winston and Clementine Churchill, when in residence at Chartwell, were only yards away. The Churchills enjoyed being close to their grandchildren, Nicholas, Emma, and Jeremy; Charlotte and Rupert were born after the Soameses left Chartwell Farm.

In late December 1952, Mary and Christopher Soames accompanied Winston and Clementine Churchill on the *Queen Mary* to the United States. They arrived in New York on 5 January 1953 and were met by General Dwight D. Eisenhower, the president-elect. Mary Soames then accompanied her mother to Jamaica the next day, where Winston Churchill, Christopher Soames, and John Colville joined them from 9–28 January.

In 1968, Mary Soames accompanied her husband, the British ambassador, to the Paris embassy, a post he held until 1972. They then went to Brussels, her husband being the first British vice president of the European Commission, 1973–1977. She also accompanied him when he was governor of Southern Rhodesia, 1979–1980.

Mary Soames has also played a substantial role in public life. She served as a justice of the peace for East Sussex, 1960–1974, and as a governor of Harrow School, 1980–1995. She was chairman of the U.K. Association for the International Year of the Child, 1979; chairman of the Royal National Theatre Board, 1989–1995; and has been chairman of the Trustees of the Winston Churchill Memorial Trust since 1991. She has written or edited several major books, including an award-winning biography of her mother and an edition of her parents' personal letters. She has been awarded honorary doctorates by Sussex and Kent universities.

Related entries:
Churchill, Clementine; Churchill, Diana Spencer; Churchill; Randolph Frederick Edward Spencer; Churchill, Sarah Millicent Hermione; Quebec Conference, First; Soames, (Arthur) Christopher John

Suggestions for further reading:
Gilbert, Martin. 1983, 1986, and 1988. *Winston S. Churchill*. Vols. 6–8. London: Heinemann.
Soames, Mary. 1979. *Clementine Churchill*. London: Cassell.
———. 1998. *Speaking for Themselves: The Personal Letters of Winston and Clementine Churchill*. London: Cassell.

Churchill, Randolph Frederick Edward Spencer (1911–1968)

He was very much "his father's son" (as his own son has emphasized), his virtues and faults written large. He aspired to match his father, Winston, just as Winston had aspired to match his father, Lord Randolph; but in his father's case, Lord Randolph Churchill had left the political stage, whereas Randolph Churchill lived under Winston's shadow. Randolph loved and admired his father and, of several loyal followers, he was the most loyal. Nevertheless, their relationship was often explosive; Randolph's extravagant living, wild gambling, and heavy drinking were often too much to bear for his parents and others close to him.

Randolph Churchill was born on 28 May 1911 at Eccleston Square, London, the only son and second child of Winston and Clementine Churchill. He was given the names Frederick and Edward after his godfathers F. E. Smith and Sir Edward Grey. Educated at Sandroyd, near Cobham, Surrey, and Eton, he went on to Christ Church, Oxford, but left after four terms to go on a lecture tour of the United States.

In the United States, his lectures were a success but, as was to be a characteristic, he spent freely. Equally alarming for his parents, he talked of marriage (to Kay Halle), although he was only nineteen. He returned to England, lost large amounts of money by gambling, and lived even more extravagantly. Then, as later, Winston Churchill paid up to save his son from the consequences of his financial folly. When Randolph turned twenty-one, Winston Churchill gave a dinner at Claridges hotel; many leading political figures and their sons were present.

Randolph Churchill wrote a series of newspaper articles on Germany in mid-1932. He perceptively warned of the threat Hitler and the Nazis posed to European peace should they achieve power. When Winston Churchill visited Marlborough's battlefields, Randolph arranged a meeting between his father and Adolf Hitler in Munich, but Hitler did not attend. Randolph joined his father in campaigning against the government's liberal policy toward India. They also gambled together on the French Riviera, in spite of Clementine Churchill's objections.

In January 1935, Randolph Churchill decided to run against the official Conservative candidate in a by-election at Liverpool, Wavertree, because he thought the candidate was unsound on India. Randolph did not consult his father, who thought his son's running foolish and damaging. Randolph did secure the support of Lord Rothermere, who had been employing him to write for the London *Daily Mail*. Nevertheless, Winston Churchill loyally and publicly wished his son success, secured a message of support

Randolph Churchill, son of Sir Winston Churchill, canvassing at Dingwall in a three-piece tweed suit and matching flat cap, January 1936 (Hulton/Archive)

At the end of 1935, the Ross and Cromarty Conservatives rebelled at having Malcolm MacDonald, National Labour, as their M.P., and invited Randolph Churchill to be a candidate. To Winston Churchill's dismay, Randolph accepted the invitation. MacDonald won easily and Randolph Churchill came in third, narrowly saving his deposit (parliamentary candidates having to make a returnable deposit to stand, then £150, returnable only if the candidate polled one-eighth or more of the valid votes cast).

Randolph Churchill returned to journalism. With war threatening, in 1938 he joined the 4th Hussars, his father's old regiment, training to be a reserve officer. That year he also published a volume of his father's speeches that he had edited, *Arms and the Covenant*. At the beginning of 1939, he and Duncan Sandys tried unsuccessfully to organize an antiappeaser political group, the Hundred Thousand.

With the outbreak of war, Randolph Churchill joined his regiment. His father sent him on HMS *Kelly* to bring the duke and duchess of Windsor back from France. Soon after his return, he met Pamela Digby; they married on 4 October 1939. In 1940, following the death of one of the Conservative M.P.s for Preston, he was invited to stand and was returned unopposed in late September. He transferred from the 4th Hussars to No. 8 Commando and was sent to Egypt in early 1941. By losing a fortune gambling on the troopship, he undermined his marriage because he left Pamela to face his creditors. In late 1941, he was appointed director of propaganda and censorship in Egypt, where he was based in Cairo.

Randolph Churchill fell out badly with his father and mother when he returned to England in spring 1942. He was outraged that they knew his wife was having an affair with Averell Harriman and seemed to take her side. Clementine banned him from their home for the remainder of the war, although he saw his father in London, at Marrakesh in 1943, and elsewhere. Ran-

from Lord Carson, and spoke at two eve-of-poll meetings. Randolph's sisters Diana and Sarah also helped. Randolph Churchill won 10,575 votes and the official Conservative candidate 13,771; but the Labour candidate won with 15,611 votes. This was not the way to launch a career in Conservative Party politics.

To Winston Churchill's horror, his son then supported an unofficial Conservative candidate at Norwood, London. Again Diana and Sarah Churchill helped their brother. However, the official candidate, Duncan Sandys, won, and later in the year he married Diana.

Before the 1935 general election, Randolph Churchill was urged to be the official Conservative candidate for Liverpool, West Toxteth, rather than be an unofficial candidate in Wavertree. He was supported by his father, who made speeches in the constituency, and by his mother and by Duncan Sandys. He lost but reduced the Labour majority by over half from a by-election earlier in the year.

dolph Churchill joined the Special Air Service and in May 1942 took part in the Benghazi raid, 400 miles behind enemy lines. In February 1944, he was parachuted into Yugoslavia, where he liaised with the partisans.

In the 1945 general election, Randolph Churchill and Julian Amery ran for the two-member Preston constituency. Winston Churchill spoke for them, addressing a crowd of 10,000 at the market square. Nevertheless, they lost. Randolph Churchill returned to journalism and giving lectures in the United States. He also edited further volumes of his father's speeches (a total of six). On 2 November 1948, he married June Osborne. They had a daughter, Arabella, the following year.

In the 1950 general election, Randolph Churchill ran as the Conservative and Liberal-National candidate for Plymouth, Devonport, against Michael Foot. Because they had both worked for the *Evening Standard* before the Second World War, they already knew each other. Winston Churchill spoke on his son's behalf on 9 February. Nevertheless, Michael Foot increased his majority. Randolph Churchill ran there again in 1951, and again his father supported him in a speech on 23 October. Again he was beaten by Michael Foot, but by a smaller majority. This was his last election contest.

Randolph Churchill again returned to journalism. He was wounded in Korea while reporting for the London *Daily Telegraph*. He also wrote books, two linked to Queen Elizabeth II's coronation in 1953, *Fifteen Famous English Homes* (1954), *What I Said About the Press* (1957), *The Rise and Fall of Sir Anthony Eden* (1959), and *Lord Derby* (1960). After the success of *Lord Derby,* Randolph Churchill turned to writing the biography of his father, assisted by a team of researchers. He still found time to fight libel cases and to write *The Fight for the Tory Leadership* (1963), *Twenty-One Years* (1965), and, with his son Winston, *The Six Days War* (1967). Before

his death, he succeeded in publishing the warmly acclaimed first two volumes of his father's biography. He died on 6 June 1968. He was buried in Bladon churchyard, next to his father and grandfather.

Related entries:
Churchill, Clementine; Harriman, Pamela Digby Churchill Hayward; Sandys, Edwin Duncan

Suggestions for further reading:
Churchill, Randolph S. 1965. *Twenty-One Years.* London: Weidenfeld.
Churchill, Winston S. 1996. *His Father's Son: The Life of Randolph Churchill*. London: Weidenfeld and Nicolson.
Soames, Mary. 1979. *Clementine Churchill.* London: Cassell.

Churchill, Sarah Millicent Hermione (Lady Audley, 1914–1982)

Sarah Churchill was Winston and Clementine Churchill's third child. To her father's surprise and initial consternation, she wished for a career in the theater and she succeeded. He nicknamed her "Mule," because of her stubbornness. She accompanied him to the major wartime conferences at Cairo, Tehran, and Yalta.

Sarah Churchill was born on 7 October 1914 at Admiralty House. Much to the chagrin of Clementine Churchill, Winston did not return from Antwerp until later that day. Sarah's godfather was F. E. Smith. She was looked after by a nanny, Miss Maryott White, Clementine's first cousin and a trained Norland nurse. Sarah and her sister Diana were sent to Notting Hill High School from the autumn of 1920 and later to a school in Broadstairs. In 1931, she was sent to a finishing school in Paris, run by three Protestant sisters named Ozanne. Clementine had ensured that her children, like her, spoke French by employing a succession of French governesses during school holidays.

Sarah Churchill loved her gramophone, passed on to her by her sister Diana. Its sound occasionally broke her father's concentration, and she was then ordered to turn the volume down. Her love of music led to her going to the De Vos School of Dancing in George Street, Manchester Square, London. After two years, with her father's approval, she was auditioned by C. B. Cochran for his 1935 revue *Follow the Sun,* and she was accepted. To the horror of her parents, she fell in love with the star of the show, Vic Oliver, an Austrian who was eighteen years older and had been married twice before. Her father successfully persuaded her to promise not to marry Oliver until he had American citizenship, warning her that otherwise she would be "married to the enemy" and would lose her British passport. Very dramatically, in a blaze of newspaper publicity, Sarah Churchill went by sea to the United States to marry Oliver, without first telling her parents.

By 1941, the marriage was crumbling. She decided to join the Women's Auxiliary Air Force (WAAF) and asked her father to get her admitted without the usual waiting period. This he did. She and Vic Oliver were in effect separated thereafter, though they saw each other occasionally when she went to his shows. She worked in the Photographic Interpretation Unit at Medmenham, not far from Chequers, for most of the war years.

In November 1943, she was given leave of absence to accompany her father as one of his aides-de-camp to the Cairo and Tehran conferences. Her brother, Randolph Churchill, also traveled with him on the *Renown,* from Plymouth to Gibraltar, Malta, and Alexandria. She accompanied her father and President Franklin D. Roosevelt to see the sphinx and the pyramids while they were in Cairo. She and Randolph also attended a dinner party given for their father on his sixty-ninth birthday. After the conferences, she flew with her father to Tunis, where he suffered from pneu-

monia. She later recalled that he told her, "Don't worry, it doesn't matter if I die now, the plans of victory have been laid, it is only a matter of time."

She was also given leave from Medmenham to accompany her father to Yalta in early 1945. She was shocked by the deterioration in Roosevelt's health since Cairo in December 1943. She was also saddened by the severe war damage in Sebastopol.

After the war, in September 1945, Sarah Churchill accompanied her father for a month's holiday to Lake Como. They stayed at Field Marshal Alexander's villa, La Rosa. There, between 2 and 19 September, they enjoyed painting and picnics.

After demobilization, Sarah worked in films, initially in Italy. Liking the Italians, she talked her father into removing derogatory remarks about them from one of his major speeches in London. She spent Christmas and New Year 1947–1948 in Marrakesh with her father. They flew out from Northolt on 10 December, stopping at Paris on the way. There, Churchill enjoyed painting and working on the proofs of the first volume of *The Second World War,* his stay funded by his American publishers.

On 18 October 1949, Sarah married Antony Beauchamp, a professional photographer whom she had first met before the Second World War. They married at Sea Island, Georgia. Her cables informing her parents reached them after they learned the news from the press. Her mother took great umbrage and snubbed the couple for some months. The marriage began to crumble in 1953 and they parted in 1955. Beauchamp committed suicide in August 1957. In January 1958, in a blaze of publicity, she was arrested at Malibu Beach and charged with being drunk. She was fined $50 on 16 January. She and her mother joined her father at the Reves's villa, La Pausa, on the French Riviera in early February.

Sarah Churchill's later theater career included a pantomime, in which she played Peter Pan, in 1958. Her parents attended, and her mother brought a party of grandchildren; her sister Diana also took a party to see the show. Sadly, there were more problems due to alcohol; these resulted in her being remanded in Holloway Prison. In July 1961, after being arrested in Lupus Street, London, for being drunk and disorderly, her probation officer told the magistrate, "She is really an alcoholic. During her probation she has had treatment and has got on very well. She has made a come-back in her profession. The trouble is that she is in with fair-weather friends. She holds parties and the friends . . . take advantage of her hospitality."

In April 1961, she married Henry Audley, the 23d Baron Audley, whom she had met in Marbella, Spain. This marriage was happy, but it ended in July 1963, when he died of a heart attack in Granada. She published a short book about her father, dedicated to her mother, after his death, *A Thread in the Tapestry* (1967), and an autobiography, *Keep on Dancing* (1981). She died on 24 February 1982.

Related entries:
Churchill, Clementine; Churchill, Diana Spencer; Churchill, Mary; Churchill, Randolph Frederick Edward Spencer

Suggestions for further reading:
Churchill, Sarah. 1967. *A Thread in the Tapestry.* London: Deutsch.
———. 1981. *Keep on Dancing.* London: Weidenfeld and Nicolson.
Gilbert, Martin. 1975–1988. *Winston S. Churchill.* Vols. 4–8. London: Heinemann.
Hough, Richard. 1990. *Winston and Clementine: The Triumph of the Churchills.* London: Bantam Press.
Soames, Mary. 1979. *Clementine Churchill.* London: Cassell.

Churchill, Winston Spencer (1940–)

Winston Churchill was delighted to have a grandson named Winston Spencer Churchill. The infant was a bright light for Churchill in the darkest days of the Second World War. At his christening, Churchill said, with tears running down his face, "Poor infant, to be born into such a world as this." His grandson followed some of his footsteps, being a journalist and a Conservative M.P. (1970–1997).

Winston Spencer Churchill was born on 10 October 1940 at Chequers; his parents were Randolph and Pamela Churchill (later the widow of Averell Harriman). He was christened at Ellesborough, near Chequers, on Churchill's sixty-sixth birthday. His godparents were Lord Beaverbrook, Brendan Bracken, Lord Brownlow, and Virginia Cowles.

In 1951, Churchill set up a family trust through which his earnings from his *The Second World War* would go to his children and grandchildren. Randolph thanked his father on behalf of Winston and Arabella for protecting "these young lions for so many years to come." When he learned that young Winston hoped to go to Christ Church, Oxford, he urged him on, warning that success would require *"sustained work."*

Churchill was delighted when Winston married Mary Caroline ("Minnie") d'Erlinger on 27 June 1964. He was unable to attend the wedding, but the bride and groom and their parents visited him. He gave his grandson a check for £1,000 and four of his paintings. There were two sons, Randolph and Jack, and two daughters, Jennie and Marina, from this marriage. It was dissolved in 1997. Later in the year, he married Luce Engelen.

Winston was educated at Eton and Christ Church, Oxford. He was a journalist who wrote for the London *Times, Observer,* and *Daily Telegraph,* and a presenter on BBC radio. He unsuccessfully contested Manchester, Gorton, in a by-election in 1967, but was elected for Manchester, Stretford (1970–1983) and Manchester, Davyhulme (1983–1997). He was parliamentary private secretary to the minister of housing and construction (1970–1972) and to the minister of state at the foreign and colonial offices (1972–1973), and a Conservative front-bench spokesman on defense (1976–1978).

His books include an autobiography, *Memories and Adventures* (1989), and a biography of his father, *His Father's Son* (1996). He has been a trustee of the Winston Churchill Memorial Trust since 1968 and was made an honorary fellow of Churchill College, Cambridge, in 1969. In 1972, he was awarded an honorary L.L.D. by Westminster College, Fulton, Missouri.

Related entries:
Churchill, Randolph Frederick Edward Spencer; Harriman, Pamela Digby Churchill Hayward

Suggestions for further reading:
Churchill, Winston S. 1989. *Memories and Adventures.* London: Weidenfeld and Nicolson.
Gilbert, Martin. 1983–1988. *Winston S. Churchill.* Vols. 6–8. London: Heinemann.
Ogden, Christopher. 1994. *Life of the Party: The Biography of Pamela Digby Churchill Hayward Harriman.* London: Little Brown.

was paid for Churchill's papers up to 1945 without also securing the copyright. Lord Rothschild, chairman of the Heritage Lottery Fund, made the case that the purchase of the papers prevented the break-up of the collection. Their sale by auction was likely to raise more money than paid by the Heritage Lottery Fund. Lord Rees Mogg even suggested that their market value might be as much as £25 million. Sir Winston Churchill's papers for the period after the Second World War became the property of his daughter, Lady Mary Soames. She donated them to Churchill College, retaining copyright.

Suggestions for further reading:
Charmley, John. 1997. "Cashing in on Winston," *Guardian* (London), 5 June, pp. 21.
Gilbert, Martin. 1994. *In Search of Churchill.* London: Harper Collins.
Johnson, Paul. 1997. "When Is a Contract Not a Contract? When a Writer's Heirs Benefit." *Spectator* (14 June): pp. 36.
Rothschild, Jacob. 1997. "The Truth Behind the Churchill Row." *Guardian* (London), 6 June, pp. 19.

The Churchill Papers (Sir Winston's)

Sir Winston Churchill's papers are housed in the archive of Churchill College, Cambridge. Weighing some fifteen tons, the Churchill Papers are a huge collection. They were used by Churchill's son Randolph Churchill and by Sir Martin Gilbert for the official life. Randolph Churchill housed them in a specially designed strong room outside his house at East Bergholt, Suffolk. Between 1968 and 1987, the papers were kept at the Bodleian Library, Oxford, while Gilbert worked on them. During this time, Sir Martin Gilbert helped many other scholars by providing information, sending out over a thousand photocopies of documents to other historians.

In June 1997, there was major controversy when £13 million of national lottery

Cigars

The large cigar was part of Churchill's image. He was very conscious of his image as a popular politician and he did not often disappoint when it came to big cigars. David Low and other cartoonists took up his cigar-smoking image and popularized it further.

Churchill already had a taste for fine Havana cigars before he visited Cuba in 1895. He informed his mother before he went that he was going to buy a good stock, many of which could be stored in the cellars of her house in London. Churchill always expected top quality cigars. His Second World War secretary, Elizabeth Layton, recalled, "It was no good trying to palm off Mr. Churchill with anything but the best cigars."

Churchill liked to have a cigar with him, often between his lips, all day except during mealtimes. He did not puff at them other than when lighting them. He kept relighting them—and if he disapproved of them for any reason, he threw them into the fire or, if it was not lit, the fireplace. He kept eight, ten, or possibly more cigars on the go all day. He also took snuff.

In late 1941, the Cuban minister presented Churchill with many boxes of the best Havana cigars. Churchill wisely had Scotland Yard check them for poison or explosives.

Clementine Churchill gave one of his Havana cigars to raise money for war victims in the Soviet Union on 4 February 1944. It was auctioned for charity in Gloucestershire, England, 54 years later. Once, when reflecting on the accusation that he smoked too much, Churchill observed, "If I had not smoked so much I might have been bad-tempered at the wrong time."

Suggestions for further reading:
Harvie-Watt, G. S. 1980. *Most of My Life.* London: Springwood.
Jacob, Sir Ian. 1968. 'Memoir.' In *Action This Day: Working With Churchill,* edited by Sir John Wheeler-Bennett. London: Macmillan.
Nel, Elizabeth. 1958. *Mr. Churchill's Secretary.* London: Hodder and Stoughton.
Thompson, Walter. 1951. *I Was Churchill's Shadow.* London: Christopher Johnson.

Claverton Manor

Winston Churchill gave his first public speech at a Primrose League rally in the park at Claverton Manor, Bath, Somerset, on 26 July 1897. His opportunity to speak at the rally was made possible by Captain Fitzroy Stewart, secretary of the Conservative Central Office, who wrote to the owner of Claverton Manor, Henry Duncan Skrine, asking him to allow Churchill, a "clever young man," to speak.

Claverton Manor, two miles outside of Bath, was designed in 1820 by Sir Jeffery Wyatville, the royal architect, and was built of Bath stone. The Skrines were a very well-connected Somerset family, and had lived at Warleigh Manor since 1634. Henry Duncan Skrine (1815–1901) was a justice of the peace and deputy lieutenant and high sheriff of Somerset.

Lord Randolph Churchill had been the most prominent founder of the Primrose League in November 1883. He termed the League "a transformation into political energy of the emotions which were aroused by Lord Beaconsfield's death and the sentiments which were excited by his career." In his speech at Claverton Manor, Winston Churchill was introduced as the son of Lord Randolph and he spoke of "Tory democracy."

At the end of July, Churchill left for India. Writing to his mother from Aden on 7 August 1897, he asked her to return to "old Mr. Skrine" a Primrose League badge that he had pinned on Churchill before his speech.

In 1961, Dallas Pratt and John Judkyn, two Americans, set up the American Museum at Claverton Manor with the intention of increasing Anglo-American understanding.

Suggestions for further reading:
Churchill, Randolph S. 1966. *Winston S. Churchill.* Vol. 1. London: Heinemann.
Pugh, Martin. 1985. *The Tories and the People 1880–1935.* Oxford: Blackwell.
Robb, Janet H. 1942. *The Primrose League 1883–1906.* New York: Columbia University Press.

Cockran, William Bourke (1854–1923)

Bourke Cockran was a great influence on the young Winston Churchill. A politician with skills in oratory and of an older generation, he was looked up to by Churchill. Cockran provided encouragement, and praise, to the fatherless aspiring politician. He was also an advocate of Free Trade.

William Bourke Cockran was born in Sligo in 1854 and emigrated to the United States in 1871. He became a successful lawyer and a Democratic member of Congress for New York in 1891–1895, 1904–1909, and 1920–1923. He was a friend of Lady Randolph Churchill and of her relatives. When Winston Churchill and his friend Reginald Barnes stopped off in New York in 1895, en route to Cuba, Cockran put them up for a week in his apartment. Winston Churchill was immensely impressed. Years later, he told Adlai Stevenson that Cockran's oratory had inspired him and he could still quote substantial excerpts from his speeches. He quoted one extract at his famous 1946 Fulton speech.

Winston Churchill proudly sent Cockran one of his Cuba articles and told him with great pride of his election to the House of Commons in 1900. Churchill sought Cockran's approval, and received it. In 1896, Cockran predicted that Churchill could take "a commanding position in public life." He also praised his "remarkable talent for lucid and attractive expression."

Churchill admired Cockran's speeches on Free Trade. In December 1903, he wrote asking Cockran to send "some good Free Trade speeches that have been made in America." Cockran invited Churchill to be his guest at the 1904 Democratic Convention, but Churchill could not spare the time away from British politics. When Cockran was in London in mid-1909, Winston Churchill wrote to his wife urging her to come to London to give them lunch. He then observed that Cockran was "perhaps the finest orator in America . . . and a mind that has influenced my thought in more than one important direction."

When Churchill reminisced in an article titled "Personal Contacts" in the *Strand,* February 1931, he wrote of Bourke Cockran second, after his father, in his account of in-

fluences on him. He wrote admiringly of Cockran's conversation, stating that it "in point, in pith, in rotundity, in antithesis and in comprehension, exceeded anything I have ever heard." He also noted with pleasure, given his own changes of party, that Cockran had left the Democrats for the Republicans and had later returned to his original party.

Related entry:
Cuba

Suggestions for further reading:
Churchill, Randolph S. 1966–1969. *Winston S. Churchill.* Vols. 1 and 2 and companion vols. 1 and 2. London: Heinemann.
Churchill, Winston S. 1932. *Thoughts and Adventures.* London: Thornton Butterworth.

Colonies, Secretary of State for the (1921–1922)

Churchill was secretary of state for the colonies from 13 February 1921 until 19 October 1922. This was a post David Lloyd George had suggested to Herbert Henry Asquith might be appropriate for Churchill after he left the admiralty in May 1915. Churchill had already been taking an interest in the Middle East as secretary of state for air. In May 1920, he had argued for the colonial office to be responsible for all the new areas controlled by Britain, instead of the India office controlling Iraq and the foreign office Palestine, with the Air Ministry responsible for their defense.

On going back to the colonial office, where he had been under secretary, 1905–1908, he organized the new Middle Eastern Department. Churchill arranged the Cairo Conference in March 1921, which discussed the future of Iraq and other Middle East matters. He secured the advice of T. E. Lawrence. After the conference, he traveled to Jerusalem, where he restated British intentions of establishing a Jewish National Home in Palestine; but he also tried to reassure the Arabs that Britain would look after their interests.

Churchill also sought to build on his East African tour of 1908 to foster economic development in the area. He sought to please the African and European populations by restricting the rights of Indian immigrants and restricting their numbers.

Otherwise, Churchill's period of office was notable for his part in securing an Irish agreement in 1921 and in supporting Lloyd George during the Chanak crisis, 1922.

Related entries:
Chanak; Lawrence, Thomas Edward

Suggestion for further reading:
Gilbert, Martin. 1975. *Winston S. Churchill.* Vol. 4. London: Heinemann.

Colonies, Under Secretary of State for the (1905–1908)

Winston Churchill's first government post was under secretary of state for the colonies in Sir Henry Campbell-Bannerman's Liberal government of 1905–1908. Churchill was initially offered the prestigious post of financial secretary to the treasury but asked for, and received, instead the post of under secretary to the colonies. While the secretary of state for the colonies, Lord Elgin, was in the House of Lords, Churchill would speak for the colonial office in the House of Commons; whereas as financial secretary to the treasury he would have been very much overshadowed by Herbert Henry Asquith, the chancellor of the exchequer. The colonial office had also enhanced political prestige after Joseph Chamberlain's tenure of the secretaryship. Moreover, after Churchill's military and journalistic experiences, he had personal knowledge of some of Britain's imperial territories, above all of South Africa, the most pressing imperial issue.

In the first session of the 1906 Parliament, Churchill was the minister who spoke secondmost (to Augustine Birrell on the Education Bill) in the House of Commons, on South Africa. He was highly active in coping with the issues of a constitution for South Africa and with the issue of indentured Chinese labor. He also became embroiled in a controversy over Lord Milner's role in South Africa.

The new Liberal government was faced with the issues of deciding when to introduce self-government to the two Boer republics and what the franchise would be. The Treaty of Vereeniging, 1902, had included the commitment that "as soon as circumstances permit, representative institutions, leading up to full self government will be introduced." The issue was put before a cabinet committee, chaired by Lord Loreburn, the lord chancellor, and which included Lord Elgin, John Morley, James Bryce, Lord Ripon, and Herbert Henry Asquith. Churchill, as colonial spokesman in the Commons, was allowed to participate.

Even before the January 1906 election, on 3 January 1906, Churchill wrote a paper arguing that the constitution for the Transvaal should go further than the proposed solution of Alfred Lyttleton, the Conservative colonial secretary (who had succeeded Joseph Chamberlain in 1903). Lyttleton had proposed a transitional phase, during which the executive would be answerable to an elected legislature. Churchill, in line with Liberal Party sentiment, argued for a speedy return to independent government. In another memorandum of 30 January 1906, he argued for franchise for white males with a property qualification of £100 (which was thought to help the non-Boers). Churchill, like other leading British politicians, did not consider extending the franchise to nonwhites. However, the government set up a committee of inquiry into the details of the constitutional settlement in the former Boer republics and this, in July 1906, recommended that there should be universal white male suffrage.

The cabinet committee recommended a speedy grant of self-government to the two former Boer states. Churchill wrote the cabinet paper of 4 February 1906 stating the case for this, which emphasized not only the pressure from within the two former states for this but also the desirability of the British government no longer being responsible for policies concerning Chinese indentured labor. The cabinet accepted the recommendations of its committee and the decision was included in the king's speech of 19 February 1906. The constitutions of the Transvaal and Orange River Colony were promulgated by Letters Patent on 6 December 1906 and 5 June 1907. For the Transvaal, Churchill, when writing to the king, had followed Sir Joseph West Ridgeway in predicting a non-Boer majority of five. The result in the Transvaal election in 1907 instead gave the Boers a five-seat majority and the former Boer commander, Louis Botha, became premier. Later in 1907, the general election in the Orange River Colony gave the Boers an overwhelming majority. However, in 1910, South Africa was unified.

Churchill became embroiled in bitter controversy over a House of Commons motion censuring Milner for authorizing the illegal flogging of Chinese laborers. Churchill attempted "to parry the blow" aimed at Milner by an amendment that condemned such floggings but expressed a desire "in the interests of peace and conciliation in South Africa, to refrain from passing censure on individuals." Churchill's speech, in which he argued that Lord Milner belonged to the past and had "ceased to be a factor in public events," caused great hostility among Conservative politicians and the Conservative press. It also angered King Edward VII, who was later more impressed by Churchill's efforts over the franchise arrangements for the Transvaal and the Orange River Colony, writing that he

was "becoming a *reliable* Minister and above all a serious politician, *which can only be obtained by putting country before party.*"

On the issue of indentured Chinese labor in South Africa, Churchill was relatively restrained in the January 1906 general election, stating the government's need to restrict the use of such labor and end abuses. In a speech in Manchester on 9 January, Churchill stated that although such labor was "servile and improper," it did not constitute slavery. He also stated the government's policy that the government would stop further recruitment but would not repudiate the licenses to import Chinese labor granted by the previous government. After the general election, Churchill faced a Conservative amendment in the House of Commons that deplored Liberal ministers' use of the term *slavery* for Chinese indentured labor, thereby bringing "the reputation of this country into contempt." Churchill in response could point to his own election comments and stated that it was not appropriate to classify such labor "as slavery in the extreme acceptance of the word without some risk of terminological inexactitude."

The issue of Chinese labor in South Africa remained controversial for Churchill and the Liberal government until the issue was passed to the newly elected Boer government. In August 1906, after allegations of "unnatural vice" among the 50,000 or more male Chinese laborers, Churchill, on behalf of the government, agreed to an enquiry. The resulting report in November 1906, which apparently produced conflicting evidence, was not published, but the issue of "catamites" (as Churchill put it) did increase the pressure to end the use of Chinese indentured labor; it was rapidly ended by Botha's Transvaal government. Half of the Chinese labor was repatriated by June 1908 and the remainder by 1910.

Churchill, as Elgin's under secretary, also played a major part at the sixth Colonial Conference, held in London in April 1907.

The conference was notable for the presence of Louis Botha, the newly installed prime minister of the Transvaal. Churchill enjoyed the several opportunities he had at associated meetings for the colonial premiers to hold forth on the merits of the British Empire. He often sounded like an elder statesman in such speeches, old beyond his then thirty-two years. After the conference, on 1 May 1907, Churchill was made a privy councillor, a mark of his growing political stature.

Related entries:
Botha, Louis; Edward VII, King; Elgin, Ninth Earl of; Milner, Alfred

Suggestions for further reading:
Churchill, Randolph S. 1967. *Winston S. Churchill.* Vol. 2. London: Heinemann.
Hyam, Ronald. 1968. *Elgin and Churchill at the Colonial Office, 1905–1908: The Watershed of the Empire-Commonwealth.* London: Macmillan.

Colville, Sir John Rupert (1915–1987)

John Colville was Churchill's much trusted private secretary during parts of his wartime premiership and all of his 1951–1955 government. "Jock" Colville was a reliable friend to Churchill in his later years. The diaries Colville kept of his years as a civil servant in Downing Street are of major interest on Churchill's life.

John Colville was born in London on 28 January 1915, the youngest of the three sons of the Hon. George Charles and Lady Helen Cynthia Colville. His father was a barrister; his mother was the daughter of the marquess of Crewe. Educated at Harrow and Trinity College, Cambridge, he entered the diplomatic service in 1937. In 1939, he became assistant private secretary to Neville Chamberlain, the prime minister. He was sorry when Chamberlain resigned, but came to admire Churchill. For most of the period October 1941 to August 1944 he served in the Royal Air Force (RAF). Thereafter, he returned to the civil service. He served briefly as one of Attlee's private secretaries, and from 1947–1949 he was private secretary to Princess Elizabeth (now Queen Elizabeth II), from shortly before her marriage. From 1949–1951, he was first secretary in the British embassy in Lisbon.

In October 1951, Churchill, wanting Colville to be again his principal private secretary, summoned him back to London from a day at the Newmarket races. He relied greatly on Colville's discretion and general good judgement. This was especially important in July 1953 when he was incapacitated by a serious stroke.

After Churchill's resignation as prime minister in April 1955, Winston and Clementine Churchill spent a fortnight at the Villa Politi at Syracuse in Sicily, with Lord Cherwell and John Colville as companions. After Churchill expressed his regret that in office he had not set up a high-quality institute of technology, Colville set about raising the money for what became Churchill College, Cambridge.

Colville remained a loyal friend during the remainder of his life and a willing defender of Churchill's reputation after his death. He published his memoirs, *Footprints in Time* (1976); a book on Churchill's inner circle, *The Churchillians* (1981); and his diaries, *The Fringes of Power* (1985). After Churchill's retirement, he became a merchant banker. He was knighted in 1974. He died on 19 November 1987.

Suggestions for further reading:
Colville, John. 1976. *Footprints in Time: Memories.* London: Collins.
———. 1985. *The Fringes of Power: Downing Street Diaries 1939–1955.* London: Hodder and Stoughton.
Gilbert, Martin. 1988. *Winston S. Churchill.* Vol. 8. London: Heinemann.
Ziegler, Philip. 1996. "Colville, Sir John Rupert." In *The Dictionary of National Biography 1986–1990,* edited by C. S. Nicholls. Oxford: Oxford University Press.

Cooper, Alfred Duff (Viscount Norwich, 1890–1954)

Duff Cooper was one of Churchill's oldest friends. He was also a political supporter of Churchill in 1924–1929 and notably after Munich, 1938. The Churchills and Coopers frequently met at social events, including those put on by themselves. Cooper was a politically brave opponent of appeasement, resigning from Neville Chamberlain's cabinet over the Munich agreement.

Duff Cooper was born in London on 22 February 1890, the fourth child and only son of Alfred and Lady Agnes Cooper. His father was a surgeon in London. His mother, formerly Lady Agnes Cecil Emmeline Duff, was the sister of the first duke of Fife. After education at Eton and New College, Oxford, Duff Cooper spent two years in Hanover, then entered the foreign office in October 1913.

Duff Cooper first met Winston Churchill in 1913, through his friendship with his sister-in-law, Nellie Hozier. He dined at Admiralty House, with Reginald McKenna, the home secretary, and Percy Illingworth, the Liberal chief whip, among those present.

Cooper was permitted to join the army in 1917. Serving with the Grenadier Guards, he showed bravery in battle and was appointed to the DSO (Distinguished Service Order). He resigned from the foreign office at the end of July 1924 and successfully ran as the Conservative candidate for Oldham in the October 1924 general election. Churchill was one of his greatest friends in Parliament. Cooper was eager to be Churchill's parliamentary private secretary, but Churchill dissuaded him, arguing that he would do better to be free to make his name through speeches in the House of Commons. Cooper did contact him before making his maiden speech and afterwards Churchill complimented him on it. He secured minor office, financial secretary to the war

office, in January 1928. Losing his seat in the 1929 general election, he was returned in a by-election in March 1931 for the safe Conservative constituency of the St. George's Division of Westminster, in spite of Lord Beaverbrook running an independent candidate. He represented the constituency until he became British ambassador to France.

Like Churchill, Cooper was a talented writer. He published the biography, *Talleyrand,* in 1932, and an official, two-volume biography, *Haig,* in 1935 and 1936. Unlike Churchill, he was given office in the National governments of the 1930s. He served as financial secretary to the war office, 1931–1934, financial secretary to the treasury, 1934–1935, secretary of state for war, 1935–1937, and first lord of the admiralty, 1937–1938.

Duff Cooper and Churchill maintained their friendship during these years and moved closer politically from 1935. They dined together at dinners arranged in the House of Commons and elsewhere by Lady Diana Cooper or at Chartwell. They shared a common alarm at the developments in Nazi Germany and the threat posed to Britain. When, in the summer of 1936, Cooper made a speech in Paris to the Great Britain-France Society in which he argued that the two countries' interests were similar and they were bound to stand together if threatened, Churchill was one of those who spoke in a House of Commons debate supporting his views. When Duff Cooper resigned from the government over the Munich agreement in 1938, Lady Diana Cooper telephoned Churchill. According to her memoirs, Churchill's voice "broke with emotion. I could hear him crying." When Cooper gave his resignation speech to the Commons, Churchill thought it one of the best speeches that he had heard there, observing, "It was admirable in form, massive in argument and shone with courage and public spirit."

With Churchill as prime minister, Duff Cooper became minister of information.

He did not enjoy the post. In his autobiography he wrote, "When I appealed for support to the prime minister, I seldom got it. He was not interested in the subject. He knew that propaganda was not going to win the war." In July 1941 he moved on to being chancellor of the Duchy of Lancaster and Churchill's representative in Singapore. He remained there until January 1942.

In October 1943, he accepted Anthony Eden's offer of becoming British representative to the French Committee of Liberation. He found Churchill suspicious of him, given that he liked General de Gaulle and Churchill distrusted him. Duff and Diana Cooper flew out to Algiers in January 1944. On 10 January, they flew to see Churchill, who was at Marrakesh; Cooper and Churchill had a lengthy and friendly talk over dinner. Cooper noted in his diary, "He is still very sticky about de Gaulle." Cooper succeeded in preventing Churchill from cancelling a meeting with the General on 12 January. Cooper and Beaverbrook were present at the meeting and Churchill was conciliatory.

Duff Cooper was formally appointed British ambassador to France on 23 October 1944. However, he and Diana Cooper flew to France on 13 September 1944 and organized the reopening of the British embassy. Cooper accompanied Churchill when he joined de Gaulle on 11 November 1944 for the victory parade in Paris. At the lunch, Cooper noted in his diary, "De Gaulle made a very good short speech and Winston replied in English. I rather wish he had tried it in French."

Churchill visited the Coopers in Paris and later at their home in Chantilly. Before Duff Cooper left his post as ambassador at the end of 1947, he and Diana Cooper gave a final ball on 10 December. Churchill, who was on his way to Morocco, attended. He was particularly pleased to meet the wartime heroine Odette Sansom at the ball.

Duff Cooper received a knighthood in 1948 and was elevated to the peerage as Viscount Norwich of Aldwick in 1952. His wife made it clear that she wished still to be known as Lady Diana Cooper. He died on 1 January 1954, while on a voyage to the West Indies.

Related entries:
Cooper, Lady Diana Olivia Winifred Maude; De Gaulle, General Charles André Joseph Marie; Eden, Sir (Robert) Anthony

Suggestions for further reading:
Cooper, Artemis. 1983. *A Durable Fire: The Letters of Duff and Diana Cooper, 1913–1950.* London: Collins.
Cooper, Diana. 1958. *The Rainbow Comes and Goes.* London: Hart-Davis.
———. 1959. *The Light of Common Day.* London: Hart-Davis.
———. 1960. *Trumpets from the Steep.* London: Hart-Davis.
Cooper, Duff. 1953. *Old Men Forget.* London: Hart-Davis.
Gilbert, Martin. 1976–1988. *Winston S. Churchill.* Vols. 5–8. London: Heinemann.

Cooper, Lady Diana Olivia Winifred Maud (Viscountess Norwich, 1892–1986)

Diana Cooper was one of the most beautiful women in English society in her age. She and her husband were long-time friends of Winston and Clementine Churchill. In her memoirs, she wrote that Churchill and poet Hilaire Belloc were the men she had known who were "nearest to genius." In the later 1930s, she was an ardent supporter of Churchill as the man who could save Britain from the Nazi menace. Throughout the interwar years, Churchill was a frequent guest at Diana Cooper's social functions.

Lady Diana Manners was born in London on 29 August 1892, the fifth of the five children of Henry John Brinsley Manners, marquess of Granby and later eighth duke of Rutland, and his wife Marion Margaret Violet Lindsay, daughter of Colonel Charles Lindsay. It was commonly believed that her real father was Harry Cust, the Conservative politician. She was educated at home. She "came out" (the term used for British debutantes on the occasion of their formal introduction to society) and was considered the "queen of beauty." She was blamed when a man drowned, swimming for a dare off a boat in the River Thames. During the First World War, she worked as a nurse. In 1916, she became informally engaged to Duff Cooper. They married on 2 June 1919. She had one child, John Julius Cooper, on 15 September 1929.

The Coopers were friendly with the Churchills. Among early common friends were Venetia and Edwin Montagu. Winston Churchill and the Montagus were among Diana's frequent dinner guests in her house at 90 Gower Street. At one of these, on 4 November 1919, Diana Cooper succeeded in bringing Churchill and Lord Beaverbrook back together as friends. The Churchills and Coopers often attended the same social events; for instance, in early 1929, Duff Cooper attended a fancy dress party and reported to Diana, who was abroad, that "Winston as Nero was good." There were further links when Duff Cooper was elected to Parliament in 1924. During the General Strike, Diana Cooper was a volunteer helper at the *Times*. On election night in 1931, Churchill was at the Coopers's party in Gower Street, Diana Cooper later recalling of him that he "cried when he heard that Randolph had been defeated."

In the mid-1930s, Duff Cooper and Churchill were often close in outlook in their concern about Nazi Germany. They were both hostile to Joachim von Ribbentrop when he was ambassador in London. Diana Cooper later recalled one luncheon, after society ladies had asked him questions about Hitler's views on Jews and he had left, "Winston and some other patriots

dancing and shouting with glee." Churchill applauded Duff Cooper's resignation from Chamberlain's government over Munich.

Diana Cooper, who had long admired Winston Churchill as a politician, from early in the Second World War saw him as Britain's potential savior. In early 1940, after dining with Churchill at the admiralty, she wrote, "Winston's spirit, strength and confidence are a beacon in the darkness, a chime that wakes the heart of the discouraged." She was delighted by Churchill's accession to the premiership, with her husband returning to office. In June 1940, when Duff Cooper feared for his life when he flew to Paris, Diana Cooper telephoned Clementine Churchill, who pressed her husband to ensure that Cooper was provided with an escort of fighter planes.

When on 21 July 1941, Duff Cooper was appointed chancellor of the Duchy of Lancaster, with additional responsibilities in the Far East, Diana Cooper accompanied her husband to Singapore and Australia. In January 1944, she accompanied her husband to Algiers, where he was British representative to the French Committee of Liberation. From November 1944 until December 1947, Cooper was British ambassador in Paris and Diana was an unconventional ambassadress, hosting social events and encouraging a group of French writers and artists. Winston and Clementine Churchill visited Paris for the great victory review on 11 November 1944. On his last night, the British embassy was reopened after the war years and General and Madame de Gaulle and the Churchills were the guests of honor at the first dinner party. The Coopers stayed on for two and a half years under Clement Attlee's Labour government. Churchill stayed with them when he was in Paris.

Diana and Duff Cooper retired to the Château St. Firmin at Chantilly, and Churchill visited them there in 1947. When Duff Cooper died, to his widow's delight Churchill attended his memorial service. She died on 16 June 1986.

Related entries:
Cooper, Alfred Duff; Eden, Sir (Robert) Anthony

Suggestions for further reading:
Cooper, Artemis, ed. 1983. *A Durable Fire: The Letters of Duff and Diana Cooper, 1913–1950.* London: Collins.
Cooper, Diana. 1958. *The Rainbow Comes and Goes.* London: Hart-Davis.
———. 1959. *The Light of Common Day.* London: Hart-Davis.
———. 1960. *Trumpets from the Steep.* London: Hart-Davis.
Gilbert, Martin. 1976–1988. *Winston S. Churchill.* Vols. 5–8. London: Heinemann.
Ziegler, Philip. 1981. *Diana Cooper.* London: Collins.

Coward, Sir Noël Peirce (1899–1973)

Churchill greatly admired Coward's songs and plays and was delighted when Coward performed his favorite songs for him. They met among the rich and famous in the South of France and occasionally at Chartwell.

Noël Coward was born on 16 December 1899 at Teddington, Middlesex, the second son of Arthur Sabin and Violet Agnes Coward. His father was a clerk. His paternal grandfather was an organist and chorister, and his maternal grandfather, Henry Veitch, was a captain in the Royal Navy. He attended the Chapel Royal choir school, Clapham. His theatrical career began when he was young, in 1911. He served briefly in the army in 1918, being discharged for ill health. He wrote plays and acted in many of them, securing success in Britain and the United States with his 1924 play, *The Vortex* (on drug addiction). In the 1930s and 1940s, he scored successes with *Private Lives* (1930), *Cavalcade* (1931), *Present Laughter* (1939), and *Blithe Spirit* (1941), among others. By the mid-1950s, he was earning so much money that he became a tax exile first in Bermuda and then in Switzerland. Author Rebecca West, a friend from his

later teens, commented of his homosexuality, "There was an impeccable dignity in his sexual life, which was reticent but untainted by pretence." He received a knighthood in 1970. He died in Jamaica on 26 March 1973.

Winston Churchill was a great admirer of Coward's work. In the dark days of the Second World War, he often sang Coward's songs, as well as more generally on the way home from The Other Club. Coward found on the few occasions he hoped for weighty conversation with Churchill, the latter wanted him to perform his favorite Coward songs, "Mad Dogs and Englishmen" and "Don't Put Your Daughter on the Stage, Mrs. Worthington." Churchill and Coward first met as fellow guests of Maxine Elliott at the Château de l'Horizon, along with the Anthony Edens and Duff Coopers, in the South of France. In the 1930s, Churchill invited him twice to Chartwell, where Churchill pressed the case for Coward painting in oils, not water colors. Coward, accompanying Robert Boothby, visited Chartwell a third time just before the outbreak of the war to seek Churchill's advice on his most useful contribution to the war effort. He was not pleased when Churchill advised him to join the Royal Navy and to sing to the sailors during action! However, he did see Churchill's point—that he was primarily an entertainer.

Coward dined with Juliet Duff, Venetia Montagu, and Churchill on 2 May 1945. He later recalled that Churchill was "at his most benign" and, with victory near, he, Juliet, and Venetia all simultaneously thought of Churchill's "foresight, courage and genius" in bringing this about: "Emotion submerged us and without exchanging a word, as simultaneous as though we had carefully rehearsed it, the three of us rose to our feet and drank Mr. Churchill's health."

Coward also supplied Churchill with much appreciated praise for the first volume of *The Second World War* (1948). He concluded an already effusive letter in a manner of which Benjamin Disraeli, in praising royalty, would have been proud: "But I do love my country and its traditions and its language and—to hell with self-consciousness. . . . Thank you deeply and sincerely for your immortal contributions to all three."

Suggestions for further reading:
Gilbert, Martin. 1986 and 1988. *Winston S. Churchill.* Vols. 7 and 8. London: Heinemann.
Lesley, Cole. 1976. *The Life of Noel Coward.* Harmondsworth, UK: Penguin.
Morley, Sheridan (introduced). 1986. *The Autobiography of Noël Coward.* London: Methuen.

Crete (May 1941)

*T*he loss of Crete was a major blow to Winston Churchill. He had hoped it could be held and felt afterwards it should have been. After the war, he took consolation in the scale of the German casualties (over 17,000 dead and wounded), observing that it had broken "the spear-point of the German lance." Many British troops felt that the Battle of Crete had been lost by poor commanders, not least in the failure to hold Maleme airport and Hill 107 overlooking it.

British control of Crete was important to Britain's role in the Mediterranean. With the German conquest of Greece well underway, British forces were moved to Crete with the intention of defending Crete vigorously. On 28 April 1941, Enigma decrypts revealed the details of the German plans to attack Crete. The big failure in Crete was the British and Allied forces' inability to win even with this advance information.

On 1 May 1941, General Freyberg, the New Zealand commanding officer, warned that the forces available on Crete were inadequate to meet such a large-scale attack. Churchill sent him a telegram stating, "Feel confident your fine troops will destroy parachutists man to man at close quarters."

The Allied forces were handicapped by having very few aircraft (according to Freyberg, "six Hurricanes and 17 obsolete aircraft"). After the Germans had landed reinforcements on Crete, the British lack of air power soon made the Allied forces' position untenable. The British navy evacuated 16,500, leaving 5,000 to be taken prisoner.

The Germans had sent in over 8,000 parachutists on some 500 airplanes on 20 May 1941. The parachutists were easy targets as they came down and they suffered very heavy casualties. In spite of this, Churchill was impressed. Although the battle was ending, he urged, on 27 May, the creation of a British parachute force of 5,000 and an Airborne Division "on the German model." After Crete, the United States also developed a large force of parachutists, some 10,000 strong. These Allied parachutists were used in Sicily and in northern Europe, most disastrously at Arnheim.

Suggestion for further reading:
Gilbert, Martin. 1983. *Winston S. Churchill.* Vol. 6. London: Heinemann. (Also note, *Timewatch* [BBC television], "Hitler, Churchill, and the Paratroops," 17 February 2001.)

Crewe, Marquess of (Robert Offley Ashburton Milnes, 1858–1945)

*L*ord Crewe was a colleague of Churchill's in the Liberal governments of 1905–1915. Crewe had come to the fore quickly in Liberal politics largely because he was one of the few Liberal peers left after Gladstone turned to Home Rule in 1885–1886. In Asquith's cabinet, Crewe carried much weight for what Lord Samuel called his "almost uncanny soundness of judgement." He did not care much for Churchill or David Lloyd George.

Robert Milnes was born in London on 12 January 1858, the third child and only son of Richard Monkton Milnes, M.P., and his wife, Annabel. His father, later Lord Houghton, was a major literary as well as political figure, best known for his biography of poet John Keats. His mother was the younger daughter of the second Lord Crewe of Crewe Hall, Cheshire. Educated at Harrow and Trinity College, Cambridge, his first employment was in 1883 as an assistant private secretary to Lord Granville, the foreign secretary. Selected as Liberal candidate for Barnsley, his father died before the next election. As Lord Houghton, he entered the House of Lords and was made a government whip there during William Gladstone's short third government. In 1886, his wife died of scarlet fever and he resigned as one of the whips. When Gladstone returned to office in 1892, he offered Houghton the post of lord lieutenant of Ireland, a post he held until 1895. After he left Ireland, Queen Victoria conferred an earldom on him and, because he had inherited his uncle's Crewe estates, he took the family name of Crewe.

In opposition, 1895–1905, Crewe was associated with Sir Henry Campbell-Bannerman and John Morley, the Gladstonian Radicals, not with Lord Rosebery and the Liberal Imperialists. With Campbell-Bannerman's government in 1905, Crewe entered the cabinet as lord president of the council. When Herbert Henry Asquith became prime minister, Crewe became secretary of state for the colonies. Churchill, who had just left the under secretaryship there, did not hesitate to give Crewe the benefit of his expertise. Crewe's biographer wrote that Churchill bombarded Crewe "with a shower of suggestions, uninvited hints and scraps of unsolicited advice." After Crewe overreacted when Churchill wound up a debate on Natal, not realizing that Asquith had asked Churchill to do so, Churchill responded with dignity. From 1908–1923 Crewe was leader of the Liberal Party in the House of Lords.

Crewe, notable for his discretion and common sense, was much respected by Asquith. In November 1910, he was appointed secretary of state for India, a post he held until the formation of the coalition government in May 1915. Churchill at the admiralty had dealings with Crewe concerning India's contributions to naval defense. Generally, after 1908, relations between Crewe and Churchill were good. Crewe was elevated to marquess in the 1911 coronation honors.

With the formation of the Asquith wartime coalition government, Crewe was again lord president of the council, 1915–1916. He was briefly president of the Board of Education from 18 August 1916 until the government's end on 5 December 1916. Crewe was no admirer of Lloyd George and was hostile to his actions leading to the ending of Asquith's premiership. He was elected chairman of the London County Council in 1917. From 1919, as leader of the Liberals in the House of Lords, he was a leader of the Opposition there. At the end of 1922, Crewe became British ambassador to France, a post he held until July 1928. His final office was as a Liberal member of Ramsay MacDonald's National government as secretary of state for war, August–November 1931 (when he retired). Nevertheless, he served again as Liberal leader in the House of Lords, 1936–1944. He died on 20 June 1945.

Suggestions for further reading:
Churchill, Randolph S. 1967. *Winston S. Churchill*. Vol. 2. London: Heinemann.
Pope-Hennessy, James. 1955. *Lord Crewe, 1858–1945: The Likeness of a Liberal*. London: Constable.

Cripps, Sir (Richard) Stafford (1889–1952)

Churchill did not care for wealthy, intellectual socialists, and generally he did not like the austere Stafford Cripps. Yet he recognized his abilities and in Britain's darkest hour, 1940, he was willing to send Cripps on a mission to Moscow to try to divide the Soviet Union from Nazi Germany. For a short time in the first half of 1942, some saw Cripps as the potential successor to Churchill.

Stafford Cripps was born on 24 April 1889 at Elm Park Gardens, Chelsea, London, the fourth son and fifth child of Charles Alfred and Theresa Cripps. Alfred Cripps was a lawyer. After Stafford's birth, he became a queen's counsel, a Conservative M.P. for three seats between 1895 and when he was made a peer in 1914 (as Baron Parmoor), and served as lord privy seal in the first and second Labour governments, 1924 and 1929–1931. His mother was a daughter of Richard Potter, her most famous sister being author Beatrice Potter, who married Sidney Webb, the socialist writer and Labour minister. Educated at Winchester and New College, Oxford, Cripps followed his father into law. In the First World War, he served for a year in the Red Cross as a truck driver. Because he had been a brilliant chemist as an undergraduate, he was recalled to work in munitions, as assistant superintendent of an explosives factory. After the war, he was highly successful at law, being made a king's counsel in 1927. He devoted much time to promoting international friendship through the churches.

He also followed his father into Labour politics. He was encouraged by the leading London Labour politician, Herbert Morrison, as well as by the Webbs. He joined the Labour Party in 1929 and was appointed solicitor general in Ramsay MacDonald's government in October 1930, with the customary knighthood. He won a by-election for Bristol East in January 1931. Cripps was one of the few leading Labour figures to hold his seat in the 1931 general election. He entered the Opposition as a leader of the party and had moved to the Left as a result of the economic and political events of 1931. Cripps became a notable left-wing rebel in the 1930s, even being expelled from the Labour Party in January 1939 for promoting the Popular Front, which was contrary to party policy; he was readmitted in 1945.

Churchill disapproved of Cripps's Popular Front activities. When Cripps was refused permission to hold a meeting in the Royal Albert Hall, he wrote letters to leading political figures complaining of a breach of freedom of speech. Churchill replied, condemning his cooperation with communists. Cripps responded, commenting that Churchill's letter showed that he was "keener on downing the communist than on supporting freedom of speech." Nevertheless, in June 1939, Cripps and Churchill met in Churchill's London apartment and discussed the need to press Chamberlain to broaden his government. Once war broke out, Cripps pressed Halifax to send a mission to Moscow to try to divide the Soviet Union from Nazi Germany. He received more sympathy when he saw Churchill at the admiralty, Churchill also wishing to separate Russia and Germany. Cripps, with some help from the foreign office, went to India, China, and Russia, where he saw Vyacheslav Molotov, the Soviet premier.

After Churchill became prime minister, his war cabinet was told by Sir Anthony Eden on 18 May 1940 that the Russians were uneasy about the German advance into France. The members agreed to send Cripps to Moscow on an "exploratory mission." He was made ambassador in early June, and spent nearly twenty months in Moscow. All he sought came about when Hitler invaded Russia in June 1941. Cripps reaped much glory, being praised for his efforts and made a privy councillor. However, Cripps was disillusioned by Stalin's tyranny. When he left Moscow finally in January 1942, he was seen by some as a possible successor to Churchill.

Cripps on his return criticized the conduct of the war and the government's attitude to Russia, popular themes when Churchill's fortunes were poor. Churchill brought Cripps into the war cabinet as lord privy seal on 19 February 1942. However, Cripps's failings were highlighted when Churchill also made him leader of the House of Commons, his schoolmasterly tone alienating many M.P.s. Cripps's mission to India in March–April 1942 to secure support for the war and to promise future independence came to nothing, which given the Congress Party's opposition and Churchill's lack of enthusiasm for Indian independence, was hardly surprising. Cripps annoyed Churchill with radical plans for postwar reconstruction and by pressing Churchill on the running of the war. In November 1942, after the victory at El Alamein, Churchill accepted Cripps's resignation from the war cabinet. Instead, he became minister of aircraft production, a post he held with success until the end of the war in Europe.

In Attlee's Labour government, Cripps was president of the Board of Trade, 1945–1947. In March–June 1946, Cripps made another mission to India to try to secure agreement on the route to independence. Again the mission failed to secure general support for its plans. When the mission's plan was published in May 1946, Churchill thought it a melancholy document. Cripps moved to be minister for economic affairs in October 1947, and a month later became chancellor of the exchequer. He was a firm, even stern chancellor. In September 1949, he was forced to devalue the pound, in spite of his earlier claims that this would not occur. Churchill denounced him, calling for his resignation. Cripps's health was always poor after the First World War, and it deteriorated in 1950. He resigned in October 1950 and died on 21 April 1952.

Related entry:
Stalin, Joseph

Suggestions for further reading:
Bryant, Chris. 1997. *Stafford Cripps.* London: Hodder and Stoughton.
Estorick, Eric. 1949. *Stafford Cripps.* London: Heinemann.
Gilbert, Martin. 1976, 1983, and 1986. *Winston S. Churchill.* Vols. 5–7. London: Heinemann.
Goredetsky, Gabriel. 1984. *Stafford Cripps' Mission to Moscow 1940–1942.* Cambridge: Cambridge University Press.

Croft, Sir Henry Page (Baron Croft, 1881–1947)

Sir Henry Page Croft was a dedicated Conservative Diehard, who even broke away to form the National Party in 1917. Croft was not a politician with whom Churchill would normally work, nor one usually sympathetic to Churchill; they came together primarily over India in the 1930s and then in opposition to Hitler's Germany.

Henry Page Croft was born at Farnhams Hall, Ware, on 22 June 1881, the second son of Richard Benyon and Anne Elizabeth Croft. His father had resigned a commission in the navy to join his wife's family maltster business. His mother was the only child of Henry Page. He was educated at Eton, Shrewsbury, and Trinity Hall, Cambridge. He joined the family firm without earning a degree. He became a zealot for tariff reform. He was elected M.P. for Christchurch in January 1910 and remained in the House of Commons until he was created Baron Croft of Bournemouth. He served in France in 1914–1916. In 1917, he formed a breakaway right-wing party, the National Party, which was ultrapatriotic and imperialistic. He returned to the Conservative Party with the collapse of David Lloyd George's coalition in 1922. In the 1920s, he resumed his campaign for tariffs. In the 1930s, he led Diehard Tories on various issues, including resisting the National government's policies on India. Croft had been an eager defender of General Reginald Edward Harry Dyer at the time of the Amritsar massacre, 1919. India brought him and Churchill together, although Churchill was less enthusiastic for General Francisco Franco of Spain, nor did he agree with Page Croft's support for Munich.

In 1940, Churchill offered Page Croft the post of joint parliamentary under secretary for war, but only on the condition that he went into the House of Lords. He served in that post from May 1940 until July 1945. He died on 7 December 1947.

Suggestions for further reading:
Croft, Lord. 1949. *My Life of Strife.* London: Hutchinson.
Gilbert, Martin. 1975. *Winston S. Churchill.* Vol. 4. London: Heinemann.
Witherall, Larry L. 1997. *Rebel on the Right: Henry Page Croft and the Crisis of British Conservatism.* Newark: University of Delaware Press.

Cromer, First Earl of (Evelyn Baring, 1841–1917)

Lord Cromer was one of many eminent public figures whom Winston Churchill came to know through his mother, Lady Randolph Churchill. Cromer was one of the great proconsuls of the late Victorian and Edwardian British Empire. Churchill gained his support for his desire to go with General Sir Herbert Kitchener to Khartoum in 1898 and Cromer also helped him with the recent history of Egypt when he was writing *The River War* (1899).

Evelyn Baring was born on 26 February 1841 at Cromer Hall, Norfolk, the sixth son of Henry Baring, M.P., and his second wife, Cecilia, daughter of Admiral William Windham of Fellbrigge, Norfolk. Educated at the Ordnance School, Carshalton, and the Royal Military Academy at Woolwich, he was commissioned and served with the artillery in the Ionian Islands. Later, he entered the war office. In 1872, he went to India as private secretary to his cousin, Lord Northbrook, the viceroy of India. In 1877, he went to Egypt as the first British commissioner to advise the Khedive Ismail on finances. He proved very effective, at least on behalf of Britain and the other bond holders. After a spell in India, he returned to Egypt in 1883 as Sir Evelyn Baring and as British agent and consul general. Mindful of the dire state of Egypt's finances, he urged withdrawal from the Sudan. General Charles George Gordon was sent to Khartoum to advise on how to carry out this policy. After Gordon's death, Baring concentrated on Egyptian finances, which he brought out of deficit by 1888.

Lord Cromer was one of Lady Randolph Churchill's influential friends. The young Winston Churchill was not reticent in making use of such connections. He tried to use Lord Cromer, the Prince of Wales, and Lord Salisbury to assist him in going to Khartoum with Kitchener's expedition in 1898.

Lord Cromer also helped him with the background for his book, *The River War* (1899). He talked with him about Egyptian politics and provided him with many introductions to many valuable contacts in Cairo. Churchill wrote to his mother in April 1899 that Cromer was "a wonderful man."

Had Cromer's health been better and had he accepted the post of foreign secretary offered him by Sir Henry Campbell-Bannerman in 1905, Churchill would have had more contact with him. Cromer retired from Egypt in 1907. In 1908, he published an account of his time there, *Modern Egypt* (2 volumes). He had been created a baron in 1899 and an earl in 1901. From 1908, he took an active role in the House of Lords. At the time of the House of Lords crisis in 1911, Cromer was one of the most prominent peers supporting the Liberal proposals.

In 1916, Cromer took on a role that was crucial for Churchill: chairman of the Dardanelles Commission. On 12 August, Churchill wrote to inform him how he intended to act in presenting his evidence and that he would conduct the case himself, without benefit of counsel. Cromer, after a meeting of the commission, told Churchill how it would proceed. However, after presiding over the early stages of the Dardanelles Commission, Cromer died on 29 January 1917.

Related entries:
Gallipoli; Kitchener, Horatio Herbert

Suggestions for further reading:
Churchill, Randolph S. 1966 and 1967. *Winston S. Churchill.* Vols. 1 and 2. London: Heinemann.
Gilbert, Martin. 1971. *Winston S. Churchill.* Vol. 3. London: Heinemann.
Hogarth, D. G. "Baring, Evelyn, First Earl of Cromer." In *Dictionary of National Biography: 1901–1911,* edited by Sir Sidney Lee. Oxford: Oxford University Press.

Cromwell, Oliver (1599–1658)

While first lord of the admiralty in 1912, Churchill came into dispute with the king over naming a Dreadnought *Oliver Cromwell.* Oliver Cromwell (1599–1658) was anathema to King George V because he had led the parliamentary forces against the Crown in the English Civil War, declaring a republic after the execution of King Charles I in 1649.

In November 1911, the king had accepted Churchill's suggestion of *Africa* for new Dreadnoughts, rejecting *Oliver Cromwell, Liberty,* and *Assiduous.* Of the king's suggestions, Churchill accepted *Marlborough,* suggested *Iron Duke* rather than *Wellington,* and opposed *Delhi* (though he yielded on this). In October 1912, Churchill suggested *Oliver Cromwell* again (backed by Herbert Henry Asquith, who agreed that Cromwell had been a major figure in the history of the British navy), as

well as *King Richard the First, King Henry the Fifth,* and *Queen Elizabeth.* The king made it clear that he had no intention of accepting the name *Cromwell,* and brushed aside Churchill's protests and the learned quotations in support of Cromwell that were prepared at Churchill's request by Lord Morley. Churchill submitted the name *Valiant* as an alternative.

In August 1913, Churchill proposed *Pitt* and *Ark Royal.* The king did not care for these, and when Churchill again argued, he was told in effect that if he submitted names for approval, he should accept the monarch's verdict. The king indicated that in the future Churchill should see him for an informal talk before formally submitting names.

Suggestion for further reading:
Churchill, Randolph S. 1967. *Winston S. Churchill.* Vol. 2. London: Heinemann.

Crookshank, Henry Frederick Comfort (Viscount Crookshank, 1893–1961)

Harry Crookshank was a cabinet minister in Churchill's 1951–1955 government. He was a senior Conservative whom Churchill could not ignore but was one of the major figures who was not always loyal to him. Churchill's successor as Conservative Party leader and prime minister, Anthony Eden, had a low view of Crookshank's abilities and his political career ended a few months after Churchill's retirement.

Harry Crookshank was born on 27 May 1893 in Cairo, the oldest child of Harry Maule and Emma Walraven Crookshank. His father, of an old Ulster family, was a physician and surgeon and inspector of Egyptian prisons. His mother was the daughter of Major Samuel Comfort of New York. Educated at Eton and Magdalen College, Oxford, he served in France and Salonika during the First World War. After the war, he served in the foreign office until 1924. He was Conservative M.P. for Gainsborough, 1924–1956. He held junior government posts, 1934–1939, was financial secretary to the treasury, 1939–1943, and postmaster general, 1943–1945. He at last reached the cabinet in 1951, as minister of health and leader of the House of Commons. From May 1952 to December 1955 he was lord privy seal and leader of the House of Commons. He was created a viscount in January 1956.

Churchill and Crookshank were not allies within the Conservative Party before 1951. Perhaps for Churchill, Crookshank was too much the supporter of Ulster Unionism and Freemasonry, while Crookshank was suspicious of Churchill's Liberal past. In 1947, Crookshank and Richard Butler (both Chamberlainites earlier) talked of trying to form a coalition government under Ernest Bevin, an idea to which Anthony Eden and Harold Macmillan were hostile.

Churchill recognized that Crookshank was a skilled debater and a master of House of Commons procedure. Hence he was given the post of leader of the House of Commons. A fastidious bachelor who liked to wear a red carnation in his button-hole, he was not a clubbable man. As early as June 1952, Crookshank was among those seeking Churchill's resignation or the date when he would go. Ironically, Churchill's continuance in the premiership kept Crookshank in office, even though Eden, the presumed successor, long held the view that Crookshank was not very competent. On 22 March 1954, Crookshank wrote in his diary that Churchill was "ga-ga." Churchill, for his part, recognized that he could not always rely on the support of Crookshank, nor that of Lord Kilmuir, Lord Salisbury, and Lord

Woolton. Crookshank died on 17 October 1961.

Related entry:
Woolton, Earl of

Suggestions for further reading:
Gilbert, Martin. 1988. *Winston S. Churchill.* Vol. 8. London: Heinemann.
Seldon, Anthony. 1981. *Churchill's Indian Summer.* London: Hodder and Stoughton.

Cuba (1895)

In 1895, Winston Churchill, in his quest for seeing military action, went to Cuba, where the Spanish were repressing a nationalist rising. He reached Havana on 20 November, ten days before his twenty-first birthday. He left Cuba on 8 or 9 December. Later, there were myths that Churchill fought on the Spanish side during the Spanish-American War of 1898. In fact, Churchill was far from Cuba then, and in an interview with the *Morning Post,* London, 15 July 1898, he called for the annexation of Cuba by the United States.

His trip to Cuba in 1895 was an early example of how he made full use of his family's influence to get what he wanted. Although he had decided to go without consulting his mother, Lady Randolph Churchill, on whom he relied for the necessary financing, she nonetheless secured the help of Lord and Lady Tweedmouth in providing letters of introduction to the governor of Jamaica. Meanwhile, Churchill approached his father's friend Sir Henry Drummond Wolff, the British ambassador to Spain, who secured the support of the Spanish minister for foreign affairs and the minister of war, as well as letters of introduction for Churchill and his companion to the Spanish military command in Cuba. He also made direct approaches to the commander in-chief of the British army, to secure permission to go. Viscount Wolseley sent Churchill and his companion, Reginald Barnes, to the director of military intelligence, who requested they collect information, including the effectiveness of a new bullet.

Churchill also arranged with Thomas Heath Joyce, editor of the *Daily Graphic,* London, 1891–1906, to write five letters and sketches of the war in Cuba for the *Graphic* for twenty-five guineas. These were published on 13, 17, 24, and 27 December 1895 and 13 January 1896. After the first four were published, Joyce informed him that they were "extremely interesting and just the kind of thing we wanted." This was his first journalism. Lord Randolph Churchill had written similar pieces for the *Daily Graphic* when he had visited South Africa in 1891.

After spending a week in New York at Bourke Cockran's apartment at 763 Fifth Avenue in Manhattan, Churchill and Barnes went by steamer from Key West, Florida, to Havana. From there, they went by train to Sancti Spiritus in the interior. He witnessed the skirmishes between the Spanish and Cuban nationalist forces near Iguara and also the Battle of La Reforma. During the battle, Churchill and Barnes were near General Juarez Valdez and after it, the general recommended them for a Spanish decoration, the Red Cross. As a result of this courtesy decoration, Churchill was much criticized for being present, the British and American press generally being on the side of the Cuban nationalists.

After his return to England, Churchill wrote three pieces on Cuba for the *Saturday Review,* "The Revolt in Cuba," "American Intervention in Cuba," and (again) "The Revolt in Cuba," published on 15 February, 7 March, and 29 August 1896. The first of these pieces mollified the Spanish, who had been upset earlier. Sir Henry Drummond Wolff had urged Churchill to "avoid saying things unpalatable to the Spaniards; having obtained the letters on your behalf which secured your good treatment I am re-proached for the unfavourable commentaries you make." Lady Randolph Churchill sent a copy of his first article to Joseph Chamberlain, who praised it as "the best short account I have seen of the problems with which the Spaniards have to deal."

Related entries:
Chamberlain, Joseph; Cockran, William Bourke

Suggestions for further reading:
Churchill, Randolph S. 1966. *Winston S. Churchill.* Vol. 1. London: Heinemann.
———. 1967. *Winston S. Churchill.* Companion vol. 1, part 1. London: Heinemann.
Churchill, Winston S. 1930. *My Early Life.* London: Thornton Butterworth.
Thomas, Hugh. 1971. *Cuba or the Pursuit of Freedom.* London: Eyre and Spottiswoode.
Woods, Frederick. 1963. *A Bibliography of the Works of Sir Winston Churchill.* London: Nicholas Vane.

Cunningham, Admiral Andrew Browne (Viscount Cunningham of Hyndhope, 1883–1963)

For Churchill, Admiral Cunningham was less easy to work with as first sea lord than his predecessor, Sir Dudley Pound. Cunningham bucked more at Churchillian interference. He was not much moved by Churchill's charisma and was not that impressed by Churchill as a strategist, even if he did recognize his qualities as a war leader.

Andrew Cunningham was born in Dublin on 7 January 1883, the third of five children of Daniel John and Elizabeth Cumming Cunningham. His father was professor of anatomy at Trinity College, Dublin. His mother was the daughter of the Reverend Andrew Browne of Beith, Ayrshire. Educated at Edinburgh Academy and Stubbington House, Fareham, he joined the *Britannia* as a cadet in January 1897. Serving at the Cape station when the Boer War broke out, he secured front-line service through his father's friendship with Lord Roberts. Unlike Churchill, Cunningham failed to secure fame or distinction as a result. In 1911, he was given command of the destroyer the *Scorpion,* serving later at the Dardanelles and in the Zeebrugge raid, 1918, during the First World War. In the interwar years, he served in various posts at sea and on land, becoming deputy chief of the naval staff at the admiralty in September 1938. In June 1939, he succeeded Sir Dudley Pound as commander in chief, Mediterranean station.

Cunningham's early wartime task was to seek to restore British naval supremacy in the Mediterranean. He secured the immobilization of the French fleet at Alexandria. He took effective action against the Italian fleet off Calabria in July 1940 and off Cape Matapan in March 1941. His determined and capable action in the Mediterranean made him acceptable to the American Joint Chiefs of Staff and in 1942 he was made Allied naval commander, Expeditionary Force under General Dwight D. Eisenhower. Cunningham's forces enabled the successful landings in North Africa, Sicily, and Salerno. He was rewarded with a baronetcy in 1942. In October 1943, he succeeded Sir Dudley Pound as first sea lord, a post he held until 1946.

Churchill was hesitant in appointing Cunningham as first sea lord, ostensibly because of his important role in the Mediterranean, but more likely because he knew that Cunningham would be less emollient than Pound. There had been friction before. Churchill had not been happy with Cunningham's peaceful solution to the French fleet at Alexandria. There had also been friction when Churchill wanted to replace Admiral Sir John Tovey as commander in chief of the Home Fleet, with Cunningham refusing unless Tovey died in post. Cunningham had also bridled against Churchill's often unwarranted promptings

for action. He complained in his memoirs, "'It was in the sort of 'prodding' message received by me . . . that Mr. Churchill was often so ungracious and hasty."

Churchill and Cunningham, nevertheless, worked well together in 1943–1945. Churchill in his resignation honors list put forward the three chiefs of staff for peerages. Cunningham accepted, but complained that the navy was otherwise inadequately recognized. In September 1945, he became Baron Cunningham of Hyndhope. In 1946, he was made a viscount and also appointed to the Order of Merit. He died on 12 June 1963.

Related entry:
Pound, Sir Alfred Dudley Pickman Rogers

Suggestions for further reading:
Cunningham, Admiral Viscount. 1951. *A Sailor's Odyssey.* London: Hutchinson.
Gilbert, Martin. 1986. *Winston S. Churchill.* Vol. 7. London: Heinemann.
Gretton, Vice Admiral Sir Peter. 1969. *Winston Churchill and the Royal Navy.* New York: Coward McCann.
Roskill, Stephen. 1977. *Churchill and the Admirals.* London: Collins.

Curzon, George Nathaniel (Marquess Curzon of Kedleston, 1859–1925)

Churchill once wrote of Curzon that he had grown up with "all the advantages of moderate affluence and noble descent," perhaps his view of himself. Both men were tremendously ambitious and both were greatly concerned about the verdict of history. Churchill was early on repelled by Curzon but came to admire him when he came to know him. They clashed over Chanak in 1922 and over loyalty to David Lloyd George.

Curzon was born at Kedleston Hall on 11 January 1859, the eldest of eleven children of the Reverend Alfred Nathaniel

Holden and Blanche Curzon. His father was the fourth Baron Scarsdale and was rector of Kedleston. Educated at Eton and Balliol College, Oxford, Curzon's life was blighted somewhat by curvature of the spine, which became apparent from 1878. He traveled abroad, supplementing his allowance from his father by writing political articles. In 1885, he was assistant private secretary to Lord Salisbury. He was elected to Parliament as a Conservative, for Southport. As a young Tory Democrat, he admired Lord Randolph Churchill; however, after Churchill's resignation, Curzon took care to align himself with Lord Salisbury. Curzon traveled widely and wrote books about his journeys. In 1891, Lord Salisbury appointed him under secretary of state at the India office. In 1895 he married Mary Victoria Leiter, the daughter of an American millionaire. Thereafter, he and his wife adopted a prosperous lifestyle.

When, in 1895, Salisbury became prime minister again, and also foreign secretary, he appointed Curzon to be under secretary of state at the foreign office. This brought Curzon to the forefront of Conservative politics in the House of Commons. In August 1898, it was announced that at the age of thirty-nine he was to be the next viceroy of India. He was created Baron Curzon of Kedleston in the Irish peerage (which would have enabled him to return to the House of Commons while his father lived).

Winston Churchill, who enjoyed expressing strong views in his letters to his mother, wrote from India in February 1897 that Curzon was, with Arthur Balfour, the Conservative leader whom he most despised and detested, adding that he was "the spoiled darling of politics—blown with conceit—insolent from undeserved success—the typification of the superior Oxford prig." Nevertheless, the following year he seriously considered applying to be Curzon's aide-de-camp. Soon after, Curzon became viceroy; Churchill stayed for a week with him in Calcutta and was de-

lighted and charmed by him. For his part, Curzon warned Churchill of the dangers of being too garrulous.

When Curzon became locked in a dispute with Lord Kitchener over their respective powers in India, Churchill believed Curzon to be right and judged that excessive powers had been given to the commander in chief, almost making him a military dictator. Curzon resigned as viceroy in 1905. Curzon's wife died in July 1906. He became busy in university reform after being elected chancellor of Oxford University in 1907. In the 1911 coronation honors, he was created Earl Curzon of Kedleston, Viscount Scarsdale (with reversion to his father and male heirs) and Viscount Ravensdale (with reversion to his daughters and male heirs).

Curzon returned to prominent political activity with the First World War. From May 1915, he was lord privy seal in Asquith's coalition government. In early 1916, he became chairman of the Shipping Control Committee and that May he became president of the air board.

Curzon opposed withdrawal from Gallipoli, fearing that this would be a very damaging reverse and be seen as such in the East. He also proposed to move troops from Salonika to Gallipoli. These views won Churchill's warm support. In February 1916, Churchill gave Curzon a tour of his part of the Western Front. Some of Asquith's supporters feared a Curzon, Lloyd George, and Churchill alliance. However, the friendship cooled, with Churchill upset that Curzon took the air board post, one he wanted as a route back into the government.

Churchill and Curzon's views were different on the issue of providing British troops in the Caucasus in 1918–1919. Churchill, as secretary of state for war, pushed hard to place available troops in Russia to fight the Bolsheviks. Curzon wanted more active intervention in the Caucasus and Persia. Churchill and Curzon also argued over who should be in charge of British policy in the Middle East. Curzon, Alfred Milner, Austen Chamberlain, and Edwin Montagu favored the foreign office, but Churchill won, with responsibility for Palestine and Mesopotamia being transferred to the colonial office just before Churchill became secretary of state there. Churchill was indignant when Curzon accepted the Milner report on Egypt and declared the British protectorate at an end in 1922.

Churchill and Curzon also took different views over the Chanak crisis in September 1922. Curzon warned against taking action against the Turkish army in the Straits area. Later, when Lloyd George, Churchill, and Frederick Birkenhead were belligerent, Curzon backed Sir Charles Harington in seeking a peaceful solution.

Curzon was not happy with Lloyd George's interventions in foreign policy nor did he wish to see another general election fought under the coalition banner. He planned to resign before the Carlton Club meeting. After the collapse of Lloyd George's government, Churchill was outraged that Curzon continued as foreign secretary under Andrew Bonar Law and condemned him in a letter to the *Morning Post,* 10 November 1922. Curzon responded by stating that his letter was marked by "copious inaccuracy and no small malevolence."

Curzon was bitterly disappointed not to succeed Bonar Law as prime minister in May 1923. He continued as foreign secretary in Stanley Baldwin's first, short government, 1923–1924. When Baldwin formed his second government in November 1924, Curzon became lord privy seal until his death on 20 March 1925.

Churchill wrote a perceptive portrait of Curzon in *Pall Mall,* January 1929, in which, when writing of the 1890s, he recalled only his favorable impressions of Curzon. He concluded it with a weighty epitaph: "The morning had been golden; the noontide was bronze; and the evening was lead. But all were solid and each was polished till it shone after its fashion." This essay on Curzon remains one of the best pieces in *Great Contemporaries* (1937).

Suggestions for further reading:
Churchill, Randolph S. 1966 and 1967. *Winston S. Churchill.* Vols. 1 and 2. London: Heinemann.
Gilbert, Martin. 1971–1976. *Winston S. Churchill.* Vols. 3–5. London: Heinemann.
Gilmour, David. 1994. *Curzon.* London: Murray.
Nicolson, Harold. 1927. *Some People.* London: Constable.
Ronaldshay, Earl of. 1928. *The Life of Lord Curzon.* 3 vols. London: Benn.
Rose, Kenneth. 1969. *Curzon: A Most Superior Person.* London: Weidenfeld and Nicolson.

D

Dardanelles Commission (1916–1917)

Churchill's wartime record at the admiralty (1914–1915) came under repeated attack from some Conservatives, notably those on the Unionist War Committee. Because Churchill believed his career would resume only when the public had detailed information about the Dardanelles campaign, in late May 1916 he asked Herbert Henry Asquith to permit major documents relating to the campaign to be placed before Parliament. Asquith agreed. Churchill consulted Admiral Lord Fisher and Sir Ian Hamilton, both also eager to be vindicated. However, on 11 July, Asquith informed Churchill that on grounds of national security, the government would not publish them after all. On 20 July 1916, two days after a House of Commons debate over the nonpublication of the Dardanelles documents, Asquith announced the setting up of a select committee of the House of Commons "to inquire into the conduct of the Dardanelles operations."

On 7 July, David Lloyd George had suggested to Churchill that such a select committee would be an alternative to publishing documents. Churchill had responded by writing that the prime minister and the government should stand by its pledge to publish but he would of course attend and assist such an inquiry.

The commission, appointed in late July 1916, was chaired by Lord Cromer. Its other members were Field Marshal Lord Nicholson; Admiral Sir William May; Judge Sir William Pickford; Sir Frederick Cawley, a Liberal M.P.; James Clyde, a Liberal Unionist M.P.; Captain Stephen Gwynn, an Irish Nationalist M.P. (who served in France); and Walter Rock, a Liberal M.P.

Churchill took immense care to prepare his statement to the Commission of Inquiry. He collaborated with Fisher over evidence. He also talked to Sir Maurice Hankey, the secretary of the cabinet, about his own evidence and consulted the Liberal M.P. Alexander MacCullam Scott and his friend F. E. Smith, a Conservative M.P. Hankey, Lloyd George (war office files), and the admiralty helped him with documents, but Asquith refused to allow him a set of war council minutes. He appeared before the commission on 28 September 1916, answering questions after having read his statement.

Churchill continued to prepare evidence for the commission into November 1916. On 19 October, he prepared a fairly detailed list of key points for Admiral Henry Francis Oliver to consider using when presenting his evidence, and Oliver made use of his guidance. Churchill carefully read other people's evidence and, where he felt it necessary, prepared rebuttals. In the case of the evidence of Sir George Arthur, private secretary to Lord

Kitchener during the war, in which he claimed Kitchener had opposed the naval attack on the Dardanelles at some conference of unspecified date, Churchill replied that his "facts" were "untrue and without foundation."

Churchill's evidence to the commission has been described by Robert Rhodes James as "A tour de force," and in his view "contributed substantially to the relative mildness with which the Commission treated his part." The commission itself commented that in his evidence Churchill had "assigned to himself a more unobtrusive part than that which he actually played." The Times, commenting when the first part of the commission's report was published in 1917, observed that Churchill had been consistent, but his was "the consistency of a dangerous enthusiast, who sought expert advice only when he could be sure of moulding it to his opinion."

Subsequently various historians have been critical of aspects of Churchill's self-vindication before the Dardanelles Commission and in The World Crisis (1923). These include Arthur Marder, Robert Rhodes James, Robin Prior, and Tuvia Ben-Moshe. Ben-Moshe has argued persuasively that some time in mid to late February 1915, Churchill came to doubt that the navy could force the Straits on its own. Hence, while Kitchener still believed he was supplying troops for the period after naval success, Churchill was asking for more (the 29th Division) so that the army could take the Gallipoli Peninsula. Churchill was reticent about this at the time as he had assured the war council the navy could succeed on its own. Ben-Moshe, like Prior, has questioned Churchill's view that he was blameless at the operational level, arguing that his mistake was not to secure early on a combined naval and military campaign.

Related entries:
French, Sir John Denton Pinkstone; Gallipoli; Kitchener, Horatio Herbert

Suggestions for further reading:
Ben-Moshe, Tuvia. 1992. *Churchill: Strategy and History.* Boulder, CO: Lynn Reinner Publishers.
Churchill, Winston S. 1923. *The World Crisis.* Vols. 1 and 2. London: Thornton Butterworth.
Marder, Arthur. 1965. *From the Dreadnought to Scapa Flow.* Vol. 2. Oxford: Oxford University Press.
———. 1974. *From the Dardanelles to Oran.* Oxford: Clarendon Press.
Prior, Robin. 1983. *Churchill's "World Crisis" as History.* London: Croom Helm.

Davidson, John Colin Campbell (Viscount Davidson, 1889–1970)

Davidson was a loyal associate and friend to Andrew Bonar Law and Stanley Baldwin. Somewhat of the respectable civil servant always, he distrusted the charismatic and colorful political figures such as Churchill, David Lloyd George, Lord Birkenhead, and Lord Beaverbrook. In the 1920s and 1930s, he viewed Churchill with a measure of doubt, even mistrust.

John Davidson was born in Aberdeen on 23 February 1889, the second child of James McKenzie and Georgina Davidson. His father was an ophthalmic surgeon and lecturer in ophthalmology at Aberdeen University. His mother was the youngest daughter of Dr. John Henderson; her brother, John Henderson, was later the Liberal M.P. for West Aberdeenshire. Educated at Westminster School and Pembroke College, Cambridge, he went on to be the unpaid private secretary to Lord Crewe, Lewis Harcourt, Andrew Bonar Law, and Stanley Baldwin. Davidson felt that Bonar Law came to treat him as a father—and Baldwin became a close friend. He was elected Conservative M.P. for Hemel Hempstead in an uncontested by-election in November 1920. When Baldwin entered the cabinet in 1921, Davidson became his parliamentary private secretary. When Bonar Law became prime minister in 1922, Davidson became his parliamentary private secretary.

With the accession of Baldwin to the premiership, Davidson became chancellor of the Duchy of Lancaster, a ministerial post, but outside the cabinet. In this role, he again served Baldwin as his efficient, confidential helper. He also took on the post of chief civil commissioner, in charge of the government's strike-breaking organization. He lost his seat in the 1923 general election but regained it in the 1924 general election. He served as financial secretary to the admiralty.

Although he ardently supported Bonar Law and Baldwin, Davidson did not admire Churchill; this feeling was reinforced when Churchill was chancellor of the exchequer, 1924–1929, and pressing hard for economies at the admiralty. Davidson later wrote, "Winston's budgets were in fact deficit budgets, balanced by odd feats of arithmetic and other manipulations. . . . He did some very clever things, and some very expedient things, but expediency was not principle." Davidson later liked to defend Baldwin over slow rearmament in the 1930s by arguing that Churchill was the architect of inadequate armaments by his policies as chancellor of the exchequer in the 1920s.

Davidson resumed his work with the government's strike-breaking Supply and Transport Committee before the General Strike, 1926. He was deputy chief civil commissioner, with particular responsibility for propaganda. He and Churchill saw representatives of the Newspaper Proprietors' Association on 3 May about the possibility of producing a newspaper during the General Strike. According to Davidson, Baldwin suggested giving Churchill the editorship of the *British Gazette* on the basis that "it will keep him busy, stop him doing worse things." Davidson came to pay tribute to Churchill's energy and commitment in running the *British Gazette*. Davidson was also involved in government dealings with the BBC during the General Strike. Davidson helped Baldwin restrain Churchill from his desire to take over the BBC and turn it into "an offshoot of the *British Gazette.*"

As early as 1921, Sir George Younger had written to Bonar Law that Davidson should be a future chairman of the Conservative Party. Davidson was an effective party chairman, one who prioritized loyalty to the party leader, Baldwin, holding the office from November 1926 until June 1930. With the formation of the National government in 1931, Davidson returned to the ministerial post of chancellor of the Duchy of Lancaster, which he held until he retired at the same time as Baldwin retired in 1937.

Davidson strongly opposed Churchill over India, even organizing a countercampaign on the subject. According to Davidson, Churchill told him that over the India Bill, "I am going to lead a Midlothian campaign against you, and the government will be out." Baldwin told Davidson that he kept Churchill out of office because of India and his threats to smash the Conservative Party on the issue. By 1936, Davidson believed Churchill should be readmitted to office, but Baldwin saw him as a disruptive as well as a dynamic force.

When Baldwin retired and received an earldom, Davidson received a viscountcy. After the outbreak of war in 1939, Davidson served in the Ministry of Information as controller of production, in particular dealing with publicity, until Brendan Bracken took over in 1941. His wife succeeded him as M.P. for Hemel Hempstead, 1937–1959. Davidson died on 11 December 1970.

Related entries:
Baldwin, Stanley; Bonar Law, Andrew

Suggestions for further reading:
Blake, Robert. 1981. "Davidson, John Colin Campbell." In *Dictionary of National Biography 1961–1970,* edited by E. T. Williams and

C. S. Nicholls. Oxford: Oxford University Press.

Rhodes, James Robert. 1969. *J. C. Davidson's Memoirs and Papers, 1910–1937*. London: Weidenfeld and Nicolson.

De Forest, Baron Arnold Maurice (Count de Bendern, 1879–)

De Forest was a lifelong friend of Churchill. A very wealthy man, he often played host to Churchill, putting his yacht, castle, or other houses at his disposal. When de Forest was subjected to smears on two occasions, Churchill rallied to his defense. De Forest, who supported David Lloyd George as well as Churchill, was a Liberal M.P., 1911–1918.

Born in 1879, Arnold Maurice Bischoffsheim was adopted by the banker Baron Hirsch. He was educated at Eton and Christ Church, Oxford. An Austrian baron, he was given royal authority in 1900 to use the title of baron in the U.K. Also in 1900, he married one of Churchill's childhood friends, Ethel Gerard. Churchill had also known de Forest since they were both children and had visited him in Paris in 1880.

Winston Churchill spent part of the summer of 1906 on de Forest's yacht *Honor* at Deauville, enjoying gambling in the casino and playing polo at Trouville. Later that summer, he stayed with de Forest at his castle in Eichorn, Austria. In March 1907, he again enjoyed de Forest's hospitality at Biarritz. When Winston and Clementine Churchill went on their honeymoon in 1908, they went to Lake Maggiore, Venice, and to de Forest's castle at Eichorn. In the summer of 1910, they went on a two-month cruise through the Mediterranean to Constantinople on de Forest's yacht *Honor*.

In 1910, de Forest unsuccessfully contested Southport as a Liberal but was successful in a by-election for West Ham North in 1911. During the First World War, he served with the Royal Naval Armoured Car Force. In the early part of the war, there were attempts to prosecute him as a German sympathizer, but with Churchill's help, he was able to show his support for the British war effort. In 1932, he became a citizen of Liechtenstein and was made Count de Bendern.

Suggestions for further reading:
Churchill, Randolph S. 1966–1969. *Winston S. Churchill*. Vols. 1 and 2, and companion vols. 1 and 2. London: Heinemann.

Gilbert, Martin. 1991. *Churchill: A Life.* London: Heinemann.

De Gaulle, General Charles André Joseph Marie (1890–1970)

With Charles de Gaulle, Churchill met his match in national pride, determination, and obstinacy. Although their relationship was often very bad, both recognized the strengths of the other. The best known anecdote of Churchill on de Gaulle—his alleged comment that of all the wartime crosses he had to bear, the heaviest was the Cross of Lorraine (the Free French symbol)—was not true. But when asked about it, Churchill replied, "No, I didn't say it, but I'm sorry I didn't, because it was quite witty . . . and so true!"

Charles de Gaulle was born in Lille on 22 November 1890, the son of Professor Henri de Gaulle and his wife Jeanne Maillot-Delannoy. He was educated at Saint-Cyr Academy, graduating in 1911. He served as an infantry officer during the First World War. He was wounded three times and taken prisoner by the Germans in March 1916. In 1921 he married Yvonne Vendroux. In the 1930s he wrote on strategy and military theory, arguing for a career army with mobile armored forces.

At the outbreak of the Second World War de Gaulle was commander of armored units in the Fifth Army. In the 1930s he had cultivated the politician Paul Reynaud. After Reynaud became prime minister in March 1940 de Gaulle became commander of the 4th Armored Division, seeing action at Laon and Abbeville in May 1940. Promotion to brigadier general on 1 June 1940 was followed by appointment as under secretary for national defense on 6 June 1940. However, Reynaud resigned on 16 June.

De Gaulle first met Churchill on 9 June 1940 when he visited London on behalf of Reynaud. Reynaud wanted Churchill to be convinced that France would remain an ally, even if her resistance to Germany was based overseas. Churchill made it clear that he would not be sending back the troops who had escaped from Dunkirk nor would he send further air squadrons to France. De Gaulle later wrote that he was impressed by Churchill as a war leader. They met again in France, when Churchill had two conferences with Reynaud, 11–13 June. Although several other French leaders were defeated, de Gaulle was not, and he spoke of guerrilla warfare over dinner on 11 June. Churchill was again impressed. However, de Gaulle was not present on 13 June when Churchill declined to agree to a French armistice and misunderstood Churchill's position when he did join the Anglo-French meeting. De Gaulle remained resolute to continue fighting, Reynaud was not.

De Gaulle left Brest for London on the British destroyer *Milan* on 15 June. On the morning of 16 June the British cabinet called for the French fleet to sail for Britain before France entered separate armistice negotiations. Churchill then had lunch with de Gaulle, who pressed for a declaration of union between Britain and France. Churchill put this to his cabinet that afternoon, securing agreement. De Gaulle flew back to France but Reynaud resigned that evening. The next morning, 17 June, de Gaulle joined General Louis Spears and

flew back to England and saw Churchill at 10 Downing Street. De Gaulle later wrote, "Washed up from a disastrous shipwreck upon the shores of England what could I have done without his help? He gave it to me at once." De Gaulle asked Churchill to be allowed to broadcast to France on BBC radio. Churchill agreed and ensured that de Gaulle was able, on 18 June 1940, to call on French people to continue the fight against Germany. France secured an armistice on 23 June. With no other substantial French political leaders in England, Churchill's government recognized de Gaulle as the "leader of all Free Frenchmen, wherever they may be, who rally to him in support of the Allied cause."

De Gaulle's willingness to cooperate was tested to the limit when the British destroyed French warships at Oran on 3 July 1940. De Gaulle, aware of French outrage at the deaths of so many sailors, broadcast to France on 8 July a speech in which he made clear his grief but stated the ships were better destroyed than used by Germany and that all Frenchmen should know "that a British defeat would seal for ever his country's bondage." Churchill, thereafter, had faith in de Gaulle's resolve, even though he was often exasperated by de Gaulle and in 1943 was willing to oust him.

In September 1940 de Gaulle was with British and Free French forces that failed to take Dakar from Vichy France. The expedition was a fiasco. Churchill resisted the option of blaming it on de Gaulle, and continued to support him and the Free French. De Gaulle was successful in Gabon later in 1940.

However, elsewhere there was friction between de Gaulle and the British. This was notably the case in Syria and Lebanon, where Vichy forces were defeated in June–July 1941. In 1941–1942 Churchill and his colleagues twice backed Vice Admiral Émile Muselier as a major force within the Free French, but were pressed successfully by de Gaulle to desist. De Gaulle's position was enhanced by the growing resistance movement within France, which mostly recognized de Gaulle's leadership.

Relations between de Gaulle and the British and Americans deteriorated when their forces landed in French North Africa in November 1942, without informing de Gaulle but having secured an agreement with Admiral Jean François Darlan, minister of marine in the Vichy government. The danger of a breach with de Gaulle was lessened when Darlan was assassinated on 24 December 1942, with British connivance. De Gaulle refused to accept second place to General Henri Giraud in North Africa, as the Americans and British wished. Several months after the Casablanca Conference in January 1943, Giraud and de Gaulle were briefly joint chairmen of the French Committee for National Liberation (from June to November 1943), but de Gaulle soon marginalized him.

Although the British were less supportive of Giraud than the Americans, Churchill became particularly angry with de Gaulle in 1943. In May he complained to Clement Attlee and Anthony Eden that de Gaulle "hates England and has left a trail of Anglophobia behind him everywhere" and even asked them "to consider urgently whether we should not now eliminate de Gaulle as a political force." Eden and Harold Macmillan were generally able to understand and sympathize more with de Gaulle's position than Churchill.

Relations thawed when de Gaulle visited Churchill, who was recuperating from ill health in Marrakesh in January 1944. De Gaulle had been angered at not being informed of the content of the discussions at Tehran between the Big Three (Joseph Stalin, Franklin Roosevelt, and Winston Churchill) and at the way Churchill treated North Africa as a British, not French, zone. Churchill feared a stormy encounter, but the meeting went well. Nevertheless, Duff Cooper wrote of de Gaulle that he was "very difficult and un-

helpful. He talked as though he were Stalin and Roosevelt combined."

More often relations were bad, with Churchill outraged at de Gaulle's attitude toward President Franklin Roosevelt and himself. There were rows before and after the Allied landings in Normandy, with de Gaulle successfully pressing for the recognition of a French government of liberation in July 1944.

By March 1944 de Gaulle was referring to the French Committee for National Liberation as the provisional government of France. De Gaulle landed in France on 14 June 1944 and ensured that this provisional government was accepted by the Allies in July. Relations between Churchill and de Gaulle improved when Churchill visited Paris for Armistice Day, 11 November 1944. The victory celebrations were moving and Churchill and de Gaulle had useful talks afterwards. Relations deteriorated again as de Gaulle pressed to be added to the Big Three conferences. Nevertheless, at Yalta, Churchill pressed that France be given a zone of occupation in Germany. De Gaulle also wrongly believed that nationalist feelings in Syria and Lebanon were due to British malevolence.

On 13 November 1945, after Churchill had left office, he visited de Gaulle in Paris. It was the day de Gaulle was elected president. Duff Cooper wrote of de Gaulle, "He was smiling and courteous and treated Winston with more deference than he ever did when Winston was Prime Minister." De Gaulle soon found the Fourth Republic unacceptable, resigning as president on 20 January 1946. He returned to power as prime minister in 1958, to draft a new constitution and to respond to France's crisis with Algeria. De Gaulle was then elected president again from 21 December 1958 to 28 April 1969.

De Gaulle presented Churchill with the *Croix de la Libération* in Paris on 6 November 1958. They both spoke of the other warmly, and over lunch the elderly Churchill reminisced. They met again on 6 April 1960, when de Gaulle visited Churchill at his London home at Hyde Park Gate and Churchill dined at the French embassy. They met for a last time in Nice on 22 October 1960, when Churchill was on vacation and de Gaulle was on an official tour. De Gaulle sent a tribute on Churchill's death and wrote on each anniversary of his death to Clementine Churchill.

De Gaulle died in November 1970.

Related entries:
Eden, Sir (Robert) Anthony; Macmillan, (Maurice) Harold; Spears, Major General Sir Edward Louis

Suggestions for further reading:
Cooper, Duff. 1953. *Old Men Forget*. London: Davis.
Gilbert, Martin. 1983, 1986, and 1988. *Winston Churchill*. Vols. 6–8. London: Heinemann.
Kersaudy, François. 1981. *Churchill and De Gaulle*. London: Collins.

Denikin, General Anton Ivanovich (1872–1947)

Churchill in 1919 had great faith in General Anton Denikin as the savior of Russia from Bolshevism. Churchill abhorred Bolshevik ideas and was determined to help the White Russians to defeat the Bolsheviks. His detestation of the Bolsheviks led him to underestimate their chances of survival. His single-minded support for British intervention in Russia led to a British public and media tired of war, dubbing the campaign "Mr. Churchill's Private War." It also exasperated David Lloyd George, the prime minister, who wished Churchill would apply his energies to reducing war office expenditure, not increasing it.

Anton Ivanovich Denikin was born in 1872, the son of a serf and a Polish housemaid. His father was conscripted into the Tsarist army at the age of thirty and retired over thirty years later with the rank of major. Anton Denikin wished to emulate his father's army career and joined the army in 1887. He succeeded in obtaining a commission and going to Staff College. He served with distinction in the Russo-Japanese war, 1904–1905. He gained a reputation for being a staunch advocate of improved conditions for soldiers. He also became an ardent supporter of the Russian Empire. During the First World War, he was a brave infantry commander, reaching the position of commander in chief of the South-Western Army Group in August 1917. He backed General Lavr Georgyevich Kornilov's attempted march on Petrograd but was imprisoned when it failed. He joined the Volunteer Army in the southeast, succeeding General Kornilov in April 1918 as joint leader with General Mikhail Vasilievich Alekseev. On Alekseev's death in October 1918, he was the sole leader of the southern White Russians until April 1920 (with General Baron von Ferdinand Petrovich Wrangel succeeding him).

Churchill had great faith in Denikin as the man who could defeat the Bolsheviks. In October 1919, he was convinced that Denikin, then advancing north to Moscow, would be the agent of an imminent Bolshevik collapse. Lloyd George backed British involvement in South Russia with a further £3 million, eager to be a clear supporter of a victorious White Russian régime. However, Lloyd George did urge Churchill to use his influence with Denikin to stop anti-Jewish atrocities by his forces. This Churchill did, warning Denikin in a letter of 10 October 1919 of the difficulties further massacres would place in the way of his securing more financial backing for the Whites in Parliament. Churchill also tried to rebut criticism that Denikin aimed to destroy Polish independence. Churchill was full of the idea that when Denikin took Moscow, he would go out to Moscow and give Denikin advice on a new Russian constitution.

However, on 23 October, when Leon Trotsky, the leading Russian revolutionary, drove Yadenitch back from the outskirts of Petrograd, Denikin was also driven further from Moscow. Churchill remained Denikin's main supporter in the cabinet. After one meeting, Arthur Balfour had complimented Churchill with "I admire the exaggerated way you tell the truth." Churchill talked Denikin up, even as Denikin and his forces retreated in chaos. Churchill did not recognize the failure of the Whites until 31 December 1919. Churchill succeeded in ensuring that Denikin kept supplies already allocated to him in mid-January 1920, but by early February it was clear to all that Denikin was comprehensively defeated. Churchill loyally did what he could to ensure the survival of Denikin and his supporters. In late March, Denikin and his forces withdrew to the Crimea.

Lloyd George took the view that the British government had backed the Whites to the sum of £100 million (some £45 million of which went to support Denikin), and at the cost of 329 British lives. In withdrawing he observed, "If the Russian people wish for freedom, we can always say we gave them the chance." As for Churchill, his critics thought his support for Denikin another military misjudgment on par with Antwerp and Gallipoli. Later, with the West horrified by Soviet misdeeds, especially under Joseph Stalin, Churchill appeared to have foresight in trying to oust the Bolsheviks in 1919–1920.

Denikin was no politician. His belief in the Russian Empire set him apart from those favoring independence for the states of the Baltic and Caucasus. He was notably unable to restrain ferocious excesses of some of his forces.

The British agent Sidney Reilly wrote of Denikin in late December 1918 that he was "a man of . . . fine presence, the dark Russian type with regular features; he has a dignified, very cultured manner, and could be classed as belonging rather to the 'higher staff officer type' than to the 'fighting type.' He gives one the impression of a broad-minded, high-thinking, determined and well-balanced man—but the impression of great power of intellect or of those characteristics which mark a ruler of men is lacking."

Denikin left the Crimea for Constantinople and then went to France, living there from 1920 to 1945. He wrote five volumes of memoirs (in Russian, titled *Sketches of the Russian Turmoil*) between 1921 and 1926. In 1945, he emigrated to the United States and died at Ann Arbor, Michigan, in 1947.

Suggestions for further reading:

Gilbert, Martin 1975. *Winston S. Churchill*. Vol. 4. London: Heinemann.
Kettle, Martin. 1992. *Churchill and the Archangel Fiasco*. London: Routledge.
Luckett, Richard. 1971. *The White Generals*. London: Longman.
Ullman, Richard H. 1968. *Britain and the Russian Civil War*. Princeton: Princeton University Press.

Dill, Field Marshal Sir John Green (1881–1944)

Dill was the first chief of the Imperial General Staff whom Churchill appointed, serving from May 1940 until December 1941. He then greatly contributed to the strengthening of Anglo-American cooperation while serving in Washington, D.C.

Dill was born on 25 December 1881 at Lurgan, County Armagh, the only son and second child of John Dill, the manager of the local branch of the Ulster Bank. After Cheltenham College and the Royal Military College, Sandhurst, he joined the Leinster Regiment. He served in the field in the final year of the Boer War. He saw much action during the First World War, including the Battles of Neuve Chapelle (1915),

Aubers Ridge (1915), and Paschendaele (1917), ending the war as a temporary brigadier general. In the interwar years, his career continued to progress. It included two years in India and then commandant of the Staff College. He was passed over as chief of the Imperial General Staff in 1937 (for General Lord Gort) and 1939 (for General William Edmund Ironside). After the outbreak of war he commanded I Corps of the British Expeditionary Force that went to France and was stationed near the Belgian border. In April 1940, he was brought back to take the new post of vice chief of the Imperial General Staff. On 27 May 1940, he succeeded Ironside.

Dill provided Churchill with professional advice. This was often too cautious for Churchill's taste, but it was salutary for Churchill's enthusiasms to be confronted with unpleasant realities. Dill also provided a buffer between Churchill and the commanders in the field. Nevertheless, the two men did not work well together, unlike General Sir Alan Brooke and Churchill. Churchill replaced Dill with Brooke as chief of the Imperial General Staff, effective on Dill's sixtieth birthday, 25 December 1941. Dill was promoted to field marshal.

Dill then was head of the British Joint Staff Mission to Washington, D.C., and acted as Churchill's representative (as minister of defense) with President Franklin D. Roosevelt and his special envoy, Harry Hopkins. He proved a very effective go-between. He was much admired and trusted by the president and by other major figures, such as the U.S. Army Chief of Staff, General George C. Marshall. After Dill died in Washington on 4 November 1944, he was given a full military funeral, with the U.S. Joint Chiefs of Staff as pall bearers, and buried in Arlington National Cemetery.

Suggestions for further reading:

Danchev, Alex. 1986. *Very Special Relationship.* London: Brassey's.
———. 1987. "Dilly-Dally or Having the Last Word: Field-Marshal Sir John Dill and Prime Minister Winston Churchill." *Journal of Contemporary History.* Vol. 22.
———. 1991. "Dill." In *Churchill's Generals,* edited by John Keegan. London: Weidenfeld and Nicolson.
Falls, Cyril. 1959. "Dill, Sir John Greer." In *Dictionary of National Biography, 1941–1950,* edited by L. G. Wickham Legg and E. T. Williams. Oxford: Oxford University Press.
Kennedy, Sir John. 1957. *The Business of War.* London: Hutchinson.

Disraeli, Benjamin (First Earl of Beaconsfield, 1804–1881)

Winston Churchill's idealized notions of Disraeli's politics were very important in his career as a Conservative politician. "Tory Democracy," or "One Nation" Conservatism, was his brand of Conservatism, at least at the outset of his political career and during his last phases after the end of the Second World War.

Born on 21 December 1804, Benjamin Disraeli was the son of Isaac D'Israeli, a wealthy Jewish literary man, and his wife, Maria Basevi. Isaac D'Israeli was a strong Tory and in 1828 he rented Bradenham, a manor house in Buckinghamshire. Disraeli was later proud of his service as a county member of Parliament. The young Benjamin Disraeli dressed as a dandy, wrote novels, and sought election to Parliament initially as a Radical. He was elected to Parliament in 1837 as a Conservative. He became the most eloquent opponent of Sir Robert Peel over his decision to repeal the Corn Laws in 1846; by 1849 he had emerged as Conservative leader in the House of Commons. In the Conservative minority governments of 1852, 1858–1859, and 1866–1888, Lord Derby, the leader in the House of Lords, was prime minister and Disraeli was chancellor of the exchequer as well as leader of the House of Commons. When Derby retired due to ill health in

Benjamin Disraeli, c. 1860 (Library of Congress)

ful, his son Winston took up "Tory Democracy" as a strong belief. In his first public speech at Claverton Manor in 1897, he observed, "British workmen have more to hope for from the rising tide of Tory Democracy than from . . . Radicalism." After the Second World War, he was again referring to Disraeli and Tory Democracy when speaking of trade unionism.

Winston Churchill never met Disraeli. He did, however, delight in working at Chartwell on an upright desk that had belonged to Disraeli.

Related entry:
Claverton Manor

Suggestions for further reading:
Blake, Robert. 1966. *Disraeli*. London: Eyre and Spottiswoode.
Feuchtwanger, Edgar. 2000. *Disraeli*. London: Arnold.
Gilbert, Martin. 1988. *Winston S. Churchill*. Vol. 8. London: Heinemann.
Smith, Paul. 1996. *Disraeli: A Brief Life*. Cambridge: Cambridge University Press.

February 1868, Disraeli became prime minister for the first time (until that December). In 1874, he became prime minister again after winning a majority of 100 seats in the general election. His major government lasted until its defeat in the 1880 general election. He died on 19 April 1881.

Disraeli delighted in promoting ideas of political links between young, enlightened aristocrats and the working class. He pursued his idea, Young England, in politics and in novels in 1842–1845 and seemed to be furthering such ideals with the social reforms enacted in 1874–1876. Lord Randolph Churchill appeared to be a younger version, with his Fourth Party campaigns of the early 1880s. He also dubbed Disraeli's social measures "Tory Democracy" and put himself forward as Disraeli's successor. He was also the key figure in the founding and promoting of the Primrose League (the primrose was believed to have been Disraeli's favorite flower).

Although Lord Randolph Churchill's belief in substantial social reform is doubt-

Dowding, Air Chief Marshal Sir Hugh Caswall Tremenheere (Baron Dowding of Bentley Prior, 1882–1970)

Churchill admired Hugh Dowding before the Battle of Britain and admired him even more as the leader of the brave fighter pilots of summer 1940. Dowding, austere and dedicated, was not a popular figure with many of his senior colleagues, who thought him conservative and resistant to new ideas. However, he was a hero to the Battle of Britain pilots, who revered his name.

Hugh Caswall Tremenheere Dowding was born at Moffat, Dumfriesshire, on 24 April 1882, the eldest son of Arthur John Caswall and Maud Caroline Dowding. His mother was the daughter of Major General

Charles William Tremenheere. Hugh Dowding studied at St. Ninian's, Moffat, and Winchester before entering the Royal Military Academy, Woolwich. He became a gunner in the Royal Garrison Artillery. From 1912 to 1913, he spent two years at the Staff College, Camberley, during which time he learned to fly; he received his certificate on 20 December 1913. He then took a three-month course at the Central Flying School, Upavon. During the First World War, he served as an observer and as a pilot. In 1915, he was commander of No. 16 Squadron at Merville. By 1917, he was a brigadier general. After the war, as a permanent officer in the Royal Air Force (RAF), he saw further active service in Iraq in the mid-1920s. From 1930–1936, he was air member for research and development, and was knighted in 1933. From 1936, he was air officer commander in chief, Fighter Command. There he played a major role in preparing Britain's air defenses.

In April 1939, Dowding went to Chartwell to discuss various air defense experiments with Churchill, a visit authorized by Kingsley Wood. Churchill also visited Fighter Command at Stanmore, where Dowding explained the control system. Churchill admired Dowding's stance during the Battle of France. Dowding repeatedly made it clear that he was strongly opposed to even one more fighter plane going to France if the RAF was to help the Royal Navy prevent a German invasion of Britain.

However, Dowding (nicknamed "Stuffy") was not so admired by several other senior figures. Sir Archibald Sinclair had wanted to retire Dowding four months before the Battle of Britain began. Churchill resisted this, writing to Sinclair to say that Dowding was one of the best men in the RAF and had his "full confidence." Dowding proved a strong and determined figure in command at Fighter Command during the Battle of Britain, and Churchill greatly admired his role.

Sinclair and his senior advisers still pressed hard for Dowding to retire. In November 1940, Churchill asked Dowding to take the leadership of a mission on war aviation to the United States. Dowding reluctantly agreed. In June and October 1941, he sought to appoint Dowding to important roles, but on both occasions Sinclair successfully opposed such moves. When in April 1941 the Air Ministry issued a booklet, *The Battle of Britain,* that omitted all mention of Dowding, Churchill complained to Sinclair of the "jealousies and cliquism" in the Air Ministry that had led to such a discreditable action. Churchill insisted Dowding take a post that involved inspecting the running of RAF establishments. Dowding and the Air Ministry continued to argue and, at his own request, Dowding retired in July 1942. In 1943 he was raised to the peerage as Baron Dowding of Bentley Priory. Dowding died on 15 February 1970.

Related entries:
Harris, Air Chief Marshal Sir Arthur Travers; Portal, Air Marshal Sir Charles

Suggestions for further reading:
Gilbert, Martin. 1983. *Winston S. Churchill.* Vol. 6. London: Heinemann.
Wright, Robert. 1969. *The Man Who Won the Battle of Britain.* New York: Scribner.

E

Eden, Sir (Robert) Anthony (Earl of Avon, 1897–1977)

Churchill and Anthony Eden had more of a love than a love-hate relationship, mostly admiring, but sometimes the relationship was one of exasperation with each other. Churchill saw Eden as his successor from early on in his first premiership. To Eden's chagrin, the succession proved elusive because Churchill, like William Gladstone earlier, went on and on. Eden and Churchill complemented each other, Eden being less successful when Churchill had gone.

Robert Anthony Eden was born at Windlestone Hall, near Bishop Auckland, on 12 June 1897, the fourth of five children of Sir William and Sybil Frances Eden. His father was the seventh baronet, a substantial landowner. His mother was the daughter of Sir William Grey and great niece of Earl Grey, prime minister, 1830–1834; Sir Edward Grey was a distant cousin. Educated at Sandroyd, near Cobham, Surrey, and Eton, Eden enlisted in the King's Royal Rifle Corps in September 1915. He served on the Western Front, including at Ploegsteert Wood, not long after Churchill had left. Eden was awarded the Military Cross for outstanding leadership and courage. In 1918, at only twenty, he was made brigade major. Two of his brothers were killed in action. From 1919–1922, he studied Oriental languages at Oxford, gaining first class honors. His time there was also notable for his enthusiasm for art and interest in Conservative politics.

In the 1922 general election, Eden ran for Spennymoor, County Durham, a strong Labour seat. In the 1923 general election, he stood for the safe Conservative seat of Warwick and Leamington, which he held until he entered the House of Lords. In October 1924, he became parliamentary private secretary to Godfrey Locker Lampson, the under secretary of state at the home office, 1924–1925, and from 1926 to 1929 he was parliamentary secretary to Sir Austen Chamberlain, the foreign secretary. With the formation of the National government in 1931, Eden was under secretary of state for the foreign office until the end of 1933, when he was promoted to lord privy seal (outside the cabinet), but he still had foreign office responsibilities. With the return of Stanley Baldwin as prime minister in June 1935, he entered the cabinet as minister without portfolio, but with responsibility for League of Nations affairs. On the resignation of Sir Samuel Hoare in December 1935, Eden achieved his early ambition of becoming foreign secretary.

Eden had viewed Churchill with disdain from the time of Gallipoli until the early 1930s. He had been critical of Churchill's

British politicians Winston Churchill and Anthony Eden on their way to the houses of Parliament during the war crisis, 29 August 1939 (Hulton/Archive)

appointment as chancellor of the exchequer in 1924 and had deplored his stance on India. Eden admired and supported Baldwin. In the early 1930s, Eden at first misjudged Adolf Hitler, deluded briefly by the camaraderie of those who had experienced trench warfare; whereas Churchill was quick to recognize the menace of Hitler but was warmer for a while toward Benito Mussolini and General Francisco Franco. Eden's resignation from the foreign office in 1938 had much to do with Neville Chamberlain's interference in foreign affairs and more to do with Mussolini than with Hitler.

Churchill had initially viewed Eden as a lightweight as foreign secretary, although he had praised his speeches on foreign affairs as early as March 1926. After Eden re-

signed on 20 February 1938, Churchill wrote to him urging that he should speak up for Britain's interests, unfettered by loyalty to his former colleagues. For a year, Eden's supporters were a separate, dissatisfied group from Churchill's circle, but with the German occupation of Czechoslovakia in March 1939, they came increasingly together.

With the outbreak of war, Churchill demanded that Eden be given office as well as himself. He went to the admiralty, with a seat in the war cabinet, while Eden became dominions secretary, a post outside the war cabinet. Churchill came to the fore in war, whereas in April 1939, an early opinion poll had shown Eden as by far the most popular choice to succeed Chamberlain. Churchill unsuccessfully pressed Chamberlain to make Eden secretary of state for war. He gave Eden that post when he became prime minister, but he remained outside the war cabinet. On 22 December 1940, he made Eden foreign secretary and a member of the war cabinet.

At the time many in high politics felt Churchill would not last long as prime minister. During the first six months of this premiership, Eden and Churchill's admiration for each other grew. Churchill, dissatisfied with General Archibald Wavell, even suggested that Eden should become commander in the Middle East, an offer Eden firmly declined. Although Eden was on occasion critical of Churchill, he rebuffed those who wished to oust Churchill in his favor. When Churchill was going to the United States in June 1942, he left King George VI a letter in which he recommended that Eden should succeed him if anything happened to him. Yet they did clash on various issues, from the effectiveness of Wavell to recognition of Charles de Gaulle and the Free French. In mid-1943, Churchill offered Eden the viceroyalty of India, but Eden, still determined to be prime minister, declined.

After 1945, Eden waited patiently, at least initially, for the succession to Churchill. He supported Ernest Bevin's foreign policy for the most part and was unenthusiastic about Churchill's Fulton speech of March 1946. With Churchill's return to office, Eden became foreign secretary again. Eden's first marriage broke down in 1946, following the death of his son Simon in Burma in June 1945. In August 1952, he married Clarissa Churchill, Winston Churchill's niece. He was ill with gallstones in 1953 and Churchill, who suffered a major stroke, stayed on until Eden had recovered. By 1954, Eden was exasperated by Churchill's refusal to retire. Eden received a knighthood in 1954.

Sir Anthony Eden succeeded Churchill as prime minister on 6 April 1955. By this time, Churchill often expressed doubts about his long-nominated political heir. Eden's government was not a success, being wrecked in the area of his expertise, foreign affairs. The invasion of the Suez Canal area was an international political disaster. Eden's health collapsed and he resigned on 9 January 1957, also leaving the House of Commons.

Eden accepted an earldom in mid-1961, becoming the earl of Avon. He died on 14 January 1977.

Related entries:
Appeasement; Churchill, Clarissa; Hoare, Sir Samuel John Gurney; Macmillan, (Maurice) Harold

Suggestions for further reading:
Barker, Elizabeth. 1978. *Churchill and Eden at War.* London: Macmillan.
Blake, Lord. 1986. "Eden (Robert) Anthony." In *The Dictionary of National Biography: 1971–1980,* edited by Lord Blake and C. S. Nicholls. Oxford: Oxford University Press.
Carlton, David. 1981. *Anthony Eden: A Biography.* London: Allen Lane.
Gilbert, Martin. 1976, 1983, 1986, and 1988. *Winston S. Churchill.* Vols. 5–8. London: Heinemann.
Rhodes James, Robert. 1986. *Anthony Eden.* London: Macmillan.

Education Act (1944)

When Churchill appointed R. A. Butler as his president of the Board of Education, he knew he was appointing an able and ambitious Tory reformer who would wish to make changes. However, he was surprised by the speed with which Butler took up reform and the scale of his proposals, given the exigencies of war. Nevertheless, when it came to the crunch, Churchill made supporting Butler and his bill a matter of confidence for his government.

The 1944 Education Act ("Butler's Education Act") was one of the major pieces of education legislation in British history. It divided primary and secondary education at eleven, with the eleven-plus exam as arbiter. Secondary education was provided by secondary modern schools, grammar schools, and technical colleges. The school-leaving age was raised to fifteen from 1947 and provision was made for a further rise to sixteen. Under the act, the president of the Board of Education was renamed the minister for education.

Within a month of his appointment as president of the Board of Education on 20 July 1941, Butler began sounding out opinions on an educational reform measure. When Butler wrote to Churchill on 12 September 1941 raising "the need for industrial and technical training and the linking up of schools with employment," "a settlement with the Churches about Church school and religious instruction in schools," and "the question of the public schools," Churchill, not surprisingly, took alarm at the probability of resurrecting again the degree of political controversy aroused in 1902 by Arthur Balfour's Education Bill. He objected to the second and third of Butler's issues. "We cannot have any party politics in war time," he told Butler.

Butler, with care, nevertheless moved ahead, aided by his under secretary, the Labour politician James Chuter-Ede. Butler secured support from the Anglicans and Nonconformists, but not from the Catholics. When Cardinal Arthur Hinsley made this clear in a letter to the *Times,* 2 November 1942, Churchill phoned Butler, complaining, "You are landing me in the biggest political row of a generation." Butler continued to make progress with his bill, and on 11 March 1943 went to Churchill's residence, Chequers, to advise Churchill on the education part of the king's speech (which outlined his government's policy for Parliament). The White Paper titled *Educational Reconstruction,* published on 16 July 1943, set out the features of the intended legislation. The Education Bill was given its first reading on 15 December 1943 and its second reading on 19 and 20 January 1944.

The upset with the bill came on 28 March 1944 when Thelma Cazalet-Keir moved an amendment to the 82d of 111 clauses, calling for equal pay for male and female teachers. Her amendment was carried by 117 to 116 votes. That evening, Butler was summoned to 10 Downing Street to see Churchill, who was in a truculent mood and determined to use this issue to bring backbenchers to heel. Butler noted afterwards that Churchill "was sorry that the issue raised had been on equal pay for women, but the issue in these cases did not much matter and he proposed to rub their noses in it." Churchill succeeded in reversing the vote by 425 votes to 23.

However, as the *Economist* commented at the time, such exercise of his power as a popular war leader in crushing social reform did his image regarding domestic policy much harm.

Related entry:
Butler, Richard Austen ("Rab")

Suggestions for further reading:
Addison, Paul. 1992. *Churchill on the Home Front 1900–1955.* London: Cape.
Gilbert, Martin. 1986. *Winston S. Churchill.* Vol. 7. London: Heinemann.
Howard, Anthony. 1987. *RAB: The Life of R. A. Butler.* London: Cape.

Edward VII, King (1841–1910)

Winston Churchill was born into the British governing elite who knew the monarch. Lord and Lady Randolph Churchill had fallen out with the Prince of Wales in the 1870s, but their friendship with the prince was renewed from 1884. The prince was attracted by the beautiful and vivacious Lady Randolph. He took an interest in Winston Churchill's career, though found his Radical politics of 1904–1910 distasteful. In 1907, the king wrote to his eldest son, "As for Mr. Churchill he is *almost more* of a cad in office than he was in opposition."

Albert Edward was born on 9 November 1841 at Buckingham Palace, the second child of Queen Victoria and her consort, Prince Albert. As the eldest son, he was given the title of Prince of Wales, on 4 December 1841. Brought up to emulate his intellectual and ascetic father, he rebelled. He enjoyed society and public adulation, and preferred dances, dinners, race meetings, and shooting parties to intellectual pleasures; he also scandalized his parents by his sexual exploits.

At last succeeding his mother on 22 January 1901, he became a wiser king than his mother had feared. He had prepared himself for the accession by playing a major part in organizing the royal pageants of Queen Victoria's Golden and Diamond Jubilees (1887 and 1897) and by taking on many public appearances during the 1890s. As king, he took a major interest in Anglo-French relations, himself being a notable Francophile. He distrusted his nephew, Kaiser Wilhelm II of Germany; the kaiser in turn despised his uncle, whom he referred to as "that vain old peacock."

As Prince of Wales, Edward had taken an interest in Winston Churchill. He had enquired after his health in 1886, when as a boy he had had pneumonia. He had taken an interest in Winston Churchill's military career, being a friend of Lady Randolph Churchill. He enjoyed *The Malakand Field Force,* and wrote to Churchill, "I have read it with the greatest possible interest, and I think the descriptions and language generally excellent." However, he wrote to Churchill to make clear his opposition to serving officers' writing about campaigns for newspapers, but was less opposed to a military history (but "not with military criticism"). The prince invited Churchill to visit him in London and, in October 1898, Churchill dined at Marlborough House.

King Edward's sympathies were usually very much with the Conservatives. He was often outraged by Winston Churchill's radical speeches, and was much angered by Churchill's denunciation of Lord Milner over his role in South Africa. He was also anxious about the Liberal government's plans for South Africa. He wrote to Churchill deploring the prospect "of losing this Colony where we have spent so much blood and money." He added to the first draft of the letter that he was "glad to see that you are becoming a *reliable* minister and above all a serious politician, *which can only be attained by putting country before party.*" The king was predictably outraged by Churchill's speeches in favor of "People's Budget" and against the House of Lords.

The king was also critical of Churchill during his phase of speaking up for peace and reconciliation in international affairs. The king deplored Churchill's speech at a miners' rally in Swansea on 17 August 1908 in which he criticized those who said "that war between Britain and Germany is inevitable." He complained to Sir Edward Grey, the foreign secretary, of such interventions in foreign affairs by both David Lloyd George and Churchill. The king died before Churchill became first lord of the admiralty in 1911 but he had noted the interest that Churchill and Admiral Sir John Fisher had in each other. He wrote from Biarritz in 1907, "Sir J. Fisher and Winston Churchill arrived here a few days ago and they are most amusing together. I call them the 'chatterers.'" King Edward VII died at Buckingham Palace on 6 May 1910.

Related entries:
Churchill, Lady Randolph; Churchill, Lord Randolph Henry Spencer

Suggestions for further reading:
Churchill, Randolph S. 1966 and 1967. *Winston S. Churchill.* Vols. 1 and 2. London: Heinemann.
Lee, Sir Sidney. 1925 and 1927. *King Edward VII: A Biography.* 2 vols. London: Macmillan.
Magnus, Sir Philip. 1964. *King Edward VII.* London: Murray.
St. Aubyn, Giles. 1979. *Edward VII: Prince and King.* London: Collins.

Edward VIII (Duke of Windsor, 1894–1972)

From 1919 until Churchill's death, Prince Edward and Winston Churchill were usually friends. Churchill liked Edward as a person and also liked to be of service to a leading member of the royal family. As king, Edward turned to Churchill for advice during the abdication crisis, and Churchill went out on a political limb for him. During the Second World War, there was some friction between them because Churchill could not prioritize the duke's sensitivities about his and the duchess's status; but generally relations were good between them.

Edward Albert Christian George Andrew Patrick David, eldest child of the then duke and duchess of York (later King George V and Queen Mary), was born at White Lodge, Richmond Park, on 23 June 1894. He was good looking, energetic, and courageous, but not well read, although he was a good linguist, speaking fluent French, German, and Spanish. In 1910, at sixteen, he was created Prince of Wales. David Lloyd George stage-managed the investiture ceremony on 13 July 1911 at Carnarvon Castle, and Churchill, as home secretary, was responsible for providing extra police from the Metropolitan force. Following two years at Magdalen College, Oxford, the prince was commissioned in the Grenadier Guards. Barred from front-line action, he spent most of the war in France, much of it spent boosting the morale of British troops.

After the First World War, the prince made very successful overseas tours, including to Newfoundland, Canada, and the United States in 1919; New Zealand, Australia, Hawaii, and Fiji in 1920; and India, Nepal, Burma, Malaya, Hong Kong, Japan, the Philippines, Borneo, Ceylon, and Egypt in 1921–1922. He continued to tour overseas until his accession to the throne. He enjoyed steeplechasing and flying as well as dancing into the night. Like his grandfather, King Edward VII, he enjoyed several affairs with married women; but unlike his grandfather, he remained an eligible bachelor. His nemesis came when, after succeeding to the crown, he became determined to marry Wallis Simpson, who was married and had also ended a previous marriage.

The prince had admired Churchill before the First World War, noting in his diary in September 1913, "He is a wonderful man and has a great power of work," but had disliked him as a politician during the First World War. After the end of the war, Churchill and the prince had much contact and became friends. They shared a common interest in polo, and Churchill advised the prince on how to improve his public speaking. The prince sat in the peers' gallery in Parliament to listen to Churchill introducing his 1927 and 1928 budgets. The prince was also one of those who contributed in 1932 to the purchase of a Daimler car for Churchill after his recovery from being seriously injured by a car in New York. After Edward's accession to the throne, Churchill drafted two speeches for him.

During the abdication crisis in December 1936, Churchill was the politician the king wished to consult. Churchill's romantic side was moved by the king's plight; he was moved by Edward's love for Wallis Simpson and Churchill had exaggerated notions about serving the Crown. After the king had decided to abdicate, Churchill continued to advise him and did what he could to enable him "to live in this country quietly as a private gentleman."

However, this was not to be. Edward left Britain for France in the early hours of 12 December 1936, the same day on which King George VI conferred on him a dukedom. Six months later, he married Wallis Simpson, and they lived in France until the outbreak of war. During this period, Churchill corresponded with the duke. When Churchill stayed in the South of France in

January 1939, he dined several times with the duke and duchess of Windsor, including one occasion when Lloyd George was also present. On 19 January 1939, Churchill and the duke argued vigorously over Spain and Churchill's call for an alliance with the Soviet Union.

The duke of Windsor appeared too sympathetic to Nazi Germany, especially when he and the duchess visited Germany in October 1937. Ostensibly the visit was to study housing and working conditions; in reality it was intended to help improve Anglo-German relations. The duke delighted in the attention paid not only to him but to the duchess. Randolph Churchill accompanied the Windsors and Winston Churchill congratulated the duke on the success of his visit. However, the Nazis made much propaganda from it and aspired to reinstall him as king in a conquered or acquiescent Britain. The duke's planned follow-on tour of the United States had to be canceled because organized labor was outraged by his apparent endorsement of the Nazi smashing of the German labor movement.

After war was declared with Germany, the duke of Windsor wrote to Churchill asking him to send a naval vessel to collect him and his party from a French channel port. Churchill sent his son, Randolph, with the destroyer dispatched to Cherbourg to bring the Windsors to Portsmouth. Soon after, they returned to France, with the duke joining the British Military Mission in Paris. After the fall of France, the Windsors went to Madrid and then on to Lisbon. From there, on 27 June 1940, the duke sent a telegram to Churchill asking to return to Britain but stipulating that he and the duchess should be given status similar to that of other members of the royal family. Churchill in effect ordered him to return, pointing out that the duke had an active military rank. Instead of returning, at the suggestion of King George VI, he was offered the post of governor of the Bahamas.

This also had the advantage of distancing him from Nazi intrigues.

Churchill was anxious then and later that the duke should not visit the United States. In March 1941, he reprimanded the duke for giving an interview to the American magazine *Liberty* that could be interpreted "as defeatist and pro-Nazi." Churchill received reports of defeatist talk by the Windsors in 1940 and 1941, but by the autumn he heard that the duke was then "very robust on war and victory." In 1942, Churchill even feared a German U-boat raid on the Bahamas to seize the duke, and called for greater security. The duke resigned the governorship shortly before the end of a normal five-year term and the Windsors left the Bahamas in May 1945. Churchill, when leader of the Opposition in late 1945, supported the duke's attempt to secure an honorary post at the British embassy in Washington, D.C. The duke and duchess of Windsor spent most of the rest of their lives living in France.

After 1945, Churchill and the duke often corresponded. In September 1948, Winston and Clementine Churchill celebrated their fortieth wedding anniversary with the duke and duchess at their villa on Cap d'Antibes. Later that year, on New Year's Eve, Churchill gave a dinner in Paris for the Windsors. He also had lunch with the duke at Downing Street in May 1954. The duke and duchess were still nonpersons with the rest of the royal family and so were the only members of the royal family not to attend Churchill's state funeral.

The duke of Windsor died at his home near Paris on 28 May 1972 and was buried on 5 June in the royal mausoleum at Frogmore. The duchess of Windsor died also at their home near Paris on 24 April 1986 and was buried beside her husband.

Related entries:
Abdication Crisis; Monckton, Walter Turner

Suggestions for further reading:
Gilbert, Martin. 1975–1988. *Winston S. Churchill.* Vols. 4–8. London: Heinemann.

Windsor, Duke of. 1951. *A King's Story.* London: Cassell.

Ziegler, Philip. 1990. *King Edward VIII.* London: Collins.

Eisenhower, Dwight David (1890–1969)

Churchill and Eisenhower respected and liked each other during the Second World War. They usually worked well together in 1953–1955, as prime minister and president. Eisenhower wrote later of the Bermuda Conference, 1953, that it was "a sort of home-coming, a renewal of an old and close relationship."

Dwight D. Eisenhower was born at Denison, Texas, one of seven sons of poor Mennonite parents. After attending West Point military academy, he joined the infantry. He created the first tank corps of United States Army. After serving on General Douglas MacArthur's staff in the Philippines in 1939, he returned to the United States. After Pearl Harbor, he became deputy chief of the War Plans Division. In June 1942, he was appointed commanding general of the European Theatre of Operations. He commanded the Allied invasion of French North Africa, 1942–1943. By December 1943, he was Allied supreme commander in the Mediterranean and early in 1944 he became supreme commander of the Allied forces invading Normandy, with General Omar Bradley, General Bernard Montgomery, and General George Patton in command beneath him.

Churchill first met Eisenhower, albeit briefly, in Washington in December 1941 when he visited President Franklin D. Roosevelt. His first substantial meeting was on 21 June 1942, a few days before Eisenhower was made commander of all U.S. forces in Europe. Churchill later recalled that he was much impressed by Eisenhower then. Churchill had his disagreements on policy with Eisenhower but always backed him publicly and also with Roosevelt. In September 1944, for instance, he emphasized to Roosevelt that he had "complete confidence" in Eisenhower. He also praised Eisenhower to his colleagues, commenting to Eden at the end of the war in Europe that Eisenhower had been "splendid throughout."

Churchill stayed at Miami Beach in January 1946. While there, he read Harry C. Butcher's articles, which became the book *Three Years with Eisenhower* (1946). He wrote to Eisenhower condemning the pieces as trivial but apologizing for keeping Eisenhower up late at night on many occasions. He wrote again to Eisenhower on 6 February 1946 expressing his concern about international relations. After his famous Fulton speech, Churchill reiterated his theme of the need for Anglo-American unity in the face of communism on 8 March 1946 at the General Assembly of Virginia, with Eisenhower present. Eisenhower invited Churchill to speak again the next day to an informal gathering of senior officers held in the office of the secretary of state for war.

In December 1950, Eisenhower became supreme commander of NATO. Churchill warmly welcomed the appointment, declaring in the House of Commons that no one else could do the job as well. In September 1951, Churchill dined at the British embassy with Eisenhower and the British ambassador, Sir Oliver Harvey. He saw Eisenhower again on 15 February 1952, at King George VI's funeral. On 15 May, Winston and Clementine Churchill gave a dinner party at 10 Downing Street for the Eisenhowers, who were returning to the United States for the presidential elections. Eisenhower delighted Churchill with talk of the special relationship between the United States and Britain.

In January 1953, Churchill visited the United States. On the way, he told John Colville that Eisenhower's victory would cause him to omit from his books on the Second World War much of the material about the United States having yielded to

Dwight D. Eisenhower giving orders to American paratroopers in England, 6 June 1944 (Library of Congress)

Russia over parts of Europe at the end of the Second World War. Eisenhower visited him the day he arrived in New York. Churchill had feared that a Republican victory would make war with the Soviet Union more likely, but he was pleased to be able to deal with Eisenhower, to whom he sent a stream of letters beginning "My dear friend." On Churchill's eighty-first birthday, Eisenhower sent him a gold medallion on behalf of the United States.

In May 1959 Churchill made his last visit to the United States. He had lunch and dined with the president on 5 May, staying overnight; and he lunched with Eisenhower again the next day. He also went with the president to his farm at Gettysburg. Churchill presented Eisenhower with one of his paintings of Morocco. In September 1959, Churchill saw Eisenhower when he was in London. Eisenhower attended Churchill's funeral service in St. Paul's Cathedral in 1965. Eisenhower died in 1969.

Suggestions for further reading:
Boyle, Peter G. 1990. *The Churchill–Eisenhower Correspondence, 1953–1955.* Chapel Hill: University of North Carolina.
Eisenhower, D. D. 1948. *Crusade in Europe.* New York: Doubleday.
———. 1963. *Mandate for Change.* New York: Doubleday.
Gilbert, Martin. 1986 and 1988. *Winston S. Churchill.* Vols. 7 and 8. London: Heinemann.

Elgin, Ninth Earl of (1849–1917)

Winston Churchill's ministerial career began at the age of thirty-one as under secretary of state for the colonies under the ninth earl of Elgin. Churchill was able to shine not only because Elgin was in the House of Lords, leaving Churchill to speak for the ministry in the House of Commons, but also because Elgin was (as Churchill put it) "such an unassertive fellow."

Victor Alexander Bruce was born on 16 May 1849 at Monklands, near Montreal, Canada, the eldest son of James Bruce, the eighth earl of Elgin (1811–1863), and his second wife, Lady Mary Louisa Lambton, daughter of the first earl of Durham. His grandfather, the seventh earl (1762–1841) is best remembered for removing marble friezes from the Parthenon in Athens; the Elgin marbles are now housed in the British Museum. His father had been governor of Jamaica, governor general of Canada, envoy to China, and viceroy of India. Educated at Glenalmond, Eton, and Balliol College, Oxford, Victor Alexander Bruce managed the family estates in Dunfermline. He served in William Gladstone's third government (1886), latterly as first commissioner of works, and was nominated by Gladstone to be viceroy of India (1894–1899). His period in India was overshadowed by that of his successor, Lord Curzon. Yet he was judged by many contemporaries to have been able and industrious, a "safe pair of hands."

As a former viceroy of India, Elgin was a big imperial figure within the Liberal Party. Arthur Balfour's Conservative government nominated him to take the chair of the Royal Commission appointed in 1902 to report on the military preparations for the Boer War. He succeeded in securing a unanimous report, presented in July 1903. He chaired another Royal Commission, set up in December 1904 to solve a Scottish ecclesiastical crisis involving the free churches of Scotland and their property. The next year, he chaired the Statutory Executive Commission that carried out the main recommendations of the earlier Royal Commission, which was embodied in the Scottish Churches Act, 1905. He was much admired by the leading Scottish Liberals, including Sir Henry Campbell-Bannerman. On forming his government in December 1905, Campbell-Bannerman considered making Elgin foreign secretary, but in the end offered him the colonial secretaryship.

Elgin proved to be a sensible, if self-effacing, colonial secretary. He was notably cautious and was not favorable to the constitutional reforms for India proposed by John Morley, the secretary of state for India. Of the Elgin-Churchill relationship, historian Ronald Hyam has observed that for Churchill "it was the only one in his political career in which Churchill experienced a restraining hand from above." This perhaps underestimates the restraint David Lloyd George at times exercised on Churchill in 1917–1922, but nevertheless makes a good point.

Elgin was not included in Herbert Henry Asquith's government in 1908. He declined the offer of a marquisate and thereafter again concentrated on his estates and Scottish politics. He died on 18 January 1917 at his home, Broomhall, in Dunfermline, Fifeshire.

Related entries:
Campbell-Bannerman, Sir Henry; Colonies, Under Secretary of State for the

Suggestions for further reading:
Brown, Frank H. 1927. "Bruce, Victor Alexander Ninth Earl of Elgin and Thirteenth Earl of Kincardine, 1849–1917." In *Dictionary of National Biography 1912–1921,* edited by H. W. C. Davis and J. R. H. Weaver. Oxford: Oxford University Press.
Churchill, Randolph. 1967. *Winston S. Churchill.* Vol. 2. London: Heinemann.
Hyam, Ronald. 1968. *Elgin and Churchill at the Colonial Office, 1905–1908: The Watershed of the Empire-Commonwealth.* London: Macmillan.

Elizabeth II, Queen (1926–)

Churchill, always a monarchist, enjoyed the role of adviser to the attractive

Elizabeth II, Queen of England, with Prince Philip leaving 10 Downing Street in London after having dinner with Sir Winston Churchill, then British prime minister, and his wife, 5 April 1955 (Hulton/Archive)

young queen. By the time of his final government, he felt he had time to enjoy himself, spending much time advising the queen and the duke of Edinburgh. She apparently enjoyed his audiences—no doubt more in the style of Benjamin Disraeli than of William Gladstone—and when he retired predicted that no successor would "be able to hold the place of my first Prime Minister."

Elizabeth Alexandra Mary was born at 17 Bruton Street, London, on 21 April 1926, the elder daughter of the duke and duchess of York. Her mother, the former Lady Elizabeth Bowes-Lyon, was the youngest daughter of the fourteenth earl and countess of Strathmore. (Princess Elizabeth was born in her maternal grandparents' home.)

She became heir to the throne in December 1936 when her uncle, King Edward VIII, abdicated. When her father, King George VI, visited Dartmouth College in July 1939, Princess Elizabeth and Princess Margaret played croquet with several senior cadets, including Prince Philip of Greece, and later that day the king and queen entertained these cadets on the *Victoria and Albert*. Princess Elizabeth and Prince Philip later married, on 20 November 1947. Princess Elizabeth was made a counselor of state at eighteen. In December 1951, the king made both Princess Elizabeth and her husband, the duke of Edinburgh, privy counselors.

Churchill, always reflective about British history, noted, in a radio broadcast the day after King George VI's death, that Queen

Elizabeth II ascended the throne at the same age as had Queen Elizabeth I. He also commented that having spent his younger years during the great Victorian era, he was pleased again to invoke "God Save the Queen." Although he did not say it in his broadcast, he was ready to play the role of elder statesman to a young queen, just as Lord Melbourne (1779–1848) had to Queen Victoria.

In April 1953, Churchill accepted the queen's invitation to become a member of the Order of the Garter. He had declined the honor when it was offered by King George VI. He preferred to be known as Mr. Churchill and would have liked to have continued as such, as would Clementine Churchill. Having accepted, he became Sir Winston Churchill, adding KG to OM and CH (Order of Merit and Companion of Honour). He wore his Garter with pride at a precoronation dinner party on 31 May 1953. He and Clementine rode in a two-horse carriage in the coronation procession on 2 June 1953, and he introduced the queen's radio broadcast that evening.

Churchill arranged a dinner party at 10 Downing Street for the queen and the duke of Edinburgh on 4 April 1955, the day before he retired as prime minister. The other guests included Clement Attlee and Herbert Morrison and their wives, and Anne Chamberlain, the widow of Churchill's predecessor as Conservative Party leader. After his retirement, he saw the queen on many state occasions, such as the Armistice Day ceremony at the Cenotaph, and also more privately, as at a dinner at Buckingham Palace on 7 November 1957.

On Churchill's death, the queen sent a message to Parliament referring to "the life and example of a national hero" and stating that she had issued instructions "that Sir Winston's body shall lie in State in Westminster Hall" and that the funeral service should be held in St. Paul's Cathedral. The queen and the royal family attended the state funeral on 30 January 1965. They stood in tribute as Churchill's coffin left the cathedral for its final journey to Bladon churchyard.

Related entries:
Edward VIII; George VI, King

Suggestions for further reading:
Gilbert, Martin. 1988. *Winston S. Churchill*. Vol. 8. London: Heinemann.
Lacy, R. 1977. *Majesty: Elizabeth II and the House of Windsor*. London: Hutchinson.
Wheeler-Bennett, John W. 1958. *King George VI: His Life and Reign*. London: Macmillan.
Ziegler, Philip. 1993. "Churchill and the Monarchy." In *Churchill,* edited by R. Blake and W. R. Louis. Oxford: Oxford University Press.

Everest, Mrs. Elizabeth Ann (1833–1895)

Mrs. Elizabeth Ann Everest was employed as the children's nurse for Winston and his younger brother, Jack, from 1875. Born in Chatham, Kent, she had earlier worked as a children's nurse looking after a young girl, Ella, for the Reverend Thompson Phillips of Carlisle. She was Winston's closest emotional support for the first twenty years of his life.

The young Winston spent far more time with his nanny, Mrs. Everest, than he did with his mother. He was an affectionate boy who sought love and reassurance. This he frequently demanded, often to no avail, from his mother. When he was ill, it was usually Mrs. Everest who sat with him. This was not unusual among the better-to-do families of the time. During the 1880s, he and his brother occasionally went with Mrs. Everest to Ventnor on the Isle of Wight. In July–August 1888 and January 1889, he and Jack stayed at 2 Verona Cottages, the home of Mrs. Everest's sister, Mrs. Balaam (the wife of a senior warder at Parkhurst Prison).

Mrs. Everest taught the young Winston reading, writing, and basic mathematics from the time he was a child in Dublin (1877–1880) until he went to St. George's School, Ascot, at the age of seven in autumn 1882. She also influenced his religious views, bringing him up in sympathy with Low Anglican views. He revolted against High Church ritual when the school attended services in the Chapel Royal, an occasion he recalled in some detail in 1930 in his account of his early life.

Mrs. Everest was housekeeper at 50 Grosvenor Square when Lord and Lady Churchill lived with the dowager duchess of Marlborough from 1892. Winston was very upset when his grandmother dismissed Mrs. Everest the next year. Mrs. Everest returned to work for her previous employer, Archdeacon Phillips of Barrow-in-Furness. Lord Randolph Churchill provided her with a small remittance, and Winston sent her money in March 1895.

Mrs. Everest died from peritonitis on 3 July 1895, at the age of sixty-two. Winston Churchill rushed to be at her side in North London when he learned of her critical condition, and engaged a nurse to look after her. He and his brother, Jack, attended her funeral on 5 July, as did Archdeacon Phillips. Winston Churchill paid for a headstone for her grave in the City of London Cemetery, Manor Park, and for the grave's upkeep thereafter.

Suggestions for further reading:
Churchill, Randolph S. 1966 and 1969. *Winston S. Churchill.* Vol. 1, and companion vol. 2, part 1. London: Heinemann.
Churchill, Winston S. 1930. *My Early Life.* London: Odhams.
Sandys, Celia. 1994. *From Winston with Love and Kisses: The Young Churchill.* London: Sinclair-Stevenson.

Farouk, King (1920–1965)

King Farouk of Egypt was pro-Italian during the early part of the Second World War, but Churchill's government succeeded in pressing him to dismiss his pro-Italian ministers in 1941. However, he appointed anti-British ministers from 1944 and, as his government was notably corrupt and he was famous for a profligate lifestyle, Churchill and his colleagues were not sorry when he was ousted in 1952.

Farouk succeeded his father, King Fuad I, in 1936. He was the grandson of Khedive Ismail, who sold the Suez Canal shares to Britain in 1875. Farouk was educated in England. His reign began with a Regency Council, headed by the Wafd leader, Nahas Pasha (the Wafd being the main nationalist party). On reaching eighteen, Farouk dismissed Nahas Pasha and his government and tried to bring about land and other economic reforms. Such measures failed, largely because of widespread corruption. In 1941, the British brought about the dismissal of Farouk's pro-Italian ministers and the return of Nahas Pasha and the Wafd. Churchill visited Farouk when he was in Egypt, notably on 8 December 1943 during the Cairo Conference.

Farouk ousted Nahas Pasha and the Wafd again in 1944 and, thereafter, until he was himself overthrown in 1952, appointed a series of anti-British ministries. When, at Yalta

in early 1945, Churchill spoke of elections taking place in Farouk's Egypt, Stalin was not impressed and commented on "a great deal of corruption there." In February 1945, Churchill expressed his dismay to Farouk at the lack of real democracy in Egypt.

When Churchill returned to office in 1951, his government was faced with terrorist activities against British troops in the Canal Zone. By the end of the year, Anthony Eden was contemplating trying to organize joint Anglo-French and U.S. action against Alexandria and Cairo. In July 1952, the Egyptian army under General Mohammed Neguib and Colonel Gamal Nasser marched on Cairo to oust Farouk, who was considered inefficient, corrupt, and profligate. Mohammed Neguib became the first president of the Egyptian Republic (1953–1954). Farouk went into exile in Italy.

Suggestion for further reading:
Gilbert, Martin. 1986 and 1988. *Winston S. Churchill*. Vols. 7 and 8. London: Heinemann.

Fisher, John Arbuthnot (Admiral Lord Fisher of Kilverstone, 1841–1920)

Viewed by many as the greatest British admiral since Lord Horatio

Nelson (1758–1805), Fisher was a major naval reformer and was much admired as such by Winston Churchill. However, Fisher's spectacular resignation as first lord of the admiralty in 1915 contributed to the stalling of Churchill's career.

Fisher was born in Ceylon on 25 January 1841, the son of Captain William Fisher, of the 78th Highlanders and aide-de-camp to the governor of Ceylon, and his wife the former Sophie Lambe. Captain Fisher left the army in 1841 to become a coffee plantation owner; but when his crops were ruined by disease, he became inspector general of the Ceylon Police. Jack (as he was known) was sent back to England at the age of six and lived with his maternal grandfather, Alfred Lambe, a London vintner. He joined the navy in July 1854 as a naval cadet. He went on to serve in the Crimean War in 1855, the China War 1859–1860, and in the Egyptian naval action of 1882. After various commands and serving as third and second sea lord, Fisher became first sea lord twice, in 1904–1910 and 1914–1915. Fisher distinguished himself by the energy and enthusiasm with which he modernized and generally made the navy more efficient. He ruthlessly pushed opposition aside and his efforts as a great naval reformer in 1904–1910 were greatly assisted by the support given to him by King Edward VII. However, Fisher's major drawbacks included his vanity and his inability to end a feud with Lord Charles Beresford, which divided the navy.

Winston Churchill first met Fisher in early April 1907 when both joined King Edward VII at Biarritz. They greatly enjoyed each other's company, and the king wrote at the time that "they are most amusing together. I call them the 'chatterers.'" Fisher was soon sending Churchill confidential documents (as he did to others).

Churchill, like so many others, was charmed and fascinated by the charismatic first sea lord. In an excellent short portrait of Fisher in his *The World Crisis* (1923),

Churchill gave the verdict that Fisher had been right nine out of ten times in his fights. He also took the view that Fisher "was maddened" by the obstructionism he faced in achieving reforms; this, Churchill thought, made Fisher combative in dealing with his fellow officers and others.

Churchill supported Fisher against Beresford. In mid-January 1908, Churchill and Fisher spent two hours together over lunch in the Ritz, with an enthusiastic Churchill promising to secure cross-party support for Fisher from several M.P.s, including F. E. Smith.

During the naval scare of 1909–1910, when there were fears of a rapid acceleration of German building of battleships, Churchill was with David Lloyd George in resisting admiralty demands for six British Dreadnoughts to be built. Fisher, with the support of the first lord of the admiralty, demanded six. This led to a temporary breach in their old friendship, although Fisher displayed humor in suggesting in a private letter to Churchill in March 1909 that the four extra Dreadnoughts should be named "Winston," "Churchill," "Lloyd," and "George," adding, "How they would fight!" The political crisis was solved by Herbert Henry Asquith's compromise of four ships in 1909–1910 and four more at the beginning of 1910–1911. With hindsight, Churchill felt that although he and Lloyd George had been right in doubting an acceleration of German Dreadnought building then, in the longer run, the British navy did benefit in the First World War from the extra Dreadnoughts.

After Fisher resigned as first sea lord on 25 January 1910, Churchill told Fisher that he regretted he (Churchill) had not pushed to be first lord of the admiralty in 1908 because then he could have backed Fisher in further naval reforms and defended him from his enemies. Churchill's arrival as first lord of the admiralty on 25 October 1911 ensured Fisher a warm welcome at the admiralty and enhanced influence on naval matters in his retirement. Although Churchill did not reinstate Fisher as first sea lord, he made him his main unofficial adviser and their friendship resumed after a two-year interval. Fisher, not wishing to undermine his successors as first, second, and third sea lords, wisely stayed in continental Europe, frequently writing Churchill long letters; but he did promise Churchill that he would return to Britain should an emergency occur.

Fisher provided Churchill with invaluable advice between 1911 and the outbreak of the First World War. Fisher was Churchill's provider of ideas for a series of important changes and reforms. These included building a class of fast battleships and bigger Dreadnoughts with bigger guns, arming merchant ships and providing naval aircraft, and creating a naval war staff in January 1912. Churchill also improved pay and conditions in the navy. He also speeded up the navy's changeover from coal to oil. In this he was assisted by Fisher's agreeing to chair the Royal Commission on Fuel Oil, the consequences of which included the British government buying and controlling shares in the Anglo-Persian Oil Company in August 1914. In 1959, Churchill contributed a brief letter as a foreword to Henry Longhurst's *Adventure in Oil: The Story of British Petroleum* (London: Sidgwick and Jackson, 1959), in which he recalled his close association with the British oil industry in 1913–1914.

Fisher replaced Prince Louis of Battenberg as first sea lord on 24 November 1914. Although seventy-three at the beginning of his second tenure, Fisher remained an energetic and dynamic force. He returned to the admiralty to take the lead in a war with Germany such as he had predicted in 1910. Like Lord Kitchener, he expected the war to be lengthy. Churchill gave Fisher the political backing he needed to get on effectively with his job and the two worked well together at first. Fisher pushed hard for the construction of the maximum possible number of ships, some 612 being arranged on 3 November 1914. Later, Churchill in *The World Crisis* paid tribute to the value of these ships when, from 1916 onward, losses from German U-boats became serious. Fisher also displayed energy and determination in dispatching without delay the necessary reinforcements for Admiral Sturdee to crush Admiral von Spee's squadron at the Battle of the Falklands, 8 December 1914.

However, Churchill and Fisher were to differ over bold plans to make use of Britain's naval supremacy. Fisher developed a grand obsession with his "Baltic Scheme" to use British naval power to land a Russian army on the Pomeranian coast. At the time and subsequently, Fisher's project was condemned as rash, even mad. The prime minister, Asquith, had Fisher's paper outlining the scheme suppressed.

Fisher was always more keen on naval initiatives against Germany than against Turkey. On 15 January 1915, the war council authorized Churchill to attack at the Dardanelles and Fisher was fully involved in the ensuing planning. However, within days, Fisher was expressing his unhappiness to others, complaining to Hankey of Churchill that "he out-argues me." Fisher was especially concerned that the battleship *Queen Elizabeth,* some battle cruisers, and submarines were to be deployed at the Dardanelles, not in the North Sea, nor would they be available if he could get his way on a Baltic campaign. In a memorandum of 25 January 1915, Fisher emphasized that dispersing major ships to the Dardanelles or elsewhere risked British naval superiority in the North Sea. Asquith refused to allow Fisher's memorandum or Churchill's response to be printed and circulated to the war council.

Fisher wrote Asquith a strong letter on 28 January in which he stated of the Dardanelles and Zeebrugge: "As purely naval operations they are unjustifiable, as they both drain our naval margin." He sent a letter of resignation to Churchill. Asquith and

Churchill saw Fisher and agreed to drop the Zeebrugge action but to continue with the Dardanelles campaign. At the war council meeting that day (28 January), Kitchener persuaded Fisher not to resign. After the meeting, Churchill saw Fisher for more than an hour and secured Fisher's support for the Dardanelles operation. Fisher later observed at the time of the Dardanelles Commission, "The attempt to force the Dardanelles, though a failure, would not have been disastrous so long as the ships employed could be withdrawn at any moment, and only such vessels were engaged, as in the beginning of the operations was in fact the case, as could be spared without detriment to the general service of the Fleet."

Fisher remained doubtful about the Dardanelles operation. On 4 March 1915 he wrote to Churchill, "The more I consider the Dardanelles, the less I like it." By the middle of the month he was informing Churchill of the need for greater speed in getting troops there. After the naval setback of 18 March, Fisher, like Churchill, saw no reason to call off the naval attack and ordered more battleships to reinforce Admiral John Michael de Robeck's fleet. However, on 23 March, when de Robeck and General Sir Ian Hamilton, the commanders on the spot, recommended suspending the naval action until military forces were available, Fisher agreed with them, although Churchill was determined there should be a second naval attack. When his senior advisers all were against him, Churchill considered resigning but did not do so. Fisher objected strongly to his continuing to pressure de Robeck to attack again and even threatened to resign. However, by 27 March, de Robeck was emphatic that further action in the Dardanelles must be a combined naval and military operation.

By this time, Fisher was more concerned about the possibility of a German invasion of the Netherlands, a fear that reinforced his fundamental concern about naval strength in home waters. In April 1915, Fisher made several attempts to avoid sending further naval reinforcements to the Dardanelles, much to Churchill's chagrin. In May, Churchill wanted limited naval action to clear mines and to advance to the Narrows, but again his proposals for action in the Dardanelles brought him into conflict with Fisher, who was against any action by the navy on its own. Fisher again threatened resignation, and on 11 May prepared a memorandum with Hankey in which Churchill was warned that if there was "purely Naval action, unsupported by the Army" it would "lead to heavy loss of ships and invaluable men." Asquith soothed Fisher with a promise that "separate naval action would not be taken without F's concurrence" and Churchill agreed to withdraw the *Queen Elizabeth,* although its withdrawal outraged Kitchener.

Fisher, feeling he was secure with Asquith's support, became more insistent in his opposition to providing naval resources for the Dardanelles. At the war council on 14 May, Kitchener complained of lack of admiralty support and, to Churchill's wrath, Fisher declared that "he had been against the Dardanelles operations from the beginning." Churchill saw Fisher for several hours later that day and left feeling they had reached acceptable compromises over their concerns.

However, Churchill's further request for more submarines to go to the Dardanelles was the last straw for Fisher. As Fisher's naval assistant, Captain Thomas Crease put it, Fisher became convinced "that there was no finality about any agreement reached with Mr. Churchill on the subject of the Dardanelles reinforcements." If Churchill was obsessed with the Dardanelles, then Fisher was equally obsessed with his Baltic scheme as well as anxious about depleting British naval supremacy in the North Sea. Fisher also had an unrealistic view of his own indispensability, wrongly feeling that Asquith would give him a veto on naval policy.

On 15 May, Fisher carried out his often-made threat of resigning. In spite of pleas from Lloyd George, Asquith, and Churchill not to do so, Fisher insisted he would resign. Churchill found on 16 May that the other sea lords were willing to continue and that Admiral Sir Arthur Knyvet Wilson was willing to succeed Fisher. However, the Conservative leader, Andrew Bonar Law, approached Lloyd George about Conservative Party disquiet about aspects of the conduct of the war and its requirement that Churchill should leave the admiralty if Fisher resigned. Lloyd George saw Asquith, who promptly agreed to the formation of a coalition government. In this, Churchill was marginalized as chancellor of the Duchy of Lancaster.

On 19 May, Fisher wrote to Asquith making an extraordinary set of demands as his conditions for his return to the admiralty. These included banning Churchill from the cabinet, vetoing Arthur Balfour as his successor, the removal of Admiral Wilson and the whole board of the admiralty and the giving to him "complete professional charge of the war at sea." Fisher's demands merely confirmed the views of the prime minister and Sir Maurice Hankey, secretary of the Committee of Imperial Defence, that Fisher was suffering from megalomania or was "unhinged." Fisher's final official appointment was chairman of the admiralty Official Inventions Board, 1915–1916. Churchill only learned of Fisher's demands twelve years later when Asquith was writing his autobiography and sent him a copy.

Fisher was critical of Churchill in his two volumes of recollections published in 1919, *Memories* and *Records*. In *Memories*, Fisher still condemned the prioritizing of the Dardanelles over the Baltic—"cutting off the enemy's big toe in the East" rather than "stabbing him to the heart in the West." Yet he paid Churchill the tribute,

"He had courage and imagination! He was a War Man!" Churchill provided his own assessments of Fisher (who died in 1920) in *The World Crisis,* vols. 1 and 2 (London: Thornton Butterworth, 1923), with excerpts from Captain Crease's notes on Fisher's resignation in 1915 being added as an appendix to the second edition (1931) of the second volume.

Churchill was taken aback by the criticisms made by Admiral Sir Reginald Bacon in *The Life of Lord Fisher of Kilverstone,* 2 vols. (London: Hodder and Stoughton, 1929), feeling that Bacon was continuing the "animosities and quarrels" that Fisher had pursued. Churchill felt especially aggrieved because he had nominated Bacon on three occasions to wartime posts. In responding to Bacon, Churchill reassessed Fisher in *Nash's Magazine,* April 1930, the London *News of the World,* 19 January 1936, and in a revised form as "Lord Fisher and His Biographer" in his *Great Contemporaries,* revised edition (London: Thornton Butterworth, 1938).

Churchill's relationship with "Jackie" Fisher was very mixed, with mutual great admiration and much disagreement and distrust. Their problem, in part, was that they held too many traits in common. They were both unusually energetic, opinionated, and egotistic, and they were both obsessed by their work. Fisher died on 10 July 1920.

Suggestions for further reading:
Bacon, Sir Reginald. 1929. *The Life of Lord Fisher of Kilverstone.* 2 vols. London: Hodder and Stoughton.
Churchill, Winston S. 1923. *The World Crisis.* Vols. 1 and 2. London: Thornton Butterworth.
———. 1938. *Great Contemporaries.* Rev. ed. London: Thornton Butterworth.
Fisher, John Arbuthnot. 1919. *Memories.* London: Hodder and Stoughton.
Hough, Richard. 1969. *First Sea Lord.* London: Allen and Unwin.
MacKay, Ruddock F. 1973. *Fisher of Kilverstone.* Oxford: Clarendon Press.
Marder, Arthur. 1952–1959. *Fear God and Dread Nought.* 3 vols. London: Cape.

———. 1961 and 1963. *From the Dreadnought to Scapa Flow.* Vols. 1 and 2. Oxford: Oxford University Press.

French, Sir John Denton Pinkstone (Earl of Ypres, 1852–1925)

Churchill and John French became friends when Churchill was first a cabinet minister in 1908. This friendship was reinforced by their difficult times in the early part of the First World War. They worked together again during the British military action in Ireland in 1919–1921.

John French was born on 28 September 1852 at Ripple, Kent, the only son and youngest of seven children of Commander John William Tracy and Margaret French. His father, an officer in the Royal Navy, died in 1854. His mother, the daughter of William Eccles, a prosperous Glasgow merchant, suffered a nervous breakdown and was committed to an asylum in 1860. He was brought up by his sisters, notably the eldest, Charlotte, who after marriage and becoming a widow, became a famous feminist and socialist as Charlotte Despard. He was educated at Eastman's Naval Academy, Portsmouth, and entered HMS *Britannia* in 1866, graduating as a midshipman. However, he desired a career in the army, and beginning in 1870 he served for four years with the Suffolk Artillery Militia. In 1874, he joined the regular army. He served with Sir Garnet Wolseley in the 1884 attempt to relieve Khartoum and General Charles Gordon. He served in India in 1889–1893. From 1895–1897 he was assistant adjutant general at the war office. He served in South Africa from September 1899 in charge of mounted troops, and he relieved Kimberley in February 1900. He was created KCB in 1900 and KCMG in 1902.

French emerged from the Boer War a national hero, unlike many of his military seniors. In 1912, he became chief of the Imperial General Staff, with the rank of field marshal from 1913. He resigned in March 1914, over the Curragh incident. He was recalled at the outbreak of the First World War to be commander of the British Expeditionary Force in France, a post he held until he resigned on 4 December 1915.

Churchill did not meet French until 1908. Earlier, at the time of the Boer War, French disapproved not only of Churchill's self-promotion and his role as a journalist but also of his support for General John Brabazon, an opponent of French. Churchill, when president of the Board of Trade, first met French at military maneuvers on Salisbury Plain and established good relations. Their mutual esteem was reinforced when they both served on the Committee of Imperial Defence before the First World War, with French often Churchill's guest on the admiralty yacht *Enchantress.* French also accompanied Churchill on his visits to many naval establishments in July 1914. After the Battles of Neuve-Chapelle, Festubert, and Loos in 1915, Churchill reinforced French's reluctance to be involved in a major autumn offensive. On the first night Churchill was in France as a serving officer, after resigning from ministerial office, French sent for him to have dinner with him at his headquarters. Churchill also joined him as his guest from 1–9 December 1915. French recommended that Churchill be promoted to brigadier general, but Herbert Henry Asquith vetoed it. French himself was dismissed, and Churchill joined French on 18 December 1915 for his last day in command.

In January 1916, French was elevated to the peerage as Viscount French of Ypres and of High Lake, County Roscommon, and made commander in chief of the Home Forces. In this role he reorganized home defenses, including against airships and airplanes. In May 1918, David Lloyd George appointed him lord lieutenant of Ireland. He and Churchill worked together during the British military campaign in Ireland until 30 April 1921, when French retired with the passing of the Government of Ireland Act, 1921. In June 1922, he was created earl of Ypres. French ended his life as captain of Deal Castle (1923–1925). He died on 22 May 1925.

Churchill kept in touch with French after his retirement. He borrowed his own letters to French of 1914–1915 when he wrote *The World Crisis*. Churchill wrote a tribute to French in the *Pall Mall,* January 1930, which was reprinted in *Great Contemporaries* (1937).

Suggestions for further reading:
Cassar, George H. 1985. *The Tragedy of Sir John French.* Newark: University of Delaware Press.
Churchill, Winston S. 1937. *Great Contemporaries.* London: Thornton Butterworth.
Holmes, Richard. 1981. *The Little Field Marshal.* London: Jonathan Cape.

Fulton Speech (5 March 1946)

Churchill gave one of his most famous speeches at Westminster College, Fulton, Missouri. In the speech, which was broadcast in the United States, he warned of communist expansionism and spoke of "an iron curtain" that had fallen across Europe.

Churchill had written to President Harry Truman in November 1945 informing him of his 1946 trip to the United States, Mexico, and Brazil, and stating that his only major speech would be at Fulton. Truman had expressed a hope that Churchill would speak in his home state.

Winston and Clementine Churchill traveled on the *Queen Elizabeth* on 9 January 1946. They stayed at Miami Beach, breaking their sojourn on 1 February, when they visited Cuba. While preparing his speech, Churchill informed Clement Attlee of its theme in a telegram on 17 February 1946. On 3 March, Churchill went to Washington, D.C., where he stayed in the British Embassy. Churchill showed his draft Fulton speech to Admiral William Leahy, James Byrnes (United States sectretary of state, 1945–1947), and, on 5 March, to Truman, all of whom liked it. At Westminster College, the president met them and they had lunch before Churchill spoke in the college gymnasium. After praising the Russian role in defeating Adolf Hitler, he complained of how Soviet control of Eastern Europe had led to political control from Moscow.

His speech led to much criticism in Britain, the United States, and the Soviet Union. Truman, although present when the lecture was given, distanced himself from it, claiming he did not know in advance what Churchill would say.

Later, Churchill's speech at Fulton was commemorated by a memorial and library at Westminster College. The memorial was founded in 1969, and is in the undercroft of the twelfth-century Church of St. Mary the Virgin, Aldermanbury, which was moved from the center of London to Fulton. World leaders have made speeches at Fulton in commemoration of Churchill's speech; notably Presidents George Bush (senior), Gerald Ford, and Ronald Reagan (U.S.), Mikhail Gorbachev (Soviet Union), and Lech Walensa (Poland), and also Prime Minister Margaret Thatcher (Britain).

Related entries:
Stalin, Joseph; Truman, Harry S.

Suggestions for further reading:
Gilbert, Martin. 1988. *Winston S. Churchill.* Vol. 8. London: Heinemann.
Muller, James W. *Churchill's "Iron Curtain" Speech Fifty Years Later.* Columbia: University of Missouri Press.

G

Gallipoli (1915–1916)

*T*he Allied invasion of the Gallipoli Peninsula in western Turkey was initially planned as a purely naval operation but became a military operation. Far from being a soft target, compared with the Western Front, Gallipoli became a bloodbath as Allied soldiers struggled to scale well-defended cliffs and to penetrate inland from their landing beaches. It also became marked by trench warfare, as both sides dug in. Admiral Lord Fisher's insistence on resignation in mid-May 1915 brought about Churchill's fall from major office and stalled his career.

The Gallipoli Peninsula dominates the northern side of the Dardanelles, the narrow sea route between the Mediterranean and the Sea of Marmora. The control of the Dardanelles affected not only a major route to Constantinople but also to the Black Sea and Russia. Turkey controlled the Dardanelles through its forts along the Gallipoli Peninsula and on the shores of Asia Minor on the southern side. Allied action in this area was expected to help Russia, both by opening up the area as a supplies route and by diverting some military pressure from the Russian armies. There were also expectations that success would lead to Turkey's leaving the war and the bringing in of Greece and Bulgaria on the Allied side.

From early in the war, Churchill considered taking action against the Turkish forts along the Dardanelles. The German battle cruiser *Goeben* and light cruiser *Breslau* evaded the navy in the Mediterranean and reached Constantinople. After the *Goeben* bombarded Odessa on 31 October 1914, Churchill ordered Vice Admiral Sackville Hamilton Carden, the commander of British naval forces in the eastern Mediterranean, to bombard, with two French battleships, the outer forts at the entrance of the Dardanelles. This was carried out on 3 November, with the fort at Sedd-el-Bahr being severely damaged. Churchill was subsequently criticized for warning the Turks of the need to improve the area's defenses; although, as Martin Gilbert has argued in his biography of Churchill, there was no need for a reminder, and the Turks did not undertake major additional fortification work in that area in the ensuing months.

After the bombardment of 3 November, Churchill and the sea lords began consideration of whether to use old battleships to force the Dardanelles. At the first meeting of the British government's war council on 25 November 1914, it was reported that a large Turkish army was moving toward the Suez Canal. Churchill was recorded in its minutes as suggesting "that the ideal method of defending Egypt was by an attack on the Gallipoli Peninsula." Later in November Churchill asked Lord Kitchener

British troops advance at Gallipoli, 6 August 1915. (Hulton/Archive)

to be prepared to provide transportation for soldiers from Egypt to the Dardanelles if necessary. Churchill was subsequently lulled into low expectations of the Turkish will to fight when the light cruiser *Doris* successfully destroyed railway lines and engines near Alexandretta, with the Turkish forces being successfully pressured into helping.

When, on 1 January 1915, Grand Duke Nicholas requested British action against Turkey to relieve the pressure on Russian forces of a Turkish attack in the Caucasus, Kitchener declared that he had no troops he could spare, but asked Churchill whether a

naval action in the Dardanelles could be carried out. Churchill took up some of Admiral Lord Fisher's ideas for a multinational combined attack on Turkey, those involving Britain's using old battleships (but disregarding Fisher's requirement for military action on Gallipoli). Carden felt that a gradual advance within the Dardanelles might work, but not one major assault, but other naval advisers were less confident. When Carden's detailed plan was discussed, Fisher proposed that the *Queen Elizabeth,* a new super-Dreadnought, be used to shell the forts from a safe distance. On 13 January, the war council decided that the navy should "bombard and take Gallipoli, with Constantinople as its objective."

Churchill himself, as Tuvia Ben-Moshe has argued, wanted action and realized that the war council would not support his other schemes (notably to take Borkum). Carden apart, the senior admiralty staff were lukewarm to a naval assault on the Dardanelles, many past appraisals of such an action being pessimistic of success. From 25 January, Fisher expressed concern, feeling it would deplete the strength of the navy in home waters and that for success it required the army to attack on land at the same time. At the war council on 28 January, Kitchener had to persuade Fisher not to leave the meeting over the issue of the Dardanelles. However, his doubts were known to most, if not all, those present. So, in spite of the widespread skepticism among the senior admiralty figures, the naval action went ahead with the support of the French minister of marine, Victor Augagneur, on 19 February.

The British fleet consisted of the *Queen Elizabeth,* three battle cruisers, twelve pre-Dreadnought battleships, four cruisers, eighteen destroyers, six submarines, twenty-one minesweeping trawlers, and the seaplane carrier *Ark Royal.* The main French contribution was four pre-Dreadnought battleships. On 25 February, they successfully shelled the outer forts but failed to demolish mobile batteries. Under Admiral John Michael de Robeck, an assault took place on the Narrows on 18 March. Two French battleships were sunk by mines and a third badly damaged by German howitzers, a British battleship and cruiser were badly damaged, later sinking, and a British battleship sank after an internal explosion. Fisher, with two further battleships en route for the Dardenelles, ordered two more to the area, and Augagneur sent another French battleship. Fisher argued that a loss of twelve battleships should be expected if the Dardanelles were to be forced open.

When de Robeck argued that they should wait until the military could attack before trying again to force the Straits, Churchill wanted to order him to attack before then but Fisher and others of the admiralty's war staff would not support this.

Before the beginning of the naval operation on 19 February, Churchill and Kitchener discussed the numbers of soldiers needed in the area after the navy had broken through the Dardanelles, with Churchill requesting the 29th Division be sent to the area. On 26 February, Churchill informed the war council that Carden was asking for troops to land on the western end of the Gallipoli Peninsula. Churchill, by this time, was contemplating landing 115,000 men to take the peninsula after 21 March should the naval attack fail. In early March, General Sir William Birdwood reported from the eastern Mediterranean to Kitchener that ground troops would be required. On 10 March, Kitchener informed the war council that he was sending the 29th Division to the area. After the failure of the naval assault on the Dardanelles on 18 March, planning for the military operations on Gallipoli were undertaken by the War Office, with the navy's role reduced to facilitating the landings. Fisher and others became more worried about a possible German occupation of the Netherlands and the need for maximum British naval power in the North Sea.

Although Fisher became more anxious about the Dardanelles, Churchill remained confident about safely landing troops on the Gallipoli Peninsula. When Kitchener argued that imperial prestige required a successful outcome, Asquith backed him and Churchill, in spite of the growing concern of Hankey and Arthur Balfour. British military forces under Sir Ian Hamilton landed on 25 April 1915, establishing beachheads at Helles and Gaba Tepe ("Anzac Cove").

By early May, with the troops on Gallipoli as static as those on the Western

Front, de Robeck raised again the issue of another naval attack. However, Fisher, concerned about the strength of the navy in the North Sea and about German submarines in the eastern Mediterranean, rejected further naval action and secured Asquith's support for his right as first sea lord to determine such matters. When Churchill continued to press for ever more reinforcements for the Dardanelles, Fisher tendered his resignation and left the admiralty building on 15 May 1915. This crisis over naval policy was a major contributor to Asquith's decision to form a coalition government. Churchill was a major loser in the change of government, leaving the admiralty for lesser office.

The Gallipoli campaign remained unsuccessful after Churchill left the admiralty. Turkish reinforcements arrived from Palestine and the Caucasus. Further landings at Suvla Bay on 6 August 1915 soon became as deadlocked as the earlier ones. With campaigns in France and Salonika receiving higher priority, large numbers of additional troops were not forthcoming. General Charles Monro (who succeeded Hamilton) recommended evacuation, a view supported on 15 November 1915 by Kitchener after visiting Gallipoli. On 7 December, the government ordered withdrawal from all three beachheads. Between 10–19 December, some 105,000 men, 5,000 animals, and 300 guns were removed from Anzac Cove and Suvla Bay; and between late December and 8–9 January 1916, some 35,000 troops and 3,700 animals were taken from Helles, all for the loss of three lives (but many munitions and supplies). Thereafter, the Allies blockaded the Mediterranean end of the Straits for the rest of the war.

The actions in the Dardanelles in February and March 1915 did succeed in forcing Turkey to divert troops from the Caucasus, thereby helping to prevent their planned April offensive against Russia. This was tangible assistance to Russia. It also delayed Bulgaria making a commitment to support the Central Powers. Otherwise, it was a dismal venture. Some 43,000 British and empire troops died, with some further 162,000 other casualties; and some 5,000 French and French Empire troops died, with some further 42,000 other casualties. The severe losses of Australian and New Zealand troops (33,600 casualties, of which a third died) left a bitter legacy in those countries.

After pressure in the House of Commons, Asquith agreed to set up a select committee (the Dardanelles Commission) to report on the conduct of the Dardanelles operations.

Related entries:
Dardanelles Commission; Fisher, John Arbuthnot; Hamilton, Sir Ian Standish Monteith; Kitchener, Horatio Herbert

Suggestions for further reading:
Ben-Moshe, Tuvia. 1992. *Churchill: Strategy and History.* Boulder, CO: Lynne Rienner.
Gilbert, Martin. 1971 and 1972. *Winston S. Churchill.* Vol. 3, and companion vols. 2 and 3. London: Heinemann.
Mackay, Ruddock F. 1973. *Fisher of Kilverstone.* Oxford: Clarendon Press.
Marder, Arthur. 1965. *From the Dreadnought to Scapa Flow.* Vol. 2. Oxford: Oxford University Press.
———. 1974. *From the Dardanelles to Oran.* Oxford: Clarendon Press.
———, ed. 1959. *Fear God and Dread Nought.* Vol. 3. London: Cape.
Prior, Robin. 1983. *Churchill's "World Crisis" as History.* London: Croom Helm.
Roskill, Stephen. 1977. *Churchill and the Admirals.* London: Collins.

The General Strike (1926)

The General Strike provided Churchill with the opportunity to do what he felt he did best: to be involved in operational decision making in a national emergency. In his eyes, the General Strike was a serious constitutional challenge against democracy and needed to be soundly defeated. His major part was in running the government's newsheet, the *British Gazette*. During the strike itself, he was a hawk, but with regard to the coal miners' dispute, which underpinned the strike, he took the view that it was a legitimate industrial struggle. Overall, his role in the General Strike reinforced the labor movement's distrust of him.

The General Strike, 1926, was a solidarity strike organized by the Trades Union Congress (TUC) in support of the coal miners. After the wartime and postwar boom years (1915–1921), when the industry had been government controlled, the price of coal tumbled and the industry was decontrolled in a hurry in 1921. When the mine owners required very substantial wage cuts and a bitter miners' lock-out ensued, the government reluctantly provided a subsidy. In 1925 when this situation was repeated, the government (under Stanley Baldwin) again provided a subsidy, which would end on 1 May 1926. In 1926, with the miners' union campaigning against wage cuts or longer working hours, the TUC supported the miners' search for alternatives, hoping, as one solution, that a further subsidy might be provided.

Baldwin, who feared Churchill might be heavy-handed in confronting the strikers in other roles, was pleased to put him in charge of preparing a government news sheet, given that the strike had closed down the national press. With volunteer labor, Churchill edited eight issues of the *British Gazette,* which began as two pages on 5 May and then on 6–8 and 10–13 May was a four-page publication, put out each day other than the Sunday. The first issue had a print run of 232,000, and the last two issues had print runs in the region of 2 million copies. In these endeavors, Churchill was assisted by J. C. Davidson, who, on Baldwin's behalf, curbed some of Churchill's excesses.

Churchill was also a prominent member of the government's strike-breaking body, the Supply and Transport Committee, which was chaired by the home secretary, William Joynson-Hicks, and ably organized by Sir John Anderson. Churchill unsuccessfully tried to press John Reith, the managing director of the BBC, into allowing the government to put its viewpoint on the radio.

After the General Strike was called off on 12 May, Churchill was an advocate of securing a moderate settlement with the miners. When his efforts failed, he was willing to restrict welfare help to miners and their families to force a speedier end to the dispute.

Related entries:
Anderson, Sir John; Baldwin, Stanley; Davidson, John Colin Campbell

Suggestions for further reading:
Gilbert, Martin. 1975. *Winston S. Churchill*. Vol.4. London: Heinemann.
Laybourn, Keith. 1996. *The General Strike 1926*. London: Arnold.
Morris, Margaret. 1976. *The General Strike*. Harmondsworth, UK: Penguin.
Phillips, Gordon. 1976. *The General Strike*. London: Weidenfeld and Nicolson.
Woods, Frederick. 1963. *A Bibliography of the Works of Sir Winston Churchill*. London: Nicholas Vane.

George V, King (1865–1936)

Churchill's relationship with King George V, "the Sailor King," was generally good. Although a deeply conservative person, George acted as fairly as he could as a constitutional monarch when he was king. Privately, his sympathies generally were Conservative, and he exulted when the Conservative candidate beat Churchill in Manchester in 1908. Yet he came to respect Churchill, not least as Churchill displayed an old-fashioned loyalty to the Crown.

George Frederick Ernest Albert was born on 3 June 1865 at Marlborough House, London, the second son of Albert

Edward, Prince of Wales, and Alexandra, daughter of King Christian IX of Denmark. His elder brother, Albert Victor, duke of Clarence, died in January 1892. However, as the younger son, he embarked on a naval career, serving from 1877 until his accession to the throne in 1910, and rising from naval cadet to admiral. After the death of his brother, Prince George, he was created duke of York and was tutored in constitutional history by the eminent historian, Professor J. R. Tanner. When his father, King Edward VII, reached sixty in November 1901, he was created Prince of Wales. George enjoyed good relations with his father and was kept informed of government matters. He enjoyed being with his family at York Cottage, Sandringham, creating a huge stamp collection and, like his father, shooting. He also read many of the latest books.

Lady Randolph Churchill met Prince George socially, through her friendship with his father, the then Prince of Wales. At Cowes in 1887, Lady Randolph and the young Winston Churchill sailed on the *Aline* with Prince George, the first time the two men met. When Sir Henry Campbell-Bannerman's government was formed in December 1905, the Prince of Wales (George) wrote to his father, "Winston Churchill, I see, is Under Secretary for the Colonies, Lord Elgin will have to look after him!"

As king, he urged Churchill in August 1911 to take firm measures, if necessary, against strikers in Liverpool, observing that "the situation there was more like revolution than a strike." After the siege of Sidney Street, the king also wanted tough action on aliens, urging him "to consider whether the Aliens Act could not be amended so as to prevent London from being infested with men and women whose presence would not be tolerated in any other country." Home Secretary Churchill took action against Edward Mylius, who had published the untrue story that George had made a secret marriage in Malta in 1890 and therefore his marriage to Queen Mary was bigamous. The action was successful and King George was grateful for Churchill's careful and considerate handling of the matter.

When taking up the post of first lord of the admiralty on 23 October 1911, he commented that "the great service of the sea . . . is one with which Your Majesty is so intimately associated by a life-time of practical experience." However, the next month he clashed with the king when suggesting names for battleships. When the king objected to "Oliver Cromwell," Churchill offered alternatives. A year later, Churchill suggested "Oliver Cromwell" again, having consulted the prime minister. The king was emphatic in his rejection, and not influenced by Churchill's further arguments, backed by reference to various historians and to Lord Morley. However, the king felt that Churchill was "sensible and fairly reasonable" over the Ulster crisis in 1914 and he thoroughly approved of Churchill's precautionary measures for the Royal Navy just before Britain entered the European war in August 1914.

There was little friction between the king and Churchill after Churchill returned to the Conservative Party. The king felt that Churchill was too belligerent as editor of the *British Gazette,* but generally approved his actions in office.

George V admired Churchill's gifts as a writer. He greatly enjoyed *The World Crisis,* reading it carefully and speculating on various might-have-beens. The king's librarian recalled how George V spoke of Churchill's biography of Marlborough: "Then here's Winston's life of his ancestor—no doubt everything he did was right! A bit heavy for me I expect, but I shall take it down to Sandringham and have a try; I daresay I shan't get far. . . . Beautiful writer he is, and a wonderful good fellow into the bargain."

George V died on 20 January 1936 at Sandringham. The next day, the *News of the*

World asked Churchill, who was in Marrakesh, to write an article on the late king. This he did in time for the next Sunday's edition, 26 January 1936. The essay is reprinted in his *Great Contemporaries* (1937).

Related entries:
Edward VII, King; George VI, King

Suggestions for further reading:
Churchill, Randolph S. 1967. *Winston S. Churchill*. Vol. 2. London: Heinemann.
Gilbert, Martin. 1971, 1975, and 1976. *Winston S. Churchill*. Vols. 3–5. London: Heinemann.
Gore, John. 1941. *King George V: A Personal Memoir.* London: Murray.
Nicolson, Harold. *King George V: His Life and Reign.* London: Constable.
Rose, Kenneth. 1983. *King George V.* London: Weidenfeld and Nicolson.

George VI, King (1895–1952)

Churchill and George VI came to like and admire each other. They both played major roles in helping to maintain British morale during the Second World War. After George VI's death, Churchill paid tribute to his courage during the Second World War and in facing serious ill health. Of the latter, he spoke memorably: "During these last months the King walked with death, as if death were a companion, an acquaintance, whom he recognised and did not fear."

Albert Frederick Arthur George was born at York Cottage, Sandringham, on 14 December 1895, the second son of the duke and duchess of York. Like his grandfather, he was known as "Bertie." Like his father, he took up a naval career. He began at the Royal Naval College, Osborne, Isle of Wight, his great grandmother's much-loved southern country home, and was an active naval officer, 1913–1917, when poor health ended his naval career. He transferred to the Royal Flying Corps (soon to be the Royal Air Force). He became a qualified pilot and in August 1919 was commissioned as a squadron leader. That autumn, he went to Trinity College, Cambridge, where he was more assiduous in his studies than his grandfather (Edward VII) or brother (Edward VIII) were. In June 1920, he was created the duke of York. Before the abdication crisis of 1936, he was most noted for his role abroad as a royal ambassador and at home for his active interest in industrial welfare.

Churchill, then first lord of the admiralty, first met Prince Albert in May 1912. The prince was on board the *Victoria and Albert* with his father, who was reviewing the fleet off Weymouth, when Churchill visited them. They met again in early October 1912, when Churchill inspected Dartmouth Naval College and Prince Albert was one of the cadets who dined with him and Clementine Churchill on the admiralty yacht. The prince was serving on the *Collingwood* at the outbreak of war in 1914, but was incapacitated by appendicitis. After recuperation from an operation, he joined the war staff at the admiralty in December 1914, being greeted by Churchill on his arrival.

Churchill and the duke of York's relationship was strained by Churchill's vigorous championing of Edward VIII during the abdication crisis. When Churchill succeeded Neville Chamberlain as prime minister, George VI was not enthusiastic. He noted in his diary on 11 May 1940, "I cannot yet think of Winston as P.M. . . . I met Halifax in the garden and I told him I was sorry not to have him as Prime Minister." However, by February 1941, the king confided in his diary, "I could not have a better Prime Minister." The king expressed this latter view to others, notably in a letter to President Franklin D. Roosevelt in June 1941 in which he declared his admiration for and confidence in Churchill. He observed, "He is a great man, & has at last come into his own as leader of this country in this fateful time in her history." The king was very taken aback when Churchill lost the 1945 general election.

British Prime Minister Winston Churchill (center) with Queen Elizabeth, King George VI, Princess Elizabeth (left), and Princess Margaret Rose on the balcony of Buckingham Palace during VE Day celebrations, 8 May 1945 (Hulton/Archive)

The king's health was often poor and it was harmed by heavy smoking. He died on 6 February 1952. Churchill was genuinely upset by his death. When John Colville went to him that morning he found Churchill "with tears in his eyes, looking straight in front of him and reading neither his official papers nor the newspapers."

Related entries:
Edward VIII; Elizabeth II, Queen; George V, King

Suggestions for further reading:
Gilbert, Martin. 1976–1988. *Winston S. Churchill.* Vols. 5–8. London: Heinemann.
Wheeler-Bennett, John W. 1958. *King George VI: His Life and Reign.* London: Macmillan.

Gibbon, Edward (1737–1794)

Edward Gibbon, the son of a M.P., was a M.P. (1774–1780, 1781–1783) and wrote *The History of the Decline and Fall of the Roman Empire* (1776–1788). His work is marked by confident judgments on all that he wrote about—from the various emperors to Christianity and the qualities of civilization. As one historian, Brian Warmington, has put it, the bases of his judgments are "those of the 'man of sense' of the Enlightenment." Such dispensing of firm judgments appealed greatly to Winston Churchill.

Before going to India in 1895, Winston Churchill planned a program of reading major historical works that would begin with Gibbon. He had read all the *Decline and Fall* by early 1897 before his return home from India on leave that May. He was much impressed by Gibbon's style, commenting that along with Macaulay he showed "what a fine language English is." In later life, he liked to reminisce of his time in India in 1895–1897, when he spent his after-lunch siestas reading Gibbon or Macaulay.

Suggestions for further reading:
Churchill, Randolph S. 1966 and 1967. *Winston S. Churchill.* Vol. 1, and companion vol. 1, part 2. London: Heinemann.
Gilbert, Martin. 1986. *Winston S. Churchill.* Vol. 7. London: Heinemann.
Warmington, Brian. 1980. "Edward Gibbon." In *The Historian at Work,* edited by John Cannon. London: Allen and Unwin.

Gladstone, William Ewart (1809–1898)

William Ewart Gladstone, 1867 (Library of Congress)

During William Gladstone's later career, Winston Churchill's father was one of his principal political opponents. After the death of his father and of Gladstone, Churchill looked back on Gladstone as one of the greatest, perhaps the greatest, parliamentarians of the nineteenth century. At the end of his career, Churchill appears to have been almost in competition with Gladstone for political longevity.

William Ewart Gladstone was born on 29 December 1809, the fourth son and fifth child of a wealthy Liverpool merchant, John Gladstone, and his evangelical wife, Anne Robertson. John Gladstone, a friend of George Canning (prime minister 1827), was a Conservative M.P. (1818–1826). W. E. Gladstone was inclined to a career in the church but his father pressed him into Conservative politics. He was elected to Parliament as a Conservative in December 1832 and served in Sir Robert Peel's 1841–1846 Conservative government. He left the Conservatives in 1846, becoming an eminent Peelite. From 1859 he became clearly committed to the Liberal Party. He was an outstanding chancellor of the exchequer, 1852–1855 and 1859–1866, notable for his careful and even parsimonious finance and reluctance to increase public expenditure ("Gladstonian finance"). He was prime minister in 1868–1874, 1880–1885, 1886, and 1892–1894. His politics were notable for a commitment to free trade, free market forces, a preference where possible for arbitration not war in international disputes, and, from the end of 1885, a commitment to Irish Home Rule.

Lord Randolph Churchill had made his reputation by vigorous opposition to Gladstone in the 1880–1885 Parliament. Winston Churchill sat in the "Distinguished Strangers" gallery of the House of Commons on 21 April 1893 to hear Gladstone's speech on the second reading of the second Home Rule Bill. When the Liberals did badly in the 1895 general election, Winston informed his mother, "I attribute the ruin of the Radical party entirely to the absence of Mr. Gladstone's sustaining power." Although Gladstone had been his family's arch political opponent (at least in the opposing party), the young Churchill recognized his greatness as a speaker and when he left for India in the summer of 1897 he insisted on having both Benjamin Disraeli's and Gladstone's speeches sent out to him.

Churchill's economic policies were built on a Gladstonian foundation. He was committed to free trade and to free market forces and, other than in war, preferred to minimize the public sector of the economy. He was prone to quote Gladstone on such matters. Also, after the Second World War, he was very aware that he was the oldest holder of the premiership since Gladstone. He liked to compare his last government (1951–1955) with that of Gladstone (1892–1894). However, Churchill suffered serious strokes before he was eighty; Gladstone remained relatively sprightly but suffered from seriously deteriorating hearing and eyesight.

Suggestions for further reading:
Churchill, Randolph S. 1966 and 1967. *Winston S. Churchill*. Vol. 1, and companion vol. 1, parts 1 and 2. London: Heinemann.
Gilbert, Martin. 1988. *Winston S. Churchill*. Vol. 8. London: Heinemann.
Matthew, H. C. G. 1986 and 1995. *Gladstone*. 2 vols. Oxford: Clarendon Press.
Shannon, Richard. 1982 and 1999. *Gladstone*. 2 vols. London: Hamish Hamilton.

Gort, Field Marshal Lord (John Standish Surtees Prendergast Vereker, 1886–1946)

Churchill admired Lord Gort as a brave soldier. He liked his company and ensured his election to The Other Club. After Gort's period as commander of the British Expeditionary Force, 1939–1940, Churchill made use of his abilities in Gibraltar, Malta, and Palestine during 1941–1945.

John Vereker was born in London on 10 July 1886, the elder son of John Gage Prendergast and Eleanor Vereker. His father was later the fifth Viscount Gort in the Irish peerage. His mother was the daughter of the novelist Robert Smith Surtees. Educated at Harrow and Sandhurst, he joined the Grenadier Guards in 1905. He succeeded his father, becoming the sixth Viscount Gort in 1902. He displayed strong leadership and bravery on the Western Front during the First World War, being much decorated and being awarded the Victoria Cross for exceptional bravery at the Canal du Nord in September 1918.

After varied service during the interwar years he was appointed military secretary to the secretary of state for war, Leslie Hore-Belisha, in 1937. Later in the year he became chief of the Imperial General Staff, a post that he held until the outbreak of war in 1939. He then commanded the British Expeditionary Force in France and made preparations to defend the Belgian border. Churchill visited his headquarters on 6 April 1940, and discussed the military situation with Lord Gort and General Sir John Dill. With the German invasion of France in May 1940, he saved his forces by withdrawing to Dunkirk. This was realistic. Characteristically, he had wished to stay with his men at Dunkirk; but on 30 May at 2:00 P.M. Churchill ordered him to return to England when the men left on the beach had fallen in number down to the equivalent of three divisions, the reason being that his capture by the Germans would be "a needless triumph to the enemy."

Although Churchill told the House of Commons on 4 June 1940 that he would be rebuilding the British Expeditionary Force "under its gallant Commander-in-Chief, Lord Gort," he was downgraded to the post of inspector general of training. However, Churchill liked and admired him. He was often seen by Churchill and was a member of The Other Club. In late June 1940, Churchill sent Duff Cooper and Gort to try to make contact with anti-German French politicians at Rabat, but they were unable to do so. In November 1941, Churchill seriously considered making Gort chief of the Imperial General Staff; and in March 1942, he pondered making him General Sir Claude Auchinleck's successor as head of the Middle East Command.

Gort was made governor of Gibraltar in April 1941. In May 1942, he was moved to the more challenging and dangerous post of governor of Malta, an island that was vital as a base for Allied convoys. Gort flew to Cairo to report to Churchill in person on 22 August 1942. Churchill visited Malta from 17 to 19 November 1942, staying as Gort's guest (though unwell and in bed much of the time), on his way to meeting President Franklin D. Roosevelt in Cairo. Gort again showed his abilities and bravery in Malta, and he was promoted to field marshal in 1943. Gort moved on to Palestine as British high commissioner in late 1944. His health declined and he was forced to resign in early 1945. In 1946, he was elevated to a British viscountcy, but he was too ill to take his seat in the House of Lords. He died on 31 March 1946.

Suggestions for further reading:
Bond, Brian. 1991. "Gort." In *Churchill's Generals,* edited by John Keegan. London: Weidenfeld and Nicolson.
Churchill, Winston S. 1948–1954. *The Second World War.* 6 vols. London: Cassell.
Colville, John R. 1972. *Man of Valour: Field-Marshal Lord Gort VC.* London: Hodder and Stoughton.
Gilbert, Martin. 1983 and 1986. *Winston S. Churchill.* Vols. 6 and 7. London: Heinemann.

Gott, William Henry Ewart (1897–1942)

Churchill admired "Strafer" Gott and was much impressed when he met him two days before Gott's death. He described him as a man who combined high ability with a "charming, simple personality." He was deeply shocked when Gott was killed flying a route that he, Churchill, had flown only a few days before.

William Gott was born at Scarborough on 13 August 1897, the elder son of William Henry and Anne Rosamond Gott. His father was a member of a Yorkshire wool-producing family. His mother was the third daughter of the Reverend William Collins of Knaresborough. Educated at Harrow and the Royal Military College, Sandhurst, he joined the King's Royal Rifle Corps in 1915. He was wounded and captured in action in 1917, later being awarded the Military Cross. During the interwar years, he mostly served in India. In 1938, he was a major and in command of the 1st battalion of the King's Royal Rifle Corps in Egypt. In September 1940, he inflicted major damage to advancing Italian forces in the western desert. He played a substantial role in the subsequent defeat of Italian forces in Libya in 1941 and then defended the Egyptian frontier against the threat from General Erwin Rommel and the German Africa Corps. Next, he served under Auchinleck in the Eighth Army.

In early August 1942 Churchill in Cairo determined to appoint Gott to succeed Field Marshal Sir Claude Auchinleck as commander of the Eighth Army. General Alan Brooke advised that Gott was exhausted from his effective campaigning and preferred General Bernard Montgomery. Churchill flew to El Alamein on 5 August and spoke with Gott. He left Gott reassured that Gott was not too tired and confirmed in his belief in his ability. He recommended him to the war cabinet. However, Gott, going in a transport plane to Cairo, was shot down and killed on 7 August 1942 by German aircraft attacking the airfield. Churchill thought his death to be the work of the hand of fate.

Suggestions for further reading:
Churchill, Winston S. 1951. *The Second World War.* Vol. 6. London: Cassell.

Gilbert, Martin. 1983 and 1986. *Winston S. Churchill*. Vols. 6 and 7. London: Heinemann.
Isham, Giles. 1959. "Gott, William Henry Ewart." In *Dictionary of National Biography, 1941–1950*, edited by L. G. Wickham Legg and E. T. Williams. Oxford: Oxford University Press.

Gough, General Sir Hubert de la Poer (1870–1963)

Gough was a brave, if sometimes rash, military officer in both the Boer War and the First World War. He was made the scapegoat for the German breakthrough on the Western Front in March 1918. Churchill appointed him to be the head of the Allied Mission to the Baltic in 1919, to liaise with White Russian forces attacking Petrograd.

Hubert Gough was born at Gurteen, County Waterford, on 12 August 1870, the elder son of General Sir Charles John Stanley and Harriet Anastasia Gough. His mother was the daughter of John de la Poer, a former M.P. for Waterford. He was educated at Eton and Sandhurst. He served in the army from 1889, in India and in the Boer War. Gough was in charge at the Curragh at the time of the incident when fifty-seven officers said that they would resign rather than impose Home Rule on Ulster. During the First World War, he rose by 1916 to command of the Reserve (later known as the Fifth Army). He unsuccessfully tried to persuade General Sir Douglas Haig to end the Passchendaele offensive in 1917 when strong resistance and heavy rain prevented speedy advances. His army faced the brunt of the German offensive of March 1918 and Gough was replaced.

Churchill had most to do with Gough when in 1919 Gough was chief of the Allied Mission to the Baltic. Then, in May 1919, he successfully recommended that Britain supply munitions to General Nikolai Nikolaevich Yudenitch. However, Yu-denitch failed to capture Petrograd as had been hoped. When Gough returned to Britain in August 1919, he had come to believe that helping Yudenitch was a waste of time and money and, moreover, warned that the White Russian leaders were more pro-German than pro-British.

Gough retired in 1922. He unsuccessfully stood as a Liberal in a by-election in Chertsey that year. He published his own account of his later campaigns, *The Fifth Army* (1931). He also published a volume of memoirs, *Soldiering On* (1954). He died on 18 March 1963.

Related entry:
Seely, John Edward Bernard

Suggestions for further reading:
Bond, Brian. 1981. "Gough, Sir Hubert De La Poer." In *The Dictionary of National Biography*, edited by T. Williams, and C. S. Nicholls. Oxford: Oxford University Press.
Gilbert, Martin. 1975. *Winston S. Churchill*. Vol. 4. London: Heinemann.

Great Contemporaries (1937)

This was one of Churchill's most popular collections of reprinted essays from journals and newspapers. The essays had been published between 1928 and 1936 in the *Pall Mall*, the *Strand*, the *News of the World*, the *Daily Mail*, and the *Sunday Pictorial*.

The first edition was published by Thornton Butterworth on 4 October 1937 at a price of 21 shillings (£1.05). With five further print runs before the end of the year, 15,000 copies were printed for Britain. It was translated into eight other languages. Further essays were added to a revised edition in 1938. When it was republished in 1943, the essays on Leon Trotsky and Franklin D. Roosevelt were omitted lest they offend Britain's powerful allies, but were reinstated in the 1958 and subsequent editions.

Suggestions for further reading:
Gilbert, Martin. 1976. *Winston S. Churchill*. Vol. 5. London: Heinemann.
Woods, Frederick. 1963. *A Bibliography of the Works of Sir Winston Churchill*. London: Vane.

Grey, Sir Edward (Viscount Grey of Fallodon, 1862–1933)

Until the First World War, Churchill generally got on well with Sir Edward Grey. Grey was a politician of integrity, a baronet whose feeling of public duty prevented him from retiring to his estate to enjoy watching birds, fishing, and other country pursuits. When Churchill was first a Conservative M.P., Grey, as a leading Liberal Imperialist, was a Liberal to whom Churchill felt politically relatively close.

Edward Grey was born in London on 25 April 1862, the eldest child of Colonel George Henry and Harriet Jane Grey. His father had served in the Crimean War and the Indian Mutiny and had been an equerry to the Prince of Wales before retiring to country life at Fallodon. His mother was the daughter of Lieutenant Colonel Charles Pearson. Grey succeeded his grandfather as baronet in 1882. After attending Winchester, he went to Balliol College, Oxford, where he was expelled for idleness in January 1884. This was no bar to his being elected chancellor of Oxford University in 1928. He was the private secretary of Sir Evelyn Baring (later Lord Cromer) and H. E. C. Childers, the chancellor of the exchequer. In 1885, he won back his grandfather's old seat, Berwick-upon-Tweed, from the Conservatives. Grey was parliamentary under secretary at the foreign office, 1892–1895, under Lord Rosebery and Lord Kimberley. Grey and his friends Herbert Henry Asquith and Richard Haldane were leading figures of the Liberal Imperialist wing of the Liberal Party, with the ex-prime minister and ex-Liberal Party leader, Lord Rosebery, as the leader. During the Boer War, David Lloyd George emerged as the most prominent "pro-Boer," "Little Englander" figure. With the return of the Liberals to office in December 1905, Grey became foreign secretary, a post he held until December 1916.

Sir Edward Grey was one of the leading Liberal Imperialists who had been courted by Churchill, Hugh Cecil, and their associates among young Conservative M.P.s. In August 1901, Grey invited Churchill to join him, Asquith, and others for dinner. After Churchill joined the Liberals, he and Grey sometimes clashed on political issues; yet Grey usually admired Churchill, recognizing his energy and ability.

Churchill recognized Grey's political weight in Asquith's Liberal government (1908–1915). When, between the two general elections of 1910, Lloyd George floated the idea of a coalition government to a few leading political figures, Churchill urged that they consult Grey. He may also have felt particularly well-disposed toward Grey, who had taken charge of the home office during August 1910 while Churchill was on holiday.

When the kaiser sent the gunboat the *Panther* to Agadir on 1 July 1911, it caused a European crisis. The British government was outraged that Germany wished to settle the future of Morocco by threats, excluding British participation. In the ensuing weeks, Churchill was among the group of ministers—Asquith, Lloyd George, Grey, and Haldane—who dealt with the crisis. Churchill and Grey still got on well, and Grey was one of Randolph Churchill's godfathers.

Churchill, however, was critical of Grey for his attitude to the militant suffragettes. Both Grey and Lloyd George were supporters of votes for women. When Lloyd George announced in November 1911 that he would move an amendment to an adult suffrage bill in favor of votes for women, Grey supported him. Churchill, who had been outraged by suffragette militant tactics, was vehemently opposed to their policy. He wrote to the Liberal chief whip warning that as his two colleagues were "working themselves up, they will have to go, if female suffrage is knocked out." Perhaps Churchill saw a possible opening for himself either at the exchequer or foreign office.

As first lord of the admiralty, Churchill, in 1913–1914, expected Grey to back for his case for building more battleships. When war came, Churchill and Grey were often in close contact, and they both were members of Asquith's war council. Churchill felt that Grey should have accepted a share of the blame for the Dardanelles failure. Grey felt that as a member of the war council he had been committed only to the purely naval action, and commented caustically to Asquith, "It appears, however, from this paper signed W. S. C. that the failure for the Dardanelles is due to Lord Kitchener and myself, though neither of us have been at the Admiralty."

With the creation of Asquith's coalition government in 1915, Grey was more upset at the ousting of his old friend Haldane than at the demotion of Churchill. Grey's ministerial career ended with Asquith's in December 1916. Later, he was often seen as a possible Liberal leader or coalition member, but he did not return to office.

He became Viscount Grey of Fallodon in July 1916. Sadly, for a man who loved to watch birds and enjoyed the countryside, his eyesight deteriorated markedly from 1914. He wrote an autobiography, *Twenty-Five Years* (1925) and *The Charm of Birds* (1927), both of which enjoyed high sales. He died on 7 September 1933.

Related entries:
Agadir; Asquith, Herbert Henry; Haldane, Richard Burdon; Rosebery, Earl of

Suggestions for further reading:
Churchill, Randolph S. 1967. *Winston S. Churchill*. Vol. 2. London: Heinemann.
Robbins, Keith. 1971. *Sir Edward Grey*. London: Cassell.
Trevelyan, G. M. 1937. *Grey of Fallodon*. London: Longmans, Green.

Guest, Frederick Edward (1875–1937)

Churchill and Frederick Guest were not only cousins but also good friends and political colleagues. Guest believed in Churchill's abilities and long hoped to see him become prime minister. He followed in Churchill's political slipstream, but he also assisted him greatly on many occasions. He was especially supportive of Churchill during his coalition Liberal years (1916–1922) and the 1930s.

Frederick Guest was born in London on 14 June 1875, the third son of Sir Ivor Bertie and Lady Cornelia Henrietta Maria Guest. His father, the second baronet, was created the first Baron Wimborne in 1880. His mother was the eldest daughter of the seventh duke of Marlborough and a sister of Lord Randolph Churchill. He was educated at Winchester and in 1894 secured a commission in the East Surrey Regiment. He served with distinction in both the Boer War and the First World War. He was awarded the DSO (Distinguished Service Order) in 1917 and appointed CBE (Commander of the British Empire) in 1919.

Winston Churchill, as he grew up, frequently saw his Guest cousins, and often stayed at their house near Bournemouth. When Churchill switched from the Conservatives to the Liberals, Frederick Guest followed. In 1908 he would have gone with Churchill to East Africa, but withdrew because his wife was due to give birth. This boy was christened Winston, with Winston Churchill as his godfather. Guest lent Churchill and F. E. Smith his car for a journey in France and Italy in September 1909.

Guest ran successfully for East Dorset in the December 1910 general election. Churchill spoke for him during the campaign. Guest followed his cousin into the coalition Liberals, 1916–1922, and was coalition Liberal chief whip, 1917–1921, and secretary of state for air, April 1921–October 1922. Churchill had proposed his cousin for that post as early as July 1919. Churchill was outraged when Lord Beaverbrook ran a successful campaign to oust Guest in the 1922 general election.

Guest was not as quick as Churchill to return to the Conservative Party, largely because he was more successful electorally, winning Stroud in 1923 and North Bristol in 1924. However, he remained loyal to Churchill, helping to organize his Westminster by-election campaign in March 1924. In the Commons, Guest supported Churchill's 1925 budget and increasingly voted with the Conservatives. After the intervention of another Liberal in Bristol in 1929 ensured his defeat, Guest announced his return to the Conservatives in 1930. He was returned to the Commons as a Conservative for the Plymouth Drake constituency in 1931 and 1935.

In the 1930s, Guest was one of the small band of loyal supporters of Churchill. As a former secretary of state for air, he took a prominent role in deputations to cabinet ministers on rearmament in the mid-1930s, along with Austen Chamberlain, Sir Robert Horne, Leo Amery, and the earl of Winterton, as well as Churchill. As Churchill's cousin, his friend, and his political acolyte, he was able to offer sensible advice to Churchill. For instance, in June 1936, he advised Churchill to stop his counterproductive attacks on Stanley Baldwin. He wrote on 19 June that Conservative backbenchers were aware of Baldwin's failings, but "they will not see the old man bullied as they are intensely and pathetically loyal to him." He added, "I need not say any more, but this is advice from someone who has been trying to help you one way and another for nearly thirty years." Churchill ignored his cousin's advice on this occa-

sion. However, he was genuinely deeply upset when Guest died of cancer on 28 April 1937.

Related entries:
Beaverbrook, Lord; Guest, Sir Ivor Churchill

Suggestions for further reading:
Churchill, Randolph S. 1967. *Winston S. Churchill*. Vol. 2. London: Heinemann.
Gilbert, Martin. 1975 and 1976. *Winston S. Churchill*. Vols. 4 and 5. London: Heinemann.

Guest, Sir Ivor Churchill (Viscount Wimborne, 1873–1939)

Churchill was on good terms with his cousin, Ivor Guest. Guest was often generous with hospitality, lending him a house on occasion, and generally wishing his career well. He was not as active politically for as long, nor politically as close to Churchill, as his brother Frederick.

Ivor Guest was born in London on 16 January 1873, the eldest son of Sir Ivor Bertie and Lady Cornelia Henrietta Maria Guest. He was the elder brother of Frederick Guest and the cousin of Winston Churchill. Churchill saw much of the five Guest boys, often staying at their home near Bournemouth. Educated at Eton and Trinity College, Cambridge, Guest served in the Boer War in the Dorset Imperial Yeomanry. He was returned unopposed as a Conservative to the House of Commons for Plymouth in a by-election in 1900 and held the seat in the general election. Committed to free trade, he crossed the floor of the Commons to the Liberals along with Churchill, his brother Frederick, and others. He remained a loyal ally of Churchill, although he was shaken by the original proposed death duties in the 1909 People's Budget; Churchill even feared that Guest might resign his seat over that issue. In

1910, he was given a peerage as Baron Ashby St. Ledgers, although he succeeded his father as Baron Wimborne in 1914. He served in the government as paymaster general, February 1910–May 1912, and as a lord-in-waiting, January 1913–February 1915. In August 1914, Churchill unsuccessfully pressed Asquith to make Wimborne civil lord of the admiralty.

In 1915, Wimborne accepted Asquith's offer of becoming lord lieutenant of Ireland, a post he held from February 1915 until May 1918, when he wisely advised against applying conscription to Ireland. He was advanced to Viscount Wimborne, June 1918. He then retired from active politics and pursued his business interests. He remained eager to see Churchill succeed in politics. Wimborne tried to secure a settlement for the miners after the 1926 General Strike, and arranged an unsuccessful meeting between A. J. Cook, the miners' leader, and the government, through Churchill, on 26 August 1926. In 1931, he agreed to be the first president of the National Liberal Party. Wimborne died on 14 June 1939.

Suggestions for further reading:
Churchill, Randolph S. 1967. *Winston S. Churchill*. Vol. 2. London: Heinemann.
Gilbert, Martin. 1971–1976. *Winston S. Churchill*. Vols. 3–5. London: Heinemann.

H

Haldane, Richard Burdon (Viscount Haldane of Cloan, 1856–1928)

Churchill, on reaching the Liberal cabinet in 1908, initially clashed with Richard Haldane when he pressed for reduced army expenditure. However, when Churchill went to the admiralty in 1911, he soon favored increased naval expenditure and worked well with Haldane. He was disgusted when Haldane was omitted from office in the coalition government of 1915 as a result of a smear campaign.

Richard Burdon Haldane was born at 17 Charlotte Square, Edinburgh, on 30 July 1856, the second, but first surviving, son of Robert and Mary Elizabeth Haldane. His father had studied law and become a writer to the signet (a legal post); and like his father and uncle, Haldane was a devout Calvinist. His mother was the daughter of Richard Burdon-Sanderson, a great-niece of Lord Chancellor Eldon and the distinguished jurist Lord Stowell, and also of a notably evangelical family. After attending Edinburgh Academy, he was educated at Göttingen University and Edinburgh University, thereby avoiding the Anglicanism of Oxford. In Germany, he was much influenced by such philosophers as Immanuel Kant and Georg Hegel. He studied law in London, being called to Lincoln's Inn in 1879. he worked as a barrister until he entered the cabinet in 1905. He was elected as a Liberal to the House of Commons for East Lothian in December 1885, a seat he held until he was created Viscount Haldane of Cloan in 1911. In the Commons he was a prominent Liberal Imperialist, a supporter of Lord Rosebery. He entered Sir Henry Campbell-Bannerman's cabinet in December 1905 as secretary of state for war.

Churchill clashed with Haldane over the 1908 Army Estimates, arguing for reductions. However, later Churchill was keen on defense expenditure. In 1911, when Churchill went to the admiralty, Haldane had wanted that post; however, he and Churchill worked well together thereafter. Soon after Churchill's appointment, Haldane wrote to his mother, "Winston is full of enthusiasm for the admiralty and just as keen as I am on the War Staff. It is delightful to work with him."

Haldane's tenure in the war office (10 December 1905–12 June 1912) was marked by major army reforms. He succeeded Lord Loreburn as lord chancellor in 1912; but when Asquith formed his coalition government in May 1915, he was the most notable casualty, being left out of the new government. This was due to a discreditable campaign to smear him as pro-German (in large part because of his taste for German philosophers). Churchill was disgusted by Haldane's treatment. Although cast down by his own demotion, Churchill wrote to express his outrage and to thank Haldane for his "unfailing kindness to me." On 26 May 1915, King George V displayed his opinion by conferring the Order of Merit on Haldane.

Haldane was very interested in education. He was a strong supporter of the Workers' Educational Association and involved himself in higher education; it was largely through this concern that he joined the first Labour government, 1924, as lord chancellor. He died on 19 August 1928.

Related entries:
Asquith, Herbert Henry; Grey, Sir Edward

Suggestions for further reading:
Churchill, Randolph S. 1967. *Winston S. Churchill.* Vol. 2. London: Heinemann.
Koss, Stephen E. 1969. *Lord Haldane: Scapegoat for Liberalism.* New York: Columbia University Press.
Maurice, Sir Frederick. 1937 and 1939. *Haldane.* 2 vols. London: Faber and Faber.
Sommer, Dudley. 1960. *Haldane of Cloan: His Life and Times, 1856–1928.* London: Allen and Unwin.

Halifax, Earl of (Edward Frederick Lindley Wood, 1881–1959)

Lord Halifax's ministerial career began under Churchill at the colonial office. Later, they held very different views on India and appeasement. Although Halifax was both friend and defender to Stanley Baldwin and Neville Chamberlain, generally his relations with Churchill were good.

Edward Wood was born at Powderham Castle, Devon, on 16 April 1881, the fourth son and sixth child of Charles Lindley and Lady Agnes Elizabeth Wood. His father was later the second Viscount Halifax, a man of strong Anglo-Catholic faith. His mother was the only daughter of the eleventh earl of Devon. He was handicapped from birth by an atrophied left arm but managed to cope without a left hand. Educated at Eton and Christ Church, Oxford, he was elected a fellow of All Souls and taught history. He was elected a Conservative M.P. in the January 1910 general election, representing Ripon until 1925 when he entered the House of Lords. He served in the army in 1914–1917, displaying bravery on the Western Front.

He first had personal contact with Winston Churchill in April 1921 when he was appointed under secretary of state at the colonial office. According to Halifax, Churchill, who was obsessed at the time with the Middle East and annoyed that Wood and not his choice had gained the post, avoided seeing him for some time. After Wood insisted on seeing Churchill and complained to him, Churchill's behavior changed. Wood later wrote, "From that day no one could have been kinder than Churchill was to me."

Wood, however, was not greatly in sympathy with those Conservatives who wished to prolong the coalition government. He entered the cabinet under Andrew Bonar Law and Baldwin as president of the Board of Education. When Baldwin returned to office in November 1924, Wood became minister for agriculture for a year while Churchill was chancellor of the exchequer.

In 1925, Baldwin recommended Wood to be viceroy of India. He was created Lord Irwin in 1925 and arrived in India in April 1926. Irwin believed that partnership, not paternalism, was the necessary policy in India. His views brought upon him the wrath of Churchill and the earl of Birkenhead. He later described Churchill as "the most formidable" of the critics of reform in India. His term ended in April 1931. That autumn, Ramsay MacDonald invited him to be foreign secretary in the National government. He declined. However, in June 1932, he agreed to return to the Board of Education. In Baldwin's last government

L–R: French Foreign Minister Georges Bonnet, British Prime Minister Neville Chamberlain, French Premier Edouard Daladier, and British Foreign Secretary Lord Halifax meeting at the French Foreign Office when the British statesmen stopped for talks en route to Rome to meet Mussolini, 10 January 1939 (Hulton/Archive)

(1935–1937), Viscount Halifax (as he had become after his father's death in January 1934) was secretary of state for war, June–November 1935, then lord privy seal and leader of the House of Lords. Under Neville Chamberlain, he was lord president of the council (1937–1938) and foreign secretary after Anthony Eden's resignation in February 1938.

Halifax was always an Establishment "insider." He got on well with Baldwin and Chamberlain, and he felt that Churchill was unfair to them at the time and in his war memoirs. He also defended himself in his autobiography *Fullness of Days* (1957) against some points Churchill had made against him. Yet, Halifax appears also to have still liked Churchill in the 1930s, even if he doubted his judgment.

In 1940, Halifax and Churchill were the alternatives as successor to Chamberlain. Halifax would have accepted the premiership if it had been thrust upon him, but, unlike Churchill, he lacked the deep belief

that it was his hour of destiny. Halifax recognized Churchill's qualities, but also felt that he would be in Herbert Henry Asquith's position in 1916, overshadowed by a dynamic figure, and in Halifax's case, not able to speak in the House of Commons. Churchill took the premiership and invited Halifax to stay as foreign secretary, a post he held until December 1940. He was also a member of Churchill's war cabinet and leader of the House of Lords (for most of the final three months of 1940). With the sudden death of Lord Lothian in December 1940, Churchill pressed a reluctant Halifax to succeed Lothian as ambassador to the United States, a post he held from January 1941 until May 1946.

Churchill usually stayed with Halifax at the British embassy for at least part of his visits to the United States. Halifax knew Churchill's deep respect for President Franklin D. Roosevelt, and when the president died he stopped Churchill from attending the funeral. Halifax's term as ambassador ended not long after Churchill's famous Fulton speech, which Halifax judged to have had a major impact in the United States. After Halifax's return, Churchill offered him a place in the shadow cabinet, which Halifax declined. Halifax died on 23 December 1959.

Related entries:
Chamberlain, (Arthur) Neville; Roosevelt, Franklin Delano

Suggestions for further reading:
Birkenhead, Earl of. 1965. *Halifax*. London: Hamish Hamilton.
Gilbert, Martin. 1976–1988. *Winston S. Churchill*. Vols. 5–8. London: Heinemann.
Halifax, Earl of. 1957. *Fullness of Days*. London: Collins.
Roberts, Andrew. 1919. *The Holy Fox: A Biography of Lord Halifax*. London: Weidenfeld and Nicolson.
Rose, Kenneth. 1971. "Wood, Edward Frederick Lindley." In *The Dictionary of National Biography 1951–1960,* edited by E. T. Williams and H. M. Palmer. Oxford: Oxford University Press.

Hamilton, Sir Ian Standish Monteith (1853–1947)

The careers of Churchill and Sir Ian Hamilton often intersected up to 1915. For the young Winston Churchill, Ian Hamilton was one of his mother's more useful connections for his career, and he benefited both in India and South Africa. For his part, Hamilton found Churchill a valuable political connection in 1900–1915. However, Churchill's pressure to put Hamilton in charge at Gallipoli led to a sad end to Hamilton's active military career.

Ian Hamilton, the elder son of Christian and Maria Hamilton, was born in Corfu on 16 January 1853. Christian Hamilton was a captain in the Gordon Highlanders. His mother, Maria Corinna Gort, was from an Anglo-Irish military family; she died in 1856. Ian and his brother were brought up by his grandfather in Argyll, Scotland. He was educated at Cheam and then Wellington College. In 1870, he passed 76th in a list of 404 successful candidates in the army's examinations for commission. In 1873, after other experiences, he went to India to join the Gordon Highlanders, but his service in India was broken by his successful request to serve in South Africa. He was wounded during the British defeat at Majuba Hill, 1881. Convalescing on the Isle of Wight, he was brought before Queen Victoria and recounted the battle; he also wrote an account of it. He returned to India as aide-de-camp to Sir Frederick Roberts, commander in chief in the Madras presidency. While in India he wrote *The Fighting of the Future,* 1885. He also enjoyed writing regularly for the *Madras Mail* as well as writing poetry. He again pushed himself forward to participate in a major action, the attempt to rescue General Charles Gordon at Khartoum. In 1886, he served in Burma. In the late 1880s, he and his wife became friends of Rudyard Kipling.

Ian Hamilton first met Winston Churchill when on leave in England in 1897; he already knew Lady Randolph Churchill socially. In 1898, when Hamilton was protecting the communication lines of the army fighting on the Northwest Frontier, Churchill used his connections with Hamilton to serve in the war zone. When Hamilton left India for service in England, he took with him the manuscript of Churchill's book *Savrola* and an article on the defense of India. He also advised Churchill to focus on one career, to decide "between the two or three avenues which radiate from your feet and lead toward fame each in its own way."

With the onset of the Boer War, Hamilton went out to South Africa to be assistant adjutant general to Sir George White in Natal, arriving on 3 October 1899. Hamilton displayed imagination and bravery in defeating Boer forces at Elandslaagte. Hamilton was with White's forces besieged in Ladysmith, and commanded the defense of the largest sector; there, he was brave and effective in repulsing Boer attacks. After the relief of Ladysmith, Lord Roberts put Hamilton in command of a 10,000 strong force, which advanced north to Johannesburg and Pretoria. Winston Churchill, as correspondent of the *Morning Post,* accompanied Hamilton; in his journalism and in his book, *Ian Hamilton's March,* 1900, Churchill expressed his admiration for Hamilton.

Hamilton left South Africa with Lord Roberts in December 1900. He was promoted to major general and received a knighthood. Roberts became commander in chief, with Hamilton as his military secretary. However, with guerrilla warfare continuing, he returned to South Africa as Lord Kitchener's chief of staff.

Hamilton had long believed that the war could be brought quickly to an end if Britain did not insist on unconditional surrender. On 20 January 1902, he wrote to Winston Churchill urging him to use his influence to secure a moderate settlement with the Boers. Hamilton took charge of the hunt for the Boer commanders in the Western Transvaal and was present at Rooiwal when a Boer column was defeated.

Back in Britain, in 1902, he became quartermaster general of the British army. In 1904 Hamilton went as an Indian army observer to Japan, rightly predicting the Japanese victory over Russia. He served as head of Southern Command, 1905–1909, being promoted to general, 1907, to adjutant general, 1909, and general officer commanding, Mediterranean, 1910–1914. Hamilton opposed his mentor, Lord Roberts, over conscription, writing a defense of a volunteer army in his book *Compulsory Service,* 1910, which had a thirty-two-page introduction by Richard Haldane. In these years, Hamilton was considered a prominent military man who favored the Liberals; he was also the most senior military man the Liberals had on their list of potential peers if they needed

to be created to break the veto of the House of Lords.

Hamilton commanded the home army when Britain entered the First World War. He was eager to see war service and his opportunity came when Churchill pressed hard for him to be appointed for the Gallipoli campaign. On 12 March 1915, Kitchener told him he was to command the expedition and he left for the Dardanelles with very little information. He asked for Jack Churchill to be assigned to him. Hamilton found Gallipoli a very difficult place to take, and when Churchill was removed from the admiralty in May 1915, Hamilton lost his major supporter. In due course, Hamilton was made the military scapegoat for Gallipoli and was recalled before the troops were evacuated. Hamilton, like Churchill, devoted much time and great effort to defending himself and his men before the Dardanelles Commission. Overall, Hamilton emerged from the Dardanelles Commission's report vindicated. Alfred Milner offered Hamilton the Northern Command in Britain, but Hamilton declined, instead taking the honorary post of lieutenant of the Tower of London until his retirement. Thereafter, he supported the British Legion, unveiled war memorials, and addressed old-comrades' associations. As a relatively radical soldier, he was apparently sounded out as a possible secretary of state for war in the first Labour government, 1924, but he declined. He was anti-Bolshevik and in favor of Anglo-German reconciliation. In August 1938, he visited Adolf Hitler at Berchtesgarden and was impressed. He remained fit until near his death on 12 October 1947.

When a memorial to Hamilton was unveiled in St. Paul's Cathedral on 6 November 1957, Churchill attended and paid tribute to his friend of sixty years, referring to him as a "brilliant and chivalrous man."

Related entries:
Gallipoli; Kitchener, Horatio Herbert

Suggestions for further reading:
Churchill, Randolph S. 1966. *Winston S. Churchill*. Vol. 1. London: Heinemann.
Churchill, Winston S. 1900. *Ian Hamilton's March*. London: Longman.
Gilbert, Martin. 1971. *Winston S. Churchill*. Vol. 3. London: Heinemann.
Hamilton, I. B. M. 1966. *The Happy Warrior: A Life of General Sir Ian Hamilton*. London: Cassell.
Hamilton, I. S. M. 1920. *Gallipoli Diary*. 2 vols. London: Arnold.
———. 1939. *When I Was a Boy*. London: Faber.
———. 1944. *Listening for the Drums*. London: Faber.
Lee, John. 2000. *A Soldier's Life: General Sir Ian Hamilton*. London: Macmillan.

Hankey, Sir Maurice Pascal Alers (Baron Hankey, 1877–1963)

Sir Maurice Hankey was at the heart of British government for over a quarter of a century. When he retired from the civil service in 1938, Churchill wrote a warm and generous letter, commenting on their lengthy friendship but also noting that they had differed over policy in the 1930s. Churchill at first kept Hankey in his wartime government, but demoted him from the war cabinet.

Maurice Hankey was born at Biarritz on 1 April 1877, the fifth child of Robert Alers and Helen Hankey. His father was for some years a sheep farmer in Australia. His mother was the daughter of William Bakewell, an Adelaide lawyer. Educated at Rugby and the Royal Naval College, he served in the Mediterranean before being transferred in 1902 to the Department of Naval Intelligence at the admiralty. In 1908, he became an assistant secretary to the Committee of Imperial Defence, and in 1912 its secretary. During the First World War, he was successively secretary of the war council, the Dardanelles committee, and the war committee. When Lloyd George became prime minister in Decem-

ber 1916, Hankey was instrumental in creating the cabinet secretariat and the efficient recording of decisions. Hankey combined the post of secretary of the war cabinet (and then the cabinet) with secretary of the Committee of Imperial Defence, and in 1923 additionally was clerk to the privy council. He retired from them on 28 July 1938.

Churchill had good relations with Hankey from the time he was first lord of the admiralty before the First World War until the 1930s. In March 1912, Hankey wrote of Churchill in comparison with his predecessor, "He is a really great man. . . . He is far more brilliant than McKenna, but probably has not such solid qualities." After Churchill left office in 1915, Churchill appears to have been aggrieved when, on 6 June 1916, Hankey did not trust him, although he was a privy councillor, with the information that the *Hampshire* had been sunk and Kitchener drowned. When, in 1917, there were discussions about appointing an air minister, Hankey favored Churchill rather than Lord Weir.

In the 1930s, Hankey deplored Churchill's stance on India and, until at least 1937, opposed his rearmament campaign. Hankey in the 1930s admired Sir Samuel Hoare, who opposed Churchill on both issues. In the mid to late 1930s, Hankey was a frequent "rubbisher" of Churchill's concerns on rearmament. After being a guest for Sunday dinner at Chartwell on 19 April 1936, Hankey even briefed Sir Thomas Inskip about Churchill's likely line of attack in the House of Commons, and on other occasions reported Churchill's conversations to ministers. Shortly before he retired in 1938, just days after he had written to Churchill expressing a hope to restore old friendly relations once he had left Whitehall, he briefed Chamberlain on how not only to rebut Churchill's criticisms but on how to counterattack.

Hankey, who became increasingly arrogant and prone to moralizing as he got older, badly overstepped the mark with Churchill in October 1937. After Hankey had expressed his own views of the need for more vigor in defense preparations, Churchill sent him a copy of an important and secret letter he had received from a Royal Air Force (RAF) officer. He stated that he trusted in "our friendship and your honour" that an investigation would not be made into who was the letter's author. Hankey, who might have briefly remonstrated about Churchill's receiving such secret information, chose instead to send an eight-page rebuke. Churchill, not surprisingly, sent a curt reply in which he said he would not confide again in Hankey in such matters.

After retiring, Hankey was created a baron. On the outbreak of war in September 1939, Chamberlain appointed Hankey minister without portfolio, with a seat in the war cabinet. When Churchill became prime minister, he kept Hankey out of the war cabinet, appointing him chancellor of the Duchy of Lancaster, May 1940–July 1941; then paymaster general, July 1941–March 1942. Hankey had been unhappy at the running of the war and in early 1942 had been grumbling with Lord Swinton and others. After his dismissal, Hankey aired his criticisms of the government. He also continued to chair two ministerial committees at the request of Ernest Bevin.

In retirement he wrote memoirs and other books. He died on 26 January 1963.

Related entries:
Hoare, Sir Samuel John Gurney; Swinton, Earl of

Suggestions for further reading:
Hankey, Lord. 1961. *The Supreme Command*. 2 vols. London: Allen and Unwin.
Naylor, John F. 1984. *A Man and an Institution: Sir Maurice Hankey, the Cabinet Secretariat and the Custody of Cabinet Secrecy*. Cambridge: Cambridge University Press.
Roskill, Stephen. 1970, 1972, and 1974. *Hankey: Man of Secrets*. 3 vols. London: Collins.

Hardie, James Keir (1856–1915)

James Keir Hardie was a pioneer of British democratic socialism, later revered within the Labour movement as something of a socialist saint. Churchill and Hardie clashed repeatedly and bitterly over the use of police and soldiers in industrial disputes in 1910–1912.

He was born on 15 August 1856 at Legbrannock, Lanarkshire, the son of a sixteen-year-old farm worker, Mary Keir (or Kerr) and probably William Aitken, a miner. He was brought up in poverty by his mother and stepfather, David Hardie, a ship's carpenter. He worked from the age of eight and began working in coal mines from 1867. He was converted to evangelical Christianity in 1878 and was a temperance advocate. An active trade unionist in 1878–1881, he was blacklisted in the Lanarkshire coal fields. He earned money from journalism, and from 1886 he was secretary of the new Ayrshire Miners' Union and the Scottish Miners' National Federation. Hardie broke with Liberal politics in 1888, fighting unsuccessfully the Mid-Lanark by-election of that year. He was a major figure in the founding of the Scottish Labour Party (1888), the Independent Labour Party (1893), and the Labour Representation Committee (1900, which became the Labour Party in 1906). He also became a major figure in international trade unionism and also in the Second International (the major socialist body).

Hardie was elected to Parliament for West Ham South, 1892–1895, during which time he earned the sobriquet of "The Member for the Unemployed," and for Merthyr Tydfil, 1900 until his death. After the 1906 general election when the parliamentary Labour Party had twenty-nine members, he was elected its first chairman (leader), 1906–1908, but in effect he temporarily retired from the leadership through ill-health in April 1907. He recuperated on a world tour, returning in April 1908.

That month, Churchill decided to stand in Dundee. Keir Hardie supported George Stuart, the Labour candidate, sending him a letter of support in which he condemned Churchill for "shameless prevarication" over Labour's "Right to Work" Bill.

In 1910–1911, Keir Hardie clashed with Churchill in the House of Commons over serious disturbances associated with strikes in the South Wales coal fields and elsewhere. In November 1910, Keir Hardie unsuccessfully pressed him hard to set up an inquiry into unrest and policing in the Tonypandy and nearby areas. In one exchange, on 24 November 1910, Hardie observed, "There is no love lost between us." To which Churchill responded, "I know perfectly well, from every act and speech of his, his life is directed to injuring and assailing the party to which I belong. As he justly says, there is no love lost between us, though I entirely respect the consistency of his career."

There were further acidic exchanges between them in 1911. After two railway workers were shot in Llanelli during the national railway strike, Hardie published a pamphlet, *Killing No Murder* (1911).

Churchill was also hostile to Hardie's encouragement of nationalist and socialist groups in the empire as well as to Hardie's campaigns for peace. In October 1910, when Charles Masterman commented that Hardie would go to heaven, Churchill responded, "If Heaven is going to be full of people like Hardie, well, the Almighty can have them to himself!"

Keir Hardie had opposed the Boer War and had received much support in his constituency, Merthyr. After the outbreak of the First World War, he was howled down there when he tried to speak for peace. Hardie died on 26 September 1915.

Suggestions for further reading:
Benn, Caroline 1992. *Keir Hardie.* London: Hutchinson.
Churchill, Randolph S. 1967. *Winston S. Churchill.* Vol. 2. London: Heinemann.
Morgan, Kenneth O. 1975. *Keir Hardie: Radical and Socialist.* London: Weidenfeld and Nicolson.

Harriman, Pamela Digby Churchill Hayward (1920–1997)

Pamela Digby, when married to Randolph Churchill, gave Winston Churchill the thing he then most wanted in his private life: a grandson. Churchill liked his daughter-in-law and was sorry that her marriage to his son lasted only a few years. Winston and Clementine Churchill continued to see her and "baby Winston" after her marriage to Randolph fell apart.

Pamela Beryl Digby was the eldest of four children of Colonel Edward Kenelm Digby of the Coldstream Guards and Constance Pamela Alice Bruce, the youngest daughter of Lord Aberdare. She was born on 20 March 1920 in Farnborough, Kent. Later that year, her father succeeded as Lord Digby and took over the family estate at Minterne Magna, Dorset, where Pamela grew up. She sometimes visited her mother's sisters in Scotland, Lady Rosebery at Dalmeny (near Edinburgh) and Lady Bradford, or her own family's estates in Ireland at Geashill and Glenamoy. She went to Downham College, 1934–1936, and then spent a year in France studying French with a family in Arcueil, on the outskirts of Paris. She then joined her parents and traveled in the United States and Canada before spending the winter of 1937–1938 in Munich. She returned to London, took part in the social season, and spent many weekends at Leeds Castle with her friend Pauline Winn. At Leeds Castle, she met several leading Conservative politicians. After the war began, she worked as a French translator. She rented a flat from Lady Mary Dunn, the daughter of the fifth earl of Rosslyn. It was through Lady Dunn that she was invited out to dinner by Randolph Churchill, then twenty-nine, on 12 September 1939.

After the first dinner together, Randolph Churchill invited her to dinner again the next night. That second evening, he asked her to marry him, and she agreed. For her, he offered an escape from country life to a London life, well-connected politically and socially. He was then also good-looking. Their son, Winston, later wrote that early in the war, "These were the days of whirlwind courtships and instant marriages," with men expecting to die as early as many of those who had gone to the Western Front in 1914–1918. Randolph Churchill desperately wanted an heir. His father liked Pamela and wrote to the duke of Westminster on 29 September that he fully approved of Randolph's wish to be married before he went to fight. They were married on 4 October 1939 at St. John's Church, Smith Square. Crowds outside the church cheered Winston Churchill when he arrived. Their honeymoon was spent at Belton, near Grantham. A year later, on 10 October 1940, Pamela gave birth to their son, Winston, at Chequers (the country residence of the prime minister). The marriage quickly began to fall apart, and the war separated them, too. More serious, Randolph drank heavily, squandered money on high living, and ran up huge gambling debts. His father and, probably, Lord Beaverbrook rescued him, and Pamela contributed by selling off their wedding presents. Pamela worked for the Ministry of Supply's Royal Ordnance factory hostel department in central London. From March 1941, she enjoyed an affair with Averell Harriman, President Franklin D. Roosevelt's special representative in London. In time, Randolph learned of this and turned for consolation to one of his female friends.

While Pamela was pregnant, she lived with Winston and Clementine Churchill at Downing Street and at Chequers. After the birth, she and Randolph set up home in Hitchin. When Randolph left on war service, she returned to central London. Pamela and her baby continued to be a part of Winston's close family circle, which constituted his main relaxation from the worries of the war. In his letters to Randolph, Winston often gave news of Pamela and his grandson. In one of 2 May 1942, he wrote that she was "a great treasure and blessing to us all." His parents' continuing closeness to Pamela and his belief that they condoned her affair with Harriman incensed Randolph and, after a row with his father, his mother banned him from their home for the duration of the war. The marriage was formally dissolved on 18 December 1945 on grounds of desertion (by Randolph), with Pamela being given custody of young Winston.

Pamela Churchill went on to marry Leland Hayward, a Broadway producer, in 1962, and, after his death, Averell Harriman in September 1971. After Averell Harriman's death in 1986, Pamela Harriman continued to be prominent in Democrat politics, especially as a notable fundraiser. She had become a U.S. citizen in 1971. In 1993, President Bill Clinton nominated her to be U.S. ambassador to France. She served in Paris from 1993 until 1996. She died on 5 February 1997.

Suggestions for further reading:
Abramson, Rudy. 1992. *Spanning the Century: The Life of W. Averell Harriman 1891–1986*. New York: William Morrow.
Churchill, Winston S. 1996. *His Father's Son: The Life of Randolph Churchill*. London: Weidenfeld and Nicolson.
Gilbert, Martin. 1983 and 1986. *Winston S. Churchill*. Vols. 6 and 7. London: Heinemann.
Ogden, Christopher. 1994. *Life of the Party: The Biography of Pamela Digby Churchill Hayward Harriman*. London: Little, Brown and Company.

Harriman, William Averell (1891–1986)

For Churchill in 1941, Averell Harriman was Britain's lifeline to President

Interpreter V. N. Pavlov, Winston Churchill, Averell Harriman, Joseph Stalin, and V. M. Molotov at the Kremlin during the Moscow Conference, 1942 (Library of Congress)

Franklin D. Roosevelt and U.S. supplies. He got on well with Harriman, enjoying playing cards with him and liking him as a very pro-British American. He quite probably cast a blind eye toward Harriman's affair with his daughter-in-law, Pamela. For Harriman, Churchill was one of the world leaders he most admired, and one whom he enjoyed visiting in later years when he was in Britain.

Born on 15 November 1891 in New York City, William Averell Harriman was the son of Edward Henry Harriman, who had made a fortune from railroads, and his wife, Mary Williamson Averell. His father died when he was seventeen, leaving an estate valued at nearly $70 million. After studying at Yale, he followed in his father's footsteps, working for the Union Pacific. During the First World War, Harriman entered shipbuilding and by 1920 he controlled a huge merchant fleet. In the 1920s, he invested in mining in the Soviet Union, steel and electricity in Poland, and in bank-

ing, and in the 1930s he invested in aviation. Like Churchill, he was an eager polo player. Harriman converted from Republican to Democrat in 1932 and helped to promote President Franklin D. Roosevelt's National Recovery Administration (NRA) in New York in 1933–1934. In October 1934, Harriman became the NRA's chief administrative officer until the Supreme Court ended its existence in 1935. Harriman's entry into wartime diplomacy stemmed from his being a protégé of Roosevelt's friend and close associate, Harry H. Hopkins.

After Harry Hopkins had spent six weeks in London as Roosevelt's special envoy, Harriman was sent by Roosevelt in March 1941 as his special "Defense Expediter," to discuss lend-lease. During 1941–1943, he traveled sixteen times to Britain, acting, as his biographer Rudy Abramson put it, as "the eyes and ears of Roosevelt and Hopkins, and he was also Churchill's principal instrument for conveying his needs to Washington." Harriman and Churchill had met before, at Cannes in 1927 and in New York in 1929.

On arriving in Britain on 14 March 1941, Harriman was taken immediately to Chequers. He delighted Clementine Churchill with a bag of tangerines and, after dinner, Churchill promised, "You shall be kept informed. We accept you as a friend. Nothing will be kept from you." Thereafter, Harriman roamed Whitehall, with access to committees and to much secret information, though Churchill kept details of shipping losses from the United States. Harriman provided Washington with detailed information about Britain's war needs and vigorously argued the case for the United States to meet these requirements. Churchill often took Harriman and J. G. Winant, the American ambassador, to see how cities were coping with enemy bombing. In mid-1941, Churchill encouraged Harriman to go on a lengthy tour of British forces in West Africa and the Middle East. He reported back to Roosevelt and joined the president at his meeting with Churchill at Placentia Bay, Newfoundland, in August 1941. The following month, Harriman went with Lord Beaverbrook to Moscow to discuss with Joseph Stalin supplies to Russia. On 7 December 1941, Harriman was with Churchill at Chequers (the prime minister's country residence) when news of Pearl Harbor was announced on the radio and confirmed by the admiralty. Later in December 1941, Harriman traveled by sea with Churchill when Churchill went to Washington, D.C., to discuss long-term strategy with Roosevelt.

Harriman was congenial company for the Churchill family. He played cards (bezique) with Churchill, croquet with Clementine Churchill, gave good advice to their children, and had an affair with their daughter-in-law, Pamela Digby Churchill. It is doubtful whether Clementine Churchill knew of this, but Randolph Churchill was convinced, perhaps rightly, that his father did know.

Harriman, who had been made an informal offer of the post of ambassador to the Soviet Union in 1941, accepted in 1943. From Moscow, he cabled Churchill in November 1943, "The essential quality of our relations with the Russians is still patience and forbearance." Harriman was present during some of meetings between Churchill and Stalin in Moscow in October 1944. His period as ambassador ended in January 1946. From April to September 1946, he was the ambassador to the Court of St. James, London.

Harriman visited Churchill when he was in the United States in 1946 and endorsed Churchill's "Iron Curtain" speech. He was also visiting Churchill at Chartwell on 22 September 1946 when President Harry Truman invited him to be his secretary of commerce. He left Truman's cabinet in April 1948 to assist European recovery through the Marshall Plan, with the official title of special representative to the Economic Co-operation Administration. In June 1950, he returned to Washington as special assistant to the president.

In 1952, Harriman was a contender for the Democrat nomination for president, but lost out to Adlai Stevenson and others. He was no more successful in 1956. However, Harriman stood successfully for the governorship of New York in 1954, holding the office from 1 January 1955 until the end of 1958. He was defeated by Nelson Rockefeller after one term. Though never to return to key government jobs, President John F. Kennedy appointed Harriman to be his ambassador-at-large, carrying out special missions and providing advice to the secretary of state. After an interval, he similarly served President Lyndon Johnson, including in Africa and in seeking peace in Vietnam. He later advised President Jimmy Carter and represented him at funerals and on other occasions.

In 1971, Harriman, a widower, met again the former Pamela Digby Churchill and they married. She sent her son to inform

Winston and Clementine Churchill. Lady Churchill responded with the comment, "My, my, an old flame rekindled." Averell Harriman died on 26 July 1986.

Suggestions for further reading:
Abramson, Rudy. 1992. *Spanning the Century: The Life of W. Averell Harriman, 1891–1986.* New York: William Morrow.
Gilbert, Martin. 1983 and 1986. *Winston S. Churchill.* Vols. 6 and 7. London: Heinemann.
Harriman, W. Averell, and Elie Abel. 1976. *Special Envoy to Churchill and Stalin, 1941–1916.* London: Hutchinson.

Harris, Air Chief Marshal Sir Arthur Travers (1892–1984)

Arthur Harris believed fervently in the power of heavy bombing of Germany to win the war. His dedication to Bomber Command and his leadership won him the loyalty of the brave aircrews. Churchill, who himself had enunciated the desirability of a bomber offensive on Germany, backed him until late in the war, by which time it was being won by other means and the cities and towns devastated were no longer prime military or economic targets.

After serving with the 1st Rhodesia Regiment, Arthur Harris joined the Royal Flying Corps. In 1918, he became a squadron leader in the Royal Air Force (RAF).

At the outbreak of the Second World War, Harris was made commander of No. 5 Bomber Group until the end of 1939. He then became deputy chief of air staff before being sent in mid-1941 as head of the Royal Air Force Delegation to the United States to advise on war preparations. In February 1942, he returned to be commander in chief of Bomber Command.

Until March 1945, "Bomber" Harris had Churchill's support in his policy of trying to win the war by area bombing. In July 1940, Churchill had argued in a minute to Lord Beaverbrook that the only effective offensive action by Britain at that time would be heavy bombing of Germany. Harris believed in the effectiveness of incendiary bombs dropped by huge numbers of aircraft, and he demonstrated it with a thousand-bomber attack on Cologne on 30 May 1942. Harris rightly judged night-time bombing to be less costly in aircrews' lives.

At the Casablanca Conference, January 1943, it was agreed to launch British and American bombing raids on key military, industrial, and transport targets. These raids proved to be inaccurate in targeting and costly in losses of aircraft. With use of fighter-plane protection and better technology, the raids became more effective in 1944. Harris, however, remained convinced that area bombing, rather than precision bombing, would win the war. He maneuvered hard for as much bombing capacity as possible to be unleashed on Germany, even arguing against focusing on the pre–invasion of French strategic targets.

Churchill's support was crucial for Harris's survival, as fewer and fewer people believed that bombing would win the war. Churchill admired the bravery of the bomber crews and felt that this policy took the war to Germans, just as the blitz had hit the British people. It was also a means of helping the Russian forces. At the first Quebec Conference, August 1943, Churchill eagerly provided Joseph Stalin with photographic evidence of the devastation caused by the British bombing of Germany. However, with Allied air supremacy, the destruction was increasingly aimed at smaller towns and cities that were not major military or industrial targets. Churchill came to feel that there was no merit in continuing such destruction, especially as the end of the war was clearly not far distant.

Arthur Harris was knighted in 1942 and, on his resignation from the RAF, promoted to marshal of the Royal Air Force. Harris and the men who had served in Bomber Command felt slighted in the end-of-war celebrations and in the refusal of Harris's request for a campaign medal to be made for Bomber Command. In January 1946, Churchill complained to Clement Attlee of the omission of Harris from the honors list. In 1951, Harris refused Churchill's offer to recommend him for a peerage, but in 1953 he accepted a baronetcy. He remained a hero to the surviving men of Bomber Command. He died in 1984.

Related entries:
Dowding, Air Chief Marshal Sir Hugh Caswall Tremenheere; Portal, Air Marshal Sir Charles

Suggestions for further reading:
Gilbert, Martin. 1983, 1986, and 1988. *Winston S. Churchill*. Vols. 6–8. London: Heinemann.
Messenger, Charles. 1984. *"Bomber" Harris and the Strategic Bombing Offensive 1939–1945*. London: Arms and Armour Press.
Saward, D. 1984. *Bomber Harris*. London: Cassell.
Webster, C., and N. Frankland. 1961. *The Strategic Air Offensive Against Germany*. 4 vols. London: Her Majesty's Stationery Office.

Harrow

Winston Churchill attended Harrow from 17 April 1888 until December 1892, leaving about a week before Christmas. There he achieved some success, winning prizes for history and recitation. Generally, however, he was a weak student and notable for "phenomenal slovenliness" (as one member of staff put it to Lady Randolph Churchill).

Harrow School, one of Britain's most famous public schools (in the United States, it would be called a private, that is, nonstate, school), was given a charter by Queen Elizabeth I in 1571, when it had already functioned for probably many years. During the headship of Dr. Joseph Drury a century earlier (1785–1805), four future prime ministers had been pupils and a fifth had been taught by him earlier at the school: Lord Goderich (1827–1828), Sir Robert Peel (1834 and 1841–1846), Lord Aberdeen (1852–1855), and Lord Palmerston (1855–1858 and 1859–1865), as well as Spencer Percival (1809–1812). The school was reorganized and revived by Dr. Charles Vaughan, its head in 1845–1859, who had been a pupil of Dr. Thomas Arnold at Rugby. Stanley Baldwin (prime minister, 1923, 1924–1929, and 1935–1937) was a pupil at Harrow from 1881 to 1885 under Vaughan's successor, Montagu Butler (1860–1885).

The headmaster during Winston's time was J. E. C. Welldon (1885–1898), who later became bishop of Calcutta, dean of Manchester, and dean of Durham. For a period, Welldon gave Winston remedial teaching in the classics, three times a week for fifteen minutes before evening prayers. Under Welldon, Harrow instituted the army class. Winston went into this class after a year and a half, but twice failed his entrance examination into Sandhurst. He was successful on the third attempt when he had improved his mathematics, his strengths being English and chemistry.

Harrow helped to foster Winston Churchill's love of British history. It also did much to mold his approach. The historian A. J. P. Taylor commented in a review of *A History of the English Speaking People*, Vol. 3 (London: Cassell, 1957) in the London *Observer*, 13 October 1957, "Its foundation, shaping the whole, is the version of English history taught at Harrow School nearly seventy years ago."

Churchill also developed his love of and fascination with the English language during his time at Harrow. Welldon commented when he was fourteen on his extraordinary love and veneration of it. Among the young Churchill's favorites was William Shakespeare, and he was adept at learning long passages from the plays. He wrote letters under the pseudonym of "Junius Junior" to the school journal, the *Harrovian*, and a lengthy poem, "The Influenza," published in the journal fifty years later in 1940.

After his return from South Africa, Churchill gave his first lecture on his experiences in the speech room at Harrow School on 26 October 1900. In an illustrated lecture, he described his capture by the Boers and his escape. Afterwards, he noted that he had badly mistimed his presentation, taking an hour and a half to work through a quarter of his notes. Nevertheless, he earned the then very good sum of £27.

He returned to Harrow School on impulse, in 1910 or 1911, a Liberal cabinet minister, at the height of the constitutional crisis and the resurrection of the issue of Irish Home Rule. He was with F. E. Smith and wished to show him the school, but the boys booed him and he did not return for many years. In 1938, when he was a Conservative M.P., he acted as the judge in the final round of the school's Bourchier Reading Prize.

Churchill warmed to his old school when it stayed put in the face of enemy action in the Second World War (other schools evacuating). From this time on, his table talk often consisted of reminiscences of his time at Harrow. During the desperate days for Britain in 1940, Churchill chose to go to Harrow to hear the songs of his youth. This he did on 18 December 1940, taking with him not only his wife, Clementine, his brother, Jack, and John Colville, but also four of the five Old Harrovians in his government: Leo Amery (secretary of state for India and Burma), J. T.C. Moore-Brabazon (minister of transport), David Margesson (chief whip), and Geoffrey Lloyd (secretary for petroleum). After the program of songs was over, Churchill asked for "Giants of Old" and "Boy." The former was written by E. E. Bowen in 1874 and the latter by E. W. Howson in 1883, both Harrow masters. After the songs, he made an impromptu speech on the songs, which he said were "one of the greatest treasures" of the school; he ended by saying that after winning the war, "the advantages and privileges" that hitherto had been enjoyed by only a few should "be far more widely shared by the men and the youth of the nation as a whole."

On 29 October 1941, Churchill returned again to Harrow School with his wife and the same contingent of colleagues as well as the fifth Harrovian in his government, Sir Donald Somervell (attorney general). Of this visit, E. D. W. Chaplin, a local historian, wrote, "For nearly two hours Prime Minister, schoolboys and Old Harrovians sang the School songs." Afterwards, he again made an impromptu speech in which he contrasted the more favorable position of Britain in the war then than at his previous visit and ended by saying that they were living in "the greatest days our country has ever lived."

After the Second World War, Churchill visited Harrow School on several occasions. He enjoyed an annual visit, each autumn, to hear and sing the school songs. He went every year from 1940 until 1960, except for 1956. Each time he made a speech. On 31 October 1945, he commented on his career and the part Britain had played in the Second world War as well as observing that it was a time when the voice of youth would be well received in the world. On 27 November 1958, he observed that the songs had inspired his action and his life. His speech on his final visit, on 10 November 1960, was the last public one he gave.

Suggestions for further reading:
Chaplin, E. D. W. 1941. *Winston Churchill and Harrow.* Harrow, UK: Harrow School Book Shop.
Churchill, Randolph S. 1966. *Winston S. Churchill.* Vol. 1. London: Heinemann.
Colville, John. 1985. *The Fringes of Power: Downing Street Diaries 1939–1955.* London: Hodder and Stoughton.
Gilbert, Martin. 1983 and 1988. *Winston S. Churchill.* Vols. 6 and 8. London: Heinemann.
Sandys, Celia. 1994. *From Winston with Love and Kisses: The Young Churchill.* London: Sinclair-Stevenson.

Hart, Sir Basil Henry Liddell (1895–1970)

*I*n the later 1920s and the 1930s, Churchill much admired Liddell Hart's writings on military history and strategy. In the 1930s, they met frequently and Churchill consulted him on several occasions.

Basil Liddell Hart was born in Paris on 31 October 1895, the younger son of the Reverend Henry Bramley and Clara Hart. His father was a Wesleyan minister in Paris, his mother the daughter of Henry Liddell, who worked for the London and South-Western Railway. He was educated at St. Paul's School, London, and for one year at Corpus Christi College, Cambridge. He served on the Western Front in 1915–1916, being wounded by a shell at Ypres, 1915, and incapacitated by gas during the Battle of the Somme, 1916. He was innovative in training soldiers in 1917–1921. After a period in the Army Education Corps, ill health forced him to retire from the army in 1927. He continued to develop his ideas in books and in newspaper articles. He was military correspondent of the London *Daily Telegraph,* 1925–1935, and the London *Times,* 1935–1939.

In the 1920s and 1930s, Churchill admired Liddell Hart's writings. On 31 August 1927, Liddell Hart was present at Salisbury Plain when Winston and Randolph Churchill viewed trials of the new mechanized force. On that occasion, according to Liddell Hart, Churchill praised his biography of Scipio Africanus (1926) "both as fresh light on history and a study in strategy," and said that following his praise in Rome the books would be published in Italian, the translation funded by Benito Mussolini's government. In March 1928, Churchill summoned Liddell Hart to 11 Downing Street to discuss with Sir Laming Worthington-Evans, the secretary of state for war, ways of modernizing the army, not least converting cavalry regiments into armored-car regiments.

Liddell Hart admired Churchill's *The World Crisis,* even quoting it against him in 1932 at the time of the Geneva disarmament conference when he criticized him in the *Daily Telegraph* for wishing to make rules to limit the use of weapons rather than limit the weapons. He was also critical of Churchill's stance on India, noting scathingly in his autobiography how Churchill told General Sir Bindon Blood that the "well-sounding" policy of Indianization "might be nullified in practice."

Liddell Hart frequently saw Churchill during the 1930s, perhaps most memorably on 14 February 1936 at Buck's Club, London. Then Duff Cooper, the secretary of state for war, invited Churchill, J. F. C. Fuller, Sir Hugh Trenchard, and Liddell Hart to dine and discuss defense problems. Liddell Hart was an unofficial adviser to Cooper's successor, Leslie Hore-Belisha.

Liddell Hart's advocacy of a compromise peace and his opposition to total war ensured that Churchill did not consult him during the Second World War. After the Second World War, Liddell Hart became something of a revered sage. He was knighted in 1966, and died on 29 January 1970.

Suggestions for further reading:
Danchev, Alex. 1998. *Alchemist of War: The Life of Basil Liddell Hart.* London: Weidenfeld and Nicolson.
Liddell Hart, Basil. 1965. *Memoirs.* 2 vols. London: Cassell.

Harvie-Watt, Sir George Steven (1903–1989)

*H*arvie-Watt served Churchill loyally as his parliamentary private secretary from 1941–1945. As an orthodox and even right-wing Conservative, he was able to keep Churchill well-informed of the views of his Conservative supporters in the House of Commons.

George Harvie-Watt was born in Bathgate, Llinlithgow, Scotland, on 23 August 1903, the son of James McDougal Watt of Armadale. He was educated at the Barthgate Academy and George Watson's Academy, Edinburgh. After school, he worked in the Atlas Steel Works for two years before going to the Royal Technical College, Glasgow (later Strathclyde University). He was commissioned into the 52d Lowland Scottish Divisional Engineers in 1924. He went on to the Inner Temple, London. While training as a barrister, he worked as secretary of the British Economic Federation and spoke for the Anti-Socialist Union, the National Citizens' Union, and the Conservative Party. He won Keighley in the 1931 general election but lost it in 1935, the same year that he was promoted to major in the Territorial Army. In 1937, as Major Harvie-Watt, he was selected for the safe Conservative seat of Richmond, Surrey. He served as parliamentary private secretary to Euan Wallace, first at the Board of Trade and then at the treasury. In 1938, he was appointed an assistant whip. At the start of the Second World War, he was commander of an antiaircraft battalion.

In autumn 1940, Churchill visited Harvie-Watt's battalion at Redhill to view experiments with rockets. He also discussed with Harvie-Watt whether or not he should become leader of the Conservative Party; Harvie-Watt advised him that it was important to do so. In July 1941, Churchill appointed him his parliamentary private secretary in succession to Brendan Bracken, with an office near the cabinet room at 10 Downing Street. As the prime minister's PPS, he acted as his eyes and ears among M.P.s in the House of Commons, though when Churchill was in a buoyant mood he would mix with M.P.s himself. Harvie-Watt later recalled, "As a rule he was a social animal and loved the Smoke Room of the House." From late 1941, Harvie-Watt wrote Churchill a weekly parliamentary report, which John Colville later praised as

excellent. He was sounded out about other posts, including governor of Bombay, but preferred to stay with Churchill for the remainder of the war. Among his many services for Churchill he arranged small dinner parties, at which backbench M.P.s spent an evening with Churchill.

In the 1945 general election, Harvie-Watt held his seat. However, Churchill had intended him to be chief whip had the Conservatives won the election. He was made a baronet in Churchill's resignation list of honors. After the defeat, Harvie-Watt for a short period continued to carry out the role of Churchill's parliamentary private secretary but he increasingly prioritized his business interests over politics. He became a director of Consolidated Gold Fields of South Africa, rising to be managing director, chief executive, and chairman of the company, and also a director of other companies. He returned to the Territorial Army as a brigade commander from 1957, and he was also appointed an aide-de-camp to King George VI and Queen Elizabeth II, until 1958. By 1951, Harvie-Watt devoted most of his time to business commitments rather than to politics, and he stood down from Parliament in 1959. He died on 18 December 1989.

Suggestion for further reading:
Harvie-Watt, G. S. 1980. *Most of My Life.* London: Springwood.

Hirohito, Emperor (1901–1989)

Although there was much popular demand for Emperor Hirohito to be tried as a war criminal, Churchill agreed with General Douglas MacArthur and the United States that it was better to use his authority to assist the development of a democratic state with a secular emperor. Hirohito, himself a scientist, had no belief in his own divinity and readily repudiated this in an Imperial Rescript, 1 January

1946. He also promulgated a new constitution, in effect from 3 May 1947, which stripped the emperor of all nonsymbolic powers.

Hirohito was born in 1901 and succeeded his father Taishô (Yoshihito) in 1926. He enjoyed research in botany and zoology, and wrote several books on marine biology. He visited Britain in 1921, when he was crown prince, and thereafter he hoped for Anglo-Japanese cooperation. He also hoped to see the role of emperor develop along the lines of constitutional monarchy in Britain, a development that occurred after military defeat for Japan in 1945.

As head of state, Hirohito was held by many people at the time as morally responsible for the declaration of war and for the manner in which it was fought. However, in practice, the emperor's political powers had long been delegated to the members of the government and to the leaders of the armed forces. Recent research has shown his reluctant support for General Tojô's expansionist policies of the 1930s and his personal opposition to war with the United States and Britain. Although he was strongly against attacking Pearl Harbor before Japan's final note to the United States was delivered in Washington, D.C., he probably saw war as inevitable by late 1941. However, from 1942, he called for a negotiated peace.

At Potsdam on 17 July 1945, Stalin told Churchill that he had received a message from Hirohito, via the Japanese ambassador in Moscow, that while Japan could not accept "unconditional surrender," it might be willing to accept other terms. This Churchill passed on to President Harry Truman. The emperor's approach was rejected by Joseph Stalin on the grounds that it offered no concrete proposals. Hirohito personally favored acceptance of the Allies' Potsdam Proclamation of 26 July 1945, which called for the immediate "unconditional surrender of Japan's armed forces."

Hirohito died on 7 January 1989, having been emperor for sixty-four years.

Suggestions for further reading:
Gilbert, Martin. 1988. *Winston S. Churchill.* Vol. 8. London: Heinemann.
Large, Stephen S. 1992. *Emperor Hirohito and Showa Japan.* London: Routledge.

A History of the English Speaking Peoples (1956–1958)

A History of the English Speaking Peoples was published in the afterglow of Churchill's retirement from active politics and when most readers could remember and revere his role in the Second World War. Not generally regarded as among his best books, they nevertheless sold well.

The work was commissioned by Walter Newman Flower, the owner and chairman of Cassell, for the then immense sum of $100,000. Churchill had long wanted to write such a history and he raised the matter while he was eagerly writing his biography of the duke of Marlborough. The two works together assured him of sizeable income for several years, though by 1937 he was considering selling Chartwell. Churchill later wrote in the preface to the first volume that he was not out to rival professional historians but "to present a personal view on the processes whereby English-speaking peoples throughout the world have achieved their distinctive position and character."

In September 1934, Keith Feiling, the Oxford University historian who had tutored Randolph Churchill and had provided advice on *Marlborough,* began work in preparing material for *A History of the English Speaking Peoples.* Churchill discussed the outlines of the volumes with Feiling at Chartwell that November. During 1935, Feiling sketched out fourteen chapters, providing Churchill with the material on which he based his work. Before Feiling withdrew in May 1936, he recommended Bill Deakin as chief researcher. In the first half of 1938, Churchill worked on the last volume of *Marlborough* alongside writing the early parts of the first volume of his *History*. By late November, he had written some 136,000 words of the *History*. In January 1939, Alan Bullock joined Deakin as a researcher for the book. Later, Maurice Ashley, John Wheldon, G. M. Young, and General James Edmonds all helped. By July 1939, the second volume was complete. Churchill continued to work on the book well into August 1939, completing a draft version up to 1865.

After the Second World War, Churchill at first returned to *A History of the English Speaking Peoples*. Traveling to the United States on the *Queen Elizabeth* in January 1946, he began revising the first volume. However, he soon turned to *The Second World War,* returning to his *History* in 1953, after his serious stroke. He was helped by Bill Deakin, Alan Hodge, Dennis Brogan, and others, with additional advice from such scholars as V. H. Galbraith, A. L. Rowse, and Robert Carson. He took particular interest in writing on the U.S. Civil War, having visited all the battlefields. This section was subsequently issued, with added illustrations, as a separate volume in 1961. Churchill began revising the proofs of the first volume within forty-eight hours of leaving Downing Street in April 1955. The first volume was published on 23 April 1956, with an initial print run of 130,000 in Britain. The other volumes were published by March 1958.

Maurice Ashley later gave the verdict that the first two volumes were the least successful as history because they covered periods that did not greatly interest Churchill. In contrast, Ashley observed, "the story lights up" in the last two volumes.

Related entries:
Gibbon, Edward; Macaulay, Thomas Babington; Trevelyan, George Macaulay

Suggestions for further reading:
Ashley, Maurice. 1968. *Churchill as Historian*. London: Secker and Warburg.
Gilbert, Martin. 1976 and 1988. *Winston S. Churchill*. Vols. 5 and 8. London: Heinemann.
Woods, Frederick. 1963. *A Bibliography of the Works of Sir Winston Churchill*. London: Nicholas Vane.
———. 1992. *Artillery of Words: The Writings of Sir Winston Churchill*. London: Leo Cooper.

Hitler, Adolf (1889–1945)

Adolf Hitler and Churchill never met. They saw each other as major adversaries. For Churchill, Hitler's Germany represented a major threat to Britain and the British Empire. He was appalled by the Nazi's anti-Semitism, terror against opponents, and general disregard for democracy and the rule of law.

Adolf Hitler was born on 20 April 1889 in Braunau, Austria, the son of Alois and Klara Hitler. His father was a customs official. After education at a monastery school at Lembach and a gymnasium at Steyr, he was a self-taught but unsuccessful artist. He served on the Western Front during the First World War. After the war, he became involved in right-wing politics, building up the National Socialist German Workers' Party. In the political turmoil of the depression of 1931–1933, he was invited to form a coalition government. He took the opportunity to take power and ruthlessly crush opponents. He soon set about undoing the Versailles Peace Treaty, rearming and seizing territory in central Europe. With his invasion of Poland in September 1939, Britain and France declared war. By 1941, the European war had become a world war. In overreaching himself in 1941, Hitler brought about a coalition of forces that led to his defeat and death in 1945.

Churchill had viewed the rise of Hitler with disquiet. On 18 October 1930, in a discussion with Prince Otto von Bismarck at the German embassy in London, he deplored the activities of the Nazis and made it clear that he did not believe Hitler's protestations that he wished for no war of aggression. Hitler and Churchill had the opportunity to meet in the late summer of 1932 when Winston, Clementine, Sarah, and Randolph Churchill visited Munich; indeed, Ernst Hanfstaengl pressed Hitler on two days to meet the Churchills, but Hitler declined.

Soon after the Nazis took power in Germany in April 1933, Churchill spoke in the House of Commons deploring the persecution of Jews in Germany, warning against German rearmament, and commenting "You have a dictatorship—a grim dictatorship." In Germany, the Nazi-controlled press denounced Churchill for his "impudence." In November, Churchill made a speech in which he warned of the Nazi's glorification of war and their wish "to inculcate a form of blood lust in their children."

In 1935, Churchill wrote a substantial essay on Hitler, published in the *Strand* in November (and reprinted in his *Great Contemporaries,* published in October 1939). In "Hitler and Choice," Churchill outlined the atrocities of Nazi Germany and asked whether he would unleash another major war or whether "we may yet live to see Hitler a gentler figure in a happier age." However, the general thrust of his article was to suggest that "this grim figure," who was encouraging "the worship of Germany under the symbols of the old gods of Nordic paganism," was more likely to opt for war.

Churchill was rightly seen by Hitler and the leading Nazis as an implacable foe. After the Munich settlement in 1938, Hitler denounced Churchill, Duff Cooper, Anthony Eden, and Arthur Greenwood. A few days later, he warned Germans against Churchill, "Tomorrow those who want war may be in the government. Mr. Churchill may be Prime Minister tomorrow." He added, "We request to be spared being supervised like a pupil by a governess."

With Churchill in power, Hitler found there would be no compromise peace. In July 1940, when Hitler made his "appeal to reason" in Britain, his vague peace offer was immediately rejected. Hitler had hopes that a different government, including Neville Chamberlain, Lord Halifax, and David Lloyd George, might discuss peace terms. Churchill, the Royal Navy, and the Royal Air Force (RAF) showed that Britain could hold on until the war widened. Whether this was in Britain's best interests has been debated by recent authors, notably John Charmley, John Lukacs, and others. Although it is clear that far greater consideration was given to a negotiated peace than the stereotype of a defiant, united Britain in 1940 allows, it seems to this author very much the case that Churchill's war leadership was soon widely admired. Also, to this author, Churchill was right to deem Hitler and the Nazis people with whom no compromises could be made, not least given the warning of what was done with their opponents and scapegoats within Germany and their conquered territories. Hitler, defeated, committed suicide on 30 April 1945.

Suggestions for further reading:
Charmley, John. 1993. *Churchill: The End of Glory.* London: Hodder and Stoughton.
Gilbert, Martin. 1976 and 1983. *Winston S. Churchill.* Vols. 5 and 6. London: Heinemann.
Kershaw, Ian. 1998 and 2000. *Hitler.* Vols. 1 and 2. London: Allen Lane.
Lawlor, Sheila. 1994. *Churchill and the Politics of War.* Cambridge: Cambridge University Press.
Lukacs, John. 1992. *The Duel: Hitler vs. Churchill.* Oxford: Oxford University Press.
Parker, R. A. C. 2000. *Churchill and Appeasement.* London: Macmillan.
Strawson, John. 1997. *Churchill and Hitler.* London: Dent.

Hoare, Sir Samuel John Gurney (Viscount Templewood, 1880–1959)

Although Churchill and Sir Samuel Hoare got on reasonably well in the 1920s, Churchill came to loathe Hoare in the 1930s. Churchill hated Hoare's liberal policy toward India and later his role as an appeaser. On becoming prime minister, Churchill omitted Hoare from his government and later vetoed his becoming viceroy of India.

Samuel Hoare was born on 24 February 1880 in London, the fifth child and eldest son of Samuel and Katharin Louisa Hart Hoare. His father, of a banking family that owned land in the Cromer area of Norfolk, was Conservative M.P. for Norwich, 1886–1906. His mother was the daughter of Richard Davis, audit commissioner. Educated at Harrow and New College, Oxford, he became the assistant private secretary to Alfred Lyttelton, the colonial secretary, in 1905. He unsuccessfully stood for Ipswich in the 1906 general election, but won Chelsea in January 1910, a seat he held until 1944. He served on the London County Council, 1907–1910. In 1915, he became the second baronet on the death of his father. He served in the army from October 1914, notably as part of the military mission to Russia, 1916–1917, and in Italy in 1918. Back in Parliament, he was chairman of the coalition government's Foreign Affairs Committee, a backbench pressure group that eagerly urged the government to support anti-Bolshevik groups in Russia. His role in this was praised by Churchill; however, by mid-1922, Hoare was disillusioned with David Lloyd George's coalition government and became a leading Conservative opponent of its continuance.

Hoare entered Andrew Bonar Law's government as secretary of state for air, initially outside the cabinet. When Baldwin succeeded as prime minister in May 1923, his office was made a cabinet post. After the brief Labour government of 1924, Hoare returned to air for the whole of Baldwin's second government (1924–1929). Hoare was one of several cabinet colleagues Churchill entertained at Chartwell in February 1926. They worked together during the General Strike that May, Hoare being re-

sponsible for the distribution of the *British Gazette* by air. Hoare also suggested that name for the government's newspaper.

Churchill and Hoare were opposed on India. Hoare was secretary of state for India, 1931–1935. Hoare was responsible for drafting a new constitution for India in the face of the vehement opposition of Churchill and the Conservative Right. Churchill accused Hoare of organizing the altering of evidence to a parliamentary joint select committee by the Manchester Chamber of Trade. This accusation led to a major inquiry by the Committee of Privileges, and Hoare was fortunate to be exonerated. However, it left a legacy of bitter animosity between the two men. Hoare succeeded in getting his Government of India Bill to the statute book in 1935.

Baldwin made Hoare foreign secretary, where he served only from June to December 1935. He resigned over what became known as the Hoare–Laval Pact. With only Britain willing to enforce collective security on Italy when it invaded part of Abyssinia, Hoare and the French foreign secretary, Pierre Laval, agreed on a plan that would have given Benito Mussolini a fifth of Abyssinia. The ensuing uproar led to Hoare's resignation. Baldwin brought him back into his government as first lord of the admiralty, June 1936. Neville Chamberlain appointed him home secretary, 1937–1939, and after the outbreak of war elevated him to lord privy seal, with a seat in the war cabinet. He remained loyal to Chamberlain until the last. He was the most prominent appeaser axed by Churchill when he became prime minister.

Sir Samuel Hoare's career ended with his becoming a special ambassador to Spain, 1940–1944. Halifax, who was instrumental in sending him, expected him to be the next viceroy of India. Churchill, who still resented Hoare's different views on India in the early 1930s, vetoed his appointment. Churchill, however, did praise Hoare for helping to keep General Francisco Franco and Spain out of the Second World War. Hoare was elevated to the peerage on 1 July 1944, as Viscount Templewood of Chelsea, Templewood being his Norfolk home. He continued to serve in Spain until the end of 1944, when he retired. He wrote several volumes of memoirs. He died on 7 May 1959.

Related entries:
Appeasement; Baldwin, Stanley; Chamberlain, (Arthur) Neville

Suggestions for further reading:
Cross, J. A. 1977. *Sir Samuel Hoare: A Political Biography.* London: Jonathan Cape.
Gilbert, Martin. 1976. *Winston S. Churchill.* Vol. 5. London: Heinemann.
Templewood, Viscount. 1954. *Nine Troubled Years.* London: Collins.
———. 1957. *Empire of the Air.* London: Collins.

Home Secretary (1910–1911)

Churchill served as home secretary from 14 February 1910 until 23 October 1911. After the January 1910 general election, Herbert Henry Asquith reshaped his cabinet, with an intention to promote Churchill. He offered him the post of chief secretary for Ireland, but Churchill asked to go to the admiralty or the home office. He was made the secretary of state for the home office.

Churchill took up prison reforms where his predecessor, Herbert Gladstone, had left off. He began by ensuring a more liberal approach to solitary confinement, to those who had not been convicted of cruelty, serious violence, indecency, or dishonesty, to providing lectures and concerts, and to assisting prisoners on their release.

Churchill also introduced the Mines Bill, which became an act in 1911 and was a major contribution to mining safety. His Shops Bill proposed a sixty-hour limit to working hours, a half-day-a-week holiday, and guaranteed mealtimes. During its pas-

sage through Parliament, the hours-of-work limitation was lost, but the half-day remained in the 1911 act. Churchill accepted the presidency of the Early Closing Association, a post he held until the Second World War.

Churchill took a higher profile when he joined the police and soldiers in the East End of London after a raid on a jeweler's shop. His part in the "Siege of Sidney Street" aroused controversy.

Because he was responsible for law and order, Churchill also became involved in industrial disputes. He was strongly criticized, mostly unfairly, for his role in responding to unrest in Tonypandy during the 1910 South Wales miners' strike. He also supplied troops during the 1911 transport strikes, notably during unrest in Liverpool and at Llanelli, resulting in two deaths at each place. On another occasion, he authorized troops to go to Manchester, where they occupied the railway stations.

Related entries:
Sidney Street, Siege of; Tonypandy

Suggestions for further reading:
Addison, Paul. 1992. *Churchill on the Home Front.* London: Jonathan Cape.
Churchill, Randolph S. 1967. *Winston S. Churchill.* Vol. 2. London: Heinemann.
Pelling, Henry. 1989. *Winston Churchill.* 2d ed. London: Macmillan.

Hopkins, Harry Lloyd (1890–1946)

Churchill came to appreciate Harry Hopkins as a dedicated supporter of Allied victory in the Second World War. Hopkins was a, perhaps the, key link between Churchill and President Franklin D. Roosevelt, particularly in 1940–1943.

Harry Hopkins was born on 17 August 1890 in Sioux City, Iowa, the fourth of the five children of David Aldona and Anna

Undated portrait of Harry Lloyd Hopkins (Library of Congress)

Pickett Hopkins. His father owned a store. His mother, a devout Methodist, had been a schoolteacher. Educated at Grinnell High School and Grinnell College, he became a social worker in New York City. Defective vision prevented him from enlisting in the First World War, but he joined the Red Cross. After further welfare work in the 1920s, he was appointed deputy chairman of Governor Franklin D. Roosevelt's Temporary Emergency Relief Agency in New York State in 1931. In 1932, Hopkins became chairman. After Franklin D. Roosevelt became president, Hopkins became director of the Emergency Relief Administration. In December 1938, Hopkins became secretary of commerce, but ill health forced him to resign in August 1940.

In late 1940, when Roosevelt expressed a wish to talk with Churchill, Hopkins offered to go to London as a special emissary. On 3 January 1941, it was announced at a press conference that Hopkins was going to England. Apparently, when Churchill heard he was coming, he demanded to know who he was. Brendan Bracken, who had met Hopkins a few years earlier, told Churchill of Hopkins's significance. Hopkins was given VIP treatment in London. He had lunch at 10 Downing Street with Churchill on 11 January 1941, informing him of the president's hope of a meeting in April 1941. Churchill gave him a frank appraisal of the war, believing that Greece was already lost but confident that Britain would successfully repel an invasion force should one come. Hopkins was impressed by Churchill and by the courage and determination he witnessed in London. He supported Churchill's request for United States aid. Hopkins stayed in England for six weeks.

Roosevelt sent Hopkins to London again in July 1941. Hopkins discussed with Churchill the forthcoming conference at Placentia Bay and the proposed United States naval support for merchant ships between the United States and Iceland. Hopkins went on to Moscow from 27 July to 1 August to try to assess how long the Soviet Union could stay in the war. He flew from Russia to Scapa Flow, joining Churchill on the *Prince of Wales* to Placentia Bay. On the journey, he briefed Churchill on his talks with Stalin.

After Pearl Harbor, Churchill visited Washington on 22 December 1941. He stayed in the White House, his large bedroom across a hall from Hopkins's room, and they frequently talked.

On 8 April 1942, Hopkins and General G. C. Marshall led a mission to London to discuss OPERATION ROUNDUP (later OVERLORD), the plan to invade France in spring 1943 in order to relieve the Soviet Union. Churchill received the proposals sympathetically and talked frankly of the problems in the Indian and Pacific Oceans. He also resisted U.S. suggestions concerning India.

In June 1942, Churchill went again to Washington to argue against the current plan to invade France in September 1942.

Roosevelt, Hopkins, and Marshall firmly argued against prioritizing North Africa and delaying the invasion of France. However, with the situation in North Africa deteriorating, Roosevelt sent Harry Hopkins, General Marshall, and Admiral Ernest Joseph King to London again. They departed on 16 and returned on 27 July. On arrival, to Churchill's fury, Marshall and King went to see Dwight Eisenhower first, but Hopkins placated Churchill by visiting Churchill immediately at Chequers. During this visit, the invasion of France was postponed and replaced with the agreement that United States troops would land in North Africa. Hopkins accompanied Roosevelt to the Casablanca Conference.

In February 1943, when Churchill further took up the contentious issue of atomic research, he corresponded with Hopkins. In May, Churchill again visited Washington and stayed at the White House. Hopkins was involved in the talks there, as he was at Quebec, Cairo, and Tehran.

Hopkins was taken ill on 1 January 1944 and spent some seven months recovering. When Hopkins's son Stephen was killed in action in February 1944, Churchill had a scroll, with an appropriate quotation from the final scene of *Macbeth* on it, sent to Hopkins in the hospital. After his illness, Hopkins could work only a few hours a day and became a lesser player in events. Roosevelt did not take him to the second Quebec Conference. Hopkins remained in contact with Churchill, keeping him informed of political and other developments in Washington.

Roosevelt regretted not having Hopkins's advice at Quebec, particularly over the plan to deindustrialize Germany, and turned again to Hopkins. In January 1945, Hopkins went again to London to discuss with Churchill issues to be covered at the Yalta conference. He reported that Churchill, who liked comfortable surroundings, had complained of Yalta, "We could not have found a worse place for a meeting if we had spent ten years on research." He went on to Paris, Rome, Naples, and Malta, where he joined Roosevelt on his journey to Yalta. After the conference, Churchill went aboard Roosevelt's ship at Alexandria on 14 February, the last time the two men met. Soon after, Hopkins was taken ill again and left the ship to recover at Marrakesh. He also did not see Roosevelt again.

After Roosevelt's death, Hopkins advised President Harry Truman for awhile, but insisted on leaving the government's service on 12 May 1945. On 8 May, he cabled Churchill, saying he had been thinking of him in victory. On 23 May, in spite of retiring, Hopkins went as Truman's special envoy to Moscow, where he had six meetings with Joseph Stalin. After Hopkins left Russia, Churchill phoned him in Frankfurt asking him to see him in London, but Truman refused Churchill's request to permit Hopkins to divert to London. On 2 July 1945, Hopkins did retire from government work, declining to go to Potsdam. He moved to New York, where he was chairman for the New York clothing industry.

In November 1945, he returned to the hospital. On 22 January 1946, he wrote to Churchill in Miami Beach, regretting he was unable to leave the hospital to join him there. Churchill wrote to President Truman on 29 January, the day Hopkins died, "I have a great regard for that man, who always went to the root of the matter and scanned our great affairs with pierceing eye."

Related entries:
Lend Lease Act; Roosevelt, Franklin Delano

Suggestions for further reading:
Gilbert, Martin. 1983, 1986, and 1988. *Winston S. Churchill*. Vols. 6, 7, and 8. London: Heinemann.
Sherwood, Robert E. 1948 and 1949. *The White House Papers of Harry L. Hopkins*. 2 vols. London: Eyre and Spottiswoode.

Hore-Belisha, Isaac Leslie (Baron Hore-Belisha of Devonport, 1893–1957)

Churchill on occasion praised Leslie Hore-Belisha while he was secretary of state for war (1937–1940). However, he was also rumored to be one of a group of politicians undermining him before 1939. Churchill did recognize the strong points of Hore-Belisha in reforming the war office and gave him office in his "caretaker" government in 1945.

Leslie Hore-Belisha was born in London on 7 September 1893. His father, Jacob Isaac Belisha, was of a Manchester cotton importing family. He died when Leslie was one. His mother, formerly Elizabeth Miriam Miers, devotedly brought him up. In 1912, she married Adair Hore, later permanent secretary to the Ministry of Pensions, and Leslie met her wishes by taking his stepfather's name. After Clifton College, Bristol, he went to Balliol College, Oxford, in 1913. He served during the First World War, leaving with the rank of major. After returning and completing his studies at Oxford, he was a successful political journalist, using his pay to fund legal studies. He became a barrister in 1923.

He ran unsuccessfully as a Liberal for Plymouth Devonport in 1922, but won the seat in 1923, holding it until 1945. In 1931, he was a prominent National Liberal, joining Ramsay MacDonald's National government as parliamentary secretary to the Board of Trade and being promoted in September 1932 to financial secretary to the treasury. In June 1934, he became minister of transport, a post he held until May 1937 (with a place in the cabinet from October 1936). He was dynamic and successful in this role, with the illuminated orange warning globes at pedestrian crossings still being known in Britain as "Belisha beacons."

When Neville Chamberlain became prime minister he made Hore-Belisha his secretary of state for war, giving him a man-date to shake up the war office. This he did, with some skill. However, he aroused much antagonism, not least from Lord Gort, commander in chief of the British Expeditionary Force, who resented his criticisms of the slow progress of defenses in France, especially in the Ardennes sector. King George VI took up Gort's complaints with the prime minister. On 4 January 1940, Chamberlain offered Hore-Belisha the Board of Trade or the Ministry of Information, but he declined, preferring to resign from the government.

Churchill later wrote that Hore-Belisha was proved right over the defective defenses in the Ardennes, but he felt that he had been inept in his relations with the senior military figures. Churchill advised Hore-Belisha to take the presidency of the Board of Trade. Later, he said that if he had still been in office in May 1940, Churchill would probably have kept him on. As it was, Hore-Belisha retired to the backbenches, and was one of those who voted for the No Confidence Motion moved by Aneurin Bevan in July 1942. Hore-Belisha's criticism during the war often stung Churchill, and on one occasion, 10 June 1941, he even led him to an empty room and warned him, "If you fight me I shall fight you back. And remember this: You are using a 4.5 howitzer, and I am using a 12-inch gun." Churchill brought him back to office as minister of national insurance in his "caretaker" government of May–July 1945.

After losing his seat in the 1945 general election, Hore-Belisha joined the Conservative Party; he unsuccessfully fought Coventry South in the 1950 general election. In 1954, he accepted a peerage. He died on 16 February 1957.

Suggestions for further reading:
Gilbert, Martin. 1983. *Winston S. Churchill.* Vol. 6. London: Heinemann.
Liddell-Hart, B. H. 1971. "Hore-Belisha, Isaac Leslie." In *Dictionary of National Biography 1951–1960,* edited by E. T. Williams and H. M. Palmer. Oxford: Oxford University Press.
Minney, R. J. 1960. *The Private Papers of Hore-Belisha.* London: Collins.

I

Industrial Charter (1947)

Churchill was lukewarm about the Industrial Charter, 1947, but was very emollient toward the trade unions after the Second World War.

The Industrial Charter was one of several drawn up by the Conservative Party after their substantial defeat in the 1945 general election. The choice of the word "charter" followed the Anglo-American Atlantic Charter of 1941 that set out broad principles for reshaping the postwar world. Also, a reassessment of policy after a substantial defeat had been carried out by Sir Robert Peel after the 1832 defeat. R. A. Butler, who chaired the Conservatives' Industrial Policy Committee, later recalled, "Peel's Tamworth Manifesto made a rallying point for Conservatism in much the same way as our charters made a rallying point." The Industrial Charter accepted much of the developments in industrial and employment policy since 1940 yet promised to "free industry from unnecessary controls and restrictions" and to restore "freedom" and "fair incentive." One section of the Industrial Charter gave what was called the "Workers' Charter." This set out a code of good practice for employers to follow if they wished, with a suggestion that in due course local authorities should accept tenders only from those who conformed to it. The "Workers' Charter" went into the 1950 Conservative general election manifesto and was a major part of the Conservatives' drive to win back working-class votes. However, by the early 1960s, at least one of those who drafted it felt that the Industrial Charter "was too concerned with the problem of the thirties—unemployment—and not sufficiently with the problem of the fifties—inflation."

Related entry:
Butler, Richard Austen

Suggestions for further reading:
Conservative Political Centre. 1947. *The Industrial Charter*. London: The Conservative Party.
Hoffman, J. D. 1964. *The Conservative Party in Opposition 1945–1951*. London: MacGibbon and Kee.
Ramsden, John. 1980. *The Making of Conservative Party Policy*. London: Longman.

Inskip, Sir Thomas Walker Hobart (Viscount Caldecote, 1876–1947)

Sir Thomas Inskip was Stanley Baldwin's choice for a major defense role in 1936 because he was considered to have sounder judgment than the charismatic but risky Churchill.

Thomas Inskip was born in Bristol on 5 March 1876, the second son of James and

Constance Inskip. His father was a prominent solicitor. Educated at Clifton and King's College, Cambridge, he went on to be a barrister. During the First World War, he served in naval intelligence. After unsuccessfully standing in the 1906 and January 1910 general elections, he was elected to Parliament in 1918 as the Conservative M.P. for Bristol, Central, a seat he held until 1929. In 1931, he was elected for Fareham, a seat he held until going to the House of Lords in 1939. From 1922 until 1936, he held a series of legal offices, except when Labour was in office.

In 1934, Sir Thomas Inskip was attorney general and a leading figure on the Committee of Privileges in the House of Commons, which investigated Churchill's complaints about Sir Samuel Hoare and India. Inskip was also a major government speaker on the India Bill in 1935. In both roles he was critical of Churchill.

In March 1936, Churchill and other politicians were surprised when Stanley Baldwin appointed Inskip, not Churchill, to be minister for coordination of defense. Neville Chamberlain's view of the appointment was that it would create no enthusiasm nor would it cause political trouble. Churchill's associate, Professor Frederick Alexander Lindemann, commented that it was "the most cynical thing that has been done since Caligula appointed his horse as consul." Churchill criticized the appointment in the House of Commons on 23 April.

On 25 May 1936, Churchill, while emphasizing that he would continue to campaign for rearmament, offered to help Inskip should he wish for his assistance. Inskip asked for Churchill's ideas on creating a Ministry of Supply and on the dangers of invasion by parachute troops. Churchill discussed the issues concerning creating a Ministry of Supply on 8 June. However, Churchill's involvement was resented by the earl of Swinton, Sir Maurice Hankey, and others. Inskip continued to be at the receiving end of Churchill's campaign for rearmament. He appears to have been more willing to carefully consider Churchill's data than were some of his colleagues.

Inskip was a "man of Munich." Earlier in the year, he had dismissed Czechoslovakia as "an unstable unit in Central Europe." In late October 1938, Chamberlain and he were still opposed to the creation of a Ministry of Supply. On 29 January 1939, Inskip became secretary of state for the dominions. His replacement at supply was a member of the House of Lords, Lord Chatfield.

At the outbreak of war, Inskip was appointed lord chancellor and created Viscount Caldecote of Bristol. When Churchill formed his wartime government, Caldecote was moved back to being secretary of state for the dominions, May–October 1940, and was also leader of the House of Lords. He was appointed lord chief justice, 1940–1946. He died on 11 October 1947.

Related entries:
Chamberlain, (Arthur) Neville; Hankey, Sir Maurice Pascal Alers; Swinton, Earl of

Suggestion for further reading:
Gilbert, Martin. 1976 and 1983. *Winston S. Churchill.* Vols. 5 and 6. London: Heinemann.

Ismay, General Sir Hastings Lionel (Lord Ismay, 1887–1965)

*I*smay was a highly able intermediary between Churchill and the generals during the Second World War. He was a great admirer of Churchill and was notably loyal and supportive. "Pug" Ismay was well liked by nearly all, including Winston and Clementine Churchill.

Hastings Ismay was born on 21 June 1887 at Naini Tal, one of the British hill stations in the Himalayas in India. His parents were Stanley Ismay (later Sir Stanley), an Indian civil servant and later chief judge of the Mysore Chief Court, and Beatrice Eileen Read. He was the youngest of four children. He was educated at Charterhouse, after which he went to the Royal Military College, Sandhurst, in 1904, and then joined the Indian army in late 1905. At the outbreak of the First World War, he was involved in military operations in Somaliland with the Somaliland Camel Corps against Mahomed bin Abdulla Hassan. With the defeat of the mullah in 1920, Ismay was appointed to the DSO (Distinguished Service Order). In 1921, he married Laura Kathleen Clegg. In 1922, he went for a year to the Staff College in Quetta, followed by just over a year at army headquarters at Simla. He returned to Britain in 1924 and was assistant secretary to the Committee of Imperial Defence, under Sir Maurice Hankey, 1925–1930.

Ismay first came into contact with Churchill during the General Strike, 1926. He was the secretary of a small committee considering how the Territorial Army could be employed on police duties, the committee consisting of Churchill, William Joynson-Hicks (the home secretary), and Sir Laming Worthington-Evans (secretary of state for war). Churchill dominated the committee. When there was a quibble as to who would pay, Churchill replied (according to Ismay), "The Exchequer will pay. If we start arguing about petty details, we will have a tired-out police force, a dissipated army and bloody revolution." Ismay was very favorably impressed by Churchill then.

Ismay became deputy secretary to the Committee of Imperial Defence in 1936, after a further period in India (1931–1933) and in the war office (1933–1936). When Hankey retired in 1938, Ismay succeeded him. He worked again with Churchill in April 1940 when Chamberlain decided that

the first lord of the admiralty would be chairman of the Military Co-ordinating Committee. In Ismay's view, the new pattern of organization would not have worked well, but Churchill's accession to the premiership transformed this and other administrative arrangements.

Churchill created for himself the post of minister of defense, which he combined with that of prime minister. As defense minister, he operated through an office run by Ismay. Ismay was his trusted assistant in a wide range of important and sensitive matters, including being his representative at Chiefs of Staff meetings and his link with the three armed services. As a result, Ismay was privy to the major decisions of war policy and he took on many highly sensitive missions abroad for Churchill. Ismay was promoted to lieutenant general in 1942 and general in 1944. He was created a baron in 1947.

Ismay retired from the army in December 1946. In March 1947, he went to India as chief of staff to Lord Mountbatten, assisting the viceroy in speeding up the granting of independence to India. In early 1948, Clement Attlee invited him to be chairman of the council for the Festival of Britain, to be held in 1951.

When Churchill won the 1951 general election, he appointed Ismay secretary of state for Commonwealth Relations. After six months, there was a widespread wish for Ismay to be the first secretary general of NATO (North Atlantic Treaty Organization). Ismay initially declined, but agreed after being pressed by Churchill in person. In his autobiography he wrote that he "would gladly do anything in the world that my revered chief asked or even advised." He took over at NATO on 4 April 1952 and served with distinction at NATO headquarters in Paris for five years. When he and his wife returned to England in May 1957, they dined with Winston and Clementine Churchill. Churchill asked, "Have you forgiven me for sending you to

NATO?" and Ismay replied, "Sir, you were right as always."

After his return from Paris, he wrote his memoirs. Churchill enjoyed reading a typescript copy of the early chapters in May 1958. Churchill contributed a letter of tribute to Ismay, published at the front of the memoirs. He was the guest of honor at a dinner in London in September 1960 after the book was published.

Ismay was appointed a Knight of the Garter in 1957. He died on 17 December 1965.

Suggestions for further reading:
Gilbert, Martin. 1983–1988. *Winston S. Churchill.* Vols. 6–8. London: Heinemann.
Ismay, Lord. 1960. *The Memoirs of General the Lord Ismay.* London: Heinemann.
Wingate, Sir Ronald. 1970. *Lord Ismay: A Biography.* London: Hutchinson.

J

Jewish Infantry Brigade

Winston Churchill was the most powerful British politician who supported accepting the offer of a Jewish brigade, fighting under its own flag and joining the British army in fighting the Nazis. Victor Cazalet and Lord Strabolgi were other supporters.

In December 1939, Churchill had prepared a draft telegram to Lord Lothian, the British ambassador in Washington, which included the comments that the government "realize to the full the value of Jewish support," not least those who were not Allied nationals, but "they would not like to feel this support was being given for any other reason but that the Jews concerned share the ideals for which the Allies are fighting, and realize that it is in the interests of the Jews of the world that the Allies should win." (This was circulated as a cabinet paper, G 161, 1939.) In 1940, he urged the acceptance of Jewish military support.

Churchill supported a secret operation in cooperation with the Zionist Agency to train Jewish men in the use of modern weapons. As a result, Arnold Lawrence (brother of T. E.), Nicholas Hammond, and Henry Barnes were sent to Jerusalem to train Haganah personnel. Those trained on Mount Carmel included Moshe Dayan and Ygal Yadin. Some of those so trained were in the advance forces in the assault on Tripoli.

Irritated by repeated procrastination by the war office and foreign office, Churchill in July 1944 insisted that a Jewish Brigade be formed. The BBC on 24 September 1944 broadcast an announcement that included the statement, "The Infantry Brigade will be based on the Jewish battalions of the Palestine Regiment." Churchill followed this up by referring to the Jewish Brigade early on in his lengthy review of the war in the House of Commons on 28 September 1944. He then commented, "I know that there are vast numbers of Jews serving with our Forces and the American Forces throughout all the Armies, but it seems to me indeed appropriate that a special Jewish unit, a special unit of that race which has suffered indescribable torments from the Nazis, should be represented as a distinct formation amongst the forces gathered for their final overthrow, and I have no doubt they will not only take part in the struggle but also in the occupation which will follow."

Churchill did his utmost to ensure that the Jewish Brigade could operate in the way that its mentors wished. He made it clear that it should fight Germans in Europe, not Japanese; that it should not be split up other than in some exceptional emergency; that he would secure the king's permission for it to have its own flag; and that political consideration would be given to what became of it after the end of the war.

The Jewish Brigade landed in Italy in November 1944, becoming part of the British Eighth Army. In March 1945, 5,500 strong, they joined the front line; in the following month, they attacked across the Senio River and then moved on to the Monte Grande area and then Milan. At the end of the war, members of the Jewish Brigade assisted Jews stranded in Austria, Poland, and elsewhere to get out and go to Palestine.

Suggestions for further reading:
Beckman, Morris. 1998. *The Jewish Brigade: An Army with Two Masters 1944–1945.* Staplehurst, Kent, UK: Spellmount.
Gilbert, Martin. 1993. *The Churchill War Papers.* Vol. 1. London: Heinemann.
Hammond, Nicholas. 1997. "British Co-operation with the Zionist Agency in Palestine 1940–1942." *The Historian* 54 (summer): pp. 21–27.

Kitchener, Horatio Herbert (First Earl Kitchener of Khartoum, 1850–1916)

Kitchener became a military hero of the British Empire through his campaigns in the Sudan and as a reassuring figure for the British people in the early stages of the First World War. Though disapproving of Churchill as a young subaltern, he and Churchill intermittently worked well together in 1914–1915.

Born on 24 June 1850 near Listowel, County Kerry, Ireland, Horatio Herbert Kitchener was the second of four sons born to Colonel Horatio and Frances Ann Kitchener. Badly educated at home, Kitchener caught up when the family moved to Switzerland, where he became fluent in French. Later, he learned Arabic. He attended the Royal Military Academy, Woolwich, in 1868. In the army, he advanced by his abilities and his courage, helped by support he gained from the foreign office, Evelyn Baring, first earl of Cromer, British agent and consul general of Egypt 1883–1907, Lord Salisbury, and even Queen Victoria. From 1892–1899 he was commander in chief (the sirdar) of the Egyptian army. Kitchener carried out all his campaigns, including the conquest of the Sudan, with financial economy, earning the reputation of a man who was hard, even autocratic.

Winston Churchill first tried to attach himself to Sir Herbert Kitchener to experience military action in November 1896. He reinforced his own applications by mobilizing his mother and her connections. In December, Kitchener wrote to Lady Randolph Churchill to inform her that he had noted Winston's name for possible special services but that he currently had no vacancies in the cavalry. Winston, in pressing for a posting with Kitchener in Egypt, told his mother that after two years there and some military action he would be in a strong position to stand for Parliament. In February 1898, Kitchener again wrote to Lady Randolph expressing the hope that he would be able to employ Winston in the Sudan. Thereafter, various of Churchill's influential supporters—including General Sir Evelyn Wood and Lady Jeune—continued to press Kitchener to take Churchill under his command.

However, as the British (as opposed to the Egyptian) part of the force was under war office control, Winston Churchill was able to become attached to the 21st Lancers. Kitchener disapproved of Churchill pushing his way into a combat zone because he rightly judged that Churchill did not intend a career in the army and was taking opportunities that were of great value to others who intended to stay in the army. Churchill met Kitchener on 1 September 1898, on the eve of the Battle of Omdurman, when Churchill reported the

Alfred Leete used the face of Lord Kitchener as a model for this recruitment poster. (Library of Congress)

advance of the dervish army toward Kitchener's forces.

Churchill wrote a history of Kitchener's campaign in the Upper Nile, 1896–1899, *The River War* (1899). In this and his newspaper reports to the *Morning Post* he was critical of Kitchener for not preventing the killing of wounded dervishes after the Battle of Omdurman and also for destroying the mahdi's tomb in Khartoum. His willingness to criticize Kitchener had not been lessened by Kitchener's forbidding Captain J. K. Watson, his aide-de-camp, from providing Churchill with information for *The River War.*

Because Kitchener resented Churchill's criticisms, it was harder for Churchill to be accepted as a newspaper correspondent at the front in South Africa with Field Marshal Lord Roberts, whose chief of staff was Lord Kitchener (ennobled in 1898). After

more pressing of his case by influential friends, Lord Roberts agreed to Churchill joining his force. In spite of much bravery on Churchill's part, neither Roberts nor Kitchener warmed to the young Churchill.

After the end of the Boer War, Kitchener served as commander in chief in India. Early on, he clashed with Lord Curzon, the viceroy, and emerged victorious. Churchill privately deplored Kitchener's stance, observing to his mother that Kitchener was an ambitious soldier who was swallowing up rivals in his drive for greater personal power.

From 1911 to 1914, Kitchener was British agent and consul general in Egypt. In this capacity, he was summoned to Malta for a conference in late May to early June 1912 to discuss the protection of the Mediterranean with Herbert Henry Asquith, the prime minister, and Churchill, first lord of the admiralty. Churchill and Kitchener came to provisional agreement on naval strength in the Mediterranean, an agreement mostly confirmed by the Committee of Imperial Defence in July 1912.

Churchill conferred with Kitchener on the 28 July 1914, the day after Kitchener had received an earldom, about the possibility of the invasion of Belgium and British participation in a general European war. They met a second time the next day, when Kitchener warned that the Germans would use large quantities of high explosive shells against the French. They met a third time at lunch on 31 July, when Kitchener predicted an imminent German attack on France and urged that Britain support France. On 4 August, Churchill successfully urged Asquith to stop Kitchener from returning to Egypt and to appoint him secretary of state for war, although quite possibly Asquith had already decided on both these courses of action.

With the First World War, the friction of earlier years between Churchill and Kitchener was gone and they worked well together, at least for some four months. When

Kitchener and Sir John French, the commander in chief of the British Expeditionary Force, clashed, Churchill worked hard at mediating between them. However, by December 1914, Kitchener felt Churchill's interventions with French were making matters worse, not better, and secured Asquith's support in stopping Churchill from visiting French in France.

Kitchener asked for admiralty help at Antwerp in September and October 1914. With German forces appearing likely to attack the city, Kitchener asked that Admiral Henry Oliver, director of the Intelligence Division of the admiralty, be sent to Antwerp to deal with thirty-eight German merchant ships that might be used for an invasion of Britain. Oliver was successful. When the situation deteriorated, on 2 October 1914, Kitchener and Sir Edward Grey consulted Churchill on whether Antwerp should be held much longer, thereby hindering the German advance along the coast in "the race to the sea" (which resulted in trenches across France and Belgium). With the agreement of Kitchener, Churchill set off that night for Antwerp, arriving after noon the next day (3 October). Churchill then explained to the Belgian prime minister Kitchener's plan for a joint British and French force to secure the relief of Antwerp. While Churchill inspected the defenses and tried to stiffen the will to resist the Germans, Kitchener arranged reinforcements. Though derided and denigrated by some of the so-called patriotic press, notably the *Morning Post,* Churchill made an heroic attempt, in line with Kitchener's wishes, to hold Antwerp and delay the German advance.

Kitchener gave wavering support to the Gallipoli campaign, which began, under Churchill, as a naval operation. Kitchener had been attracted to the idea of a naval demonstration in the Dardanelles in early January 1915 when the Russians called for Britain to put pressure on Turkey, but he was then firmly against providing troops that otherwise would go to the Western Front. In mid-February, Kitchener came to believe that some troops would be necessary after the navy had forced the Narrows. However, due to a misunderstanding between him and Churchill over the offer of a naval division to Sir John French, Kitchener changed his offer from British regular troops, the 29th Division, to Australian and New Zealand troops stationed in Egypt. After a war council discussion on 19 February, there was a vague commitment to take British regular troops to the Mediterranean if needed. At the war council on 24 February, Churchill was still reiterating that the action in the Dardanelles was purely naval but, in reply to Kitchener's queries, he stated that it was wise to have a military force to use if it would ensure success, not failure. Although Kitchener resisted committing the 29th Division to the Dardanelles, he was convinced that "the effect of a defeat in the Orient would be very serious." Nevertheless, at a further meeting of the war council on 26 February, Kitchener, fearing Russian defeat in the east, would not release the 29th Division for the Dardanelles. Churchill vigorously declared that if disaster followed in this area because of insufficient troops, it would not be his responsibility. At the war council on 10 March, Kitchener declared he would now send the 29th Division to the Dardanelles, although it would take a month for them to arrive.

After this, Kitchener, who had previously belittled the capabilities of the Turkish troops on the Gallipoli Peninsula, was cautious, wanting no military action until the 29th Division arrived. When the naval force fell back after losses due to mines, both Churchill and Kitchener wanted a renewed advance up the Straits, but the senior naval officers led by Admiral Lord Fisher refused to agree to ordering Admiral John de Robeck to make a second naval attack. When troops did go in at Gallipoli on 25 April, Kitchener was determined to secure victory.

On 25 May 1915, when Churchill's replacement by Arthur Balfour as first lord of the admiralty was imminent, Kitchener visited Churchill in the admiralty, spoke warmly to him and commented that nobody could take away from him the fact that the fleet was ready at the outbreak of the war.

By September 1915, like many others, including David Lloyd George and George Curzon, Churchill had lost all belief in Kitchener's competence. On 4 October, he wrote to Asquith urging that Kitchener be removed from the war office and put in command of the British armies in France. Churchill and other critics of Kitchener were appalled by his secretiveness and his failure to argue for coherent and consistent policies in Gallipoli and on the Western Front. In November, Asquith removed Kitchener temporarily by sending him to report on the situation at Gallipoli.

When Churchill came to prepare a defense of his role in the Dardanelles, he felt that the records of the time cast Kitchener in a poor light. However, as he prepared a submission to those whom he expected soon to be preparing an official selection of documents on the Dardanelles (in line with a government promise later not honored), Kitchener was drowned off Marwick Head, Orkney, on 5 June 1916, when, en route to Russia, HMS *Hampshire* hit a mine. Churchill felt that Kitchener was fortunate to die while he was still a national hero, before his reputation with the public crumbled.

Suggestions for further reading:
Arthur, Sir George. 1920. *Life of Kitchener.* 3 vols. London: Macmillan.
Cassar, Sir George. 1977. *Kitchener: Architect of Victory.* London: Kimber.
Churchill, Randolph S. 1966 and 1967. *Winston S. Churchill.* Vols. 1 and 2. London: Heinemann.
Churchill, Winston S. 1899. *The River War.* 2 vols. London: Longmans, Green.
Magnus, Sir Philip. 1958. *Kitchener: Portrait of an Imperialist.* London: Murray.

L

Lansbury, George (1859–1940)

Churchill was out of sympathy with George Lansbury's pacifism and his left-wing Christian socialism. He was outraged by Lansbury's efforts to foster trade unionism among troops at the end of the First World War and his opposition to intervention against Bolshevik Russia. Lansbury in his 1928 autobiography denounced Churchill as "the champion political contortionist of our time" and condemned "the foulness of this electoral campaign of lies," referring to Churchill's comments on South Africa in the 1906 general election.

Born on 21 February 1859, Lansbury was the son of a railway timekeeper. Lansbury and his wife emigrated to Australia in 1884, but returned after two years. He then worked in his father-in-law's timber business. Lansbury was active in East End London Liberal politics but became an active socialist from 1892. From 1892, he was also an active member of the Poplar Board of Guardians (who were responsible for the workhouse). He was elected M.P for Bow and Bromley in December 1910. A strong supporter of women's suffrage, he resigned his seat in 1913 to fight a by-election on the issue, but lost. He did not reenter Parliament until 1922, then remaining until his death on 7 May 1940.

Lansbury made his name as a left-wing socialist (and a Christian socialist). He was the editor of the fiery London *Daily Herald,* 1913–1922. Lansbury, a pacifist, ensured that the newspaper took an antiwar stance during 1914–1918 as well as campaigning against profiteers and for trade union action to maintain real wages. At the end of the First World War, he supported nationalism in Egypt, India, and Ireland, and condemned Allied intervention in Russia.

Churchill's enthusiasm for stamping out Bolshevism in Russia was anathema to Lansbury, as were Lansbury's efforts to block intervention anathema to Churchill. Lansbury was also highly critical of the continuation of the Allied blockade on Germany and Austria after the Armistice of November 1918 into mid-1919, which led to severe privations for many of the urban populations. He also supported the campaign for men enlisted into the army until six months after the end of the war to be demobilized in May 1919, six months after the Armistice rather than after the signing of the peace treaty at Versailles. Churchill and the government were especially annoyed that Lansbury published in the *Herald* on 13 May 1919 one of Churchill's war office circulars to commanding officers in which they were required to find out and report whether their men would assist in breaking strikes or would volunteer for overseas service, especially in Russia, and whether there was evidence of the spread of trade unionism among them.

When Lansbury and the Labour movement's Council of Action in 1920 organized to block armaments going to help the Poles fight the Red Army, Churchill was very angry. He wrote a minute in which he expressed fears that leading soldiers might resign. He also specifically instructed MI5, the British intelligence agency, to gather information against Lansbury, writing on one official file, "My object is to secure in one document the complete statement of the case against Mr. Lansbury." On 19 August 1920, the government released claims that the *Daily Herald* was being subsidized by Soviet Russia. However, Lansbury could publish the details of his newspaper's finances and rebut the claims under the headline, "Not a bond, not a franc, not a rouble." It later turned out that, unknown to either Lansbury or the British authorities, a young director of the newspaper, Francis Meynell, had smuggled Russian jewels into Britain, hidden in a box of chocolates. Lansbury did go to prison in 1921, as one of the Poplar Guardians who clashed with the central government over levels of relief for those unemployed.

When the first Labour government was formed in 1924, Ramsay MacDonald kept Lansbury out of the cabinet. In the second Labour government, 1929–1931, MacDonald gave him the office of first commissioner of works, a post where it was felt he could do no harm to the government's moderate image. In the 1931 election, Lansbury was one of only forty-six Labour candidates elected. He became leader in the House of Commons, with Arthur Henderson as party leader in 1931–1932, and then succeeded Henderson in 1932–1935. However, with pacifism looking increasingly quaint in the face of international moves to war throughout the 1930s, Lansbury resigned in 1935. Yet again in these years, he and Churchill were far apart in their views and policies. Lansbury died on 7 May 1940.

Suggestions for further reading:
Lansbury, George 1928. *My Life.* London: Constable.
Postgate, Raymond. 1951. *The Life of George Lansbury.* London: Longmans, Green.
Schneer, Jonathan. 1990. *George Lansbury.* Manchester, UK: Manchester University Press.
Shepherd, John. 2002. *George Lansbury.* Oxford: Oxford University Press.

Lavery, Lady Hazel (1880–1935)

Hazel Martyn was born on 14 March 1880 in Chicago. Her father, Edward Jenner Martyn, was a chief adviser to the leading meat-packaging firm, Armour and Co. Her mother, Alice Louise Taggart, was the only child of John and Susan Taggart, who owned a substantial hardware business in Ripon, Wisconsin.

After her father's death in 1897, Hazel, her mother, and her younger sister Dorothea traveled in Europe. Hazel studied etching in Paris and her early work received some acclaim. While in Brittany in 1903, she first met the artist John Lavery (1856–1941), a widower. Though greatly attracted to Lavery, she consented to marry the surgeon Edward Trudeau in December 1903, a man of her own age group who fit her mother's social aspirations. He died after suffering from pneumonia in May 1904. Their daughter Alice was born that October. After her mother's death in 1909, Hazel married John Lavery. He received a knighthood in 1918.

The Laverys entertained London society at their home, 5 Cromwell Place, Kensington, and John Lavery painted many of the society and political figures of the day. Before 1914, his portraits included Gwendoline Churchill (wife of Jack) and Elizabeth Asquith (later the Princess Bibesco). In 1915, he painted Winston Churchill (the painting is now in the Hugh Lane Municipal Gallery of Modern Art, Dublin).

The Laverys became friendly with Winston and Clementine Churchill after they moved to 41 Cromwell Road to live with Gwendoline Churchill and her two sons in late June 1915 (Jack being at Gallipoli). It was in the period following his departure from the admiralty (late May 1915) that Churchill took up painting. In his chapter "Painting as a Pastime" in his *Thoughts and Adventures* (1932), he recounted how the gifted Hazel Lavery showed him how to be bold with brushes and paint. On another occasion, when he ran out of turpentine while at Hoe Farm in Surrey, she took a taxi and delivered him a supply. Later, when Sir John Colville wrote *The Churchillians* (1981), he observed that few women impressed Churchill and mentioned Hazel Lavery first among exceptions, for the hours she devoted to teaching him how to paint. One way Churchill repaid the help that both she and her husband gave him was by writing the introduction to the catalog of their joint exhibition in the Alpine Club Gallery, 1921.

Lady Lavery strongly supported Irish nationalism, especially in 1918–1929. She and her husband took great pains to host social events and make introductions for the leading Irish nationalists, especially Michael Collins. She provided valuable information concerning the views of Collins and others to Churchill and other British ministers, and of the government to Collins and others. The Churchills were among her guests at a dinner party she held in honor of Michael Collins, Eamon Duggan, and Kevin O'Higgins on 23 January 1922. She also tried to build bridges with Lord Londonderry, of the Northern Ireland government, and Collins. Londonderry and Collins did meet in Churchill's room at the colonial office on 30 March 1922. She arranged further meetings for Collins in early June 1922, including one with Churchill.

After 1922, Lady Lavery continued to write to Churchill about Irish matters. The Churchills and Laverys remained on friendly terms. For instance, the Churchills attended one of her dinners in honor of Irish politicians in June 1923, and the Churchills and Laverys were fellow guests at a weekend party in 1929.

Lady Lavery died on 3 January 1935. Winston Churchill attended her funeral at Brompton Oratory on 7 January 1935.

Suggestion for further reading:
McCoole, Sinéad. 1996. *Hazel: A Life of Lady Lavery 1880–1935*. Dublin: Lilliput Press.

Lawrence, Thomas Edward (1888–1935)

For Churchill, T. E. Lawrence epitomized much that he admired. He was an old-fashioned romantic hero, an individual leading and displaying bravery. He was also modest in his bearing after the First World War. Perhaps he was also a puzzle; unlike Churchill, Lawrence after 1918 did not seek power or position. Churchill admired Lawrence as an author and Lawrence reciprocated this esteem.

Thomas Edward Lawrence was born on 15 August 1888 at Tremadoc in North Wales, the second of five sons of Thomas Robert and Sarah Lawrence. His father, whose surname was originally Chapman, was of an Anglo-Irish landowning family. His mother was the daughter of a Sunderland engineer named Maden. Educated at Oxford High School and Jesus College, Oxford, in 1910–1914, he participated in archaeological expeditions in Syria and Mesopotamia, during which he learned some Arabic. After the outbreak of war, he spent two years in military intelligence in Egypt, monitoring Arab nationalist activities. After going to Jiddah in October 1916, he was sent to liaise with Feisal Ibn Hussein and then entered legend as Lawrence of Arabia when he played a substantial role in the Arab revolt. He found his loyalties to Feisal and the Arab nationalists conflicted with Anglo-French imperialist plans for the area. He left Arabia after the fall of Damascus in October 1918 and advised Feisal at the Paris Peace Conference.

Churchill first met Lawrence at the peace conference. He invited him to lunch, during which he rebuked him for discourtesy to the king (in declining to accept honors). Later, he learned that Lawrence had not rejected the honors in front of others. When Churchill was preparing to become secretary of state for the colonies in early 1921, he made it clear to David Lloyd George that he wished to have responsibility for Mesopotamia and Palestine. On 8 January, Edward Marsh brought Lawrence to see Churchill in Whitehall and Lawrence agreed to be his adviser, working in the Middle East department of the colonial office, February 1921 to July 1922. Lawrence provided detailed advice on Feisal. In March 1921, Lawrence was among Churchill's advisers at the Cairo Conference, where Churchill moved toward a political settlement favorable to Feisal as well as substantial savings by using the Royal Air Force (RAF) and fewer troops to defend the mandated area. Later, Lawrence paid tribute to Churchill's role, observing, "His was the imagination and courage to take a fresh departure and enough skill and knowledge of political procedure to put his political revolution into operation in the Middle East, and in London, peacefully." When Lawrence resigned from the colonial office, he declined offers of other jobs. Instead, he joined the RAF under the pseudonym of J. H. Ross, then T. E. Shaw, serving until February 1935.

Churchill saw Lawrence when he was in the air force; he sometimes rode to Chartwell on his motorbike for Sunday afternoon tea with the Churchill family. Lawrence admired Churchill's books, praising *Lord Randolph Churchill, The World Crisis,* and *My Early Life,* and in 1929 urged him to write a biography of the duke of Marlborough. According to Liddell Hart, Lawrence was critical of Churchill's pursuit of his own interests, commenting, "If Winston's interests were not concerned in a question, he wouldn't be interested." However, to others, he praised Churchill for his political courage.

Lawrence was killed in a motorbike accident on 19 May 1935. Churchill attended his funeral on 21 May, and was reduced to tears. On 3 October 1936, Churchill spoke at the unveiling of a memorial to Lawrence at the Oxford High School for Boys. He later wrote, "Here was a man in whom there existed not only an immense capacity for service but that touch of genius which everyone recognizes that no one can define."

Suggestions for further reading:
Churchill, Winston S. 1937. *Great Contemporaries.* London: Thornton Butterworth.
Graves, Robert. 1927. *Lawrence and the Arabs.* London: Jonathan Cape.

Lend Lease Act (March 1941)

The U.S. Lend Lease Act, signed by President Franklin D. Roosevelt on 11 March 1941, resulted in massive aid to Britain and the other allies of the United States (some $41 billion by the end of June 1945).

Churchill and Roosevelt maintained a correspondence from the time of Churchill's return to the admiralty in September 1939. On 8 December 1940, Churchill wrote that the danger of a German invasion of Britain had receded but that Britain could be broken if she did not secure sufficient supplies of food and munitions. He suggested that the United States would suffer if Britain was defeated before the United States was ready to defend itself against aggression. He asked for aid on the

Two English women of the Auxiliary Territorial Service move armfuls of American rifles just arrived from the United States under the Lend Lease Act. (Library of Congress)

most generous terms the United States could agree upon.

Roosevelt considered that a meeting between him and Churchill would be useful. When Harry Hopkins offered to go to London, Roosevelt agreed after some hesitation. Churchill, briefed by Brendan Bracken on Hopkins's role as the president's confidant, made a big effort to impress him. The first met on 7 January 1941. They discussed a Churchill-Roosevelt meeting in March or April. Hopkins was taken by Churchill on tours of military bases and munitions factories, and he was also invited to Chequers, the prime minister's country residence.

In March 1941, Roosevelt secured the passage of the Lend Lease Act, marking the president's commitment to "all aid short of war" and being the "arsenal for democracy." It also provided aid to China and Greece.

After its passage, Roosevelt felt he might have pushed Congress too far and gone too much ahead of U.S. public opinion.

Roosevelt and other prominent figures in the United States administration continued to harbor doubts about whether Britain really was in dire economic straits. With the end of the war in the East on 14 August 1945, the Lend Lease Act abruptly ended on 15 August 1945. The United States' total wartime foreign assistance amounted to a net $41 billion.

Related entries:
Quebec Conference, Second; Roosevelt, Franklin Delano

Suggestions for further reading:
Brown, W. A., and R. Opie. 1953. *American Foreign Assistance.* Washington, DC: Brookings Institution.
Dobson, A. P. 1986. *U.S. Wartime Aid to Britain.* London: Croon Helm.

Stettinius, E. R. 1944. *Lend-Lease: Weapon for Victory.* Harmondsworth, UK: Penguin.

Liberalism and the Social Problem (1909)

iberalism and the Social Problem was published by Hodder and Stoughton in London at 3s 6d (17.5p) in November 1909 and in the United States by Doubleday, Doran, at $1.50. Hodder and Stoughton printed 5,000 copies.

The book brings together twenty-one of Churchill's major speeches given in his first four years in government office. He revised them in October 1909, observing to his wife on 25 October that he wanted the book published very quickly. This was because it was becoming increasingly probable that there would be a general election soon over the House of Lords. The book was published on 26 November 1909, a week before Parliament was prorogued and M.P.s returned to their constituencies to campaign for the general election of January 1910.

The speeches printed in the volume exhibit Churchill's reverence for the British constitution as well as his wish to bring about social reforms for the most needy. His speeches were imbued with a sense of British history, which he thought had evolved sensibly toward democracy. In dealing with South Africa's development, his touchstone was the British parliamentary tradition. Indeed, on several themes—imperial preference (with the issue of the control of taxation), the role of the House of Lords, and South Africa—he expounded a series of lucid statements on British constitutionalism. He condemned the Conservative Party for moving away from championing church, king, and constitution when constitutionalism no longer suited the party.

Churchill also expounded in the speeches his beliefs in a property-owning democracy and a mixed economy. He wanted a middle way between individualism and collectivism. He advocated that the state should nationalize services that were in effect monopolies. Such services would include railways and canals and "an ever-widening area of municipal enterprise."

He argued for state intervention to ensure "the universal establishment of minimum standards of life and labour." One tangible achievement was to restrict the workings of the free market to protect sweated labor by the Trade Boards Act, 1909. He also called for—and secured—greater state action on behalf of those unemployed.

Liberalism and the Social Order is especially interesting for Churchill's views concerning the need for social reforms to stabilize British society. He was an advocate of the competitive economic system; as he put it, "I do not want to see impaired the vigour of competition, but we can do much to mitigate the consequences of failure."

Related entries:
The People's Rights; Trade Boards Act

Suggestions for further reading:
Churchill, Randolph S. 1967. *Winston S. Churchill.* Vol. 2. London: Heinemann.
Churchill, Winston S. 1909. *Liberalism and the Social Problem.* London: Hodder and Stoughton.
Woods, Frederick. 1963. *A Bibliography of the Works of Sir Winston Churchill.* London: Nicholas Vane.

Lindemann, Frederick Alexander (Lord Cherwell, 1886–1957)

*indemann, widely known by his nickname "The Prof," was one of Churchill's closest advisers. He was ambitious to advise on scientific policy at the national level, and became prominent through his friendship with the earl of Birkenhead, then Churchill. Churchill admired him as a scientific expert and liked him as a person, as did Clementine Churchill.

Frederick Lindemann was born at Baden-Baden, Germany, on 5 April 1886, the son of Adolphus Frederick Lindemann, an engineer and scientist, and his American wife, Olga (formerly Noble). The Lindemanns were an aristocratic family from Alsace. After the Franco-Prussian War, 1870, the Lindemanns moved to a large house in Sidmouth, Devon, inherited by Frederick's mother, where Frederick and his brother, Charles, were brought up. He was born in Baden-Baden because his mother had rented a villa there to take the waters. After attending a preparatory school in Scotland, he was educated in Darmstadt, then Hochschulef, and Berlin University.

In 1915, he was a scientist employed at the Royal Aircraft Establishment at Farnborough. He worked on finding a way a pilot could survive if his aircraft went into a spin. Having found a solution, he learned to fly and tested his theory himself. In 1919, he was appointed to the chair in experimental philosophy at Oxford University. He also revived the Clarendon Laboratory. He invited many Jewish scientists to leave Germany and to work at Clarendon. Lindemann was quick to grasp and lucid in explaining scientific developments and, although he did not make great original contributions to physics, it was precisely these abilities that Churchill needed.

Lindemann was a keen sportsman, his tennis playing being of top quality, and he was also proficient at squash and golf. These attributes helped him gain acceptance in English society, notably at weekend house parties.

It was through the duke of Westminster that Lindemann first met Churchill, on 18 August 1921, in London. Their friendship soon grew. During the General Strike, 1926, Lindemann took charge of the volunteer labor that ran the printing presses of the *British Gazette*. Lindemann also undertook minor intellectual labors for Churchill, providing factual information for some of Churchill's essays and even calculating the heights needed for the flows of water to Churchill's water gardens at Chartwell. He was also a very welcome guest in the eyes of Clementine Churchill.

Lindemann was firmly Conservative in his politics. He stood as an independent Conservative Party candidate in the 1937 by-election for an Oxford University seat, with Churchill speaking in his support. Lindemann won nearly as many votes as the official Conservative candidates, but came third. He enjoyed striking right-wing poses, including over India, but he was more moderate on domestic issues. He had substantial inherited money and he did not hesitate to use it, even to flaunt it.

When Churchill and Archibald Sinclair met Konrad Henlein, leader of the Sudeten Germans, on 13 May 1938, Lindemann was the interpreter. All three were unduly impressed by Henlein, feeling he was more independent of Hitler than he was.

However, Lindemann was very alert to the Nazi danger. Sir Maurice Hankey consulted him on air defense in 1927, and from mid-1934 Lindemann was vocal on the need for Britain to update its preparations for responding to aerial attacks. With Churchill and Austen Chamberlain, he pressed for a small committee, half its ordinary membership consisting of scientists, to investigate ways of preventing night bombers from reaching their targets. He was dismissive of his old friend Henry Tizard's Committee for the Scientific Survey of Air Defence because he felt it was without power. Eventually, he joined it and embarked on what was to be a lengthy feud with Tizard. Tizard was outraged that Lindemann had aired his criticisms to Churchill, who then raised them at a higher committee (the Air Defence Research subcommittee of the Committee of Imperial Defence). Tizard later condemned Churchill for uncritically accepting anything Lindemann said on air defense. In November 1936 Tizard's committee was reconstructed, with Lindemann omitted.

Lindemann's time came with Churchill's return to office in September 1939. He was first Churchill's personal adviser, but in 1941 he became a peer, Lord Cherwell, and in 1942 entered the cabinet as paymaster general. Lindemann's skills included the ability to write brief abstracts of substantial documents. He provided Churchill with advice on a wide range of issues, not just on matters of air power. Lindemann set up and headed a statistical branch at the admiralty. When Churchill became prime minister, the statistical section moved with him. Lindemann offered bad advice to Churchill over German rockets, repeatedly arguing that technical difficulties and the likely small damage done by them made it unlikely that the Germans would develop them. He was nevertheless right on the relatively small damage they caused. He did predict the earlier flying bombs. After the United States entered the war, Cherwell favored Anglo-American talks on the future liberal economic policies. He opposed the advocates of continuing Imperial Preference, such as Leopold Amery and Lord Beaverbrook.

Cherwell served in Churchill's shadow cabinet, 1945–1951, and was Conservative economic spokesman in the House of Lords. He was also a warm supporter of developing atomic energy. In 1951, at Churchill's insistence, he returned to office as paymaster general again. Churchill secured him two years' leave of absence from Oxford University. With Beaverbrook and Brendan Bracken retired, Cherwell was Churchill's last close friend in office with him in 1951–1953. He was a strong opponent of making sterling convertible, with a floating exchange rate, playing a major part in 1952 in securing the rejection of this plan (OPERATION ROBOT). Cherwell was also successful in pressing for the setting up of an independent atomic energy authority, a cause in which he argued a case in opposition to Churchill's views. In October 1953 he resigned, to return to Oxford University.

Cherwell was appointed a Companion of Honour in October 1953, after his resignation. In 1956, Sir Anthony Eden put his name forward for a viscountcy. He died on 3 July 1957. Churchill attended his funeral service, held in Christ Church Cathedral, and insisted on going to the cemetery and walking to the grave.

Suggestions for further reading:

Birkenhead, the Earl of. 1961. *The Prof in Two Worlds: The Official Life of Professor F. A. Lindemann, Viscount Cherwell*. London: Collins.
Gilbert, Martin. 1976–1988. *Winston S. Churchill*. Vols. 5–8. London: Heinemann.
Harrod, R. F. 1959. *The Prof: A Personal Memoir of Lord Cherwell*. London: Macmillan.
Wilson, Thomas. 1995. *Churchill and the Prof*. London: Cassell.

Lloyd George, David (Earl of Dwyfor, 1863–1945)

David Lloyd George was the major influence on Winston Churchill during Churchill's Liberal phase. This was especially so in 1904–1911. The men were also friends, although there was occasional friction. For instance, Churchill, and even more so his wife, felt that Lloyd George was unduly slow in restoring him to senior political office after becoming prime minister in 1916. Yet, throughout their political careers, Churchill was one of the few public figures whom Lloyd George invited into his home, the others including F. E. Smith, Sir Philip Sassoon, the marquis of Reading, Lord Lee of Fareham, and Lord Riddell. Lloyd George was Britain's great war leader of the First World War, Churchill the great war leader of the Second World War.

David Lloyd George, described after his death by Churchill as "the greatest Welshman . . . since the age of the Tudors," was born not in Wales but in Chorlton-upon-Medlock, Manchester, 17 January 1863. However, from the age of four months he grew up in Wales. After the early death of his father, William George, a schoolmaster and tenant farmer, he was brought up by his uncle, Richard Lloyd, a shoemaker, in the North Wales village of Llanystumdwy. He was educated in the village school and then by his uncle, who succeeded in getting him and his brother trained as solicitors. His uncle was an unpaid minister in the Baptist sect, the Disciples of Christ. The key thing about David Lloyd George's politics up to 1905 was that he was a spokesperson for Nonconformity.

Unlike Churchill, Lloyd George began as a grassroots politician, involved in a range of Nonconformist and Radical pressure groups before winning his selection as Liberal candidate for Carnarvon Boroughs. Though a backbencher, 1890–1905, he increasingly came to the fore on such Nonconformist issues as opposition to the Conservative government's 1902 Education Bill, as well as through being a leading opponent of the Boer War (1899–1902). With the return of the Liberals to office in 1905, he entered the cabinet as president of the Board of Trade (1905–1908), and when Herbert Henry Asquith became prime minister, he succeeded him as chancellor of the exchequer (1908–1915).

Churchill made his maiden speech in the House of Commons on 18 February 1901 on the South African War, carefully choosing to follow and to criticize Lloyd George. After his speech, as he recounted in his *My Early Life* (1930), he met and talked with Lloyd George for the first time. When he crossed the floor of the House of Commons on 31 May 1904, he sat next to Lloyd George, who welcomed him. On 4 June 1904, he spoke with the Liberal leader, Sir Henry Campbell-Bannerman, and Lloyd George at a meeting to mark the centenary of the birth of the Free Trader

Richard Cobden. In the period before the resignation of Arthur Balfour's Conservative government in December 1905, he often acted with Lloyd George in the House of Commons; and in speeches in the country, he associated himself with Lloyd George, "the best fighting man in our party" (as at Cheetham Hill, 9 October 1905). Churchill later recalled (in *The World Crisis,* vol. 1 [1923]) that he and Lloyd George had been in "close accord" during Sir Henry Campbell-Bannerman's government (1905–1908).

They combined to form a powerful partnership for social reform during the early part of Herbert Henry Asquith's peacetime governments (1908–1914). In these years, they formed a political friendship that lasted, with varying degrees of strength, until Lloyd George died in 1945. They had several similarities. They were both fully absorbed by politics, their various friendships contributing to their political careers—or at least being linked to them. They were both men in a hurry, both hypochondriacs who felt they would die young. They had also set out with things to prove to those at home: Lloyd George to his Uncle Lloyd, Churchill to his mother and his father's memory. They were also both blunt about the importance of their political ambitions to their wives, who had few doubts that they took second place. Lord Riddell observed of Lloyd George in November 1912 that criticism did not hurt him: "He is pretty case-hardened. What he dislikes is being ignored." Both Lloyd George and Churchill were highly egocentric, expecting to be the center of attention.

Churchill clearly greatly admired Lloyd George's dynamism and innovative approach to social issues. He told Lord Riddell in June 1911 that "L. G. has more political insight than any other statesman." According to Riddell, he added that they were both agreed upon the "necessity for a constructive social policy" and that "L G has selected and 'imported' with great skill from Germany (1) the labour exchanges (2) the sweated trades wages scheme (3) the Insurance Bill and (4) the Unemployment Bill." Although Lloyd George gained much from his German visit, the ideas concerning insurance also drew on British trade union and friendly society experience. Moreover, Churchill himself made the major contributions to introducing the national labor exchange scheme of 1909 and the Trade Boards Act 1909, as well as developing the proposals for unemployment insurance. He had even been urging on Asquith a "Germanised network" of state regulations five months before Lloyd George went on his fact-finding trip to Germany in 1908.

Whether national insurance was electorally popular has been doubted by Henry Pelling and other historians. It was even doubted at the time. When Churchill spoke enthusiastically in June 1911 to Riddell about Lloyd George's imported social policies from Germany, Riddell responded, "I was not enthusiastic and told him that the people want more wages to spend as they like, and that schemes of this sort will not satisfy them and will make it more difficult for employers to increase wages" (Riddell Papers, British Museum MS 62969, f. 85). Nevertheless, the Lloyd George-Churchill combination did make the running in the politics of social policy before the First World War. On 30 November 1910, Beatrice Webb commented in her diary that since 1908, "Lloyd George and Churchill have practically taken the *limelight* not merely from their own colleagues, but from the Labour Party."

Even during these years, there were tensions between Churchill and Lloyd George. In the autumn of 1909, Churchill was initially unenthusiastic about the People's Budget (Lloyd George's radical tax proposals), and in a letter to his wife on 3 November 1909, he commented that his relations with Lloyd George, though friendly, were "more formal and independent than before." This was a minor blip in their rela-

tionship. There were more substantial differences when Churchill moved from social policy into the home office, and then into the admiralty.

The most serious clashes between Lloyd George and Churchill came over naval spending, when in 1914 it looked as if one of them would resign from the government. In an earlier clash over naval estimates, in 1909, Churchill had backed Lloyd George. As first lord of the admiralty, and increasingly alarmed by the intentions of Kaiser Wilhelm and Germany, Churchill insisted on higher spending than Lloyd George wished. With Asquith's support, Churchill's view prevailed.

However, with the entry of Britain into the European conflict, both Churchill and Lloyd George became leading proponents of tough measures to secure victory. Although Lloyd George was attracted to the plan of a naval attack in the Dardanelles, he favored more taking action from Salonika against Austria-Hungary. As a result, he escaped the opprobrium that Churchill suffered as the Gallipoli campaign failed. When Churchill was ousted from the admiralty at the time when Asquith formed a coalition government (May 1915), he was hurt that Lloyd George did not fight to prevent his demotion. Lloyd George had accepted that Churchill should leave the admiralty, but had suggested that he should go to the colonial office. Warm relations soon resumed, with Churchill well aware that his return to the forefront of politics depended on Lloyd George's support, not Asquith's.

Churchill felt his hour had come with Lloyd George's accession to the premiership in December 1916. He underestimated the hostility of the Conservatives, whose support was crucial for Lloyd George to form a coalition government. Lloyd George was more politically acute. In May 1917, Lloyd George still took a political risk when he revived Churchill's political career by making him minister of munitions.

When postwar demobilization of Britain's huge army led to serious unrest, Lloyd George promoted Churchill to the war office to sort out the muddle.

After the First World War, Churchill swung politically to the Right, alarmed by revolution and communism. Although Lloyd George was hostile to communism, he was less apprehensive of its subversive powers than Churchill and was unwilling to wage a crusade against it in the aftermath of the Great War. He and Churchill clashed over intervention in Russia. That apart, Lloyd George was pleased to have Churchill as one of the very few politically weighty Liberals in his government. In 1920, he moved Churchill to the colonial office. During Lloyd George's postwar coalition government (1918–1922), Churchill, along with F. E. Smith, was seen as one of the stars who outshone less colorful and more orthodox politicians.

Although Churchill repositioned himself politically and became a Conservative chancellor of the exchequer (1924–1929) under Stanley Baldwin, he was much distrusted within the Conservative Party. Part of this was because many Conservatives feared a return of Lloyd George and coalition politics, with Churchill as a key supporter. Early in 1929, the two did discuss Lloyd George's terms for supporting a minority Conservative government after the forthcoming general election. Lloyd George, as Liberal leader in the House of Commons 1926–1931, achieved a measure of recovery for his party in 1929.

Churchill remained in the political wilderness for a decade from 1929. Lloyd George's career ebbed markedly from 1931, although he remained a significant parliamentarian. The two men maintained their friendship, and Churchill even spent a long holiday with Lloyd George in Morocco in December 1935–January 1936. Churchill opposed appeasement earlier than Lloyd George. Lloyd George voted against the Munich agreement, but Churchill abstained.

During the early part of the Second World War, Lloyd George felt that Britain could not win alone and for a while favored peace by negotiation. Churchill, on forming his coalition government felt, as Lloyd George had done in December 1916, that he could not risk losing Conservative support by offering major office to his political friend. However, when he did offer Lloyd George a place in the war cabinet and later the post of ambassador to Washington, D.C., the now elderly Welsh politician declined. In 1942, although frail, Lloyd George agreed to chair a joint session of the House of Commons and the House of Lords when General Jan Smuts addressed the M.P.s and peers. Churchill and Lloyd George remained friends and, after Lloyd George's death on 26 March 1945, Churchill made a glowing tribute to him in the House of Commons.

Suggestions for further reading:
Churchill, Randolph S. 1967. *Winston S. Churchill*. Vol. 2. London: Heinemann.
Gilbert, Martin. 1971–1983. *Winston S. Churchill*. Vols. 3–6. London: Heinemann.
Grigg, John. 1978. *Lloyd George: The People's Champion, 1902–1911*. London: Methuen.
———. 1985. *Lloyd George: From Peace to War, 1912–16*. London: Methuen.
———. 1993. "Churchill and Lloyd George." In *Churchill*, edited by R. Blake and W. R. Louis. Oxford: Oxford University Press.
Riddell, Lord. 1934. *More Pages from My Diary*. London: Country Life.
Wrigley, C. J. 1992. *Lloyd George*. Oxford: Blackwell.

Londonderry Arms Hotel

Winston Churchill inherited the Londonderry Arms Hotel, Carnlough, in 1921. Carnlough, on the Antrim coast, was developed after the Irish famine by Frances Arne Vane Tempest, marchioness of Londonderry, and her husband, the third marquis of Londonderry. He was half brother to Lord Castlereagh (British foreign secretary, 1812–1822) and was ambassador to Austria at the time of the Congress of Vienna, 1815. The marchioness had inherited land, including Carnlough, from her mother, the countess of Antrim, and built the hotel as a coaching inn in 1848.

The marchioness's eldest daughter married Churchill's grandfather, the seventh duke of Marlborough. Under the terms of the marchioness's will, Churchill inherited the hotel as part of the Garron Tower estate on the death of his second cousin, Lord Henry Vane-Tempest (1862–1921). Vane-Tempest was one of seventeen killed on 26 January 1921 when an express train from Aberystwyth collided with a local train.

Winston Churchill sold the Garron Tower estate, including the Londonderry Arms Hotel, in 1924. He used £5,000 of the £57,000 raised by the sale to buy Chartwell.

Suggestion for further reading:
Gilbert, Martin. 1977. *Winston S. Churchill.* Companion vol. 4, parts 1 and 2. London: Heinemann.

Low, Sir David Alexander Cecil (1891–1963)

There was a very long love-hate relationship between Churchill and Low; this was marked by real admiration for the abilities of the other but also by long periods of detesting the other's politics. Low was probably the most admired political cartoonist in Britain during the interwar and Second World War years.

David Low was born in Dunedin, New Zealand, on 7 April 1891, the third son of David Brown and Jane Low. His father was a Scot, a successful businessman. His mother, formerly Jane Caroline Flanagan, was of Irish descent. Educated at Christchurch Boys' High School and briefly at a local school of art, he was largely self-taught in drawing. He developed his talent for cartoons in Melbourne from 1911, becoming an effective critic of the Australian prime minister, William Hughes. From November 1919, he worked in London for the *Star*, where the early butt of his cartoons was David Lloyd George. Although he was radical in politics, from 1926 to 1949 he worked for Lord Beaverbrook's *Evening Standard*, but with a contract guaranteeing him freedom of comment. He became a notably effective critic of the European dictators, annoying Joseph Goebbels and other leading Nazis by his satires of Adolf Hitler. He also caricatured an imaginary archetypal reactionary "Colonel Blimp," as well as the real political equivalent "Jix" (William Joynson-Hicks), the Conservative home secretary of 1924–1929.

Churchill, though often the butt of Low's pen, described him as "the greatest of our modern cartoonists" in the essay "Cartoons and Cartoonists," published in the *Strand*, June 1931 (and reprinted in *Thoughts and Adventures*, 1932). Low had caricatured Churchill as a shabby imitation Napoleon when he was the leading advocate of intervention in Russia. He went on to mock him as chancellor of the exchequer. Churchill was sometimes outraged by Low, but often amused and even flattered by his attention. For his part, Low observed, "I always try to find Winston Churchill out in something cartoonable mainly because he is so plump and because he likes it and encourages one. He hangs my most vicious works around the Treasury Office."

Low was not above baiting Churchill in person. He recorded of one occasion when he wished to draw him, "I suggested that the British Empire was an unnatural combination and that the Dominions would not fight its wars in future." Churchill responded, Low commenting, "Mr. Churchill's face seemed to rise and hang in the heavens."

Low mocked the European dictators from early on, with the result that the

Evening Standard was banned in both Italy and Germany. Churchill won Low's support against appeasement and Low supported Churchill as a war leader, although he was critical of aspects of the war effort. Low helped portray Churchill as a popular politician, making his cigar, various hats, and his V-sign automatically identifiable. Churchill, always keen to promote himself, made much of these caricaturable features.

After the end of the Second World War, Low returned to the attack on Churchill and the Conservatives. From 1950, Low worked for the London *Daily Herald* and then the *Guardian.* For Churchill's eightieth birthday, he produced a colored cartoon for the *Illustrated London News,* the original of which was presented to Churchill. His final cartoon of Churchill was published when Churchill was eighty-eight.

Low received a knighthood in 1962. He died on 19 September 1963.

Suggestions for further reading:
Benson, Timothy. 2000. "Low and Churchill." *History Today* (February) p. 50.
Churchill, Winston S. 1932. *Thoughts and Adventures.* London: Odhams.
Low, David. 1935. *Ye Madde Designer.* London: Studio.
———. 1956. *Low's Autobiography.* London: Joseph.
Seymour-Ure, Colin, and Jim Schoff. 1985. *David Low.* London: Secker and Warburg.

Lyttelton, Oliver (Viscount Chandos, 1893–1972)

Churchill admired Oliver Lyttelton as an efficient businessman and was pleased to bring him into politics. Lyttelton played a major role in ensuring ample supplies of materials for the war effort. Churchill had known his father, also a secretary of state for the colonies.

Oliver Lyttelton was the only surviving son and elder child of Alfred and Edith Sophie Lyttelton. His father was M.P. for War-wick and Leamington, 1895–1906, and for St. George's, Hanover Square, 1906–1913; he was colonial secretary from 1903 to 1905. His mother was the daughter of Archibald Balfour. Educated at Eton and Trinity College, Cambridge, Lyttelton served in the Grenadier Guards during the First World War, winning the Military Cross (MC) and being appointed to the Distinguished Service Order (DSO). After a year as a merchant banker, he worked for the British Metal Corporation. He advised the director of army contracts on buying copper in 1935, when Benito Mussolini invaded Abyssinia; and at the outbreak of war in 1939, he was made controller of nonferrous metals.

In June 1940, Churchill made Lyttelton his liaison with all munitions production, with membership in the supply council. In October 1940, he appointed Lyttelton president of the Board of Trade, and secured him a seat in the House of Commons for Aldershot. Later in the year, Churchill seriously considered appointing Lyttelton ambassador to the United States, but chose Lord Halifax instead. In June 1941, Churchill set up a new Middle East authority, with Lyttelton as minister of state in the Middle East, and gave him a place in the war cabinet. In Cairo, Lyttelton organized supply and dealt with the Vichy officials in North Africa and the shah of Persia as well as the Egyptian government.

In March 1942, Churchill appointed Lyttelton minister of production, with a seat in the war cabinet. As such, he oversaw production, especially important as Allied forces went on the offensive. He also made several visits to Washington to arrange more supplies for Britain.

After the 1945 election, Lyttelton was the front bench Conservative speaker on trade and industry. He vigorously opposed the Labour government's nationalization measures. On returning to office, Churchill offered him the post of minister of materials and rearmament. Lyttelton did not care for that and was offered, and accepted, the post of colonial secretary, the post his father had held. He dealt with substantial crises in Malaya, Kenya, and Uganda. By 1954, he was eager to return to industry, primarily for financial reasons, and he resigned from the government in July 1954.

Lyttelton was created Viscount Chandos in 1954. He returned to Associated Electrical Industries, serving as chairman until he retired in 1963. He died on 21 January 1972.

Suggestions for further reading:
Chandos, Viscount. 1962. *The Memoirs of Lord Chandos.* London: Bodley Head.
Fraser, Hugh. 1986. "Lyttelton, Oliver." In *The Dictionary of National Biography: 1971–1980,* edited by Lord Blake and C. S. Nicholls. Oxford: Clarendon Press.
Gilbert, Martin. 1983, 1986, and 1988. *Winston S. Churchill.* Vols. 6–8. London: Heinemann.

Lytton, Pamela (Countess of Lytton, 1874–)

For Churchill, Pamela Plowden was his first love, "the most beautiful girl I have ever seen" (as he wrote to his mother). Like many first loves, Pamela Plowden remained special in his affections. She married Victor Bulwer-Lytton (1876–1947), the second earl of Lytton and grandson of the eminent novelist. She was a close family friend of the Churchills until the end of his life.

Pamela Frances Audrey Plowden was born in 1874, the daughter of Trevor and Millicent Chichele-Plowden. Her father was in the Indian Civil Service, was knighted in 1898, and retired in 1900. She was living with her father at Hyderabad when Churchill met her in November 1896. His mother, who had met her, drew her to her son's attention. He was taken with her, describing her to his mother as "very beautiful and clever." They were close friends for several years, with Lady Randolph and others expecting them to marry. This close relationship waned after 1900, but they remained friends for the rest of Churchill's life.

Pamela Plowden appears to have been a good but critical friend of Churchill. She accused him early on of being incapable of affection. Later, after she had married the earl of Lytton in 1902, she observed to Edward Marsh, "The first time you meet Winston you see all his faults, and the rest of your life you spend in discovering his virtues." Churchill informed her when he became engaged to Clementine Hozier.

He maintained a somewhat nostalgic friendship with her into old age. He invited her to Chartwell on occasions, including during the summer of 1956. She noticed his birthdays with small presents and sent her condolences when Diana Churchill died in 1963.

Suggestions for further reading:
Churchill, Randolph S. 1966 and 1967. *Winston S. Churchill.* Vols. 1 and 2. London: Heinemann.
Gilbert, Martin. 1988. *Winston S. Churchill.* Vol. 8. London: Heinemann.

M

Macaulay, Thomas Babington (Baron Macaulay, 1800–1859)

Churchill greatly admired Macaulay's historical works, other than when he criticized the duke of Marlborough. Churchill read Macaulay in India when he was in the army. He enjoyed rereading his books and frequently cited Macaulay in his letters and other writings.

Thomas Macaulay was both a historian and a whig politician. He was elected to the House of Commons in 1830–1834, then sought to make his fortune in India in the service of the East India Company, 1834–1838. He returned to England and was elected again to the House of Commons in 1839–1847, 1852–1856, and 1857, when he accepted a peerage. He published his *History of England* in five volumes in 1849–1861, his coverage ending in 1702. Churchill was outraged by Macaulay's attacks on his ancestor, the duke of Marlborough, and appears to have decided in 1924 to write a defense. Ten years later, when Churchill had drafted the first volume of his biography of Marlborough, Professor Lewis Namier of Manchester University commented that he had spent far too much space in rebutting Macaulay.

Nevertheless, he frequently drew on Macaulay and his own oral and written style was influenced by Macaulay, among others.

Related entry:
Gibbon, Edward

Suggestion for further reading:
Clive, John. 1973. *Thomas Babington Macaulay: The Making of an Historian.* New Haven: Yale University Press.

Macmillan, (Maurice) Harold (Earl of Stockton, 1894–1986)

Churchill recognized Macmillan's abilities from early on in his parliamentary career. For a period in the late 1920s, Macmillan was in Churchill's circle of bright young Conservative M.P.s. But, unlike, say, Brendan Bracken, Macmillan did not wish to follow wherever Churchill went because he had his own Tory democrat ideas. Although Churchill fostered Macmillan's ministerial career from 1940, he was never fully sure about Macmillan and did not put his career on a fast track.

Harold Macmillan was born on 10 February 1894 at Cadogan Place, London, the youngest of three sons of Maurice Crawford and Helen Artie Macmillan. His father was a publisher in the famous firm that his father, Daniel Macmillan, had founded. His mother was the daughter of Joshua Tarleton Belles, a surgeon in Indianapolis. He was educated at Summerfields, Oxford from

Harold Macmillan, April 1955 (Library of Congress)

1903 to 1906, Eton from 1906 to 1909, by private tuition from 1909 to 1912 when ill health forced him to leave Eton, and Balliol College, Oxford University from 1912 to 1915, where he gained first class honors in classics. He served on the Western Front during the First World War. He was wounded on three occasions, the last time more seriously during the Battle of the Somme. In 1919, he was aide-de-camp to the duke of Devonshire, governor general of Canada. He married Devonshire's daughter, Lady Dorothy Evelyn Cavendish, on 21 April 1920. He worked as a junior partner in the family publishing firm.

In the 1923 general election, Macmillan ran as a Conservative candidate for Stockton-on-Tees, losing by only 73 votes. In the October 1924 general election, he won the seat by 3,215 votes. Macmillan, moved by his experiences of contact with working-class soldiers during the First World War, now represented an industrial working-class town. This reinforced his inclination to liberal Conservatism, to Churchill's "Tory Democracy." With Robert Boothby and others, he published *Industry and the State* (1927), which argued for an interventionist Conservatism, including advocating greater industrial democracy. During this period, he saw much of Churchill, his friend Boothby being the chancellor of the exchequer's parliamentary private secretary. Churchill took up one idea in *Industry and the State,* to derate industry, which Macmillan argued was a "constructive policy other than Protection."

Macmillan lost his seat in the 1929 general election. He drifted away from Churchill, who was moving to the Right. He was appalled by Churchill's views on India. Macmillan continued to be the embodiment of socially concerned Conservatism, publishing in 1938 *The Middle Way.* He was firmly against the appeasers, even resigning the Conservative whip for a year from 1936 when sanctions against Benito Mussolini were abandoned. Macmillan was of Anthony Eden's circle, not Churchill's. This was partly because Boothby, who was having a long-lasting affair with Macmillan's wife, was someone Macmillan preferred to avoid after 1929.

Macmillan came in from the cold with Churchill's accession to the premiership. He was appointed parliamentary under secretary at the Ministry of Supply. There he acted on the ideas of economic planning and organization that he had propounded in the 1920s and 1930s. He was promoted to under secretary at the colonial office in February 1942. At the end of the year, Churchill made him minister resident in Northwest Africa, a post of cabinet rank; but he did not give him a seat in the small war cabinet.

When Churchill urged Macmillan to wear uniform, Macmillan suggested that his

1919 demobilization rank of captain would not impress the generals in North Africa. Churchill agreed, and Macmillan wore civilian uniform. General Dwight D. Eisenhower did not warm to his appointment until Macmillan spoke of his mother from Indiana, a point that Churchill made in a letter to President Franklin D. Roosevelt on 27 December 1942. Macmillan was soon in attendance to Churchill and Roosevelt at the Casablanca Conference. Macmillan, like Anthony Eden, staunchly supported General Charles de Gaulle, and argued against Churchill when he wished to dispense with the French general.

Macmillan attended the Cairo Conference in 1943. Churchill spoke to Macmillan of his fears about the Soviet Union after victory over Germany. He again tried to mitigate Churchill's angry attitude to de Gaulle. In November 1944, Churchill made Macmillan the head of the Allied Control Commission in Italy. Macmillan then moved on to Greece, where the British army was fighting Greek communists, and paved the way for Churchill to visit in December and arrange an anticommunist government, with Archbishop Damaskinos as regent. Macmillan ended the war dealing with Yugoslavia, where, controversially, Soviet citizens who had been captured by the Germans were repatriated. Macmillan returned to Britain in May 1945 and served as minister for air in Churchill's caretaker government.

In the 1945 general election, Macmillan lost his seat but was fortunate to be selected for the first Conservative seat contested in a by-election. He won Bromley in November 1945 and held it until he retired. Macmillan made a mark as a leading Opposition speaker, with some commentators speaking of him as a possible successor to Churchill. He played his part in reformulating Conservative Party policy, and, like Churchill, he advocated Conservative and Liberal Party unity. Macmillan was a prime mover behind the Industrial Charter, 1947, which drew on his interwar books. Churchill was less than enthusiastic.

With Churchill's return to power in 1951, Macmillan was summoned to Chartwell. Churchill offered him the Ministry of Housing and Local Government, commenting that taking on a mass house-building program would make or break his career. In it, he was a success. Churchill moved him to be minister of defense in October 1954, a frustrating position because Churchill liked to oversee defense, having combined the post with the premiership for four months when resuming office.

Macmillan increasingly felt that it was time for Churchill to retire after he suffered a severe stroke in 1953. Churchill was reluctant to go, telling Macmillan he had doubts about Eden's ability to take over and a belief that he, Churchill, could secure peace with the Soviet Union. Macmillan pressed Churchill to retire before October 1954 and, after that date had passed, urged him to fix an early definite date. While others complained, Macmillan acted.

Macmillan was foreign secretary, then chancellor of the exchequer under Sir Anthony Eden. He succeeded Eden as prime minister from 10 January 1957 until 13 October 1963. He left the House of Commons in 1964. He published six volumes of memoirs between 1966 and 1973. In 1984, he accepted an earldom, taking the title the earl of Stockton. He died on 29 December 1986.

Related entries:
Boothby, Robert John Graham; Butler, Richard Austen; Eden, Sir (Robert) Anthony

Suggestions for further reading:
Blake, Lord. 1996. "Macmillan, (Maurice) Harold." In *The Dictionary of National Biography: 1986–1990,* edited by C. S. Nicholls. Oxford: Oxford University Press.
Horne, Alistair. 1988 and 1989. *Macmillan: The Official Biography.* 2 vols. London: Macmillan.

Turner, John. 1994. *Macmillan*. London: Longman.

Marlborough (1933–1938)

From his youth, Winston Churchill was fascinated by the career of his ancestor John Churchill, the first duke of Marlborough (1650–1722). Having worked for James II as king (1685–1688) and earlier when he was the duke of York, John Churchill transferred his allegiance to William of Orange (King William III, 1688–1702). As a military commander he won great victories in the wars against France: Blenheim (1704), Ramillies (1706), Oudernarde (1708), and Malplaquet (1709). Dependent on Whig political support, he was dismissed from office in 1711 after the Tories gained power. His wife Sarah was a major power in the Whig interest.

After the publication of Churchill's *The Malakand Field Force* in 1898 Charles Mallet of Nisbet invited Churchill to write biographies of Lord Randolph Churchill and the first duke of Marlborough. Writing a biography of Marlborough appealed to Churchill but he only took up the matter thirty years later. In June 1929 he met Maurice Ashley and employed him to work half time on the biography of his ancestor, which he hoped to complete within two years.

Although subject to criticism when published and subsequently, *Marlborough* remains a major biography. Churchill was too prone in the book to overreact to the old criticisms made by Thomas Macaulay. He overstated the case for Marlborough's integrity in his relationship with King James II. Also, although there was substantial archival research carried out for the book, the historian J. H. Plumb was later critical of the number of important archives that were not used. Yet Churchill expended much effort and money in preparing the book, it was written in his memorable style and Churchill drew on his own experience of "high politics" to provide insights into the politics of Marlborough's time.

Churchill drew heavily on the expertise of Edward Marsh for improving the style and content of his biography. Between 16 May 1933 and 25 February 1938 Marsh devoted much time to the proofs of the *Marlborough* volumes. Churchill wrote in mid-1933 that he found Marsh's corrections "invaluable," adding, "I told Ashley that it was an education in itself to read a proof corrected by you." With the last proofs completed, Churchill informed Marsh, "There is hardly one of your comments that I have not accepted, and I could easily explain the two or three exceptions to you."

In Britain the first volume of *Marlborough* was published on 6 October 1933 in a limited edition of 155 copies and a general edition, which after reprintings and revision, numbered 17,000 by 1939. By 12 October 1933 some 8,500 copies were sold and Churchill's bank overdraft was eliminated. The further three volumes were also published in limited editions of 155. The second volume reached 15,000 copies in two impressions and the third and fourth volumes were published in print runs of 10,000.

Related entries:
Ashley, Maurice Percy; Marsh, Sir Edward Howard; Trevelyan, George Macaulay

Suggestions for further reading:
Ashley, Maurice. 1968. *Churchill as Historian*. London: Secker and Warburg.
Hassall, Christopher. 1959. *Edward Marsh: Patron of the Arts*. London: Longmans.
Plumb, J. H. 1969. "Churchill the Historian." In A. J. P. Taylor et al., *Churchill: Four Faces and the Man*. London: Allen Lane.
Woods, Frederick. 1963. *A Bibliography of the Works of Sir Winston Churchill*. London: Nicholas Vane.
———. 1992. *Artillery of Words: The Writings of Sir Winston Churchill*. London: Leo Cooper.

Marlborough, Ninth Duke of (1871–1934)

Winston Churchill and his cousin were warm friends from childhood until Marlborough's death in 1934. Churchill corresponded with his cousin, often confiding in him his feelings concerning current politics. Winston and Clementine Churchill and their children often stayed with Marlborough at Blenheim Palace. He was one of Churchill's closest friends.

Charles Richard John Spencer-Churchill was born at Simla on 13 November 1871. He was the only son of the eighth duke and his wife, Alberta, daughter of the first duke of Abercorn. He succeeded his father in 1892. In 1895, he married Consuelo Vanderbilt. They separated in 1906 and divorced in 1920, when he married Gladys Deacon, also an American. Winston Churchill remained a friend of Consuelo Vanderbilt Balsan after her divorce and remarriage.

The ninth duke's nickname, "Sunny," stemmed from his earlier courtesy title of Sunderland. From a young age, "Sunny" and Winston Churchill were often in each other's company at Blenheim. When Churchill was elected to Parliament, his cousin lent him rooms at 105 Mount Street, London, which he occupied from 1900–1905. However, from 1905, Churchill outdistanced his cousin politically (although there was no sense of rivalry).

Marlborough was paymaster general, 1899–1902, and served with the Yeomanry Cavalry in South Africa; he was aide-de-camp to Lieutenant General Ian Hamilton. From 1903 to December 1905, he was under secretary of state for the colonies, his successor being his cousin. He returned to minor office in the wartime David Lloyd George coalition government, as parliamentary secretary to the Board of Agriculture, 1917–1918.

The ninth duke spent much of his life restoring and improving Blenheim, which had been neglected by his predecessors. He encouraged Winston Churchill to write a biography of their great ancestor, and he closed his archives even to the eminent historian G. M. Trevelyan until this work was completed.

Related entries:
Blenheim Palace; Marlborough, Tenth Duke of; Trevelyan, George Macaulay

Suggestions for further reading:
Gilbert, Martin. 1976. *Winston S. Churchill*. Vol. 5. London: Heinemann.
Soames, Mary. 1979. *Clementine Churchill*. London: Cassell.

Marlborough, Tenth Duke of (1897–1972)

Winston and Clementine Churchill continued to enjoy frequent hospitality at Blenheim from the son of his cousin "Sunny." "Bert" and Mary Marlborough were among the few friends and relations they enjoyed visiting often.

John Albert Edward William Spencer-Churchill, born on 18 September 1897, was the eldest son of the ninth duke and his first wife, Consuela (née Vanderbilt). He served in the Life Guards, 1916–1927. He married Mary Cadogan, the daughter of Viscount Chelsea, in 1920. He succeeded his father in June 1934. During the Second World War, he was a lieutenant colonel and liaison officer with the U.S. forces, 1942–1945.

Like his father, he and his family were frequent hosts to Winston and Clementine Churchill and their family at Blenheim. He died in 1972. His son, the eleventh duke, has been a member of the Winston Churchill Memorial Trust since 1966.

Related entry:
Marlborough, Ninth Duke of

Marsh, Sir Edward Howard (1872–1953)

Edward ("Eddie") Marsh was one of Winston Churchill's closest friends and associates. He served as Churchill's private secretary when Churchill held government office in 1905–1915, 1917–1922, and 1924–1929.

Edward Howard Marsh was born on 18 November 1872, the son of the surgeon, Frederick Howard Marsh. His father was later professor of surgery at Cambridge University and, from 1907 to 1915, master of Downing College. His mother, June Perceval, was the granddaughter of Spencer Perceval, prime minister from 1809 to 1812. Marsh was educated at Westminster School and Trinity College, Cambridge, where his friends included the philosophers G. E. Moore and Bertrand Russell. In London, the young Marsh joined the literary circle of Edmund Gosse and regularly attended Gosse's social gatherings.

Having come second in the civil service examinations in 1896, Marsh was appointed a junior clerk in the colonial office. In 1900, he was promoted to assistant private secretary to the colonial secretary, a post he held under both Joseph Chamberlain and his successor, Alfred Lyttelton. By the time Churchill was appointed under secretary of state, Marsh had been promoted to first class clerk.

Churchill first met Marsh in December 1904 at a house party at Hartham, given by the Poynder family. He met him a third time at a party given on 14 December 1905 by Lady Granby (later the duchess of Rutland). After he and Marsh spoke, Churchill discussed Marsh with his aunt Leonie (Mrs. John Leslie) and the next day invited him to be his private secretary. Marsh asked for advice from Churchill's friend, Lady Lytton (the former Pamela Plowden), who, he recalled in his memoirs, told him, "The first time you meet Winston you see all his faults, and the rest of your life you spend in discovering his virtues." After dining with Churchill that evening (15 December), Marsh accepted the offer.

Marsh accompanied Churchill on most of his major endeavors of subsequent years. This began with Churchill's 1906 general election campaign, when they stayed at the Midland Hotel, Manchester. According to Marsh, when they walked around a poor area of Manchester, Churchill commented, "Fancy living in one of these streets, never seeing anything beautiful, never eating anything savoury, never saying anything *clever!*" He also journeyed with him in Northeast Africa in 1907–1908. In 1910, Marsh twice declined the offer from Herbert Gladstone, newly appointed governor of South Africa, to be his secretary in Pretoria. Marsh declined, partly because he liked working for Churchill and partly because his life outside of work was centered on the literary and society circles in London.

When Churchill much admired John Galsworthy's play *Justice,* at Churchill's request, Marsh wrote to the playwright to say that the home secretary looked forward to his future writings on the subject. Lady Randolph Churchill then arranged a dinner party to which she invited Galsworthy and Marsh, as well as her son. Marsh often enjoyed the company of Lady Randolph Churchill in subsequent years.

When Churchill went to the admiralty, Marsh acted as an intermediary between Churchill and Admiral Lord Fisher, the dynamic retired former first sea lord. Among other issues, Fisher pressed the issue of replacing coal with oil for the navy via Marsh. Marsh's travels with Churchill as first sea lord included the cruise on the *Enchantress* with the prime minister and his wife and daughter Violet Asquith (later Bonham Carter) in the Mediterranean in May 1913, and a trip to Spain with Winston and Clementine Churchill in April 1914. On 5 December 1914, Marsh attended the christening of Sarah Churchill as her godfather.

When Churchill resigned from the government in November 1915, Marsh joined Herbert Henry Asquith's staff as an assistant private secretary at 10 Downing Street. Churchill and Marsh corresponded during Churchill's time on the Western Front. When Asquith fell from office in December 1916, Marsh reverted to working as a clerk in the West African department of the colonial office, a price he had to pay for having linked his own fortunes to those of Churchill.

With Churchill's return to office as minister of munitions in July 1917, Marsh resumed working as his private secretary. He was in the car with Winston and Clementine Churchill when in the summer of 1917, after a visit to a munitions factory, another car crashed into the side of their car, turning it over. Apart from cuts to two of Churchill's fingers, they were unharmed. Marsh also accompanied Churchill on his wartime visits to France as minister of munitions. Marsh continued as his private secretary when Churchill moved to the war office and then the colonial office.

Marsh helped Churchill with *The World Crisis,* probably from August 1922 when he was with the Churchills in Biarritz. He later helped him with articles and other books. After Churchill left office in October 1922, Marsh continued to see much of the Churchills. This included spending New Year's Eve, 1922–1923, with them. Marsh continued to work as private secretary to Churchill's successors as secretary of state for the dominions and colonies, the duke of Devonshire and Labour's J. H. Thomas, during 1922–1924. He returned to Churchill during his time as chancellor of the exchequer, 1924–1929, when his main task was looking after Churchill's private correspondence.

After the fall of Stanley Baldwin's government and Churchill's loss of office for a decade, Marsh worked again as private secretary to J. H. Thomas (1929–1935) and Malcolm McDonald (1935–1937) at the colonial office. He received the KCVO (Knight Commander of the Royal Victorian Order) when he retired in 1937. Churchill was among the 140 who attended his retirement dinner at the Mayfair Hotel, London, on 17 March 1937, and he proposed a toast to "Eddie the Man." Churchill also attended a further dinner at Brook's, London, on 22 April 1937, organized by Marsh's former civil service colleagues.

After Churchill's departure from government in 1929, Marsh remained friendly with the Churchills and continued to help Churchill with his books. He greatly assisted him with *Thoughts and Adventures, Marlborough, A History of the English Speaking Peoples,* and *The Second World War.* Marsh died on 13 January 1953. Churchill, on holiday in Jamaica, cabled a short tribute that was published in the *Times,* 14 January 1953. He was represented at Marsh's funeral by Brendan Bracken.

Marsh's biographer, Christopher Hassall, wrote of him, "His stern refusal ever to breathe a word concerning his official relations with Mr. Churchill had already won him [by 1919] the popular title of 'The perfect Private Secretary.' He never relaxed that discipline." Max Beerbohm drew two cartoons of Churchill with Marsh, and Churchill himself painted a portrait of him. H. G. Wells savagely portrayed Marsh as "Mr. Mush," along with Churchill in his book, *Men Like Gods.*

Related entries:
Asquith, Herbert Henry; Churchill, Lady Randolph; *My African Journey*

Suggestions for further reading:
Churchill, Randolph S. 1967. *Winston S. Churchill.* Vol. 2. London: Heinemann.
Gilbert, Martin. 1971, 1975, and 1976. *Winston S. Churchill.* Vols. 3–5. London: Heinemann.
Hassall, Christopher. 1959. *Edward Marsh: Patron of the Arts.* London: Longmans.
Marsh, Edward. 1939. *A Number of People.* London: Heinemann.

Masterman, Charles Frederick Gurney (1874–1927)

Charles Masterman played a major part in bringing about the Liberal social reforms of the 1908–1911 period. Not only was he a major source of advice but he worked hard for both Churchill and David Lloyd George. He was one of Churchill's political allies within the Liberal Party, especially in 1907–1911.

Charles Masterman was born at Spencer Hill, Wimbledon, on 25 October 1874, the fourth son of Thomas William and Margaret Hanson Masterman. His father was an unsuccessful farmer. His mother was the daughter of Thomas Gurney, of the Quaker family. Educated at Weymouth College and Christ's College, Cambridge, he became a fellow of his college. He edited *The Heart of Empire* (1901). He wrote books, journal articles, and newspaper essays on social problems. After unsuccessfully contesting Dulwich in a by-election in 1903, he was elected for West Ham, North, in the 1906 general election.

When Herbert Henry Asquith became prime minister, he appointed Masterman parliamentary secretary of the Local Government Board (April 1908–July 1909). In 1909, Masterman moved to the home office, where as under secretary of state he served under Churchill for part of his time. In February 1912, he became financial secretary to the treasury, where he worked with Lloyd George. During these years, Masterman was closely associated with Churchill and Lloyd George and made an important contribution to bringing forward major social legislation. Churchill and Masterman had talked much about social policy in 1907, and that September Churchill had insisted on helping Masterman finish an article, "A Party in Ruins" for the London *Daily News*. In 1909, Masterman published a classic social study, *The Condition of England*. In February 1914, Masterman was promoted to chancellor of the Duchy of Lancaster, with a seat in the cabinet. Until 1918, such promotions involved a by-election, and Masterman was unfortunate in losing his seat and then failing to win another. He resigned in February 1915, having been a year without having a seat in the House of Commons.

In the early part of the First World War, Masterman was in charge of British war propaganda. He operated from Wellington House, his base when he had been developing the national insurance system. When he organized propaganda, he made a great effort to conceal the government's role in it. From early 1917, he worked under John Buchan, director of the Department of Information. When he failed to win a seat in the 1918 general election, he returned to freelance journalism and also wrote more books. In the 1923 general election, he was elected for Manchester, Rusholme, but was defeated a year later. His health deteriorated, damaged in part by too much alcohol.

He died on 17 November 1927. His widow, Lucy, drew on his and her own diaries for her biography of her husband; her book provides many fascinating accounts of Churchill and Lloyd George during the years of Edwardian social reform.

Suggestions for further reading:
Addison, Paul. 1992. *Churchill on the Home Front.* London: Jonathan Cape.
Hopkins, Eric. 1999. *Charles Masterman: Politician and Journalist: The Splendid Failure.* New York: Edwin Mellen.
Masterman, Lucy. 1939. *C.F.G. Masterman: A Biography.* London: Cass.
———. 1959. "Recollections of David Lloyd George." *History Today* (March and April) p. 9.

Mawdsley, James (1848–1902)

James Mawdsley ran with Winston Churchill in his first electoral contest in 1899, but they failed to hold two Conservative seats in Oldham at a double by-election. Mawdsley was one of the first, possibly the first, trade unionist with whom Churchill had any substantial contact. Mawdsley was antisocialist but wanted cotton trade unionists to have representation in Parliament; he was also in favor of collectivist regulation in his industry.

James Mawdsley was one of the few heavyweight trade unionists who supported the Conservative Party. Born in 1848, he became assistant secretary to the Preston Spinners' Association. After chaotic financial organization had damaged the Amalgamated Association of Operative Cotton Spinners, Mawdsley took over as its general secretary and was very effective in that role until his death in February 1902. Mawdsley emphasized the need for financial strength, not romantic rhetoric, in trade union affairs. He was a skillful negotiator, and within his own organization he was autocrat. He was also a delegate to Manchester Trades Council until 1890.

As a leading cotton trade unionist, Mawdsley played his part in the Trades Union Congress (TUC). He served on the parliamentary committee of the TUC (in effect, its executive body), 1882–1883, 1884–1890, and 1891–1897, and was the TUC's chairman in 1886. He was a notable antisocialist. He resigned from the parliamentary committee in 1890 in protest against the growing influence of New Union socialists in the TUC. He considered socialist ideas fit only for the "scum of London." In 1895, he was instrumental in forging a cotton and mining unions' alliance at the TUC to disenfranchise trades councils, to exclude those no longer working in their trades, and to introduce the block vote—all of which were designed to exclude socialist and other political activists. Mawdsley was appointed a member of the Royal Commission on Labour, 1891–1894, and signed a Minority Report drawn up, at least in part, by Sidney Webb.

Although Mawdsley, like many of his contemporary trade unionists of all political persuasions, favored resolving industrial disputes by joint committees, he was ready and willing to fight if necessary. He expressed such sentiments in 1885: "We can fight the employers to the bitterest of endings . . . let it be . . . so that whichever wins we may at its close be able to shake hands with them, knowing that neither side had forfeited that self-respect which constitutes the highest dignity of mankind." Mawdsley was involved in industrial disputes, above all in one of the biggest of the late nineteenth century: the cotton lock-out of 1892–1893. He led the union side at the meeting with the employers on 23 March 1893 at the Brooklands Hotel, which led to the long-lasting system of conciliation for cotton, the Brooklands Agreement.

Mawdsley and other cotton union leaders were dissatisfied with the efforts of M.P.s representing cotton towns. They wanted more labor regulation, including from 1894 a statutory eight-hour working day. After a ballot on parliamentary representation in his association in 1894, there had been talk that Mawdsley would run as a Conservative, and David Holmes, president of the Amalgamated Weavers' Association, would run as a Liberal in the 1895 general election. This came to nothing, largely because Mawdsley declined to run, finding divided political loyalties among his members. However, with by-elections for both seats in the two-member constituency of Oldham, Mawdsley agreed to run.

For the Conservatives, he was the most attractive trade union candidate, a long-established and much respected major figure in the main skilled trade union organization of Oldham. The Conservative candidate who had topped the poll in 1895, Robert Ascroft, had been solicitor to another major cotton trade union organization, the Amalgamated Association of Card Blowing and Ring Room Operatives. Ascroft had played a key role in negotiating wage agreements in 1889 and 1890 and had been the initial mover in resolving the 1892–1893 lock out.

Mawdsley seemed to be the most appropriate replacement.

Winston Churchill appeared to be the other part of what later would be called a "dream ticket." He was the lively young aristocrat, son of the "Tory Democrat" Lord Randolph Churchill. Together they could appear as the embodiment of Benjamin Disraeli's romantic notions of "Young England," benevolent aristocrats working with working-class people.

However, Churchill and Mawdsley failed to hold the marginal constituency. Four years after the big Conservative win in the 1895 general election and two months before the Boer War boosted Conservative political fortunes, it was not surprising that they lost. Churchill lost by 1,293 votes and Mawdsley by 1,321 votes. For both to have been elected they would have needed to win some 13 percent more votes.

Suggestions for further reading:

Clegg, H. A., A. Fox, and A. F. Thompson. 1964. *A History of British Trade Unions since 1889.* Vol. 1. Oxford: Clarendon Press.
Fowler, A., and T. Wyke, eds. 1987. *The Barefoot Aristocrats.* Littleborough, UK: Kelsall.
Turner, H. A. 1962. *Trade Union Growth, Structure and Policy.* London: Allen and Unwin.

McKenna, Reginald (1863–1943)

During 1905–1915 Churchill and McKenna were upwardly mobile Liberal politicians, aspiring for high office. McKenna disliked David Lloyd George, who was the same age, and also Churchill, feeling that both were unduly pushy and both colorful competitors for the top political posts.

Reginald McKenna was born in London on 6 July 1863, the fifth son and youngest child of William Columban and Emma McKenna. His father was a civil servant, who had come from County Monaghan, Ireland. His mother was the daughter of Charles Hanby. He was educated in Saint Malo, France, and Ebersdorf, Germany, before attending King's College, Cambridge. After working as a barrister, he was elected Liberal M.P. for Monmouth in a by-election in 1895, and held the seat until 1918. He was a close associate of the former Radical cabinet minister, Sir Charles Dilke. With the formation of Sir Henry Campbell-Bannerman's government, McKenna became financial secretary to the treasury. In January 1907, he was promoted into the cabinet as president of the Board of Education. Churchill had to wait until Asquith's premiership in 1908 to enter the cabinet.

McKenna became first lord of the admiralty under Herbert Henry Asquith, from 12 April 1908 until when Churchill succeeded him on 23 October 1911. Churchill, then president of the Board of Trade, pressed McKenna in 1908 to bring forward naval construction planned for 1909 to the autumn of 1908 to reduce seasonal unemployment. As an engineers' strike had delayed expenditure, it was easily possible for McKenna to provide such employment that autumn. In proposing this, Churchill was following the earlier Radical policies of politicians such as Joseph Chamberlain and the winter relief work put on by some Progressive municipalities.

Churchill joined Lloyd George in 1908 in trying to reduce the increase in naval spending proposed by McKenna. On 21 December 1908, Lloyd George wrote to Churchill thanking him for "the assistance you rendered me in smashing McKenna's fatuous estimates." The efforts to reduce the numbers of Dreadnoughts to be built in the 1909 naval estimates (four, not six) led to a major political crisis for the Liberal government. In the end, only four were started in 1909, but there were plans to begin work on eight more before April 1910.

However, Churchill and Lloyd George's belief in the lack of need for such an increase in naval building was undercut by the German emperor's dispatch of a gunboat to Agadir in July 1911. By 1913, with Churchill as first lord of the admiralty, it was he who was under serious attack from cabinet colleagues (notably John Simon, Herbert Samuel, and Walter Runciman) over his proposed increased naval expenditure.

Asquith replaced McKenna with Churchill as first lord of the admiralty in October 1911. This was partly due to Churchill's being more willing to follow the army's example and set up a naval war staff and partly due to Churchill's being a more determined arguer for the post than Richard Haldane, who also wanted it. Also, McKenna, with his legal training and by representing Monmouth, was better suited to be in charge of the Welsh Disestablishment Bill that was planned to come before Parliament.

Churchill as a naval big spender did pay tribute to his predecessor. In Glasgow, in February 1912, Churchill spoke warmly of McKenna's "foresight and resolution." Nevertheless, they did disagree over naval dispositions. In June 1912, Churchill pressed for the major concentration of British naval forces to be in home waters; McKenna supported those who wished to divide the forces between the Mediterranean and the North Sea.

McKenna did not care for either Lloyd George or Churchill. He staunchly supported Herbert Henry Asquith, and with the formation of Asquith's coalition government in May 1915, McKenna became chancellor of the exchequer. He was unhappy with the introduction of conscription, arguing that it would entail financial ruin for Britain, and even offered his resignation. His first budget was notable for the introduction of duties of a third on certain imports considered luxury goods (thereby boosting the automobile industry), in order to save on shipping space and currency. This breach of free trade was known as "the McKenna duties." McKenna left office with

Asquith in December 1916, and lost his seat in the 1918 general election.

He turned to banking. He joined the board of the London City and Midland Bank in 1917 and was chairman of the Midland Bank, 1919–1943. In 1922, he was invited by Andrew Bonar Law to be chancellor of the exchequer, but he declined. Invited a second time, he made the unreasonable condition that he be given the safe City of London parliamentary seat to stand as an Independent (the incumbent had no desire to resign). He died on 6 September 1943.

Suggestions for further reading:
Churchill, Randolph S. 1967. *Winston S. Churchill.* Vol. 2. London: Heinemann.
McKenna, Stephen. 1948. *Reginald McKenna, 1863–1943: A Memoir.* London: Eyre and Spottiswoode.

Menzies, Robert Gordon (1894–1978)

For Churchill in 1941 Robert Menzies was important as the premier of one of the dominions supporting the war effort. Earlier Menzies had supported Chamberlain's appeasement policies, and in 1941 he was often bluntly critical of Churchill. It has been suggested that he may even have had hopes of succeeding Churchill as prime minister. After the Second World War, Menzies was one of several wartime figures who was in power, and Churchill warmed to Menzies, loyal to the Commonwealth and reliably anticommunist.

Robert Gordon Menzies was born on 20 December 1894 at Jeparit, the son of James Menzies. He was educated at Grenville College, Ballarat, Wesley College, Melbourne, and Melbourne University. In 1920 he married Pattie Maie. He practiced as a barrister in Victoria. Menzies began his political career in the United Australia Party (later the Liberal Party) in Victoria in

1928. After election to the federal Parliament, his rise was quick. He became attorney general, 1934–1939, and party leader and prime minister in April 1939. Menzies supported the appeasement of Germany and in July 1939 his government expressed its concern to Neville Chamberlain that Churchill was a warmonger. Once Britain was at war, Menzies brought Australia in as well, but with little enthusiasm. Not unreasonably, Menzies became increasingly alarmed by Japanese expansionism. Menzies favored a negotiated peace, and in January 1940 he sent a telegram to Chamberlain asking that no decision on action concerning Norway be taken until the dominions had been consulted.

After Churchill became prime minister, Menzies still expected Britain to be defeated, and he requested that President Franklin D. Roosevelt help Britain. Menzies was outraged by the failure to inform him of the attack on Dakar and by its failure, acidly observing that it was essential to do better in the Middle East. Churchill replied sharply. More generally, Churchill refused to inform the dominions of secret operations, but did make an exception in the case of General Jan Smuts. Menzies responded to Churchill by pointing to the Australian forces in the Middle East and pledging his country's and his own support.

In January 1941, Menzies traveled to London at the invitation of the war cabinet. He visited Singapore, where he was dismayed by the poor state of the defenses, and the Middle East on the way. He reached England in February and stayed at Chequers for the weekend of the twenty-second, the first of several visits there. Menzies gave rousing speeches and a radio broadcast in which he pledged empire support until Britain was victorious. Churchill pressed Menzies into agreeing to the use of Australian troops in an attempt to defend Greece, a decision confirmed by the first war cabinet meeting he attended.

Menzies, rightly concerned about British policy in the Far East and Greece, became critical of Churchill, especially over Singapore. Menzies stayed on in London, pressing Churchill over reinforcements for Singapore, aircraft for Australia, and better relations with Ireland. He made common cause with those critical of Churchill, notably Lord Beaverbrook and David Lloyd George. It has been argued by David Day that Menzies expected Churchill to fall and that he would succeed Churchill. This is doubtful, or, at least, if Menzies had thoughts of this, they were unrealistic. The House of Commons was unlikely to approve as premier a nonmember of Parliament and a leader from another country. Nevertheless, Menzies, in London on Australia's behalf, was often ready to speak bluntly to Churchill. However, Menzies returned to Australia in May 1941 and, faced with inadequate reliable parliamentary support, resigned as prime minister in August. He was sufficiently impressed by Churchill to send him birthday greetings that November.

Robert Menzies became prime minister of Australia again from 1949 to 1966, leading a Liberal-Country Party coalition. Churchill and Menzies were both present at the Commonwealth prime ministers' meeting in June 1953. Menzies then expressed concern that the United States might intensify its operations in Korea. Menzies sent Churchill Australian black swans for his lake at Chartwell, for the last time in June 1964. In thanking him, Churchill's reply remarked on "our long comradeship." Even though the letter was drafted by another, it probably expressed Churchill's attitude in his later years toward "Bob" Menzies. Menzies died in 1978.

Suggestions for further reading:
Day, David. 1986. *Menzies and Churchill at War.*
    London: Angus and Robertson.
———. 1988. *The Great Betrayal.* London: Angus
    and Robertson.
Gilbert, Martin. 1983 and 1988. *Winston S.*
    Churchill. Vols. 6 and 8. London: Heinemann.

Menzies, Robert. 1965. *Afternoon Light*. London: Cassell.

Milner, Alfred (Viscount Milner, 1854–1925)

Milner was the subject of one of Churchill's early political controversies. In 1906, as a junior minister, he was dismissive of Alfred Milner, in particular over permitting the flogging of Chinese laborers. For many Conservatives, this was offensive, given Churchill's eagerness to see Milner in South Africa some six years earlier when he was aspiring to be a Conservative politician. Later, the two men got on reasonably well in David Lloyd George's coalition governments in 1917–1921.

Alfred Milner was born in Giessen, Hesse-Darmstadt, on 23 March 1854, the only son of Charles and Mary Ierne Milner. His father, a member of a Lancashire business family, was a doctor. His mother was the daughter of Major General John Ready and the widow of St. George Cromie, assassinated in Ireland. He grew up partly in Germany and partly in England. He spent three years at the gymnasium of Tubingen. He studied at King's College, London, and Balliol College, Oxford. Milner became a barrister, briefly wrote for the *Pall Mall Gazette,* lectured in Whitechapel, and was a founder of Toynbee Hall (and chairman of its governors, 1911–1925). In 1884–1885, Milner was private secretary to G. J. Goschen. Milner stood unsuccessfully as a Liberal in the 1885 general election. Like Goschen, Milner became a Liberal Unionist and was elected to the new party's general committee. When at the end of 1886 Goschen succeeded Lord Randolph Churchill as chancellor of the exchequer, he made Milner his private secretary again. In 1889–1892, Milner displayed much ability as an administrator in Egypt, writing *England in Egypt* (1892) while he was there.

He returned to England to be chairman of the Inland Revenue. He was knighted in 1895.

In 1897, Milner was sent to the Cape as high commissioner for South Africa. After nearly a year there, he came to the conclusion that there would have to be either substantial changes in the Transvaal, one of the two Boer republics, or war. Milner proved as inflexible as the Transvaal's leader, President Paulus Kruger, and war followed. When Milner went back to Britain on leave in May 1901, he was raised to the peerage as Baron Milner of St. James's, London, and given the freedom of the City of London. In July 1902, after Lord Kitchener and he signed the treaty of Vereeniging on 31 May, he was made a viscount and appointed governor of the Transvaal and Orange River Colony in addition to being high commissioner. Milner, with the assistance of able young men from Oxford and Toynbee Hall, set about reconstruction. Most controversial of his policies was the bringing in of indentured Chinese labor. He was offered the post of colonial secretary by Arthur Balfour, but declined so that he could continue his work in South Africa.

Milner returned to Britain in July 1905. He soon faced criticism of his record in South Africa, not least the permitting of flogging Chinese laborers. One of his foremost critics was Winston Churchill. Churchill had eagerly met Milner in early November 1899, using a letter of introduction from Joseph Chamberlain. Nine months later on 4 July 1900, Churchill had further conversation with Milner and also went fox hunting with him. In his maiden speech in the House of Commons on 18 February 1901, he had praised Milner. Five years later, in a memorandum of 30 January 1906, he again praised some of Milner's characteristics; but Churchill thought Milner highly unsuitable to be high commissioner after the 1902 peace treaty because he was seen as the enemy of the Boers. In the House of Commons, Churchill said that Milner had committed a grave dereliction of duty by permitting the floggings. Later, he delivered a patronizing judgment of Milner that caused considerable offense; King Edward VII in a private letter referred to his conduct as "simply scandalous." The House of Lords responded by passing a motion praising Milner's record in South Africa.

Milner opposed the Liberal government on the big political issues: tariff reform, the People's Budget, 1909, the House of Lords crisis, 1910, and Home Rule, 1911–1914. However, when Churchill returned to office under Lloyd George in 1917 he served with Milner until Milner retired in 1921. Milner was a member of Lloyd George's war cabinet, December 1916–April 1918, secretary of state for war, April 1918–January 1919, and colonial secretary, January 1919–February 1921. Churchill succeeded him in both of his last two government offices.

Milner had opposed Churchill's return to office in 1917, and even considered resigning. His view of Churchill improved over the next three and a half years. When he retired from the colonial office, he wrote in a private letter that Churchill was "keen, able and broad-minded" and a "powerful backer," but felt his weakness was in coming to conclusions before fully understanding a subject. Milner died on 13 May 1925.

Related entries:
Chamberlain, Joseph; Smuts, Jan Christian

Suggestions for further reading:
Churchill, Randolph S. 1966 and 1967. *Winston S. Churchill.* Vols. 1 and 2. London: Heinemann.
Gilbert, Martin. 1975. *Winston S. Churchill.* Vol. 4. London: Heinemann.
Gollin, Alfred. 1964. *Proconsul in Politics.* London: Anthony Blond.
Marlowe, John. 1976. *Milner: Apostle of Empire.* London: Hamish Hamilton.
Wrench, John Evelyn. 1958. *Alfred Lord Milner: The Man of No Illusions.* London: Eyre and Spottiswoode.

Monckton, Walter Turner (Viscount Monckton of Brenchley, 1891–1965)

Churchill generally found Walter Monckton a sagacious and reliable adviser. He joined Monckton in advising King Edward VIII during the abdication crisis. After falling-out with Monckton over his advice on the governorship of Malta in 1942, Churchill made a reconciliation in 1944 and brought Monckton into his last government as minister of labor.

Walter Monckton was born on 17 January 1891 at Reed House, Plaxtol, Kent, the elder son of Frank William and Dora Monckton. His father's family owned paper mills and was actively Conservative in politics. His mother was the daughter of William Golding. Educated at Harrow and Balliol College, Oxford, he trained as a barrister. Although nearly blind in one eye, he was commissioned into the Queen's Own West Kent Regiment, 1914–1919, serving on the Western Front in 1917–1918 and being awarded the Military Cross. After the war, he flourished as a barrister, becoming a king's counsel, 1930, recorder of Hythe, 1930–1937, and attorney general to the Prince of Wales and the Duchy of Cornwall, 1932–1947, 1948–1951. He was also constitutional adviser to the nizam of Hyderabad and to the nawab of Bhopal, which involved him visiting India in 1935 and 1936. His second Indian visit was cut short so that he could advise King Edward VIII during the abdication crisis.

On 7 July 1936, before going to India, Monckton consulted Winston Churchill at Churchill's London flat at Morpeth Mansions. Monckton recorded that Churchill was "extraordinarily sympathetic and ready to help," advising against a divorce and that the king should not flaunt his friendship publicly. On 4 December, the king asked Stanley Baldwin, the prime minister, whether he could consult Churchill "as an old friend with whom he could talk freely." In the next few days, Churchill joined Monckton as one of the king's main advisers, giving some assistance to revising his abdication speech (mostly drafted by Monckton). Monckton was knighted in the New Year's honors list in 1937. He subsequently helped the duke of Windsor, the title given Edward VIII after his abdication, and his successor, King George VI, resolve financial matters. He also encouraged Churchill, as well as Neville Chamberlain, Lord Halifax, and Duff Cooper, to visit the duke.

In October 1939, Monckton became director general of the Press and Censorship Bureau and also chairman of the Aliens Advisory Committee. In December 1940, Churchill upgraded him to director general of the Ministry of Information. Monckton undertook several overseas missions in 1940–1942. In July 1940, Churchill sent him to Lisbon to speed up the departure of the duke and duchess of Windsor to the Bahamas. In October 1941, he was sent to Moscow to try to improve the release of information to the British press. On the way, he formed a poor view of the governor of Malta, General Sir William Dobbie, and urged Churchill to replace him because he was exhausted. Churchill took offense at this advice, and after 1942 gave Monckton no new tasks until 1945. After Russia, Monckton went on to Cairo, where he served as the director general of Propaganda and Information Services. After the departure of his friend Oliver Lyttelton, he was acting minister of state for the Middle East, February–May 1942.

In July 1944, when both Churchill and Monckton were guests of the duchess of Kent, Churchill ended the bad feelings over Dobbie. According to Monckton, Churchill said, "It has been our only difference; you were right and I was wrong." He also spoke of Monckton's entering his government, even though he was not a Conservative. When Churchill formed his caretaker gov-

ernment, he appointed Monckton solicitor general, May–July 1945.

In January–May 1946, Monckton visited India to advise the nizam of Hyderabad on the coming of independence. From there, he wrote to Churchill about the concerns of the Indian states and the various treaties they had made with Britain. He returned to India that November to participate in discussions with the viceroy on the future of Hyderabad. Monckton continued to advise the nizam, but eventually the state was forcibly taken by the Indian army.

Churchill urged Monckton to enter Parliament. He was unsuccessful in seeking the nomination for South Oxfordshire in 1949, partly because he had divorced his first wife and married the former Lady Carlisle. In February 1951, he was elected for Bristol West in a by-election.

When Churchill formed his last government, Monckton was made the minister of labor, a post that Churchill described as the worst in the cabinet. As Churchill intended, Monckton was against confrontations between the state and the trade unions. Early on, Monckton declared, "I am a firm believer in government by consultation and consent." As sterner Conservatives became concerned about inflationary wage levels, Monckton, backed by Churchill, resolved several disputes with concessions. At the time this was very popular, Monckton receiving an ovation in the House of Commons in 1953 when he avoided a pre-Christmas rail strike. Monckton continued in this post under Anthony Eden until December 1955.

Monckton's last major post was secretary of state for defense, December 1955–October 1956. He had been opposed to the military intervention at Suez, but loyally remained silent and did not risk undermining the government by resigning. He ended his ministerial career as paymaster general, October 1956–January 1957.

After he retired from office, he was created a viscount. He was chairman of the

Midland Bank, 1957–1964, and chairman of the Iraq Petroleum Company, 1958–1965. In 1959–1960, he was chairman of the Commission of Inquiry into the Constitution of the Federation of the Rhodesias and Nyasaland. The Monckton report probably spelled the death-knell of the federation. Monckton died on 9 January 1965.

Related entries:
Abdication Crisis; Edward VIII

Suggestions for further reading:
Birkenhead, Lord. 1969. *Walter Monckton*. London: Weidenfeld and Nicolson.
Gilbert, Martin. 1976 and 1988. *Winston S. Churchill*. Vols. 5 and 8. London: Heinemann.
Hyde, H. Montgomery. 1991. *Walter Monckton*. London: Sinclair-Stevenson.

later Nonie Chapman, and from 1981 Lady Sargant) was Clementine Churchill's private secretary from 1964 until the latter's death in December 1977.

After Winston Churchill's death, Browne worked in the Queen's Private Office before working in the City of London for, among others, International Life Insurance and Gerrard and National. He is a founder-member of the board of trustees of the Winston Churchill Memorial Trust.

Suggestions for further reading:
Gilbert, Martin. 1988. *Winston S. Churchill*. Vol. 8. London: Heinemann.
Montague Brown, Anthony. 1995. *Long Sunset*. London: Cassell.
Soames, Mary. 1979. *Clementine Churchill*. London: Cassell.

Montague Browne, Anthony (1923–)

Anthony Arthur Duncan Montague Browne, the son of an Ulsterman who had been a regular army officer, grew up in Switzerland. He joined the Royal Air Force in 1942 and was awarded the Distinguished Flying Cross. He joined the foreign office in 1946. In 1952, when Churchill required a new private secretary, he asked for someone from the foreign office with active war service, and Montague Browne was selected.

He worked for Churchill during his final premiership, returned briefly to the foreign office, and then was seconded as private secretary to Churchill until the latter's death in 1965 (his salary being paid by Churchill). He became Churchill's right-hand man for the last decade of Churchill's life, handling his affairs carefully and protecting Churchill from excessive intrusions as his health declined. He was with the family when Churchill died and with them at Churchill's funeral.

Anthony Montague Browne's first wife Nonie (née Noel Evelyn Arnold-Wallinger,

Montgomery, Bernard Law (Viscount Montgomery of Alamein, 1887–1976)

Churchill admired Bernard Montgomery as a dynamic general, one who maintained the morale of his troops and was prepared to fight to the end if necessary. Yet, like so many others, he was sometimes outraged by Montgomery's predilection for self-advertising and bragging, which damaged Anglo-U.S. military relations on occasion. On one occasion, Churchill observed that soon British soldiers would be nicknamed "Monties" instead of "Tommies."

Bernard Montgomery was born on 17 November 1887 in St. Mark's vicarage, Kennington Oval, the third of six sons and the fourth of the nine children of Henry Hutchinson and Maud Montgomery. His father, the Reverend Henry Montgomery, was the son of a lieutenant governor of the Punjab. His mother was the daughter of Dean Frederick William Farrar, author of *Eric, or Little by Little* (1858). In 1889, his father became the bishop of Tasmania, and

Field Marshal Bernard Law Montgomery with Winston Churchill at a British airfield (Library of Congress)

Bernard received his earliest education in Hobart. When his father became secretary of the Society for the Propagation of the Gospel in Foreign Parts in 1902, the family returned to Britain. Educated at St. Paul's School and Sandhurst, he was commissioned in 1908 into the Royal Warwickshire Regiment. After service on the Northwest Frontier, he saw active service in the First World War. He was wounded in the first Battle of Ypres and appointed to the Distinguished Service Order. His later service included the Somme and Passchendaele. After various posts, he consolidated his reputation by tough action against terrorism in Palestine in 1938–1939. He returned to take command of the 3d (Iron) Division just before the outbreak of the Second World War. He distinguished himself in France in 1939–1940, especially in the retreat to Dunkirk. He returned to England highly critical of Lord Gort.

When Churchill visited the 3d Division on the south coast on 2 July 1940, Montgomery impressed on him the need for mobility for his division, so that it could counterattack invaders. His demand for buses was met. When Montgomery dined with Churchill he refused alcohol, to Churchill's surprise. When Montgomery asserted he neither drank nor smoked and was 100 percent fit, Churchill replied that he drank and smoked and was 200 percent fit.

When General Gott was killed in August 1942, Montgomery replaced him in command of the Eighth Army at El Alamein. He was efficient and highly confident, and spread reassurance among his forces. From the end of August he fought an effective defensive battle at Alum Halfa. He then gave Churchill his first substantial victory of the war at El Alamein. After this battle, he was promoted to a full general and was knighted. Montgomery advanced into Tunisia. Churchill, who usually complained of his generals' cautiousness, urged Alexander in December 1942 to stop Montgomery from making statements about how he would outwit Erwin Rommel until after he had done so. After attending the Casablanca Conference, Churchill visited the Eighth Army on 3 February 1943, spoke to officers and men in an amphitheater, and spent the night in one of Montgomery's caravans. He went on into Tripoli and ate a picnic lunch with Montgomery.

Montgomery made a substantial contribution to the invasion of Sicily by improving the plan of attack. However, in its execution, General George Patton's American force was quicker to break through. At the end of 1943, he was taken away from the Italian campaign to command the Twenty-First Army Group in the invasion of France. Churchill discussed the plans with him in Marrakesh on 31 December 1943 and 1 January 1944, and Montgomery further discussed the plans with General Dwight D. Eisenhower when he visited

Churchill there. As with the Sicily campaign, he improved the plans considerably. Churchill saw Montgomery in London, including for dinner on 29 March 1944. However, back in England, Montgomery was enjoying the adulation he received, and in April, Churchill urged that the army council should tell Montgomery "to bring to an end his public tours and civic receptions" and spend the time on staff work before the invasion.

After the D-Day landings, Churchill was soon impatient with the speed of Montgomery's progress in France. However, on 10 July 1944, he telegraphed congratulations to Montgomery for the capture of Caen. On 30 August 1944, Montgomery was created a field marshal, backdated to the capture of Rome on 4 June 1944. His promotion made him even less willing to be cooperative with Eisenhower and the American forces.

On 2 March 1945, Churchill flew to Eindhoven, where he dined with Montgomery. The next day, he visited the U.S. Ninth Army with Montgomery and Field Marshal Alan Brook and visited the Siegfried Line. Churchill returned eager to publicize more the contribution of the British armed forces to the advance into Germany. At Luneburg Heath on 3 May 1945, Montgomery received the unconditional surrender of all German forces in Denmark, the Netherlands, and northwest Germany.

Montgomery was appointed commander in chief of the British forces of occupation in Germany. In the 1946 New Year's honors list, he was elevated to the peerage as Viscount Montgomery of Alamein and Hindhead (in the county of Surrey), and that December he was installed as a Knight of the Garter. Also in 1946 he became chief of the Imperial General Staff, proving to be as difficult to work with as ever. In 1948, he was "promoted out of Whitehall," to be chairman of the Western Union commanders in chief; in December

1950, he became deputy supreme commander of Allied forces of NATO (North Atlantic Treaty Organization) in Europe under General Dwight D. Eisenhower. He retired from his activities in NATO in 1958. That year he published his *Memoirs,* which outraged Eisenhower, among others.

Churchill saw much of Montgomery after 1945. He stayed at Chartwell several times up to August 1961 and even visited Churchill in the south of France in 1958. They also had lunch or dinner together occasionally in London. When Churchill died, Montgomery was not well enough to be a pallbearer, but he was well enough to be a pallbearer at Field Marshal Lord Alexander's funeral in 1969. Montgomery died on 25 March 1976.

Related entries:
Auchinleck, Field Marshal Sir Claude John Eyre; Eisenhower, Dwight David; Gott, William Henry Ewart

Suggestions for further reading:
Carver, Michael. 1991. "Montgomery." In *Churchill's Generals,* edited by John Keegan. London: Weidenfeld and Nicolson.
Gilbert, Martin. 1983, 1986, and 1988. *Winston S. Churchill.* Vols. 6–8. London: Heinemann.
Hamilton, Nigel. 1981, 1983, and 1986. *Monty.* 3 vols. London: Hamish Hamilton.
Montgomery, Field Marshal Viscount. 1958. *Memoirs.* London: Collins.

Moran, First Baron (Charles McMoran Wilson, 1882–1977)

*L*ord Moran became Churchill's doctor on 24 May 1940. He took great care of his patient, helping him to recover from his strokes and stay on in office until 1955. Moran felt that Churchill's interest in life would dwindle once he had left active politics. When Moran published his record of conversations with his patient, the book caused great controversy as a breach of confidentiality and a breach that disregarded the widow's views.

Charles Wilson was born at Skipton, Yorkshire, on 10 November 1882, the youngest of three children born to John Forsythe and Mary Jane Wilson. His father was a doctor. His mother was the daughter of a Presbyterian minister, the Reverend John Julius Hannah. Educated at Pocklington Grammar School and St. Mary's Hospital Medical School, Wilson became a medical registrar at St. Mary's Hospital in 1913. During the First World War, he served in the Royal Army Medical Corps, receiving the Military Cross (1916) for bravery at the Battle of the Somme and ending the war as a major. After the war, he returned to St. Mary's Hospital and was instrumental in greatly upgrading the quality of its medical school.

Wilson was also active in promoting the improvement of medical practice through the Royal College of Physicians. He was president of the Royal College of Physicians, 1941–1950. He was knighted in 1938 and, when he became a peer in 1943, he spoke up on major medical issues in the House of Lords.

When he became Churchill's personal physician in 1940, Wilson gave up his medical practice. He attended Churchill at Downing Street, Chequers, Chartwell, and elsewhere, often making notes of his conversations with Churchill and writing them in diary form in the evening. According to Moran, he was urged to publish his diaries by Brendan Bracken, Field Marshal Jan Smuts, and, later, G. M. Trevelyan. This Moran did after his patient was dead.

Churchill usually saw Moran very briefly when he was well. The diaries naturally often focus on Churchill's illnesses and physical decline, and so provide only a part of the picture of his life from at least 1942 to 1953. Nevertheless, they record Churchill's conversations and provide much information on Churchill's health during the latter part of the Second World War and after.

That Moran kept a diary was well known. Sir John Colville, Sir Pierson

Dixon, and he even read to each other passages from their diaries concerning Churchill's meeting in Athens with Greek rebels in December 1944. However, the publication of the diaries created much outrage as a serious breach of the confidentiality due to patients by doctors. This was the case with Clementine Churchill: she wrote to Moran indicating her disapproval and unsuccessfully asked to see the proofs of his book. When it was published, she was upset. The family's disapproval was made very clear by Randolph Churchill in the *Times* amidst much correspondence on the matter in April 1966. The edited version of the essays, *Action This Day: Working with Churchill,* edited by John Wheeler-Bennett (1968), were intended in part to redress the balance. Lord Moran died on 12 April 1977.

Suggestions for further reading:
Colville, John. 1976. *Footprints in Time.* London: Collins.
Kemp, T. A. 1986. "Wilson, Charles McMoran." In *The Dictionary of National Biography, 1971–1980,* edited by Lord Blake and C. S. Nicholls. Oxford: Oxford University Press.
Moran, Lord. 1966. *Winston Churchill: The Struggle for Survival 1940–1965.* London: Constable.
Soames, Mary. 1979. *Clementine Churchill.* London: Cassell.

Morton, Sir Desmond (1891–1971)

Desmond John Falkiner Morton was born on 13 November 1891. He was the only son of Colonel Charles Falkiner Morton, Royal Dragoons, and his wife Edith (formerly Leather) of Middleton Hall, Bedford, Northumberland. After attending Eton and the Royal Military Academy, Woolwich, he joined the Royal Horse and Royal Field Artillery in 1911. Shortly before the First World War, he converted to Roman Catholicism and remained devoted to the Roman Catholic Church.

Churchill first met Morton on the Western Front in 1917. As an aide-de-camp to Field Marshal Sir Douglas Haig, he escorted Churchill, then minister of munitions, to the front line on several occasions. In 1919, Churchill supported David Lloyd George (prime minister) and Sir Eyre Crowe (senior foreign office official) in appointing Morton to establish industrial intelligence in the foreign office.

Morton lived at Edenbridge in Kent, a mile from Chartwell, which Winston and Clementine Churchill bought in September 1922. He assisted Churchill in writing *The World Crisis* (five volumes, 1923–1931), by sorting and assessing documents as they arrived. Later, he also helped Churchill write his four-volume *Marlborough* (1933–1938). From 1929, Morton, with the successive agreement of the prime ministers Ramsay MacDonald, Stanley Baldwin, and Neville Chamberlain (according to Robert Rhodes James), briefed Churchill on rearmament matters in Europe. From January 1929 to September 1939, Morton was head of the Committee of Imperial Defence's Industrial Intelligence Centre, which had as its terms of reference, "To discover and report the plans for manufacture of armaments and war stores in foreign countries." Sir Martin Gilbert in the fifth volume of the official biography commented on the advice on secret defense matters given by Morton from 1934, Ralph Wigram in 1935–1936, and Wing Commander Torr Anderson from 1936 that it was crucial in enabling Churchill to be effective in keeping up "his sustained pressure on the government, to have kept himself so fully informed . . . on the true defence situation in all its aspects, to have aroused public opinion through his detailed and accurate warnings."

When Churchill became prime minister, Morton became Churchill's personal assistant in his private office. At first he occupied the room adjacent to the cabinet office, previously occupied by Neville Chamberlain's powerful eminence grise Sir

Horace Wilson. Initially he was Churchill's liaison officer with the intelligence services and with the Free French and other free governments resident in Britain during the war. Sir John Colville later recalled that his loud voice and frequent laughter reverberated through 10 Downing Street and that he "provided a genial antidote to the gloomiest news and the noisiest bombs." As the war went on, Morton was eased away from his central role through working at the annex to 10 Downing Street.

After the end of the war, Churchill secured him a knighthood and the Order of the Bath. According to R. W. Thompson, Morton felt strongly that Churchill should have retired in 1945. Morton worked at the treasury and then the Ministry of Civil Aviation until he retired in 1953. He moved from Kent to Kew, Surrey, in 1947. Thereafter, he was busy as a governor of the Hammersmith group of hospitals; he died in Hammersmith Postgraduate Hospital, 31 July 1971.

In his letters to author and journalist R. W. Thompson, he was critical of Churchill to such an extent that historian Ronald Lewin has described the letters as having "almost a vengeful character." A. J. P. Taylor, a reviewer for the London *Observer*, also commented with some surprise on his lack of charity, quoting, among others, Morton's comments on "the depths of childish brutality to which he could sink" in relation to Churchill's sacking of Wavell. Morton appears to have become embittered from 1943, when Churchill turned more to Sir Stuart Menzies, head of the Secret Intelligence Service. One of his wilder comments was that Churchill liked President Franklin D. Roosevelt so much that he felt "almost homosexual" feelings for him! The explanation for such bitterness may have been that Morton was a lonely unmarried man who was disappointed that Churchill's one-time close friendship did not last. Morton commented bitterly of Churchill, "The idea of having a friend who was of no practical use

to him, but being a friend because he liked him, had no place."

Suggestions for further reading:
Colville, John. 1981. *The Churchillians.* London: Weidenfeld and Nicolson.
———. 1985. *The Fringes of Power: Downing Street Diaries 1939–1955.* London: Hodder and Stoughton.
Gilbert, Martin. 1976, 1983, and 1986. *Winston S. Churchill.* Vols. 5, 6, and 7. London: Heinemann.
James, Robert Rhodes. 1973. *Churchill: A Study in Failure 1900–1939.* London: Weidenfeld and Nicolson.
Lewin, Ronald. 1978. *Ultra Goes to War.* London: Hutchinson.
———. 1986. "Morton, Sir Desmond John Falkiner." In *Dictionary of National Biography 1971–1980,* edited by Lord Blake and C. S. Nicholls. Oxford: Oxford University Press.
Taylor, A. J. P. 1976. "Churchillian Chit-Chat" (review of Thompson). *Observer* (London), 25 July, pp. 21.
Thompson, R. W. 1976. *Churchill and Morton: Correspondence between Major Sir Desmond Morton and R. W. Thompson.* London: Hodder and Stoughton.

Mr. Brodrick's Army (1903)

This small book contains six of Churchill's speeches on the proposed army reforms of St. John Brodrick, the secretary of state for war. Three of the speeches were given in the House of Commons, the others at the Cambridge University Carlton Club, Oldham and Wallsend. He dedicated the book "To The Electors of Oldham."

As a Conservative M.P. opposing his own government, he was careful to align his views with the great leaders of the recent past, Benjamin Disraeli and Lord Salisbury. Above all, he made it clear that he was taking up the baton from his father in opposing excessive military expenditure, the cause on which his career collapsed in December 1886.

The book was published by Arthur Humphreys, London, in April 1903 at a price of one shilling (5p).

Suggestions for further reading:
Churchill, Randolph S. 1967. *Winston S. Churchill.* Vol. 2. London: Heinemann.
Woods, Frederick. 1963. *A Bibliography of the Works of Sir Winston Churchill.* London: Vane.

Wrigley, Chris. 1982. "The Ministry of Munitions: An Innovatory Department." In *War and the State,* edited by K. Burk. London: Allen and Unwin.

Munitions, Minister of (1917–1919)

Churchill was minister of munitions from 17 July 1917 until 10 January 1919, and he was delighted to be back in office. He had been disappointed and angry when David Lloyd George, upon becoming prime minister in December 1916, had not brought him back into the government. Churchill felt that Lloyd George had betrayed him, only realizing when there was a political storm over his appointment that Lloyd George had told the truth when he said the Conservative leaders would not permit him to give Churchill office when he formed his coalition government.

Lloyd George had formed the Ministry of Munitions in June 1915 and had succeeded in securing huge quantities of munitions before the start of the Battle of the Somme, 1 July 1916. As with the Board of Trade in 1908, Churchill found that Lloyd George was a hard act to follow (albeit a year after Lloyd George had left munitions). Yet he did energize munitions, providing political flair that his two immediate predecessors, Edwin Montagu and Christopher Addison, lacked. Although Churchill was generally successful as minister of munitions, he did blunder into the minefield of wage differentials, in spite of civil service warnings. On granting in 1917 a 12.5 percent pay rise for skilled men on time rates, he was faced with a wave of unrest from unskilled piece-rate workers and others, which led to a lesser raise for them.

Suggestions for further reading:
Gilbert, Martin. 1975. *Winston S. Churchill.* Vol. 4. London: Heinemann.

Murray, Edmund (1917–1996)

Sergeant Edmund Murray was Winston Churchill's bodyguard from 1950 until 1965. He shared Churchill's enjoyment of painting and was notably solicitous of Churchill's wellbeing in his declining years.

Born on 18 August 1917 at Friarside, County Durham, he was the third of five children of the deputy overman at Friarside mine and gamekeeper of Friarside Woods, owned by the Bowes-Lyon family. After attending Alderman Wood secondary school, West Stanley, Murray moved to London. There he worked in a series of casual jobs until 1937, when he went to France and joined the French Foreign Legion for eight years. He was involved in fighting Japanese soldiers in Indochina. After his contract ended, he worked for the British military authorities training agents to operate behind enemy lines in Burma and Malaya. After the Second World War, he worked as a courier for a travel company before joining the Metropolitan Police in 1947. After eighteen months he became a member of the Special Branch.

Churchill admired Murray for his adventurous past, and was usually happy with him in his entourage. Murray helped in all manner of menial ways, including setting up Churchill's easel and paints; Murray even gave advice to Churchill on his painting. When the first volume of *A History of the English Speaking Peoples* (1956) was published, Churchill gave Murray one of his first copies. Although Murray admired Clementine Churchill, there was occasional friction. In January 1958 she gently warned him not to give the press stories about

Winston Churchill's health or other private matters. Generally though, Murray was appreciated for the job he did for Churchill.

After Churchill's death, Murray and his wife (the former Beryl Häfliger, whom he married in 1947) ran a hotel in Devon. Later, he was briefly curator of the Wookey Hole Caves and worked for the Ministry of Defence. He died in December 1996.

Suggestions for further reading:
Daily Telegraph (London),Obituary, 24 December 1996.
Gilbert, Martin. 1988. *Winston S. Churchill.* Vol. 8. London: Heinemann.
Murray, Edmund. 1987. *I Was Churchill's Bodyguard.* London: Thomas Allen.

Mussolini, Benito Amilcare Andrea (1883–1945)

Churchill admired Benito Mussolini as a staunch anticommunist, being much impressed when he met him in 1927. Even into the late 1930s he hoped that Mussolini might support Britain and France against Germany, which he rightly judged to be the greater menace to world peace. However, he became increasingly disillusioned with Mussolini, especially from 1938.

Benito Mussolini was born on 29 July 1883 in Verano di Costa, the elder son of the three children of Alessandro and Rosa Mussolini. His father was a socialist blacksmith, his mother a devout Catholic schoolmistress. He was named after his father's revolutionary heroes: Benito Jaurez, president of Mexico; Amilcare Cipriani, who marched on Rome with Giuseppe Garibaldi and fought for the Paris Commune; and Andrea Costa, an Italian revolutionary who turned to constitutional means. Alessandro Mussolini followed Costa's example, serving on the Predappio district council, 1889–1907. He was educated at his mother's school in Dovia, a boarding school in Faenza, and, most importantly, the Collegio Carducci, Forlimpopoli. At eighteen, he became an elementary school teacher and then a journalist. He was a committed socialist until 1914. He was expelled from the Socialist Party in October 1914, after he suddenly reversed his antiwar views and advocated Italian entry in the war on the side of the Allies. Mussolini served in the Italian army as a corporal, then lance sergeant, until he was wounded in 1917 and discharged. In March 1919, he founded the Fascist Party. He became prime minister of a coalition government in 1922. In 1925, he assumed dictatorial powers, banning all opposing parties in 1926.

Churchill was outraged when Mussolini ignored the League of Nations and occupied Fiume, commenting in a letter to his wife, "What a swine this Mussolini is." Churchill was happier with Mussolini's government when he secured agreement in January 1926 on a schedule of war debt repayments to Britain. In January 1927, he visited Italy with his son, Randolph, and brother, Jack. He commented in a letter to his wife that Italy was like a "happy, strict school." In Rome, he had further talks with the Italian minister of finance about war debts. He also briefly met Mussolini twice, once at a ball and the other occasion after dinner at the British embassy. Churchill afterwards said he found him charming and was convinced he was committed to the long-term interests of the Italian people. He even said that if he had been Italian he would have been with him in the struggle against "the bestial appetites and passions of Leninism." These comments caused outrage on the Left in Britain. Churchill also had an audience with the pope, the ice being broken when they both denounced the Bolsheviks at length.

In February 1933, speaking at the twenty-fifth anniversary meeting of the Anti-Socialist and Anti-Communist Union, he contrasted Oxford undergraduates and their motion against fighting for king and country to the martial enthusiasm of youth in Germany and Italy. Although rejecting Fascism for Britain he praised Mussolini as "the Roman genius."

As the 1930s went on, Churchill saw Hitler and Nazi Germany as the greatest threat to peace and to the British Empire, although he still respected Mussolini and hoped he would be an ally. However, he was angered by Mussolini's invasion of Abyssinia; he felt the Mediterranean fleet should be strengthened and that Britain should support League of Nations collective action. As well as making public warnings to Italy, he also made them to the Italian ambassador, Count Grandi, on 28 September 1935. He continued to see the Italian action as "an absolutely shameful adventure."

Nevertheless, Churchill still had hopes that Mussolini might enter a Mediterranean pact for mutual support in the event of aggression. With the Spanish civil war, Churchill favored neutrality, wanting to back neither pro-Germans nor communists. However, in July 1937 he expressed concern about Mussolini's anti-British propaganda in the Middle East. Nevertheless, in a piece titled "The Great Dictators" in the *News of the World,* 10 October 1937, he praised Mussolini's strong qualities and noted that even if liberty had been sacrificed, Italy had been safeguarded from communism.

When Sir Anthony Eden resigned in February 1938, Churchill complained that he had been ousted at the behest of Mussolini. Churchill was even more concerned when the Fascist deputies in the Italian Chamber on 30 November 1938 chanted for Nice, Tunisia, and Corsica, all French territories. In April 1939, Mussolini invaded Albania, and Churchill regretted that the British navy had not been deployed to prevent it.

In May 1940, Churchill resisted talk of entering peace negotiations supervised by Mussolini. Halifax was the main proponent within the government; another advocate was the Australian high commissioner (who suggested President Franklin D. Roosevelt as well). However, on 10 June 1940, Mussolini declared war on Britain. Churchill was unconcerned, observing, "People who go to Italy to look at ruins won't have to go so far as Naples and Pompeii again."

The Allied campaigns in North Africa and Sicily hit the Italian forces hard. The Allied advance up Italy undermined Mussolini. In July 1943 he was forced to resign by the Fascist Grand Council, but in September German parachutists seized him and he was installed as the puppet head of an Italian Fascist government on Lake Garda. On 27 April 1945, he and his mistress were captured by partisans at Lake Como as they tried to flee to Switzerland; they were shot the next day.

Related entries:
Eden, Sir (Robert) Anthony; Hitler, Adolf

Suggestions for further reading:
Gilbert, Martin. 1976, 1983, and 1986. *Winston S. Churchill.* Vols. 5–7. London: Heinemann.
Mack Smith, Denis. 1981. *Mussolini.* London: Weidenfeld and Nicolson.
Ridley, Jasper. 1997. *Mussolini.* London: Constable.

My African Journey (1908)

While under secretary of state for the colonies, Winston Churchill went on a tour of northeastern Africa. He was especially interested in seeing the intended railway connection between Lakes Victoria, Chioga, and Albert. Before departing, he had secured a contract to supply five articles to the *Strand* magazine and a longer account, including the *Strand* material, as a book. He was paid well for the magazine articles: £750, which more than covered the costs of his journey.

The articles in the *Strand* were published between March and November 1908. In the book these became the first nine chapters. The book had in addition his account "Down the White Nile" and his reflections on the potential for economic development of the areas he had visited. The book was published in December 1908 by Hodder and Stoughton at 5 shillings (25p), with an initial print run of 12,500. A cheap paperback edition followed in March 1910. It was published in the United States in April 1909 by Doubleday, Doran, at $1.50.

In his preface, Churchill stated that he had mostly written his accounts of his journey in Uganda "in a long hot afternoon, after the day's march was done." He hoped that they would help to strengthen the British people's interest in their northeastern African empire.

The book is written in powerful, ornate prose, and it is notable for its colorful cameo accounts. He was full of admiration for the Uganda Railway (running then from Mombasa to the edge of Uganda) not only as a scenic route but also on account of the quality of its construction and that it made a profit. He admired also the near paradise of the kingdom of Uganda, but spelled out the deadly insect dangers of the area, not least from infected tsetse flies. He also detailed the opportunities for shooting animals, which he did with great gusto, including three rare white rhinoceroses, other rhinoceroses, a hippopotamus, lions, buffalo, warthogs, and antelope.

Churchill, although not questioning assumptions of white men's superiority in East Africa, nevertheless did not wish for unrestrained white-settler rule. He considered the prospects for the Indians as well as the Black Africans, and he argued that there was sufficient land to provide for all. He also favored state development of hydroelectric power and more railways.

Yet, he held the prejudices of the time. He hoped the government would encourage natives to move toward "civilized at-tire," away from "primary squalor, without religion, without clothes, without morals." He warmly approved of the kabaka of Baganda's adoption of many British ways. In best Victorian style, Churchill took the view that the natives had no right to live in idleness but should be industrious.

Churchill enjoyed being received as a government minister on his travels. He participated in welcoming ceremonies along the way, and he also saw numerous deputations of local people. Given his marginal Manchester parliamentary seat, he also made several mentions of Manchester and cotton or of Manchester settlers in Kenya in his narrative. The concluding moral of his book was "concentrate upon Uganda," where he judged there would be big returns on small investments. In particular, he saw Uganda as a superb area for the expansion of cotton plantations financed by external capital.

The journey ended with major misfortune at Khartoum. Churchill's servant, George Scrivings, was taken ill (probably of Asiatic cholera) and died within fifteen hours. Churchill saw that Scrivings, who had been a yeoman, was buried with full military honors. Churchill's other traveling companions were Colonel Gordon Wilson, an uncle (married to Lady Sarah), and Edward Marsh, his private secretary. Marsh wrote an account of the journey, published in the *Manchester Guardian,* 11 January 1908.

Related entries:
Colonies, Under Secretary of State for the; Marsh, Sir Edward Howard

Suggestions for further reading:
Churchill, Randolph S. 1967. *Winston S. Churchill.* Vol. 2. London: Heinemann.
Hassall, Christopher. 1959. *Edward Marsh: Patron of the Arts, a Biography.* London: Longmans.
Woods, Frederick. 1963. *A Bibliography of the Works of Sir Winston Churchill.* London: Nicholas Vane.

O

Onassis, Aristotle Socrates (1906–1975)

Churchill first met Onassis in January 1956, possibly through his son, Randolph. After dining with him at La Pausa, the home of Emery and Wendy Reves, he wrote to Clementine that he had been much impressed by him. He dined on Onassis's yacht *Christina* on 6 February 1956, the first of many occasions he enjoyed Onassis's hospitality. Aristotle Onassis was a Turkish-born Greek shipowner; in 1932, he had launched what became the largest independent shipping line in the world.

Churchill availed himself of Onassis's luxurious hospitality. He first cruised in the Mediterranean with him in September 1958. In February 1959, he joined Onassis for a cruise to the Canary Islands and along the Mediterranean coast. In July–August of that year, they cruised in Greek and Turkish waters, passing Gallipoli, calling at Istanbul, and sailing back to Monte Carlo. He joined Onassis for two cruises in 1960: in March to the West Indies and Puerto Rico, and in July in the Adriatic and eastern Mediterranean. In March–April 1961, they cruised again in the West Indies on their way to New York. In March–April 1962, Churchill went for the last time, cruising in the Mediterranean. On these journeys, Onassis often sat on deck near Churchill and talked with him. Clementine Churchill rarely accompanied him, but he took a small entourage with him. On the earlier trips in particular, there were also celebrities such as Maria Callas, the celebrated opera singer, among the other passengers—and various dignitaries joined Churchill and Onassis at ports. In New York in April 1961, he even received an invitation to join President John F. Kennedy, a trip he had to decline for health reasons. Churchill also enjoyed Onassis's hospitality on land.

Onassis's daughter, Tina, who had joined some of the cruises, married the marquis of Blandford in October 1961. As Blandford was Churchill's cousin, Churchill enjoyed commenting, "So, Ari, we are related at last!" Churchill took Onassis to The Other Club as a new member on 1 November 1962. On another occasion there, Selwyn Lloyd, the leading Conservative politician, later remembered how he and Onassis talked with some difficulty (because of Churchill's deafness) with Churchill about the Middle East.

Related entries:
The Other Club; Reves, Emery

Suggestions for further reading:
Coote, Colin R. 1971. *The Other Club.* London: Sidgwick and Jackson.
Gilbert, Martin. 1988. *Winston S. Churchill.* Vol. 8. London: Heinemann.

The Other Club

The Other Club played a major part in Churchill's life between 1911 and 1964. It met his need for good dining with good male company, perhaps a taste he had acquired in the army. His sponsorship for membership indicated that he not only liked someone but that he felt that person would be good company, that he would fit into Churchill's social club.

The Other Club was founded in May 1911 by Churchill and F. E. Smith, then Liberal and Conservative M.P.s respectively. Apparently they both had failed to win election to "The Club," whose cofounders were Sir Joshua Reynolds and Dr. Samuel Johnson, and which for a period was known as "The Literary Club." The club's members included Herbert Henry Asquith, Arthur Balfour, and Lord Hugh Cecil.

The Other Club was set up as a dining club with no more than fifty members. Its rule that there should be no more than twenty-four M.P.s among the fifty was soon broken. It soon became for most a matter of prestige to be elected to it. Aneurin Bevan and Sir Stafford Cripps were elected, but declined membership; others, such as Sir Samuel Hoare, were nominated but rejected. The original fee upon joining was £5, with an annual subscription of £7.10s. The club met on alternate Thursday evenings when Parliament was sitting, with M.P.s present paired (so that they could miss votes). Its rules included, "Nothing in the rules of the Club shall interfere with the rancour or asperity of party politics."

The Liberals in the original forty members included Churchill's associates and connections, including David Lloyd George, Charles Masterman, Freddy Guest, and Neil Primrose (son of Lord Rosebery). The Conservatives included Andrew Bonar Law and Admiral Charles Beresford. There were major figures of the court: Sir Francis Hopwood and Sir Arthur Bigge; of Fleet Street: Lord Riddell, J. L. Garvin, and W. H. Massingham; and of the army: Lord Kitchener and Sir John French. Clearly Churchill and F. E. Smith felt that they could match or even outdo "The Club."

Churchill greatly enjoyed selecting members for The Other Club. Although he much admired Edward Bridges, he put up his successor as cabinet secretary, Norman Brook, not Bridges, for membership. Similarly, though he respected Clement Attlee's wartime work as his deputy, he was not "clubbable" in Churchill's eyes. Those he added early on included John Lavery, Professor Frederick Lindemann, Archibald Sinclair, Lord Beaverbrook, and Sir Edward Spears.

An unwritten rule of The Other Club was no speeches. Churchill broke this when thirty-four members dined after the death of his cofounder, F. E. Smith, the Earl of Birkenhead. He paid tribute to his friend, who had attended seventy-eight of the ninety-four dinners since the club was founded.

Sir Colin Coote, a member from about 1938, later recalled that Churchill dominated The Other Club. He observed that although Churchill was not a one-man executive committee, he suspected that "If he wanted you to get in, you did; and, if he didn't, you didn't." He added, "It cannot be too often stressed that The Club did not consist only of Churchillian cronies or toadies, but of people who liked him—at least intermittently—and whom he liked."

Churchill loved attending The Other Club, traveling up from Chartwell to the Savoy hotel in London for its meetings. Mostly only major political meetings or illness kept him away. In old age, he still ate and drank champagne and brandy lavishly, and always sang in his chauffeur-driven car on the way back to Chartwell. He last attended The Other Club on 10 December 1964. The Other Club continued after Churchill's death.

Suggestions for further reading:
Campbell, John. 1983. *F. E. Smith: First Earl of Birkenhead.* London: Cape.
Coote, Colin R. 1971. *The Other Club.* London: Sidgwick and Jackson.

P

Painting as a Pastime (1948)

*P*ainting as a Pastime was published as a separate small book in December 1948 by Ernest Benn at ten shillings and sixpence in a print run of 25,000. A further 12,000 were printed in June 1949, followed by 20,000 in October 1949. A further 20,000 went to the United States, where the book was published by Whittlesey House, New York. The book also appeared in French, Finnish, German, and Japanese.

Winston Churchill painting beside Lake Geneva, October 1946 (Hulton/Archive)

The book consists of two of Churchill's 1920s essays and color reproductions of eighteen of his paintings. The essays are "Hobbies," first published in *Nash's Pall Mall,* December 1925; and "Painting as a Pastime," first published in the *Strand,* December 1921–January 1922. "Hobbies" was one of thirty-two pieces written by Churchill that *Nash's Pall Mall* published between 1924 and 1930. The *Strand,* inaugurated by Sir George Newnes, published many of Arthur Conan Doyle's Sherlock Holmes short stories.

The book proved to be very popular. When Churchill was writing his *A History of the English Speaking Peoples,* he observed to his wife that he hoped the book would be as effective for encouraging people to read history as *Painting as a Pastime* had been in encouraging people to paint.

Suggestions for further reading:
Churchill, Winston S. 1948. *Painting as a Pastime.*
     London: Odhams and Ernest Benn.
Gilbert, Martin. 1988. *Winston S. Churchill.* Vol. 8.
     London: Heinemann.
Woods, Frederick. 1963. *A Bibliography of the
     Works of Sir Winston Churchill.* London:
     Nicholas Vane.

The People's Rights (1910)

*T*he People's Rights was published by Hodder and Stoughton during the second week of January 1910. It sold at one shilling (10p). A second version replaced the index with an appendix, "Labour Exchanges and Unemployment Insurance" (in addition to one titled "The Principles of the Trade Boards Bill"). It was reissued with both appendices and the index by Jonathan Cape in 1970.

Churchill, in his preface to the book, dated 29 December 1909, stated that much of it was drawn from his early December 1909 speeches in Lancashire, with additional extracts taken from his *Liberalism and the Social Problem.* The book provides para-

graphs from speeches on the 1909 budget, free trade, land, and welfare, with an opening section, "The People's Rights," and a concluding section, "The People's Choice."

In spite of Churchill and the printers' efforts to avoid repetition, there is overlap between the various extracts, and in places his arguments seem to go round in circles. Nevertheless, like *Liberalism and the Social Problem,* the book made a strong case for constitutional and social reform and so added usefully to the general election publications supporting the Liberal Party.

Suggestions for further reading:
Churchill, Randolph S. 1967. *Winston S.
     Churchill.* Vol. 2. London: Heinemann.
Hazlehurst, Cameron. 1970. "Introduction" to
     The People's Rights by Winston S. Churchill.
     London: Jonathan Cape.
Woods, Frederick. 1963. *A Bibliography of the
     Works of Sir Winston Churchill.* London:
     Nicholas Vane.

Placentia Bay Conference (August 1941)

*C*hurchill and President Franklin D. Roosevelt met on board their ships at Argentia, Placentia Bay, Newfoundland, in August 1941. They discussed the threats from Japan and those of a German invasion of the Iberian Peninsula and agreed to publish a joint statement of broad principles, the Atlantic Charter. The meeting had been postponed from March or April 1941 primarily due to Churchill's concerns over Greece and Crete.

Harry Hopkins, Roosevelt's special envoy, visited Churchill in London in January 1941 for preliminary discussions about a meeting. He returned in July 1941 to finalize details. Roosevelt made it clear that he wished for no economic or territorial deals to be raised, nor the issue of United States entry into the war.

Churchill traveled to Placentia Bay in the *Prince of Wales,* a battleship recently re-

American President Franklin D. Roosevelt with British Prime Minister Winston Churchill, on board the **Prince of Wales** *for their Atlantic meeting, 14 August 1941 (Hulton/Archive)*

States giving Japan a warning, as well as discussion of a possible German invasion of Spain and Portugal. As a result, the Atlantic Charter was drawn up. Roosevelt also agreed that the United States Navy would look after merchant ship convoys as far north as Iceland.

The *Prince of Wales* left Placentia Bay in the late afternoon of 13 August. It reached Iceland on 16 August, where Churchill and his party visited Reykjavik. Churchill went to the Althinghus, the Icelandic parliament. With Roosevelt's son, Franklin Junior, Churchill reviewed British and American troops. On 18 August, the *Prince of Wales* returned to Scapa Flow.

Related entries:
Atlantic Charter; Hopkins, Harry Lloyd;
    Roosevelt, Franklin Delano

Suggestions for further reading:
Gilbert Martin. 1983. *Winston S. Churchill.* Vol. 6.
    London: Heinemann.
Morton, H.V. 1943. *Atlantic Meeting.* London:
    Methuen.
Wilson, Theodore A. 1969. *The First Summit:
    Roosevelt and Churchill at Placentia Bay, 1941.*
    London: MacDonald.

fitted after fighting the *Bismarck.* Although Roosevelt had intended few advisers to be present, Churchill preferred to take a strong contingent. These included the service chiefs, Admiral Sir Dudley Pound, Field Marshal Sir John Dill, and Air Vice Marshal Wilfred Freeman, and the head of the foreign office, Sir Alexander Cadogan. Churchill's favored adviser, Lord Cherwell, also went. The *Prince of Wales* left Scapa Flow on 4 August, reaching Placentia Bay on 9 August.

That day, Churchill joined Roosevelt on the *Augusta* for lunch and presented a letter of introduction from King George VI. Roosevelt and Churchill had talks then and on ensuing days; the service chiefs and diplomats had substantial discussions separately. There was much talk of Japanese aggression in the Far East and of the United

Plumb, Sir John Harold (1911–2001)

J. H. Plumb was one of the eminent historians Churchill turned to when preparing *A History of the English Speaking Peoples.* Plumb helped with the third volume. He wrote about Churchill as a historian in 1969.

J. H. Plumb was born in Leicester on 20 August 1911, the third son of James Plumb. He was educated locally at Alderman Newton's School and then at University College, Leicester, where he gained first class honors in history in 1933. He went on to Christ's College, Cambridge, for his doctoral research. He was influenced by G. M. Trevelyan and Herbert Butterfield. During the Second World War, he worked in the foreign office (1940–1945). He was a research fellow at King's College, Cambridge (1939–1946), and then a fellow of Christ's College until his retirement. He rose from university lecturer (1946–1962) to reader (1962–1965) to professor of modern English history (1966–1974) and master of Christ's College (1978–1982). He was elected a fellow of the British Academy in 1968 and was created a knight in 1982.

When Alan Hodge, a joint editor of *History Today,* helped Churchill polish the draft version of *A History of the English Speaking Peoples* from August 1953, Plumb was one of the experts enlisted to help. Jane Hodge later recalled of mid-1955, "Immense drafts were turned in by J. H. Plumb and other historians and worked over by Churchill and Alan." Plumb also helped check chapters in proof. Churchill sent him a copy of the first volume shortly before it was published on 23 April 1956. Plumb wrote warmly of the *History* in a review in the London *Daily Telegraph,* praising "its narrative power, its fine judgement of war and politics, of soldiers and statesmen, and even more because it reflects a tradition of what Englishmen in the hey-day of their empire thought and felt about their country's past." Plumb was more direct in his 1969 essay "Churchill: The Historian," and in his comments in his collected essays. In his essay on Churchill as a historian, he wrote of *A History of the English Speaking Peoples,* "It was like an apparition from the nineteenth or early twentieth century," and, "As history, it fails, hopelessly fails; as a monument to a great Englishman's sense of the past, it is a brilliant success."

Plumb died on 21 October 2001.

Suggestions for further reading:
Ashley, Maurice. 1968. *Churchill as Historian.* London: Secker and Warburg.
Gilbert, Martin. 1988. *Winston S. Churchill.* Vol. 8. London: Heinemann.
Plumb, J. H. 1988. *The Making of an Historian: The Collected Essays.* Vol. 1. Brighton, UK: Harvester-Wheatsheaf.

Portal, Air Marshal Sir Charles (1893–1971)

Churchill had great confidence in Portal, whom Churchill later described as "the accepted star of the Air Force." Portal succeeded in persuading Churchill not to pursue some of his wilder ideas for the Royal Air Force and maintained the prime minister's confidence in his bomber policies.

Charles Portal was born in Hungerford on 21 May 1893, the first child of Edward Robert and Ellenor Kate Portal. His father was a country gentleman, with income from a family wine business, and a former barrister. His mother was the daughter of Captain Charles Hill, governor of Winchester Prison, and Portal's second wife. Charles Portal was known to his family and friends by the nickname of "Peter." Educated at Winchester and Christ Church, Oxford, he enlisted in the Royal Engineers in 1914. In 1915, at his request, he was seconded to the Royal Flying Corps. He flew many sorties and was decorated three times for bravery. In 1919, he was promoted to major (and soon squadron leader). After various posts, in 1934 he took command of British forces in Aden and demonstrated the effectiveness of air power. At the outbreak of the Second World War, he was promoted to temporary air marshal. In April 1940, he was put in charge of Bomber Command before becoming chief of the British air staff from October 1940 to December 1945. He was honored with a knighthood in July 1940.

Portal supported Churchill's desire for area bombing, motivated by the belief that it was morale-raising retaliation for the blitz on British cities. Some in the Royal Air Force believed that area bombing could demolish German civilian morale and bring a speedy end to the war (a somewhat similar argument to the later use of atomic weapons). When in September 1940, Churchill wanted counterattacks on German towns, Portal drew up a list of twenty large towns that should be bombed; he proposed that a statement be broadcast "that as a reprisal for each night of indiscriminate bombing by the enemy, one of these towns would be selected for indiscriminate bombing by the RAF." By early 1944, Portal was impressed by the American preference for precision bombing and ordered the Royal Air Force (RAF) to conduct nighttime operations aimed at oil targets. This proved successful. The precision bombing diverted resources away from area bombing, leading Arthur Harris, commander in chief of Bomber Command, to offer his resignation in January 1945 (an offer that Portal declined).

Portal was described in the official history of the RAF in the Second World War as "a man of quiet but powerful resolution whose polite address, discretion and immense ability made an immediate impression on all who met him." Its authors also wrote, "To him as much as to any man is due the success in battle of the RAF." Portal wrote memoranda to the prime minister two or three times a week and they also regularly conferred. He succeeded in talking Churchill out of several unrealistic proposals for the RAF. Churchill appreciated Portal's qualities, and others also admired Portal. General Dwight D. Eisenhower even commented that he was the greatest British war leader, "greater even than Churchill." Sir Arthur Harris commented, "Anything you could do, Peter Portal could do better."

Churchill, as retiring prime minister in 1945, recommended Portal for a peerage, and in August 1945, he became Baron Portal of Hungerford; in the New Year's honors list, 1946, he became first Viscount Portal of Hungerford and was admitted to the Order of Merit.

Portal retired from the RAF at the end of 1945. He had been kept informed of atomic developments during the later part of the war, and in early 1946, at Clement Attlee's request, he became controller of production in the atomic energy directorate of the Ministry of Supply. In January 1950, with the reorganization of atomic research, he became controller of atomic energy. After the British atomic bomb was made, Portal resigned in August 1951. He declined Churchill's offer to make him the minister of defense if the Conservatives won the next election. Instead he took on more directorships: the British Match Corporation, of which he was chairman, 1959–1964, and the British Aircraft Corporation, of which he was its first chairman, 1960–1968. Portal died on 22 April 1971.

Related entries:
Dowding, Air Chief Marshal Sir Hugh Caswall Tremenheere; Harris, Air Chief Marshal Sir Arthur Travers

Suggestions for further reading:
Carver, Michael. 1993. "Churchill and the Defence Chiefs." In *Churchill*, edited by R. Blake and W. R. Louis. Oxford: Oxford University Press.
Gilbert, Martin. 1983 and 1986. *Winston S. Churchill*. Vols. 6 and 7. London: Heinemann.
Richards, D., and H. Saunders. 1953–1954. *Royal Air Force 1939–1945*. 3 vols. London: Her Majesty's Stationery Office.
Richards, Denis. 1977. *Portal of Hungerford*. London: Heinemann.

Potsdam Conference (July 1945)

Churchill and Clement Attlee met President Harry Truman and Joseph Stalin at the Potsdam Conference in July 1945. In case he lost the 1945 general election, Churchill invited Attlee, leader of the Labour Party. The results were announced on 26 July and Churchill resigned that day. The conference dealt with a wide range of issues, the defeat of Japan being the most important.

Churchill enjoyed a short holiday at the Château de Bordaberry, south of Bordeaux, before flying to Potsdam on 15 July. On the sixteenth, he toured Berlin, where he visited

Clement Attlee, Harry Truman, and Joseph Stalin at the Potsdam Conference, July 1945 (Library of Congress)

Adolf Hitler's bunker. On the seventeenth, he was informed by Henry Stimson, the U.S. secretary of war, of the successful experiments with atomic bombs in New Mexico earlier in the month. On the eigh-

teenth, he had very full discussions with Truman; and a further discussion, with Anthony Eden and James Byrnes also present, on 22 July. Churchill entertained Truman, Stalin, and the senior members of their parties to dinner on 23 July. He flew back to England on 25 July, not to return to the conference.

At the conference Churchill, Roosevelt, and Truman were concerned not only with the defeat of Japan but with ensuring free elections in Poland; the freedom of Greece, Persia, and Turkey; the future of Yugoslavia; the nature of Allied control of Germany; and the disposal of the German fleet. During his time at the conference, Churchill was informed of the first atomic bomb test in New Mexico. Churchill left the conference at 12:15 P.M. on 25 July 1945. At that stage, he had failed to gain concessions on Poland but had secured Stalin's agreement to allow British and American forces to share in the occupation of Vienna, for all Allied troops to withdraw from Persia, and for the Soviet Union to recognize the eastern frontier of Turkey.

Related entries:
Stalin, Joseph; Truman, Harry S.; Yalta Conference

Suggestions for further reading:
Gilbert, Martin. 1988. *Winston S. Churchill.* Vol. 8. London: Heinemann.
Mee, Charles L., Jr. 1975. *Meeting at Potsdam.* London: Deutsch.
Truman, Harry S. 1955. *Memoirs.* Vol. 1. New York: Doubleday.

Pound, Sir Alfred Dudley Pickman Rogers (1877–1943)

Churchill and Alfred Pound worked well together in 1939–1943. Pound was no Admiral "Jackie" Fisher, whose resignation as first sea lord in 1915 undercut Churchill's early career; he was never going to overturn all in exasperation with Churchill. Pound on the whole handled Churchill well, but there have been criticisms that as first sea lord he should have stood up to Churchill. He was undoubtedly loyal to Churchill, not least in shouldering the responsibility for the loss of the *Prince of Wales*

and *Repulse* in 1941, although the admiralty had opposed sending them to the Indian Ocean.

Dudley Pound was born at Wroxall, Isle of White, on 29 August 1877, the eldest child of Alfred John and Elizabeth Pickman Pound. His father was a barrister, his mother was American, the daughter of Richard Saltonstall Rogers of Boston, Massachusetts. Wanting a career in the Royal Navy, he joined the *Britannia* as a cadet in January 1891. Thereafter, he rose quickly. He qualified as a specialist torpedo officer and later served on the torpedo side of the naval ordnance department. In 1913, he went as an instructor to the new Naval Staff College. In 1914, before the war, he took command of the *St. Vincent.* In 1916, he took part in the Battle of Jutland as flag captain in the *Colossus,* and was commended. After the First World War, he held various posts at the admiralty and at sea, reaching the post of second sea lord in 1932. From 1936, he was commander in chief, Mediterranean station. In June 1939, he was appointed first sea lord, and the following month he was promoted to admiral of the fleet.

Pound's period as first sea lord saw some notable failures as well as successes. He and the admiralty were criticized for inadequate action during the Norway campaign of early 1940, for the loss of the *Prince of Wales* and the *Repulse* off Malaya in December 1941, and for the escape of the German cruisers *Scharnhorst* and *Gneisenau* from Brest in February 1942. His successes included reclaiming control of the Mediterranean and the successful landings in North Africa and Sicily.

That Pound and Churchill worked well together owed much to Pound's patience and humility. However, even he was moved to comment to A. V. Alexander, "At times you could kiss his feet—at others you could kill him." On 1 December 1940, Pound wrote to Admiral Andrew Cunningham of Churchill's being difficult, "One has to take

The American and British chiefs of staff meet at the Casablanca Conference. Left: Admiral E. J. King, General Marshall, and Lieutenant General Arnold. Right: Field Marshal John Dill, Air Chief Marshal Sir Charles Portal, General Sir Alan Brooke, Admiral Sir Dudley Pound, and Lord Louis Mountbatten (Library of Congress)

a broad view because one has to deal with a man who is proving a magnificent leader, and one just has to put up with his childishness as long as it isn't dangerous."

Churchill was genuinely upset when Pound suffered a severe stroke and resigned in September 1943. Churchill paid generous tribute to him in a published letter, in which he praised "your fortitude in times of anxiety and misfortune, your resourcefulness and readiness to run the risks with-

out which victory can never be won." Pound died on 21 October 1943.

Suggestions for further reading:

Brodhurst, Robin. 2000. *Churchill's Anchor: The Biography of Admiral Sir Dudley Pound.* London: Pen and Sword.

Churchill, Winston S. 1952. *The Second World War.* Vol. 5. London: Cassell.

Gilbert, Martin. 1983 and 1986. *Winston S. Churchill.* Vols. 6 and 7. London: Heinemann.

Roskill, Stephen. 1977. *Churchill and the Admirals.* London: Collins.

Q

Quebec Conference, First (August 1943)

Churchill and Roosevelt met at Quebec in August 1943, a conference hosted by the Canadian government. This conference was given the code name Quadrant. There was some friction over when France would be invaded and over retaking Burma to aid China.

Churchill left for Halifax, Nova Scotia, on the *Queen Mary* on 5 August and arrived on 9 August. Churchill's large party included General Sir Alan Brooke, Lord Mountbatten, Lord Leathers, Major General Sir Hastings Ismay, and Averell Harriman. In addition, he had brought Brigadier Orde Wingate to advise on Burma. Clementine and Mary Churchill also accompanied him. On 12–14 September, before the conference began, Churchill visited President Franklin D. Roosevelt's home, Hyde Park, in New York State; on the way he again visited Niagara Falls, which he had viewed in 1900.

Churchill favored the invasion of Italy and also Norway; the Americans wanted to prioritize the invasion of France. The British Chiefs of Staff predicted that if the invasion of France went ahead, it would take place a few weeks later than the planned date of 1 May 1944. With regard to the Far East, Churchill wanted to attack the main Japanese islands from Russia; however, encouraged by Wingate, he agreed to an advance into Burma. At the conference there was also Anglo-American agreement on the exchange of atomic information and on informing each other before using an atomic bomb.

After the Quebec Conference, Churchill went fishing at the Lac des Neiges, 26–31 August, and then stayed with Roosevelt at the White House, 1–11 September. He received an honorary degree at Harvard University on 6 September, and returned to Britain on the battleship *Renown,* 11–19 September 1943.

Related entries:
Roosevelt, Franklin Delano; Wingate, Major General Orde Charles

Suggestion for further reading:
Gilbert, Martin. 1986. *Winston S. Churchill.* Vol. 7. London: Heinemann.

Quebec Conference, Second (September 1944)

Churchill and President Franklin D. Roosevelt met for a second time in Quebec in September 1944, the conference being given the code name Octagon. The discussions centered on defeating Japan, the British insisting on a major role that would start with fully recovering Burma. They also dealt with the division of Germany.

Accompanied by a large party, Churchill left England on the *Queen Mary,* sailing from Greenock on 5 September and arriving at Halifax on 10 September. His entourage included Lord Cherwell, Major General Sir Hastings Ismay, and General Sir Alan Brooke. Again, Clementine and Mary Churchill accompanied him.

The British wanted to maintain Allied forces in Italy. At the conference, they agreed to prioritize retaking Burma. There was also much discussion of postwar policies, including the allocation of occupation zones in Germany and also the future governments of France and Greece. Churchill and Roosevelt agreed to the plan to de-industrialize Germany after the war, a plan put forward by Henry Morgenthau, the U.S. secretary of the treasury, but this was later dropped by both of them.

Winston, Clementine, and Mary Churchill visited Roosevelt's home at Hyde Park, New York State, on 18–19 September. They returned to Britain on the *Queen Mary,* which sailed from New York on 20 September, arriving at Greenock on 26 September 1944.

Related entries:
Quebec Conference, First; Roosevelt, Franklin Delano

Suggestion for further reading:
Gilbert, Martin. 1986. *Winston S. Churchill.* Vol. 7. London: Heinemann.

R

Reves, Emery (1904–1981)

He was born Imre Révész in Bacs-foldvar, Hungary, the only child of Simon and Gizela Révész (his father's surname originally being Rosenbaum). He was educated in Budapest, Berlin, and Zurich (where he earned a doctorate in economics). In 1930, he set up an organization, Cooperation Press Service, in Berlin to publish articles by leading politicians and writers in newspapers in many countries. Fleeing the Nazis in 1933, he relocated in Paris before moving on to London in late 1939. His British nationality application was supported by Churchill, Sir Anthony Eden, Clement Attlee, and Sir Herbert Samuel. In 1941, he again created his press business in New York. After the end of the Second World War, Reves arranged the overseas sales of rights to Churchill's war memoirs (1948–1954) and his *A History of the English Speaking Peoples* (1956–1958).

Emery Reves was important in assisting the transmitting of Churchill's anti-Nazi message through many countries between 1937 and September 1939 (when Churchill entered Neville Chamberlain's government). Reves claimed that he succeeded in getting Churchill's views prominently published in newspapers in twenty-five languages with circulations of 15 to 20 million copies.

After the Second World War, Reves made an editorial contribution to Churchill's war memoirs. This included convincing Churchill of the need to change the title of the first volume from *The Downward Path*. Reves also ensured that the war memoirs and *A History of the English Speaking Peoples* were translated into many languages and published in many countries.

After retiring from office, Churchill stayed eleven times with Emery and Wendy Reves at their villa, La Pausa, at Roquebrune in the South of France between January 1956 and April 1959. La Pausa, a former lavender farm, was 600 feet above sea level and had superb views of the coast. According to Emery Reves's estimates, Churchill spent some 400 days at La Pausa. There he finished *A History of the English Speaking Peoples*, painted, discussed painting, listened to classical music, and generally relaxed. He considered his stays there among the most enjoyable times of his life.

Related entries:
A History of the English Speaking Peoples; Onassis, Aristotle Socrates

Suggestions for further reading:
Gilbert, Martin. 1976, 1983, and 1988. *Winston S. Churchill.* Vols. 5, 6, and 8. London: Heinemann.
———, ed. 1997. *Winston Churchill and Emery Reves: Correspondence 1937–1964.* Austin: University of Texas Press.

Montague Brown, Anthony. 1995. *Long Sunset*. London: Collins.

Riddell, Lord (George Allardice Riddell, 1865–1934)

George Riddell became a friend of David Lloyd George through his newspaper connections, and through Lloyd George he came into frequent contact with Churchill. Riddell kept records of his conversations with Churchill and other leading politicians. Unlike Lord Beaverbrook, Riddell was not a politician and his records are not notably politically biased, although he was often perceptive on the politicians of his day.

George Riddell was born in Brixton, London, on 25 May 1865, the only child of James and Isabel Riddell. His father, a photographer, died before his son was two. The boy was brought up by his mother, whose maiden name was Young, and her parents. Educated privately, his first job was as a clerk to a firm of solicitors. His uncle, D. W. Allardice, provided the funds so that Riddell could be articled and become a solicitor. He became legal adviser to the London *News of the World,* and in 1903, its chairman. He became friendly with David Lloyd George and through him he met other leading politicians.

Riddell kept notes about his many meetings with Lloyd George, Churchill, and other politicians. About half of these notes (now in the British Library, London) were published in three volumes of "diaries" in 1933–1934, at the end of his life. These volumes provide fascinating accounts of Churchill's conversations and those of other politicians. However, Riddell added to the published version and, not surprisingly, omitted much that in 1933–1934 could cause offense or even litigation.

Riddell did much to help Lloyd George, even providing him with a house by a golf club at Walton Heath, Surrey. Before the First World War, Riddell often played golf with Churchill as well as with Lloyd George. Lloyd George secured Riddell a knighthood in 1909 and a baronetcy in 1918.

During the first World War and after it, he came to greater prominence. He was vice chairman of the Newspaper Proprietors' Association and with the war became a member of the admiralty, the war office, and the press committee. At the Paris Peace Conference in 1919, he served as the principal liaison officer between the press and the British delegation, headed by his friend Lloyd George. He took on the same role at the other peace conferences and at the Anglo-U.S. Naval Conference in 1921. Although he was the guilty party in a divorce case in 1900, Lloyd George nevertheless secured him a peerage in the New Year's honors list, 1920.

Riddell and Lloyd George remained friends after 1920, but the friendship cooled over differences on foreign policy. As a result, Riddell's contacts with front-rank politicians, including Churchill, lessened. Nevertheless, Riddell's diaries, according to Professor J. M. McEwen, contain 74 substantial conversations with Churchill (against nearly 700 with Lloyd George).

During the General Strike, Riddell was unwilling for the press to be a mouthpiece for the government. After Churchill and John Colin Davidson, deputy chief civil commissioner, saw representatives of the Newspaper Proprietors' Association on 3 May 1926, Davidson wrote, "Riddell throughout behaved, whether from design or because it is in his nature, in a most obstructive manner." Lord Riddell died on 5 December 1934.

Related entry:
Lloyd George, David

Suggestions for further reading:
Fyfe, Hamilton. 1949. "Riddell, George Allardice." In *The Dictionary of National Biography 1931–1940,* edited by L. G. Wickham Legg. Oxford: Oxford University Press.

McEwen, J. M., ed. 1986. *The Riddell Diaries 1908–1923*. London: Athlone Press.

Riddell, Lord. 1933. *Lord Riddell's Intimate Diary of the Peace Conference and After, 1918–1923*. London: Gollancz.

———. 1933. *Lord Riddell's War Diary, 1914–1918*. London: Ivor Nicholson and Watson.

———. 1934. *More Pages from My Diary, 1906–1914*. London: Country Life.

Roosevelt, Franklin Delano (1882–1945)

Undated photo of Franklin Delano Roosevelt (Library of Congress)

Churchill and President Franklin D. Roosevelt struck a warm friendship during the Second World War, perhaps warmer on Churchill's part. Yet the men showed great consideration for each other and maintained a friendly, often informal relationship.

Franklin Delano Roosevelt was born at Hyde Park, New York, on 30 January 1882, the only son of James and Sara Delano Roosevelt. He grew up at Hyde Park, and was educated at Groton School, Massachusetts; after attending Harvard and Columbia, he became a lawyer. His father died at seventy-two, when Roosevelt was nineteen. He became a lawyer. A Democrat, he was elected to the New York State senate for Dutchess County in 1910. He held office under President Woodrow Wilson as assistant secretary of the navy, 1913–1921, and was the Democratic vice presidential candidate in 1920. He was seriously affected by poliomyelitis from 1921. Roosevelt was governor of New York State, 1929–1932, and became president of the United States on 4 March 1933. He responded to the Great Depression with the New Deal, a mixture of interventionist economic and social measures.

Churchill and Roosevelt first met in London in 1918 at a dinner at Grays Inn when Roosevelt was assistant secretary of the navy. When they next met at Placentia Bay in August 1941, Roosevelt was put out when Churchill made it clear that he did not remember their first meeting.

Churchill sent Roosevelt a copy of the first volume of his biography, *Marlborough*, on 8 October 1933. His inscription wished the president success in "the greatest crusade of modern times." Roosevelt initiated their correspondence on 11 September 1939. In his first letter, he invited Churchill and Neville Chamberlain to keep in touch with him personally "with anything you wish me to know about," warmly welcomed Churchill's return to office, and commented that he had enjoyed reading *Marlborough*. They were soon having conversations by telephone.

Churchill desperately needed Roosevelt's support, especially during the period when Britain was at war with Germany, but neither the United States nor the Soviet Union were belligerents. Roosevelt, who had no intention of buttressing the

British Empire nor of funding Britain if the country was more solvent than Churchill claimed, did provide fifty old destroyers in mid-1940, an important symbol of U.S. support. More vital to the war effort, Roosevelt launched the huge Lend Lease program from the spring of 1941.

Churchill and Roosevelt met at a series of conferences beginning with the one at Placentia Bay, Newfoundland, in August 1941, and ending with the Yalta Conference in February 1945. At the Casablanca Conference in January 1943, the two leaders agreed on the policy of "unconditional surrender" toward Germany. Churchill characteristically presented the president with one of his paintings of Marrakesh. By the time of the Tehran Conference in late 1943, Churchill was becoming anxious about Joseph Stalin's intentions. In 1944, Roosevelt continued to treat Churchill in a friendly and respectful manner; but it was increasingly apparent that the Soviet Union remained a major power, whereas Britain was now declining into a second-class power.

By 1945, Roosevelt's health was fading fast. Churchill and his party were deeply shocked by the decline in Roosevelt's appearance and his mobility when he arrived in the Crimea on 3 February 1945. After Yalta, Roosevelt's correspondence with Churchill was more formal, prepared by government officials and not by the president. Churchill was genuinely upset by the news of Roosevelt's death on 12 April 1945.

Although Churchill decided he would not leave Britain to attend Roosevelt's funeral at Hyde Park, New York, he was present at the British memorial service held in St. Paul's Cathedral, London, on 17 April 1945. There, as so often, Churchill was in tears. He paid a characteristically memorable tribute to Roosevelt, "the greatest American friend we have ever known," in the House of Commons later that day.

Related entries:
Cairo Conference; Casablanca Conference; Lend Lease Act; Placentia Bay Conference; Quebec Conference, First; Quebec Conference, Second; Tehran Conference; Yalta Conference

Suggestions for further reading:
Gilbert, Martin. 1983 and 1986. *Winston S. Churchill.* Vols. 6 and 7. London: Heinemann.
Kimball, Warren F. 1984. *Churchill and Roosevelt: The Complete Correspondence.* 3 vols. Princeton, NJ: Princeton University Press.
Lash, Joseph. 1976. *Roosevelt and Churchill, 1939–1941: The Partnership That Saved the West.* New York: W. W. Norton.
Sainsbury, Keith. 1994. *Churchill and Roosevelt at War.* London: Macmillan.
Stafford, David. 1997. *Roosevelt and Churchill: Men of Secrets.* London: Little and Brown.

Rosebery, Earl of (Archibald Philip Primrose, 1847–1929)

Archibald Rosebery was a major influence on the political development of the young Winston Churchill. Churchill looked up to Rosebery, a Centre politician who was a friend of his father. Churchill could identify with Rosebery's enthusiasm for the British Empire and his interest in social reform.

Archibald Philip Primrose, later Lord Dalmeny and later still the fifth earl of Rosebery, was born in London on 7 May 1847, the elder son of Archibald and Catherine Lucy Wilhelmina Primrose. His father died in 1851. His grandfather was the fourth earl. His mother was the daughter of the fourth earl of Stanhope and great-niece of William Pitt. Educated at Eton and briefly at Christ Church, Oxford, he succeeded to the earldom in March 1868. He famously left Oxford in 1869 when he was given the choice of selling his racehorse (which came in last at that year's Derby) or staying to take his degree. Rosebery was later the proud owner of three Derby winners.

In the 1870s, Rosebery rarely spoke in the House of Lords; however, he was an effective critic of Benjamin Disraeli's policies toward the Eastern Question. His own wealth was greatly reinforced with that of his wife, when in 1878 he married the heiress Hannah de Rothschild. As a leading Scottish Liberal, he invited William Gladstone to make Dalmeny, his stately home near Edinburgh, the headquarters for his Midlothian campaigns, 1879 and 1880. Rosebery spent large sums in support of Gladstone. Back in office in 1880, Gladstone offered Rosebery the under secretaryship at the India office, but Rosebery declined on the grounds that it might appear he had bought his post. In August 1881, he accepted the under secretaryship at the home office, resigning in 1883 due to dissatisfaction with the government's progress with Scottish issues. He entered the cabinet in February 1885 as lord privy seal. In Gladstone's brief 1886 government, Rosebery served as foreign secretary.

With most of the Liberal Party's aristocrats departing in 1886 over Gladstone's Irish Home Rule policy, Rosebery became even more important in the Liberal Party. In 1889, he was elected in the first London County Council elections and became the first chairman of the London County Council. He served again as foreign secretary, 1892–1894, and succeeded Gladstone as prime minister, 1894–1895. In 1896, when Gladstone emerged from retirement to denounce Turkish massacres in Armenia, he resigned as leader of the Liberal Party. By the turn of the century, he was the leader of Liberal Imperialism and the most notable exponent of "national efficiency." However, his denigration of party politics and his increasing criticisms of the Liberal Party ensured that he did not return to office in 1905.

Rosebery had been at Eton with Lord Randolph Churchill. At Oxford, he maintained his friendship with Lord Randolph, who was at Merton College, and other Etonians. They saw more of each

other as rising stars of politics in the houses of Parliament.

The young Winston Churchill looked up to Rosebery as a great political figure who had been his beloved father's contemporary. By November 1896, he was writing to Lady Randolph that Rosebery was "a great man," and that he hoped one day Rosebery and Joseph Chamberlain would lead "the Tory Democracy." For five or six years, Churchill saw Rosebery almost as a political father figure and admired him as a man who combined a commitment to imperialism and social reform. Churchill spoke warmly of Rosebery in many speeches.

Churchill and Rosebery first met in 1900 when they were both staying with Lord Tweedmouth at his home, Guisachan. Although Rosebery had been unfavorably impressed by Churchill's egotistic garrulousness at that time, he came to like and admire Churchill. When in 1902 Churchill began writing the biography of his father, Lord Randolph Churchill, he turned to Rosebery for help and support. He needed that support because his father had decreed that Rosebery should be given a copy of a biography to ensure there was no breach of confidentiality in using official papers. When Churchill sent Rosebery a set of proofs in January 1905, he was surprised by the amount of criticism Rosebery made. Rosebery also wrote a short memoir about Lord Randolph that he had intended for Churchill's use, but he decided to publish it himself, *Lord Randolph Churchill* (1906).

Nevertheless, Churchill and Rosebery remained friends. Churchill often visited Rosebery and enjoyed political discussion with him during the Campbell-Bannerman government. As Rosebery grew older and preferred solitude, Churchill was one of the few visitors he welcomed. Rosebery died on 21 May 1929.

Related entries:
Asquith, Herbert Henry; Grey, Sir Edward

Suggestions for further reading:

Churchill, Randolph S. 1966 and 1967. *Winston S. Churchill.* Vols. 1 and 2. London: Heinemann.

Crewe, Marquess of. 1931. *Lord Rosebery.* 2 vols. London: John Murray.

Rhodes James, Robert. 1963. *Rosebery.* London: Weidenfeld and Nicolson.

S

Salisbury, Lord (Robert Arthur Talbot Gascoyne-Cecil, 1830–1903)

Lord Salisbury represented for Winston Churchill not only aristocratic power and patronage but one of his father's generation of Conservative politicians. Although he was critical, even bitter, about how his father had been treated, Churchill did not hesitate to avail himself of Salisbury's influence to help him.

Lord Robert Cecil was born at Hatfield house on 3 February 1830, the second son of the second marquess. Educated at Eton and Oxford, he was elected, unopposed, for the pocket borough of Stamford in 1853. He was also elected a fellow of All Souls College, Oxford. Against his father's wishes, he married Georgina Alderson. Unfortunately, Cecil's family boycotted the wedding and cut him off financially, which meant that he had to earn money from journalism. However, when his brother died in 1868, he inherited the title and Hatfield House.

Salisbury was a notably intellectual and capable peer. He served as secretary of state for India in 1866 and 1874–1876, and foreign secretary in 1878–1880 before succeeding Benjamin Disraeli as leader of the Conservative Party in the House of Lords, 1881–1885. He led the Conservative Party from the Right, yet was successful in maintaining its unity and attracting to its support politicians leaving the Liberal Party under William Gladstone's leadership. He was as big a Victorian political figure as Disraeli and Gladstone, and served longer as prime minister (1885–1886, 1886–1892, and 1895–1902).

Winston Churchill's attitude toward Salisbury was ambivalent because he felt that Salisbury had been unfair to his father. For Churchill, the two had held major political differences rather than being divided by personal dislike and, on Salisbury's part, justified distrust in the other's judgement. The young Winston Churchill also saw Salisbury as the embodiment of a reactionary, old-fashioned Conservatism. In 1897, when Salisbury failed to espouse the cause of the Greeks for independence for Crete against Turkey, Churchill complained to his mother, "I look on this question from the point of view of right and wrong: Lord Salisbury from that of profit and loss."

Yet Winston Churchill, the grandson of a duke, was pleased to avail himself of Salisbury's influence. His mother, Lady Randolph, was on friendly terms with Salisbury. When he published *The Story of the Malakand Field Force* (1898), he placed a quotation from Salisbury at the front of the book: "They (Frontier Wars) are but the surf that marks the edge and the advance of the wave of civilisation." Salisbury, who was curious to see his old party opponent's son, read the book and invited the young Churchill to visit him on 5 July 1898. After the meeting, Churchill requested that Salisbury help him join Sir Herbert Kitchener's staff at Khartoum, but Churchill secured his aim without Salisbury's aid. He put a flattering dedication to Salisbury in the resulting book, *The River War*, which included "under whose wise direction the Conservative Party have long enjoyed power and the nation prosperity."

Later, Winston Churchill turned to his father's erstwhile friends and colleagues, Salisbury and Sir Henry Drummond Wolff, as useful contacts in his Conservative political career. He also turned to them for information when he wrote his father's biography. In February 1901, he called on Lord Salisbury at the foreign office. Salisbury then, or later, lent him letters he had received from Lord Randolph Churchill.

Salisbury resigned as prime minister on 11 July 1902. He died just over a year later on 22 August 1903.

Suggestions for further reading:
Churchill, Randolph S. 1966 and 1967. *Winston S. Churchill.* Vols. 1 and 2. London: Heinemann.
Foster, R. F. 1981. *Lord Randolph Churchill.* Oxford: Clarendon Press.
Roberts, Andrew. 1999. *Salisbury: Victorian Titan.* London: Weidenfeld and Nicolson.
Steele, E. D. 1999. *Salisbury: A Political Biography.* Oxford: Oxford University Press.

Sandys, Edwin Duncan (Baron Duncan-Sandys, 1908–1987)

Duncan Sandys was an able young Conservative politician in the late 1930s and 1940s who had the substantial asset of being Churchill's son-in-law. He was vigorously opposed to the appeasers in the late 1930s, and after the Second World War he was deeply committed to the European Movement. George Harvie-Watt wrote of him that he "had a tremendous lust for power."

Duncan Sandys was born on 24 January 1908 at Sandford Orcas, Dorset, the son of Captain George and Mildred Sandys. His father, Captain George J. Sandys, was Conservative and Unionist M.P. for Wells, 1910–1918. His mother was the daughter of Duncan Cameron of Ashburton, New Zealand. Educated at Eton and Magdalen College, Oxford, Sandys entered the diplomatic service in 1930 and served in the foreign office and in the British embassy in Berlin. In March 1935, he was the successful official Conservative candidate in a by-election for Norwood in South London, even though Randolph Churchill supported a rival Conservative candidate (to Winston Churchill's wrath). Sandys met Churchill's daughter Diana during the campaign, and they married later in the year. Churchill soon came to like his son-in-law and Sandys became one of his political associates. Like his father-in-law, Sandys was outraged by the German occupation of the Rhineland in 1936 and he was also anxious about British preparedness for a major war. Commissioned in the Territorial Army in 1937, there was an attempt to discipline him for asking parliamentary questions based on secret information. This led to a parliamentary inquiry into whether such a move against an M.P. was a breach of parliamentary privilege. After the Munich settlement in 1938, to Winston Churchill's chagrin, his son and son-in-law tried to launch a new antiappeasement movement, aiming to gain 100,000 members who were preparing for war. It quickly folded.

When Churchill became prime minister, Sandys acted as his "special liaison" with the home office and Air Raid Precautions. Sandys served in Norway and then in France in 1940. He and Diana were frequently with Churchill at Chequers or at 10 Downing Street, the prime minister's official residence. On one visit to Chequers, on 7 March 1941, John Colville noted in his diary that Sandys was "very blood-thirsty" because he argued for tough treatment for Germany after the war. Churchill was firmly against such revenge.

In the summer of 1941, Sandys was seriously injured in a car crash when his driver fell asleep and the car hit a bridge. Both his feet were smashed and his spine was injured, leaving him with a limp for the rest of his life.

In 1943, General Ismay recommended that Sandys be put in charge of finding out what Germany was doing in regard to long-range rockets and preparing countermeasures. By late June 1943, Sandys had prepared a dossier confirming that rocket manufacture was well advanced and the bombing of Peenemunde was authorized. He remained chairman of the war cabinet's committee for defense against rockets until 1945.

Churchill gave Sandys a minor office in February 1943, appointing him parliamentary secretary to the Ministry of Supply. He was promoted to minister of works, in charge of housing, a post he held from 21 November 1944 until the defeat of Churchill's caretaker government in July 1945. After the serious war damage, this was a high-priority area.

Sandys lost his seat in the 1945 general election. He worked closely with his father-in-law, in particular in promoting a united Europe. When Churchill tried to open informal talks with General de Gaulle about the Soviet Union in November 1946, he suggested his part be done through Sandys. Sandys was a founder of the European Movement in 1947, referring to it to Churchill as "our movement." He was one of the British participants, with Churchill, at the European Conference at the Hague, 7–10 May 1948, and they both were Opposition members of the British representatives at the first meeting of the Council of Europe at Strasbourg, 12 August 1949.

Sandys was reelected to Parliament in the 1950 general election, winning the London seat of Streatham. With Churchill's return to office in 1951, Sandys was given ministerial office outside the cabinet, as minister of supply. Apparently, Churchill had considered giving him the war office, but Clementine Churchill had warned that it might prove embarrassing to have his son-in-law in such a senior post, not least if he had to dismiss him. Sandys, however, performed well, and in October 1954 he was promoted to minister of housing and local government, in succession to Harold Macmillan.

After Churchill's retirement, Sandys remained in the cabinet during the governments of Anthony Eden, Harold Macmillan, and Alec Douglas-Home. He held the posts of defense (1957–1959), aviation (1959–1960), commonwealth relations (1960–1962), and the combined colonies and commonwealth relations (1962–1964). After 1964, he focused on business interests, becoming chairman of Lonrho in 1972. He retired from the House of Commons in 1972, and in 1974 was made a life peer, Baron Duncan-Sandys.

His marriage to Diana Churchill ended in divorce in 1960. They had one son and two daughters: Julian, Celia, and Edwina. In 1962, he married again. He died on 26 November 1987.

Suggestions for further reading:
Gilbert, Martin. 1976–1988. *Winston S. Churchill.* Vols. 5–8. London: Heinemann.
Lamb, Richard. 1996. "Sandys, (Edwin) Duncan." In *Dictionary of National Biography: 1986–1990,* edited by C. S. Nicholls. Oxford: Oxford University Press.

Sassoon, Siegfried Lorraine (1886–1967)

Although Siegfried Sassoon's First World War poetry was critical of the war, Churchill greatly admired his verse and delighted in quoting it. Sassoon was a war hero and a considerable writer, both attributes appealing to Churchill.

Siegfried Sassoon was born on 8 September 1886 at Matfield, Kent, the second son of Alfred Ezra and Theresa Sassoon. In 1889, his father left Theresa and their three sons. Thereafter, Siegfried was devoted to his mother and closer to her family, the Thornycrofts. He was educated at home until he was almost fourteen, when he, like his two brothers, went to New Beacon School. He went on to Marlborough College and Clare College, Cambridge. Comfortable on an income of £400 per annum left to him by his father, Sassoon left the university without graduating. He wrote poetry and enjoyed golf, cricket, and hunting. Through Edmund Gosse, Sassoon and his poetry encountered Edward Marsh, who encouraged Sassoon to improve his poetry. Marsh included poetry by Sassoon in his *Georgian Poetry 1916–1917* collection. Sassoon, who enlisted at the beginning of the war and won the Military Cross early on, became disillusioned with the war by 1916. In 1917, Sassoon issued an antiwar statement, expecting to be court-martialed. Instead, he was treated as suffering from a nervous disorder and sent to Craiglockhart Hospital, near Edinburgh.

Sassoon's second collection of publicly available poems, *Counter-Attack* (1918) was admired by Churchill, who surprised many people by enthusiastically quoting Sassoon's poems. In August 1918, Lord Esher inquired who Sassoon was, noting that "Winston knows his last volume of poems by heart, and rolls them out on every occasion." Through Edward Marsh, Churchill met Sassoon at the Ministry of Munitions on 3 October 1918 and made clear his admiration for Sassoon's poems. They met again on the night of the Armistice, at an after-dinner party given by Lady Randolph Churchill, where Winston Churchill again expressed his enthusiasm for Sassoon's work.

The war changed Sassoon's outlook and he emerged from it with radical views. He spoke for Philip Snowden, the antiwar Socialist, during the 1918 general election. In early 1919, he went to Glasgow to write about the engineering strike for the radical newspaper, the *Nation,* published in London. From April 1919, he was the literary editor of the London *Daily Herald.* He supported the miners in the 1921 coal dispute, reporting from South Wales for the *Herald* and also the *Nation.* He also supported the miners and the other trade unions during the General Strike, 1926.

With the publication of *Memoirs of a Fox-Hunting Man* in 1928, Sassoon enjoyed success in prose as well as poetry. He followed this success with *Memoirs of an Infantry Officer,* 1930, and *Sherston's Progress,* 1936, as well as three volumes of autobiography.

Sassoon met Churchill again at a house party in May 1934. Sassoon was impressed by Churchill's view that another major war was inevitable. In May 1939, he wrote to Edward Marsh asking Churchill, through him, what "a supposedly influential writer" could contribute to the war effort, once war occurred.

After the Second World War, Sassoon continued to write poetry. In 1956, he was awarded the Queen's Medal for Poetry. In August 1957, Sassoon was received into the Catholic Church, after some years of spiritual questing. He died on 1 September 1967.

Suggestions for further reading:
Gilbert, Martin. 1975. *Winston S. Churchill.* Vol. 4. London: Heinemann.
Roberts, John S. 1999. *Siegfried Sassoon.* London: Richard Cohen Books.

Savrola (1900)

Savrola: A Tale of the Revolution in Laurania was Churchill's only novel. It was published in the United States at $1.25 on

3 February 1900 and in the United Kingdom at six shillings on 13 February 1900.

Savrola is a boy's own action tale, full of action and battles, the hero based on the author. Its mixed reviews praised the action but criticized the weak characterization. When, in November 1898, Churchill invited his grandmother, the duchess of Marlborough, to comment on the character of the heroine, she readily agreed that "Lucile is a weak and uninteresting personality" and commented that her grandson clearly had no knowledge of women nor any experience of love. However, more favorable comments were made among the reviews, including interesting comparisons with Benjamin Disraeli and also comments on his stylistic debts to Thomas Macaulay.

When *Savrola* was published in book form, Churchill wrote in a prefatory note that it had been written in 1897. He had written half of it in India, before he joined the Malakand Field Force. He completed it while in England, in October and November 1898. He dedicated the book to the officers of the 4th Queen's Own Hussars "in whose company the author lived for four happy years."

Churchill accepted £100 for the novel to be serialized in *Macmillan's Magazine* (May–December 1900). After Churchill became prime minister it was again serialized, twice in the London *Sunday Dispatch* (from January 1942 and from November 1954). It was also serialized in France, Canada, and the United States. When it was issued in cheap paperbacks in Britain and the United States in 1957, A. L. Rowse wrote in the *New York Times Book Review* that "the story holds one's attention for its own sake, is even exciting," and added that it "is well written and well constructed."

Suggestions for further reading:
Churchill, Randolph S. 1966. *Winston S. Churchill*. Vol. 1. London: Heinemann.
Woods, Frederick. 1963. *A Bibliography of the Works of Sir Winston Churchill*. London: Nicholas Vane.

Scrymgeour, Edwin (1866–1947)

Two very different worlds came into collision when Churchill and Edwin Scrymgeour were repeatedly electoral opponents (1908, January 1910, December 1910, 1918, and 1922). Scrymgeour was very much the local politician, a Dundee phenomenon. He represented fundamentalist religious views, rigid prohibitionism, and left-wing socialism, all alien to Churchill.

Edwin Scrymgeour, the son of a former Chartist (the radical working-class movement, which in the 1830s and 1840s sought a widening of parliamentary representation), was born in Dundee on 28 July 1866. His family were prominent in Dundee, and in particular in the Tally Street Wesleyan Chapel. After school, he worked as a clerk. An early member of the Independent Labour Party (ILP), he was elected as an ILP parish councillor in 1895 and 1898. He left the ILP but always remained on the Left. He combined intense, even millennial, religious feelings with a deep belief in temperance. He urged his followers, "Vote as you pray." He was a founder of the Scottish Prohibition Party and its organizing secretary. He was elected to the Dundee Town Council in 1905, where he was a fiery, radical presence.

In the 1908 by-election, Scrymgeour, who described his politics as "Prohibition and Labour," stood against Churchill, the Liberal candidate, and also the Conservative and Labour candidates, and came bottom of the poll with 655 votes. In the January 1910 general election, he received 1,512 votes, and in the December 1910 election, 1,825 votes, but remained bottom of the poll.

With the First World War, Scrymgeour opposed the war, as he had the Boer War. He spoke out for conscientious objectors, representing several at military tribunals. In the 1918 general election, Scrymgeour's vote rose again, to 10,423. By this time he was attracting many Irish and women's votes. In the 1922 election campaign, nine days after Benito Mussolini's rise to power, Scrymgeour observed that it would not surprise him in the event of civil war "if Mr. Churchill were at the head of the Fascisti party." Generally, however, Scrymgeour's appeal lay in his socialist and temperance politics. When the votes were counted, Scrymgeour topped the poll in the two-member constituency, the famous conscientious objector and radical E. D. Morel (Labour) came second, with Churchill fourth.

Scrymgeour was reelected in the general elections of 1923, 1924, and 1929, standing always as a Scottish Prohibition Party candidate. In the House of Commons, he voted with the Labour Party, other than on the issue of prohibition. He was defeated in the 1931 general election. He died on 1 February 1947.

Suggestions for further reading:
Churchill, Randolph S. 1967. *Winston S. Churchill.* Vol. 2. London: Heinemann.
Gilbert, Martin. 1975. *Winston S. Churchill.* Vol. 4. London: Heinemann.
Knox, W., and J. Saville. 1984. "Scrymgeour, Edwin." In *Dictionary of Labour Biography,* edited by J. Bellamy and J. Saville. Vol. 7. London: Macmillan.
Paterson, Tony. 1980. *A Seat for Life.* Dundee, UK: David Winter.
Walker, W. M. 1970. "Dundee's Disenchantment with Churchill: A Comment upon the Fall of the Liberal Party." *Scottish Historical Review* 49, pp. 85–108.
———. 1979. *Juteopolis: Dundee and Its Textile Workers 1885–1923.* Edinburgh: Edinburgh University Press.

The Secret Service

Throughout his career, Churchill took a considerable interest in intelligence matters. The extent of his interest became more apparent in the 1980s and 1990s as the British records relating to Ultra and to the Special Operations Executive (SOE) were opened. Churchill's interest has also been made clear by the historian David Stafford, who concluded that "Churchill stood head and shoulders above his political contemporaries in grasping the importance of intelligence and harnessing it to his cause."

From early on in his career, Churchill was familiar with military intelligence. When he and his friend Reginald Barnes went to Cuba in 1895, Churchill was briefed by the director of military intelligence and asked to report back, taking particular care to assess the effectiveness of a new bullet. He learned more of military intelligence on the Northwest Frontier of India as well as in the Sudan and South Africa.

As a cabinet minister, 1908–1915, Churchill supported the establishment of Britain's secret service. Soon after the Secret Service Bureau was set up in 1909, with the two divisions that became MI5 and MI6, John Spencer Ewart, the director of military intelligence, saw Churchill after he had attended the annual German army maneuvers. Churchill provided much information about Germany's finances. When Churchill became home secretary in 1910, he chaired two Committee of Imperial Defence subcommittees concerned with surveillance, tighter controls over secret information, and the monitoring of aliens. In April 1910, Churchill as home secretary had to defend the pension of Sir Robert Anderson, who had run espionage operations against the Fenians and Charles Stuart Parnell and had published memoirs. Churchill was also involved in the rushing through Parliament of the Official Secrets Act, 1911, and in securing police action in secretly compiling a register of aliens and in opening the mail of suspect individuals or organizations. In June 1912, Churchill was instrumental in introducing the "D-notice" system, whereby a committee of the admiralty and war office advised the

Reinhard Heydrich, head of the German secret police, speaking with Vermer von Blomberg (Library of Congress)

press not to publish specific stories that were considered detrimental to the security of the country.

As first lord of the admiralty, Churchill was susceptible to alarmist talk of threats to naval supplies. He was also fearful that German agents were funding the 1911 railway strike and threatened South Wales coal supplies. Repeatedly Churchill took action on Captain Vernon Kell's alarmist reports of German spies, which were made more credible by the prewar arrest of several actual German spies. Churchill even employed the colorful "Captain" Tupper, a

right-wing trade union organizer, to provide him privately with lists of spies.

After the outbreak of war, Winston and Clementine Churchill showed that they were not immune from spy fever. Clementine Churchill passed on stories of foreigners walking on the cliffs near her holiday cottage near Cromer, leading to fears of a German plot to kidnap her. Winston Churchill, visiting a remote loch in northwest Scotland, took high-handed action when a searchlight was spotted on Loch Rosque Castle, the home of a Conservative M.P., Sir Arthur Bignold. Churchill and others, armed with guns, rejected Bignold's explanation that it was used to locate deer for hunting, and insisted on immobilizing it immediately.

In both the world wars, Churchill was alert to the importance of intercepting German naval and military messages. Churchill, having been initially skeptical that the Germans could intercept British radio messages, became an eager supporter of cryptography, which became based in room 40 of the admiralty building (and thereafter was known as "Room 40"). The British, Russians, and Australians secured copies of the German navy's three code books, giving the Allies a similar advantage to that of Enigma in the Second World War. While Churchill was on the Western Front in 1916, he met and became friends with Major Desmond Morton.

When Churchill became minister of munitions, he inherited the Ministry of Munitions Labour Intelligence Division. It went beyond its initial purpose of protecting munitions factories from sabotage to investigating militant workers. Opposition to the continuance of the war was also countered by the National War Aims Committee, chaired by Churchill's cousin Frederick Guest, by Special Branch, and by the Ministry of Information, headed by John Buchan (whose anti-Bolshevism and anti-pacifism is well displayed in his novel *Mr. Standfast,* 1919).

When Churchill became secretary of state for war and air in January 1919, he was centrally placed to combat Bolshevism abroad and what he considered its equivalent at home. Churchill formed an army secret intelligence department, MO4(X), which worked with MI5 and Special Branch to monitor and combat subversion and disorder. One of Churchill's targets was George Lansbury and his socialist newspaper, the *Herald*. After the First World War, a major focus for Room 40 was Russian secret messages. Where these could be used to discredit Lansbury, they were leaked to the right-wing *Morning Post* and to the ultrapatriot (and crooked) Horatio Bottomley, M.P. In 1920, Churchill and the secret service chiefs discussed publishing transcripts of Moscow messages to secure the expulsion of the Russian trade delegation and advised the cabinet to authorize this. To Churchill's rage, the cabinet rejected this advice and continued trade negotiations.

Churchill was deeply interested in anti-Bolshevik espionage in Russia. He may well have colluded with his cousin Clare Sheridan's trip to Moscow in 1920, when she made sculptures of Vladimir Lenin, Leon Trotsky, Feliks Dzerzhinsky, and Grigory Zinoviev. He backed Boris Savinkov's guerrilla activities against Bolshevik forces, in spite of secret service doubts about him. Churchill arranged for Savinkov to see David Lloyd George and Lord Birkenhead. Churchill included an essay on Savinkov in his *Great Contemporaries,* after Savinkov had gone to Moscow, been imprisoned, and probably murdered in 1925. Churchill also backed Sidney Reilly, the most famous British spy of the period, who was often his link with Savinkov. Reilly also died in Russia, probably in late 1925. Churchill also had links with Savinkov and Reilly through his friends Archie Sinclair and Louis Spears.

Churchill, as secretary of state for war, was at the fore in the British war with Sinn Fein in Ireland after the First World War. He backed the Black and Tans, and was vigorous in defending their outrages. However, British intelligence in Ireland was unimpressive.

In the 1930s, Churchill built up private networks of information. As well as Desmond Morton, his sources included Squadron Leader Torr Anderson, Sir Robert Vansittart, Ralph Wigram of the foreign office, and Sir Hugh Sinclair, director of MI6. When Neville Chamberlain became prime minister in 1937, there was a more determined attempt to curtail Churchill's access to secret information. However, the attempt to threaten his son-in-law,

Duncan Sandys, with the Official Secrets Act failed when a select committee of the House of Commons gave the verdict that M.P.s had immunity from prosecution for raising issues in the House of Commons.

Churchill returned to the admiralty at the outbreak of the Second World War. Again, he keenly supported Naval Intelligence and the admiralty's Operational Intelligence Centre, a successor to Room 40. However, it was not until spring 1941 that British intelligence could read the Enigma cipher. Churchill took a keen interest in all security matters concerning Ireland, approving the use of an armed merchant ship disguised as a trawler to search the Irish coast for German submarines.

Churchill took a particular interest in securing British nationality for Imre Révész, a Hungarian Jew who had fled from the Nazis in Berlin to Paris in 1933 and who faced substantial obstruction from the British secret service. Churchill succeeded in bringing Révész to Britain in October 1939. He changed his name to Emery Reves before going to New York to help with British propaganda.

As well as reading intercepts for military and naval information, Churchill was greatly interested in diplomatic intercepts. He took special interest in those relating to Turkey, one of the most important neutral countries, and these gave him additional information for when he sought to bring Turkey into the war on the Allied side.

Churchill was quickly disillusioned by Vernon Kell and MI6 after several bungled operations in the early part of the war. Churchill, soon after becoming prime minister, set up the Special Operations Executive (SOE) under Hugh Dalton. His spy mania matched that he had had in the First World War; as prime minister he ordered the mass internment of aliens, and sent some to Canada (many of whom drowned when their ship was torpedoed). Churchill had Kell sacked. His successor, Sir David Petrie, was more effective. Chur-

chill kept an eye on intelligence matters, not least the use of double agents to misinform the Germans. Churchill, in the early part of his wartime premiership, relied on Lord Swinton and Desmond Morton to supervise and advise him on intelligence matters.

From 22 May 1940, the British could read the German messages in cipher on the Enigma machines, as a result of the skills of the code breakers at Bletchley Park. Churchill was as eager to read these intercepts as he had been to read those available in the First World War. These reports, given as coming from Ultra, were sent to Churchill via Stewart Menzies. Through them Churchill learned much crucial information, including the ending of Hitler's plans to invade Britain, Hitler's plans to invade Greece, and German strength in North Africa. Churchill shared Enigma information with the United States and the United States shared with him its Purple machine that could read Japanese cipher messages. Anglo-American intelligence was also promoted by links between MI6 and the FBI and later the Office of Strategic Services (OSS), initiated in May 1940 by William Stephenson. Churchill also passed on information from Ultra, as if from conventional secret sources, to Stalin before the German invasion, as well as for the rest of the war.

Churchill strongly supported SOE and its objective of setting Europe ablaze. In May 1942, Czech agents, trained and equipped in Britain, assassinated Reinhard Heydrich, head of the German secret police, in Prague. It is probable that British agents assisted the assassin of Admiral Jean Darlan in December 1941. Churchill was also kept informed of the SOE and Norwegian resistance's heroic and effective actions in 1943 against the Norsk Hydro plant at Vemork, near Rjukan, and the destruction of its output of heavy water (deuterium oxide), which obstructed Germany's development of atomic weapons. In the case of

Yugoslavia, Churchill sent his own emissary, Fitzroy Maclean, to Josip Tito. Churchill also ensured the Marquis in France received far more ammunition and supplies.

Churchill received intercepts concerning German massacres of Jews from June 1941 onward. He spoke of massacres in Russia, not specifically of Jews, in a radio broadcast on 24 August 1941. He was shocked by news of extermination camps. In 1944, Moshe Shertok saw Randolph Churchill, urging him to secure his father's support for the creation of Jewish SOE groups to organize resistance in Hungary and the Balkan states. Churchill liked the idea but it was not implemented.

Churchill's relationship with Desmond Morton declined from 1943. Morton resented Stewart Menzies's growing importance to Churchill in intelligence matters. Alan Hillgarth, a naval intelligence officer who had served in Spain and the Far East during the Second World War, remained in contact with Churchill after his defeat in the 1945 general election and provided him with information on the Soviet Union.

With Churchill's return to office in 1951, he permitted spy-plane flights over Russia. He was also fully supportive of the joint Anglo-American secret services action that toppled Dr. Mohammed Musaddiq of Iran, after he had nationalized the Anglo-Iranian oil company's refinery at Abadan.

Related entries:
Morton, Sir Desmond; Swinton, Earl of

Suggestions for further reading:
Andrew, Christopher. 1985. *Secret Service.* London: Heinemann.
Denniston, Robin. 1997. *Churchill's Secret War: Diplomatic Decrypts, the Foreign Office and Turkey, 1942–1944.* New York: St. Martin's Press.
Foot, M. R. D. 1984. *SOE: The Special Operations Executive, 1940–1946.* London: BBC.
Jones, R. V. 1979. *Most Secret War: British Scientific Intelligence 1939–1945.* London: Cornet.
Lewin, Ronald. 1979. *Ultra Goes to War.* London: Hutchinson.
Stafford, David. 1997. *Churchill and the Secret Service.* London: Murray.

Seely, John Edward Bernard (First Baron Mottistone, 1868–1947)

Jack Seely was a Unionist Free Trader who, like Churchill, switched to the Liberals and became a cabinet minister under Asquith. He and Churchill were close political associates in the decade or so before the First World War.

Seely was born on 31 May 1868 at Brookhill Hall between Derby and Nottingham, the fourth son and seventh child of nine of Sir Charles and Emily Seely. The Seelys were wealthy coal owners. Jack Seely's grandfather was Radical M.P. (1861–1885) for Lincoln; his father was Liberal M.P. (1869–1874 and 1880–1885) for Nottingham and Liberal Unionist M.P. for Nottingham West (1892–1895); and his brother was Liberal Unionist M.P. (1895–1906) for Lincoln. Hence when Jack Seely went from the Conservative and Unionists to the Liberals with Churchill, he was returning (on the Free Trade issue) to familiar politics for his family, unlike Winston Churchill.

Seely, like Churchill, was educated at Harrow. He went on to Trinity College, Cambridge, before becoming a barrister. A member of the Hampshire Yeomanry before the Boer War, he saw service during it commanding his Yeomanry and displaying great bravery. He was appointed to the DSO (Distinguished Service Order) in 1900. He was elected Conservative M.P. for the Isle of Wight in a by-election in May 1900; he vacated his seat over tariff reform in 1904 but was returned unopposed as an Independent Conservative. He was Liberal M.P. for Liverpool Abercromby, 1906–1910, and from March 1910 for Ilkeston, Derbyshire. In 1908, Asquith appointed him to succeed Churchill as under secretary of state for the colonies and, like Churchill, his superior, Lord Crewe, was in the House of Lords. Clearly he and Churchill had much in common.

Although Churchill was much younger, Seely and he dated their friendship back to Harrow. In South Africa, Churchill visited Seely at the front at Dewetsdorp, where they shared a meal the night before an expected battle. The next morning, realizing that the Boers had retreated, Churchill rode on his own to the British objective, a hill that overlooked an important ridge, to the delight of Seely but to the wrath of some of Seely's superiors.

In the House of Commons in 1903, Churchill organized a small group of Conservative and Unionist opponents to the army reform proposals put forward by the secretary of state, St. John Brodrick. Seely was prominent in this, as were Lord Hugh Cecil, Ivor Guest, and Ernest Beckett. Seely later declared that this active opposition had begun the disintegration of the Conservative Party that ended in its heavy defeat in 1906. Seely was also one of the sixty Conservative and Unionist M.P.s who joined the Free Food League, of which Churchill was the prime mover.

When, in 1904, Seely vacated his Isle of Wight seat to appeal to his constituents over his opposition to tariffs, Churchill wrote "all the best parts" of his address. He later wrote of Churchill, "He was, indeed, a trusty friend and doughty champion during these troublous times." Seely also felt that Churchill played a major role in the 1906 general election "in winning votes for Free Trade, not only in Manchester, but throughout the country" and deemed it to be "one of the most remarkable electoral performances of our time."

Churchill championed Seely and successfully suggested to Herbert Henry Asquith that Seely should become secretary of state for war. Seely, when taking this office in June 1912, was already convinced that war between Britain and Germany was inevitable. He secured Churchill's cooperation in creating a small committee to ensure cooperation between the army and navy. This consisted of Seely and Churchill,

the chief of the Imperial General Staff (Sir John French), the first lord of the admiralty (Prince Louis of Battenburg), the permanent secretaries, and Maurice Hankey (as a link with the Committee of Imperial Defence). This committee successfully planned ahead the swift transportation of the British Expeditionary Force in the event of war. After Seely's resignation over the handling of a potential mutiny of senior army officers at Curragh (Ireland), he continued to serve with Churchill on the Committee of Imperial Defence.

During the First World War, Seely served in France. When sent by Sir John French to Dunkirk on 25 September 1914, he was surprised to find Churchill with his naval force at Dunkirk. He was also sent to Antwerp when Churchill was there. Seely later wrote, "He dominated the whole place, the King, ministers, soldiers, sailors." After Churchill went, Seely displayed great coolness and much bravery in evacuating troops from Antwerp. He was the last to cross the major bridge of boats route out of the city. He later gave the judgment that Churchill and his naval men were crucial in securing the escape of the Belgian army.

When Churchill joined his regiment on the Western Front near St. Omer in November 1915, he arranged to meet Seely. By this time Seely was a general, in charge of a Canadian mounted brigade. Seely admired Churchill's activities as a battalion commander and was outraged when French's promise of a brigade to Churchill was not acted upon by his successor, Sir Douglas Haig. For Seely, "It was an extraordinary instance of the rigid exclusiveness of the old-fashioned military mind." Seely himself displayed much bravery until he was gassed in April 1918, being mentioned five times in dispatches and receiving further awards, and ending the war as a major general.

While minister of munitions, Churchill set up a tank board to plan an expansion in production of tanks; after Seely had recovered from the gas, Churchill persuaded him to take charge of it. Seely was Churchill's parliamentary secretary of munitions from 10 July 1918. In the 1918 general election, Seely campaigned for Churchill in Dundee. After polling in the election, Churchill urged David Lloyd George to make Seely minister of pensions, commenting that Seely's wartime service made him ideal to gain the confidence of ex-servicemen; or if not minister of pensions, then postmaster general.

When Churchill moved from munitions to become secretary of state for air as well as secretary of state for war on 10 January 1919, Seely went with him as under secretary for air. Seely attended the Paris Peace Conference of 1919, representing the Air Ministry on the Aviation Committee. Seely was greatly impressed by Lloyd George's abilities there and he also commented, "Winston's buoyancy upheld the interests of our country, and Birkenhead's practical sagacity saved her from many pitfalls." As under secretary for air and the most senior politician other than Churchill in that ministry, Seely presented the 1919 Air Estimates in the House of Commons in March 1919 and presented it on many occasions at cabinet meetings.

On 10 November 1919, Seely resigned, wanting an independent Air Ministry, not one that was "an annexe" of the war office. Seely was also disappointed that his two junior posts had not resulted in a return to the cabinet. Churchill wrote a personal reply to his resignation, observing that he had done all he could to restart his political career and that had it been in his power to give him a cabinet post he would have done so. He also indicated that he felt Seely was ill-advised to resign if he hoped for further political preferment.

Seely remained a coalition Liberal M.P. until defeated in the 1922 general election. He was reelected as a Liberal for his original seat, the Isle of Wight, in the 1923 general election, but his political career ended when he was defeated in the October 1924 general election. In his later years as an M.P., he remained a Churchill supporter. When Churchill was moving ever closer to the Conservatives, he wrote to Stanley Baldwin on 10 May 1924 naming Seely as one of his group of Liberal M.P.s who would vote against the Labour government. A month later he was mentioning Seely as a likely Liberal Conservative. Seely's political trajectory was similar to Churchill's. Seely, for example, was also vehemently hostile to the General Strike, 1926. When Churchill was chancellor of the exchequer, Seely was appointed chairman of the National Savings Commission, 1926–1943. Churchill wrote to Stanley Baldwin on 4 June 1929, pressing that both Jack Seely and Freddy Guest be given peerages in his resignation list of honors. Seely was created Baron Mottistone four years later, in 1933. Churchill certainly did his best for his "oldest friend."

Seely was a courageous, loyal, and good-natured man. He was a genuine hero in both the Boer War and the First World War. In his introduction to Seely's autobiography, *Adventure,* the Earl of Birkenhead wrote that "the hero, and writer, of the present volume is as outstanding as the greatest of the Musketeers." He was very much one of Churchill's political supporters and, in turn, he benefited from Churchill's patronage. He died on 7 November 1947.

Related entries:
Air, Secretary of State for; Cecil, Lord Hugh Richard Heathcote; Guest, Frederick Edward; Guest, Sir Ivor Churchill

Suggestions for further reading:
Churchill, Randolph S. 1967. *Winston S. Churchill.* Vol. 2. London: Heinemann.
Gilbert, Martin. 1971, 1975, and 1979. *Winston S. Churchill.* Vols. 3 and 4, and companion vol. 5, part 1. London: Heinemann.
Seely, J. E. B. 1930. *Adventure.* London: Heinemann.
———. 1931. *Fear and Be Slain.* London: Hodder and Stoughton.

———. 1932. *For Ever England*. London: Hodder and Stoughton.

Sidney Street, Siege of (1911)

Winston Churchill was much criticized at the time for his high-profile involvement as home secretary in the police operation in the East End of London against an armed and very dangerous band of burglars. One reporter present, Hugh Martin, later observed, "It is not so much that he consciously seeks the limelight as that the limelight follows him."

On 16 December 1910, the police were called to a shop in Houndsditch, East London, where a group of armed men were breaking into a Mr. Harris's jeweler's shop. When the police intervened, three were shot dead and a further two wounded. It was believed that those involved were anarchists from Latvia, led by Peter Straume ("Peter the Painter") from Riga. Ten days later, the police found a pistol, cartridges, and chemicals for making explosives when raiding the house in Gold Street that belonged to the one burglar fatally wounded in the burglary, a Mr. Morountzeff (or Gardstein).

On 3 January 1911, armed police surrounded a house, 100 Sidney Street, where the surviving members of the gang were believed to be hiding. When they called on those inside to surrender, shots were fired from inside, wounding a sergeant.

Churchill, as home secretary, was contacted by the home office to formally authorize the use of soldiers in the siege. As well as further numbers of armed police, Scots Guards from the Tower of London had already been summoned to the scene because those besieged brandished weapons more powerful than those the police carried. Churchill readily gave the authorization and then drove to Houndsditch; there, he reconnoitered the rear of the building

under siege to check that there was no escape route that way.

After the house caught fire, Churchill was asked by a junior officer of the fire brigade to confirm that they should not try to put the fire out. This he did, feeling that fire brigade staff should not put their lives at risk. When the building had burnt out, the bodies of Fritz Svaars and Jacob Fogel were found; one had been shot by the besiegers, the other had been asphyxiated. Afterwards, Churchill was subjected to much criticism from the Conservatives and the press for going to the "siege of Sidney Street" and even for taking operational command there (which he did not, other than taking responsibility for confirming that the fire brigade should not approach the burning building). When a newsreel film of Churchill at Sidney Street was shown at London's Palace Theatre and elsewhere, he was booed by the audiences. However, the local police in the East End were appreciative of his unequivocal support.

Afterwards, Churchill was willing to propose tougher restrictions on aliens, something he had opposed in 1904–1905. On 19 January 1911, Churchill recommended to the cabinet that a bill be introduced that would make aliens convicted of an offense liable to expulsion and impose stronger penalties on those found guilty of harboring illegal immigrants; under the proposed bill, aliens would also be required to secure special permission to carry firearms. Though introduced into the House of Commons on 18 April 1911, the measure was not given sufficient parliamentary time and fell.

Contrary to the view at the time, those involved in the jewelry robbery had tenuous links with British anarchism. Some had been in the Jewish Anarchist Club in Jubilee Street, but otherwise there seems to have been no notable involvement by them in British anarchist politics. The historian John Quail has suggested that "the men involved were either unpolitical or connected with the Leftist Social Democrat combat groups."

Related entry:
Home Secretary

Suggestions for further reading:
Churchill, Randolph S. 1967. *Winston S. Churchill.* Vol. 2. London: Heinemann.
Churchill, Winston S. 1932. *Thoughts and Adventures.* London: Thornton Butterworth.
Martin, Hugh. 1932. *Battle: The Life Story of the Rt. Hon. Winston S. Churchill.* London: Sampson Low.
Quail, John. 1978. *The Slow Burning Fuse: The Lost History of the British Anarchists.* London: Paladin.
Rogers, Colin. 1981. *The Battle of Stepney: The Siege of Sidney Street.* London: Robert Hale.

Sinclair, Sir Archibald Henry MacDonald (Viscount Thurso, 1890–1970)

Sinclair was one of Churchill's oldest friends. Before the First World War they shared interests in Liberal politics, polo, and flying. They remained friends after the Second World War, Sinclair staying at Chartwell in December 1949 and at 10 Downing Street in January 1954. Churchill was Sinclair's mentor in the First World War and after, but Sinclair stayed with the Liberals after 1922, becoming Liberal leader in 1935–1945 and the last Liberal leader to hold ministerial office (1940–1945).

Archibald Sinclair was born on 21 October 1890, the only child of Clarence Granville and Mabel Sinclair. By the age of five he was an orphan, brought up by his grandfather and other relatives. Educated at Eton and Sandhurst, he was commissioned in the 2d Life Guards in 1910. He was a very keen aviator and a polo player. He became a friend of Winston Churchill. During the First World War, he was aide-de-camp to Jack Seely, one of Churchill's friends. When Churchill went to serve at the Western Front, he asked for Archie Sinclair or Edward Spears to serve under him, and Haig arranged for Sinclair's transfer to Churchill's battalion as second in command.

Before the First World War, Churchill had introduced Sinclair to Liberal Party officials in the hope that he could gain a parliamentary seat. By the end of the First World War, Sinclair was unenthusiastic for David Lloyd George's coalition government, but he was not eager to join Labour. He helped Churchill in Dundee in the 1918 general election. When Churchill was secretary of state for war, Sinclair accepted the post of his military secretary. When Churchill became colonial secretary, Sinclair left the army and became his assistant in that post. In the 1922 general election, Sinclair ran as a National Liberal in Caithness and Sutherland, his home constituency, successfully fighting the incumbent Independent Liberal. Sinclair held his seat through his hard work in his large constituency. With Lloyd George's return to a united Liberal Party in 1923, Sinclair became involved in the new policymaking on land, being a founder member of the Land Committee and chairing its Scottish sister committee that produced the "Tartan book." In 1930, as the Liberal Party split three ways, Sinclair became chief whip. He was neither pro-Tory nor pro-Labour, but devoted to Liberal independence.

With the formation of the National government in August 1931, Sinclair became secretary of state for Scotland (with the post in the cabinet from November 1931), until those Liberals led by Sir Herbert Samuel resigned when the government ended free trade. When Sir Herbert Samuel was defeated in the 1935 general election, Lloyd George supported Sinclair to succeed as leader, a post he held in 1935–1945.

Sinclair opposed appeasement. He believed a Liberal revival would occur and championed its independence. He did participate in other groupings, including Focus, funded by Eugen Spier, which helped promote Churchill and opposition to Nazism. Sinclair also joined with Walter Citrine, the TUC secretary, and Churchill to launch the Arms and the Covenant movement (in support of the League of Nations and collective security) on 3 December 1936. Before Munich, Sinclair and other Liberal leaders called on Neville Chamberlain to defend Czechoslovakia. Sinclair denounced the Munich agreement and thereafter called for Churchill to be brought into the government.

With the outbreak of war, Chamberlain offered Sinclair a cabinet-rank office, but outside the war cabinet. He declined. When Churchill became prime minister, Sinclair reluctantly accepted the Air Ministry, but without a place in the war cabinet. Sinclair was capable and worked long hours, but remained subordinate to his old mentor, Churchill. Sinclair declined Churchill's offers of ambassador to Washington, 1941, and viceroy of India, 1942. Sinclair's role was squeezed by Churchill, himself determining the main features of air strategy; production being under Lord Beaverbrook and his successors. Churchill did nothing to stop the bickering between Beaverbrook and the less abrasive Sinclair.

In the 1945 general election Sinclair lost his seat and failed to recover it in the 1950 general election. When Churchill returned to the premiership in 1951, Sinclair was elevated to the House of Lords as Viscount Thurso. His health deteriorated soon after. He died on 15 June 1970.

Suggestions for further reading:
De Groot, Gerard J. 1993. *Liberal Crusader: The Life of Sir Archibald Sinclair.* London: Hurst.
Gilbert, Martin. 1971–1988. *Winston S. Churchill.* Vols. 3–8. London: Heinemann.

Slim, Field Marshal Sir William Joseph (Viscount Slim of Burma, 1891–1970)

As time has passed Slim has been judged to have been one of the greatest of British generals in the Second World War, being the key figure in the successful Burma campaign, 1942–1945. He had not been one of Churchill's favorite generals. Indeed, Churchill's joke, at Alanbrooke's suggestion that Slim be promoted, is well remembered: "I cannot believe that a man with a name like Slim can be any good." However, to his troops in the Burma campaigns Slim was known as "Uncle Bill."

Slim was born at Bishopstone, Bristol, on 6 August 1891 but from 1903 lived in Birmingham. He was the second son of John Slim, a wholesale hardware merchant. His mother, Charlotte, was a devoted Catholic and he was educated at St. Philip's Edgbaston, a Catholic grammar school. He lapsed from the Catholic Church but always held a basic Christian faith. He was an eager member of the Officer Training Corps (OTC). At the outbreak of the First World War he was appointed a second lieutenant in the Royal Warwickshire Regiment. He served on Cape Helles, Gallipoli, from July 1915, being seriously wounded on 9 August when advancing on part of the Sari Bair ridge. Although deemed still unfit for active service, he managed to serve with General Sir Stanley Maud in Mesopotamia in 1916–1917, being wounded again at Duqma on 27 March 1917. From November 1917 he served in India, succeeding in receiving a transfer to the Indian Army. He served with the 4th Gurkhas, including at Malakand, 1922–1924. After an outstanding performance at the Staff College at Quetta, 1925–1927, he served in various staff positions until the outbreak of the Second

World War. To boost his income and for enjoyment he wrote, under the pseudonym Anthony Mills, many short stories drawing on his soldiering experiences on the northwest frontier for British newspapers and journals, some of which were collected in his *Unofficial History* (1959).

In the Second World War Slim first saw action in November 1940 against the Italians on the Sudanese border at Gallabat and Metemma. Through a lack of boldness he failed to take Metemma. He was wounded for a third time in January 1941 when Italian fighter planes strafed his truck in Eritrea. In May 1941 he was appointed to command the 10th Indian Division in its advance into Iraq and then into Syria. In March 1942 he was appointed commando of 1st Burma Corps, with the task to save the army in Burma (if, as was probable, it was impossible to hold Burma). Wavell also called on Slim to defend Upper Burma to safeguard the oil fields at Yenangyaung and to maintain contact with the Chiang Kaishek's troops in eastern Burma. Slim found himself in charge of part of the harrowing retreat northward, giving instructions on 14 April for the successful destruction of the oil field installations. Slim succeeded in enabling the fighting troops to withdraw from Burma with their morale intact in May 1942.

Churchill, requiring success in southeast Asia, successfully urged the setting up at the Quebec Conference, August 1943, of an Anglo-American Southeast Asia Command. Louis Mountbatten was appointed supreme commander and put Slim in charge of the new Army (14th) for the Burma campaign. Although Churchill and Mountbatten expected amphibious campaigns along the coasts, Slim produced results inland. Slim succeeded in raising morale and recreating a belief in the British and Indian ability to defeat the Japanese. When the Japanese attacked again in February 1944 Slim was ready, with air supplies prepared for troops and substantial

troop reserves at the ready. At the second Battle of Arakan, Slim turned defensive measures into offensive ones, and broke the myth of Japanese invincibility. In the Battles of Imphal and Kohima in March 1944 Slim, fully backed by Mountbatten and Churchill, engaged Japanese forces where their lines of communications were long and poor, and won, though the Japanese general retreat only began on 10 July. Slim was knighted in December 1944. He followed this victory at Imphal by advancing after the Japanese, deceiving them into thinking that he was going to attack Mandalay but instead seized Meiktila, which was crucial to Japanese operations in central and northern Burma. Slim defeated the Japanese forces when they counterattacked and then took Mandalay. Slim's forces then raced to Rangoon, arriving on 2 May 1945 shortly after the monsoon arrived. Slim's offensive against the Japanese, in which they lost some 350,000 men, was probably the greatest land victory against Japanese forces in World War Two. On a month's leave in England, Slim and his wife, Aileen, were invited to Chequers in late June 1945. Churchill wished to assess Slim before approving his promotion to commander in chief of Southeast Asia Command. When Churchill spoke over lunch of the general election, his wife commented that the armed forces' ballot was doubtful. To this, Slim responded somewhat tactlessly, "I know one thing. *My* Army won't be voting for you." In this he was probably right (the view being firmly echoed to the author by a Burma campaign officer some 25 years later). Churchill, nevertheless, warmly approved of Slim, paying generous tribute to Slim and the Burma campaign in his *The Second World War* (vol. 6).

When Slim returned to Southeast Asia on 16 August 1945 the war had nearly ended. Slim was kept busy with the releasing of Allied prisoners, the formal receiving of swords at regional Japanese surrenders, and responding to Asian nationalism in the liberated lands. In December 1945 Slim returned to Britain to become commandant of a revived Imperial Defence College in London. He blossomed as a radio broadcaster for the BBC, making a highly successful talk on "Courage" in autumn 1946. He declined a request from Pandit Nehru to become commander in chief in India and one from Jinnah to be governor of East Bengal. He retired from the Indian Army on 1 April 1948. After a brief period as deputy chairman of the Railway Executive, Prime Minister Attlee brought Slim back to succeed Montgomery as Chief of the Imperial General Staff (CIGS) in November 1948.

Slim began his time as CIGS by threatening to resign if the government did not add six months to the term of National Service. Thereafter, his task was readjusting the army to the postwar world, with the cold war and the ending of empire major concerns.

When Churchill returned to office in October 1951 he combined the premiership with being minister of defense for six months. Slim accompanied him from 31 December 1951 on a trip to the United States, traveling over on the *Queen Mary*. At one point Churchill was critical of the first sea lord, Admiral Sir Rhoderick McGrigor, but observed, "Slim is quite different. I can work with him." Slim also played an important role for Churchill when in 1952, as chairman of the Chiefs of Staff Committee, he oversaw the major strategic review, which was published as "Defence Policy and Global Strategy."

In late 1952 Sir Robert Menzies successfully sought Slim's appointment as governor general of Australia, aware that Slim was nearing the end of his term as CIGS. This was announced, but in March 1953 Churchill pressed Menzies to release Slim temporarily to deal with a crisis in Egypt. However, the crisis passed and Slim and his wife left for Australia in April 1953. He was sworn in on 8 May 1953. Alongside carrying out his duties, Slim wrote most of his

account of the Burma campaign, *Defeat into Victory* (1956), which was to become a best-seller. His term of office was renewed for a further two years, ending in 1960, when he was created a viscount. Then, back in London, he joined the board of Imperial Chemical Industries (ICI) and other companies. He also was committed to promoting the Burma Star Association. In 1963 he was appointed deputy constable and lieutenant governor of Windsor Castle, and took up residence in its Norman Tower. He was also made a member of the Order of the Garter. He retired through ill health in mid-1970. He died on 14 December 1970.

Suggestions for further reading:
Anderson, Duncan. 1991. "Field-Marshal Lord Slim." In *Churchill's Generals,* edited by John Keegan. London: Weidenfeld and Nicolson.
Evans, Lieutenant General Sir Geoffrey. 1969. *Slim as Military Commander.* London: Batsford.
Gilbert, Martin. 1988. *Winston S. Churchill.* Vol. 8. London: Heinemann.
Lewis, Ronald. 1976. *Slim: The Standardbearer.* London: Leo Cooper.
Slim, Field Marshal the Viscount. 1956. *Defeat into Victory.* London: Cassell.

Smuts, Jan Christian (1870–1950)

*T*he lives of Churchill and Jan Smuts often intersected, especially in war: in the Boer War, the First World War, and the Second World War. They became friends during the First World War. They shared beliefs in the British Empire and were strongly anticommunist. Smuts even upbraided Churchill for being willing to support a republican India joining the British Commonwealth, which he feared set a precedent for South Africa.

Jan Smuts was born on a farm near Riebeeck West, Cape Province, South Africa, on 24 May 1870, the second child of Jacobus Abraham and Catharina

Jan Smuts talking to troops in South Africa (Library of Congress)

Petronella Smuts. They were descendants of an employee of the Dutch East India Company who settled in the Cape in 1692. Jan Smuts's father was a farmer and a member of the Cape legislature. Educated at "Die Ark," Riebeeck West, Victoria College, Stellenbosch, and Christ's College, Cambridge (1892–1895), he returned to the Cape to practice law. The Jameson Raid, 1895, alienated him from Cecil Rhodes and he moved to Johannesburg. President Stephanus Kruger appointed him state attorney in June 1898. When Churchill was captured in the Boer War, on 15 November 1899, Smuts interrogated him. After the fall of Pretoria in 1900, Smuts became a Boer general and the very effective commando leader. He was one of the Boer negotiators of the peace treaty at Vereeniging, 1902.

After the Boer War, Smuts returned to his legal practice, which he located in Pretoria. With Louis Botha and Koose de la Rey, Smuts formed the Het Volk party to campaign for responsible government and reconciliation between the Boers and British. In January 1906, Smuts visited London to influence leading Liberal politicians to grant self-government to the former Boer republics. Smuts contacted Churchill, meeting him on 19 January. Liberal politicians were already moving in favor of self-government, and Smuts's lobbying perhaps added to the momentum. Smuts left for South Africa on 10 February 1906. When the Union of South Africa was established, he became minister of the interior, 1910–1912, and minister of defense, 1910–1920. With the First World War, Botha and Smuts opposed pro-German Boers and by December 1914 had crushed them. Smuts and Botha moved against German forces in Southwest Africa in 1915, defeating them quickly. In 1916, he accepted command of British Empire troops in East Africa. In 1917, Smuts went to England where he participated in the war cabinet and the imperial war cabinet, 1917–1918. Churchill greatly admired Smuts and his sagacious advice, and the two men became friends for the rest of Smuts's life. At the end of the war, Smuts shared Churchill's anxieties about Bolshevism, observing in the war cabinet that it was "a danger to the whole world." Smuts attended the Paris Peace Conference and deplored its treat-

ment of Germany, signing the peace treaty under protest. In August 1919, Smuts returned to South Africa. He was prime minister, 1919–1924, minister of justice, 1933–1939, and prime minister, 1939–1948.

Smuts also helped the British war effort in the Second World War. In October 1940, he visited the war in East Africa. In September 1941, he was given the rank of field marshal. In August 1942, he flew from Cape Town to Cairo to advise Churchill on military commanders in North Africa. In October 1942, he flew to Britain to discuss strategy in North Africa and the Middle East. He attended meetings of the war cabinet, with Churchill exhorted a large gathering of miners to produce more coal, and he addressed both houses of Parliament on 21 October (an address that was broadcast on radio by the BBC).

In September–October 1943, he again flew to Cairo and visited Allied forces in North Africa. He went on to Britain, where he stayed with Churchill at Chequers, attended war cabinet meetings, made a major speech on 19 October in London in the Guildhall, and broadcast on the radio.

In April–June 1944, Smuts again flew to Cairo and then traveled on to Britain. He again stayed with Churchill, attended the first Commonwealth prime ministers' conference, went with Churchill to Portsmouth to watch troops embarking for the invasion of France, and later went with him to Normandy. He made a fourth wartime visit to Britain in April 1945 to attend another Commonwealth prime ministers' conference. He flew on to the United States for the San Francisco Conference, which inaugurated the United Nations. Smuts, like Churchill, took a grim view of the Soviet Union, observing that appeasement would not work with the Russians but rather frank talking backed up by military might.

After the war, Smuts returned to London for a Commonwealth prime ministers' conference in April 1946. He returned to

Europe in August for the Paris Peace Conference and visited Churchill at the Villa Choisi on Lake Geneva. In September, Smuts and Churchill met in the British embassy in Paris. Smuts returned to London for the wedding of Princess Elizabeth in November 1947. In the 1948 South African general election, Smuts was defeated heavily, even losing his own seat. Smuts was made chancellor of the University of Cambridge in 1948.

Smuts died on 11 September 1950. Churchill paid a fulsome tribute to him at The Other Club, breaking the custom of no speeches. On 7 November 1956, Churchill unveiled a statue of Smuts in Parliament Square.

Suggestions for further reading:
Gilbert, Martin. 1983, 1986, and 1988. *Winston S. Churchill*. Vols. 6–8. London: Heinemann.
Hancock, William Keith. 1962. *Smuts*. Cambridge: Cambridge University Press.
Smuts, J. C. 1952. *Jan Christian Smuts*. London: Cassell.

Soames, (Arthur) Christopher John (Baron Soames, 1920–1987)

Christopher Soames married the Churchills' youngest daughter, Mary, in 1947. Although Clementine had reservations about him at first, they both became very fond of him. As Churchill's parliamentary private secretary in his last premiership, Soames was his eyes and ears in the House of Commons. Soames introduced his father-in-law to horse racing, a major pleasure for Churchill in his later years.

Christopher Soames was born at Ashwell Manor, Penn, Buckinghamshire, the youngest child of Captain Arthur Granville and Hope Mary Woodbyne Soames. His father, a distant figure, served in the Coldstream Guards. His mother was the daughter of Charles Woodbyne Parish. Educated at Eton and the Royal Military College, Sandhurst, he followed his father into the Coldstream Guards in 1939. He served with distinction in the Middle East, Italy, and France, being awarded the croix de guerre in the Second World War. In 1946, he was assistant military attaché at the Paris embassy. There he met Mary Churchill, and they married on 11 February 1947. For ten years they and their growing family lived at Chartwell Farm, very close to Winston and Clementine Churchill. Soames was Churchill's farm manager initially.

In 1950, Christopher Soames was elected Conservative M.P. for Bedford, a seat he held until 1966. He acted as his father-in-law's parliamentary private secretary during his final premiership. He traveled frequently with him, including on his December 1952–January 1953 trip to the United States and Jamaica. He played a major role with John Colville in concealing the seriousness of Churchill's health in mid-1953, after Churchill had suffered a major stroke on 23 June. They also dealt with much routine government business while he recovered. Clementine Churchill made Christopher Soames promise to inform her if support in the House of Commons fell away from her husband.

After resigning as prime minister, Churchill made one of his few general election speeches in support of Christopher Soames in Bedford, on 17 May 1955. He was delighted that his son-in-law was reelected and hoped he would achieve government office.

He enjoyed going to horse races with his son-in-law. To the initial horror of Clementine Churchill, Christopher Soames had made her husband enthusiastic about racing. From 1949, he had owned racing horses, registering in his own name Lord Randolph Churchill's colors. In June 1957, Christopher Soames wrote, "Winston is well and wanting to go racing constantly—in fact more often than the horses do."

Churchill lived long enough to see Christopher Soames's rise to ministerial posts. He served under Eden and Macmillan as under secretary at the Ministry of Air, December 1955–January 1957, parliamentary and financial secretary at the admiralty, January 1957–January 1958, secretary of state for war, January 1958–July 1960, and minister for agriculture, July 1960–October 1964. After Churchill's death, Soames lost his seat in the 1966 general election. He became the British ambassador to Paris, 1968–1972; the first British vice president of the European Commission, and commissioner for external affairs, 1973–1977; lord president of the council and leader of the House of Lords, May 1979–September 1981; and also governor of Rhodesia, 1979–1980. After leaving office, he was chairman of ICL and a director of N. M. Rothschild's and the National Westminster Bank. He died on 16 September 1987.

Related entry:
Churchill, Mary

Suggestions for further reading:
Colville, John. 1985. *The Fringes of Power.* London: Hodder and Stoughton.
Gilbert, Martin. 1988. *Winston S. Churchill.* Vol. 8. London: Heinemann.
Renwick, Robin. 1996. "Soames (Arthur), Christopher (John)." In *The Dictionary of National Biography: 1986–1990,* edited by C. S. Nicholls. Oxford: Oxford University Press.
Soames, Mary. 1979. *Clementine Churchill.* London: Cassell.

Spears, Major General Sir Edward Louis (1886–1974)

Edward Spears was long a friend of Churchill. More than that, he was first a soldier and then a politician who tied his fortunes to those of Churchill. He became a member of Parliament and then something of a proconsul in the Levant during the Second World War largely on the strength of the Churchill connection. He also wrote books concerning his experiences in both world wars that were admired by Churchill and by many others.

Edward Louis Spiers (he changed his surname to Spears in 1918) was born at Passy, near the Bois de Boulogne in Paris. He was the son of a French father and English mother. His grandfather, Alexander Spiers, had been a notable scholar, publishing an English-French dictionary; his father was a commission agent. As his parents' marriage broke up, he saw little of his father. Edward Spears's biographer, Max Egremont, believes that Spears later sought father figures, one of whom was Winston Churchill.

Edward Spiers joined the Kildare Militia in 1903 and served in the 8th Hussars from 1906 and the 11th Hussars from 1910. Injured in a polo match by a ball to the head, he was operated on and convalesced on half pay. From late 1909, his language skills (he was bilingual) were used by General G. M. W. Macdonogh, head of the war office's intelligence department (MO5). From 1911, on and off, Spiers worked on an Anglo-French military codebook. He first met Winston Churchill at the home of a war office colleague, Captain Anthony Henley, and his wife, Sylvia, the sister of Venetia Stanley. In May 1914, he was sent to Paris to the Ministry of War to work with the French and to contact British intelligence agents in Belgium. Once war was declared, he served as a liaison officer between the British and French armies. Wounded four times, decorated with the Military Cross and the croix de guerre with three palms, he was promoted to brigadier by 1917, when he became head of the British military mission to Paris.

Spiers had contact with Churchill from 1915. On 21 April, he accompanied Churchill to the front. He warned him that the French military saw the Dardanelles operation as risky because it would divert troops from the Western Front. However, he liked Churchill. He was pleased to see Churchill on 5 December, after Churchill had left office to serve in France. Churchill invited him to be his brigade major. However, Asquith vetoed Churchill being given a brigade and he was given only a battalion. He was not permitted to take Spiers with him. Spiers saw much of Churchill in December 1915 and was fascinated by his brilliant conversation. On 7 December, Spiers noted in his diary aspects of their conversations, including Churchill saying "some fine things about democracies," and on religion that "he believes he is a spirit which will live, without memory of the present, in the future." Thereafter, they remained friends, often writing to each other.

Churchill and Spiers saw each other frequently again in 1918. Churchill went to France on 18 March, his fifth visit as minister of munitions, and was at Nurlu on 21 March when the Germans began their great offensive. In the succeeding days, Spiers was one of those whom he consulted. He returned in the company of David Lloyd George on the night of 2–3 April 1918. Churchill also saw Spiers on his visit to France in August 1918. Then Spiers took him to dine with General Henri Pétain, where they discussed future changes in warfare, including tanks replacing cavalry and the need for large numbers of light lorries to transport the infantry.

When Churchill became secretary of state for war in January 1919, Spears, still head of the British military mission to Paris, was viewed by some as "Winston's spy." Spears eagerly supported Churchill in his crusade against Bolshevism in Russia and supplied Churchill with memoranda of the kind that reinforced Churchill's views. Spears returned to civilian life in 1920. In June 1921, the Churchills visited Edward and Mary Spears at Ightham Mote.

Churchill fully backed Spears in his wish to enter Parliament. Churchill arranged for him to see the organizer for the coalition Liberals, and he was recommended to try for the Loughborough nomination; this he secured in December 1921. Churchill spoke for him in the town hall on 4 March 1922, a speech in which he called for a new and permanent National Party that would be antisocialist and anticommunist. In the October 1922 general election, Spears was elected unopposed because the Labour candidate was late with his nomination papers. As a result, he was free to help Clementine Churchill campaign for her husband, who was recuperating from an appendix operation. When Churchill lost, Spears offered to resign his seat and let Churchill stand in the by-election. Churchill declined this "splendid proof of your friendship." Spears held Loughborough in the December 1923 general election but lost in October 1924.

Spears followed Churchill into the Conservative Party, joining in April 1925 and informing his mentor, "Once more I have nailed my colours to your mast." When he stood in the 1927 Bosworth by-election, Churchill sent a letter of support, but Spears lost. He won Carlisle at the second attempt, in the 1931 general election.

In Parliament, Spears joined Churchill in warning against Nazi Germany. He was the first chairman of the cross-party European study group, begun in March 1934, which initially included Clement Attlee, Robert Boothby, and Josiah Wedgwood, with Harold Macmillan, Leo Amery, Ronald Cartland, Ronald Tree, Harold Nicolson, and Hugh Dalton joining later. Spears was also joint chairman of the Anglo-French Parliamentary Group, with Pierre-Etienne Flandin his cochair.

With the furor over the proposed Hoare–Laval Pact in December 1935, Spears was prominent among Conservative M.P.s opposed to appeasing the dictators. In February 1936, he took the chair at the first meeting of the December Club, of those prepared to ignore the Conservative Party whip, which included again Macmillan, Boothby, Cazalet, Nicolson, Cartland, and Tree. In 1938, this group of rebel Conservatives looked to Anthony Eden for leadership, Churchill having alienated many people over India and the abdication crisis. Spears was among those Conservatives who abstained in the vote of confidence in the House of Commons that followed the Munich agreement.

After Munich, Churchill and Spears worked more closely together again. There had been friction, particularly over the abdication of King Edward VIII, with Churchill caustically singing "God save our other King" in front of Spears and others. With war imminent, in August 1939 Spears arranged for Churchill to visit the Maginot Line and he accompanied him. Churchill was not convinced that the French defenses were secure against a strong armored attack.

After Churchill returned to office, in February 1940, he sent Spears on a mission to France to argue for the mining of the Rhine River. In April 1940, he traveled with Churchill to Paris, where Churchill saw prominent French politicians. After becoming prime minister, Churchill, in May 1940, sent Spears as his personal representative to Paul Reynaud, the French premier. Spears was depressed by the lack of fighting spirit in Paris, a contrast with 1914. Oliver Harvey wrote in his diary of Spears, "He bucks up the French and is a useful contact with the P.M." When Churchill and Attlee flew to Paris on 31 May 1940 for a meeting of the Supreme War Council, Spears was part of the British group, looking after Churchill. At the time of Dunkirk, Spears defended Churchill to the French leaders, arguing that Churchill was "the best friend the French ever had." On 7 May, Spears returned to London in Churchill's plane and reported to Churchill at 10 Downing Street. He dined with Winston and Clementine Churchill that evening and on 10 May. On 11 May, he flew back to France with Churchill, Eden,

Sir John Dill, and Hastings Ismay, meeting the French leaders near Orleans. On 17 June 1940, Spears and Charles de Gaulle flew out of France together.

Spears was assigned to liaise with de Gaulle, recognized by the British government as the leader of free France. He accompanied de Gaulle on the Dakar expedition, with the right to report directly to Churchill as minister of defense. After the failure of the attack on Dakar, Churchill, Spears, and de Gaulle were much criticized. Churchill continued to have confidence in Spears, even if de Gaulle increasingly did not. Spears accompanied de Gaulle in March 1941 to visit the French forces in Eritrea and traveled with him in the Middle East for several months.

In early 1942, Churchill approved the appointment of Spears as minister to Syria and Lebanon. He went with a mission to bring about independence for these countries from the French. He ruffled many feathers, but was secure because he had Churchill's support. Spears reported to Churchill at Chequers on 26 June and also saw him in London on 7 July 1943. Spears reached the zenith of his career when resisting successfully a French attempt to restore their power in the Levant. However, Spears seemed to many to be going too far in promoting independence and had become "definitely, if not violently, francophobe" (as Duff Cooper wrote to Churchill, 21 February 1944). Eventually, in late November, Churchill told Spears to resign by 15 December 1944.

When Spears was defeated in the 1945 general election at Carlisle, he returned to his business interests. His main postwar business was Ashanti Goldfields (in Ghana). He was made a baronet in 1953, there being too much hostility to him for him to be elevated to the peerage.

Spears also continued to write. He had published two much-praised books about the First World War, *Liason 1914: A Narrative of the Great Retreat* (London: Heinemann,

1930) and *Prelude to Victory* (London: Heinemann, 1939). Churchill contributed a preface to each volume. He wrote a much more personal account of 1940 in the two volumes, *Assignment to Catastrophe: Prelude to Dunkirk* and *The Fall of France* (London: Heinemann, 1954). Churchill again much admired the volumes, but declined to write a foreword as he was prime minister again and the book would upset the French.

Spears was also active in the Institute of Directors, taking a vigorously antisocialist stance. He was chairman in 1948–1966 and then given a new honorific post, chancellor, until his death on 27 January 1974.

Suggestions for further reading:
Egremont, Max. 1997. *Under Two Flags: The Life of Major General Sir Edward Spears.* London: Weidenfeld and Nicolson.
Gilbert, Martin. 1971–88. *Winston S. Churchill.* Vols. 3–8. London: Heinemann.
Spears, Major General Sir Edward. 1954. *Assignment to Catastrophe.* 2 vols. London: Heinemann.

Stalin, Joseph (Joseph Vissarionovich Djugashvili, 1879–1953)

Churchill hated communism and Joseph Stalin fulfilled his fears of Red Tyranny. Yet in the Second World War, he needed the Soviet Union, as well as the United States, to enable Britain to survive the Nazi threat. During the war, he came to admire Stalin as a leader, noting even that he had a sense of humor. However, toward the end of the war, his old apprehensions were aroused again and he came to see Stalin and the Soviet Union as the threat of the future.

Joseph Djugashvili was born in Gori, Georgia, on 21 December 1879, the first surviving child of Vissarion Ivanovich and Ekaterini Djugashvili. His father was a shoemaker. His mother was the daughter of George Gheladze, a poor peasant. She worked as a washerwoman. He was educated at the ecclesiastical school, Gori, 1888–1893, and the Theological Seminary, Tiflis, 1894–1899, working in a shoe factory with his father in between. At Tiflis, he engaged in Marxist discussion circles. Expelled from the seminary in May 1899, he worked for the Tbilisi Physical Institute, 1899–1901. He moved to Batumi on the Black Sea, and his political activities resulted in his being put in jail in 1902 and exiled to Siberia in 1903. He escaped from Siberia in 1904, and aligned himself with the Bolsheviks. He attended the Social Democratic Party congress in London in April–May 1907. Thereafter, he was in and out of exile until March 1917, when he arrived in Petrograd.

Before Lenin's arrival in Leningrad in 1917, Stalin took the more moderate Bolshevik line. He was a Bolshevik leader at the time of the October Revolution, but played a minor role compared to Vladimir Lenin and Leon Trotsky. Nevertheless, he was a leading Bolshevik, becoming commissar for nationalities in 1921 and general secretary of the Communist Party in 1922. By 1928, Stalin was the undisputed successor to Lenin and he embarked on the modernization of Russian industry and agriculture at a terrible cost in human suffering. In spite of Stalin's purges of Red Army leaders and his pact with Adolf Hitler in 1939, the Soviet Union was able to respond to the German invasion of 1941.

Churchill was vehemently opposed to the Bolsheviks and was the most determined major Western politician to support White Russian forces against the Bolshevik government. Churchill spoke of Stalin and Soviet Russia as preparing for war during a House of Commons debate on disarmament in June 1931.

In July 1934, Churchill began to moderate his statements concerning the Soviet Union when he said that its inclusion in the League of Nations would be welcome.

However, he deplored Soviet intervention in Spain. He also expressed his basic anti-communist feelings in the House of Commons when he said on 14 April 1937, "I will not pretend that, if I had to choose between Communism and Naziism, I would choose Communism." However, in 1938, faced with Hitler's expansionism, Churchill preferred war to humiliation, and wanted the support of France and the Soviet Union. This was not achieved; instead there was the Nazi–Soviet agreement of 24 August 1939. In the early stages of the Second World War, Churchill remained cool initially in the face of the Soviet attacks on Poland and Finland. Finnish resistance evoked his admiration and by late 1939 he could envisage Britain being at war with Russia as well as Germany. By the time he became prime minister, Churchill again thought the support of Stalin and the Soviet Union would be important for Britain, even if he underestimated it, and he sent Sir Stafford Cripps to Moscow to improve relations.

With the German invasion of Russia in June 1941 and the United States not yet in the war, Churchill saw supporting Stalin as important provided help did not denude Britain of war materials. During 1941–1943, Churchill believed that Stalin was a trustworthy ally and that the Soviet Union could be brought back into international relations. Also, the Red Army was increasingly defeating German forces. Churchill and Stalin met at the Tehran, 1943, and the Yalta and Potsdam conferences, 1945.

Churchill, however, became increasingly alarmed about Stalin's intentions by 1944. He was soon warning colleagues that the next threat to world peace would be the Soviet Union. Stalin was always suspicious of Churchill. Stalin had been angered by Churchill's failure to open up "the Second Front" in Europe in 1942 or 1943 to relieve pressure on the Red Army. He also distrusted Churchill's intentions, observing in 1945, "I think that Roosevelt will not break

the Yalta agreements, but Churchill, that one might do anything." Churchill, for his part, conceded that Stalin kept his word with regard to postwar spheres of influence in Eastern Europe.

Nevertheless, Churchill's apprehensions of Stalin's postwar intentions continued to grow in 1945, especially over Poland. After falling from office, his attitude was hardened by further developments in Eastern Europe, notably in Roumania and Bulgaria. Hence his warning (in his famous "Iron Curtain" speech) about the Soviet Union at Fulton on 6 March 1946. After the Second World War, Churchill returned to his deeply held anticommunist sentiments, so often expressed in the period 1917–1933 and sometimes later. Stalin died on 5 March 1953.

Related entries:
Potsdam Conference; Tehran Conference; Yalta Conference

Suggestions for further reading:
Carlton, David. 2000. *Churchill and the Soviet Union.* Manchester, UK: Manchester University Press.
Deutscher, Isaac. 1949. *Stalin.* Oxford: Clarendon Press.
Folly, Martin H. 2000. *Churchill, Whitehall and the Soviet Union, 1940–1945.* London: Macmillan.
Gilbert, Martin. 1983 and 1986. *Winston S. Churchill.* Vols. 6 and 7. London: Heinemann.
McNeal, Robert H. 1988. *Stalin: Man and Ruler.* London: Macmillan.

Sutherland, Graham Vivian (1903–1980)

Graham Sutherland was liked by Winston and Clementine Churchill; Sutherland's major portrait of Churchill, however, greatly upset them, so much so that Clementine Churchill had it destroyed, an action that caused great controversy after her death.

Graham Sutherland was born on 24 August 1903 in Streatham, London. His father was a barrister and a senior civil servant at the Board of Education. After an unhappy period as an engineering apprentice, he studied at Goldsmiths College's school of art. After specializing in etching, in the early 1930s he turned to painting. He was an official war artist, 1940–1945. After the Second World War, he began painting portraits, his first two being of Somerset Maugham and Lord Beaverbrook. These led to an all-party committee of both houses of Parliament to commission a portrait of Sir Winston Churchill to mark his eightieth birthday.

Sutherland saw Churchill at Chartwell from mid-August 1954, with a final session at Chequers in mid-November 1954. Clementine Churchill was much taken by both Graham Sutherland and his wife, Kathleen, deeming him to be "a most attractive man" ("A 'Wow'"). The portrait, with a commemorative bound book containing the signatures of the parliamentarians who had contributed to the cost of the portrait, was presented to Churchill in a unique ceremony on 30 November 1954.

Churchill had seen the painting two weeks earlier and greatly disliked it, thinking it malignant. However, he graciously accepted it, recognizing the generous intentions of those who had commissioned it. Also Churchill himself, mostly a kind and generous man, did not wish to hurt people's feelings by denouncing it or rejecting it.

Clementine Churchill first saw the portrait in late October, when it was with Sir Kenneth and Lady Clark at Saltwood Castle. Her first reaction was to praise its truthfulness. However, she came to feel it portrayed her husband as "a gross & cruel monster." She had destroyed other depictions of her husband that she felt were detrimental, sketches by Walter Sickert and Paul Maze (in 1927 and 1944 respectively). She had the Sutherland portrait destroyed in 1955 or 1956, a matter the family made public soon after her death in December 1977. Not surprisingly, the destruction of a

portrait by a major artist and one presented by members of Parliament caused much controversy. Sutherland's preliminary study of his portrait of Churchill was bought from Sutherland by Lord Beaverbrook and is in his collection in New Brunswick, Canada. It was exhibited in Britain for the first time in London and Sheffield, September 1999–January 2000.

Sutherland's later work included portraits of Konrad Adenauer and Lord Goodman, self-portraits, and the design for the huge tapestry "Christ in Glory" for Coventry Cathedral. Sutherland was admitted to the Order of Merit in 1960. He died on 17 February 1980.

Suggestions for further reading:
Berthoud, Roger. 1982. *Graham Sutherland.* London: Faber.
Gilbert, Martin. 1988. *Winston S. Churchill.* Vol. 8. London: Heinemann.
Hayes, John. 1980. *The Art of Graham Sutherland.* London: Phaidon.
Soames, Mary. 1979. *Clementine Churchill.* London: Cassell.

Swinton, Earl of (Philip Cunliffe-Lister, 1884–1972)

Churchill generally regarded Philip Swinton as a "safe pair of hands" in office. They shared a certain camaraderie of having both served at Ploegsteert on the Western Front, Swinton shortly after Churchill had left. Even when Churchill was denouncing the Stanley Baldwin and Neville Chamberlain governments over rearmament, he was less critical of Swinton, secretary of state for air, 1935–1938, than of others.

Philip Lloyd-Greame was born on 1 May 1888 at East Ayton, Yorkshire, the third son of Yarburgh George and Dora Letitia Lloyd-Greame. His father, a member of a large landholding family, had taken the name Greame on succeeding to his mother's estate. His mother was a daughter of Bishop O'Brien, the Irish Anglican bishop of Ossory. He was educated at Winchester and University College, Oxford, where he studied law. He became a barrister. He was adopted as a prospective Conservative candidate for his home area, Buckrose in the East Riding of Yorkshire. He served on the Western Front, but was invalided out of France in November 1916. In 1917–1918 he worked under Auckland Geddes, the minister of national service, often attending war cabinet meetings with Geddes.

Lloyd-Greame abandoned Buckrose for Hendon in 1918, being elected as a coalition Conservative. It proved to be a very safe seat. He was a founder-member of the British Commonwealth Union, a pressure group funded by business and committed to defeating "Bolshevism" and the British Labour Party. From July 1918 to August 1920, he was its vice chairman. From January 1920, he was a member of the executive committee of the Federation of British Industries. In August 1920, he was appointed parliamentary secretary to the president of the Board of Trade, Robert Horne, who was another major figure in the British Commonwealth Union. He was in charge of the government's propaganda for its strike-breaking body, the Supply and Transport Committee, during the 1920 and 1921 coal disputes. From 1 April 1921 until the fall of David Lloyd George's coalition government he was secretary of the Department of Overseas Trade. With the fall of the Lloyd George coalition government, he served as president of the Board of Trade in the governments of Andrew Bonar Law (1922–1923) and Stanley Baldwin (1923–1924 and 1924–1929). In December 1924, he and his wife changed their names to Cunliffe-Lister to inherit (through her) the Swinton estates near Ripon.

Churchill and Lloyd-Greame had much contact in 1917–1918, when the latter worked for the Ministry of National Service. They both served on the Supply and Transport Committee, both being vigorous opponents of Bolshevism. After the Conservative victory in the October 1924 general election, Lloyd-Greame and Samuel Hoare pressed Baldwin to include Churchill in his government. During the 1925 coal mining negotiations, Cunliffe-Lister offered to resign from the government, given his wife's ownership of coal mines, but Baldwin, Churchill, and others persuaded him not to, but to take no part in negotiations. In 1928, he strongly backed Churchill's proposals for the derating of industry.

Cunliffe-Lister was one of four Conservatives who took cabinet posts in August 1931 in Ramsay MacDonald's National government. He returned to the Board of Trade until November 1931, when he became colonial secretary. Like Baldwin, unlike Churchill, he took a liberal view of developments in India. When Baldwin became prime minister again in 1935, he appointed Cunliffe-Lister secretary of state for air, by this time a highly critical area of government policy. Later in the year, he was elevated to the House of Lords as Viscount Swinton. Eventually, on 16 May 1938, given disquiet over the government's aircraft program, Swinton resigned. Churchill soon after paid tribute to what he had achieved, stating he was one of the least blameworthy of those responsible for defense in the cabinet.

During the early part of the Second World War, Swinton was chairman of the United Kingdom Commercial Corporation, which operated on behalf of the Ministry of Economic Warfare. In May 1940, Churchill appointed him to the additional post of chairman of the Security Executive, dealing with state security and preparations to resist an invasion. From June 1942 until October 1944, he was minister resident in West Africa. He returned to London to another ministerial post outside the cabinet, minister for civil aviation, a post he held until Churchill's defeat in the 1945 general election.

Before the election, Churchill appointed Swinton chairman of the Emergency Business Committee, a joint ministerial and Conservative Central Office body, which gave policy advice to candidates. As in 1924 and 1929–1931, he was a member of the shadow cabinet during 1945–1951 and was deputy leader of the Opposition in the House of Lords. Swinton donated part of Swinton to be a Conservative College in 1947. Swinton became deputy chairman of the Conservative Party's Advisory Committee on Policy in March 1950. With Churchill's return to office in 1951, Churchill omitted Swinton from the cabinet but was pressed by several senior Conservatives to offer him an office. While still deputy leader in the House of Lords, he was appointed chancellor of the Duchy of Lancaster and minister of materials. He gave valued advice to colleagues on such matters as ending the fixed exchange rate for sterling and on housing. He returned to the cabinet as secretary of state for commonwealth relations from 24 November 1952 until the end of Churchill's final premiership. During his final years of office, Swinton was widely viewed by colleagues as a wise, efficient, and dependable colleague, including by Churchill. Churchill made clear to Swinton that he was sorry Sir Anthony Eden replaced him when he succeeded Churchill as premier. Swinton was elevated to an earldom.

Swinton remained active in the House of Lords and in the Conservative Party. He died on 27 July 1972.

Suggestions for further reading:
Cross, J. A. 1982. *Lord Swinton.* Oxford: Clarendon Press.
Swinton, Earl of. 1966. *Sixty Years of Power.* London: Hutchinson.
Swinton, Viscount. 1948. *I Remember.* London: Hutchinson.

T

Tehran Conference (November–December 1943)

*T*he conference (code name Eureka) was held in Tehran, Iran, at the end of November and the beginning of De- cember 1943. Churchill flew from Cairo to Tehran on 27 November and stayed in the British legation, the grounds of which ad- joined those of the Soviet embassy. The conference sessions began on 28 November and ended on 1 December. On 2 Decem- ber, Churchill flew back to Cairo, where he

Marshal Joseph Stalin, President Franklin D. Roosevelt, and Prime Minister Winston Churchill on the portico of the Russian embassy, 1943 (Library of Congress)

had further talks with President Franklin D. Roosevelt from 4 December.

Joseph Stalin successfully physically divided his Western allies, by housing Roosevelt and the American delegation within the grounds of the Soviet embassy. He also began talks with Roosevelt an hour before Churchill joined them. Stalin also refused to allow Chiang Kai-Shek to participate in the conference.

Stalin promised to declare war on Japan after the defeat of Germany. He secured approval for Russia to retake eastern Poland and for the Polish western border to extend westwards into Germany. He also secured recognition for Marshal Josip Tito as the major resistance leader in Yugoslavia. The Big Three also agreed to guarantee the independence of Iran. Churchill and Roosevelt agreed to the cross-channel invasion (OPERATION OVERLORD) and to an attack on southern France by 1 June 1944, with Stalin pledging a simultaneous Soviet offensive in the east. The three leaders avoided conflict over the postwar settlement, leaving it to the future to define what would constitute ample opportunities for the "expression of the will of the people."

Churchill spoke with Stalin after Roosevelt had retired to bed on 28 November. They discussed the possibility of a German recovery, as after 1918, and spoke of the need to supervise Germany after the war. They also discussed new frontiers for Poland.

Churchill gave the conference dinner on 30 November, his birthday. Sarah and Randolph Churchill were present, and Stalin was in a genial mood. When Churchill toasted "the proletarian masses," Stalin responded by toasting "the Conservative Party."

Related entries:
Cairo Conference; Roosevelt, Franklin Delano; Stalin, Joseph; Yalta Conference

Suggestions for further reading:
Gilbert, Martin. 1986. *Winston S. Churchill.* Vol. 7. London: Heinemann.

Kimber, Warren F. 1984. *Churchill and Roosevelt: The Complete Correspondence.* Vol. 2. London: Collins.

Thompson, Walter H.

Walter Thompson served as Winston Churchill's bodyguard twice. He served first from 1921–1929, and accompanied Churchill to the United States in December 1931. He was recalled from retirement to be his personal bodyguard from August 1939 until May 1945. During the Second World War, Churchill was usually protected only by two Scotland Yard men, Thompson being the senior man.

Thompson worked as PC549 at Paddington Green Police Station until spring 1913, when he joined the Special Branch at Scotland Yard. He had been involved in watching militant suffragettes and foreign anarchists and revolutionaries before the outbreak of the war. During 1914–1917, he was among those who effectively rounded up German agents in Britain and took precautions generally against spies. From 1917–1920, he served as the bodyguard of David Lloyd George, the prime minister.

Walter Thompson was transferred to guarding Churchill in early 1921 when Churchill was still secretary of state for war and air. He continued to be his bodyguard when Churchill moved to the colonial office. Thompson later recalled that Churchill "was in daily danger of assassination from the Sinn Feiners, dangerous men at any time but now provoked beyond endurance by the work of the 'Black and Tans.'" Thompson continued to guard Churchill after he lost his parliamentary seat in 1922. Churchill, with his usual aristocratic disdain for job specifications, readily made use of Thompson as extra labor when preparing Chartwell for the Churchills to live there. Thompson continued to protect Churchill when he was chancellor of the exchequer (1924–1929) and was with him in the United States in December 1931, when he was injured by a car.

After leaving Churchill, Thompson was assigned to guarding major foreign dignitaries visiting Britain. These included the crown prince of Saudi Arabia and Marshal Gustaf von Mannerheim. He retired at the rank of detective-inspector in 1936 and opened a grocery business in Norwood, London. When he visited Churchill at Chartwell in April 1939, he later recalled, Churchill told him that Britain would be at war within six months and he would probably return to the cabinet.

On 22 August 1939, Thompson received a telegram from Churchill summoning him to meet him at Croydon airport the next day at 4:30 P.M. on his return from Paris. Churchill told him to collect his baggage and follow him to Chartwell in a second car. There he told Thompson that an eminent French statesman had warned him that the Germans were likely to try to assassinate him. He asked Thompson to protect him at night as a private bodyguard (paid £5 per week). He provided Thompson with his own Colt automatic. This arrangement was short-lived, Thompson returning to the police force after a state of emergency was declared on 26 August, and immediately being assigned to Churchill, at Churchill's request. He relinquished the Colt automatic for a Webley .32. Once he was appointed first lord of the admiralty, Churchill secured Thompson again as his permanent bodyguard.

In both the 1920s and the Second World War, Churchill came to feel comfortable with Thompson in attendance, not only as his bodyguard but also as a factotum. Sir John Colville later recalled of Thompson that "he knew all his foibles and could, at appropriate moments of crisis, be an effective substitute as valet, secretary, friend and nanny." Once, when, in June 1940 while traveling on a French train, Thompson was not around to ensure that a bath was ready for Churchill the moment he got up, Churchill burst in upon two French officers in his night clothing, demanding "Uh ay ma bain?" Churchill loved two hot baths a day for relaxation.

Thompson was with Churchill when he went to Buckingham Palace to be appointed prime minister. Then, according to Thompson's recollections, when he commented on the enormity of his task, Churchill replied, "God alone knows how great it is. All I hope is that it is not too late. I am very much afraid it is. We can only do our best."

Churchill felt he could protect himself if necessary. He had small arms and practiced with them and with rifles. Thompson later wrote of Churchill's skills at a firing range that he was "a first-class shot with his Mannlicher rifle, his .45 Colt automatic and a service .38 Webley." Thompson added, "He was most deadly with the Colt and there would be little chance for anyone who came within range," Churchill also told Thompson that he did not intend to be captured alive.

Thompson had an uphill task in trying to make Churchill be cautious during the bombing of London. He could not talk Churchill out of going on to the roof of the Annexe to 10 Downing Street to watch the German bombing raids.

He also accompanied Churchill on his wartime overseas journeys. He was in Churchill's group that joined President Franklin D. Roosevelt on the *Augusta* at Placentia Bay on 9 August 1941, when the two leaders met and discussed the Atlantic Charter. The next day, after Churchill had personally introduced Thompson to the president, Roosevelt concluded his comments with, "Look after the Prime Minister. He is one of the greatest men in the world." Thompson's other travels with Churchill included his visit to Moscow in August 1942. When Churchill made a supposedly secret visit to President Ismet Inönu of Turkey in January 1943, they were warned by the British ambassador that the Germans knew of the meeting, so Thompson and a colleague sat inside Churchill's locked railway coach with their guns at the ready. Churchill and Thompson were also fearful of assassination attempts at the Cairo Conference, November 1943, and moved the meetings of Churchill, Roosevelt, and Joseph Stalin into the Russian embassy. After the conference, Thompson let a heavily escorted procession go ahead but followed with Churchill in a battered old army car that attracted no attention.

Thompson's second marriage was to one of Churchill's wartime secretaries, Mary Shearburn. His three sons by his first marriage all served in the Royal Air Force (RAF); one of them, Flight Lieutenant Frederick D. J. Thompson, was lost on his forty-third mission as a pathfinder for bombers on the night of 11–12 March 1943. In his second retirement, Thompson ran a garage with one of his sons, was a Romney municipal councillor, and wrote three volumes of memoirs, the second, *I Was Churchill's Shadow* (1951), giving an intimate account of Churchill during the Second World War. His account is especially interesting for its testimony to Churchill's scrupulousness on paying for travel costs that could be considered unofficial visits and for ensuring that customs duty was paid on all personal purchases made overseas.

Suggestions for further reading:
Colville, John. 1981. *The Churchillians.* London: Weidenfeld and Nicolson.
Gilbert, Martin. 1986. *Winston S. Churchill.* Vol. 7. London: Heinemann.
Thompson, W. H. 1938. *Guard from the Yard.* London: Jarrolds.
———. 1951. *I Was Churchill's Shadow.* London: Christopher Johnson.
———. 1953. *Sixty Minutes with Winston Churchill.* London: Christopher Johnson.

Tito, Josip Broz (1892–1980)

Churchill admired the courage and effectiveness of Josip Tito and his partisans in pinning down German troops. However, he probably underestimated Tito's loyalties to the Comintern and Moscow during the Second World War, though Churchill was pleased when Tito went his own way from 1948 onward. Churchill's support for Tito, rather than for the royalist partisans, has been a matter of controversy since the Second World War.

Josip Broz was born near Klanjec in Croatia in 1892. During the First World War, he served in the Austrian army and was captured by the Russians. He served in the Red Army during the Russian civil war. He returned to Yugoslavia in 1923 and was a leading revolutionary, using various pseudonyms, but Tito lasted. In the mid-1930s, he worked for the Comintern in Moscow. From 1937, he was the effective leader of the Communist Party of Yugoslavia, being confirmed as its secretary in 1940. Yugoslavia was attacked by Germany in April 1941 and occupied. When Germany invaded Russia in June 1941, Tito launched guerrilla warfare against the Germans, rivaling General Mihailovic's Chetnik guerrillas, who operated in conjunction with the Yugoslav government in exile.

At the end of January 1943, Churchill, while in Cairo, reviewed British policy toward the resistance forces in Yugoslavia. He was advised by the head of the Special Operations Executive (SOE) in the Middle East, Colonel Keble, and by his former research assistant, Captain F. W. D. Deakin. Although Mihailovic's forces were effective in Serbia, other groups (led by Tito's supporters) were resisting the Germans in Croatia and Slovenia. In deciding to supply both resistance groups, Churchill was primarily concerned about maintaining their pressure on the Germans and so keeping German forces away from other fronts, but he also wanted to ensure that they received support from the British, not from Russia or the United States, thereby maintaining British influence in the area. Deakin was dispatched in May 1943 to Yugoslavia to work with Tito's partisans. Churchill monitored the effectiveness of the partisans through the Enigma decrypts.

In June 1943, Churchill authorized further supplies to Tito's forces. Then the Enigma information suggested that Tito's forces were responsible for forcing the Axis Powers to maintain thirty-three divisions in Yugoslavia. In late July, with discussions taking place concerning an Italian armistice, Churchill strengthened the British military mission with Tito by sending Fitzroy MacLean, a Conservative M.P.

At the Cairo Conference with President Franklin D. Roosevelt in November 1943, Churchill spoke warmly of Tito and his 220,000 partisans, saying that they "were holding as many Germans in Yugoslavia as the combined Anglo-American forces were holding in Italy south of Rome." While there he consulted with both Deakin and MacLean, while planning further support for Tito. In January 1944 Randolph Churchill accompanied MacLean when he returned to the British mission to Tito's partisans. On 8 January 1944 Churchill informed Tito that the British government would give no further support to Mihailovic, that it had "no desire to dictate the future government of Yugoslavia" but would continue recognizing King Peter II. In the survey of the progress of the war that he delivered to the House of Commons on 22 February 1944, Churchill explained the decision to back Tito's forces as being due to them being "the only people who are doing any effective fighting against the Germans now." Churchill was very taken aback in April 1944 when he discovered that the United States was about to send a mission to Mihailovic; he successfully pressed Roosevelt not to send it.

In June 1944, Churchill encouraged Ivan Subasic, the former governor of Croatia, to visit Tito at Vis to discuss unity of opposition to the Germans. On June 17, an agreement was signed concerning collaboration between King Peter II's supporters and Tito's National Liberation Committee.

Churchill met Tito when the latter visited him in Naples at the Villa Rivalta on 12 August 1944. Churchill told Tito that Britain would not tolerate the arms supplied to Tito being used against other groups in Yugoslavia. He also urged that after the war Yugoslavia should adopt a democratic system of government. Tito said that he agreed, having no intention of setting up a communist state. At the ensuing lunch in Tito's honor, Churchill praised his courage.

In September 1944, when the Russian forces advanced into Romania and Bulgaria, Churchill was anxious to maintain good relations with Tito lest he be given an "excuse to throw himself into the hands of the Russians." The following month, when Churchill and Anthony Eden went to Moscow, the British insisted on fifty-fifty postwar influence in Yugoslavia, Eden observing to Vyacheslav Molotov that Churchill was especially interested in Yugoslavia. Churchill urged that there should be joint action by Britain and Russia to create a united Yugoslavia, avoiding nationalistic strife within the area.

By the end of 1944, Churchill was already disillusioned with the fifty-fifty formula. He observed to Jan Smuts that Tito had gone a long way in turning Yugoslavia into a communist state and was endeavoring to secure Trieste, Fiume, and Istria for it. In January 1945, King Peter II rejected an agreement between Subasic and Tito for joint participation in a government. As a result, Churchill took the view that, until there were free elections, Britain would support a Tito–Subasic government under a regency. At Yalta, Joseph Stalin agreed to the Tito–Subasic government and an anti-Fascist Assembly of National Liberation that included all prewar members of Parliament except those who had collaborated with the Germans. However, by late April, Churchill was complaining that Tito had become a dictator and that only six of thirty-one ministers were from the former royal government in exile.

Also in April 1945, Churchill opposed Tito's claims to Trieste and Istria. He saw these claims as a useful means of embarrassing, and probably splitting, the Italian Communist Party. Churchill pressed for British and American forces to occupy Trieste and Istria first. New Zealand troops entered Trieste and some Istrian towns only shortly ahead of Tito's forces. Churchill urged General Harold Alexander to ensure that he had a show of military strength in the area to ensure that Tito's forces were not tempted to try to take over Trieste and Istria. Churchill even telegraphed Tito warning him not to attack Alexander's forces. President Harry Truman supported Churchill in taking a firm line with Tito. Churchill went on to insist to Alexander that he oust Tito's forces from the port of Pola, if necessary by attacking the town. However, by mid-June, Tito had withdrawn from Pola.

Churchill welcomed Tito's distancing of Yugoslavia from Moscow's influence. In March 1953, Churchill saw Tito when he visited London: Tito felt that the recent death of Stalin would not end the cold war but expected the new rulers of Russia to be cautious in their policies for a while. Their last meeting was on 14 July 1960. Then Winston and Clementine Churchill were cruising in the Adriatic in Aristotle Onassis's yacht *Christina* and called in to the port of Split to visit President Tito.

Tito had become president of a federal Yugoslavia in 1953. After falling out with Moscow in 1948 over his form of communism (based on profit-sharing workers' councils), he became a leading figure of the nonaligned countries during the cold war. He died in 1980.

Suggestions for further reading:
Auty, Phyllis. 1970. *Tito: A Biography*. London: Longman.

Deakin, F. W. D. 1971. *The Embattled Mountain*. Oxford: Oxford University Press.
Gilbert, Martin. 1986 and 1988. *Winston S. Churchill*. Vols. 7 and 8. London: Heinemann.
Pavlowitch, Stevan. 1992. *Yugoslavia's Great Dictator, Tito: A Reassessment*. London: Hurst and Blackett.

Tonypandy (1910)

Winston Churchill's name became associated with repression of miners in Tonypandy, South Wales, in November 1910, just as Herbert Henry Asquith's name was long linked with Featherstone, Yorkshire, after two miners were killed there by soldiers in 1893. Like Asquith before him, Churchill was involved because as home secretary he was responsible for law and order. However, unlike Asquith, no miners were killed in Tonypandy in the period of Churchill's involvement. The incidents at Tonypandy arose during a bitter mining strike in the mines of the Rhondda Valley and its vicinity over the rates to be paid for working a new coal seam. After recent hard times, the miners were in no mood to compromise. Bitter feelings led to efforts to bring out the safety men (who prevented the mines from flooding). As feelings became inflamed, damage was done to colliery property. The local authorities called for troops, but Churchill and Richard Haldane, the secretary of state for war, agreed to send in London police to reinforce the 1,400 police available in the area and to keep soldiers available nearby for use if police action proved not to be sufficient. In all, 800 London police were sent to the area.

The local police successfully defended the various pits from somewhat halfhearted attacks. When, on 21 November, there was rioting with those involved attacking shops on the main street of Tonypandy, they were dispersed by the Metropolitan Police. Later anti-Churchill feeling in Tonypandy stemmed from the toughness of the response from London, not local, police. According to later folk memory, these police, in chasing rioters up the streets on the steep hill above the main road, were not too particular whom they batoned. Moreover, on at least one occasion infantry cleared youths from the high side streets, prodding them in the rear with their bayonets.

Nevertheless, in deciding to use police, not troops, Churchill ensured there was far less likelihood of fatalities than had the army been used. The myth of Churchill and deaths at Tonypandy represents a confusion between the action there in November 1910 and unrest at Llanelli during the national rail strike of August 1911. Then Churchill readily agreed to the use of troops to protect the railways, to keep supplies moving, and to maintain order. In Llanelli, two people were killed by troops when a train was stopped and the engine driver was attacked.

Suggestions for further reading:
Churchill, Randolph S. 1967. *Winston S. Churchill*. Vol. 2. London: Heinemann.
Clegg, Hugh. 1985. *A History of British Trade Unions since 1889*. Vol. 2, 1911–1933. Oxford: Clarendon Press.
Macready, General the Rt. Hon. Sir Nevil. 1924. *Annals of an Active Life*. 2 vols. London: Hutchinson.

Trade Boards Act (1909)

*I*n introducing the Trade Boards Bill into the House of Commons in March 1909, Winston Churchill took up the issue of sweated labor. A House of Lords committee had investigated the matter in 1888, but without tangible results. Sir Charles and Lady Dilke, Sidney and Beatrice Webb, and the Anti-Sweating League were among major advocates for state intervention on behalf of the most vulnerable in the workforce.

The Trade Boards Act of 1909 provided for the setting up of boards to fix minimum wage rates that became legally enforceable when confirmed by the president of the Board of Trade. The boards were made up of representatives of the employers, the workpeople and independent members nominated by the minister. As the boards, not the minister of Parliament, fixed the wage rates, the system has been described as one of compulsory collective bargaining in sectors where labor was too weak to negotiate more than poverty-level wages. In so doing, the act was building on earlier interference in rates of wages in private industry in the form of fair wages resolutions of the House of Commons.

The act initially led to the setting up of trade boards in ready-made tailoring, cardboard box-making, machine-made lace finishing, and chain-making trades. The president of the Board of Trade was given powers to extend coverage to other trades marked by notably low wages. In 1913, trade boards were extended to a further five industries. The trade boards legislation helped women not only gain a little better pay but also to unionize. Initially, the act was applied to 200,000 workers, 70 percent of whom were women. The 1913 extensions covered a further 170,000 workers.

In arguing for trade boards, Churchill was emphatic that the sweated industries were exceptions "as sick and diseased industries." In defining sweated industries, he spoke not only of especially low wages but also of "conditions prejudicial to physical and social welfare."

The trade boards lasted most of the twentieth century, until the governments of Margaret Thatcher and John Major. Known as wages councils, they were weakened by the Wages Act of 1986 and those under twenty-one were removed from their scope. They were abolished by the Trade Union Reform and Employment Rights Act of 1993. However, the lowest paid, who were preponderantly women, benefited under

Tony Blair's government's 1999 minimum-pay legislation.

Suggestions for further reading:
Churchill, Randolph S. 1967. *Winston S. Churchill.* Vol. 2. London: Heinemann.
Clegg, H. A., A. Fox, and A. F. Thompson. 1964. *A History of British Trade Unions since 1889.* Vol. 1, 1889–1910. Oxford: Clarendon Press.
Phelps Brown, E. H. 1959. *The Growth of British Industrial Relations.* London: Macmillan.
Sells, Dorothy. 1923. *The British Trade Boards System.* London: King.

Tree, (Arthur) Ronald Lambert Field (1897–1976)

Ronald Tree was a Conservative M.P. who was an early opponent of Nazi Germany and a strong supporter of Anthony Eden in the late 1930s. He came into repeated close contact with Churchill when the Churchills and their entourage stayed at Tree's home, Ditchley Park, on thirteen occasions in 1940–1943, when Chequers was not safe from German bomber aircraft.

Ronald Tree was born on 26 September 1897, the oldest son of Arthur and Ethel Tree. The Trees were an American family, originally stemming from Somerset, and Arthur Tree chose to live in England. Ronald's mother was the daughter of Marshall Field, who made a large fortune from his department store and then from property. His parents divorced, his mother marrying the future admiral, David Beatty, and he was brought up by his father. Educated at Winchester, he went to the United States after his father died in 1914. When the United States entered the First World War, Tree joined the Naval Air Service and served in Italy and France.

After the war, he lived in the United States. From 1922 to 1926, he was managing editor of *Forum Magazine* in New York. He returned to Britain in late 1926. He became joint master of the Pytchley hounds in Northamptonshire, 1927–1933, which, as he later recollected, "put me in contact with a great many well established and influential Tories in the country." In 1933, he was elected Conservative M.P. for Market Harborough in a by-election, a seat he held until the 1945 general election.

Ronald and Nancy Tree bought Ditchley Park in North Oxfordshire in 1933. Tree visited Nazi Germany in 1934, visiting Berlin, Trier, and the Saarland. He returned deeply opposed to Hitler and to appeasing him. Tree served as parliamentary private secretary to Robert Hudson when he was minister of pensions, then minister of overseas trade, 1936–1938. He resigned at the end of 1938 because he frequently abstained from supporting Neville Chamberlain's government over foreign affairs.

Tree was a core member of the Edenite group. It was led by Anthony Eden and Lord Cranborne (later Salisbury), with Duff Cooper, Leo Amery, Harold Macmillan, J. P. L. Thomas, and Ronald Cartland among its members. Tree later recalled, "We shared the views and objectives of the people surrounding Winston Churchill; nevertheless our two groups remained distinct." He also recollected that Churchill, on his infrequent visits to the House of Commons, "sat in a corner of the smoking-room, with a few of his intimates, drinking whisky-and-sodas, and making no attempt to solicit adherents to his side."

Tree's association with Eden made him suspect to Chamberlain's supporters. Like Churchill, Tree's telephone was tapped, apparently on the instructions of Sir Joseph Ball of the Ministry of Information. Tree was one of thirty-three Conservative back-benchers who voted against Chamberlain's government in the decisive debate on 8 May 1940 that resulted in Churchill's premiership. Tree's Anglo-American connections led Eden to take Tree with him to New York in December 1938 and to his being sent by Lord Macmillan, minister of information, to report on British Information Services in the United States soon after the outbreak of war in 1939. From January 1940, he served as parliamentary private secretary to Sir John Keith, Lord Macmillan's successor as minister of information, and then under his successors, Duff Cooper and Brendan Bracken, until he resigned in early 1943.

Ronald Tree had had friendly contact with Churchill in the late 1930s, and Churchill had visited Ditchley Park on one occasion. In November 1940, Churchill summoned Tree to his room in the House of Commons and asked whether he could be accommodated at Ditchley for weekends when the "moon is high." At that time, Chequers was in danger of being bombed by German aircraft. Tree asked Churchill to choose his fellow guests and arranged for a film to be shown on the Saturday evenings of Churchill's visits. He was delighted by the first choice, *Lady Hamilton,* which he subsequently watched several more times. On 14 December 1940, the film was *The Great Dictator,* starring Charlie Chaplin, and the next night it was *Gone with the Wind.*

Churchill usually arrived about 5:00 P.M. on Friday and departed late on Monday morning. He took no exercise, yet ate large breakfasts, drank much brandy, and had an unlit cigar in his mouth much of the time. On one visit, after heavy bombing raids on Coventry, Churchill went up to show his support for the people of that city.

Churchill visited Ditchley on thirteen occasions in 1940–1943. These were on 9–11 November, 16–18 November, and 14–16 December 1940; 10–13 January, 15–17 February, 19–21 April, 9–11 May, 6–8 June, 6–8 September, and 1–3 November 1941; 28 February–2 March and 26–28 September 1942; and finally one day in March 1943. He was accompanied by his wife on all but one occasion when she declined to spend a weekend with Sir Samuel and Lady Hoare. Their daughter Mary was with them on seven occasions, and her sister Diana, with her husband Duncan Sandys, on one occasion. Brendan Bracken went every time except the final one-day visit, and F. A. Linde-

mann joined Churchill from Oxford for part of the weekend on the first five visits. Other visitors included Anthony and Beatrice Eden, Duff and Diana Cooper, Oliver and Moira Lyttelton, Peter and Jean Portal, Archibald Sinclair, John Colville, and Venetia Montagu. Important overseas visitors included Harry Hopkins, Averell Harriman (three occasions), and General Wladyslaw Eugeniusz Sikorski, the Polish leader in exile.

After leaving the Ministry of Information in late 1942, Tree was a founder of the Tory Reform Committee. He and his colleagues were warm supporters of the Beveridge Report. Tree frequently spoke in the House of Commons on postwar reconstruction issues. He was briefly parliamentary secretary at the Ministry of Town and Country Planning before the Conservatives were defeated in the 1945 general election and he lost his seat.

He left Britain, having homes in Barbados and New York. Churchill invited the Trees to dine with him when he visited New York in January 1952. Tree was a member of the Council of the University of the West Indies and president of the Barbados National Trust. He wrote *A History of Barbados,* 1972, as well as his memoirs, *When the Moon Was High,* 1975. He died on 14 July 1976.

Related entries:
Cartland, John Ronald Hamilton; Colville, Sir John Rupert; Cooper, Alfred Duff; Eden, Sir (Robert) Anthony

Suggestions for further reading:
Gilbert, Martin. 1983 and 1988. *Winston S. Churchill.* Vols. 6 and 8. London: Heinemann.
Tree, Ronald. 1975. *When the Moon Was High: Memoirs of Peace and War, 1897–1942.* London: Macmillan.

Trevelyan, George Macaulay (1876–1962)

Both Churchill and Trevelyan wrote narrative history with style. Trevelyan was as eager to defend his ancestor, Thomas

Balington Macaulay, from Churchill's criticisms as Churchill was keen to vindicate his ancestor, the first duke of Marlborough. Trevelyan helped Churchill in correcting his life of Marlborough.

George Macaulay Trevelyan was born on 16 February 1876 at Welcombe, Warwickshire, the third and youngest child of George Otto and Caroline Trevelyan. His great uncle was Thomas Babington Macaulay. His father, a Liberal cabinet minister under William Gladstone and Lord Rosebery, published a biography of Thomas Macaulay the year G. M. was born. Educated at Harrow and Trinity College, Cambridge, he won a fellowship in that college in 1898 and taught at Cambridge University until 1903. Financially secure, he became a gentleman scholar, devoting himself to writing history. In 1927, he became the Regius Professor of History at Cambridge University.

Historian David Cannadine, in his biography of G. M. Trevelyan, has commented on the similarities between Trevelyan and Churchill. These included being members of "governing families," being of patrician outlook, being advocates of New Liberalism, and being disconcerted by the impact of the First World War and becoming more conservative after it. In their younger days, they both admired Giuseppe Garibaldi, Trevelyan writing a multivolume biography and Churchill in April 1898 planning to write two historical studies, one on Garibaldi, the other on the American Civil War. In terms of writing history they both favored narrative and they both took a highly favorable view of the evolution of British parliamentary democracy (an attitude often referred to as "the whig interpretation of history").

Trevelyan was genuinely impressed by Churchill's style. He praised *My Early Life, Great Contemporaries, Marlborough,* and *A History of the English Speaking Peoples.* Of *Great Contemporaries,* Trevelyan wrote in a letter to Churchill, "there is profundity of political and historical wisdom, perfectly expressed. I wish I had your gift of historical writing."

Trevelyan read the proofs of *Marlborough* for Churchill. On 21 August 1936, he praised the third volume, observing, "The great battle at Ramillies is about as good a description of a battle as can be given," and he added that "the politics of the reign were never told more truly or more clearly." Earlier, he was robust in defending his ancestor, Macaulay, from Churchill's criticism over his negative portrait of Marlborough. However, in the 1930s he was critical of Churchill politically, being a supporter of the National government and its appeasement of Adolf Hitler. By June 1940, he was confessing to his brother, "We have all been great fools" and praised Churchill's government, especially the leading Labour ministers.

Churchill admired Trevelyan as a historian. Trevelyan's *History of England* (1926) was one of the volumes he kept close at hand for reference when he was writing *A History of the English Speaking Peoples.*

In the autumn of 1940, Churchill put forward Trevelyan's name for the mastership of Trinity College, Cambridge. He was master until 1951. He was elected a fellow of the British Academy in 1925. He was president of the Historical Association, 1946–1949, and president of the English Association, 1951–1954. In 1956, Churchill was one of the signatories of an appeal to raise a lectureship in his honor. In 1961, Churchill and Trevelyan were among the first Companions of Literature. Trevelyan died on 21 July 1962.

Suggestions for further reading:
Cannadine, David. G. 1992. *Trevelyan: A Life in History.* London: Harper-Collins.
Gilbert, Martin. 1976 and 1982. *Winston S. Churchill.* Vol. 5, and companion vol. 5, part 3. London: Heinemann.

Truman, Harry S. (1884–1972)

Although Churchill and Truman liked and respected each other, there was

Harry S. Truman talks with Winston Churchill, 20 March 1952 (Library of Congress)

not the warmth of Churchill's relationship with Roosevelt. Churchill was out of office for most of Truman's presidency, though when Churchill was leader of the Opposition, Truman accompanied Churchill to Westminster College, Fulton, for his "iron curtain" speech.

Harry Truman was born on 8 May 1884 in Lamar, Missouri, the eldest child of John Anderson and Martha Ellen Truman. His father was a farmer, working with his father. His mother, the daughter of pioneer farmers Solomon and Harriet Louisa Young, lived to her nineties and saw him elected president. He was educated at Noland School, Independence. He worked as a timekeeper for the Santa Fe Railroad, later for the National Bank of Commerce, Kansas City, then worked on the family farm, 1906–1917. He served in the army in 1917–1918, going to France in March 1918 and in action in the Vosges Moun-

tains from early September until the Armistice. After the war, he married Bess Wallace, a school friend, and opened a haberdashery store, which went into liquidation during the 1921–1922 recession. Truman was paying creditors until 1934. A Democrat, he was elected a judge in 1922–1924 and 1926–1934. In 1934, he defeated a Republican to be senator for Missouri. In 1944, Franklin D. Roosevelt supported Truman for the Democratic vice presidential nomination, which he secured at the Democratic Convention. He was sworn in as U.S. vice president on 20 January 1945. He succeeded Roosevelt as president on 12 April 1945.

On becoming president, he received a State Department briefing that noted that Churchill's policy was "based fundamentally on cooperation with the United States" and commented that "the British government has been showing increasing apprehension of Russia and her intentions." Truman replied to Churchill's message after Roosevelt's death by affirming that he wished to maintain the "loyal and close collaboration" between the two countries.

Churchill telephoned Truman on 25 April 1945 to give the war cabinet's response to Heinrich Himmler's offer to negotiate peace on the Western Front. Truman published a transcript of the conversation in the first volume of his memoirs. In early May, Churchill and Truman argued that they wanted Joseph Stalin to propose a Big Three meeting and that it would be held in Germany. Truman sent Harry Hopkins to see Stalin in Moscow, and Joseph Davies, the former U.S. ambassador to Moscow, to see Churchill in London. Davies had meetings with Churchill on 26–29 May.

Although Truman had seen Churchill in Washington earlier in the war, he met and first spoke with him on 16 July 1945. He wrote later, "I had an instant liking for this man." Truman and Churchill attended the Potsdam Conference from its opening on 17 July until Churchill returned to Britain on 26 July for the general election result the next day.

On 8 November 1945, Churchill informed Truman that he would be visiting the United States in 1946 and that his sole major speech would be at Westminster College, Fulton, Missouri. Truman accompanied Churchill to his home state and attended Churchill's speech. On the way, he was shown a copy of the speech and approved of its arguments but rightly predicted that "it would make a stir." The stir was sufficiently great for Truman to deny having read it in advance.

In April 1949, Churchill traveled to the United States, with his wife and son, to speak at the Massachusetts Institute of Technology. He visited Truman in Washington. Truman originally intended to join Churchill for two days in Boston, but withdrew. Churchill's speech included further condemnation of Soviet Russia, which he deemed "something quite as wicked but in some ways more formidable" than Hitler's regime.

After becoming prime minister again, Churchill visited the United States from 5 to 22 January 1952. He had major talks with Truman in Washington, 5–8 January.

Churchill visited the United States again in January 1953. He arrived on 5 January, and twice met Dwight D. Eisenhower in New York. He flew to Washington on 8 January, visiting Truman in the White House, then giving a dinner in his honor in the British embassy.

After both men had retired, Truman visited Britain in June 1956. He visited Chartwell, having lunch with the Churchills and Lord Beaverbrook. After Churchill recovered from illness, Truman wrote from Independence, Missouri, "How happy I am that you fooled the doctors, just as I did." Truman died on 26 December 1972.

Related entries:
Fulton Speech; Potsdam Conference

Suggestions for further reading:
Gilbert, Martin. 1986 and 1988. *Winston S. Churchill*. Vols. 7 and 8. London: Heinemann.
McCullough, David. 1992. *Truman*. New York: Simon and Schuster.
Truman, Harry S. 1955. *Memoirs*. Vol. 1: *Years of Decisions*. New York: Doubleday.
———. 1956. *Memoirs*. Vol. 2: *Years of Trial and Hope*. New York: Doubleday.

War, Secretary of State for (1919–1921)

Churchill was secretary of state for war from 10 January 1919 until 13 February 1921. It was very much a post that suited him and he held it during tumultuous times in Russia, Ireland, India, and Egypt.

Churchill took over when there was substantial unrest in the army over demobilization. Mutinies among some troops were not revolutionary manifestations but expressions of a determination to return quickly to civilian life and impatience with the existing demobilization plans. Churchill boldly scrapped the demobilization system and substituted one more defendable and more in line with the soldiers' views, which took into account length of service, injuries, and age.

Churchill vigorously supported intervention in Russia and was the most powerful British supporter of the White generals. David Lloyd George did not care for Bolshevism, but he was highly critical of Churchill's judgment on occasion on Russia. Although no friend of constitutional change in India, Churchill was lucidly and vigorously critical of General Reginald Dyer and the Amritsar massacre of 1919. He made it clear in the House of Commons that he felt British rule in India was secure and not under serious threat.

In Ireland, the threat was greater. Churchill, as in violent industrial disputes, was particularly anxious for the safety of the troops exposed to danger. Faced with an overall shortage of soldiers for Britain, India, Egypt, and elsewhere, Churchill urged the raising of a special force of ex-soldiers. Churchill thereafter remained robust in his efforts "to break the murder campaign and to enforce the authority of the law."

He was also concerned about the Middle East. He left the war office for the colonial office, taking over responsibility for British policy in that area.

Related entries:
Air, Secretary of State for; Denikin, General Anton Ivanovich

Suggestions for further reading:
Gilbert, Martin. 1975. *Winston S. Churchill.* Vol. 4. London: Heinemann.
Townshend, Charles. 1975. *The British Campaign in Ireland 1918–1921.* Oxford: Clarendon Press.

Wavell, Field Marshal Archibald Percival (Early Wavell, 1883–1950)

Churchill got on badly with Archibald Wavell. He thought him to be a pessimist, to lack fire, and generally to be too cautious. He also did not care for his long silences and brevity in conversation. Nevertheless, he recognized Wavell's achievements in defeating the Italians in North Africa. He also secured him the viceroyalty of India, in spite of Wavell's views being more liberal than his own.

Archibald Wavell was born on 5 May 1883 at Colchester, the son of Major Archibald Graham and Lillie Wavell. His father's side had a tradition of army service, and Wavell's father pressed him into the army. His mother was the daughter of Richard Percival of Springfields, Bradwell, Cheshire. Educated at Winchester and the Royal Military College, Sandhurst, he served in the Black Watch, his father's regiment, in the later stages of the Boer War (1899–1902). In the First World War, he lost an eye at Ypres, 1915. Later he served Sir Edmund Allenby in the Middle East. In the interwar years, he served at the war office, Aldershot, and in Palestine. In July 1939, he was sent to the Middle East to form the new military command there. When war broke out with Italy, Wavell received reinforcements from India and the dominions, but was still outnumbered.

Churchill and Wavell first met in August 1940. Churchill was angered by Wavell's failure to take decisive action in the desert, apparently not impressed by the superior numbers of Italian troops. However, the war cabinet did approve Wavell's list of military needs. Churchill did not like Wavell's advice to evacuate Somaliland, but he did agree that the defense of Egypt was the top priority. Wavell was reinforced by tanks, sent via the Cape for safety. In December 1941, Wavell, whose caution was enraging Churchill, launched an offensive that resulted in the defeat of Italian forces and the taking of Cyrenaica. This was followed by a successful campaign from Kenya into Italian Somaliland.

Wavell's fortunes changed thereafter. His participation in the Greek campaign was quickly followed by the need to evacuate British troops. General Erwin Rommel advanced in Libya. Churchill felt Wavell's preparations for defending Crete were insufficiently dynamic. He was angered by Wavell's failure to take action against a German coup in Iraq or to use Free French forces in Syria. Churchill determined in May to replace Wavell with Auchinleck. After the failure of two offensives against Rommel in May and June 1941, Wavell was sent to India to replace General Sir Claude Auchinleck as commander in chief in India, Churchill arguing that Wavell was tired.

Wavell asked that Burma be under his command, a request that was granted after the Japanese attack on Pearl Harbor, December 1941. At the start of 1942, he became supreme allied commander for the Southwest Pacific Theater. Wavell presided over the loss of Singapore and the retreat from Burma. Even during the Burmese retreat, Wavell began planning an offensive to retake Burma and he supported Wingate's operations. However, Churchill was unimpressed when the Arakan offensive of December 1942 to May 1943 failed. Churchill promoted him out of his command, securing him the post of viceroy of India.

Wavell was promoted to field marshal on 1 January 1943. With his appointment as viceroy he was raised to the peerage as Viscount Wavell. He served as viceroy from October 1943 until March 1947, when Attlee dismissed him. He was then elevated to an earl.

Wavell became constable of the Tower of London in 1948 and lord lieutenant of London in 1949. He died on 24 May 1950.

Related entries:
Auchinleck, Field Marshal Sir Claude John Eyre; Slim, Field Marshal Sir William Joseph; Wingate, Major General Orde Charles

Suggestions for further reading:
Beckett, Ian. 1991. "Wavell." In *Churchill's Generals,* edited by John Keegan. London: Weidenfeld and Nicolson.

Connell, John. 1969. *Wavell: Supreme Commander.*
London: Collins.
Gilbert, Martin. 1983 and 1986. *Winston S.
Churchill.* Vols. 6 and 7. London: Heinemann.
Lewin, Ronald. 1980. *The Chief.* London:
Hutchinson.

Wingate, Major General Orde Charles (1903–1944)

To his admirers Orde Wingate seemed something of a later Lawrence of Arabia, and T. E. Lawrence was a distant relative. Churchill praised him in 1943 as "a man of genius and audacity" and commented that some people referred to him as "The Clive of Burma." When Wingate died, Churchill described himself as "deeply grieved and stricken" by the news.

Wingate was born in India on 26 February 1903 into a three-generation military family. His parents were Plymouth Brethren. After being educated at Charterhouse and the Royal Military Academy, Woolwich, he was commissioned into the Royal Artillery in 1923. He learned Arabic at the School of Oriental Studies, London, in 1926 and was assigned to the Sudan defense corps in 1928. He followed T. E. Lawrence in relying on camels, rather than motor vehicles, when he went on a Royal Geographical Society-sponsored search for the legendary lost oasis of Zerzura in the Libyan Desert in 1932. After passing the qualifying examination to the Staff College, but not being admitted in 1935, he went to the top (a characteristic trait) and protested to the chief of the Imperial General Staff. As a result, he was posted to the general staff of the British forces in Palestine, 1936–1939.

There Wingate began his unorthodox career. He became a supporter of Zionism. He organized and trained irregular combat groups, the Special Night Squads. These proved very effective in countering Arab at-tacks on Jewish settlements and oil supplies. Wingate won a DSO and attracted the support not only of Archibald Wavell, the commander in Palestine, but also of Basil Liddell Hart, the defense expert of the London *Times*. Wingate wanted to meet Churchill, and made his approach via Liddell Hart. Wingate and Churchill first met on 30 November 1938, at Churchill's sixty-fourth birthday party.

In the autumn of 1940, Wingate became a part of substantial British special operations in the Middle East. He was assigned to foster guerrilla warfare in support of Emperor Haile Selassie against the occupying Italians. Wingate's irregulars succeeded in diverting Italian troops away from preparing to fight the main British forces. Haile Selassie was restored in Addis Ababa in May 1941, and Wingate received a bar to his DSO (Distinguished Service Order).

After the action was over, Wingate fell into depression. Suffering from malaria he took too high dosages of quinacrine hydrochloride and attempted to commit suicide with a sheath knife on 4 July 1941. Having recovered, he was called to the Far East by Wavell, then still commander in chief, India. Arriving in Burma in March 1942 Wingate was put in charge of British guerrilla operations against the Japanese. Wingate set up Long Range Penetration Groups of soldiers to disrupt communications deep in Japanese-occupied territory. The 3,000 men in these groups became known as the Chindits. In February 1943, the first Chindit expedition began, going into enemy territory on foot and there hitting rail and road networks. They succeeded also in keeping much of two divisions of Japanese troops busy. After they returned (some 800 fewer), Wingate was awarded a second bar to his DSO; Churchill was impressed, even talking of making Wingate commander in Burma.

In August 1943 Churchill insisted on taking Wingate and his wife in his party traveling on the *Queen Mary* to Canada for the Quebec Conference. Churchill clearly believed that Wingate would be evidence of British determination to defeat the Japanese in Burma. Wingate was very much the man of action and courage that Churchill craved. At the Quebec Conference, Churchill and President Franklin D. Roosevelt set up the Southeast Asia Command under Lord Louis Mountbatten and confirmed Wingate as the head of the Long Range Penetration Group. They also spoke of Wingate in their Far East plans at Cairo in November 1943. With such powerful backing, General William Slim and other commanders knew they had to include a role for Wingate in their military plans.

In March 1944, Wingate's Chindits went into action again, this time being taken by gliders deep into Japanese-occupied territory. However, Wingate was killed in an air crash in the jungle on 24 March 1944. Wingate's Chindits boosted morale and demonstrated that the Japanese were not invincible in the jungle, even if such operations were highly costly in resources.

Suggestions for further reading:

Gilbert, Martin. 1986. *Winston S. Churchill*. Vol. 7. London: Heinemann.
Gordon, John W. 1991. "Wingate." In *Churchill's Generals,* edited by John Keegan. London: Weidenfeld and Nicolson.
Sykes, Christopher. 1959. *Orde Wingate*. London: Collins.
Tulloch, Major General Derek. 1972. *Wingate in Peace and War.* London: MacDonald.

Winterton, Earl of (Edward Turnour, 1883–1962)

Eddie Winterton was a long-term friend of Churchill, in spite of periodic strong political differences. Although a vigorous opponent during Churchill's Liberal years, Winterton was a founder member of The Other Club. He and Churchill were particularly in sympathy over the Middle East (1921–1922) and the earlier years of the campaign for rearmament (1934–1937), but Winterton's support for Neville Chamberlain (1937–1939) damaged his later political career.

Edward Turnour was born on 4 April 1883, the only child of Edward Turnour, the fifth Earl of Winterton and his wife, Lady Georgiana Susan Hamilton, a daughter of the duke of Abercorn. Educated at Eton and New College, Oxford, he was elected to Parliament when in his third year as an undergraduate. He was elected in a by-election in November 1904 for Horsham, Sussex, a seat he held until 1951. He was the first candidate to stand in support of Joseph Chamberlain's tariff reform policy and he held a safe Tory seat after a run of such seats had been lost in by-elections. He succeeded his father to become sixth earl of Winterton in 1907, but as an Irish peer he could stay in the House of Commons. In 1905, he was made parliamentary private secretary to E. G. Pretyman, financial secretary to the treasury, and after the Conservative defeat in 1906, he carried out that role for Joseph Chamberlain.

In Opposition, Winterton proved a vigorous opponent of the Liberal government. On one occasion in 1911 he and Churchill nearly came to blows. He was highly critical of Churchill's penal reforms when he was home secretary. Nevertheless, he was a founder-member of The Other Club that year. Winterton served in Gallipoli and Egypt, and then with T. E. Lawrence before the fall of Damascus. Winterton greatly admired Churchill's Middle East policies, 1921–1922, on one occasion eulogistically praising him in the House of Commons. In early 1921, Churchill had suggested that Winterton become an under secretary in the government, and Winterton did become under secretary for India, March–October 1922; but by mid-1922, he was one of many Conservative junior ministers hostile to David Lloyd George's coalition government. Winterton continued to hold that post under Andrew Bonar Law and

Stanley Baldwin (1922–1924 and 1924–1929). Although on the right of the Conservative Party, he supported Baldwin, not Churchill, over India in the early 1930s.

Winterton strongly supported Churchill over rearmament. Alongside Churchill he signed motions critical of British air defenses in 1934 and 1936 and called for the Territorial Army to be expanded.

However, when Neville Chamberlain became prime minister in 1937, Winterton became chancellor of the Duchy of Lancaster. In March 1938, he entered the cabinet when he was given the additional post of deputy to Lord Swinton, the secretary of state for air. In the cabinet, Swinton, Duff Cooper, and he unsuccessfully spoke up for an expansion of aircraft production. In May 1938, he clashed with Churchill over rearmament. At his request he switched his additional responsibilities from air to the home office. When Swinton and Duff Cooper resigned, Winterton stayed in office, discrediting himself in the eyes of Churchill's circle. In January 1939, he was demoted to paymaster general, a post outside the cabinet, which he held until November 1939.

Churchill offered Winterton no ministerial post but did offer other posts overseas, which he declined. Instead he criticized the government when he judged it necessary. Churchill in 1941 saw Winterton, along with Leslie Hore-Belisha, as a leading member of the Opposition of "the left-outs of all parties." When Lloyd George accepted a peerage on 1 January 1945, Winterton became the father of the House of Commons (the longest continuous serving M.P.). After the Conservatives' 1945 general election defeat, Churchill made him a member of his shadow cabinet.

In 1951, Winterton retired from the House of Commons. In 1952 he became a peer, Baron Turnour of Shillinglee, and so entered the House of Lords. He was a keen fox hunter, calling his favorite hunting horse Churchill. He died on 26 August 1962.

Related entry:
Appeasement

Suggestions for further reading:
Brodrick, Alan Houghton. 1965. *Near to Greatness: A Life of the Sixth Earl Winterton.* London: Hutchinson.
Gilbert, Martin. 1975, 1976, and 1983. *Winston S. Churchill.* Vols. 4–6. London: Heinemann.
Rose, Kenneth. 1981. "Turnour, Edward." In *The Dictionary of National Biography: 1961–1970,* edited by E. T. Williams and C. S. Nicholls. Oxford: Oxford University Press.
Winterton, Earl of. 1953. *Orders of the Day.* London: Cassell.

Woolton, Earl of (Frederick James Marquis, 1883–1964)

*L*ord Woolton was that much sought-after thing in twentieth-century Conservative politics: the businessman in politics. Brought in by Neville Chamberlain in 1940, he impressed Churchill as reliable and efficient. Churchill shrewdly used the skills Woolton had shown during the Second World War to reorganize the Conservative Party's organization after the 1945 election defeat.

Frederick Marquis was born in Salford on 23 August 1883, the only child of Thomas Robert and Margaret Marquis, née Ormerod. His father was a saddler. Educated at Ardwick Higher Grade School, Manchester Grammar School, and Manchester University, he taught mathematics at Burnley Grammar School and also taught two evenings a week at the local technical school. He was then a Fabian socialist, and his concern about the causes of poverty led him to the Manchester University settlement at Ancoats Hall and then to the wardenship of the David Lewis Hotel and Club Association in Liverpool. He went on to be warden of Liverpool University's settlement, which also gave him the opportunity to lecture on industrial history in the university.

In 1912, he married Maud Smith, who was also active in philanthropic work; together they wrote a book on employment opportunities for young people. Rejected as unfit for military service, Marquis worked as a civil servant during the war, organizing the leather and boot industries to meet war needs among other work. In 1917, he resigned from the Fabian Society and accepted an invitation to be secretary of the trade federation for the boot industry. He later became a director of the department store chain of Lewis, becoming managing director in 1928 and chairman in 1936.

Marquis was known and respected in the civil service. He served on advisory councils to the Overseas Development Committee, 1928–1931, the Board of Trade, 1930–1934, and the post office, 1933–1947. He was made one of the three commissioners for areas of special distress, responsible for Lancashire and the northeast. He was knighted in 1935 and created a baron in 1939, becoming Lord Woolton. From 1936 onward he was also involved in war preparations, ranging from the problem of responding to the bombing of civilians to organizing ample supplies of clothing for the army. He became the director general of the Ministry of Supply when war broke out.

In April 1940, he moved from a civil service role into a political one, becoming minister of food. When Churchill took over a few weeks later, Woolton wrote to him and offered to stand down. When Churchill saw him, he wondered whether Woolton could manage large numbers of civil servants; nevertheless, he kept him in the post until November 1943. Woolton was doubtful about Churchill, believing he had lacked judgment in the First World War. They eventually came to respect each other, Woolton later writing of Churchill's success in securing cooperation between generals and politicians that "I am sure his hardest-won victory was over himself."

After a successful period as minister of food, Churchill promoted Woolton to

minister of reconstruction with a seat in the war cabinet, a post he held until the end of the war in Europe. When Churchill pressed him over lunch to accept the post, he pointed out that as a nonparty figure he was acceptable to chair the Reconstruction Committee. Clement Attlee was deputy chairman. Woolton's proposals included a comprehensive health service but one that left the medical profession to operate as they wished. Woolton described this as "a half-way house to the system of nationalized service." He also introduced the White Paper on Employment Policy, which sought a "high and stable level of employment."

When Churchill formed his caretaker government after the ending of the coalition government, he appointed Woolton lord president of the council. After the Conservatives' defeat, Woolton, who was opposed to nationalization and who greatly admired Churchill personally, joined the Conservative Party. Churchill was much moved by this action in the hour of defeat. With Lord Cranborne away, Woolton led the Opposition in the House of Lords and was a member of the shadow cabinet. Churchill invited him to become chairman of the Conservative Party, saying that he had the skills to reorganize the party organization and make it efficient. Woolton saw much of Churchill, discussing with him the reformulation of Conservative policy. Woolton was in charge during the 1950 and 1951 elections, in which he tried to avoid attacks on Labour figures in order to concentrate on policies.

With Churchill's return to office in 1951, Woolton returned to the post of lord president of the council. He also became deputy leader in the House of Lords while remaining chairman of the Conservative Party. When food subsidies were cut, the Labour Party quoted Woolton's pledges that the Conservatives would not cut them, and he offered to resign. Churchill refused to accept his resignation. After a serious illness

Woolton moved to be chancellor of the Duchy of Lancaster, a post he held until December 1955. From September 1953 until August 1954, he was also minister of materials, with the task of closing down a ministry set up during the Korean War. After Churchill's retirement, he agreed to stay on in office and as party chairman until after the general election. He retired at his own insistence, and was honoured with an earldom and an additional viscountcy.

He died on 14 December 1964. Lord Redcliffe-Maud later wrote, "He was frankly scared of Churchill and never became intimate . . . with him."

Suggestions for further reading:
Redcliffe-Maud, Lord. 1981. "Marquis, Frederick James." In *The Dictionary of National Biography: 1961–1970,* edited by E. T. Williams and C. S. Nicholls. Oxford: Oxford University Press.
Woolton, Earl of. 1959. *Memoirs.* London: Cassell.

The World Crisis (1923–1931)

*T*he World Crisis was a great boost to Churchill's precarious finances. The work enabled him to buy Chartwell. Apparently Churchill had intended to call his study *The Great Amphibian,* to mark the importance of the war at sea as well as on the land. The publishers were not attracted by that title, and the title *The World Crisis* was adopted.

The writing of these huge volumes is another testimony to Churchill's powers of hard work. He wrote much of them while in office, under David Lloyd George while at the war and then colonial offices and later when chancellor of the exchequer, 1924–1929. When Sir George Riddell talked to him about the book in January 1921, Churchill had written much of the first volume. According to Riddell, Churchill commented that it was "very exhila-rating to feel that one was writing for half a crown a word!"

Churchill revised his draft chapters in 1922, adding documentary detail. He had been much criticized by Lord Esher. *The Tragedy of Lord Kitchener,* published in August 1921, was highly and unfairly critical of Churchill at the admiralty. In the cabinet on 30 January 1922 he asked, and received, permission to defend himself by drawing on official documents in his possession. The use of such documents helped ensure that for long later historians frequently cited Churchill's books. Churchill's inside knowledge on naval matters, 1914–1915, strengthened the first volume, whereas he had less that was novel to offer in the fifth volume on the Eastern Front.

The book received criticism for its mixture of autobiography and history under the grand title, *The World Crisis.* There was some detailed criticism made in the late 1920s, published by Lord Sydenham and others as *The World Crisis: A Criticism* (1928). More recently, Robin Prior subjected the main volumes, 1911–1918, to telling criticism, especially the large portion of the work given to the Dardanelles campaign. He also points to Churchill's frequent references to the "fates," which Prior observes he uses "not to explain events but to explain them away." He is also critical of Churchill's selective use of documents. However, Prior praises Churchill for his analysis of casualty statistics, his account of the Battle of the Somme, and for the "thread of humanity" that runs through the books.

The World Crisis was a great success when published and has proved popular ever since.

Suggestions for further reading:
Gilbert, Martin. 1975 and 1976. *Winston S. Churchill.* Vols. 4 and 5. London: Heinemann.
Prior, Robin. 1983. *Churchill's "World Crisis" as History.* London: Croom Helm.

Yalta Conference (February 1945)

The conference (code name Argonaut) was held in Yalta in the Crimea in February 1945. Churchill flew to the Crimea from Malta on 3 February, arriving soon after President Franklin D. Roosevelt. At Yalta he stayed in the Vorontsov villa. Churchill left Yalta in the evening of 11 February, traveling to the *Franconia,* anchored off Sebastopol. He flew on to Athens on 14 February. Although the Yalta Conference was one of the most important of the war, for Churchill and the British it marked a further slide (begun at Tehran) from there being a Big Three to a Big Two.

Churchill left Northolt for Malta on 29 January 1945, with his daughter Sarah, Lord Moran, and Sir Edward Bridges in his party. Anthony Eden, General Alan Brooke, and Sir Alexander Cadogan flew in another aircraft. On 2 February, Roosevelt arrived in Malta by sea. Churchill and Roosevelt had lunch together, attended a meeting of the Combined Chiefs of Staff and dined together in the evening. Churchill pressed the president to ensure that they should both be clear of the key issues to put to Stalin at what Churchill deemed to be "a decisive conference." Roosevelt avoided substantive talks with Churchill. Churchill pressed for the Allies to occupy as much of Austria as

possible, rather than let the Russians encroach further into Western Europe.

On 3 February, the president and Churchill flew separately to the Crimea. They did not have private talks together again until 6 February, three days into the Yalta Conference. The Yalta Conference elaborated on many matters agreed at the Tehran Conference. With Soviet forces only forty miles from Berlin, the Yalta Conference discussed the nature of the Polish government, the Polish frontier, and arrangements for the occupation of Germany and Austria. With the defeat of Japan expected to take a further eighteen months, the Americans were keen to see Soviet forces involved in fighting the Japanese and offered what later appeared to be generous terms. There was also discussion at Yalta on voting rights at the United Nations and providing France with an occupation zone in Germany.

Among the documents agreed at Yalta was the "Declaration on Liberated Europe." This pledged America, Britain, and Russia to help the liberated peoples of Europe "to solve by democratic means their pressing political and economic problems" during the postwar instability.

On 12 February, Churchill was shown Sebastopol, including the tomb of Lord Raglan, the British Crimean War commander, and also the battlefield of Balaklava. On 14 February, he flew to Athens, diverting his plane to circle the island of Skyros, where Rupert

Prime Minister Winston Churchill, President Franklin D. Roosevelt, and Marshal Joseph Stalin at the palace in Yalta, where the Big Three met, February 1945 (Library of Congress)

Brooke was buried. In Athens, the Acropolis was floodlit in his honor, the first time since the German occupation of April 1941.

Related entries:

Roosevelt, Franklin Delano; Stalin, Joseph; Tehran Conference

Suggestions for further reading:

Clemens, Diane Shaver. 1970. *Yalta.* New York: Oxford University Press.

Gilbert, Martin. 1986. *Winston S. Churchill.* Vol. 7. London: Heinemann.

Kimball, Warren F., ed. 1984. *Churchill and Roosevelt: The Complete Correspondence.* Vol. 3. London: Collins.

1874   *November 30.* Born at Blenheim Palace

1880   *February 4.* His brother, John, born

1882   *November 3.* Educated at St. George's School, Ascot (1882–21 July 1884)

1884   *September 16.* Educated at Misses Thomson School, Hove (1884–29 March 1888)

1885   *June 23.* Lord Randolph Churchill becomes secretary of state for India

1886   *July 25.* Lord Randolph Churchill becomes chancellor of the exchequer (resigns in December)

1888   *April 17.* Educated at Harrow (1888–1893)

1893   *February.* Educated at Captain James's "crammer," London (February–June)

1893   *September 1.* Enters the Royal Military College, Sandhurst

1895   *January 24.* Lord Randolph Churchill dies

        February 20. Commissioned and joins 4th Hussars

        November–December. Visits the United States (9–18 November) and Cuba (20 November–7 December and returns via New York on 14 December)

1896   *October 1.* Posted to India, arrives in Bombay (1) and Bangalore (9)

1897   *May–August.* On leave in England. First political speech, Primrose League meeting, Bath (26 July)

        September 1. Joins Malakand Field Force

1898   *March 14.* *The Story of the Malakand Field Force* published

        August 2. Joins 21st Lancers and Lord Kitchener's expedition to the Sudan

        September 2. In cavalry charge at the Battle of Omdurman

1899   *March.* Departs from India (mid-March)

        June–July. Fights unsuccessful by-election, Oldham

        October 14. Departs for the Cape, arriving on 30 October

        November 6. *The River War* published

        November 15. Captured by Boers, imprisoned in Pretoria

        December 11. Escaped from Boers, reaches Durban (23)

1900   *February 3.* *Savrola* published (U.S. publication date; U.K., 13)

        February 28. With General Sir Redvers Buller at relief of Ladysmith

        May 15. *London to Ladysmith* published

        June 2. Cycles through Johannesburg ahead of British troops

        June 8. Enters Pretoria with British troops

        July 28. Lady Randolph Churchill marries Lieutenant George Cornwallis-West

        October 1. Elected M.P. for Oldham (1900–1906)

        October 12. *Ian Hamilton's March* published

        November. Lecture tour in the U.K.

December. Lecture tour in the United States. Christmas in Canada

1901 *January.* Lecture tour in Canada

1903 *April (n.d.). Mr. Brodrick's Army* published

1904 *January.* Conservative whip withdrawn for two weeks

May 31. Joins the Liberal Party in House of Commons

1905 *December 12.* Parliamentary under secretary of state for the colonies (1905–1908)

1906 *January 2. Lord Randolph Churchill,* 2 volumes, published

January 13. Elected M.P. for Manchester, Northwest (1906–1908)

1907 *April–May.* Imperial Conference, London

October–January. Travels via Malta and Cyprus to Kenya and Uganda; returns via the Sudan and Egypt

1908 *April 12.* Enters cabinet, president of the Board of Trade (1908–1910)

May 8. Elected M.P. for Dundee (1908–1922)

September 12. Marries Clementine Hozier, St. Margaret's, Westminster

December (n.d.). My African Journey published

1909 *March 24.* Speaks on Trade Boards Bill (second reading, House of Commons)

June 16. Introduces Labour Exchanges Bill (second reading, House of Commons)

July 11. Birth of Diana

November 26. Liberalism and the Social Problem published

1910 *January 14. The People's Rights* published

February 14. Home secretary (1910–1911)

November 8. Sends police to Tonypandy

1911 *January 3.* Present at siege of Sidney Street, East London

January. Responsible for the National Insurance Act, Part 2, Unemployment Insurance

March 17. Speaks on the Mines Bill (second reading, House of Commons)

March 31. Speaks on the Shops Bill (second reading, House of Commons)

May 28. Birth of Randolph Frederick Edward Spencer

August. Soldiers kill two men at Llanelli during railway strike

October 23. First lord of the admiralty (1911–1915)

1912 *February 8.* Speaks in Ulster, at Celtic Road football ground, Falls Road, Belfast

1914 *July 30.* Churchill orders the fleets to take up battle stations

August 4. Britain at war with Germany (1914–1918)

October 3–6. At Antwerp

October 6. Birth of Sarah

October 29. Admiral Sir John Fisher appointed first sea lord

1915 *February 19.* Naval bombardment of Turkish forts, Dardanelles

May 25. Chancellor of the Duchy of Lancaster

November 12. Resigns from government

November 18. Leaves for France

November 19. Joins Guards at Merville (November–December)

1916 *January 1.* Given command of 6th Battalion, Royal Scots Fusiliers

January 26. Moved into line at Ploegsteert

May 9. Resumes political activities in London

September 28. Examined on his evidence at Dardanelles Commission

1917 *March.* Dardanelles Commission's first report mostly exonerates him

July 17. Minister of munitions (1917–1919)

1918 *November 15.* Birth of Marigold Frances (dies August 1921)

1919 *January 10.* Secretary of state for war and air (1919–1921)

February 14. Sees President Woodrow Wilson in Paris with proposals for Allied intervention in Russia

1921 *February 13.* Secretary of state for the colonies (with air until April), 1921–1922

March 12–22. Cairo Conference on future of Iraq and British policy in the Middle East

June 29. Death of Lady Randolph Churchill

September 15. Birth of Mary

September 24. Buys Chartwell Manor, Kent

1922 *September–October.* Supports David Lloyd George in Chanak crisis

November 15. Defeated in general election at Dundee

December. In a villa in Cannes (until May 1923)

1923 *April 10.* The World Crisis, vol. 1, published (the last volume, 1931)

October 30. The World Crisis, vol. 2, published

December 6. Defeated in general election at Leicester West

1924 *March 19.* Defeated as Independent Anti-Socialist candidate, Westminster Abbey by-election

October 29. Elected in general election as Constitutionalist candidate, Epping (1924–1964)

November 6. Chancellor of the exchequer (1924–1929)

1925 *April 28.* Returns Britain to the Gold Standard at the prewar parity

1926 *May 5–13.* Edits British Gazette during the General Strike

1927 *January 14.* Visits Benito Mussolini (and the pope) in Rome

March 3. The World Crisis, vol. 3 (in two parts), published

1929 *March 7.* The World Crisis, vol. 4, published

August–October. Tours Canada and the United States

October 19. Visits President Herbert Hoover in the White House

1930 *October 20.* My Early Life published

1931 *January 27.* Churchill resigns from Conservative shadow cabinet over India

May 27. India published

November. The World Crisis, vol. 5, published

December 13. Injured by a car in Manhattan, early in lecture tour

1932 *January 2–22.* Recuperates at Nassau, Bahamas

January–March. Lecture tour in the United States (28 January–early March)

November 10. Thoughts and Adventures published

1933 *October 6.* Marlborough, vol. 1, published

1934 *March 8.* In Parliament calls for much greater spending on Royal Air Force

October (n.d.). Marlborough, vol. 2, published

1935 *July 9.* Joins the Air Defence Research Subcommittee of Committee of Imperial Defence

1936 *October 23. Marlborough,* vol. 3, published

November–December. Abdication crisis, King Edward VIII and Mrs. Simpson

December 3. "Arms and the Covenant" meeting, Albert Hall

1937 *October 4. Great Contemporaries* published

1938 *June 24. Arms and the Covenant* published

September 2. Marlborough, vol. 4, published

1939 *June 27. Step by Step* published

September 3. First lord of the admiralty (1939–1940)

1940 *May 10.* Prime minister and minister of defense

May 14. In House of Commons offers nothing but "blood, toil, tears, and sweat"

June 4. In House of Commons after Dunkirk pledges, "We shall fight on the beaches . . ."

June 16. Cabinet approves a Declaration of Union for Britain and France

August 13. Roosevelt agrees to supply fifty destroyers; Britain leases bases in West Indies, Bermuda, and Newfoundland for ninety-nine years

August 20. In House of Commons pays the tribute, "Never in the field of human conflict has so much been owed by so many to so few"

1941 *February (n.d.). Into Battle* published

August 9–13. Meets Roosevelt at Placentia Bay, Newfoundland. Atlantic Charter drafted

December 8. Declares war on Japan (the day after Pearl Harbor)

December 10. Sinking of *Prince of Wales* and *Repulse*

December 22. In United States, based at the White House (22 December–14 January) and addresses both houses of Congress (26)

December 29–31. Visits Canada, addresses Canadian Parliament (30)

1942 *January 5.* Stays at Palm Beach, Florida (5–10)

February 15. Fall of Singapore

September 24. The Unrelenting Struggle published

1943 *January 15–24.* Casablanca Conference with Franklin D. Roosevelt; afterwards they visit Marrakesh together (24–25)

July 29. The End of the Beginning published

August 17–24. First Quebec Conference with Franklin D. Roosevelt. Before conference, visits Hyde Park (12–14) Afterwards stays at Snow Lake (26–31)

September 1–11. Stays at White House; receives honorary degree, Harvard (6)

November–December. Cairo Conference with Franklin D. Roosevelt; Tehran Conference with Joseph Stalin also.

December 12. Ill in Tunis, convalesces at Marrakesh (27 December–January 1943)

1944 *June 29. Onwards to Victory* published

August 10–28. Flies to Algiers, then to Italy. Based in Naples and Rome (sees Marshal Tito and the pope)

September 13–16. Second Quebec Conference with Franklin D. Roosevelt. Afterwards stays at Hyde Park (18–19)

October 9–19. Moscow Conference with Joseph Stalin

November 10–14. In Paris with Charles de Gaulle. Made honorary citizen of Paris (12)

December 25–29 .   In Athens

1945   *February 4–11.*   Yalta Conference with Franklin D. Roosevelt and Joseph Stalin

July 15–25.   Potsdam Conference with Harry Truman and Joseph Stalin

July 26.   Announcement of Conservative general election defeat

July 26.   The Dawn of Liberation published

1946   *January–March.*   In United States and Cuba. With Harry Truman to Missouri (4–5 February) for "Iron Curtain" speech at Westminster College, Fulton

July (n.d.).   War Speeches published

August–September.   In Switzerland. Receives honorary degree at Zurich. Spoke of "a kind of United States of Europe" (19 September)

September 26.   Secret Session Speeches published

1948   *May 7.*   Gave a speech and chaired foundation meeting of the "United Europe" campaign, The Hague

June 21.   The Second World War, vol. 1, published (U.K. edition in October)

August 19.   The Sinews of Peace published

1949   *March 29.   The Second World War,* vol. 2, published (U.K. edition in June)

August.   Delegate to first meeting of Consultative Assembly to establish a Council of Europe, Strasbourg

1950   *February 3.   Europe Unite* published

July 20.   The Second World War, vol. 3, published (U.K. edition in July)

August 10–17.   Delegate to Consultative Assembly of Europe at Strasbourg

1951   *August 3.   The Second World War,* vol. 4, published (U.K. edition in August)

October 18.   In the Balance published

October 26.   Prime minister and minister of defense (prime minister, 1951–1955; minister of defense 1951–March 1952)

November 23.   The Second World War, vol. 5, published (U.K. edition 3 September 1952)

1952   *September 3.   The War Speeches* (definitive edition), 3 volumes, published

1953   *June 23.*   Suffers serious stroke

June 25.   Stemming the Tide published

November 30.   The Second World War, vol. 6, published (U.K. edition in April 1954)

December 4–8.   Bermuda Conference with Dwight D. Eisenhower and Joseph Laniel (France)

1954   *June 25–29.*   Visits Dwight D. Eisenhower in Washington

June 29–30.   Visits Louis St. Laurent in Canada

1955   *April 5.*   Retires as prime minister

1956   *April 23.   A History of the English Speaking Peoples,* vol. 1, published

November 26.   A History of the English Speaking Peoples, vol. 2, published

1957   *October 14.   A History of the English Speaking Peoples,* vol. 3, published

1958   *March 17.   A History of the English Speaking Peoples,* vol. 4, published

1961   *April 27.   The Unwritten Alliance* published

1963   *April 8.*   The two houses of Congress vote to confer honorary citizenship of the United States on him

October 19.   Death of his daughter Diana

1965   *January 24.*   Dies on seventieth anniversary of his father's death

January 30.   State funeral and burial at Bladon churchyard

BIBLIOGRAPHY

The Official Biography

Winston S. Churchill. 8 vols. London: Heinemann, 1966–1988.
(Vols. 1 and 2 by R. S. Churchill;Vols. 3–8 by M. Gilbert)
Vol. I:Youth. 1874–1900 (1966)
Vol. II:Young Statesman. 1900–1914 (1967)
Vol. III: 1914–1916 (1971)
Vol. IV: 1917–1922 (1975)
Vol. V: 1922–1939 (1976)
Vol. VI:Their Finest Hour 1939–1941 (1983)
Vol. VII:The Road to Victory 1941–1945 (1986)
Vol. VIII: Never Despair 1945–1965 (1988)

Companions to the Official Biography
Edited by Randolph S. Churchill:
Winston S. Churchill. Vol. I, companion vol. 1: 1874–1896 (1967)
Winston S. Churchill. Vol. I, companion vol. 2: 1896–1900 (1967)
Winston S. Churchill. Vol. II, companion vol. 1: 1901–1907 (1969)
Winston S. Churchill. Vol. II, companion vol. 2: 1907–1911 (1969)
Winston S. Churchill. Vol. II, companion vol. 3: 1911–1914 (1969)

Edited by Martin Gilbert:
Winston S. Churchill.Vol. III, companion vol. 1:August 1914–April 1915 (1972)
Winston S. Churchill. Vol. III, companion vol. 2: May 1915–December 1916 (1972)
Winston S. Churchill. Vol. IV, companion vol. 1: January 1917–June 1919 (1977)
Winston S. Churchill.Vol. IV, companion vol. 2: July 1919–March 1921 (1977)
Winston S. Churchill. Vol. IV, companion vol. 3: April 1921–November 1922 (1977)
Winston S. Churchill. Vol. V, companion vol. 1: The Exchequer Years (1979)
Winston S. Churchill. Vol. V, companion vol. 2: The Wilderness Years, 1929–1935 (1981)
Winston S. Churchill. Vol. V, companion vol. 3: The Coming of War, 1936–1939 (1982)

Winston S. Churchill. The Churchill War Papers: Vol. 1:At the Admiralty (1993)
Winston S. Churchill. The Churchill War Papers: Vol. 2: Never Surrender (1994)
Winston S. Churchill. The Churchill War Papers: Vol. 3:The Ever-Widening War (2000)

The Collected Speeches:
James, R. R., ed. 1981. *Churchill Speaks: Collected Speeches, 1897–1963.* New York: Chelsea House and Bowker.

Select Bibliography of Works on Churchill

Addison, Paul. 1992. *Churchill on the Home Front, 1900–1955.* London: Jonathan Cape.

Alldritt, Keith. 1992. *Churchill the Writer.* London: Hutchinson.

Amery, L. S. 1953–1955. *My Political Life.* 3 vols. London: Hutchinson.

Arthur, Sir George C. A. 1940. *Concerning Winston S. Churchill.* London: Heinemann.

Ashley, M. 1968. *Churchill as Historian.* London: Secker and Warburg.

Atholl, Duchess of. 1958. *Working Partnership.* London: Arthur Baker.

Avon, Earl of. 1962 and 1965. *The Eden Memoirs.* Vols. 1 and 2. London: Cassell.

Bardens, Dennis. 1968. *Churchill in Parliament.* London: Robert Hale.

Barker, Elizabeth. 1978. *Churchill and Eden at War.* London: Macmillan.

Barnes, J., and D. Nicholson, eds. 1980. *The Leo Amery Diaries 1896–1929.* London: Hutchinson.

———. 1988. *The Empire at Bay:The Leo Amery Diaries 1929–1955.* London: Hutchinson.

Ben-Moshe, Tuvia. 1992. *Churchill: Strategy and History.* Hemel Hempstead, UK: Harvester Wheatsheaf.

Berlin, I. 1965. *Mr. Churchill in 1940.* London: John Murray.

Best, G. 2001. *Churchill: A Study in Greatness.* London: Hambledon.

Bibesco, Princess. 1957. *Sir Winston Churchill: Master of Courage.* London: Robert Hale.

Birkenhead, Earl of. 1989. *Churchill, 1874–1922.* London: Harrap.

Blake, R., ed. 1952. *The Private Papers of Douglas Haig, 1914–1919.* London: Eyre and Spottiswoode.

Blake, R., and R. W. Louis, eds. 1993. *Churchill.* Oxford: Oxford University Press.

Blunt, W. S. 1919 and 1920. *My Diaries 1884–1914.* London: Secker.

Boadle, D. G. 1973. *Winston Churchill and the German Question in British Foreign Policy, 1918–1922.* The Hague: Martinus Nijhoff.

Bonham-Carter, V. 1965. *Winston Churchill as I Knew Him.* London: Eyre and Spottiswoode with Collins.

Boothby, R. 1947. *I Fight to Live.* London: Victor Gollancz.

———. 1978. *Recollections of a Rebel.* London: Hutchinson.

Boyce, D. G., ed. 1987. *The Crisis of British Unionism: The Domestic Political Papers of the Second Earl of Selborne, 1885–1922.* London: Historians Press.

———. 1990. *The Crisis of British Power: The Imperial and Naval Papers of the Second Earl of Selborne, 1895–1910.* London: Historians Press.

Boyle, P. G., ed. 1990. *The Churchill-Eisenhower Correspondence 1953–1935.* Chapel Hill: University of North Carolina.

Brendon, P. 1984. *Churchill: An Authentic Hero.* London: Secker and Warburg.

Brett, M. V., ed. 1934. *Journals and Letters of Reginald, Viscount Esher.* Vol. 2: 1903–1910. London: Ivor Nicholson and Watson.

———. 1938. *Journals and Letters of Reginald, Viscount Esher.* Vol. 3: 1910–1915. London: Ivor Nicholson and Watson.

Broad, L. 1941. *Winston Churchill.* (Revised editions: 1943, 1946, 1951, 1952, 1956). London: Hutchinson.

———. 1960. *The War That Churchill Wages.* London: Hutchinson.

Brock, M., and E. Brock, eds. 1982. *H. H. Asquith, Letters to Venetia Stanley.* Oxford: Oxford University Press.

Bryant, A., ed. 1957. *The Turn of the Tide 1939–1943.* London: Collins.

———. 1959. *The Triumph in the West 1943–1946.* London: Collins.

Buchan, W. 1940. *Winston Churchill.* London: Pilot Press.

Bullard, F. Lauriston. 1914. *Famous War Correspondents.* Boston: Little Brown.

Burbridge, W. F. 1943. *The Rt. Hon. Winston Leonard Spencer Churchill.* London: Crowther.

Butler, R. A. 1971. *The Art of the Possible.* London: Hamish Hamilton.

———. 1982. *The Art of Memory.* London: Hodder and Stoughton.

Callahan, R. 1984. *Churchill: Retreat from Empire.* Newark: University of Delaware Press.

Captain X. 1924. *With Winston Churchill at the Front.* Glasgow: Cowans & Gray.

Carlton, David. 2000. *Churchill and the Soviet Union.* Manchester: Manchester University Press.

Cazalet-Keir, Thelma. 1967. *From the Wings.* London: Bodley Head.

Chamberlain, Sir Austen. 1937. *Politics from the Inside.* London: Cassell.

Chandler, D., et al., eds. 1970. *The Eisenhower Papers.* Vol. 2. Baltimore: Johns Hopkins University Press.

Chandos, Lord. 1962. *The Memoirs of Lord Chandos.* London: Bodley Head.

Chaplin, E. D. W., ed. 1941. *Winston Churchill and Harrow: Memoirs of the Prime Minister's Schooldays 1888–1892.* Harrow, UK: Harrow School.

Charmley, J., ed. 1987. *Descent to Suez: The Diaries of Sir Evelyn Shuckburgh 1951–1956.* London: Weidenfeld and Nicolson.

———. 1993. *Churchill: The End of Glory.* London: Hodder and Stoughton.

———. 1995. *Churchill's Grand Alliance.* London: Hodder and Stoughton.

Chown, J. L. 1945. *Life and Times of Winston S. Churchill.* Wolverhampton, UK: Whitehead Brothers.

Churchill, R. S. 1965. *Twenty-One Years.* London: Weidenfeld and Nicolson.

Churchill, R. S., and H. Gernsheim, eds. 1955. *Churchill: His Life in Photographs.* London: Weidenfeld and Nicolson.

Churchill, Sarah. 1981. *Keep on Dancing.* London: Weidenfeld and Nicolson.

Churchill, Winston S. 1996. *His Father's Son.* London: Weidenfeld and Nicolson.

Clarke, A., ed. 1974. *"A Good Innings": The Private Papers of Viscount Lee of Fareham.* London: Murray.

Cockett, R., ed. 1990. *My Dear Max: The Letters of Brendan Bracken to Lord Beaverbrook, 1925–1958.* London: The Historians Press.

Colville, J. 1981. *The Churchillians.* London: Weidenfeld and Nicolson.

———. 1985. *The Fringes of Power: The Downing Street Diaries, 1939–1955.* London: Hodder and Stoughton.

Connell, J. 1956. *Winston Churchill.* London: Longmans Green for the British Council and National Book League.

Coote, Colin R. 1971. *The Other Club.* London: Sidgwick and Jackson.

Cosgrave, Patrick. 1974. *Churchill at War: Alone, 1939–1940.* London: Collins.

Cowles, V. 1953. *Winston Churchill: The Era and the Man.* London: Hamish Hamilton.

Cunningham-Reid, Captain. 1942. *Besides Churchill: Who?* London: W. H. Allen.

Dalton, H. 1957. *The Fateful Years.* London: Muller.

D'Arcos, J. P. 1957. *Churchill: The Statesman and Writer.* London: The Caravel Press.

David, E., ed. 1977. *Inside Asquith's Cabinet.* London: John Murray.

Davis, R. Harding. 1941. *The Young Winston Churchill.* New York: Scribner.

Dawson, R. M. 1940. *Winston Churchill at the Admiralty, 1911–1915.* Oxford: Oxford University Press.

Day, David. 1986. *Menzies and Churchill at War.* North Ryde, NSW, Australia: Angus and Robertson.

De Gaulle, Charles. 1956. *Mémoires de Guerre: tome II, l'unité.* Paris: Plon.

De Mendelssohn, P. 1961. *The Age of Churchill: Heritage and Adventure 1874–1911.* London: Thames and Hudson.

Dilks, D., ed. 1971. *The Diaries of Sir Alexander Cadogan 1938–1945.* London: Cassell.

Dixon, P., ed. 1968. *Double Diploma: The Life of Sir Pierson Dixon.* London: Hutchinson.

Duff Cooper, A. 1953. *Old Men Forget.* London: Hart-Davis.

Eade, C. 1953. *Winston Churchill by His Contemporaries.* London: Hutchinson.

Eden, G. 1945. *Portrait of Churchill.* London: Hutchinson.

Ephesian [Bechofer Roberts]. 1927. *Winston Churchill.* London: Mills and Boon.

European Movement. 1949. *European Movement and the Council of Europe.* London: Hutchinson.

Evans, T., ed. 1972. *The Killearn Diaries.* London: Sidgwick and Jackson.

Fedden, R. 1969. *Churchill at Chartwell.* Oxford: Pergamon Press.

Feis, H. 1957. *Churchill, Roosevelt, Stalin.* Oxford: Oxford University Press.

Ferrier, N. 1955. *Churchill: The Man of the Century.* London: Photocron Midget Books.

Fishman, Jack. 1963. *My Darling Clementine.* London: W. H. Allen.

Gardner, Brian. 1968. *Churchill in Power: As Seen by His Contemporaries.* Boston: Houghton Mifflin.

Garnett, D., ed. 1938. *The Letters of T. E. Lawrence.* London: Cape.

Germains, H. V. 1931. *The Tragedy of Winston Churchill.* London: Hurst and Blackett.

Gilbert, M. 1974. *Churchill: A Photographic Portrait.* London: Heinemann.

———. 1981. *Churchill's Political Philosophy.* Oxford: Oxford University Press.

———. 1991. *Churchill: A Life.* London: Heinemann.

———. 1994. *In Search of Churchill.* London: Heinemann.

———, ed. 1997. *Winston Churchill and Emery Reves: Correspondence 1937–1964.* Austin: University of Texas Press.

Gordon, P., ed. 1986. *The Red Earl: The Papers of the Fifth Earl Spencer.* Vol. 2, 1885–1906. Northampton, UK: Northampton Record Office.

Graebner, Walter. 1965. *My Dear Mr. Churchill.* London: Michael Joseph.

Gretton, Sir Peter. 1969. *Winston Churchill and the Royal Navy.* New York: Coward McCann.

Grey, Sir Edward. 1925. *Twenty-Five Years.* 2 vols. London: Hodder and Stoughton.

Grigg, P. J. 1948. *Prejudice and Judgement.* London: Cape.

Guedalla, P. 1941. *Mr. Churchill: A Portrait.* London: Hodder and Stoughton.

Hagberg, Knut. 1929. *Kings, Churchills and Statesmen: A Foreigner's View.* London: Bodley Head.

Halifax, Earl of. 1957. *Fullness of Days.* London: Collins.

Halle, Kaye, ed. 1971. *Randolph Churchill: The Young Unpretender.* London: Heinemann.

Harvey, J., ed. 1970. *The Diplomatic Diaries of Oliver Harvey 1937–1940.* London: Collins.

————. 1978. *The War Diaries of Oliver Harvey 1941—1945.* London: Collins.

Harvie-Watt, G. S. 1980. *Most of My Life.* London: Springwood.

Hawthorn, H. 1942. *Long Adventure: The Story of Winston Churchill.* New York: Appleton-Century-Crofts.

Hay, M. V. 1934. *Winston Churchill and James II: A Criticism of Marlborough.* London: Harding and More.

Henderson, H. W. 1946. *The Truth about the Churchill-Stalin Controversy.* Glasgow: John S. Burns.

Henderson, Sir Nevile. 1940. *Failure of a Mission.* London: Hodder and Stoughton.

Higgins, T. 1957. *Winston Churchill and the Second Front.* Oxford: Oxford University Press.

————. 1963. *Winston Churchill and the Dardanelles.* London: Heinemann.

Hilditch, N. 1946. *In Praise of Churchill.* London: Muller.

Hill, M. 1999. *Churchill: His Radical Decade.* London: Othila Press.

Home, Lord. 1976. *The Way the Wind Blows.* London: Collins.

Hough, R. 1985. *Former Naval Person: Churchill and the Wars at Sea.* London: Weidenfeld and Nicolson.

————. 1990. *Winston and Clementine: The Triumph of the Churchills.* London: Bantam Press.

Howells, Roy. 1965. *Simply Churchill.* London: Robert Hale.

Hughes, E. 1950. *Winston Churchill in War and Peace.* Glasgow: Unity Publishing Co.

————. 1955. *Winston Churchill: British Bulldog.* New York: Exposition Press.

Hyam, R. 1968. *Elgin and Churchill at the Colonial Office.* London: Macmillan.

Irving, D. 1987. *Churchill's War: The Struggle for Power.* Bullsbrook, Australia: Veritas.

Ismay, Lord. 1960. *The Memoirs of General the Lord Ismay.* London: Heinemann.

Jablonsky, David. 1991. *Churchill: The Great Game and Total War.* London: Cass.

James, R. R., ed. 1967. *Chips: The Diaries of Sir Henry Channon.* London: Weidenfeld and Nicolson.

————. 1969. *Memoirs of a Conservative: J. C. C. Davidson's Memoirs and Papers, 1910–1937.* London: Weidenfeld and Nicolson.

————. 1970. *Churchill: A Study in Failure.* London: Weidenfeld and Nicolson.

————. 1976. *Victor Cazalet.* London: Hamish Hamilton.

————. 1981. *Churchill Speaks.* London: Hamish Hamilton.

Jeffrey, K., ed. 1985. *The Military Correspondence of Field Marshal Sir Henry Wilson 1918–1922.* London: Army Records Society and Bodley Head.

Jeffreys, Kevin. 1987. *Labour and the Wartime Coalition: From the Diary of James Chuter Ede 1941–1945.* London: Historians Press.

Jog, N. G. 1944. *Churchill's Blind-Spot: India.* Bombay: New Book Co.

Kavanagh, D. 1974. *Crisis, Charisma and British Political Leadership: Winston Churchill as the Outsider.* London: Sage.

Keegan, John, ed. 1991. *Churchill's Generals.* London: Weidenfeld and Nicolson.

Kersaudy, F. 1981. *Churchill and De Gaulle.* London: Collins.

Kettle, M. 1992. *Churchill and the Archangel Fiasco.* London: Routledge.

Keynes, J. M. 1925. *The Economic Consequences of Mr. Churchill.* London: Hogarth Press.

Kiernan, R. H. 1942. *Churchill.* London: Harrap.

Kilzer, L. C. 1994. *Churchill's Deception.* New York: Simon and Schuster.

Kimball, W. F. 1984. *Churchill and Roosevelt: The Complete Correspondence.* 3 vols. Princeton: Princeton University Press.

————. 1997. *Forged in War.* London: Harper Collins.

King, J. 1919. *The Political Gambler.* Glasgow: Reformer's Bookstall.

Kraus, R. 1940. *Winston Churchill.* New York: J. B. Lippincott.

————. 1941. *The Men Around Winston Churchill.* Philadelphia: J. B. Lippincott.

————. 1944. *Winston Churchill in the Mirror.* New York: Dutton.

Lamb, R. 1977. *Roosevelt and Churchill, 1939–1941: The Partnership That Saved the West.* London: Deutsch.

————. 1991. *Churchill as War Leader.* London: Bloomsbury.

Lawlor, Sheila. 1994. *Churchill and the Politics of War, 1940–1941.* Cambridge: Cambridge University Press.

Le Vien, J., and J. Lord. 1962. *The Valiant Years.* London: Harrap.

Lee, J. M. 1980. *The Churchill Coalition, 1940–1945.* London: Batsford.

Leech, H. J. 1907. *Mr. Winston Churchill, M.P.* Manchester: Abel Heywood.

Lewis Broad, C. 1940. *Winston Churchill, Man of War.* London: Hutchinson.

Lockhart, J. G. 1951. *Winston Churchill.* London: Duckworth.

Longford, Elizabeth. 1974. *Winston Churchill.* London: Sidgwick and Jackson.

Lukacs, John. 1991. *The Duel: Churchill and Hitler.* New York: Ticknor and Fields.

Mackenzie, N., ed. 1978. *The Letters of Sidney and Beatrice Webb.* Vol. 2. London: Virago.

Mackenzie, N., and J. Mackenzie, eds. 1984. *The Diaries of Beatrice Webb.* Vol. 3. London: Virago.

Macleod, R., and D. Kelly, eds. 1962. *The Ironside Diaries 1937–1940.* London: Constable.

Macmillan, H. 1966. *Memoirs.* Vol. 1, *Winds of Change.* London: Macmillan.

———. 1984. *War Diaries.* London: Macmillan.

MacNalty, Sir A. 1949. *The Three Churchills.* London: Essential Books.

Manchester, W. 1983. *The Last Lion: Winston Spencer Churchill: Visions of Glory 1874–1932.* London: Michael Joseph.

———. 1988. *The Caged Lion: Winston Spencer Churchill 1932–1940.* London: Michael Joseph.

Manning, P., and N. Bronner. 1941. *Mr. England: The Life Story of Winston Churchill.* Toronto: J. C. Winston.

Marchant, Sir J., ed. 1954. *Winston Spencer Churchill: Servant of Crown and Commonwealth.* London: Cassell.

Marsh, J. 1955. *The Young Winston Churchill.* London: Evans.

Marsh, Sir Edward. 1939. *A Number of People.* London: Heinemann with Hamish Hamilton.

Martin, Hugh. 1932. *Battle.* London: Sampson Low. (Also 1940 updated edition, London: Victor Gollancz).

Martin, J. 1991. *Downing Street: The War Years.* London: Bloomsbury.

McCabe, J. 1944. *Winston Churchill: The Man and His Creed.* London: Watts.

McCallum Scott, A. 1905. *Winston Spencer Churchill.* London: Methuen.

———. 1916. *Winston Churchill in Peace and War.* London: Newnes.

McEwan, J. M., ed. 1986. *The Riddell Diaries 1908–1923.* London: Athlone Press.

McGowan, N. 1958. *My Years with Churchill.* London: Souvenir Press.

Middlemas, K., ed. 1969–1970. *Whitehall Diary.* 3 vols. Oxford: Oxford University Press.

Miner, S. M. 1988. *Between Churchill and Stalin.* Chapel Hill: University of North Carolina.

Minney, R. J., ed. 1960. *The Private Papers of Hore-Belisha.* London: Collins.

Moir, P. 1941. *I Was Winston Churchill's Private Secretary.* New York: Wilfred Funk.

Montague Browne, A. 1995. *Long Sunset.* London: Cassell.

Moon, P., ed., 1973. *Wavell, the Viceroy's Journal.* Oxford: Oxford University Press.

Moore, R. I. 1979. *Churchill, Cripps and India.* Cambridge: Cambridge University Press.

Moorehead, A. 1960. *Churchill: A Pictorial Biography.* London: Thames and Hudson.

Moran, Lord. 1966. *Winston Churchill: The Struggle for Survival 1940–1965.* London: Constable.

Morgan, Ted. 1982. *Churchill: 1874–1915.* London: Jonathan Cape.

Morton, H. V. 1943. *Atlantic Meeting.* London: Methuen.

Muller, J. W., ed. 1997. *Churchill as Peacemaker.* Cambridge: Cambridge University Press.

Murray, E. 1987. *I Was Churchill's Bodyguard.* London: Edmund Murray.

Neilson, F. 1954. *The Churchill Legend.* Appleton, WI: CC Nelson Publishing Co.

Nel, E. 1958. *Mr. Churchill's Secretary.* London: Hodder and Stoughton.

Nicolson, N., ed. 1966–1968. *Harold Nicolson: Diaries and Letters.* 3 vols. London: Collins.

Nott, S. 1941. *The Young Churchill.* New York: Coward McCann.

Ogden, Christopher. 1994. *The Life of the Party: The Biography of Pamela Digby Churchill Hayward Harriman.* London: Little, Brown and Company.

Page Croft, Sir H. 1948. *My Life of Strife.* London: Hutchinson.

Paneth, P. 1943. *The Prime Minister Winston Churchill: As Seen by His Enemies and Friends.* London: Alliance Press.

Parker, R. A. C., ed. 1995. *Winston Churchill: Studies in Statesmanship.* London: Brasseys.

———. 2000. *Churchill and Appeasement.* London: Macmillan.

Paterson, Tony. 1980. *Churchill: A Seat for Life.* Dundee, UK: David Winter.

Pawle, Gerald. 1963. *The War and Colonel Warden.* London: Harrap.

Pearson, John. 1991. *Citadel of the Heart: Winston and the Churchill Dynasty*. London: Macmillan.

Pedraza, Howard. 1986. *Winston Churchill, Enoch Powell and the Nation*. London: Cleveland Press.

Pelling, H. 1974. *Winston Churchill*. London: Macmillan.

Pilpel, Robert H. 1976. *Churchill in America, 1895–1961*. New York: Harcourt, Brace, Jovanovich.

Pimlott, B., ed. 1986. *The Political Diary of Hugh Dalton, 1918–1940*. London: Jonathan Cape.

———. 1986. *The Second World War Diary of Hugh Dalton, 1940–1945*. London: Jonathan Cape.

Ponting, Clive. 1994. *Churchill*. London: Sinclair-Stevenson.

Prior, R. 1983. *Churchill's "World Crisis" as History*. London: Croom Helm.

Rabinowicz, O. K. 1956. *Winston Churchill on Jewish Problems*. Vol. 1. London: Lincolns-Prager.

Ranft, B. M., ed. 1989. *The Beatty Papers: Selections from the Private and Official Papers of Admiral of the Fleet Earl Beatty*. Vol. 1, *1902–1918*. London: Naval Records Society.

Reith, J. W. 1949. *Into the Wind*. London: Hodder and Stoughton.

Reynolds, E. E. 1944. *Four Modern Statesmen*. Oxford: Oxford University Press.

Richardson, C. 1991. *From Churchill's Secret Circle to the BBC: The Biography of Sir Ian Jacob*. London: Brasseys.

Robbins, Keith. 1992. *Churchill*. London: Longman.

Roberts, A. 1994. *Eminent Churchillians*. London: Weidenfeld and Nicolson.

Roberts, Brian. 1970. *Churchills in Africa*. New York: Taplinger.

Roberts, C. E. B. 1928. *Winston Churchill*. London: Newnes.

Rose, N., ed. 1973. *Baffy: The Diaries of Blanche Dugdale* London: Valentine, Mitchell.

———. 1994. *Churchill: An Unruly Life*. London: Simon and Schuster.

Rowse, A. L. 1945. *The English Spirit*. London: Macmillan.

———. 1958. *The Later Churchills*. London: Macmillan.

Sainsbury, Keith. 1994. *Churchill and Roosevelt at War*. London: Macmillan.

Sandys, Celia. 1994. *From Winston with Love and Kisses: The Young Churchill*. London: Sinclair-Stevenson.

———. 1999. *Churchill: Wanted Dead or Alive*. London: Harper Collins.

Schoenfeld. 1972. *The War Ministry of Winston Churchill*. Ames: Iowa State University Press.

Seldon, Anthony. 1981. *Churchill's Indian Summer: The Conservative Government, 1951–1955*. London: Hodder and Stoughton.

Sencourt, R. 1940. *Winston Churchill*. London: Faber and Faber.

Seth, H. L. c.1942. *Churchill on India*. Lahore, Pakistan: Hero Publications.

Simon, Lord 1953. *Retrospect*. London: Hutchinson.

Soames, Mary. 1979. *Clementine Churchill*. London: Cassell.

———. 1982. *A Churchill Family Album*. London: Allen Lane.

———. 1990. *Winston Churchill: His Life as a Painter*. London: Collins.

———, ed. 1998. *Speaking for Themselves*. London: Doubleday.

Stafford, David. 1997. *Churchill and Secret Service*. London: John Murray.

Stansky, Peter, ed. 1973. *Churchill: A Profile*. London: Macmillan.

Stewart, H. L. 1954. *Winston Churchill as Writer and Speaker*. London: Sidgwick and Jackson.

Strang, Sir W. 1956. *Home and Abroad*. London: Deutsch.

Stuart, C., ed. 1975. *The Reith Diaries*. London: Collins.

Tatlock Miller, N., and L. Sainthill. 1958. *Churchill: The Walk with Destiny*. London: Hutchinson.

Taylor, A. J. P. 1969. *Churchill: Four Faces and the Man*. London: Allen Lane.

———. 1971. *Lloyd George: A Diary by Frances Stevenson*. London: Hutchinson.

———, ed. 1975. *My Darling Pussy: The Letters of Lloyd George and Frances Stevenson 1913–1941*. London: Weidenfeld and Nicolson.

Taylor, R. L. 1952. *Winston Churchill*. New York: Doubleday.

Temple-Patterson, A., ed. 1968. *The Jellicoe Papers: Selections from the Private and Official Correspondence of Admiral of the Fleet Jellicoe*. Vol. 2, *1913–1935*. London: Naval Records Society.

Templewood, Lord. 1954. *Nine Troubled Years*. London: Collins.

Thomas, D. A. 1995. *Churchill: The Member for Woodford*. London: Cass.

Thompson, R. W. 1963. *The Yankee Marlborough*. London: Allen and Unwin.

————. 1974. *Generalissimo Churchill*. London: Hodder and Stoughton.

————. 1976. *Churchill and Morton*. London: Hodder and Stoughton.

Thompson, W. H. 1938. *Guard from the Yard*. London: Jarrolds.

————. 1951. *I Was Churchill's Shadow*. London: Christopher Johnson.

————. 1953. *Sixty Minutes with Winston Churchill*. London: Christopher Johnson.

Thomson, G. M. 1968. *Vote of Censure*. London: Secker and Warburg.

Thomson, M. 1945. *The Life and Times of Winston Churchill*. London: Odhams.

Thornton-Kemsley, Colin. 1974. *Through Winds and Tides*. Montrose, Scotland: Standard Press.

Trukhanovsky, V. G. 1978. *Winston Churchill*. Moscow: Progress Publishers.

Tucker, B. 1945. *Winston Churchill*. London: Sagall Press.

Van der Poel, J., ed. 1973. *Selections from the Smuts Papers*. Vol. 6. Cambridge: Cambridge University Press.

Vansittart, Sir R. 1958. *The Mist Procession*. London: Hutchinson.

Vincent, J., ed. 1984. *The Crawford Papers*. Manchester: Manchester University Press.

Watchman. 1939. *Right Honourable Gentleman*. London: Hamish Hamilton.

Weidhorn, M. 1974. *Sword and Pen: A Survey of the Writings of Sir Winston Churchill*. Albuquerque: University of New Mexico.

————. 1979. *Sir Winston Churchill*. Boston: Twayne.

Wheeler-Bennett, J. 1968. *Action This Day: Working with Churchill*. London: Macmillan.

Williamson, P., ed. 1988. *The Modernisation of Conservative Politics: The Diaries and Letters of William Bridgeman, 1904–1935*. London: Historians Press.

Wilson, Thomas. 1995. *Churchill and the Prof*. London: Cassell.

Wingfield-Stratford, E. 1942. *Churchill: The Making of a Hero*. London: Gollancz.

Wood, I. S. 2000. *Churchill*. London: Macmillan.

Woods, Frederick. 1963. *A Bibliography of the Works of Sir Winston Churchill*. London: Nicholas Vane.

————. 1992. *Artillery of Words: The Writings of Sir Winston Churchill*. London: Leo Cooper.

Woolton, Earl of. 1959. *The Memoirs of the Rt. Hon. the Earl of Woolton*. London: Cassell.

Wyatt, Woodrow. 1958. *Winston Churchill: Distinguished for Talent*. London: Hutchinson.

Young, John. 1996. *Winston Churchill's Last Campaign*. Oxford: Oxford University Press.

Young, Kenneth. 1966. *Churchill and Beaverbrook*. London: Eyre and Spottiswoode.

Young, K., ed. 1973, 1980. *The Diaries of Sir Robert Bruce Lockhart*. 2 vols. London: Hutchinson.

Ziegler, P., ed. 1988. *Personal Diary of Admiral the Lord Louis Mountbatten, Supreme Allied Commander South-East Asia 1943–1947*. London: Collins.

ABOUT THE AUTHOR

Chris Wrigley is professor of modern British history at the University of Nottingham and has spent most of his academic career studying Winston Churchill and David Lloyd George.

Lightning Source UK Ltd.
Milton Keynes UK
UKHW051158070419
340525UK00012B/41/P